KU-506-651

WITHDRAWN

THIRD EDITION

ELECTRONIC COMMERCE

FROM VISION TO FULFILLMENT

Elias M. Awad

McIntire School of Commerce
University of Virginia

THE LEARNING CENTRE
HAMMERSMITH AND WEST
LONDON COLLEGE
GLIDDON ROAD
LONDON W14 9BL

PEARSON

Prentice
Hall

 HAMMERSMITH WEST LONDON COLLEGE

327718

Upper Sad... ...w 07458

Library of Congress Cataloging-in-Publication Data

Awad, Elias M.
  Electronic commerce: from vision to fulfillment / Elias M. Awad.— 3rd ed.
    p.   cm.
  Includes bibliographical references and index.
  ISBN 0-13-173521-7 (pbk.)
  1. Electronic commerce—Handbooks, manuals, etc.   I. Title.
HF5548.32.A93 2006
658.8′72–dc22   2005026161

AVP/Acquisitions Editor: Bob Horan
VP/Editorial Director: Jeff Shelstad
Editorial Assistant: Ana Cordero
AVP/Marketing Manager: Debbie Clare
Marketing Assistant: Joanna Sabella
Senior Managing Editor (Production): Cynthia Regan
Production Editor: Melissa Feimer
Permissions Supervisor: Charles Morris

Manufacturing Buyer: Michelle Klein
Design/Print Production Manager: Christy Mahon
Cover Design: Karen Salzbach
Cover Image: Getty Images
Manager, Print Production: Christy Mahon
Composition/Full-Service Project Management:
  Thistle Hill Publishing Services, LLC
Printer/Binder: R.R. Donnelley

Credits and acknowledgments borrowed from other sources and reproduced, with permission, in this textbook appear on appropriate page within text.

Microsoft® and Windows® are registered trademarks of the Microsoft Corporation in the U.S.A. and other countries. Screen shots and icons reprinted with permission from the Microsoft Corporation. This book is not sponsored or endorsed by or affiliated with the Microsoft Corporation.

Copyright © 2007, 2004, 2002 by Pearson Education, Inc., Upper Saddle River, New Jersey, 07458.
Pearson Prentice Hall. All rights reserved. Printed in the United States of America. This publication is protected by Copyright and permission should be obtained from the publisher prior to any prohibited reproduction, storage in a retrieval system, or transmission in any form or by any means, electronic, mechanical, photocopying, recording, or likewise. For information regarding permission(s), write to:
Rights and Permissions Department.

Pearson Prentice Hall™ is a trademark of Pearson Education, Inc.
Pearson® is a registered trademark of Pearson plc
Prentice Hall® is a registered trademark of Pearson Education, Inc.

Pearson Education LTD.
Pearson Education Singapore, Pte. Ltd
Pearson Education, Canada, Ltd
Pearson Education—Japan
Pearson Education Australia PTY, Limited
Pearson Education North Asia Ltd
Pearson Educación de Mexico, S.A. de C.V.
Pearson Education Malaysia, Pte. Ltd

HAMMERSMITH AND WEST
LONDON COLLEGE
LEARNING CENTRE

/ 9 SEP 2008

327718   £44·99
658 051678 AWA
BUSINESS
3 WKS

This book is not for sale or distribution in the U.S.A. or Canada.

10 9 8 7 6 5 4 3 2 1
ISBN 0-13-173521-7

ABOUT THE AUTHOR

Dr. Elias M. Awad is the Virginia Bankers Association Professor of Bank Management at the University of Virginia. Dr. Awad has more than 40 years of IT experience in the academic, publishing, and consulting areas. He is one of the world's leading IT instructors and seminar presenters in the banking industry here and abroad. He is also the CEO of International Technology Group, Ltd., an IT consulting group with offices in Chicago, New York, Geneva, and Charlottesville, Virginia. Dr. Awad's consulting work has taken him to 26 countries, including Russia, Korea, Hong Kong, Cambodia, Canada, Mexico, Kazikhstan, Moldova, Uzbekistan, Armenia, Ukraine, Slovak Republic, Philippines, Belize, Saudi Arabia, Lebanon, Jordan, and Egypt.

E-Commerce is one of Dr. Awad's most recent books. He has been writing since the early 1960s and has authored several bestsellers across the IT discipline about such topics as systems analysis and design, database management, knowledge management, management information systems, human resources management, building knowledge automation systems, human resources information systems, and building expert support systems. His publications have been translated into German, Spanish, Portuguese, Chinese, Arabic, Russian, and Braille. They have earned international recognition for lucidity, logical flow, and presentation of material based on experience in the field.

Dr. Awad may be reached at International Technology Groups, LTD, Suite 100, 3015 Old Lynchburg Road, North Garden, Virginia 22959; e-mail: ema3z@virginia.edu; voice: (434) 924-3423; private: (434) 984-AWAD.

Dedicated to Dr. Houston "Tex" Elam,
long-time colleague and friend

CONTENTS

PART III　E-STRATEGIES AND TACTICS

PREFACE

Welcome to the world of online, real-time, just-in-time e-commerce and e-business via the Internet—the superhighway of today's commerce here and abroad. Whether it is e-commerce, e-business, supply chain, or networking global business, the goal of this maturing industry is to improve the quality of life and the quality of time. There is virtually nothing today that is not affected by the electronics that bring people, technologies, and processes together in the interest of time saving, efficiency, productivity, and human comfort. Even the nonprofit sector from churches to schools, has adopted the World Wide Web to establish a presence.

The Internet is the foundation for a new industrial order. *It is a noose for mediocrity.* The e-corporation is combining computers, the Web, and enterprise software to change everything about how it operates. The Net is about choice, freedom, and control. The Net is about pull (not push) advertising and marketing goods and services. Consumers can now shop and get the truth. Retailers come to customers *not* like the old days and ways. Everything is an auction. It is the end of geography. Products and information about goods and services come to my place, during my convenient time.

The famous scientist Albert Einstein once said, "I prefer imagination over knowledge." If e-commerce were there during his time, he probably would have said, "I prefer creativity through imagination, knowledge through experience, and profitability through competitive advantage." E-commerce offers all these. It is an American invention and will go down in history as the mark of leadership through creativity, adding value to customers worldwide. Whether you are a student or a venture capitalist, you should benefit from the fundamentals and technologies that make e-commerce a reality. This is what this edition is all about.

As you begin reading this text, you will find that the Internet and the World Wide Web are not that safe or sound. The number one concern is security of navigation. For clean and intact messages, purchase orders, and business traffic, you have to build firewalls and install software that is anti-spam, anti-spyware, anti-adware, anti-pop up ads, and anti-phishing, relying on encryption to secure sensitive traffic. You can expect hackers, cookies, and intelligent "agents" to monitor your pattern of navigation and your preferences for certain sites so they can send you junk e-mail or refer your profile to unwanted ads that often bring nothing but headache and chaos to the privacy of your office, home, or business. All these problems and how to eliminate them are explained in this edition.

Speaking of security, we discuss the USA Patriot Act approved by Congress as a result of the tragic events of September 11, 2001, to show how terrorists and the criminal community use the Internet to prosper and promote the traffic of evil and money laundering. Criminals and hackers do more than their share to blemish the goodness of the Internet. Unfortunately, these events are all part of the total picture surrounding e-commerce.

WHY THIS BOOK?

This edition is designed to provide you the necessary tools and technology to enter the maturing commerce on the Internet. The book is designed around a "front end," "back end," and a lot in between. The "front-end" is what you see—the Web site, the information displayed to attract you to shop for goods and services. The "back end" explains how the e-merchant connects to the supplier, wholesaler, or manufacturer to ensure "ready to ship" products through the supply chain and add to the value chain. What is in between is the technology and the architecture that network customers to retailers, retailers to banks for payments, and retailers to suppliers for delivery night and day.

Boxes and tables have been updated to reflect recent or current events. The entire book has been revisited, reedited, or reworked. New topics such as spyware, blogging, adware, phishing, CRM, and the USA Patriot Act have been introduced. There is more text and better content than what you will find in the competition. The focus is on learning and doing as we explore e-commerce in a serious way. What is more, the entire work is integrated around a life-cycle approach from "vision" or strategic planning to "fulfillment" for delivery of products and service on time—all with the goal of customer satisfaction.

Clearly, we are in the midst of exciting events. E-commerce has reached a level of maturity that separates the men from the boys. The methodology is becoming standardized and the technology is gaining credence so that those who enter e-commerce tend to stay longer, relying on professionals and facing informed customers. This leading-edge industry is already complementing established IT courses and business practice at the undergraduate and graduate levels. Additionally, this edition incorporates in writing style and content over four decades of the author's academic and industrial experience.

This edition stands out in terms of lucidity, ease of learning, and the approach taken to integrate concepts, methodologies, processes, and technologies via a life-cycle approach to e-commerce. It is truly exciting to know how to strategize reality and potential, how to evaluate and design Web sites, how to launch an e-commerce site or link to e-business from scratch, and how wireless technology is making it easier to shop and communicate with people and businesses everywhere.

As a prospective e-entrepreneur, you will begin to learn how to market your products or service, how you are assured of payments, the goodness of security, the laws and ethics of the new industry, and the building blocks that protect your business through the maze of the Internet. Managerial and organizational implications are cited at the end of each chapter to note the relationship between the business and technology that makes it possible.

WHO SHOULD READ THIS BOOK?

This edition is an ideal choice for undergraduate students majoring in IT, management, finance, marketing, accounting, or e-commerce. Students majoring in computer science or systems engineering also will find the approach, content, and treatment of the technology in a business environment an appropriate addition to their fields of concentration. First-year MBA or MS students will benefit from the technology and practical orientation presented in the text.

Likewise, professionals, general managers, and practitioners in general can use this text as a reference or as a way to learn e-commerce. They include Webmasters, ISP technicians, CIOs, systems designers, project managers and planners, e-commerce sales staff, suppliers, vendors, and e-commerce consultants.

BOOK ORGANIZATION

This text is organized into five parts. Each part represents a key step in the e-commerce process. An index is provided at the end of the text.

Each chapter begins with a set of learning objectives and "In a Nutshell," which highlights the main points of the material and what to expect in the chapter. Chapter content includes boxes, easy-to-read figures, and tables designed to help to summarize essential details. Definitions of key terms are available in the margin where first cited. Each chapter ends with a comprehensive summary, terms to learn, review (Test Your Understanding) questions, discussion questions, and Web exercises. References for further review are provided at the end of the book.

PART I: FIRST THINGS FIRST

Chapter 1 is a refreshing overview of e-commerce—the good life in blogging, the digital divide, e-learning, definitions of e-commerce and its main drivers, myths worth noting, pros, issues, and constraints related to security, data integrity, fulfillment and customer relations problems, cultural and language issues, and the high risk of Internet startup. Also covered is the value chain and integrating e-commerce. The latter topic includes supply chain management, business-to-business, business-to-consumer, business-within-business, and business-to-government. A number of commerce business models such as storefront, click-and-mortar, service provider, subscription-based access, broker, advertiser, portal site, free access, virtual mall, virtual community, and infomediary are also discussed. The chapter ends with implications for management practice.

Chapter 2 focuses on the World Wide Web—Web search elements, the search engine, search engine optimization, Internet service providers and their functions and offerings, Web fundamentals and the role of URLs and HTTPs in helping you navigate on the Internet, and Internet services and languages. A distinction between the Internet and the WWW also is made throughout the chapter.

PART II: THE TECHNOLOGY OF E-COMMERCE

Chapter 3 presents comprehensive coverage of Internet architecture. It begins with a description of a network and how information is transferred via standards and protocols from the browser to the Web server and back. The chapter also talks about video and movie standards, how to pick and register a domain name, and the basics of the OSI reference model. A summary of the necessary network hardware, cable types, and network components (hubs, switches, routers, and gateways) is included toward the end of the chapter. A section on the key steps in designing a network and how to manage the corporate network also is included.

Chapter 4 covers the makeup, design, and contributions of intranets and extranets. More specifically, it explains the technical infrastructure, how to plan for an intranet installation, and whether a company should build it or outsource it. E-mail, spamming, e-mail etiquette, blogging, and instant messaging are also covered. For extranets, heavy emphasis on the role of supply chain management concludes the chapter.

Chapter 5 shows how to host your Web site—how ISPs really work, types of ISPs, their structure and services, how to choose an ISP, what to consider, and how to register your domain name. Application service providers are also discussed.

Chapter 6 is devoted to mobile (wireless) business: why wireless is gaining in popularity, the role of Wi-Fi as a standard, how wireless technology is employed, with special emphasis on Bluetooth protocols and applications, wireless security issues and concerns, wireless application protocol, along with security and legal issues. Finally, mobile banking as an evolving technology is also covered.

PART III: E-STRATEGIES AND TACTICS

Chapter 7 addresses Web site design. Specifically, it begins with the justification for a Web site, the life cycle of site building, how to build Web sites, creating user profiles, the importance of cultural differences, design criteria such as appearance, viewability, scalability, and security, and what to look for in hiring a Web designer. This is a critical chapter that sets the tone for the user-merchant interface.

The focus of Chapter 8 is on how to evaluate Web sites and manage Web traffic. It begins with an anatomy of a Web site, and discusses the use of color and its psychological effects, color and cultural age, gender, and class differences, geometric shapes and gender differences, and what to consider for the color blind and those with impaired vision. The chapter also covers site evaluation criteria, how to delete and reject cookies, and the criteria that make a Web site usable. Web site content and traffic management also are discussed. At the end of the chapter, reliability and user testing and the role of Web site administration is explain in detail.

Chapter 9 is about the skills and techniques that are unique to Internet marketing. It begins with the pros and cons of online shopping, Internet marketing techniques, the concept of permission marketing, and the marketing cycle. The second part of the chapter explores ways of marketing presence, how to promote your site on the Internet, how to attract customers, how to account for cultural differences, and how to predict buying behavior. Customization and personalization issues are also covered. Finally, customer relationship management (CRM) is discussed in detail to emphasize the increasing role of this area of service in e-commerce.

Chapter 10 is about Web portals and Web services. Specifically, the chapter begins with the evolution and key characteristics of portals, portals and business transformation, and enterprise portal technologies, including key functionalities, collaboration, content management, and use of intelligent agents. Knowledge portals, Web services and portals, and mobile Web services are also covered. The chapter concludes with brief coverage of who is building enterprise portals, who sponsors enterprise portals, and portal product selection.

Chapter 11 is a comprehensive coverage of Web-based business-to-business e-commerce. Supply chain management, B2B building blocks and integration challenges, building models, and tools are heavily emphasized.

Chapter 12 addresses ethical, legal, and international issues related to e-commerce. In the ethical issues section, we cover major threats to ethics, the privacy factor, and the role of the professional ethicist. Legal issues relate to tort law on the Internet, copyrights, trademarks, and trade names. The taxation issue, online gambling, encryption laws, and legal disputes on the Internet are especially emphasized. International issues, especially the ones affecting developing countries, and the issue of intellectual property make up the bulk of the material.

PART IV: SECURITY THREATS AND PAYMENT SYSTEMS

Chapter 13 devotes full attention to the concept and serious nature of e-security. The critical components include security in cyberspace (ID theft, "phear of pharming," and the many woes of the password), how to design for security, how much risk a company can afford (keeping in mind hackers, viruses, and cybercrime), the privacy factor, how to protect against various types of viruses, and how to recover from security failure. The role of biometric security, how to build a response team, security protocols resulting from the USA Patriot Act, and money laundering are also discussed.

Chapter 14 is about encryption. The focus is on cryptographic algorithm, authentication and trust, digital signatures, major attacks on cryptosystems, digital certificates, and Internet security protocols and standards. Government regulations that relate to encryption are also covered.

Chapter 15 is about e-payments and how merchants get paid. The chapter explains money properties, Internet-based systems requirements, and electronic payment media such as credit cards, debit cards, smart cards, digital cash, e-cash, and the e-wallet. Electronic funds transfer and Automated Clearinghouse processes are also covered.

PART V: MANAGERIAL AND CUSTOMER-RELATED ISSUES

Chapter 16 focuses on the procedure and mechanics of launching a new business on the Internet. It begins with strategizing reality (planning), followed by considering the necessary hardware, software, security, and setup phase. The next step is the actual design phase, which brings up Web site design, the storefront, and whether the work should be done by the company's IT staff or outsourced to professionals. The last three steps are marketing, fulfillment, and maintenance. Each step is covered in some detail in the chapter.

ACKNOWLEDGMENTS

As this author sees it, a textbook is a project, not a document. Once a prospectus has been adopted, an editor takes the lead, assembling a team of reviewers, a copyeditor, a production manager, and others on the staff to see to it that the manuscript gets the best treatment before it becomes a text. This author is grateful to see this text adopted by an experienced team and a premiere publisher.

I wish to acknowledge with gratitude the following reviewers, whose comments and wisdom ensured a respectable edition: Cihan Cobanoglu, University of Delaware; Thomas Dillon, James Madison University; Anthony Gauvin, University of Maine; Cherie Henderson, University of Texas, Austin; Mirza Murtaza, Middle Tennessee State University; Alan Paradise, Washington Unviersity, St. Louis; Dien Phan, St. Cloud State University; Catherine Roche, Rockland Community College; Ming Wang, California State University, Los Angeles.

Bill Beville, editor and sales representative at Prentice Hall, a friend, and a coach deserves special recognition for years of encouragement in my publishing career. I acknowledge with appreciation my colleague Tony Feghali of the School of Business at American University of Beirut, for his contributions to the CRM material in Chapter 9. Lama Ghrawi, also of the School of Business at American University of Beirut, contributed many hours of valuable time transforming the second edition from stubborn read-only Acrobat into a readable format in Word under time constraints.

Transforming a manuscript into a respectable text is never an easy task. I want to thank Melissa Feimer, Production Editor at Prentice Hall Business Publishing, for a great job managing this project from the home office. I am especially thankful to Amanda Hosey Dugan, Senior Project Editor at Thistle Hill Publishing Services, for her diligence, communication skills, and for the professional treatment of this manuscript through the production process.

This edition is dedicated to Dr. Houston "Tex" Elam, a long-time colleague and a special friend, who in 1962 foresaw the potential of computers in industry and government. His vision at the time was shared by only a handful of people nationwide. His invaluable advice led to my first publication, *Business Data Processing* (Prentice Hall, 1965) and set my academic and consulting IT career ever since.

CHAPTER 1

THE DAWN OF A MATURING INDUSTRY

Learning Objectives

The focus of this chapter is on several learning objectives:

- Conceptual understanding of e-commerce, e-business, and e-strategy
- Drivers
- The rise of specialized Web sites such as blogs
- Value-chain and supply-chain management and how they relate to e-commerce and e-business
- Business models of the e-environment
- A trend toward integrating e-commerce

IN A NUTSHELL

If you have a personal computer (PC) with a browser, you can connect to the Internet and do business online. No more worries about programming. No more looking for phone numbers, paying long-distance charges, or keeping the store open late into the evening. Just get on the Web, launch an online store, and watch your business grow. It is that straightforward.

Welcome to the wired world of business, where technology, human talent, and a new way of doing business make up today's growing worldwide economy. The backbone of electronic commerce is the Internet. The wired world is not about technology; it is about information, decision making, and communication. The wired world is changing life for everyone—from the individual household to the largest corporation. No business can afford to ignore the potential of today's connected economy.

If you look closely at the changes that have taken place during the past two decades, you find that computers, information technology, and networking have joined together to replace labor-intensive business across industries and in government. In banking, for example, the change has been seen in the widespread use of automated teller machines

(ATMs), credit cards, debit cards, smart cards, and Internet lending. This type of computer-based, bank-to-bank, bank-to-consumer, and consumer-to-consumer transactional and informational exchange is what electronic commerce is all about.

More recently, wireless transmission paved the way for consumers to shop, to trade, and to access information from *anywhere* at *any time* in a matter of seconds using a cell phone. Mobile commerce has taken on the "business of time," as we shall see in Chapter 6. It is already showing savings and adding value in business-to-business transactions and other Internet-based areas as well.

In this chapter we cover the essence of electronic commerce—what it is, what it is not, where it is used, its benefits and limitations, and its impact on the value chain and supply chain management concepts of doing business.

FIRST THINGS FIRST

Welcome to the new world of electronic commerce (e-commerce or EC)—an industry that has matured in the United States in less than a decade. It is the industry of the twenty-first century, where you can now do business electronically and via satellite from virtually anywhere in the world that has a computer. Electronic commerce has brought dramatic changes to business firms, markets, and consumer behavior. In 2004 alone, e-commerce generated well over $100 billion in retail business and over $1.5 trillion business-to-business traffic. Nobody knows how much more mature it will become, but it has already been recognized as the fastest growing form of commerce on the planet.

This book is about modern electronic commerce and how it has revolutionized the way we do business in the U.S and abroad. It is the new breed that grew out of the explosive growth period of 1995 to 2000. That time was a period of exploration, cost justification, and risky investment by big business with deep pockets like Wal-Mart, General Electric, and General Motors. It was also the beginning of early birds like eBay, Amazon.com, and Expedia that survived the recession of 2001–2003. For each survivor, dozens have failed. That is one reason why we have Web trash on the Internet. Hundreds of the once high-flying dot-com firms that entered the fray failed to make money, abandoned their Web sites, failed to update them, or simply lost interest in the whole venture.

Before delving into this exciting industry, you should know what precipitated the revolution. It was the **Internet**—an international network of independent computer systems. It is the fastest superhighway of unmonitored information ever built. It is also the fastest-maturing tool for free enterprise. Speed and momentum are giving us a new way of doing business, saving time and energy in virtually all walks of life.

Despite security, privacy, and other problems, the Internet has permeated virtually every phase of society—economic, social, psychological, political, and military. It is in households, in schools, in police cars, and aboard airplanes. A decade ago, it was a novelty; today, it is a necessity. We can now learn much faster and far more than we could before.

THE GOOD LIFE IN BLOGGING

The rise of specialized Web sites and Web logs (blogs) generated opportunities to read and write on a vast array of topics. You can chat, share, collaborate, and communicate knowledge (not just information) about virtually any topic any time, 24 hours a day, year round. My hobby is online backgammon. On command, a specialized Web site (zone.com) lines up an opponent from another country at my "expert" level, turns on the chat, sets up the backgammon table on the screen, keeps the score, and declares the winner—I never have to leave the comfort of my office at the farm.

blog: a shared online journal for posting diary entries about hobbies and personal experiences.

A **blog** is a shared online journal where people post entries about their hobbies or personal experiences on the job, on vacation, and so forth. (See www.blogger.com.) Blogs are available on the Internet exactly like any other Web page. They are automatically indexed by search engines like Yahoo.com and Google.com. There are eight million personal blogs in the United States, according to the Pew Internet & American Life Project. People write blogs to talk about their days, family outings, or days gone awry. But certain types of news or views can also get you in hot water, as reported in Box 1.1.

On the international scene, blogging in China is causing the Chinese Communist Party some discomfort. This wrestling match of history is evidenced by self-appointed journalist Li Xinde's www.yulunch.com. Xinde started the Chinese Public Surveillance Net, one of four million blogs in China. Some 100 million Chinese citizens now surf the net, use e-mail, and visit chat rooms. A growing number of Web dissidents have been arrested, but there just aren't enough police to control the Internet (Kristof, 2005).

BOX 1.1

Free Expression Can Be Costly

Under the pseudonym of Sarcastic Journalist, Rachel Mosteller wrote this entry on her personal Web log one day last April:

> I really hate my place of employment. Seriously. Okay, first off. They have these stupid little awards that are supposed to boost company morale. So you go and do something "spectacular" (most likely, you're doing your JOB) and then someone says "Why golly, that was spectacular." Then they sign your name on some paper, they bring you chocolate and some balloons.
>
> Okay two people in the newsroom just got it. FOR DOING THEIR JOB.

This post, like all entries in Mosteller's online diary, did not name her company or give her name. It did not name co-workers or bosses. It did not say where the company was based. But apparently, Mosteller's supervisors and co-workers at the Durham (N.C.) *Herald-Sun* were well aware of her Web log. The day after that posting, she was fired.

Usually bloggers have little protection. In most states, if an employer doesn't like what you say or share, they can simply let you go. It seems that blogging is a good way to improve communication between the employer and the employee and help community building. Google Inc., the search engine company, has a blog for employees that shares such things as stories about the company dog and the person who creates the holiday art at Google.com. It sort of turned into a very informal access to the public. But Google had its own controversy recently when a blog by employee Mark Jen suddenly went dark, sparking a flurry of speculation on what had happened to him. Google confirmed that Jen is no longer an employee, but the company would not discuss why.

Source: Amy Joyce, "Free Expression Can Be Costly When Bloggers Bad-Mouth Jobs," story.news.yahoo.com/news?tmp1=story&cid=1804&ncid= 1804&e=1&u= wash . . . , February 12, 2005, 1–5.

Today's Internet promotes individualism. Consumers can personalize and customize their own products and their own communications universe. This means a dramatic increase in individual control over content and an obvious decrease in the power of intermediaries like newspapers and broadcasters. One positive side effect is to encourage collaboration and teamwork on special projects. The overall result is to widen our horizons and open the door for creativity and energy not experienced before.

The 2004 presidential campaign was fought and advertised on specialized Web sites that could be accessed worldwide. Military personnel in Iraq and Afghanistan had no problem staying tuned into ongoing political activities at home. Internet-based political strategies included e-mail solicitations, donations, and online advertising. This is just one slice of the Internet pie.

THE DIGITAL DIVIDE

On the surface, everything about e-commerce seems rosy. One thing worth keeping in mind, however, is that computers are increasingly conditioning the country. The **digital divide** refers to the gap between the haves and the have nots in computers, Internet access, access to information, and e-commerce. The divide has widened social gaps, especially among young people. The gap is slowly leveling off, but not fast enough.

digital divide: gap between the haves and the have nots in computer use, Internet access, and being part of e-commerce.

The Digital Divide Network (www.digitaldividenetwork.org) is the Internet's largest environment in which concerned citizens and activists can build their own online community, publish blogs, share documents, and announce news and events. The connection allows 115 countries to share ideas and educational resources with underdeveloped communities. Once developed, e-commerce should begin to involve such communities and beyond.

E-LEARNING

Today, students find applications and opportunities on the Internet. Doing academic research on the Internet is a common practice. Students can easily access methodology, white papers, and research material at all levels. Internet portals provide access to the highest quality content on the Web. Accuracy and reliability continue to be a problem, but several solutions have been offered for determining the accuracy of the information found. Students at many universities are given lists of approved online sources for Internet research.

e-learning: technology-based learning; learning materials are delivered via the Internet to remote learners worldwide.

E-learning is technology-based learning. Learning materials are delivered via the Internet to remote learners worldwide. In 2001, MIT decided to make materials from virtually all of its courses freely available on its Web site for noncommercial use. In 2002, the University of Phoenix enrolled over 50,000 students online. Today, the offerings are worldwide.

E-learning's increasing popularity comes from its learner-centricity and self-paced learning environment. It is also known for letting students acquire knowledge just-in-time, enabling continuous interaction between the e-system and the learner,

TABLE 1.1 Traditional classroom learning and e-learning		
	Traditional Classroom Learning	*E-Learning*
Advantages	• Immediate feedback • Familiar to both instructors and students • Motivates students • Cultivation of a social community	• Learning-centered and self-paced • Time and location flexibility • Cost-effective for learners • Potentially available to global audience • Unlimited access to knowledge • Archival capability for knowledge reuse and sharing
Disadvantages	• Instructor-centered • Time and location constraints • More expensive to deliver	• Lack of immediate feedback in asynchronous e-learning • Increased preparation time for the instructor • Not comfortable for some people; requires more maturity and self-discipline • Potentially more frustration, anxiety, and confusion

Source: D. Zhang, et al., "Can E-Learning Replace Classroom Learning?" *Communications of the ACM*, May 2004, 76.

providing students with flexible control over the learning process and content, and monitoring each individual's learning progress. It is ideal for homemakers, full-time employees who want to move ahead in their careers, and others who cannot afford to quit their jobs and leave their families to get a traditional classroom education. Table 1.1 summarizes the comparison of traditional learning and e-learning.

Today's knowledge-based economy has exhibited an increasing demand for innovative ways of delivering and acquiring education. With the expanding economy requiring more people to learn new knowledge and skills in a timely way, advanced computer technology and networking deliver e-learning in a more personalized, portable, and on-demand form on a global basis.

Multimedia technology allows an e-learner to "learn by asking"—typing in questions in keywords or conversational English. The answers or content are displayed immediately to the learner. So today's real-time learning environment is becoming best known for just-in-time knowledge acquisition, self-directivity, interactivity, and giving flexibility over the learning process. Yet not every student is attracted to this approach to learning. Some find it boring or intimidating.

MARKS OF MATURITY

This author has experienced five generations of computer system growth dating back to 1960 when the first business computer (IBM 1401) and computing language (COBOL) were born. Each generation brought improved speed, an easier English-like programming language, smaller-size hardware, and more user-oriented information systems. The move from the giant mainframe that once occupied entire floors of buildings to the personal computer that can be tucked under a standard office desk took two decades. In contrast, the move of e-commerce from infancy to maturity took less than a decade—quite an accomplishment.

Briefly, there are unique characteristics to early e-commerce that began in the early 1990s:

- Slow dial-up modems ran at 28K bits per second using voice (telephone) lines. Late in 1998, the 56K bits per second modem appeared, but that was still slow for the exponential growth in Web traffic.
- E-mail used as a tool for communication by convenience was a novelty. There was no structured purpose behind the attempt.
- From the e-merchant's end, inventory, parts, and components were scanned using bar codes for the fulfillment phase of the e-commerce life cycle.
- Digital products were a challenge to sell on the Internet. They spawned the beginning of digital piracy, especially in music.
- Big business reigned supreme, because it took deep pockets to set up Web sites and the accompanying technical infrastructure. Small business was mainly on the sidelines.
- E-commerce activities were primarily national, with limited international transactions beyond Canada or Mexico.

The mark of maturation for today's e-commerce is exemplified in several ways:

- The digital subscriber line (DSL) is now more common and is available at an attractive monthly rate. A DSL connection uses a piece of networking hardware similar to a network switch. The increase in broadband connections to homes is fulfilling the ultimate mission of e-commerce; that is, to do business from the home around the clock.
- E-mail is now the very connectivity of e-commerce—from customer to e-merchant to sellers and beyond. It is also the backbone of marketing and customer communication systems.
- Bar code scanning is on the way out, replaced by sophisticated biometric technology (fingerprint scanning and retina scanners) on smart cards to handle human and product traffic in a variety of situations.
- Legal downloading and distribution of music, video, and other digital products via the Web is increasing. Legal issues are covered in Chapter 12.
- Big business, as well as small- and medium-sized firms, can afford to develop a Web presence quickly, reliably, and at an affordable cost. Web sites range from the most complex, like Dell.com, to the simplest two- to four-page Web site of the local grocery store.
- E-commerce has gone international. With high-speed satellite communications, broadband, and the like, access and response times have shrunk down to two seconds or less.

WHAT IS E-COMMERCE?

Box 1.2 profiles an e-commerce legend, Jeff Bezos of Amazon.com. By careful evaluation of buying patterns, promotions, and selling, Bezos fine-tuned Amazon.com to become a highly respected Internet business. It has also become the model success story of e-commerce.

There are several ways of looking at e-commerce:

1. From a *communications* perspective, it is the ability to deliver products, services, information, or payments via networks like the Internet.

2. From an *interface* view, e-commerce means information and transaction exchanges: business-to-business (B2B), business-to-consumer (B2C), consumer-to-consumer (C2C), and business-to-government (B2G). (These are covered later in the chapter.)

3. As a *business process,* e-commerce means activities that support commerce electronically by networked connections. For example, business processes like manufacturing and inventory and business-to-business processes like supply chain management are managed by the same networks as business-to-consumer processes. (Supply chain management is covered later in the chapter.)

BOX 1.2

E-Commerce Trends: The Story of Amazon.com

In 1994, a young financial analyst by the name of Jeff Bezos was full of hope about the potential of doing business on the Internet. He sat down one evening and came up with a list of 20 products he believed would sell well on the Internet. Books were number one. Three years later he formed Amazon.com.

Bezos had never sold a book in his life, but he figured that books were small-ticket items that would be easy and inexpensive to ship. They are the type of product customers do not have to inspect before they decide to buy. Bezos figured that there were probably over five million book titles worldwide in a given year, and that no bookstore could conceivably stock more than a fraction of the total. He developed a strategic plan for selling books online.

You know the rest of the story. Bezos improved on the initial plan of selling books by capturing the comments and recommendations of buyers on the site—like the friendly salesperson in a store offering advice on which books to buy. The Web site tracks customer traffic, the number of visitors who access the site, how long they stay, what pages they click on, and so forth. By carefully evaluating buying patterns, promotions, and selling, Bezos fine-tuned Amazon.com to become a highly respected Internet business.

Surviving the 2001–2003 recession, Amazon.com began to expand beyond books into music, hardware, and electronics. In January 2003, Amazon experienced soaring sales and declared a second quarterly profit that shot its stock to $25 per share. For the first time since its inception in 1994, it began to have abundant cash flow to sustain day-to-day operations.

Today, the company has added a wide range of products, including cakes, cheese, and coffee. The food department features lobsters from Virginia's Chesapeake Bay and Omaha's famous steaks. Amazon's Web sites list over 200 merchants in its food department alone. Orders for food items are electronically sent to food merchants for delivery. Amazon takes a commission for simply being an intermediary. It is also an intermediary for products from companies such as Target, Toys "R"Us, and Office Depot.

4. From an *online* perspective, e-commerce is an electronic environment that allows sellers to buy and sell products, services, and information on the Internet. The products may be physical, like cars, or services like news or consulting.

5. As a *structure,* e-commerce deals with various media: data, text, Web pages, Internet telephony, and Internet desktop video.

6. As a *market,* e-commerce is a worldwide network. A local store can open a Web storefront and find the world at its doorstep—customers, suppliers, competitors, and payment services. Of course, an advertising presence is essential.

E-COMMERCE IS NOT E-BUSINESS

Ask any number of information technology professionals what e-business is and chances are you will get as many definitions. **E-business** is the conduct of business on the Internet, in supply-chain planning, tracking, fulfillment, invoicing, and payment. It includes buying and selling as well as servicing customers and collaborating with business partners (www.primode.com/glossary.html). Electronic information is used to boost performance and create value by forming new relationships between and among businesses and customers.

e-business: connecting critical business systems and constituencies directly via the Internet, extranets, and intranets.

E-business goes beyond a Web site on the Internet to affect all aspects of business, from strategy and process to trading partners and the ultimate consumer. It combines the resources of traditional information systems with the global reach of the Web.

In e-business, organizations have several goals in mind:

1. Reach new markets.

2. Create new products or services.

3. Build customer loyalty.

4. Enrich human capital.

5. Make the best use of existing and emerging technologies.

6. Achieve market leadership and competitive advantage.

One example of e-business is SAP—the world's leading provider of business software solutions, addressing the needs of small and midsize businesses as well as enterprise-scale suite solutions for global organizations. SAP has customers with an interest in integrating the major facets of the business, but such customers are brick and mortar businesses that want to integrate information within their divisions and applications. Further elaboration on e-business brings up the value-chain concept and supply-chain management, which is covered later in the chapter.

In contrast, **e-commerce** is selling goods and services on the retail level with anyone, anywhere, via the Internet. It includes new business opportunities that result in greater efficiency and more effective exchange of goods and services. The crux of the exchange is transactions—blocks of information exchanged between an e-merchant and a customer via the corporate Web site. An example of e-commerce is www.crutchfield.com or www.amazon.com; each e-firm uses a Web site to sell goods and services via the Internet.

transaction: a block of information exchanged between the merchant and its customers via the corporate Web site.

One reason why it is difficult to understand electronic commerce is the speed with which it has grown. It happened so quickly and in so many ways that even experts cannot compare it to anything from the past. Its impact has already exceeded that of radio in the 1920s, television in the 1950s, and personal computers in the 1980s. Every indicator points to a profound long-term impact on the world economy.

Unlike the traditional ways of doing business, EC has broken ground in several ways:

- Companies share information with competitors.
- Suppliers share information with buyers.
- Corporate procurement is no longer determined solely on price.
- Financial transactions occur with the involvement of banks.

Nowhere is EC changing the rules more profoundly and rapidly than in the banking industry. The surge of online banking calls into question the role of banks: Businesses and consumers now have more choices about how and where to pay bills. See www.uvacreditunion.org for a look at basic online banking services. They include money transfer from one account to another, looking up past history of deposits and withdrawals, and loan inquiries. Many larger banks like www.wachovia.com provide an image of the front and back of any check you may have written.

Cost savings, opportunism, and threats drive action and innovation even in the most conservative companies. These factors have influenced how companies reposition themselves to take advantage of opportunities that include establishing new service delivery channels and new markets for existing services. Leveraging the power of the Web means a shift from static pages to dynamic applications. For example, Web services that give merchants real-time access to bank card payment information rather than waiting for hard-copy bank statements are already available. J. P. Morgan has already replaced hardware codes with digital certificates that verify the identity of the sender, place a seal on a message, and provide proof that a transaction has occurred. The service saves the company at least $1 million in the process. Other Web benefits for a changed world are exemplified in Box 1.3.

BOX 1.3

E-Trade Beats the Clock

E-trade Financial Corporation and other online stock brokerages are at war over how fast they can execute a trade. Ameritrade Holding Corporation kicked off the execution promise game in 2001 by guaranteeing a turnaround of 10 seconds or less. E-trade countered with a nine-second guarantee, and since then it has all been downhill.

Last year, Ameritrade promised to complete trades within five seconds, and in March, E-trade lowered its pledge to two seconds. A spokesman said the firm will forgo less than $1 million in trading commissions this year as a result of the guarantee. The company collected $191 million in commissions in the first six months of this year.

E-trade has 3.5 million customer accounts and completes more than 100,000 trades each day, on average. The company says most of its trades are completed in less than a second, a remarkable achievement for a complex operation that spans multiple computers, routers, and applications, not all of them controlled by E-trade.

Source: Excerpted from Gary H. Anthes, "E-trade Beats the Clock," *Computerworld*, Sept. 27, 2004, 27.

THE DRIVERS

E-commerce firms operate in a volatile and highly competitive environment that forces change in business strategies and in the distinctive competencies required to stay in business. Unpredictable change in competitors' products and in customers' needs and expectations represent market volatility. Several drivers support e-commerce survival and growth:

1. **Digital convergence.** The digital revolution has made it possible for digital devices to communicate with one another. The Internet's massive growth during the past decade — a creation of market forces — will continue. Steady increase in computer power and decreasing cost made navigation on the Internet a reality (see Figure 1.1).

2. **Anytime, anywhere, anyone.** Today's e-commerce is available to anyone, anywhere in the world, 24 hours a day, seven days a week (24/7). E-commerce ties together the industrial sector, merchants, the service sector, and content providers using text, multimedia, video, and other technologies (see Figure 1.2).

3. **Changes in organizations.** More and more of today's businesses empower front-line workers to do the kind of work once performed by junior management. The trend is toward partnering owners and managers across departments to develop a chain of relationships that adds value to the enterprise. Downsizing large organizations, outsourcing specialized tasks, shortening product life cycles, and encouraging cross-functional business processes all require better communication between the departments that perform these functions. E-commerce, which makes communication easy, is an ideal method of making these connections (see Figure 1.3).

4. **Increasing pressure on operating costs and profit margins.** Global competition and the proliferation of products and services worldwide have added unusual

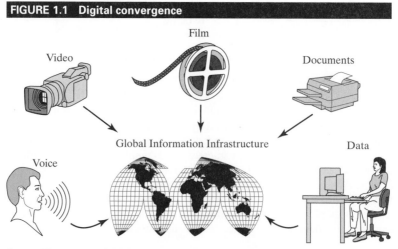

FIGURE 1.1 Digital convergence

Film

Video

Documents

Global Information Infrastructure

Data

Voice

Source: The concept of EC business drivers is courtesy of Dr. Richard Welke, professor of CIS, Georgia State University.

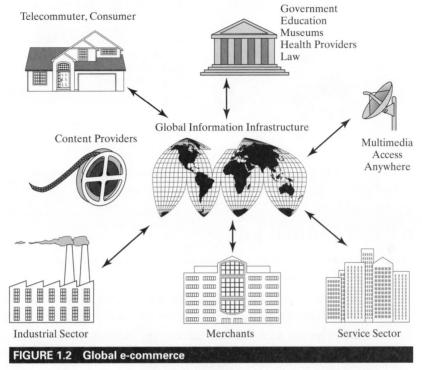

Telecommuter, Consumer

Government
Education
Museums
Health Providers
Law

Content Providers

Global Information Infrastructure

Multimedia
Access
Anywhere

Industrial Sector   Merchants   Service Sector

FIGURE 1.2   Global e-commerce

Source: Courtesy of Dr. Richard Welke, professor of CIS, Georgia State University.

pressure on operating costs and profit margins. E-commerce addresses these concerns quickly, efficiently, and at low cost (see Figure 1.4).

5. **Demand for customized products and services.** Today's customers are collectively demanding higher quality and better performance, including a customized way of producing, delivering, and paying for goods and services. Mass customization puts

- Empowerment of front-line workers
- Informating of key business activities
- Outsourcing and downsizing of large organizations
- Partnering
- Cross-functional business processes
- Virtual designs

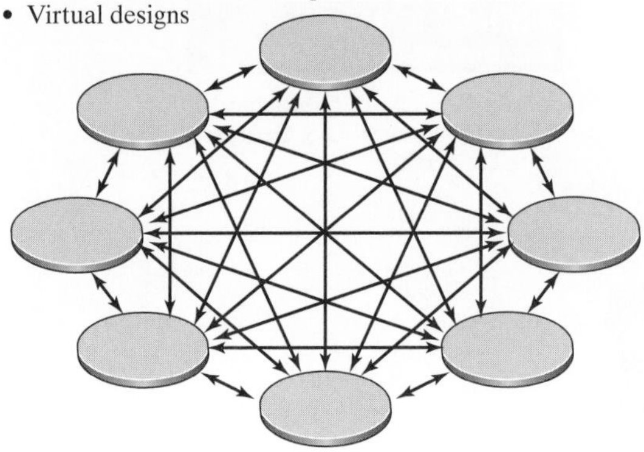

FIGURE 1.3   Changes in organizational makeup

Source: Courtesy of Dr. Detmar Straub, professor of CIS, Georgia State University.

- Global competitors
- Proliferation of commodity-like
  products and services

FIGURE 1.4   Increasing pressure on costs and margins

Source: Courtesy of Dr. Richard Welke, professor of CIS, Georgia State University.

pressure on firms to handle customized requests on a mass-market scale. Firms that don't move with the trend will eventually lose out (see Figure 1.5).

MYTHS YOU SHOULD KNOW

There is still confusion about what e-commerce can or cannot do. The following are myths that need to be addressed:

1. **Setting up a Web site is easy.** True, except it is not easy to ensure performance. There are technology, networking infrastructure, and design criteria to consider.

2. **E-commerce means no more mass marketing.** The Web is the first commercial channel that enables cost-effective, one-to-one marketing on a large scale, but a business must still market its Web presence.

3. **E-commerce means a new economy.** There is no "new" economy, but there is something new in the real economy.

4. **E-commerce is revolutionary.** Inasmuch as Internet technology created a new way to shop, most rules of retailing still apply. Merchandise is obtained from vendors, warehoused, and shipped to customers. Some of it is returned. Unfortunately, many Internet retailers (i-tailers) spend a disproportionate amount on the "revolutionary" tasks of Web site construction and marketing and too little on customer support and fulfillment.

5. **E-commerce is a commercial fad that crashed in 2000.** No question, the dot-com frenzy crashed in 2000. But the Internet continues to reshape businesses and the

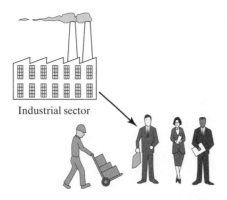

Industrial sector

FIGURE 1.5   Mass customization

Source: Courtesy of Dr. Richard Welke, professor of CIS, Georgia State University.

information systems that run them. It is an infrastructure for a new way of doing business.

6. **All products can be sold online using identical business models.** Different products require different selling techniques and customer support. What works for book selling does not work as well for furniture, although it is getting better with improved screen color, texture clarity, and guaranteed returns. Internet sales should still follow different business models depending on the product.

7. **Build it and they will come.** Web sites have to be promoted just like any other business. Customers bought with price promotions and giveaways are rarely loyal customers. The moment a competitor lowers the price, customers click over to that site.

8. **The middleman is out.** Intermediaries are the traditional organizations that deliver products to the retailer from the manufacturer or the wholesaler. Web intermediaries are resellers of products. Despite a direct interface between consumers and merchants, new intermediaries continue to surface on the Web.

ADVANTAGES AND ISSUES IN E-COMMERCE

The digital age and the digital revolution affect everyone. Like the telephone and the fax machine, PCs and printers have become essential ingredients in doing business; as have e-mail, Web storefronts, and integrated digital communications. The much-talked-about "digital convergence" will drive all these pieces of hardware into one digital platform, whether it is a computer connected to the Internet or a computer interacting with other computers, because such connectivity will prove to be more efficient and effective. The case of Amazon.com versus Barnes & Noble, in which Barnes & Noble sued Amazon for billing itself as the largest bookstore, demonstrates that the very definition of "store" must be reevaluated.

Any way you look at it, e-commerce has become a mature industry and is still growing. As soon as you click onto the Net, some attractive banner advertisement invites you to its Web site and tries to sell you products or services. Areas that are growing by leaps and bounds are financial services, entertainment, travel, medicine, and retailing. Even Uncle Sam wants e-commerce (see Box 1.4). The Office of Management and Budget (OMB) projects the federal government will spend nearly $65 billion on technology and Web service in fiscal 2006. That is a 40 percent increase from just two years ago. Most of the federal agencies that make up the Homeland Security Department proposed technology infrastructure spending increases for fiscal 2006. The federal government has become a "click-and-mortar" enterprise, from customer interfaces to supply chain.

ADVANTAGES

The 2000 burst of the e-bubble certainly tarnished the once glamorous dot-com economy. Today's journalists and many investors cringe at the thought of more e-inspired goods and services. Yet the pros in large companies like Wal-Mart and Ford see opportunity and hope in a better tomorrow for e-commerce. In 2004 when Google.com went public, the initial offer of $85 per share surged to over $200 in less than three months.

BOX 1.4

Uncle Sam Wants E-Commerce

For all the complaints about government being behind the times, the era of e-government is here: Government agencies are optimizing their internal computer operations. As a logical next step, the possibilities of B2G (business-to-government) e-commerce are emerging as governments look at moving procurement online. The initiatives span all levels of government: The Clinton administration pushed to move federal procurement online by 2003, and even local school districts are buying supplies online.

The Gartner Group projects rapid growth, with online government procurement increasing by 400 percent, to $6.2 billion, in five years. The market for providing these B2G services is wide open; a clear leader has yet to emerge. However, success in the government arena requires several adjustments for potential market entrants accustomed to fast-moving, market-driven clients.

The government of the state of Washington provides a good example of the cost savings potential. The state shifted its procurement to what it calls its Buysense system, designed by American Management Systems (AMS), a Fairfax, Virginia-based consulting firm with strong ties to the government. Washington is saving money by buying in greater bulk, controlling renegade purchasing, and reducing paperwork; AMS charges a small transaction fee to each side. Although the program started only last June, Washington is already a model for other governments to follow.

Source: Excerpted from John Furth, "Uncle Sam Wants e-Commerce," www.line56.com.

Three in five customers make online purchases on a regular basis. That is double the number who said so four years ago. Among the drivers behind the growth in Web shoppers is convenience. Most e-shoppers go online to check prices before they buy. Travel reservations or tickets are the most popular purchases, while the least popular online activities today are downloading books. The bottom activities in the ranking continue to be home grocery deliveries and buying pet food or stamps online.

E-commerce provides several advantages.

LOWER COST TO THE E-MERCHANT. Other factors considered, doing e-business on the Internet is cost effective; it reduces logistical problems and gives small business equal visibility with giants like Amazon.com, General Motors, or Bank of America. In a commercial bank, a basic over-the-counter transaction costs $1.10 to process; over the Internet, the same transaction costs about one penny. Every financial transaction eventually turns into an electronic process. The sooner it makes the conversion, the more cost-effective the transaction becomes.

ECONOMY. By any standard, e-commerce is economical. Unlike the brick-and-mortar environment, there is no rental of physical store space, insurance, or infrastructure investment. All you need is an idea, a unique product, and a well-designed Web storefront to reach your cyber-customers, and a partner to make the delivery.

HIGHER MARGINS. E-commerce means higher margins. For example, the cost of processing a conventional airline ticket is $8. According to a local travel agency, processing the same ticket (called an e-ticket) over the Web costs $1. Along with higher margins, businesses can gain more control and flexibility and save time when manual transactions are done electronically.

BETTER CUSTOMER SERVICE. E-commerce means better and quicker customer service. Web-based customer service makes customers happy. Instead of calling a company on the phone, holding for 10 minutes, then connecting to a clerk to tap into your account, customers have direct access to their accounts over the Web. It saves time, even though it might not be cheap. Competitive distinction alone could easily outweigh the cost of maintaining the Web infrastructure. In the long run, it is a win-win proposition.

For companies that do business with other firms, adding customer service to the Web is a competitive advantage. The overnight package delivery service, where tracking numbers allow customers to check the whereabouts of a package online, is one good example.

QUICK COMPARISON SHOPPING. E-commerce helps consumers to comparison shop. Automated online shopping assistants called *hopbots* scour Net stores and find deals on everything from applesauce to printer ribbons. For example, mySimon (www.mysimon.com) "learns" the navigation preferences of its runner (a tool that fills out the request form asking the bot to search Web pages for solutions). It lets you enter basic keywords such as "lady's dress" to search its database of Web stores for the best buys.

hopbot: automated online shopping assistant.

PRODUCTIVITY GAINS. E-commerce means productivity gains. Weaving the Web throughout an organization means improved productivity. IBM incorporated the Web into every corner of the firm—products, marketing, and practices. It figured it would save over $800 million by letting customers find answers to technical questions via its Web site (see www.IBM.com for recent details).

TEAMWORK. E-commerce means working together. E-mail is one example of how people collaborate to exchange information and work on solutions. It has transformed the way organizations interact with suppliers, vendors, business partners, and customers. More interaction means better overall results. The more interactive and collaborative-rich the Web site is, the higher the payoff for the business.

GROWTH IN KNOWLEDGE MARKETS. E-commerce helps create knowledge markets. Small groups inside big firms can be funded with seed money to develop new ideas. DaimlerChrysler has created small teams to look for new trends and products. A Silicon Valley team is doing consumer research on electric cars and advising car designers.

INFORMATION SHARING, CONVENIENCE, AND CONTROL. Electronic marketplaces improve information sharing between merchants and customers and promote quick, just-in-time deliveries. Customers and merchants save money; are online 24 hours a day, 7 days a week; experience no traffic jams, no crowds, and do not have to carry heavy shopping bags.

Control is another major driving factor. Instead of banks controlling the relationship with the customers, they can have more control of their banking needs via Web sites. Banks like Bank of America and Wells Fargo now give customers access to their accounts via the Web.

CUSTOMIZATION.   Digital products are highly customizable. They are easy to reorganize, revise, or edit. With information about consumer tastes and preferences, products can be differentiated (customized) and matched to individual needs.

ISSUES AND CONSTRAINTS

With advantages and benefits are problems and issues to consider before plunging into the Web business.

THE COST FACTOR.   To set up an e-commerce infrastructure, you need cash. Beyond a sophisticated interactive Web site, you need networks, servers, terminals, software, staffing, and training. Transaction costs are another issue. The electronic marketplace appears to be a perfect market, where worldwide sellers and buyers share information and trade without intermediaries. New types of intermediaries like electronic malls that guarantee product quality, mediators for bargaining, and certification authorities to ensure the legitimacy of transactions add to transaction costs..

SECURITY.   With spamming, spying, file corruption, and malicious misuse, no company can afford to do business online without protection via firewalls, specialized antivirus products, and the like. For millions of potential cyber-customers, the fear of credit card theft and identity theft continues to be a concern. The goal of an online merchant is to assure customers secure lines and secure sites that will protect their privacy, whatever the transaction.

SYSTEM AND DATA INTEGRITY.   Data protection and the integrity of the system that handles the data are serious concerns. Computer viruses are rampant, with new viruses discovered every day. Viruses cause unnecessary delays, file backups, storage problems, and the like. The danger of hackers accessing files and corrupting accounts adds more stress to an already complex operation.

SYSTEM SCALABILITY.   A business develops an interactive interface with customers via a Web site. After a while, statistical analysis determines whether visitors to the site are one-time or recurring customers. If the company expects two million customers and six million shows up, Web site performance is bound to experience degradation, slowdown, and eventually loss of customers. To keep this problem from happening, a Web site must be scalable or upgradable on a regular basis.

scalability: ability of a computer system, database infrastructure, or network to be upgraded to new standards.

E-COMMERCE IS NOT FREE.   For a long time, success stories in e-commerce have favored large businesses with deep pockets and smart funding. Small retailers that go head-to-head with e-commerce giants could be in for a surprise. As in the brick-and-mortar environment, they simply cannot compete on price or product offering.

Brand loyalty is related to this issue. Brands are expected to lower search costs, build trust, and communicate quality. Users remain suspicious of search engines for locating product information; instead, they rely on recognized dot-com brands for purchases.

FULFILLMENT AND CUSTOMER RELATIONS PROBLEMS.   Tales of shipping delays, merchandise mix-ups, and Web sites crashing under pressure continue to be problems in e-tailing. Customer confidence in e-commerce's ability to deliver during heavy shopping seasons continues to be a concern. Even happy customers say the experience could be improved. Customer relations management (CRM) is taking on high priority as more and more e-merchants have found that without prompt delivery of products and quick response to customer complaints, they are not going to make any headway in the e-industry. CRM is covered in some detail in Chapter 9.

The interpersonal part of e-commerce between e-merchants and customers continues to be a setback. Many Web sites lack a phone contact to discuss order problems with humans. This is also the case with help desks that are designed to help customers wade through technical problems. The lines are either busy or simply do not answer. This is directly related to fulfillment problems, when customers have a difficult time receiving or returning items purchased over a merchant's Web site. The best approach is to have customers who purchase items via the company's Web site go to the nearest company's brick-and-mortar store and settle the complaint in person. This is what has been recently called "click'n brick" business.

PRODUCTS PEOPLE RESIST BUYING ONLINE.   Think of the Web sites furniture.com or living.com, whose venture capitalists invested millions in selling home furnishings online. Furniture.com's site enabled browsers to design floor plans using existing furniture on the Web site. But in the case of a sofa, you'd want to sit on it, feel the texture of the fabric, and so on. Besides the "sofa road test" factor, online furniture stores faced costly returns and deliveries that could not be expedited via FedEx or UPS. Living.com folded in August 2000 and Furniture.com followed a few months later.

From this lesson we learned to focus on specific business models that process standardized items with strong brand identity and require no inspection or comparative analysis. Examples are airline tickets, books, office supplies, and brand-name hardware. Each commodity item is standardized and well known. They are hard to distinguish from the same products or services provided by brick-and-mortar sellers. Buying these items on the Internet becomes a matter of price and convenience.

We also learned that when personal selling skills are required, such as in selling real estate, traditional commerce continues to be a better way to sell. A combination of electronic and traditional commerce strategies is ideal in situations when the business process involves a commodity that requires personal inspection. For example, people looking for a standardized item like a Sony 52" TV first visit a retailer like Best Buy. Then they shop on the Internet for the same item, hoping to buy it for significant savings.

In today's growing e-commerce business, the trend is to look more for value than price. The key question is what value to get by purchasing an item via the Internet compared to buying from a local dealer. More and more local dealers are beginning to match Internet prices to stay alive. They explain to the consumer the value they're getting such as processing rebates, local service or in-house repairs, 30-day guaranteed returns, and so on, at the same price as the Internet. Of course, the customer saves on shipping charges, but pays the sales tax.

CULTURAL, LANGUAGE, AND TRUST ISSUES.   In addition to these generic problems and drawbacks, there are global issues as well. When e-commerce and the Internet went global, there was an obvious pressure to adapt e-marketing, e-products, and interfaces to cultural expectations and constraints. *Culture* is the set of norms and innate values of a community, a society, or a region. For example, in the Middle

East, where the norm is to buy a house with cash rather than a cashier's check or via a loan, it is difficult to trust electronic transactions via credit cards. Similarly, when it comes to purchasing flowers, in eastern European countries, the bouquet should contain an odd number of flowers. The North American concept of a dozen roses simply doesn't fly because the number is even.

A firm launching a business in a new country must be aware of the culture as well as the language of that culture. Trust is another issue that needs to be addressed. When the Internet is perceived to be an unreliable environment with a great number of anonymous users, customers are cautious in communicating via the Internet. Since the Internet and the Web are essentially an information space that reflects not just human knowledge but also human relationships, it will soon become obvious that trust relationships among people, organizations, and computers are too complex to ignore. Culture, language, and trust issues are expanded in Chapters 2 and 8.

CORPORATE VULNERABILITY. The availability of product details, catalogs, and other information about a business through its Web site makes it vulnerable to access by the competition. The idea of extracting business intelligence from the competition's Web pages is called *Web farming*, a term coined by Richard Hackathorn.

Web farming: systematically refining information resources on the Web for business intelligence gathering.

LACK OF A BLUEPRINT FOR HANDLING E-COMMERCE. There is a continuing shortage of *e-literate* people in the workplace. Most of the surveys conducted in 2003 and 2004 conclude that few key managers have e-commerce skills, Internet experience, or foresight. They also have a tough time attracting people wanting to take advantage of online opportunities. Traditional organizational structures and cultures were also found to inhibit progress in e-commerce.

HIGH RISK OF INTERNET START-UP. Many stories unfolded in 1999 and 2000 about successful executives in established firms leaving for Internet start-ups, only to find out that their "get rich" dream with a dot-com was just that—a dream. With the recession over, many retailers are rethinking re-entry.

BENEFITS AND LIMITATIONS OF THE INTERNET

The Internet is the enabler of e-commerce, just as the highway is the enabler for the automobile. Managers use it to glean intelligence about rivals, monitor sales, and so on. At Cisco Systems, for example, the company's chief executive required executives from various departments to demonstrate how they would use the Web. Cisco and other companies like Dell Computers and Microsoft's Expedia Travel Service use Internet technology in their businesses: Dell, for example, sells more than $8 million worth of computers a day from its Web site, and Expedia's service generates more than $16 million a month the same way.

MAIN BENEFITS

MARKETING AND SELLING PRODUCTS AND SERVICES. The "buy and sell" aspect of Internet commerce has attracted more media attention than any other networked activity to date. The highest sales volume was in business-to business commerce, and it is growing. The next highest sales were to government agencies, followed by colleges and universities. In terms of revenue, business-to-consumer ranks fourth in Internet revenue.

When it comes to advertising and reaching customers quickly and cheaply, the Internet is "marketing heaven." You can reach anyone, anywhere, without paying extra for distance or duration. The Internet is host to thousands of electronic publications that provide promotional opportunities for any business. Web sites attract millions of readers on a daily basis. Companies use the Internet to send electronic mass mailings to customers and prospects. They also send surveys to selected customers, notices about special sales, and the like.

DOING BUSINESS FAST.   E-selling is conducted in minutes rather than hours or days. Can you imagine having to wait on the phone to place an order or fill out a form for mailing? Speed compresses business processes and promotes the growth of a customer base.

GATHERING OPINIONS AND TRYING OUT NEW IDEAS.   The Internet is an ideal place for trying out new ideas at low cost. Interactive surveys provide quick feedback. Many online opinion polls provide real-time statistics to the user after a computer package analyzes the user's response in real time.

Companies unsure about going all out to do business on the Internet can start small by designing a "who we are" Web site to gain online experience and exposure. The site can be used for sales promotions and to build customer awareness of the company's people, products, and services.

LEVELING THE PLAYING FIELD.   Even mere presence is a benign way of expanding a business and creating new selling opportunities to customers who otherwise would have gone to the competition. In an interview session with a client, here is what one merchant said about her experience in Web commerce: "The Internet is a great equalizer. It makes me feel as big as the guy next door. I might still be small, but it encourages me to be very good at what we do in the business that we're in."

PROMOTING A PAPER-FREE ENVIRONMENT.   In addition to cutting down on the paper used for catalogs and promotional material, company memos, employee handbooks, and reports can be placed on the company's intranet and retrieved or circulated electronically at any time by authorized personnel.

PROVIDING SUPERIOR CUSTOMER SERVICE AND SUPPORT RESOURCES. Most Web sites generate customer feedback via comments, suggestions, and complaints. The challenge for the online merchant is to have adequate staff to address feedback in a timely fashion. Customer relationship management (CRM) is picking up a lot of slack in this area. CRM is covered in Chapter 9.

frequently asked questions (FAQs): answers to repeatedly asked questions that a business places in a simple list on the Web site so users can find solutions any time.

A common support resource is the **frequently asked questions (FAQ)** list. An FAQ list eliminates having staff answer the same questions over and over again. If a new question comes up, the answer is added to the list. Using e-mail to handle customer support also frees company personnel from being tied to a telephone.

EFFICIENCY AND UNEQUALED COST-EFFECTIVENESS. For many niche products and services, the Web is the only cost-effective sales method available. A commercial Web site also can provide addresses, directions, online order tracking, and the like, reducing phone calls, phone interruptions, and staff time. From a marketing view, the Web site provides user information more quickly, in a more timely fashion, and at the convenience of the user, regardless of location or distance.

SUPPORTING MANAGERIAL FUNCTIONS, SPREADING IDEAS, EASE OF TECHNICAL SUPPORT. The traditional managerial functions of planning, organizing, directing, and controlling require managers to collect, evaluate, and distribute management information, especially in organizations with branches worldwide. The Internet sends business information through a company's networks and across networks around the globe. E-mail is a convenient tool for managers to reach employees, bosses, customers, and suppliers quickly and at no charge.

The Internet has spawned discussion groups, chat rooms, and online interactive sessions in which technical and managerial staff evaluate products and processes, and arrive at value-added decisions that result in lower costs and increased performance.

Better technical support is one of the key benefits of linking to the Internet. IBM, for example, offers customer and technical support, fixes bugs, and handles software upgrades on the Internet. Thousands of free software programs are available for anyone to download.

Market research firms are a natural for the Web. Credit bureaus, lawyers, private detectives, accountants, baby-sitters, and teachers are all examples of people or agencies that use the Internet for scheduling or advertising their services. The Internet continues to deliver thousands of databases of research data, ranging from topics such as medicine, vehicles, and food preparation, to suggestions for the ideal baby diaper, to hundreds of research and development (R&D) discussion groups. For thousands of research journals, automated searches through current and back issues are available in minutes rather than the days and weeks it once took to find the information in a brick-and-mortar library. White papers that research centers place on their Web sites provide current information about the latest developments in various fields.

Company research is no different. Companies use the Internet to seek information about customer tastes and preferences, to profile a customer base for a new product, or to test a new concept to see if it is worth developing. All of this can be done in a matter of days rather than the months it once took to get the same results.

TRIGGERING NEW BUSINESSES. Mere Web presence is bound to trigger one type of business activity or another. This includes business-to-business, business-to-government agencies at all levels, business-to-colleges and universities, as well as business-to-consumers. For example, a tiny commercial filter maker in Lynchburg, Virginia, landed a $6 million contract with the government of Saudi Arabia from the Internet.

PROVIDING WEB SERVICES. Technology is the enabler of e-service or Web service. Web services are essentially business services, composed of standards that allow different platforms, operating systems, and languages to exchange information or carry out a business process together. They also make it easier for people to construct and integrate applications via the Web. The whole concept is a customer-centric concept. It is based on reducing costs through automation and increased efficiency and an emphasis on maximizing revenue by improving customer relationship. Web services are covered in Chapter 10.

LIMITATIONS

Like any system with unique benefits, the Internet and the World Wide Web also have unique limitations. The following discussion highlights the importance of continuing to work on these limitations in the interest of advancing use of the Internet in general and the Web in particular.

SECURITY AND PRIVACY.   Key questions that are brought up continually by online consumers are: "How do I know I am paying for a product on a secure line? How do I know the Web site assures me privacy for the product I am buying?" Various devices have been embedded into Web storefronts to ensure security. (For a full discussion of Internet security, see Chapter 13.)

In terms of privacy, according to a September 2003 study of major Web sites by the Federal Trade Commission (FTC), only 20 percent met FTC standards for protecting consumer privacy, but the study also found a 90 percent compliance rate by Internet companies for posting their privacy policies.

FAKES AND FORGERIES.   The availability of the Internet has spawned the online sale of fake passports, Social Security cards, driver's licenses, college diplomas, birth certificates, and even IDs for police officers and FBI agents. Some of them are so authentic looking that it takes a real expert to detect the forgery. This new and growing Internet problem accounts for more than 30 percent of all fake ID documents in the United States.

There are three levels of fake-ID procurement: Some Web sites sell authentic-looking documents in the customer's name. Others sell templates that allow customers to make their own phony documents. The third level is the do-it-yourself counterfeiter. Thomas W. Seitz, who used phony documents to get car loans, currently is serving a three-year state prison term for theft by deception and forgery.

CYBER TERRORISM.   The September 11, 2001, terrorist attacks struck fear in the heart of America and made us rethink our safety, security, and well-being. The attacks of Al-Qaeda inspired a newfound sense of vulnerability, demonstrating that terrorists of all types may be knocking on our door and threatening us.

A new generation of Al-Qaeda members and of other terrorist organizations— foreign and domestic—is growing up with technology. Cyberspace, which is an invaluable tool for economic growth and promotion of civil liberties, and a tool to improve everyday life, can also be at a forum for expressing malcontent against governments, businesses, and people, potentially in devastatingly harmful ways. To protect against attacks, intrusion detection systems, firewalls, and encryption methods may provide adequate shields to stymie terrorist endeavors. These tools are covered in detail later in the text.

PROBLEMS AND STRESS.   Growing e-business has put increasing demand on existing network infrastructures. Managers have been under pressure to upgrade and maintain more complex networks to ensure site performance, while at the same time keeping costs from skyrocketing. Regardless of what tools are used, there is still the nagging headache of deciding whether to add a second and third shift to address network problems when they occur.

Many of today's Internet companies continue to have problems processing and fulfilling online customer orders. The main cause is the merchant's link with the vendor and the vendor's responsiveness. For example, the faulty technical infrastructure between a high-visibility online mail-order company and its vendors resulted in shipping duplicates of thousands of customer orders before the error was found months later. The company went bankrupt, with losses in the millions.

For the small retailer, it is a struggle to compete with the giants on the Internet. Many barely break even; others show a profit, but at a high cost. Small businesses cannot afford the cost of maintaining and upgrading Web sites and the security and other issues that must be addressed around the clock.

Despite sophisticated FAQs, e-mail, and other technologies, customers still have problems with simple issues like returning unwanted items and securing information (e.g., "No one told me your company gives a discount for items received past the promised delivery date"). The heavy demand for customer service also puts added pressure on customer service personnel.

In addition, people will not buy certain products online. Items like houses, cars, and diamonds have yet to make headway on the Internet. Diamonds are best seen before purchase. People have found that they can't pick a dream house and close on the property with a mouse click. Even if they were to do so, a slew of state and local regulations require physical presence and legal processing in person.

A thicket of state and federal regulations about shipping alcohol over state lines poses a serious constraint to selling wine on the Net. WineShopper.com, a San Francisco start-up backed by Amazon.com, is tailoring its business model to the interlocking regulatory framework, but so far, the going has not been easy.

Despite this success, or perhaps because of it, the surge of e-commerce and e-business on the Internet has far outgrown the availability of qualified technical people to handle the technology and the traffic.

ABUSES IN THE WORKPLACE. In addition to being a channel for communication and commercial exchange, the Internet provides employees with the world's greatest playground and provides distractions in cubicles and the workplace. One way of looking at non-work-related surfing (also called *cyberloafing*) is that a certain amount of playful use of computer applications can contribute to learning, which could have potential value to the job or to the organization. The deviation from the immediate job might be the break that makes happy and productive workers.

Yet a conservative organization is likely to look at it differently. Any time spent away from the job is unnecessary waste and should be addressed in a serious way. In fact, some psychologists have suggested that Internet access in the workplace could transform some employees into Internet junkies.

In either case, Internet abuse has become rampant. This is especially the case when employees are caught using the Internet to download pornography and other illicit or immoral material. The question then is, does the company have the right to regulate, snoop at, or monitor employee Internet traffic? This issue along with work/play ethics will be addressed in Chapter 12 on legal, ethical, and international issues.

One conclusion is that Internet access must be managed properly and profession-ally based on policies and standards. If an employer is to monitor employee e-mail traf-fic, for example, employees should be informed in what ways they are being monitored. Companies also should back up policies with consistent disciplinary action. The IT department that carries out the monitoring should establish an open line with company managers to keep them abreast of developments, violations, and the like.

ROLE OF E-STRATEGY

The road map for a successful e-commerce business is identifying the critical success factors (CSFs) and developing a realistic strategy for the business. IBM identified four CSFs that make e-commerce work in any industry:

1. A sound strategy that has the full support of top management
2. A clear goal of long-term customer relationships and value
3. Making full use of the Internet and related technologies
4. A scalable and integrated business process and infrastructure

We shall see in Chapter 16 that the first step to becoming an e-commerce business is adopting a sustainable business strategy based on unique opportunities to provide value for the firm. To do so requires a clear understanding of the company, the industry in which it does business, and available Internet technologies. As a matter of common sense, the strategy should be difficult to duplicate, have high barriers to entry for com-petitors, and high switching costs for customers.

To ensure a successful e-commerce business, a realistic strategy is a must. The objectives of the business should be based on the technology in use at the time and a working budget. The resulting Web site should reflect the company's current image, because e-commerce is an extension of any business. In the final analysis, you need to build a community of loyal customers, keep track of their needs and preferences, and make your site responsive, easy to use, and easy to navigate.

VALUE CHAIN IN E-COMMERCE

In e-commerce, many business processes and activities go unnoticed by the consumer and are often taken for granted. Within an online merchant's business, value-added activities work together to make the business-to-consumer (B2C) interface operational. The adoption of e-commerce tools has led to the e-commerce value chain. In this section, we systematically analyze a company's **value chain** and how it makes commerce on the Internet a reality.

value chain: a way of orga-nizing the activities of a business so that each activ-ity adds value (*value-added* activity) or productivity to the total operation of the business.)

In 1985 Michael Porter wrote a book called *Competitive Advantage: Creating and Sustaining Superior Performance.* In the book, he introduced the concept of the value chain. It is a strategic tool for identifying how the critical components of a business tie together to deliver value for the business across the value-chain process. Businesses receive raw materials as input, add value to them through various processes, and sell the finished product as

The Value Chain for American Airlines

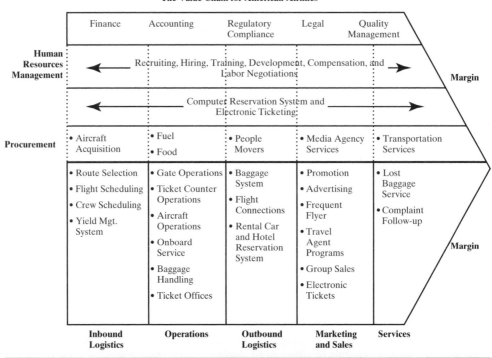

FIGURE 1.6 Value chain—an example

output to customers. This means that organizations are *open systems*. They do not consist of isolated sets of functions. They are a chain of value-creating activities that assure competitive advantages by the way they deliver value to the customer. A communication process that extends from a firm backward to suppliers and forward to customers ties all sorts of activities together—therefore, the value chain. (See Figure 1.6.)

Competitive advantage is achieved when an organization links the activities in its value chain more cheaply and more effectively than its competitors. For example, the purchasing function assists the production activity to ensure that raw materials and other supplies are available on time and meet the requirements of the products to be manufactured. The manufacturing function, in turn, has the responsibility to produce quality products that the sales staff can depend on. The human resource function must hire, retain, and develop the right personnel to ensure continuity in manufacturing, sales, and other areas of the business. Bringing in qualified people contributes to stability, continuity, and integrity of operations throughout the firm.

With all this in mind, communication plays a key role in developing linkages to improve value within the broader spectrum of the supplier's and the customer's value chain activities. For example, an order from marketing creates information for manufacturing, public relations, and service. These connectivities or linkages are passed backward to the supplier(s) and forward to the customer to inform him or her of expected shipping and delivery times.

There is no time sequence or special sequence of activities before a business is considered successful or effective. The idea is to link different activities in such a way that the value-added output of one activity (department, process, etc.) contributes to the input of another activity. The integration of these activities results in an organization fine-tuned for profitability, growth, and long-term relationships with customers.

> Value Activities: The physically and technologically distinct activities a firm performs, including both primary and support activities. Value-chain analysis reveals opportunities to add value by improving cost, responsiveness to customers, efficiency, quality, reliability, and integrity.
>
> Support Activities: Activities that support primary activities and each other by providing purchased inputs, technology, human resources, and other firm functions.
>
> Primary Activities: Activities involved in the physical creation of a product or service and its sale, transfer to buyer, and after-sale assistance.

PRIMARY ACTIVITIES

According to Porter, the primary activities of a business are:

1. **Inbound logistics.** These are procurement activities—vendor selection, comparative shopping, negotiating supply contracts, and just-in-time arrival of goods. They represent the supply side of the business. In e-commerce, the business must be capable of exchanging data with suppliers quickly, regardless of the electronic format.

2. **Operations.** This is the actual conversion of raw materials received into finished products. It includes machining, packaging, assembly, equipment maintenance, testing, printing, and facility operations. This production activity provides added value for the marketing function. Operational activities are the point in the value chain where the value is added. These happen in the back office where the pizza is baked, the PCs are assembled, or the stock trades are executed. Data are shared at maximum network speed among internal and external partners involved in the value-adding processes.

3. **Outbound logistics.** This activity represents the actual storing, distributing, and shipping of the final product. It involves warehousing, materials handling, shipping, and timely delivery to the ultimate retailer or customer. The output of this activity ties in directly with marketing and sales.

4. **Marketing and sales.** This activity deals with the ultimate customer. It includes advertising, product promotion, sales management, identifying the product's customer base, and distribution channels. The output of this activity could trigger increased production, more advertising, and so forth.

5. **Service.** This activity focuses on after-sale service to the customer. It includes testing, maintenance, repairs, warranty work, and replacement parts. The output of this activity means satisfied customers, improved image of the product and the business, and potential for increased production, sales, and so on.

Primary activities are not enough. A business unit needs support activities to make sure the primary activities are carried out. Imagine, for example, a manufacturing concern with no people or with poorly skilled employees.

SUPPORT ACTIVITIES

The key support activities in the value chain are:

1. **Corporate infrastructure.** This activity is the backbone of the business unit. It includes general management, accounting, finance, planning, legal services, and quality management. It is most often pictured in an organization chart showing the relationships among the different positions, the communications network, and the authority structure. Obviously, each position holder must add value to those above as well as below.

2. **Human resources.** This is the unique activity of matching the right people to the job. It involves recruitment, retention, career path development, compensation, training and development, and benefits administration. The output of this activity affects virtually every other activity in the company.

3. **Technology development.** This activity adds value in the way it improves the product and the business processes in the primary activities. The output of this activity contributes to the product quality, integrity, and reliability, which make life easier for the sales force and for customer relations.

4. **Procurement.** This activity focuses on the purchasing function and how well it ensures the availability of quality raw material for production.

There are several questions to consider when analyzing value chain activities:

- What type of activity is being performed? Does it add value? Does it ensure the quality of other activities?
- How does the activity add value to the customer?
- Could the same activity be reconfigured or performed in a different way?
- What inputs are used? Is the expected output being produced?
- Is the activity vital? Could it be outsourced, deleted completely, or combined with another activity?
- How does information flow into and out of the activity?
- Is the activity a source of competitive advantage?
- Does the activity fit the overall goals of the organization?

E-COMMERCE VALUE CHAIN

The value chain depicts the series of interdependent activities of a business. A business evaluates its value chain (purchasing, accounting, finance, human resources are links) to find opportunities for improving the *value activities*. Optimizing internal fit will add value to customers and lower a firm's costs and improve profits.

Where does e-commerce fit in? The value chain is a useful way of looking at a corporation's activities and how the various activities add value to other activities and to the company in general. E-commerce views information technology as part of a company's value chain, adding to its competitive advantage. To address the e-commerce value chain means identifying the competitive forces within the company's e-commerce environment, the business model it will use, and then identifying the value activities that help the e-commerce value chain do its homework. This means we need to know how to incorporate communication technologies within a company's business model.

E-commerce can play a key role in reducing costs, improving product quality and integrity, promoting a loyal customer base, and creating a quick and efficient way of selling products and services. By examining the elements of the value chain, corporate executives can look at ways of incorporating information technology and telecommunications to improve the overall productivity of the firm. Companies that do their homework early and well ensure themselves a competitive advantage in the marketplace.

A generic e-commerce model is shown in Figure 1.7. Web sites are used to provide and collect information between the e-merchant and the customer. Competitive pricing information contributes to variable pricing like that found in auctions. Invoicing facilitates online payment flows. Customized products or orders can be shipped and delivered by independent shippers directly to the customer. This way, warehousing and inventory storage is kept at a minimum. Managers who can leverage technology to improve the efficiency of the e-value chain can realize significant savings for their company.

The trend in e-commerce is to integrate the entire transaction life cycle, from the time the consumer purchases the product on the Web site to the time the product is actually received. This life cycle centers around three major e-commerce applications: business-to-consumer (B2C), done on the Internet; business-to-business (B2B), done on the Internet and extranets; and business-within-business, done on the intranet (see Table 1.2).

FIGURE 1.7   A generic e-commerce model

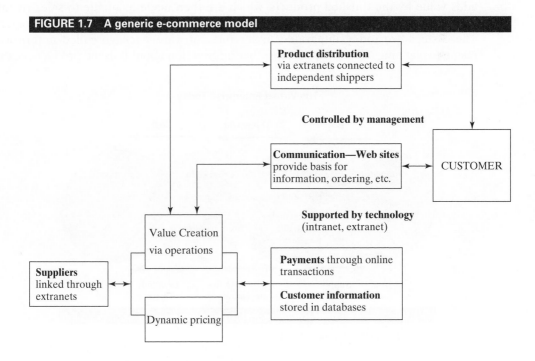

TABLE 1.2	Key elements of Internet, extranet, and intranet e-commerce		
Element	*Internet*	*Extranet*	*Intranet*
E-commerce type	Business-to-consumer (e.g., mail order via the Web)	Business-to-business (procurement and fulfillment)	Internal procurement and processing
Access	Unrestricted (anyone can access a URL address)	Restricted to company employees, staff, and business partners	Restricted to company customers, employees, and staff
Security	Generally minimal, except for verifying credit cards and financial transaction integrity	Firewalls and restricted access to data and applications	Firewalls to eliminate noncompany employees
Payment method	Credit card or electronic cash	Predefined credit agreement between businesses	Within-business charges

INTEGRATING E-COMMERCE

The path to success is integration of the various links (departments) in the chain to work together for a common objective—profitability and customer satisfaction. As shown in Figure 1.8, the supplier links with the manufacturing division of the firm (back office) via a supply chain that keeps manufacturing in business. Manufacturing adds value by the finished products, which are then made available to sales (front office). Sales, in turn, add value by advertising and selling the products to the customer. These steps are today integrated under one software package called enterprise resource planning (ERP) that ties together information about finished products, costs,

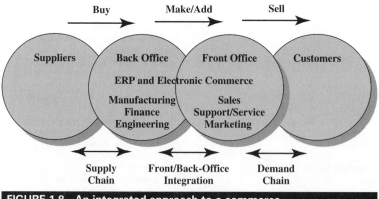

The Virtual Enterprise Today

FIGURE 1.8   An integrated approach to e-commerce

Source: The Yankee Group

sales figures, accounting, and human resources and makes it available to any authorized personnel in the firm.

BUSINESS-TO-CONSUMER (INTERNET)

shopping cart: online order form supported by the appropriate software.

The focus of this e-commerce application is on the consumer's use of a merchant's Web storefront or Web site. Consumers anywhere can browse and order goods or services online at any time. This approach is modeled on the traditional shopping experience found in stores like Safeway, Kroger, and K-mart. For example, a shopping cart is used to hold goods until the customer is ready to check out. Checkout is order and payment processing. B2C is the electronic equivalent of the traditional mail-order or telephone-based ordering system.

BUSINESS-TO-BUSINESS (INTERNET AND EXTRANET)

Having a Web storefront is not a big deal anymore. Everyone has one. The real power of e-commerce lies not in the direct sale of products to consumers, but in the integration of relationships among merchants and suppliers for prompt, quality customer service. Business-to-business e-commerce is industrial marketing: among the processes it handles are fulfillment and procurement. As soon as an online purchase is entered and payment is approved through a credit card clearance procedure, a message is generally displayed saying, "Thank you for your order. The amount of $xxx will be charged to your credit card. The product should reach you within 5 to 7 working days." The moment the message is displayed on the customer's monitor, an electronic order is sent to the vendor to fill the order and ship it directly to the customer. Doing this electronically means reduced inventory and quicker service.

However, B2B is more than fulfillment: there is the potential for the Internet to become like a central computer system for all industries. Companies can conveniently and quickly check their suppliers' inventories or make instant purchases. Overhead should decline as Web-driven systems eliminate many of the traditional workers who do the faxing and handle purchase orders. Competing online should also force prices for materials and supplies to drop dramatically. An **extranet** is a shared intranet deploying e-commerce within the larger community of an organization, including its vendors, contractors, suppliers, and key customers.

SUPPLY-CHAIN MANAGEMENT

supply-chain management: integrating the networking and communication infrastructure between businesses and suppliers to ensure having the right product in the right place, at the right time, at the right price, and in the right condition.

The concept of supply-chain management (SCM) is having the right product in the right place, at the right time, at the right price, and in the right condition. It means delivery of customer and economic value through integrated management of the flow of physical goods and related information, from raw material to delivery of finished products to consumers. SCM is designed to improve organizational processes by optimizing the flow of goods, information, and services between buyers and suppliers in the value chain (Singh et al., 2005, 109).

SCM is an integral part of the business-to-business framework. It cuts across application infrastructures and business relationships. It transforms the way companies deal with suppliers, partners, and even customers. The goal is to improve efficiency and profitability, but it also means creating new opportunities for everyone involved.

Supply-chain management employs powerful tools that allow companies to exchange information (inventory levels, sales trends, etc.) in an effort to reduce cycle times, to have quicker fulfillment of orders, to minimize excess inventory, and to improve customer service. This communication is done quickly from one database to another. According to an *InformationWeek* research survey of 300 IT executives using supply-chain systems, the majority of respondents said the most important strategic advantages of supply-chain systems are better collaboration with business partners, lower operational costs, and reduced cycle times (see Box 1.5).

In SCM, the name of the game is *collaboration* among business partners, *coordination* of logistics for timely delivery of goods or products, *cooperation* among businesses and suppliers to make sure orders and inquiries are filled correctly, and *connectivity* through networking infrastructure to ensure speed and good response time at all times. More and more, companies are extending their focus from internal

---

BOX 1.5

E-Commerce Trends: Killer Supply Chains

For most retailers, one of the trickiest links in the supply chain is moving goods from the supplier to the warehouse, then on to the store. Home Depot Inc. has found a simple way around that problem: Remove it. The Atlanta-based building supplies retailer now moves 85 percent of its merchandise—nearly all of its domestic goods—directly from the manufacturer to the storefront. Product no longer languishes in warehouses, saving both suppliers and Home Depot money. "We're treating each of our stores as if it were a distribution center," says CIO Ron Griffin. Because of Home Depot's high volume—its stores average $44 million in sales and $5^1/2$ full inventory turns a year—the products frequently ship in full truckloads, making the system even more cost-effective.

Associates walk store aisles, watching for goods that need replenishment. As they enter orders directly into mobile computing devices, called the Mobile Ordering Platform, the request can go almost instantly via EDI connections to more than 80 percent of Home Depot's manufacturers, which can respond immediately. Home Depot offers its partners recognition incentives to get them on board.

Short-term forecasting is handled locally, with up to 65 weeks of data at the store level, and store managers are given latitude to adjust for demand based on merchandising programs. Home Depot prepares long-range forecasts of three to five years on a national level for its suppliers; they contain product-volume data, of course, as well as where growth is expected and where Home Depot plans to build new stores. That helps suppliers decide where to build new plants and distribution centers, and it puts Home Depot in the position of helping determine facility location instead of simply working around it. "Rather than assume fixed capacity, we help shape it," Griffin says.

Home Depot opens up even more data to its biggest partners. Electric-tool manufacturer Black & Decker is Home Depot's largest supplier, and Home Depot is its largest customer. So it benefits both companies to share information. Home Depot passes point-of-sale data to Black & Decker, which helps the Baltimore company analyze sales and determine future manufacturing volume.

operations like scheduling and enterprise resource planning to relationships with external customers and suppliers. They are looking for the perfect virtual enterprise that will link their supplier's suppliers to their customer's customers to operate together under one umbrella with seamless connections among databases, manufacturing, inventory systems, and Web servers.

Supply-chain management is beginning to address perhaps the most critical link in the value chain—the end customer. The integration between sales-force automation applications and between consumers and business customers means all partners can now configure and order online what they need, when they need it. This means better business value, with tighter collaboration between customers and suppliers, and ultimately with the end user.

What about everyone in the middle—the wholesaler, the jobber, intermediaries in general? Middlemen are probably the most vulnerable to the killer supply chain. Based on various reports, dramatic changes are transforming the business of many intermediaries. Today's wholesaler is taking a hard look at its current activities and extracting valuable skills it can offer outside the traditional way of doing business. Wholesalers are becoming financiers, logistics specialists, outsourced presales and postsales support providers, and the like. What all this means is that they are wrapping information around the products they handle and adding significant value in the process.

As you can see, B2B exchanges pave the way for a new business model for the digital economy. It is a distinct network of suppliers, distributors, Internet service providers, and customers that use the Internet for communications and transaction handling. As communication tools get better and cheaper, transaction costs should drop. With the Internet, many transaction costs are approaching zero. People around the world can now quickly and cheaply access the information they need almost instantly. Companies can also add value to a product or service from any location, at any time, day or night.

To illustrate, General Motors, Ford, and DaimlerChrysler announced in early 2000 that they were moving all their business-to-business activity, involving more than $250 billion and 60,000 suppliers, to the Internet. The new system will replace a mammoth procurement process built on phone calls and fax processing. For GM, the average processing cost of a purchase order is $125. With the Internet, the cost has dropped to below $1. Bidding will also drive down the cost of some goods. Parts such as tires and headlights are already purchased through online reverse auctions, where the automaker names the price of the part it needs, leaving it to a supplier to accept the price. It is much like Priceline.com. This approach should capture millions of dollars in savings.

This is all well and good, but installing the necessary SCM software can be a big challenge. The serious task is overhauling the way work gets done in a company, which for large corporations can take years and cost hundreds of millions of dollars. For example, Ford wants to revamp its manufacturing plants to begin building customized cars for consumers in just two weeks. This means major changes for employees, dealers, and suppliers worldwide. Early in 2000, General Motors launched an SCM project with similar goals. The work is scheduled for completion by 2003 and will cost well over $100 million. It could mean reengineering almost all GM's business processes and a big investment in new technology, but the payback has already been in the hundreds of millions. Select e-business leaders and innovators are shown in Table 1.3.

TABLE 1.3 Select e-business leaders and innovators

Rank	Company	URL Address	E-Business Leader	E-Business Profile
1	Office Depot	www.officedepot.com	Monica Luechtefeld, Sr. V.P., "Our success is measured not by traffic, but by sales"	Office-supply company integrates e-business technology across all channels of its business, increasing customer self-service and order sizes while reducing transaction costs.
2	eBay	www.ebay.com	Meg Whitman, CEO, "predicts eBay will host $30 billion in gross sales by 2005"	Turned eBay into the largest site for e-commerce, with over 30 million registered users. Except during the 2000–2003 recession, the site has been profitable since it began in 1996.
3	AOL Time Warner, Inc.	www.aol.com	Steve Case, Chairman, "His goal is to make sure new rules for the Internet won't inhibit his company, or the growth of the Net"	AOL Time Warner is arguably the most powerful company on the Net since the merger. Case is moving beyond the role of company visionary to industry statesman.
4	Dell Computer Corp.	www.dell.com	Michael Dell, Chairman, "He must find growth in the midst of shrinking PC demand"	Wrote the book on e-business, tapping the Net to do everything from handling customer orders to linking suppliers.
5	General Electric Co.	www.ge.com	Gary Reiner, CIO, "The challenge is to push cultural change among GE's 340,000 employees and getting customers to buy GE stuff online"	Helped make GE the e-business leader among large manufacturers, with savings of $2.8 billion in 2004.
6	Amazon.com, Inc.	www.amazon.com	Jeff Bezos, CEO, "Keeps a relentless focus on customer satisfaction creating a gold standard for other online outfits to meet"	The world's biggest consumer e-commerce company. Bezos has made Amazon more efficient, turning over inventory faster and closing some facilities in an effort to show profit.

(Continued)

TABLE 1.3 Continued				
Rank	*Company*	*URL Address*	*E-Business Leader*	*E-Business Profile*
7	Microsoft Corp.	www.microsoft.com	Rick Belluzzo, COO, "Challenge is building a new Web business by adding subscription services like stock trading alerts through Microsoft's Net technologies"	Reversed the fortunes of Microsoft's consumer Web business, making MSN the second most-popular family of Web sites on the Net after five years of fits and starts.

Another problem with business-to-business e-commerce is in understanding the technology and making it work. Many companies are relying on in-house talent to do the job rather than bringing in specialists from outside. The upside of this is that insiders know the business, the products, and the customers. The downside is the time-consuming learning curve. It is like building a business from scratch. It is one thing to create an in-house Web site and sell to business customers and buy supplies, but it is quite a different thing to try to link Web sites together, integrate internal inventory and accounting, and manage them in a global e-marketplace. SCM is covered in Chapter 12.

BUSINESS-WITHIN-BUSINESS (INTRANET)

The intranet plays a role as a corporate and product information center but is strictly a "within company" type of information exchange. This networked environment is restricted to internal employees and customers, with firewalls to keep out nonemployees. E-mail replaces paper for the communication of messages, order acknowledgment and approvals, and other forms of correspondence within the firm. In terms of requisitions and procurement, the intranet makes it possible to link a company's requisition system to Web-based supplier catalogs or shipment-tracking systems for quick and responsive delivery.

In an intranet, there is no true payment process. Transfers of funds or charges against budget accounts are purely an accounting transaction as part of the intra-company billing procedure. In effect, an intranet becomes a facilitator for the exchange of information and services among the departments or divisions of a large company. For example, using a Web browser, a regional manager of a retail chain can inquire about the status of his or her region's quarterly sales. The query is sent to the company server dedicated to its intranet. To get such information, the system verifies the authenticity of the request and then transmits the requested information to the manager's monitor via the company intranet.

Different departments with different PCs or local area networks can interact on an intranet. For example, the human resources department can use the company's intranet to post employee handbooks, company policies, job openings, and state and government employment regulations. The company can also post white papers, special announcements to all employees, corporate phonebooks, and online training courses so employees can do their training anytime, anywhere, at their convenience. The benefits of an intranet are many:

1. Low development and maintenance costs
2. Environmentally friendly because it is company-specific
3. Availability and sharing of information
4. Timely, current information
5. Quick and easy dissemination of information

There is one thing to remember, though: An intranet is not free. It costs money to install and takes regular maintenance to monitor reliability and integrity. As information becomes more abundant, there is a tendency for the intranet to contribute to congestion, especially in e-mail traffic. Employees are always being reminded to purge their e-mail files and work within the space allotted to their e-mail box.

Intranet software is hardware-independent and runs well on a PC, a Macintosh, or in a UNIX-based environment. The intranet infrastructure generally includes a Transmission Control Protocol/Internet Protocol (TCP/IP), Web server hardware and software, and a firewall server. (Intranets are covered in detail in Chapter 4.)

BUSINESS-TO-GOVERNMENT (B2G)

Federal and state government business is an institution by itself. E-commerce has emerged as governments look at moving procurement online. Today, even local school districts are buying supplies online. The government market is strikingly similar to B2B. Most of the software and technology are directly usable. Some said if the 20 percent cost savings claimed by B2B proponents can be replicated in B2G, the ramifications for tax-payers as well as market entrants will be enormous in this $1.8 trillion market. State and local government procurement expenditures represent another $1 trillion.

Like any new entrant, B2G comes with its own set of difficulties. Changing the status quo in government is not so easy. Process efficiencies could mean job cuts and powerful unions may not view the change in a positive light. Also, the tax savings potential of B2G is not easily recognized by the taxpayers or government officials. At the same time, committing to technology means constant need for upgrades and additional costs.

To date, government-to-consumer has done well. For example, paying for speeding tickets and renewing one's driver's license online has paid dividends to government agencies as well as customers. E-procurements is the latest stage, where government agencies announce requests for proposals on their Web sites for suppliers to bid on each proposal by e-mail or through the Web site. The potential savings from e-procurement in time and costs could be quite impressive.

E-COMMERCE BUSINESS MODELS

Web sites are not free; every one costs money to develop and maintain. The cost and potential revenue constitute a **business model.** It is a way of doing business to sustain a business—generate revenue. Free e-mail service has a business model. Free home pages fit into a business model. The business model spells out how a company makes money by showing where it is in the value chain.

There are different business models in e-commerce. Each model has its own unique features and offerings.

STOREFRONT MODEL

This is a true e-commerce site that offers products or goods for a price. The business provides a Web site with product information, a shopping cart, and an online ordering mechanism. Users select the products they want to buy and place an order through the shopping cart. The product price is usually fixed, but can be negotiable. The merchant makes money the same way as traditional brick-and-mortar shops: through the profit margin in the product price.

The storefront model is typical of physical goods and services like books, computers, or a pizza delivery service. The merchant reaches customers directly and sells without retailers or intermediaries.

CLICK-AND-MORTAR MODEL

A "click-and-mortar" shop combines a Web site with a physical store. The additional advantages are that it already has an established brand name, and that it can use its physical store to promote the Web site. Further, users can return unwanted or defective items simply by going to the store rather than mailing it to a Web site operator.

BUILT TO ORDER MERCHANT MODEL

A manufacturer such as a computer vendor can use this model by offering goods or services and the ability to order customized versions. The customized product is then assembled individually and shipped to the customer. This provides added value to consumers and allows the manufacturer to create only those products that will be sold.

SERVICE PROVIDER MODEL

A pizza delivery service can operate on a pay-per-item basis, but many Internet-based services cannot easily operate this way. It is often difficult to define the "product" sold or to what price to charge. For instance, a news site can offer the service of access to its archive, but even one dollar is probably too much for retrieving one article. There is also the cost of processing the charge through a third party. Some service providers provide advertising-based access to their service, hoping to recover the costs through revenue from the advertisers. Few ad-driven sites bring enough income to stay alive; Yahoo! is one of the few successful ones.

SUBSCRIPTION-BASED ACCESS MODEL

Many service operators provide subscription-based access to their service. A visitor pays a fixed fee per month or year in return for unlimited access to the service. Access beyond a certain limit is subject to a surcharge. This model is typical for accessing databases with articles, news, and patents as well as online games or adult Web sites. However, the viability of subscription-based models is doubtful. This model is slowly gaining acceptance, because many Internet users are reluctant to pay to view content on the Web.

PREPAID ACCESS MODEL

Services like telephony offer payment by the minute and are handled via a subscription. A viable alternative is prepaid access, where users pay a certain amount for access to the service for a certain time period or content. It is similar to paying for a prepaid telephone card, which can be renewed for the same charge. In most cases, the card is a smart card that stores the minutes purchased. The available credit on the smart card is reduced during usage of the service. Prepay schemes give users greater control over how much to spend on the service.

BROKER MODEL

Brokers are market makers. As intermediaries, they bring buyers and sellers together and facilitate transactions between them. Those can be business-to-consumer (B2C), business-to-business (B2B), or consumer-to-consumer (C2C) markets. A broker makes money by charging a fee for every facilitated transaction or a percentage of the price of the transaction.

There are variations of this business model:

- Group buying model—Brings potential buyers into a group to trigger volume discounts that benefits each buyer in the group.
- Bounties—The broker offers a reward for finding a person, thing, idea, or other desired but hard-to-find item. The broker may list items for a flat fee or charge a percentage of the reward if the item is found. An interesting example is BountyQuest, which offers rewards for uncovering prior art for particular patents.
- Search agent—A software agent or "robot" that looks for price and availability for a good or a service specified by the buyer. An example is www.MySimon.com.
- Transaction broker—Provides a third-party payment mechanism for buyers and sellers to settle transactions. An example is www.Paypal.com.
- Demand collection—A prospective buyer makes a final bid for a good or a service. The broker arranges fulfillment. An example is www.priceline.com.

ADVERTISER MODEL

Advertising-driven sites are currently one of the cornerstones of e-commerce. A site offers free access to something and shows advertisements on every page. A user clicks on an advertisement and goes to an advertiser's page. The advertiser pays the site operator for showing the advertisement ("eyeballs") or for every time someone clicks on the advertisement (click-through).

There are two main types of business advertiser models—targeting advertisers and updating advertisers. An advertisement related to the topic at hand on the site gets higher exposure and click-through. The site operator earns more money if it places targeted advertisements. For example, a spreadsheet shows advertisements for a stock brokering service. Racing games, soccer games, and the like commonly show billboards in the game to emulate the look of the real playing field. The advertisements thereon can be chosen as "real" advertisements.

Search engines use the same idea, but relate the advertisements to the keywords entered in a query. For instance, if you are searching information on holidays, an advertisement pops up about a hotel chain with search results. In addition, the advertisement can relate to the visitor profile doing the search. For example, if the profile shows the visitor likes to golf, an advertisement is shown for a hotel near a golf course.

DoubleClick is one company that uses the advertising-driven concept as a business opportunity. It captures ads from many sources and facilitates their placements on different sites. The sources pay DoubleClick for the placement effort and this revenue is then shared with the site owners. As a side job, DoubleClick builds a user profile based on the ads that the user watches. This profile helps in refining the match of visitors and ads.

It is desirable to be able to present users fresh advertisements periodically, even when they are not connected to the network. To this end, the browser or other client can download multiple advertisements simultaneously and display them one at a time when users are offline. A screensaver can also present advertisements when the system is idle. The screensaver periodically downloads updated advertisements and/or news messages and presents them to the user.

PORTAL SITE MODEL

In this business model, a portal offers one-stop access to specific content and services like news, stock information, message boards, or chat. Allowing the visitor to personalize the interface and content (for example, see www.my.yahoo.com or www.my.cnn.com) makes it easier for the visitor to identify with the portal. The portal site can then target its ads based on the personalization.

FREE ACCESS MODEL

Users are given something for free, but with advertisements. A free Web space provider typically provides advertising banners at the top or bottom of its sites. Electronic greeting cards are sent with a personal message and an advertisement. Since the visitor base is diverse, it is hard to target the right advertisements, making the revenue low.

VIRTUAL MALL MODEL

A virtual mall is a hosting site for many merchants, service providers, brokers, and other businesses. The virtual mall operator charges a fee for setting up and maintaining the merchant's "booth" and for including the merchant in the sitewide catalog. The operator may also charge a fee for every transaction the merchant performs. Virtual malls can operate within the context of a larger site, such as a portal.

virtual mall: a site that hosts many merchants, service providers, brokers, and other businesses.

The virtual mall can act as an intermediary between customers and the business it hosts by facilitating payment and guaranteeing a full refund if a merchant does not deliver in time. When such service is offered, it can aggregate customer profiles to be used later in forming specialized malls oriented at, for example, kids or sports lovers.

virtual community: a Web site that attracts a group of users with a common interest who work together on the site.

VIRTUAL COMMUNITY MODEL. Also called a vanity site, a virtual community is a Web site that attracts a group of users with a common interest who work together on the site. Users share information and make contributions in other ways. Since they have contributed to it themselves, users feel highly loyal to the site and will visit it regularly. This offers possibilities for advertising.

The largest virtual community can be found on Slashdot, a Linux-oriented site on which users share news articles and Web sites. A specialized type of virtual community is the knowledge network or expert site, where laymen and experts share expertise. These sites operate like a forum. Participants get questions answered or raise topics for discussion. Usenet newsgroups are a good example of such a community.

One way to monitor a virtual community is to require registration and a fee for access to the site. This allows intersession tracking of visitors' site usage patterns, which generates data of potential value in targeted advertising campaigns. Unregistered visitors are often attracted by offering "teasers" to entice registration.

INFOMEDIARY MODEL

An infomediary collects, evaluates, and sells information on consumers and their buying behavior to other parties who want to reach those consumers. Initially, a visitor is offered something for free, like free hardware or free Internet access, which allows the infomediary to monitor the visitor's online activities. The information gathered can be extremely valuable for marketing purposes.

The infomediary needs to keep track of its users. A simple way to achieve this is to require registration for access to the site, preferably for free. This allows intersession tracking of users' site usage patterns and thereby generates data of greater potential value in targeted advertising campaigns. Registration can be made more attractive by offering limited access or "teasers" to unregistered users by offering the option to customize the site after registration.

MANAGERIAL IMPLICATIONS

When it comes to success in this emerging field, it is people and managerial talent that matter. It takes people with a vision of the future and with innate ability to handle the speed of change. The person who figures out how to harness the collective genius of the organization will blow the competition away.

With change now accepted as a way of life, the human resources department has the option of getting new people or changing the people already on staff. There is a new focus on building a productive organizational culture, managing change and results, building intellectual capital, creating future leaders, managing organizational learning, and pushing for growth and innovation. As someone said, "If you are not the lead elephant, you'll never charge."

For success in today's digital economy, the real asset is not money; money is just a commodity. The real asset is information and how it is used to create value for the customer. More than half of doing business no longer depends on the brick-and-mortar side of commerce; it depends on the core personnel of the firm and the customer.

Having employees be part of the organization and improving their skill sets adds value and contributes to the success of the firm.

The top challenge in managing an e-business is understanding the consumer. Most successful companies form a 360-degree consumer view by gathering data from every possible source and analyzing it to shed light on the details that mark the way consumers shop and buy. Obviously, companies that better understand their customers' preferences can sell more. They know which customers are most important, most profitable, and most loyal.

Finally, a visitor like you should know the many ways companies on the Internet try to pull you into their sites to solicit exchange, trade, or information. It is becoming extremely important to gain knowledge of these companies through learning about the business models they represent.

Summary

1. Electronic commerce (EC) is the ability to deliver products, services, information, or payments via networks such as the Internet and the World Wide Web. From a structural perspective, EC involves various media—data, text, Web pages, Internet telephony, and Internet desktop video.

2. Electronic business connects critical business systems directly to key constituents—customers, vendors, and suppliers—via the Internet, intranets, and extranets.

3. The rise of specialized Web sites and Web logs (blogs) generated opportunities to read and write on a vast array of topics. You can chat, you can share, you can collaborate, and you can communicate knowledge (not just information) about virtually any topic any time, 24 hours a day, year round.

4. Several drivers promote EC: digital convergence, 24/7 availability, changes in organizational makeup, increasing pressure on operating costs and profit margins, the demand for customization, and the need for speed.

5. Advantages of EC: low cost; economical; higher margins; better and quicker business service; easy comparison shopping; productivity gains; creation of knowledge markets; information sharing, convenience, and new customer control; ability to swap goods and services; customization.

6. Limitations of EC: security issues; concerns about data protection and the integrity of the system that handles the data; system scalability; fulfillment (delivery) problems; customer relations problems; products people won't buy online; Web site access by the competition; high risk of Internet start-ups.

7. A value chain is a way of organizing the activities of a business so that each activity provides added value or productivity to the total operation of the business. Supply-chain management (SCM) means having the right product, in the right place, at the right time, and in the right condition. The goal is to improve efficiency and profitability so as to add value to each link in the chain.

8. The transaction life cycle includes three major e-commerce applications: business to consumer (B2C), business to business (B2B), and business within business.

9. An intranet wires the company for information exchange. E-mail replaces paper. An intranet links a company's requisition system to Web-based supplier catalogs or shipment-tracking systems for quick and responsive delivery.
10. Success in the e-commerce field depends on attracting and keeping qualified technical people and managerial talent. Attracting qualified technical people is a challenge; finding ways to retain them is a full-time job.
11. There are several types of specialized Web sites on the Internet. Each site is based on a business model as a way of doing business to sustain a business—generate revenue.

Key Terms

- **blog** (p. 3)
- **business model** (p. 34)
- **digital divide** (p. 4)
- **electronic business (e-business)** (p. 8)
- **electronic commerce (e-commerce)** (p. 8)
- **electronic learning** (p. 4)
- **extranet** (p. 29)
- **frequently asked questions (FAQs)** (p. 19)
- **hopbot** (p. 15)
- **Internet** (p. 2)
- **scalability** (p. 16)
- **shopping cart** (p. 29)
- **supply-chain management (SCM)** (p. 29)
- **transaction** (p. 8)
- **value-chain** (p. 23)
- **virtual community model** (p. 38)
- **virtual mall model** (p. 37)
- **Web farming** (p. 18)

Test Your Understanding

1. What indicators suggest e-commerce is here to stay? Explain.
2. What is a blog? Does it make sense to share personal information with others by blogging? Explain.
3. There are several definitions of e-commerce. Give a definition of your own.
4. How would one distinguish between e-commerce and e-business?
5. The chapter mentions drivers in e-commerce. In what way(s) do they serve as drivers?
6. What is meant by digital convergence? Is it the same as the digital divide? How?
7. Several myths about e-commerce were discussed. Can you think of others?
8. Of the advantages listed in the chapter regarding e-commerce, can you think of others? Do you think the advantages outweigh the limitations?
9. In what way is security a limitation of e-commerce?
10. Of the benefits and limitations of the Internet, what final impression do you have of the potential of the Internet in your career?
11. Distinguish between:
    a. Value-chain and supply-chain management
    b. Intranet and extranet
    c. Storefront and service-provider models
12. Where does a shopping cart fit in B2C e-commerce? Explain.
13. Is the intranet necessary in every type of business? Why?

14. Distinguish between:
    a. Virtual mall and virtual community models
    b. Broker and portal site models
    c. Infomediary and service provider models
15. What is so unique about e-learning?

Discussion Questions

1. "E-banking will have a more profound effect on banking than ATMs ever did." Do you agree? Surf the Internet, investigate the topic, and defend your answer.
2. "EC means the end of mass marketing." Do you agree? Surf the Internet and try to bring recent opinions to the discussion.
3. It has been said, "In almost all cases, EC does not change some fundamental rules of banking." Contact a local commercial bank and explore the likelihood that this statement is true. Write a one-page report of your findings.
4. Is the Internet different from other media? Discuss.
5. One of the factors for success in doing business on the Internet is to deliver personalized service. How can this be done?
6. Find a company that chose not to use EC in its business. What factors or problems did it consider in staying away from EC?
7. Explore two industries that can greatly benefit from EC in reducing production cycle time.
8. Give an example of how EC can help a firm reach its customers in a very low-cost fashion.
9. Do you think a team can solve problems through blogging? Discuss.

Web Exercises

1. Check the following Web sites to learn more about these practices in EC:
    a. Let customers help themselves: www.got.com, www.edmunds.com
    b. Nurture customer relationships: www.amazon.com
    c. Streamline customer-focused business processes: www.onsale.com
    d. Target markets of one: www.wsi.com
    e. Build a community of interest: www.cnet.com
2. Discuss the value chain by visiting the FedEx Web site at www.fedex.com. Discuss the company's automated package tracking, virtual ordering, and shipping activities.
3. Visit the following sites on the Internet, analyze them, and report your findings. Include the title of each site with your report:
    a. www.sportszone.com for live interviews, play-by-play calls, and other interesting audio and animated information
    b. www.cai.com for animations from engineering automation
    c. www.paris.org/musees/louvre for exhibits at the Louvre
    d. www.virtualproperties.com for video tours of real estate

4. Internet transactions will alter the traditional form of money as security and privacy solutions allow for extensive use of digital cash. Review the literature and report.

5. Look up Amazon.com on the Internet (www.amazon.com) and report the number and types of EC books available for sale.

6. Interview a business or a technical person who is involved with EC. What has been his or her experience in incorporating the technology into the company's day-to-day operations? What performance criteria are used to judge the success (or failure) of EC in the business? Write a short news release for the college or university newspaper to share your findings.

7. Locate a Web site for each of the following items:

   a. Airline tickets
   b. Personal computers
   c. Clothes
   d. Books
   e. Automobile tools
   f. Road maps
   g. Looking up the address and phone number of a friend

   Explain how you looked up the Web site (by subject, URL address, etc.). Write the Web address and company name. Would you go back to the site or, if you had more time, would you look up a better one? Explain.

8. You have decided to upgrade to a new laser printer. Let's say you have decided to purchase a Hewlett Packard inkjet color printer via the Web sites of e-merchants like Office Depot or Staples. Use the Internet to look up three such Web sites and report on the outlet from which you have chosen to buy the printer. Include your reasoning for your final choice.

9. You are an Internet consultant to a company that wants you to make a one-hour presentation to top management about the importance and potential of the Internet in the company's business. What information do you need before you prepare the presentation? Write a three-page report detailing the content of your speech.

CHAPTER 2

THE WORLD WIDE WEB

Learning Objectives

The focus of this chapter is on several learning objectives:

- The rising tide of the Internet—what it is, how it began, and how it paved the way for the World Wide Web
- The makeup of the Web—key protocols, physical structure, and what one needs to search the Web
- The main Web search elements—browser, plug-ins, multimedia, and the search engine
- The main elements of Web research and Web research tips
- The search process and some important facts to remember about Web research
- How to optimize Web sites
- The role of the ISP
- Web fundamentals, including the makeup of the URL
- Internet services

IN A NUTSHELL

Since 1960, when the first business computer appeared, information technology has changed the way commerce is conducted around the globe. The personal computer (PC) revolution, local area networks, electronic data interchange, client/server design, and enterprise resource planning have all had a hand in shaping today's business organization. The past few years have been World Wide Web (WWW) years, as companies worldwide have embraced a change without equal. It is a change that has had more impact and has been more lasting than anything that has occurred to date. This technology is setting the pace for how a company does business, how it launches new products and enters a new market, how it deals with suppliers, and how it communicates with customers and others in the new marketplace. Any way you look at it, business will never be the same.

The primary technology for this transformation is the WWW, which became a reality with the advent of the **Internet**—a universal global data network that moves closer and closer to the ubiquity of the telephone. What makes the Internet so powerful is that it is more about information and communication than it is about technology. It is a medium and a market. As a result of the Internet, transaction and communication costs have been reduced dramatically. It is virtually unstoppable, forcing all kinds of businesses to reexamine their practices and their future. This chapter covers the World Wide Web—its functions, contributions, and potential within the framework of the Internet.

THE INTERNET TODAY

For all the directions the Internet has taken and all the companies it has spawned, this "superhighway" was first developed as a tool for people (originally scientists) to keep in touch with one another. This is the way many people use the Internet today. The greatest strength of the Internet is its ability to bring together individuals, governments, and businesses, and facilitate the exchange of information among them. (See Box 2.1.) It allows users to entertain children, buy a house, fill prescriptions, make new friends, find new music, learn a foreign language, get driving directions, keep romance alive, or engage in a political discussion.

On the personal side, the Internet is giving people power they never had before, and they are enjoying it. Sophisticated Web tools let people assess medical treatments. For example, the Heart Profiler site (www.americanheart.org) is one of the many sophisticated and personalized tools consumers can use to figure out their risk of serious disease such as heart failure or coronary artery disease, and to make life-and-death treatment decisions once they are diagnosed by their specialist. The number of such tools is growing.

On the business side, the rise of the Internet as the enabler of e-commerce is changing how companies manage their business. Closed-enterprise systems are giving way to open-system environments, where customers connect to the company's Web site and trading partners connect via an **extranet** and the Internet.

The WWW is the fastest growing and most commercially popular technology to date. Anyone with a PC connected to the Internet, a **browser,** and few **plug-ins** can surf Web sites and do business round the clock. A **Web site** is a unique representation of a company's products or services on the Internet. It consists of pages connected to one another by links. A page from one Web site can be linked to a page on another Web site halfway around the globe. The idea is to make information, products, and services available anytime, anywhere, to anyone 24 hours a day, seven days a week (24/7). The sharing and integration of information means improved decision making and efficiency of operations for everyone.

One feature of the Internet is not available on the telephone. The Net allows you to send messages to multiple persons at the same time, much like television or radio broadcasting. It began with message communication, but now it is possible to transmit and receive computer data containing graphics, voice, photos, and even full-motion

---

BOX 2.1

Web-Based Conferencing: Listen Up

Netspoke Inc. provides companies with more sophisticated Web-based conferencing and collaboration options. One of the unique features of this setup is the way the technology organizes task-oriented features such as polling, as both menu items and subcomponents of the broader Web-conference-creation task. The system also does a good job of managing reports around individual Web conferences, collecting meeting, quiz, and survey data from each session. One could record and play back meetings via a downloadable playback client.

Compared to the competition, Netspoke's conferencing hub tries to balance the simplicity of a single toolbar across the top of the application with floating applets that manage features such as chat, audio conferencing, and polling. The balancing act does not quite work, but many of these tools are used infrequently, so presenters should be OK.

One of the more interesting new wrinkles in Web conferencing is the Web and Audio Conferencing feature in the Intranet Suite offered by Intranets.com Inc. Customers of this service rent Web conferencing capabilities based on Netspoke Inc.'s Conferencing Hub application, as part of Intranets.com's eponymously named hosted collaborative team-room application suite. The service is priced at $150 per month for up to 25 simultaneous participants. As part of the service, Intranets.com also offers audio conferencing at 12 cents per minute per connection.

Source: Michael Caton, "Web-Based Conferencing: Listen Up," *eWeek,* Nov. 15, 2004, 47–50.

videos. The part of the Internet that can accomplish these tasks is called the World Wide Web, also known as WWW or the Web.

More than two-thirds of American adults now surf the Web. The definition of "Internet user" is subject to interpretation. Some companies count a 2-year-old as a Net surfer, but others count those as young as age 16 or 18. The latest reported demographic profile information from Mediamark Research shows that 40 percent of surfers are college graduates, 40 percent have household incomes above $75,000, and 63 percent hold white-collar jobs. The trend, however, is toward a rapid increase in use among lower-income and less educated demographic groups.

One of the unanticipated problems of the Internet is that it is littered with abandoned Web sites. One study of 3,634 blogs found that two-thirds had not been updated for at least two months and a quarter not since they began. Having extra junk there makes surfing for good stuff harder and harder. Neglected sites are:

- Web sites that do not respond when one clicks on the URL because the site is no longer active.
- New e-business that begin with Web sites, but are abandoned on the Internet when the business fails.
- Simple boredom—pasting pictures, changing text, and updating products often lead to Web site neglect.

As long as business keeps pouring in, the Web site becomes a fixture with no motivation to update. When orders begin to shrink, it is often too late to save the Web site from major overhaul. In addition, limited-time Web sites for political, social, or special events die quickly after the event. Unfortunately, most of them stay gone for lack of funding, interest, or care.

As a result of the increasingly heavy Internet traffic, Internet companies have found value in recycling misaddressed Web traffic. Some common errors are misspelling simple Web addresses like www.bestby.com (instead of www.bestbuy.com), typing a plain English word into a Web browser, including erroneous punctuation in a Web address (an apostrophe in Companies'.com), or omitting the dot in addresses that should end in .com or .net. As explained in Box 2.2, "trash traffic" is now directed to the companies' Internet search engines, where they display advertisements. This means money for sending traffic to another site.

THE BEGINNINGS OF THE INTERNET

Basically, the Internet is the infrastructure that links thousands of networks together. No one knows exactly how many computers are connected to the Internet. It is certain that the number is in the millions and is increasing at a rapid rate. By linking the large computers that manage individual networks, the Internet becomes an information highway that makes the information stored on thousands of computers

---

BOX 2.2

Value in Trash Traffic

One person's online trash is an e-company's treasure. Every day, millions of online users erroneously punch Internet addresses that don't exist into their Web browsers (by mistakes in spelling, format, and so forth). This "trash traffic" seems worthless, but a growing number of companies are finding creative ways to recycle it.

In a potentially significant development, VeriSign Inc. is privately directing large portions of trash traffic to Web sites of its choosing. VeriSign sends users who flub an address—say by typing bestby.com into their browsers instead of bestbuy.com—to another Web site, most likely an Internet search engine. In effect, it will be capturing error-prone users before the software from companies like Microsoft and AOL can nab them, potentially shifting significant sums of traffic away from those sites.

AOL no longer gives users error messages when they attempt to reach a nonexistent Web site. The service automatically funnels those users to AOL Search, which uses Google's search engine. AOL then examines the spelling of the Web address and suggests sites that users might have been trying to reach. Users who type in Newyrker.com, for instance, are sent to an AOL Web page that asks, "Do you mean Newyorker.com?" Users who click on the Web address in that question then go to an AOL Search page with various hyperlinks, including ads selling *New Yorker* magazine subscriptions.

Some software programs from the Internet may also change which Web sites they are sent to when they make Web address errors. Other online companies exploit users' typing errors in an entirely different fashion: by setting up Web sites at addresses that resemble popular online destinations. In early September 2003, federal agents arrested a man who allegedly ran pornographic Web sites that exploited misspelled addresses for Disneyland, Teletubbies, and other online destinations for children.

Source: Nick Wingfield, "Internet Companies See Value in Misaddressed Web Traffic," *Wall Street Journal,* Sept. 5, 2003, B1ff.

worldwide available to millions of people everywhere. The Internet transmits messages among servers using satellites, dedicated and fiber-optic cables, microwaves, and other technologies, including the simple phone line used in every-day conversation.

One interesting thing about the Internet is that no one is in charge: No governing body is in control. The Internet backbone through which Internet traffic flows is owned by private organizations. The Internet owes its existence to the Pentagon and the cold war. The original networked sites were military installations, universities, and business firms with defense department contracts. Fearing that centralizing computer operations under one roof might make systems vulnerable to bomb attack, in 1964 scientists at the RAND Corporation developed the concept of connecting thousands of computers in the same way the human brain is built, so that the loss of a few neurons does not disrupt normal function.

The initial goal was to design a network that would maintain the safe transition of data between military computers at select sites through redundant communication routes. The built-in redundancy meant that in case of war, military data transfer would continue uninterrupted. It also meant that no single site would be the vulnerable one. Five years later, two nodes (in this case, computers) were connected to a network on ARPAnet (Advanced Research Projects Agency), which was the sponsor of the research. This was the beginning of what we now call the Internet.

packet: a short message sent through a network.

Researchers at Stanford Research Institute, Massachusetts Institute of Technology (MIT), University of California at Los Angeles, and the British National Physical Lab devised a way of bundling information into **packets** that carried the **network address** of the recipient. Such a packet is sent into a so-called "cloud" across the vast array of computers on the network. Each computer checks to see if the information belongs to any of its clients and forwards it to the next computer to which it might belong. Once claimed by the right computer, the packet is opened to reveal the message. This message delivery system is moved by a **protocol.** (This technology is covered in greater detail in Chapter 3.)

protocol: a set of rules for ordering and formatting data across a network.

ARPAnet was decommissioned in 1969. In 1984, it split into two interconnected networks. The military part was named MILNET. The educational part, which kept the name ARPAnet, became known as the Internet. Since the mid-1980s, the National Science Foundation (NSF) and other agencies of the U.S. government have controlled access to the Internet. At first, Internet traffic was government related and government subsidized: No ordinary person or company could use the Internet. In fact, the story is told that in 1994, a consultant informed a firm inquiring about the potential uses of the Internet that if it used the Internet for commercial purposes, its officials could be shot by the military. Things changed in April 1995 when the U.S. government relinquished control of the Internet to independent governing bodies, which relaxed entry for almost everyone.

The Internet today offers a variety of services including e-mail, file transfer, interest group membership, multimedia displays, real-time broadcasting, shopping opportunities, access to remote computers, and the quick and easy transmission of information among computers worldwide. Many federal agencies now allow anyone to access timely information. The agencies include the Social Security Administration, Veterans Administration, and the U.S. Postal Service.

The Internet is sustained by interested parties, private and public. It grew of its own accord to meet the expanding needs of its users. The rapid development of the PC and local area networks in the 1980s and the 1990s also contributed to its growth. Part of the Internet is a variety of access protocols featuring programs that allow users to search for and retrieve information made available by the protocol. More information on protocols is provided in Chapter 3.

THE MAKING OF THE WORLD WIDE WEB

In 1990, Tim Berners-Lee, a programmer who worked in the European Particle Physics Laboratory, wrote a program called a *hypertext editor* that allowed information highlighted in a document to link to other documents on a computer network with a mouse click. Soon, physicists associated with the lab began to use the hypertext editor and the Internet to send papers to each other. Later, their electronic mail became more elaborate as they built links that crossed the Internet to transmit information and documents. This virtual space became known as the World Wide Web.

hypertext: any text that contains links to other documents.

link: also referred to as hyperlink; connects current document to another location in the same document or to another document on the same host computer.

Hypertext is text that contains keywords to connect to other documents. Such keywords, called **links,** are selected by the designer of the Web site. Hypertext for the Web can be generated with a language called HyperText Markup Language (HTML). With HTML, the designer places tags within the text to do page formatting, italics, bold, font size, and hypertext links. The language is upgraded regularly, and new tags are added with each upgrade. To access a Web page, you do the following

- Enter an Internet address to retrieve a page.
- Browse through Web pages and select links to move from one page to another.
- Enter a search statement at a search engine to retrieve pages on the designated topic.

World Wide Web, WWW, the Web: an organization of files designed around a group of servers on the Internet programmed to handle requests from browser software on users' PCs.

The **World Wide Web** (also known as the Web) is the universe of network-accessible information and the embodiment of human knowledge. Technically, it is a cluster of software, protocols, and standards. It is an organization of files designed around a group of Internet servers programmed to handle requests from browser software that resides on users' PCs. The name is based on the fact that the sound, text, animation, pictures, or information that make up a document may come from anywhere in the world. A single document can be perceived to stretch—weblike—throughout the world. (See www.w3.org/www.)

Through hypertext and multimedia, it is easy for anyone to use, surf, browse, and exchange information night and day. When a document is accessed in Washington or Singapore or Madrid, the components are pulled from different computers worldwide and integrated in the document displayed on the user's screen. The request is received

TABLE 2.1 Major events in the creation of the World Wide Web	
Date	*Event*
March 1989	WWW project originated by Timothy Berners-Lee
November 1990	Revised version of the project developed NeXT computer
March 1991	WWW released to a select group for testing
September 1993	National Center for Supercomputing Applications (NCSA) released first working version of Marc Andreesen's Mosaic for all common platforms
October 1993	More than 500 known HTTP servers in operation
October 1994	More than 10,000 known HTTP servers in operation; today, there are hundreds of thousands worldwide
June 1995	Sun formally announced Java at SunWorld '95
October 1998	XML (Extensible Markup Language) introduced
June 2003	Spread of broadband allows the Net to reach its full commercial potential (See Box 2.3)

by one computer, which interprets its content to see if it has what is requested. If not, the request hops across other computers until the entire document is assembled.

A brief summary of the key events in the creation of the World Wide Web is shown in Table 2.1. Note that when you are on the Web, you are on the Internet, but not the other way around. For example, those sending e-mail are not on the Web unless they are sending e-mail via a Web browser.

BOX 2.3

At Last, the Web Hits 100 MPH

Experts are increasingly optimistic that high-speed Internet access really, finally, will help deliver the full promise of the Web. With broadband charges steadily decreasing, it is forecast that broadband will reach enough people to kick off a round of changes on the Web.

Broadband connections are always on, so people don't have to think twice about turning to the Net for news or a quick peek at airline fares. That is one reason people spend two-thirds more time online each day—around two hours—after signing up for broadband. And once there, they are big shoppers, spending 29 percent more annually, or around $523. Speed demons also are more likely to create art on the Web, download music, and try out online gaming.

Over the next five years, the impact of broadband will show itself in stages. One reason it won't happen all at once is that it will take three years for speedy access to surpass dial-up. Until then, businesses will cater primarily to those with poky connections.

Downloading a two-hour film is nearly impossible over an old, creaky connection, taking upwards of 14 hours. With broadband, that drops to 45 to 75 minutes, luring more film buffs to the Web. Also, as more consumers have fast access at home, they'll also shop less at work. Buy.com Inc. is making the most of that by offering four-hour sales that give consumers a reason to also shop at night and on weekends once they have a fast connection at home. As a result? Buy.com's best promotions boosted sales 40 percent.

Source: Tim Mullaney, "At Last, the Web Hits 100 MPH," *BusinessWeek,* June 23, 2003, 80–81.

architecture: hierarchical physical structure of the Internet.

backbone: the main network of connections that carry Internet traffic.

network access point (NAP): primary connection point for access to the Internet backbone.

TCP/IP: a set of protocols or rules that provide the basis for operating the Internet.

The physical structure, or **architecture,** of the Internet is hierarchical: High-speed **backbones** are at the top, with regional and individual networks at the bottom. The bulk of Internet traffic is fed onto the backbone via **network access points (NAPs)**, which are maintained by Sprint and other service providers at strategic locations throughout the United States. (See Figure 2.1.) This grand network of networks shares a common set of communication protocols called a **TCP/IP** (transmission control protocol/Internet protocol) suite, which is covered in Chapter 3.

The Web supports hypertext to access several Internet protocols on a single interface. Internet protocols are specific rules that make it possible to conduct "between machine" communications on the Internet. Protocols are covered in greater depth in Chapter 3.

The key protocols accessible on the Web are as follows:

- E-mail—The protocol for e-mail is Simple Mail Transport Protocol, or SMTP. The major job is to distribute electronic files and messages to one or several e-mail boxes. Also, electronic files can be attached to an e-mail message. MIME (Multimedia Internet Mail Extension) enables users, for example, to send a document created in Microsoft Word to another party, who retrieves it with the appropriate e-mail program.

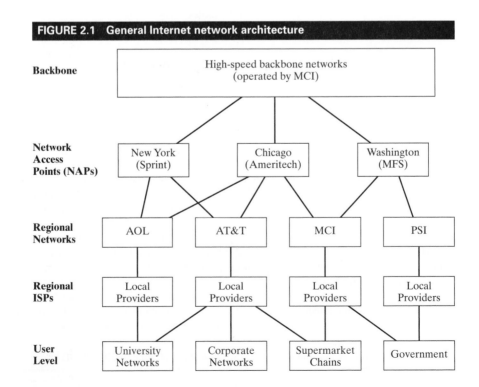

FIGURE 2.1 General Internet network architecture

- HTTP—HyperText Transfer Protocol makes possible transmission of hypertext over networks. HTTP has been designated as the protocol of the World Wide Web.

- **VoIP—Voice over Internet Protocol** makes it possible to place a telephone call over the Web.

The newness of the Web—along with its rapid, phenomenal growth—has been a challenge for corporations that want to create a presence on the Internet. They have found it difficult and too costly to invest employees' time in doing professional

Webmaster: a person who is skilled in Web design, Web maintenance, and Web upgrade.

Web design work. The demand has created a new industry specializing in Web design and Web mastering. Because of the increasing number of Web sites, **Webmaster** is a lucrative new career.

WEB SEARCH ELEMENTS

The Internet contains thousands of Web sites dedicated to tens of thousands of topics. Many of us know how to search, but are not quite as knowledgeable about the elements that make the search process feasible. Therefore, it is a good idea to know what makes the search process happen.

THE BROWSER.   To access the Web, you need a Web browser. A *browser* is a piece of software that allows users to navigate the Web. Netscape Navigator and Microsoft Internet Explorer are examples of popular browsers. Technically, a browser is a **Web client** program that uses Hypertext Transfer Protocol (HTTP) to make requests of **Web servers** throughout the Internet on behalf of the browser user. See www.webjunction.org:980/w/components/glossary.html.

There are two types of browsers:

- *Text-only mode* such as Lynx. You navigate the Web by highlighting emphasized words on the screen with the up and down arrow keys and pressing the forward arrow (or Enter) key to follow the link. For more information, see "Guide to Using Lynx" (library.albany.edu/internet/www.html).

- *Graphic mode* involves a graphical software program that retrieves text, audio, and video. Examples are Netscape Navigator and Internet Explorer. You navigate the Web by pointing and clicking with a mouse on highlighted words and graphics. Navigator is available for downloading on Netscape's Web site, home.netscape.com. Microsoft's Internet Explorer can be downloaded from Microsoft's Web site, www.microsoft.com.

Because of the increasing popularity of surfing and doing business on the Internet, more and more browsers appear on the market each year. For example, in 2005 when this edition was being completed, several browsers were added:

- *WinWap for Windows*—uses Wireless Application Protocol services on a PC over any connection. Introduced in May 2005.

- *Mozilla Pop*—an open-source browser with a pop-up killer. Introduced in April 2005.

- *Opera 8.0 pop*—allows browsing with a multiple-document interface, mouse gestures, keyboard shortcuts, and zooming functions. Introduced in April 2005.
- *Pathfinder 1.0 pop*—browser that renders Web pages and blocks pop-ups. Introduced in April 2005.

PLUG-INS.   Software programs are configured to a Web browser to improve its capabilities. For example, when a browser senses a sound, an image, or a video file, it passes the data to other programs, called *plug-ins,* to run or display the file. Working together with plug-ins, browsers today offer seamless multimedia experiences. Many plug-ins are available on the Internet free of charge. Examples of plug-ins introduced in 2005 are Greasemonkey pop, MetaProducts Inquiry Professional Edition, EZ Save MHT, and Wi-Fi Desktop Search Toolbar pop, which searches for Wi-Fi hotspots, cleans your computer of unwanted files, and searches the Web.

A popular plug-in on the Web is Adobe Acrobat Reader. This program allows the user to view documents created in Adobe's Portable Document Format (PDF). When Acrobat Reader is configured to your browser, the program will display the requested file when you click on a hyperlinked file name with the suffix .pdf. Once configured to your browser, a plug-in will become active automatically when you choose to access a file type that it uses.

Microsoft developed software called **Active X,** which makes plug-ins unnecessary. This software makes it possible to embed animated objects and data on Web pages. For example, one can use Active X to view the three-dimensional **Virtual Reality Modeling Language (VRML)** world in a Web browser without a VRML plug-in. Being a Microsoft product, Active X works best with Microsoft's Internet Explorer browser.

MULTIMEDIA.   Since 1999, the Web has become a broadcast screen. It is now common to use the Web to listen to audio and watch video—prerecorded or live off the Internet. Even the nightly television news can be watched on one's PC monitor. The old problem of slow download time is answered by a multimedia capability called **streaming media.** With this technology, audio or video can be played as they are downloaded (streaming) into your computer. **Buffering** is used to minimize the wait time between downloading and actual viewing of the material on the monitor. Netscape Communicator includes a Cosmo viewer for experiencing a three-dimensional world.

RealPlayer and **Windows Media Player** are alternative options for the broadcast of real-time (live) events. Beyond that, **Shockwave** is multimedia software that allows for an entire multimedia display of audio, graphics, animation, and sound. This means that sound files containing music also can be heard on the Web with the appropriate plug-ins.

Active X: a Microsoft program that embeds animated objects and data on Web pages.

Virtual Reality Modeling Language (VRML): a Microsoft product that allows a three-dimensional view of objects in a Web browser.

streaming media: audio or video that begins to play as it downloads (streaming), done through buffering.

buffering: a PC feature that minimizes the wait time between downloading and actual viewing of the material on the monitor.

RealPlayer: an alternative option or program for broadcast of real-time (live) events via Microsoft's Windows operating system.

Windows Media Player: an alternative option or program for broadcast of real-time (live) events via Microsoft's Windows operating system.

Shockwave: multimedia software that allows for an entire multimedia display of audio, graphics, animation, and sound.

Live Cam: software that is essentially a video camera that digitizes images and transmits them in real time to a Web server.

A unique aspect of the multimedia experience on the Web is **Live Cam.** This software is essentially a video camera that digitizes images and transmits them in real time to a Web server. From there, the video can be downloaded off any PC connected to the server.

chat program: a facility that makes it convenient for people to "talk" to each other in real time by typing messages and receiving a response.

Finally, in terms of real-time collaborative communication, **chat programs** make it convenient for people to "talk" to each other in real time by typing messages and receiving responses. An example of such software is America Online's Instant Messenger.

search engine: a Web site or a database and the tools to search it.

THE SEARCH ENGINE.   A search process begins with a **search engine**—a Web site or a database, along with the tools to generate that database and search its contents for "keywords" that describe what you're looking for. Google.com and Yahoo.com are examples of search engines. There are other definitions as well:

- A software program that collects and indexes Internet resources (Web pages, Usenet Newsgroups, programs, graphic images, etc.) and provides a keyword search system allowing the user to identify and retrieve resources based on words, phrases, or patterns within those documents. Google is one of the best-known search engines. See www.library.queensu.ca/webisi/survivalguide/glossary.html.

- A Web-based system for searching the information available on the Web. Some search engines work by automatically searching the contents of other systems and creating a database of the results. Other search engines contain only material manually approved for inclusion in a database, and some combine the two approaches. See www.unitedyellowpages.com/internet/terminology.html.

- An automated system that relies on a software agent (otherwise known as spiders, robots or crawlers) that explores the World Wide Web following links from site to site and catalogs relevant text and content, storing Web pages and creating a customized index based on the user's query of the search engine's database. See www.proshay.com/glossary.s.html.

The collection part of a search engine (also known as automated robots like Wanderer, Spider, Harvest, and Pursuit) roams Internet sites; retrieves messages; and sorts, indexes, and creates a database from them. Web robots keep a list of Web pages to index and download the pages one by one. On a well-connected Web, a robot can index every page it reads.

index: a database that stores a copy of each Web page gathered by the spider.

The two main elements of Web research are indexes and search engines. Searching by index can help a writer who has a general topic but does not yet have a specific focus within the topic. An **index** can help a searcher acquire general information or gain a feel for the general topic. Steps to follow, for example, could be:

- Go to Google (an index).
- Think of a topic that is of interest (e.g., "universities").
- Follow it through specific type or level (e.g., "private universities," "private small universities," "private small Virginia universities").

Search engines have some type of index attached to them. An index can be hierarchical or alphabetical. Hierarchical indexing leads from general to specific topics; alphabetical indexing contains sources that focus on a specific topic or area of concern. A search engine sends inquiries to Web sites without evaluating them. The results found by various search engines differ. Because search engines maintain tens of thousands of sites, narrowing your topic is necessary to get the kind of information you need. Otherwise, you could end up with page after page set of sources, which is costly in time and timeliness.

To illustrate the powers of an index, Yahoo! Inc.'s online search engine index spans more than 20 billion Web documents and images, nearly double the material scanned by rival Google, Inc. By comparison, Google tracks 11.3 billion objects. Yet Google is better known for producing more useful results, depending on what one is looking for (Daily Progress 2003).

In addition to an index, there are two other components of a Web search engine.

spider: a software tool that prowls the Internet looking for new sites where information is likely to reside.

- A **spider** is a program that roams the Web from link to link, identifying and scanning pages. The index contains a copy of each Web page gathered by the spider.
- Software unique to a search engine allows users to query the index and returns results in relevancy-ranked order (alphabetical).

second-generation search engine: a search engine that organizes search results by peer ranking, concept, domain, or site rather than by relevancy; also called "off the page" information.

first-generation search engine: a search engine that returns results in schematic order, constructing a term relevancy rating of each hit and presenting search results in this order; also called "on the page" ranking.

It is important to remember that a spider cannot tell whether a resource is good or bad, current or outdated, inaccurate or incomplete. It is up to you to evaluate each resource and decide how relevant it is to your research. A new, **second-generation search engine** technology orders search results by concept, keyword, links, site, domain, or level of popularity. These search engines are more reliable in the ranking of results. A Web page becomes highly ranked if it is linked to other highly ranked pages. For example, Google derives its results from the behavior and judgment of millions of Web users. In contrast, with **first-generation search engines,** the engine merely searches its index and generates a page with links to resources that contain your terms, and the results are presented in term-ranked order.

A checklist of Web research tips is summarized in Figure 2.2. A summary of the major shopping search engines is shown in Table 2.2.

Many of the newer search engines differentiate themselves by providing a "best-of-breed" search offering, which adds ease-of-use features to the search process, making it easier for users to surf the Internet. Some search engines use a spider. The quality of a search site today, however, depends on the number of sites to which it is linked. Search engines such as Yahoo!, Lycos, Excite, and others have gone beyond simple search capabilities, adding everything from free e-mail to games and chat rooms. Their goal is to become a **portal,** or an all-purpose home base for Web users. How easy it is to surf the Net has a lot to do with the quality and attractiveness of the Web site.

portal: a location on the Web that acts as a launching point for searching for and retrieving information.

For a surfer, knowing where to look, how to phrase a search term, and how to make use of sites returned by the search engine are what make the difference between successful surfing and utter failure.

To illustrate the search process, take the author's first-choice search engine—Google. Google is an established resident of the Internet that quickly captured the preference of surfers and researchers alike. It is today's number one search engine for thoroughness of search, speed, ease of use, and convenience. Google and Yahoo! were the first search engines to introduce a virtual mall and comparison shopping.

One of the unique features of Google is its ability to search for all the words you type in. You don't need to customize the entry by + or − or place words in quotes, and so on. For example, to search for Civil Liberty Union, you'd search for "Civil Liberty Union" rather than the individual words "Civil" "Liberty" "Union." Every phrase that matches the quote is listed.

In addition, Google allows you to exclude certain terms from Web searches by adding a minus sign before the word to be deleted (−). For example, to find pages that present Professor Andersen's publications but not Andersen Consulting, try searching for Andersen Consulting. For more tips on how to search on Google, go to Google's online help pages.

FIGURE 2.2   Checklist of Internet research tips

1. Evaluate everything on the Internet for its appropriateness for research use.
2. Try out a handful of sites when researching a topic on the Internet. Do not reply on only one site or one type of site.
3. When searching for a proper name, capitalize the first letter of each word.
4. When searching for several names that are linked together, use a comma to separate them(e.g., George Bush, President).
5. Use quotation marks when doing a phrase search (e.g., "Congressional E-Mail Addresses"). If you leave out the quotation marks, the engine will search for all documents with the word *congressional,* all documents with the word *e-mail,* and all documents with the word *address.* You will get tens of thousands of hits. With the quotation marks, you will get only documents with those three words exactly as you have placed them.
6. Use hyphens when searching for words that must appear within one word of each other (e.g., cable-networks). The words can otherwise have numerous connotations.
7. Use brackets to find words that appear within 100 words of each other (e.g., [bus safety]).
8. Use a plus sign to find two or more words that must be in the documents together (e.g., bus schedule +SEPTA. No space should be placed between the + sign and the second word.
9. If you have a multiple-term search, decide on the logical relationship between them. For example, a search about the relationship between Bush and terrorism would be formulated as: +bush+terrorism on many Web search engines for AND logic to apply.
10. If you want images, place a colon between the word *image* and the image topic name (e.g., image: comet).
11. Use an asterisk to find all combinations of a word or word fragment (e.g., edu*). This will yield pages containing *education, educator,* etc.
12. To find URLs, use *url:* and the address fragment (e.g., url:mciu.kl2). This will match pages with the words *mciu* and *Kl2* together in the URL.
13. Keep in mind that phrases are strings of words that are adjacent in a document.
14. Take advantage of capitalization if the search engine is case sensitive.
15. Check your spelling. You'd be surprised how important correct spelling is.
16. Work with different search engines, as no two engines work from the same index.
17. If you are unhappy with the results, repeat the search using alternative terms.

Source: Excerpted from phoenix.liunet.edu/~jberger/websearch.html. Accessed April 2003. See also Laura Cohen, "Conducting Research on the Internet," library.albany.edu/internet/research.html (July 2002, 1–14). Accessed April 2003.

TABLE 2.2	Selected shopping search engines	
Search Engine	*URL*	*Description*
BizRate	www.bizrate.com	Allows you to search for products from hundreds of online vendors. Features include merchant ratings, reviews, tax and shipping information, as well as a list of your own past searches and recently viewed products.
Froogle	www.froogle.com	Comparison-shopping search engine from Google. Gathers listings from crawling the Web and accepting product feeds from vendors.
Kelkoo	www.kelkoo.co.uk	Major comparison-shopping search engine for the United Kingdom and other European countries; 16 out of the top 20 e-commerce sites in the U.K. are currently advertising through Kelkoo.
MSN Shopping	shopping.msn.com	Formerly known as eShop; offers Buyer's Guides with tips and tools, editor's suggestions, and other features beyond the price comparisons offered by other shopping search sites.
mySimon	www.mysimon.com	One of the oldest comparison-shopping sites on the Web, featuring the ability to search for products from thousands of merchants or browse by product category.
PriceGrabber.com	www.pricegrabber.com	Comparison-shopping search engine with ability to see member ratings of products. Available in English or Spanish, including specialized product searches for retailers in Mexico and Brazil.
Yahoo Shopping	shopping.yahoo.com	Connects you with thousands of merchants—traditional retail stores, name-brand catalog companies, small boutiques, and specialty vendors. Listings come from merchants hosted in Yahoo Store and through partnerships with others, in addition to online merchants throughout the Web. Provides access to user reviews.

FACTS TO REMEMBER

An online merchant should know some basic facts.

1. **People look up Web sites with search engines.** A frequently visited Web site is one that appears on several search engines. Other sources include printed media, Web site addresses on business cards, and inserts in customers' monthly statements. Make sure that search engines and other sites bring up your site in their top 10 or so sites. As will be explained later in the text, you need to embed many metatags in the homepage. A *metatag* is a word that is similar to your company's

product, service, or mission. For example, a commercial bank's Web site would use metatags such as "commercial bank," "financial institution," or "loan" so that Web surfers can access the bank by a number of synonyms—metatags.

2. **People usually use bookmarks to visit their favorite Web sites. Bookmarking,** or saving URL addresses for future use, is one of three methods people use to search for sites. The other two methods are entering the URL address or entering a subject on the search engine homepage. When you advertise a Web site, encourage users or customers to bookmark the site. It is easy, quick, and the most convenient way of getting visitors to make a habit of visiting your Web site.

bookmarking: action taken on a facility of a Web browser that allows you to save URL addresses for future quick access and use.

3. **A Web site must be quick and current.** Study after study has shown that more than two-thirds of visitors cite Internet speed as a major problem. Users simply click away if the information they seek is not displayed on the screen within a few seconds. Slow speed, broken links, and difficulty in finding a given site do not promote loyalty. The trick is to keep a Web site simple and easy to maintain. Because Web sites are set up in a single physical location, performance is limited by the speed of that single connection. It is up to the Internet service provider to expand its Internet network and hardware to accommodate more data performance and minimize latency (delay).

4. **A Web site should address the privacy and navigation concerns of the user.** Various studies have shown that censorship is the leading concern of Internet users, followed by privacy concerns. Ease of navigation is an added concern for Web traffic. For a commercial Web site to build customer loyalty, it is important to protect user information and ensure ease of use of the Web site at all times, regardless of the amount of traffic.

5. **The "bottleneck" problem.** Anyone who uses a 56-kbps modem knows the so-called "last mile" bottleneck. A modem tapping into the Internet via a narrow-band connection is bound to cause frustratingly slow performance. Connecting to a DSL line or high-speed line would help, but as more and more people go that route, congestion is bound to happen.

6. **People are reluctant to pay to surf a Web site.** Very few sites that began to charge for visits have stayed in business. This is similar to the early 1970s, when banks started charging customers for making withdrawals through the ATM. Today, most banks offer this service free of charge with a minimum balance in checking or savings accounts. Foreign customers (customers from other banks), however, continue to be charged a fee for using ATMs that are not their bank's machine. On the Web, about the only exceptions to the no-pay rule are specialized services such as online stock market quotations, adult-oriented material, and the like. Charges also are associated with retrieval of full text from many research sites.

SEARCH ENGINES ARE GETTING SMARTER

Search engines are getting smarter. Some sites have different languages to draw in more users worldwide. Others have enhanced conversational language to make it easier for novice surfers to wade through the ever-growing volume of online information. Before too long, search engines literally will converse with surfers, speak their language, and produce the desired information within seconds. To illustrate, Ask Jeeves has powerful smart search capabilities that help in all phases of the shopping process. Results are produced only when the search engine determines that a query is shopping-related. Such query analysis attempts to determine where a shopper is in the purchase process.

Ask Jeeves' smart search offers a rich variety of different types of information in addition to price comparison. This includes product reviews, feature comparisons, and links to online stores that have the products for sale. The way the smart search adapts to the user's intent is what makes Ask Jeeves unique.

If you were searching for a laptop computer, Ask Jeeves generates a series of related categories that are actually links that help Jeeves refine a query to a more specific level, such as "notebooks and accessories" and "memeory." A user's click on Notebooks and accessories generates further refinement links like notebooks, batteries, Y adapters, tablet PCs, and so forth. Graphic displays of actual products are shown with links to additional information about each product.

Today's search engines can miraculously take your topic of the day, scan millions of Web pages, and in seconds present you with the information you want. But as powerful as they are, search engines are not without weaknesses. For example, a random search on Google for "ERP" took less than one second, but it produced 90 million hits. The answer to your query could have been number 20,000 on the list.

Experts are working feverishly at making search engines more intelligent. One approach taken is to personalize the search engine so it will know you are, for example, an IT professor, and when you search for "hard disk," it will know it is more likely you want information about a computer device than about a medical problem in your lower back.

An example of incorporating "intelligence" into search engines is a software agent called Query Tracker, built by a computer science professor in 2004. The Query Tracker supplements a user's query with its own, and it gains in performance with prolonged use and feedback. As shown in Figure 2.3, the Query Tracker sits between the user and a conventional search engine. Once it receives the user's query, it begins to look for information of recurring interest to the user query. Then, once a day it submits to the search engine a query of its own and returns results accordingly. Daily queries are automatically generated with steady improvements in the quality of the queries. In essence, it learns enough from preceding queries to improve on the quality of succeeding queries. After the Query Tracker filters the results of queries for reliability and relevance, it sends them back to the user for final action.

Another intelligent search engine application is IBM's WebFountain. This project centers on a huge Linux infrastructure that runs 9,000 programs at the same time and crawls 50 million new Web pages every day. The system uses natural language analysis concepts to extract and tag meaning from text. The unique feature about WebFountain is its capability to determine whether an entity is a person's name, a corporate logo, a product, a discount, and so on. Then it goes ahead and attaches a metadata tag to it. This is tantamount to extracting opinions from online text documents (Anthes 2004).

On the drawing board is "thinking in pictures" as an alternative way to search the Web. When you type a search phrase into www.kartoo.com, you face a screen dominated by a flowchart. The chart is filled with words related to the search phrase. You can simply click on the term(s) to add them to your phrase and focus your search. Such an approach is designed to appeal to creative learners and children.

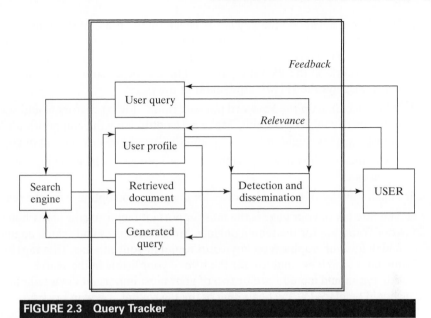

Feedback

Relevance

FIGURE 2.3   Query Tracker

Source: Adapted from Gary H. Anthes, "Search For Tomorrow" *Computerworld*, April 5, 2004, 26.

SEARCH ENGINE OPTIMIZATION

Have you ever noticed that most visitors choose the top five or six Web sites listed by a search engine? Search engine optimization (SEO) is a way of trying to increase the number of visitors to a Web site by ranking high in the search results displayed by a search engine. The closer the Web site is to the top of the list, the greater the chance of attracting more visitors.

One way to optimize is via hyperlinks. Text-based hyperlinks can improve your listing in the search engines. Search engines usually figure out that linking anything to your Web page is likely to be closely related to the content of the page. This means you should include the most important keyword phrases in the link itself and surrounding text for optimization of your Web site. Each page of the site you want listed should be optimized to the best of your ability. Choosing the right keywords makes a difference. The keyword phrases should be included within the hyperlink itself and in the text that immediately precedes or follows the hyperlink.

Knowing how important the keywords are for optimizing your pages, consider these tips before submitting them to the search engine:

1. General keywords are nowhere as good as specific keyword phrases. If they are too general, chances are they won't rank well in the search engines. Here is an example of a Web site selling tires:

Too General	Much Better
a. Tires	Michelin performance tires
b. Auto tires	Auto all-weather tread
c. Truck tires	Truck heat-resistant quality

2. Before you decide on the keywords, check the Web site of the competition for ideas. Do a search by applying the keywords you want to use on those sites. Go to the source HTML code and view the keywords included in their metatags. To do so, right-click on the Web site page and then choose "source" or "page source," which displays the HTML equivalent of the page.

3. When deciding on the keyword phrases, think of what visitors would search for in the page you're optimizing. Make sure not to copy the competition's keyword phrases, as they might not fit right, and that would be in violation of copyright.

4. Try to include the most important keyword phrases in heading tags on your page if you can.

5. Finalize the list of keyword phrases for the pages you optimize for the search engine.

6. The title tag of your page is the most important factor to consider when optimizing your Web page for the search engines. Most directories and search engines place a high level of emphasis on keywords found in your title tag. Title tags are actually the ones search engines use for the title of your listing in the search results. Your title tag should include one or two of your most important keyword phrases and should be placed at the beginning of the tag so that you won't risk having them cut off. The title tag should be between 50 and 80 characters long, including spaces. This is a safe range for most search engines.

7. Visitors as well as search engines read your pages by looking at keywords to see what you have to offer. When it comes to optimizing your pages, each page should have at least 200 words of copy on it. The text should include the most important keyword phrases, yet remain readable.

8. Many people have a false impression that good metatags are all that is needed to achieve good listings in the search engine. Metatags are always part of a well-optimized page, but they are not the be-all and end-all of optimizing pages. Search engines have changed. They now look at a combination of things, not just your metatags.

9. There are two metatags that can help in listing your Web site: meta keywords and meta descriptions. Meta keywords look like this:

```
<META NAME="keywords" content="keywords phrase 1, keyword phrase 2,
keyword phrase 3, etc.">
```

Meta descriptions look like this:

```
<META NAME="description" content="description of what is on your page.
The most important keyword phrases should appear here"
```

For a meta description, make sure the content of each page optimized is described accurately and three or four of the most important keyword phrases are included, especially those used in the title tag and page copy. For meta keywords, make sure you use the keyword phrases placed in the title tag, meta description, copy of your page, and other tags. Watch out for repeats—including the most important phrases. For example, "Alaska tour" and "Alaska tours" are two different phrases, but the word "Alaska" appears twice. This is OK, but be careful not to repeat the same word too many times (more than four or five times).

While you're optimizing your Web site, one thing to stay away from is "spamming" the search engines. Since traffic to your Web site comes through search engines, they are the last ones you'd want to antagonize. Here are some things that search engines consider spamming:

- Anything to trick search engines into listing your site in a more favorable position
- Listing keywords anywhere other than in your keywords metatag
- Using the same color text on your page as the page's background color
- Submitting identical pages
- Using multiple instances of the same tag, such as using more than one title tag
- Submitting the same page to any search engine more than once within 24 hours

How long does it take to get listed? Much depends on the search engine you are submitting your page to. Here is a general guideline of selected search engines:

Google	Up to four weeks
AOL	Up to two months
MSN	Up to two months
HotBot	Up to two months
Excite	Up to six weeks

INTERNET SERVICE PROVIDERS

To link the rapidly growing commercial Internet landscape, the Internet Service Provider (ISP) industry was born in the mid-1990s. As we discuss in detail in Chapter 7, the ISP industry offers a variety of services, including:

1. Linking consumers and businesses to the Internet (e.g., America Online, Microsoft Network)
2. Monitoring and maintaining customers' Web sites
3. Providing network management and system integration
4. Providing backbone access services for other ISPs (like PSI and UUNET)
5. Offering payment systems for online purchases

As public demand for access to the Internet surged, ISPs began to add more lines and better access to accommodate the traffic. Initially, the cost for Internet access often exceeded $1,000 per month, but with new ISP arrivals and competition, prices plummeted. Many of today's ISPs offer unlimited access for as low as $5 per month. Many local governments are funding the use of the Internet because of its political, educational, and commercial benefits. Once on the Internet, no additional charges are accrued. You can contact anyone, anywhere, anytime for that monthly fee. The exceptions are Web sites that charge a membership fee or a fee for access to privileged information.

Almost everything one needs on the Internet is free. The following are among the free services.

- Hotlists that tell the user what is popular and what is not
- Comics that focus on entertainment events
- Software archives that list the latest free software available
- Weather services that provide free weather forecasts for anywhere in the world
- Magazines and broadcasting stations that constantly update the news
- Searchers that help locate items or subjects on the Internet
- Dictionaries that include thesauruses and "fact" books on almost all subjects
- Government services that publicize what is available from them

The problem for some ISPs is sudden growth without advance planning to accommodate that growth. As a result, response time slows down, triggering customer complaints. The challenge is to maintain profitability and meet or beat the competition, while maintaining customer satisfaction. To do all this well requires professional management, a highly skilled technical staff, and a healthy budget to bring the technology in line with the voracious appetite of today's consumer. The trick is to ensure a balance between creativity and control and between managing growth and a stable technical infrastructure.

STABILITY AND RELIABILITY OF THE WEB

No one single agency or company owns the Internet. Each company on the Internet owns its own network. The links between these companies and the Internet are owned by telephone companies and ISPs. The organization that coordinates Internet functions is the Internet Society. It does not operate any of the thousands of networks that make up the Internet but works with ISPs by providing information to prospective users. This association's Internet Architecture Board consists of work groups that focus on TCP/IP and other protocols. Various committees also handle technical issues and day-to-day operational aspects of the Internet.

The Web itself, because it resides everywhere and nowhere at the same time, simply cannot cease functioning by itself. Also, because it is based on the Internet, its stability is as good as that of the Internet, which is fairly good so far. The Internet is designed to be indefinitely extendable. Reliability depends primarily on the quality of service providers' equipment. Inadequate phone lines or bandwidth, or mediocre computers can affect the reliability of the overall service.

WEB FUNDAMENTALS

The World Wide Web is a global network of millions of Web servers and Web browsers connected by the **hypertext transfer protocol (HTTP)** and its many derivatives. The World Wide Web is like a client/server system: Content is held by Web servers and requested by clients or browsers. Clients display the information sent by the Web server on their monitors. Web servers provide pages of multimedia

hypertext transfer protocol (HTTP): an Internet protocol designator that allows transfer and display of Web pages.

information in seconds. The most important element of a Web site is its links to other pages within the site or across sites. By clicking on the link, a user can navigate from page to page without having to worry about the location of the information or how it travels across the network.

Web history dates back to the Berlin airlift in June 1948, when U.S. Army Master Sergeant Edward A. Guilbert developed a standard manifest system to track thousands of tons of cargo per day until the main road to Berlin was reopened a year later. In 1965, Holland-America Steamship Line sent shipping manifests as telex messages that automatically converted into computer data. The next major step was in 1982, when General Motors (GM) and Ford mandated Electronic Data Interchange (EDI) for suppliers. EDI became popular in several industries, especially in banking. In 1994, Netscape Navigator 1.0 introduced "cookies" to recognize repeat customers to Web sites. Finally, in 2000, GM, Ford, and DaimlerChrysler formed the Covisin B2B exchange, which created supply-chain management.

URLs AND HTTP

Uniform Resource Locator (URL): a name that represents the address of a specific Web site.

Uniform Resource Locators (URLs) are central to the Web in e-commerce.

As we discuss in detail in Chapter 4, a URL such as http://www.virginia.edu consists of two key parts:

1. http:// (Hypertext Transport Protocol) is a protocol designator. It is a special method used in moving files that contain links to other documents related to the material requested across the Internet. It simply tells the browser what protocol to use in connecting to the Web server (in this case, http). Web browsers also can use other protocols, such as FTP (file transfer protocol) for file transfer and SMTP (simple mail transfer protocol) for electronic mail.

2. www.virginia.edu is the server name. The series *www* after the double slash tells the network that the material requested is located on a dedicated Web server somewhere; *virginia* is the name of the Web site requested; and *edu* is a code indicating that the site is an *edu*cational institution. Other codes like *org* (*org*anization; e.g., www.ACM.org), *gov* (*gov*ernment; e.g., www.Whitehouse.gov), and *mil* (*mil*itary; e.g., www.defenselink.mil) also are used. The most common code is *com* (*com*mercial; e.g., www.dell.com). (HTTP and networking are covered in detail in Chapter 3.)

secure sockets layer (SSL): a protocol for transmitting private information in a secure way over the Internet.

To locate a resource on the Internet, the user simply enters an address in the standard format discussed here.

secure HTTP (S-HTTP): an extension to HTTP that provides various security features such as client/server authentication and allows Web clients and servers to specify privacy capabilities.

SECURITY PROTOCOLS

There are two main security protocols. The first is **Secure Sockets Layer (SSL)**, developed by Netscape Communications Corporation. To date, it is the most widely used security protocol on the Internet, providing security services for messages or streams of data. The second security protocol is **Secure HTTP (S-HTTP)**.

INTERNET SERVICES AND LANGUAGES

In order to learn from this course, you need to focus on Internet literacy. Like many areas of computing, the Internet and the World Wide Web have terms, languages, and services that are unique to the field. Here are some key terms that will make it easier to understand the technology covered in Chapter 3.

Internet service provider (ISP): a company that links users to the Internet for a fee; the entrance ramp to the Internet.

A *provider* (also called an **Internet service provider** or **ISP**) is an organization whose specialty is to provide an entrance ramp to the Internet. The ISP purchases expensive, high-speed Internet feed from a major Internet source and a number of telephone lines from a local phone company. By placing computers at the site that interface the phone lines with the Internet, the ISP can begin to sell online commercial access. The faster the Internet feed is, the more data or users it can accommodate simultaneously. More data means more users or more revenues coming from users. The ISP recoups its investment by selling Web services, providing service to many people simultaneously, and selling major Internet hookups to large corporations in their area of operation.

When you purchase Internet access from an ISP, you first receive an account that allows you to store files and do your Internet work. You are connected to a NetNews feed that brings you thousands of interest groups on virtually any topic imaginable. You also receive an e-mail address that links you with the world at large and provides access to the entire Internet.

browser: a program designed to search for and display Internet resources.

A *browser* is a software program loaded on a PC that allows you to access or read information stored on the Internet. It is the vehicle that enables you to interface with the Internet. The browser takes your instructions and converts them into a language and a format that can be sent to a remote site and executed.

A *server* is the destination point on the Internet. It is where the information you are seeking is stored. We will see in Chapter 4 that when you send a message to retrieve a piece of information through the Internet, the browser picks up the message, reformats it, and sends it through various layers to the physical layer, where cables and wires transmit the message to the appropriate server. Once there, the server retrieves the information and sends it back to the browser to be viewed by the user. There are all kinds of servers, depending on the information sought by the user. Because most of the focus in this book is on the World Wide Web, we will use the word *server* to refer to Web servers.

Electronic mail (e-mail) is probably the most popular and abused network application across all user categories. E-mail is best known through the use of programs like Microsoft Outlook or Eudora that allow you to send, receive, edit, and store e-mail messages. You can also send a message to multiple recipients and attach voice, video, or graphics to the message.

Telnet: a protocol that allows users to log on to a computer and access files from a remote location.

Telnet is a basic Internet service that allows you to access remote computers as if they were local. To use Telnet, you must have the Internet address of the remote computer. Once you transmit the computer address, you are asked to **log in** before being allowed to access computer files or use the computer. Once you are logged in, the information you read and the actions you take are acted upon by the remote computer.

A **file transfer protocol (FTP)** is a standard protocol that allows you to copy files from computer to computer. Like Telnet, FTP allows you to access remote computers. When you FTP to a remote computer, you log in as *anonymous*, which means simply entering your e-mail address as the password. The Web makes heavy use of FTP protocol. Most browsers know how to access information from FTP sites. This feature allows you to store Web homepages at low-cost FTP sites anywhere in the world.

People often confuse **bulletin board systems (BBS)** and pay services. A BBS generally has a simple interface to the Internet for users to access services like e-mail and NetNews. By calling a BBS via your PC, you can locate all kinds of information. The e-mail part of this system, for example, accepts e-mail during the day, compiles it, and sends it once or twice a day as a batch. It also receives incoming e-mail the same way. This is probably satisfactory service for small-time users or those with no time requirements.

bulletin board system (BBS): a computer-based meeting and announcement system that allows local people to exchange information free of charge.

An alternative type of BBS is service by subscription. These systems are so popular that system owners have added better computer hardware, better storage, more phone lines, and so on. The cost of keeping the system current requires users to pay a set fee per month. Pay services like America Online and Prodigy have become household names, offering millions of users access to popular telecommunications offerings that include stock quotes, Internet access, setting up your stock portfolio, and other specialized services.

Many pay services follow a similar procedure. First, you subscribe for a fee, which covers basic access to the service. The fee allows you to have e-mail, interactive real-time communication, watch the news, and the like. Pay services offer other options that are hard to get on the Internet. For example, a live news feed and free online (no delay) stock quotes are available for a membership fee; some are free. Security software also is included to ensure privacy, confidentiality, and integrity of the exchange process.

Web pages are written in a language called **Hypertext Markup Language (HTML).** The language specifies the display features that visually structure a page. Go to any homepage on your monitor, right-click, click on "source" and the homepage is converted to the equivalent in HTML format. Links on Web pages are specified by their URLs that identify the location and the protocol used to access it.

HTML is best known for publishing static (information flows in one direction) Web pages and making them easily accessible. As electronic business applications became more pervasive, there was greater pressure to come up with a way to allow the user to interact with the Web site. For example, to order a book from Amazon.com, you must inform the e-firm about the specific book you want, release your credit card information, specify the shipping address, and state how you want the book to be shipped. This is all done by filling out the information on an online form provided by Amazon. Such communication is made possible by *common gateway interface (CGI)*. Special programs called CGI scripts execute the process on the server. When executed, it passes the data (posted form) provided by the customer for verification and action.

With steadily increased interaction traffic on the Web, Sun Microsystems came out with a new, stronger language called *Java programming language* or *Java*. Java makes it possible for the customer to interact directly with the program on the screen. Java is also used to develop interactive multimedia applications, which we see on the market today.

MANAGERIAL IMPLICATIONS

The Web has changed the way business and information technology work together. The two are becoming equal partners. The best partnership takes place when the technical staff understands the business, and business users are technology-literate. Today companies seek out techies with business acumen and look for businesspeople who, by background or experience, understand technology. The fundamental skills that IT people bring to the new corporate world are useful if they get the proper managerial and technical training. Then they become the true problem solvers of e-commerce.

E-commerce is transforming the Internet from a "browse-and-surf" environment into a mammoth information exchange. In just a few years, the Internet has moved from novelty to necessity. It is a dynamic entity with a life of its own. The standards that help make the Internet work mean that a company's business has a good chance of surviving entry and competing on an equal footing with those already in the marketplace.

The important thing to remember is to keep an eye on the technologies as they evolve and to be familiar with the changes before taking a dive into the Internet. If your business does not have internal expertise in developing Web-based systems, hire this expertise after investigating the competence of the Web design agency. In the meantime, try to learn as much as possible about the process so you eventually can bring these activities in-house.

Critics often warn that the Internet has been oversold. Many businesses have entered the Web with fancy sites and injected millions in start-up money, only to learn that they would have been better off to stick to the brick-and-mortar environment. Many have pulled out poorer but wiser. The bottom line is to strategize first, test the waters, and be sure you have a unique product supported by qualified staff to follow up on the Web traffic that it attracts.

The implication behind the IT staff shortage is that less than 10 percent of a company's qualified IT staff is safe from recruiters and headhunters. According to a 2000 study, 40 percent of those interviewed said they plan to be with the company no more than one year. The reasons given were "lack of adequate training," "not enough money," "broken promises," "unappreciated and taken for granted," and "management indifference"

In another study reported by *Computerworld* (Watson 2000), companies hired IT employees as salaried professionals, planning to work them overtime and on weekends with no bonuses and no overtime pay. When there is little pay and no respect, it is the end of job loyalty and the beginning of a job search.

Summary

1. The Web is the fastest growing, most user-friendly, and most commercially popular technology to date. Anyone with a PC connected to the Internet through an Internet service provider (ISP), a browser, and a few plug-ins can surf the Internet and download text, graphics, and even voice. The part of the Internet that can accomplish these tasks is called the World Wide Web, WWW, or the Web. When you are on the Web, you are on the Internet, but not the other way around.

2. The Internet owes its existence to the Pentagon, where it originally was created for military research. It linked military labs, universities, and business firms with defense department contracts. Two nodes were connected to a network of Advanced Research Projects Agency (ARPAnet), which was the sponsor of the research. ARPAnet was decommissioned in 1969. In 1984, it split into MILNET and ARPAnet, which became known as the Internet. In 1995, the U.S. government relinquished control of the Internet to independent governing bodies and relaxed entry to the Internet for anyone.

3. The Internet is physically hierarchical. High-speed backbones are at the top, with regional and individual networks at the bottom. The bulk of Internet traffic is fed onto the backbone via network access points (NAPs).

4. Internet service providers link commercial traffic to its destination. This involves paying for transactions, managing networks, and linking consumers and businesses to the Internet. Some of the free services are hotlists, comics, weather services, dictionaries, and government services.

5. As the enabler of e-commerce, the Internet has many uses; it also has many limitations. It can be a tool for marketing and selling products and services; doing business at high speed; gathering opinions and trying out new ideas; providing equal opportunity for all businesses; and as a vehicle for inexpensive, easy mass distribution of information, products, and services, among other advantages. There are limitations as well: security and privacy issues; fakes and forgeries; hackers, worms, Trojan horses, and viruses; fulfillment and customer relations problems; products that are not candidates for online selling; and a shortage of e-literate people in the marketplace.

6. The World Wide Web is a global hypertext network of millions of Web servers and browsers connected by hypertext transfer protocol (HTTP) and its many derivatives. The most important element of a Web site is its hypertext links to other pages within the site or across sites.

7. It is important to learn the language of the Internet before starting an e-commerce project.

8. The Internet and the Web have changed the way business and technology work together; the two are becoming equal partners. Managers need to be knowledgeable about the technology before diving into the Internet with their business. They also need to know when to outsource and how to hire the right people.

Key Terms

- **Active X** (p. 52)
- **architecture** (p. 50)
- **backbone** (p. 50)
- **bookmarking** (p. 57)
- **browser** (p. 44)
- **buffering** (p. 52)
- **bulletin board system (BBS)** (p. 65)
- **chat program** (p. 53)
- **extranet** (p. 44)
- **File Transfer Protocol (FTP)** (p. 65)
- **first-generation search engine** (p. 54)
- **hypertext** (p. 48)
- **hypertext markup language (HTML)** (p. 65)
- **hypertext transfer protocol (HTTP)** (p. 62)
- **index** (p. 53)
- **Internet** (p. 44)
- **Internet service provider (ISP)** (p. 64)
- **link** (p. 48)
- **Live Cam** (p. 53)
- **log in** (p. 64)
- **network access point (NAP)** (p. 50)
- **network address** (p. 47)
- **packet** (p. 47)

- **plug-in** (p. 44)
- **portal** (p. 54)
- **protocol** (p. 47)
- **RealPlayer** (p. 52)
- **search engine** (p. 53)
- **second-generation search engine** (p. 54)
- **secure HTTP (S-HTTP)** (p. 63)
- **secure sockets layer (SSL)** (p. 63)

- **Shockwave** (p. 52)
- **spider** (p. 54)
- **streaming media** (p. 52)
- **Telnet** (p. 64)
- **transmission control protocol/Internet protocol (TCP/IP)** (p. 50)
- **Uniform Resource Locator (URL)** (p. 63)
- **Virtual Reality Modeling Language (VRML)** (p. 52)

- **Voice over Internet Protocol (VoIP)** (p. 51)
- **Web client** (p. 51)
- **Web server** (p. 51)
- **Web site** (p. 44)
- **Webmaster** (p. 51)
- **Windows Media Player** (p. 52)
- **World Wide Web** (p. 48)

Test Your Understanding

1. The Internet is a medium and a market. Could one say the same about the Web? Discuss.
2. What do you make of the history of the WWW in terms of tomorrow's business?
3. How does the World Wide Web differ from the Internet? Which one implies the other?
4. What were the key events in the building of the Web?
5. What is a Webmaster? If you were to write a job description, what would you say?
6. How are second-generation search engines different from their first-generation counterparts?
7. Distinguish between the following:
   a. Search engine and Internet service provider (ISP)
   b. HTTP and URL
   c. Web client and Web server
   d. SEO and metatags
8. Briefly describe some uses of the Web.
9. In what way does the Web provide equal opportunity for all businesses? Elaborate.
10. Do you see any limitations of the Web? What are they? Explain in detail.
11. What security and privacy issues are limitations of the Web? Discuss.
12. Write a brief procedure for optimizing Web pages.
13. How would one look up a Web site? Explain.
14. Explain the makeup of a URL address.

Discussion Questions

1. How does the Web fit with company strategy? Discuss.
2. What does the Web mean to a company's competitive situation?
3. If you were asked to sell a first-time business on the Web's potential advantage for that business, what would you need to know first? What would you say?
4. How does the Web affect our traditional sales channels, partners, and suppliers? Explain in detail.
5. How would you show a company how it can best prepare to use the Web as a profitable venture?
6. What do you find in the World Wide Web that adds value to your academic life that you did not have before?

7. Of the major events in the creation of the WWW, what event do you think was the most significant? Discuss with your team and report your findings.
8. How is buffering related to Windows Media Player? Do your surfing on the Internet to answer this question. Discuss your findings with your team.
9. Do you believe there is a "last mile" bottleneck? Look up a solution via the Internet and report your findings to class.
10. How do you explain the increasing "smartness" of the search engine? Discuss.

Web Exercises

1. At the end of an e-commerce course, five business students and a computer science student got together and decided to start a catering business for students, faculty, and administration within the university. This is a "party" school, so every weekend is busy with socials at fraternities and sororities and other activities. The students formed a partnership, designed a Web site on one of the business school servers, and advertised their presence in the daily student newspaper. They contracted with a local restaurant to supply the food, drink, and other needs customized to the special requirements of the client.

   a. Devise ways that this new student-run business can deliver warm, personalized service.
   b. What information and services should be included in the Web site?
   c. How would the university community be encouraged to place orders and become loyal customers?

2. Look up two car manufacturers' Web sites on the Internet (e.g., www.ford.com/ and www.toyota.com). Configure the car of your choice and report your findings. Make sure to include payment options, shipping charges, financing (if any), and delivery schedule.

3. Evaluate four high-volume items that are sold on the Internet (e.g., www.dell.com for PCs, www.amazon.com for books). What makes these e-merchants so successful? Elaborate.

4. If you were talking with a first-time surfer who is a student in your school, what advice or tips would you give to help the person get started researching the Internet for a term paper?

5. One of the recommendations for success in doing business on the Internet is to deliver personalized service. How can this be done?

6. Find a company that chose not to use e-commerce in its business. What factors or problems did it consider in staying away from e-commerce?

7. Go on the Internet and look up a tutorial on the World Wide Web. Review the tutorial and explain why you think it is easy (or difficult) to use as a learning tool.

8. What implications does the Web have for managing a small e-business?

CHAPTER 3

INTERNET ARCHITECTURE

Learning Objectives

The focus of this chapter is on several learning objectives:

- Types of networks required to conduct e-commerce
- The technical backbone behind accessing information on Web sites
- How information is transferred between a customer's browser and a Web site on the Internet
- How a message is handled in transit on the Internet
- Hardware and software requirements to support a Web site for e-commerce
- Factors to consider in designing and managing networks

IN A NUTSHELL

The building blocks of e-commerce are the technologies of the World Wide Web—protocols, standards, browsers, and servers. Applications like telecommunication networks and wireless networks are made possible by the underlying Internet infrastructure—servers, software, and storage that enable the working functions of the Internet: load balancing, firewall security, backup, and content distribution and management. Every time customers order a product, check a stock quote, or transfer funds online, they are relying on the integrity of the architecture to deliver. It is crucial and timely apparatus.

Satellite companies offer broadband networks to reach people where telephone service is not available. Cable television providers have prepared their networks for two-way Internet traffic via boxes that act as converters for inbound and outbound traffic, for data other than video or voice. Telecommunications companies provide new technologies for higher-bandwidth communication across existing networks. Wireless networks are being converted for Internet use and mobile-commerce. Providers for each technological area play a major role in the expansion of the Internet. As Figure 3.1 shows, they form the overall building blocks of electronic commerce.

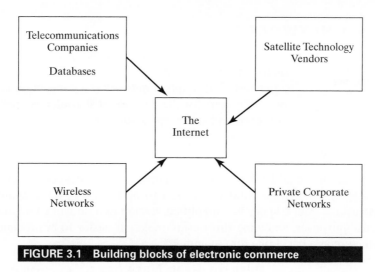

| FIGURE 3.1   **Building blocks of electronic commerce** |

The Internet is a network of networks. A network is any-to-any communication. This communication is made possible by assigning a unique address to each station (called a **node**) on the network. This technical architecture is like the telephone network connecting your phone to any other phone. All you need is the other party's phone number. Intermediary nodes (normally special computers) forward traffic between network segments. These nodes include routers and switches. Linking the nodes together within a network and among networks is called *data communications*.

node: station or component linked as part of a network.

This chapter is about the technologies of the Internet. Technologies are specified by protocols, meaning rules that govern the way a network operates, how applications access the network, how data travel in packets, and how electrical signals represent data on a network cable. In Internet terminology, any computer of any size attached to the Internet is a host—servers as well as home PCs. Each host has an assigned number to identify it to other hosts, much like a phone number. This is called an IP address. Throughout the chapter, we use the term *host* when we explain the various aspects of the technology and how it works.

To understand how the Internet works for e-commerce, you need to know the mechanics of networking. The chapter begins by reviewing some core networking concepts; how data are sent from one place to another; and the standards used when you dial into the Internet from home, from the office, or on the road. We will also look at the TCP/IP-OSI standards architecture that governs the Internet worldwide.

As an information technology (IT) student or a student of business, you will not need to learn how to program switches or routers, but you will need to understand how they work and the functions they perform in an e-commerce environment. This background will help you work with planners and network designers to know what you're getting in return for financial investment in the infrastructure.

WHAT IS A NETWORK?

Before we get into the technical aspects of the Internet and how computers communicate on the Internet, it is important to have a clear idea of the concept of a network. Put simply, a **network** is a connection between at least two computers for the purpose of sharing resources. All networks are based on the concept of sharing.

network: a connection between at least two computers for the purpose of sharing resources.

TYPES OF NETWORKS

In this section, we address two types of networks: peer-to-peer or client/server networks. The latter type is what you expect to find in every e-merchant's technology infrastructure. Peer-to-peer is a simplified version of a network for small business for in-house purposes. Knowing this design makes it easier to appreciate client/server architecture as a backbone for e-commerce.

peer-to-peer network: the linking of several PCs (usually fewer than 10) so that each acts as a peer, sharing and exchanging information without the need for a centralized server.

PEER-TO-PEER NETWORKS. Computers in **peer-to-peer networks** are linked together as equals, with no centralized server or control. Any computer can share its resources with any other computer on the same network in any way and whenever it chooses to do so. Users are network administrators in that they control access to the resources that reside on their own computer. Because of the flexibility of this arrangement, peer-to-peer networks can result in institutionalized chaos, and security can be a problem (see Figure 3.2).

FIGURE 3.2   A basic peer-to-peer network

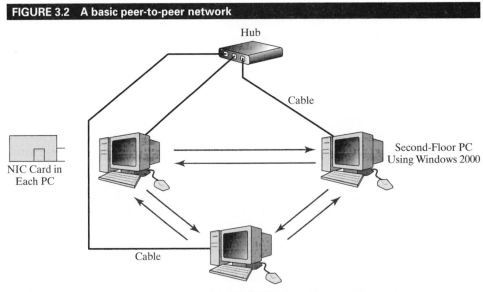

Hub

Cable

NIC Card in
Each PC

Second-Floor PC
Using Windows 2000

Cable

Downstairs PC Using Windows NT

As a rule, a peer-to-peer setup connects fewer than 10 computers. It is appropriate for a dental clinic or a travel agency, for example. As the number of users increases, the peer-to-peer environment becomes impractical. The more users that try to access resources on any particular computer, the worse the performance of the user's machine being accessed across the network. For example, if a user's printer is network accessible, it slows down every time another user in the network sends a job to that printer.

Another drawback is the status of information. With each machine behaving like a server, it is difficult for users to know what information is on which computer. Backing up files is also difficult. Each network computer has to back up its own data, which makes the whole process inefficient and unwieldy. The flip side of these disadvantages is the distinct benefits of low cost and ease of installation, ability to protect one's own resources, and allowing users to act as their own network administrator. Table 3.1 is a summary of the benefits and drawbacks of peer-to-peer networks.

server: special-purpose computer or specialized hardware and software designed for one function.

client: any computer or workstation connected to the server within a network.

client/server network: a cluster of computers (called clients) connected to one or more servers to form a network.

CLIENT/SERVER NETWORKS. A **server** is simply a special-purpose computer or specialized hardware and software designed for one function—to address a client's requests. A **client** is any computer or workstation connected to the server within a network. One of the main advantages of **client/server networks** is centralized control over network resources.

All programs or applications reside on the server. For example, a client might send a request to the server to use Microsoft Word. The server allows the client to download the executable portion of Word. When the work is finished, the program is uploaded onto the server for storage and future use. A client/server system is a multi-user environment. More than one authorized user can access any program or application that resides on the server (see Figure 3.3).

Servers are usually fast computers with physical and logical security capable of controlling who accesses what resource. They provide centralized verification of user passwords and current accounts. To access an application on the server, a user must

TABLE 3.1 Pros and cons of peer-to-peer networks	
Key Benefits	*Key Drawbacks*
Users can control their own shared resources. Easy to install. Easy to configure the system.	Network security is applied to one computer at a time. Every time a computer in the network is accessed, performance suffers.
Inexpensive to purchase and operate. No dependence on a dedicated server. Ideal for small businesses of 10 users or fewer. All you need to set up this network is an operating system and a few cables. No need for a full-time network administrator.	Backup is performed on each machine separately to protect shared resources. Users have to use a separate password on each computer in the network. No centralized setup to locate, manage, or control access to data.

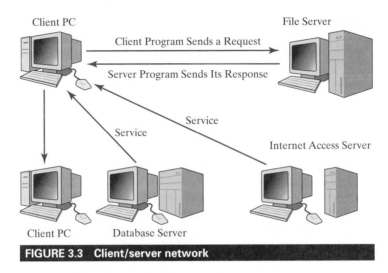

FIGURE 3.3 Client/server network

provide a name and password to the server's domain controller, which checks the user's credentials. The whole setup is monitored by a network administrator, who is the only person authorized to make changes in passwords or to issue passwords. The pros and cons of client/server design are summarized in Table 3.2.

Compared to peer-to-peer designs, a client/server network costs more, requires more knowledgeable staff to manage it, and causes problems for everyone should it go down. A client/server design is appropriate when more than 10 users must share network resources, when centralized security and control are required, and when users require access to specialized servers on a regular basis.

IP ADDRESSES

IP address: a host number represented by strings of 32 bits.

A Web site's address includes the name of the host computer the Web site resides on. The address looks like this: www.wachovia.com. Each host is identified by a host number (called an **IP address**), which identifies it to other hosts, and by a name that is easier to remember than the number. To transmit a message, a source host (the sender) needs to know only the official IP address of the destination host, regardless of location.

TABLE 3.2 Pros and cons of client/server network

Key Benefits	*Key Drawbacks*
Ideal for more than 10 users.	Network failure means clients are almost
Centralized security access and control.	helpless.
Simpler network administration	Specialized staff needed to manage
than peer-to-peer networks.	the specialized hardware and software.
Users remember only one password.	Higher costs than peer-to-peer network
Ideal when user computers are not	because of the specialized hardware and
in close proximity.	software architecture.
More scalable (upgradable) than	
peer-to-peer networks.	

An IP address consists of strings of 32 bits (ones and zeros). Because it is nearly impossible to remember this many bits, the same address is written in dotted decimal notation. Here are the three main steps in creating an IP address in decimal notation.

1. Take an IP address in raw form: 10111111010101010100000000001100

2. Divide the 32-bit string into four 8-bit blocks or four octets.

10111111 01010101 01000000 00001100

(In computer memory, a collection of 8 bits is called a byte; in data networking, it is called an octet.)

3. Represent each.

The IP address contains four number groups separated by dots. The decimal numbers represent the bits and are easier to remember. These numbers may be computer friendly, but they are not human friendly. For this reason, another type of Internet address, called a **host name**, was introduced. It consists of several text labels separated by dots. Operationally, it serves the same purpose: It represents a host computer. For example, 191.170.64.12 has the host name peersbrewer@net.net.

host name: Internet address consisting of text labels separated by dots.

router: network hardware that links a network to other networks.

Internet Service Provider (ISP): a company whose router connects a user to the Internet, usually for a fee.

In the United States, transmission lines and **routers** are owned by commercial organizations. To use the Internet, your computer must be connected to an organization called an *Internet Service Provider (ISP)*. When you send a message or request information from another host computer, you dial into an ISP, whose router connects you to the router of the other host computer. This might involve intermediary routers that bounce your message across routers to its eventual destination (see Figure 3.4).

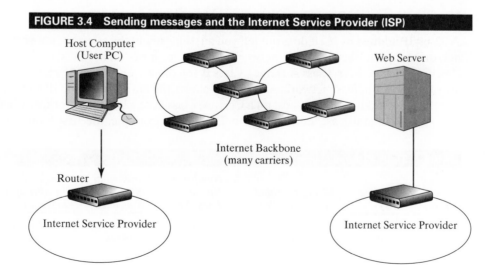

FIGURE 3.4   Sending messages and the Internet Service Provider (ISP)

Host Computer (User PC)

Web Server

Internet Backbone (many carriers)

Router

Internet Service Provider

Internet Service Provider

NETWORKS AND NUMBERS

Take a look at this phone number: 434-924-3423. What do you see? The first six digits identify the location of the phone exchange. In this example, it is Charlottesville, Virginia. The last four digits are a unique phone number in the exchange. Internet host numbers are organized in a similar way. Our host number 191.170.64.12 is divided into two parts: the *network part* and the *local part*. The first two numbers are the network part and represent the organization's unique IP address. The remaining two numbers are two levels of IP addresses assigned by the organization to computers within its area of operation.

To illustrate, the University of Virginia's unique IP address network part is assigned by an IP address registrar as 191.170.0.0. The first two decimal numbers are the network part of the address. Each of that network's host IP addresses must begin with that network sequence. They become the first 16 bits in every host IP address in the university. The university then assigns a unique third decimal number (also called an 8-bit subnet) to each of its colleges, schools, or divisions. For example, the School of Commerce might be assigned 64 as the third part of the IP address or 191.170.64.0. From the university's view, 64 is a local part of the university's IP address.

The School of Commerce, in turn, assigns a unique IP address (fourth decimal number) to each of the PCs within its operations (faculty, lab PCs, etc.). So a particular faculty member's PC as a host computer might be 191.170.64.12. Every other faculty member in the commerce school will have an IP address that has a unique fourth decimal number plus the preceding three decimal numbers. This is like a *child-parent relationship*, where the fourth decimal number (e.g., 12) is the *child* of 64 (the commerce school). The commerce school's decimal number 64 is the child of the parent—the University of Virginia—191.171. Reading the IP address from right to left:

191. 171	**.64**	**.12**
(network part)	(local part or the subnet)	
University	commerce	Bob Johnson's PC
of Virginia	school	

NETWORKS AND SIZES

A 32-bit IP address by itself does not tell you anything about the size of its network, subnet, or host part. Because some networks have more hosts than others, networks are classified in three sizes: Class A (large), Class B (medium), and Class C (small). There is also a Class D multicast network. As Table 3.3 shows, the initial bits of the IP address tell whether an IP address is for a host on a Class A, Class B, or Class C network, or whether it is a Class D multicast address. In our IP address example, the first 8-bit octet is

TABLE 3.3 IP address classes					
Class	*Beginning Bit(s)*	*Bits in Remainder of Network Part*	*Number of Bits in Local Part*	*Maximum Number of Networks*	*Maximum Number of Hosts in Network*
A	0	7	24	136	16 million
B	10	14	16	16,000	65,000
C	110	21	8	2 million	254

10111111. The first 2 bits (10) indicate that the IP address is a Class B address, with 14 remaining bits in the network part, 16 bits (2 octets) in the local part, and a maximum of 65,000 possible hosts in the network.

CLASS A NETWORKS.   You can tell the IP address represents a host in a Class A network if the beginning bit of its first octet is 0. This leaves 7 bits or 216 (2^7) possible Class A networks. Each of these networks could hold up to 16 million hosts.

CLASS B NETWORKS.   An IP address that represents a host in a Class B network begins with 10 in its first octet, leaving 14 bits in the network part to specify more than 16,000 Class B networks. With 16 bits left in the host part, there are more than 65,000 hosts in each of the Class B networks. Because of the even distribution of 16 bits for the network part and 16 bits for the local part, this class of network has been popular from its inception. It is now virtually exhausted. More and more IP address assignments are now being made in a new scheme called *Classless InterDomain Routing (CIDR)*. With CIDR, an IP address can be used to designate several IP addresses. A CIDR IP address ends with a slash followed by a number called the IP prefix. For example, the CIDR IP address 147.200.0.0 would be displayed as 147.200.0.0/12. The IP prefix of /12 can address 2^{12} or 4,096 Class C addresses.

CLASS C NETWORKS.   An IP address that represents a host in Class C networks begins with 110 bits. The network part is 24 bits. With 3 bits used to represent the class, there are 21 remaining unoccupied bits, allowing more than 2 million Class C networks. With an enormous number of networks, Class C networks leave only 8-bit (2^8) or 254 hosts in each network. In the 1970s and 1980s, when mainframes were popular, a small number of hosts was reasonable. With the growing use of PCs as hosts, a limited number of hosts per network is almost useless. CIDR was developed to address this problem.

CLASS D NETWORKS.   Class D addresses begin with 1110 and are used for multicasting. Unlike unicasting, where the packet goes to only one host IP address, IP multicasting means the packet is broadcast to all the hosts on that subnet.

ZONES AND DOMAIN NAMES

An Internet name is decoded from right to left. Take, for example, the Internet name www.Virginia.edu. The rightmost part, edu, is a **zone name;** it tells us that the site is an educational site. The next part, Virginia, is the name of the University of Virginia. The host naming system is also somewhat egalitarian. In it, virginia.edu, a university of 18,000 students, is right up there with other schools like Harvard, Dartmouth, and Yale. In the eye of the Internet, they are all the same, regardless of size or halo. In contrast to a zone name is a domain name. An address like www.virginia.edu is called a **domain name.** It contains two or more word groups separated by periods. The most specific part of a domain is the leftmost part (in this example, Virginia). The www means it is a Web address.

zone name: the last (rightmost) part of a domain name preceded by a dot, specifying the type of domain name.

domain name: a Web address that contains two or more word groups separated by periods.

Zones are classified in two ways: three-letter zone names and two-letter zone names (see Table 3.4). In the United States, most Internet sites fall into one of the two categories. Two-letter zone names are codes of countries and are the last ones shown in

TABLE 3.4 Sample zone names	
Popular Three-Letter Zones	
com	Commercial organizations
edu	Colleges and universities
gov	U.S. government agencies and departments
int	International organizations
mil	Military agencies or sites
net	Network access providers
org	Any other sites or organizations, but primarily professional societies
Common Geographical Two-Letter Zone Names	
au	Austria
be	Belgium
ca	Canada
dk	Denmark
fl	Finland
fr	France
de	Germany
in	India
il	Israel
it	Italy (Italian Republic)
jp	Japan
lb	Lebanon
ru	Russian Federation
es	Spain
sy	Syria
ch	Switzerland
uk	United Kingdom
us	United States

Source: Used with permission of Slashdot.org.

the Internet name. For example, the American University of Beirut (Lebanon) is www.aub.edu.lb. Three-letter zone names are types of organizations. For example, www.Dell.com is the name of a commercial organization.

HOW TO PICK AND REGISTER A DOMAIN NAME

Virtually every business has a Web site. What you pick for a domain name will affect how busy your site is and how well you rank with a search engine. If you sell bananas, put bananas in your domain name. Think of ice-skating. Because search engines use a scoring system called algorithms, your domain name is equivalent to landing a triple jump. If your domain name contains the most important aspects of your business, you will rank higher than if you don't include it. Here are some pointers to consider:

- If you sell bricks, pick a domain name containing a word like brick (e.g., www.brickstore.com). If someone is looking for bricks, you score higher.

- Consider name length and ease of remembering the name. Remember that although a domain name like www.readybrickandsupplies.com is too long to put on a business card or to remember, it is given a higher ranking by search engines.

- One or more hyphens in the domain name forces the search engine to see keywords in your domain name so that your Web site does better in search engine results.

- Make sure the domain name is easy for Web users to remember and find.

- The domain name should suggest the nature of your product or service.

- The domain name should serve as a trademark to discourage your competition from using it as a business name.

- The domain name should be free of legal conflicts with trademarks belonging to other businesses.

In short, a domain name should be short, easy to find, easy to pronounce, clever, and memorable. When it comes to ownership, make sure you are the registrant of the domain name. Often, a Web site design firm will register the domain name for you and will register it in their name rather than in your name.

Several sites will tell you if the domain name you propose has been taken. For example, go to www.8.95domains.com. Enter your proposed domain name in the space indicated to learn if the name is available. Another site, www.FasterWhois.com, will also tell you if the proposed name is taken. To register your domain name cheaply, look up www.registerwizards.com or www.data393.com and you should have no difficulty registering the domain name. The site this author uses for registration is www.internic.net/alpha.html. It is one of the most popular and reliable registration sites.

INFORMATION TRANSFER

In e-commerce, messages, invoicing, and other information transmission is made possible by protocols, standards, and other software that transmit information via packets through a cable to its destination. Look at the U.S. Postal Service. When you mail a package to someone, you wrap the goods in a box and supply the recipient's address, and also your return address in case it is refused, proves to have the wrong address, or has to be returned. The U.S. Postal Service routes the package from a local post office to a central facility by truck. The package goes from one office to another by plane or by truck until it reaches the local office closest to the recipient's address. From there, it is carried and delivered by hand.

The Internet works much the same way. When you send a message to another host, the message is sandwiched in one or more packets and forwarded via routers that identify its destination and send it from one router to another until it reaches the host computer. Forwarding messages electronically from one part of a net to another is common. To standardize the way electronic traffic is managed, rules have been developed to ensure successful transmission and delivery.

PACKETS AND PROTOCOLS

Let's use the U.S. Postal Service analogy again. Suppose you want to send a 5-pound package to a friend in Uzbekistan. On the last segment of the trip from Frankfurt, the package can be flown only on Uzbek Air, which restricts the weight of any package to

2 pounds. You split the package into three smaller packages, label them in some sequence, and send them off. When they arrive, the recipient reorganizes them based on the way they are labeled.

packet: the grouping of data for transmission on a network.

In Internet terms, all data sent through the Internet are sent as packets. Technically, a **packet** is a sequence of bits that carries identifying information for transmitting the data as well as the data itself. A single packet contains a header to keep track of the actual data it carries. The general size of a packet is between 100 and 2,000 octets (bytes), with a typical size of 1,536 octets per packet. This happens to be the limit of an Ethernet network (Ethernets are discussed later in the chapter). Messages that are larger than the standard packet size are split into a series of packets for transmission. Putting the packets back together at the destination is no problem.

network: any-to-any communication or connectivity system. Any station (PC) can communicate with any other station on the network.

Internet protocol (IP): a set of rules used to pass packets from one host to another.

Packets and **Internet protocols (IP)** have one thing in common: One cannot function without the other. For example, when A dials B, B answers the phone by saying "Hello." So the term *Hello* is the protocol for answering the phone. **Protocols** are pieces of software that run on every node or computer and allow every pair of computers to communicate directly without having to know much about each other, except for the IP address.

protocol: a rule that governs how communication should be conducted between two parties, two computers, or a source and a destination.

More specifically, protocols govern communication between peer processes on different systems. The different systems are the user PC and the Web server. The Internet is named as the collection of networks that pass packets to one another using Internet protocols or IP.

Protocols used in connection with the IP include many functions. They are called an Internet protocol suite, or Transmission Control Protocol, or TCP/IP. This is the most widely used protocol suite on the Internet and is explained later in the chapter.

Packet switching is a basic Internet communication term. It refers to the way data are exchanged between two communicating computers. The technology divides data into packets (datagrams), which also contain control information like Internet addresses of the source and destination computers. Once loaded, they are sent independently through the network and reassembled at the destination computer into the original message. Bandwidth is the medium that makes packet transmission possible.

As you can imagine, packet switching makes it possible to enable multiple communicating computers to share the network efficiently, quickly, and accurately. The main problem with such a setup is possible loss of packets during network congestion. Congestion causes delay (latency) and compounded loss of packets during the process. This is why it is quite a feat to implement Internet telephony (telephone calls over the Internet), considering the likely distortions it causes.

Remember that the Internet is not a single large network, but a series of interconnected networks (hence its name), using specialized devices called routers that pass packets from one network to another.

INTERNET PROTOCOLS: THE OSI REFERENCE MODEL

Now that you have an idea of what a protocol is, you need to know the protocols and standards employed for e-commerce. In 1978, the International Standards Organization

OSI Reference Model: a seven-layer model that defines the basic network functions.

(ISO) created a seven-layer model that defines how the Internet works. This model is called the **OSI Reference Model;** OSI stands for Open-Systems Interconnection. Each layer handles a different portion of the communications process with specific network functions. This means that two different networks supporting the functions of a related layer can exchange data at that level. The model was revised in 1984 and became the international standard for networked communication.

The best way to understand the OSI reference model is to assume you are requesting information from a merchant's Web server via your PC. The message that carries the IP address of the Web server goes through a series of layers from the application layer down to and across the physical layer (where it is carried across electrical cables) and up the same layers to the Web server (see Table 3.5). Once the information is found and verified, it is sent back to your PC in reverse sequence in a matter of seconds. One way to remember the sequence of the layers is to remember the phrase "**P**lease **D**o **N**ot **T**hrow **S**ausage **P**izza **A**way" (PDNTSPA), where the letters represent physical, data link, network, transport, session, presentation, and application layers, respectively. (See Table 3.5.) The first letter of each word should remind you of each layer in sequence. Now let's examine each layer.

THE APPLICATION LAYER. The application layer communicates with the actual application in use. It is simply two useful programs talking to each other. For example, an e-mail client browser program talks to the e-mail server program, saying: "Deliver this message to ema@Georgia.com." Remember that each type of program (e-mail) has its own protocol. As in a relay event, the application level protocol assumes the next layer down (presentation layer) will take care of passing the message along to its destination.

hypertext transfer protocol (HTTP): technology that allows the browser on the user's PC to look at a standard set of codes called HTML to decide how the text or graphics should be displayed.

hypertext markup language (HTML): a standard set of codes representing text or graphics.

Standards at the application layer specify how two application programs should communicate. The main standard on the application layer is **hypertext transfer protocol (HTTP).** It governs requests and responses between the browser and the Web server applications program. HTTP also allows the browser on the user's PC to look at a standard set of codes called **hypertext markup language (HTML)** to decide how text and graphics should be displayed. HTTP decides how an HTML document transfers from a Web server to your PC (see Figure 3.5).

The application layer is where the user begins to do something useful—browse a Web site, send e-mail, or transfer a file between file servers

TABLE 3.5 The OSI reference model		
Layer	*Information Transacted*	*TCP/IP Protocols*
7. Application layer	Application messages	HTTP, SNMP, FTP DNS
6. Presentation layer	Compressed data, encrypted data	
5. Session layer	Session messages	
4. Transport layer	Multiple packets	TCP
3. Net (Internet) layer	Packets	IP
2. Data link layer	Frames	Ethernet, PPP
1. Physical layer	Bits	Wiring, cables

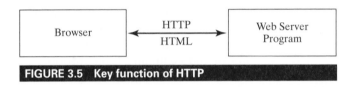

FIGURE 3.5   Key function of HTTP

simple network manage-
ment protocol (SNMP):
protocol that controls
network devices at the
application layer.

domain naming service
(DNS): software that
converts IP addresses into
easy-to-remember names
for the user.

and client computers. This is where File Transfer Protocol (FTP) plays a major role. FTP is another member of the TCP/IP protocol suite. **Simple network management protocol (SNMP)** is a TCP/IP protocol used for controlling network devices at the application layer. **Domain naming service (DNS)** converts IP addresses into easy-to-remember names for the user. It is easier to enter www.virginia.edu than the IP address 191.172.54.12. Like a dictionary, DNS takes the name and looks up the equivalent IP address, which it sends along for processing.

Although all layers are important to make your interface with the e-merchant's Web site possible, it is the application layer that is the most important for conducting business on the Internet.

THE PRESENTATION LAYER. The presentation layer is the network's translator. It converts data into a format for network transmission. For incoming messages, it converts the data into a format the receiving application can understand.

THE SESSION LAYER. This layer facilitates a "session" between two parties to communicate across a network. Applications on each end of the session are able to exchange data for the duration of the session. This layer keeps track of the status of the exchange and ensures that only designated parties are allowed to participate. It enforces security protocols for controlling access to session information.

THE TRANSPORT LAYER. The transport layer manages the transmission or flow of data between two computers or across a network. It makes sure that the program on one computer connected to another program on another computer receives and sends information accurately. The way it manages the data flow is by segmenting data into multiple packets (see Table 3.5). If a lot of traffic is flowing, it tells other computers to pause.

The transport layer also acknowledges successful transmissions and requests retransmission if packets are damaged or arrive in error. It breaks the connection when transmission ends.

The standard for the transport layer is the **transmission control protocol (TCP).** TCP relies on the next level down (the Internet layer) to take care of moving packets of data on to their destination without a problem. TCP is the most popular standard in use on the Internet. When you use a Web server, it does not matter if it is a PC or a mainframe. Your PC can communicate with it using TCP. HTTP also requires the use of the TCP standard at the transport layer.

transmission control
protocol (TCP): protocol
that specifies how two host
computers will work
together.

In addition to ensuring data delivery from one computer to another, TCP performs flow control. Sometimes a fast computer sends data at a rate that the slower, receiving computer cannot process. TCP moderates data flow to the speed of the slower computer to avoid network congestion and ensure reliability of data transmission.

THE INTERNET LAYER.   The Internet layer routes messages across multiple nodes. It also handles network congestion. A typical message is, "Send this packet to computer number 190.172.63.08 via computer number 123.32.12.14, which is on a network one hop away."

The standard at the Internet layer specifies how hosts and routers will route packets from source host to destination host across several subnets or single networks connected by routers. At this layer, messages are called packets. The standard for routing packets is the Internet Protocol (IP). You can see now why Internet addresses are called IP addresses.

TCP and IP are actually two standards, but they are shown as TCP/IP, because one standard cannot do its homework without the other. **TCP/IP** is the most widely used protocol on the Internet. If packets get lost, it resends them automatically. It defines how data are subdivided into packets for transmission across a network and how applications can transfer files and e-mail. TCP/IP provides the basis for high-performance networking.

TCP/IP: a set of protocols that guarantee data delivery.

THE DATA LINK LAYER.   The data link layer is the "basement" of the Internet. It takes care of the actual transfer of data between two computers located on the same network. A typical message is, "Send this packet to computer number 110.42.21.13, which I can see right next door."

point-to-point protocol (PPP): a standard at the data link layer used for framing and error detection.

When we dial in with a telephone line and a modem, the main standard at this layer is the **point-to-point protocol (PPP).** Its main job is framing and error detection. Framing marks the boundary between packets. Messages at the data link layer are called data **frames.** At the receiving end, the data link layer packages bits of data from the physical layer into data frames for delivery to the Internet layer. This data frame is the basic unit of Internet traffic. Data from upper layers are placed for sending, and data are sent from it to the upper layers.

frame: basic unit of Internet traffic.

Ethernet: a protocol that makes it possible for personal computers to contend for access to a network.

A better way of sending packets is over an **Ethernet.** Ethernet is a protocol that makes it possible for PCs to contend for access to a network. Framing and error detection are handled automatically by Ethernet hardware. A typical Ethernet has 100 computers linked to it. There must be a way to tell which of these computers the packet is intended for. A commonsense way to do it is to place the IP address of the destination computer in front of the packet. As each packet whizzes by, only the computer with the correct address receives it. Although the Ethernet broadcasts a message to all the computers linked to it, only the computer with the right address broadcasts an answer. The rest ignore both the question and the answer.

THE PHYSICAL LAYER.   The physical layer is the lowest layer in the journey of a message from source to destination. It converts bits into signals for outgoing messages and signals into bits for incoming messages. This is where cables begin to do their homework.

SUMMING UP

If you are going through this material for the first time, it probably seems incredibly complicated. It is, but all you need to keep in mind is how your message from your PC makes it to the merchant's Web server to conduct business over the Internet. Can you imagine a highway without street signs, speed limits, or police to enforce traffic rules? The Internet is the same. For message traffic to flow smoothly and reliably, we need standards for communication and ways for systems from different vendors to work together. We also need protocols or rules of transmission at each layer of the communication cycle.

Here is an example: A user sends a request via PC to access a company's Web page (e.g., Dell.com). The PC's browser activates the application layer to communicate between the client program on the user's PC and the Web server application program. At the application layer, for the Web the standard is HTTP. The application layer reviews the message and its destination and *stamps* it or *tags* it with a special identifier to keep track of it before it is sent to the next layer (transport) for processing.

The transport layer ensures that the user's computer and the host computer (Web server) can work together, regardless of the vendor or make of the two computers. HTTP mandates the use of TCP at the transport layer. Before the message is sent to the Internet layer, the transport layer divides it into chunks (packets) if it is too large and provides checks to make sure it is error free when delivered. The chunks are resequenced at their destination (see Figure 3.6).

At the Internet layer, the packet will be routed to the destination host (Web server), using IP as a standard. It translates the network address and names into their physical equivalents and uses one or more routers connected by single networks to do the job. This layer handles packet switching and ensures the best way to route a packet. It also handles network congestion and delivery priorities to minimize unnecessary delay in packet delivery. Once it leaves the Internet layer, the packet is in the hands of the physical layer.

The physical layer uses modems and telephone network standards to transmit the message as raw data to its destination. It actually converts bits into signals for outgoing messages and signals into bits for incoming messages. Modems are used only to link a user host to the first router. By now the message is halfway to its destination. The physical layer is at the bottom in the data communication model. The data link layer picks up the raw data (incoming message) from the physical layer and converts it into frames for delivery upward to the Internet layer.

The standard used between the user's PC and the first router is the point-to-point protocol (PPP). It checks to make sure the message is intact before sending it to the Internet layer. At the Internet layer, the frame is encapsulated into an IP packet. This layer decides on the best way to route the message to the destination host computer (Web server). At the transport layer, the IP packet is received, de-encapsulated, checked for errors, and the content is sent to the next-higher level—the session layer.

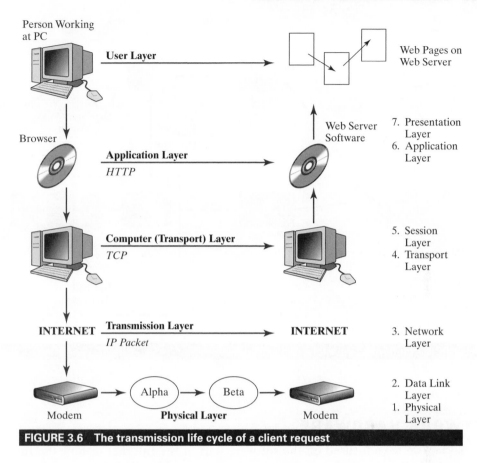

FIGURE 3.6 The transmission life cycle of a client request

At the session layer, the message is checked to determine which host computer should get it. The presentation layer merely decides on the format the message should have before it reaches the Web server. When the message reaches the application layer of the Web server, it is acknowledged and responded to, and the homepage of the firm (in our example, www.dell.com) is displayed on the user's monitor—the journey from beginning to end takes less than 2 seconds.

OTHER NETWORKS

TCP/IP protocols are not restricted to the Internet. Companies have found them useful in creating **intranets,** or internal company networks using TCP/IP to share information within an organization. Companies wishing to connect with vendors and suppliers establish shared databases and use TCP/IP to form **extranets.** This infrastructure is part of business-to-business e-commerce. Figure 3.7 shows the connections among the Internet, an intranet, and an extranet. (Intranets and extranets are covered in detail in separate chapters later in the text.)

intranet: a network using TCP/IP to share information within an organization.

extranet: a network that connects separate companies with a shared database.

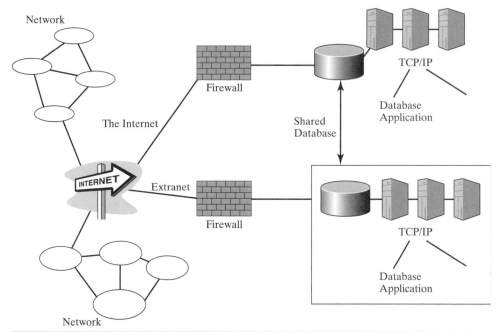

FIGURE 3.7 Internets, intranets, and extranets

NETWORK HARDWARE

So far, we have focused on the software part of the Internet or how the Internet works. In systems design, software is the first consideration. The second step is to assess the hardware required to drive the software. Network hardware plays a crucial role in helping information flow through the Internet. In its simplest form, a computer network includes two or more PCs connected to a printer. In some multinational organizations, it means thousands of PCs, printers, servers, firewalls, routers, switches, repeaters, and gateways. It's like comparing a two-bedroom apartment to a sky-scraper. Each piece of hardware serves a special function, such as connecting a PC to the network, managing and routing traffic, boosting performance, and connecting different parts of a network.

Complex networks require people with specialized skills to manage them effectively. The level of technical skill and the size of the technical staff depend largely on the size of the network, the time requirements of the organization, and the type of information transmitted. Unless a company has a network with fewer than 20 users, companies need at least one full-time network administrator.

CABLE TYPES

Network connectivity means speed of data transfer, network size, and ease of installation. Briefly, there are three types of cable (twisted pair, optical fiber, coaxial), plus wireless technology.

twisted-pair cable: two pairs of insulated wires twisted around each other, then enclosed in a plastic sheath.

TWISTED-PAIR CABLE.   **Twisted pair** is probably the most commonly used type of networking cable in the United States. It originally was used to connect a telephone to a wall jack. Two pairs of insulated copper wires are twisted around each other, then enclosed in a plastic sheath. Twisting the wires protects against cross talk or natural signal overflow and interference from one wire to another.

Twisted pair is the least expensive cable medium. But it is susceptible to noise and distance limitations. It is also the least secure, which means it is the easiest to tap.

SHIELDED AND UNSHIELDED TWISTED PAIR.   The cheapest LAN transmission medium is the copper wire. Ensuring a complete electrical circuit requires only a pair of copper wires. A pair of wires usually is twisted to reduce interference problems but does not have shielding against electrical interference. Therefore, it is called **unshielded twisted-pair** cabling, or UTP.

unshielded twisted pair (UTP): a pair of wires twisted to reduce electrical interference but without the shielding.

UTP cabling is defined in terms of five cable categories, with category 5e (enhanced) used for handling data transfer rates of 100 Mbps. UTP cabling is vulnerable to electromagnetic interference and cross talk. It is also subject to attenuation, which means weakening of the signal beyond 100 meters. Attenuation makes signals unreadable after a specified distance unless a repeater (a device that regenerates and retransmits the signal) is used.

In contrast to UTP cabling, **shielded twisted pair (STP)** cabling has an electrically grounded woven copper mesh or aluminum foil wrapped around each twisted pair and another metal mesh wrapped around a multiple bundle of wires. This cable type reduces electromagnetic interference, but the wiring is thick and difficult to lay and maintain.

shielded twisted pair (STP): cable with an electrically grounded, woven copper mesh or aluminum foil wrapped around each twisted pair.

fiber-optic cable: transmission system that uses light rather than voltage to transmit data.

FIBER-OPTIC CABLE.   **Fiber-optic cable** uses light rather than voltage to carry data. Fiber optics relies on the principle that light can travel in a glass medium and carry more information than other predecessors of data communication. The fiber enables digitized light signals to be transmitted more than 60 miles without being amplified. This medium has a number of benefits that outperform copper and coaxial media such as fewer transmission losses, lower interference, and higher bandwidth.

When light reaches the central glass core, it hits a layer of glass cladding, resulting in internal reflections at the boundary. Because no light escapes, there is little attenuation and zero interference or eavesdropping (see Figure 3.8).

Fiber-optic speed for data transmission ranges from 100 Mbps to 2 Gbps (gigabits per second). Data are reliably transmitted over a distance of 2 kilometers (1.4 miles) without a repeater. Unlike other cable types, fiber-optic cable supports voice and video as well as data transmission. These features make fiber-optic cabling a good candidate for networks that must be very secure and require fast transmission over long distances. Its main drawbacks are:

- It is the most expensive of all network media types.
- Each segment that transmits incoming and receiving data must contain an incoming cable and an outgoing cable.
- It requires highly skilled installers and special connectors.

(a) Cross-Talk Interference: A Termination Problem

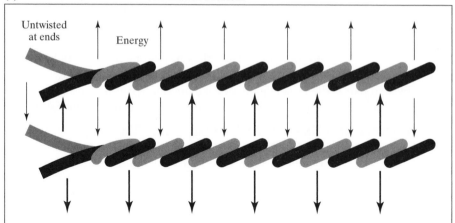

Untwisted at ends

Energy

Each pair radiates into the environment. Each pair receives radiation from the environment. Signals in adjacent pairs interfere with one another (cross talk). Twisting each pair helps reduce this cross-talk interference. Cross-talk interference is worst at the ends, where the wires are untwisted. This is terminal cross talk.

(b) Unshielded Twisted Pair (UTP) Wire Bundle

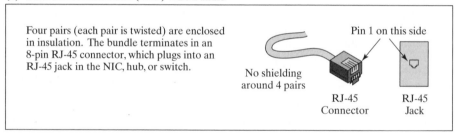

Four pairs (each pair is twisted) are enclosed in insulation. The bundle terminates in an 8-pin RJ-45 connector, which plugs into an RJ-45 jack in the NIC, hub, or switch.

No shielding around 4 pairs

Pin 1 on this side

RJ-45 Connector

RJ-45 Jack

(c) Optical Fiber

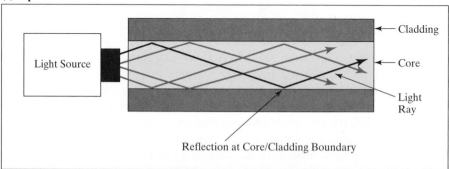

Cladding

Light Source

Core

Light Ray

Reflection at Core/Cladding Boundary

Figure 3.8   Fiber-optic cable

Source: Adapted from Panko, Raymond, *Business Data Communications and Network* (3rd ed.), Upper Saddle River, NJ: Prentice Hall, 2001, p. 278.

SELECTION CRITERIA. According to the International Engineering Consortium for fiber optics, there are three factors to consider in deciding whether or not to use fiber-optic cable:

- *Attenuation* or delay, the reduction of signal strength due to gravitational pull. For fiber optics, reduction of light is measured in decibels per kilometer. Optical fiber is superior to other transmission media, because it provides higher bandwidth with low attenuation that requires fewer amplifiers and allows the signal to be transmitted over longer distances.
- *Dispersion,* the time distortion of an optical signal that results from discrete wavelength components traveling at different rates, causing distortion of wavelengths and limiting data rates as well as the capacity of a fiber.
- *Mode-field diameter (MFD),* the functional parameter that determines optical performance when a fiber is coupled to a light source, spliced, or bent.

In summary, fiber optics has proven itself as the networking technology of the future. It is reliable, because the data delivered over this medium are the least susceptible to the propagation effects witnessed in traditional networking media. Advanced fiber-optic technologies are expected to provide for greater network capabilities than ever seen in the past.

coaxial cable: a cable consisting of a copper center shielded by a plastic insulating material, which allows high data transmission rates over long distances.

COAXIAL CABLE. **Coaxial cable** is an early version of the way computers were connected to a network, and it worked well. It is the cable in cable TV. This cable has a copper core that is much thicker than twisted-pair cable, so it allows higher data transmission rates over long distances. The core is shielded by a plastic insulating material surrounded by a second conductor that looks much like woven copper mesh or aluminum foil. The outer shield is used as an electrical ground that simultaneously protects the inner core from interference.

Coaxial cable can transmit up to 10 Mbps for a distance of up to 500 meters. The main drawback of this type of cable is its inflexibility and low security, but it requires little maintenance and is simple to install. It also provides better resistance to electrical noise over long distances, and its electronic support components are affordable.

wireless data transmission technology: data transmission without physical attachments; microwave, radio wave, and infrared.

WIRELESS TECHNOLOGY. Going wireless is like scuba diving wearing lightweight gear and not being linked to a ship by a long umbilical cord for air. Wireless transmission is data communication without physical attachments. At present, it varies in speed, signal type, transmission distance, and frequency (the higher the frequency, the higher the transmission rate).

The three types of **wireless data transmission technology** are microwave, radio wave, and infrared. *Microwave* transmission is used to connect LANs in separate buildings (e.g., two skyscrapers) where physical media are impractical. The transmitter and receiver must be within the line of sight of each other, usually 30 miles apart. For global transmission, the technology relies on satellites and ground-based satellite dishes to meet the line-of-sight requirements.

Radio technology transmits by radio frequency with no distance limitations. It is susceptible to atmospheric and electronic interference and is subject to government regulation. Because of security limitations and the potential for eavesdropping, most radio transmission is encrypted.

Infrared transmission operates at frequencies approaching the speed of light. Because of interference from bright light, infrared is limited to line-of sight or short-distance applications. It is commonly found in department stores or office buildings. A summary of the pros and cons of network cabling is shown in Table 3.6.

TABLE 3.6   Pros and cons of cabling types

Cabling Type	Advantages	Disadvantages
Twisted pair	Protects against cross talk and interference Easy to add computers to network Well-understood technology Less expensive than other cabling media	Susceptibility to noise Least secure Distance limitations Requires more expensive hubs
UTP	Inexpensive Easier to install than STP	Interference from outside electromagnetic sources Cross talk Vulnerable to tapping Subject to attenuation
STP	Reduces EMI High-speed transmission	Difficult to lay and maintain Delicate cable
Optical fiber	Reliable transmission High security Supports voice, video, data Smallest in size Longest in longevity	Most expensive medium in terms of installation and maintenance Requires incoming and outgoing cable Requires special connections
Coaxial cable	Can transmit up to 10 Mbps over 500 meters Low maintenance Simple to install Good resistance-to-noise ratio Inexpensive electric support components	Inflexible, thick cable Low-security cable is rigid Limited distance Susceptibility to tapping
Wireless technology	Convenient alternative to network cabling connections	Relatively new
Microwave	Connects two buildings where physical media are impractical	Transmitter and receiver must be within line of sight
Radio wave	No distance limitations	Susceptible to atmospheric and security limitations
Infrared	Operates at speed of light Wireless data transfer	Limited to short distance and line-of-site applications

Network Components

A typical network has several pieces of critical components—network interface card (NIC), switches, routers, and gateways.

Network Interface Card.   At the user's end of the network, the most direct physical connection from the PC is through the **network interface card (NIC).** A NIC card is installed in a slot in the PC, with a cable plugged into the back (see Figure 3.9). The other end of the cable is plugged into a wall-jack connection or directly into the hub or switch for a small network (see following text). Another cable runs from the switch to the route to complete the connections.

network interface card (NIC): a card installed in a slot in the PC to allow communication between the PC and other PCs in the LAN and beyond.

To communicate over a telephone line, the PC needs a **modem,** which has the dual function of converting digital signals into analog form for transmission across the telephone line, and converting incoming analog signals into digital signals. Computers represent data in bits or digital format; the telephone line is analog. (See Figure 3.10.)

modem (modulator/demodulator): a device that converts digital signals into analog format for outgoing transmission and converts incoming messages from analog to digital format for computer processing.

Hubs and Switches.   A **hub** is a piece of hardware that operates at the OSI physical layer and acts as a connecting point—like a one-way road where all cars share the same lane. Hubs are a party line on which everyone talks at once (see Figure 3.9).

hub: a piece of hardware that operates as a connecting point for many PCs in a network.

Switches are like a highway where every car has its own lane. This means no traffic congestion. Unlike a hub, where everyone talks at once, a switch offers direct connection to a particular PC. Hubs are phasing out because they do not offer the same efficiency as switches.

switch: a piece of hardware that offers a direct connection to a particular PC.

Routers.   A *router* is a piece of hardware that operates at the OSI Internet layer, linking the network into little chunks called *network segments*, so users on different LAN segments can talk to one another. Routers are usually "intelligent": They evaluate the network traffic and can stop local traffic from entering and causing

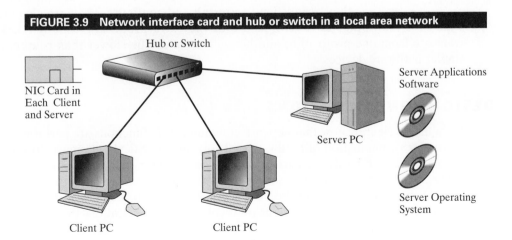

FIGURE 3.9   Network interface card and hub or switch in a local area network

Hub or Switch

NIC Card in Each Client and Server

Server Applications Software

Server PC

Server Operating System

Client PC

Client PC

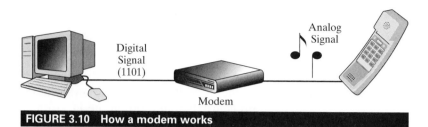

FIGURE 3.10   How a modem works

congestion on other local area networks. Routers can also make intelligent path choices. They can filter out packets that need not be received. In this way, they can reduce network congestion and boost data performance. Because routers can select an alternative path for a packet if the default route is down, they make data delivery more reliable.

Routers have drawbacks. They are expensive and difficult to operate. At times they are slow, because they must perform additional processing on the data packet. Some advanced routers also can add excessive traffic to the network because of constant messages to one another when updating their routing tables.

A **routing table** on a router is a log of the pattern of traffic coming from neighboring routers so that the next time the router sends out or receives packets, it can tell whether to take a certain route based on information stored in its routing table. Every few seconds, each router on the Net consults the router to which it is directly connected (its neighbor). By comparing notes, the router can decide which way to send packets to each of the hundreds of routers on the Internet. The goal for the router is to minimize the number of *hops* a packet must take before it reaches its destination.

routing table: software that logs the pattern of traffic coming from neighboring routers.

GATEWAYS.   A **gateway** is a special-purpose computer that facilitates communications between dissimilar systems connected to a network, TCP/IP, or IBM's System Network Architecture (SNA). Gateways operate primarily at the application layer of the OSI. They have many advantages, but they are difficult to install and configure. They are also more expensive than other devices. Because of the extra processing time it takes to translate from one protocol to another, gateways can be slower than routers and similar hardware devices.

Gateway: a special-purpose computer that allows communication between dissimilar systems on the network.

DESIGN CONSIDERATIONS

It should be clear by now that network communication functions are performed primarily by a combination of hardware and software specifically designed to support the network. The hardware part typically includes the network interface card, the cables, and the switches that connect the workstations to the router and beyond. Your Web site is the front of the network architecture. To implement the network, you need to think about the various protocols and the applications that will support the hardware.

STEP 1: FACTORS TO KEEP IN MIND

When designing a network, you need to consider several factors.

- Location—Where will the network be installed? How convenient is the location? How easy is it to install—the cabling, space allocation, and other issues?
- Capacity—What is the optimum traffic capacity of the network? How scalable (upgradable) is it? How efficient is its performance at that capacity?
- Distance limitations—What is the distance of the farthest PC to the server? How does distance affect network performance during peak hours? How does distance compromise security?
- Cost—What is the estimated cost of the proposed network installation? Is the cost within the client's budget? What are the hidden costs? Given the cost, how would you justify the return on investment?
- Potential growth—How easily and how well can the network be expanded to meet the growing demands of the client organization? What is the expected cost of such growth?
- Security—How secure is the proposed network? What security measures should be incorporated? Who will be in charge of monitoring security?

STEP 2: HARDWARE AND SOFTWARE CONSIDERATIONS

The next step is to consider these factors when selecting network architecture.

HARDWARE REQUIREMENTS.   Hardware includes servers, workstations, printers, switches, routers, minicomputers, and backup systems. Amount of usage is also important. For example, it makes no sense to install a high-powered networked environment for a company with limited usage and low growth potential. If network utilization is high and the organization expects rapid growth, it makes sense to replace aging terminals and hubs with intelligent workstations and intelligent routers.

SOFTWARE REQUIREMENTS.   These requirements depend largely on the hardware and applications available. For example, if the company has mission-critical applications with high performance requirements, the only choice would be to bring in the software that can meet immediate needs. The choice of network architecture will depend on the factors cited earlier.

DISASTER RECOVERY AND FAULT-TOLERANCE REQUIREMENTS.   Recovery from disaster depends on the sensitivity of data, size of the files, and reliability of the network. The network infrastructure must be protected by an Uninterruptible Power Supply (UPS), which takes over in the event of a blackout or loss of power. All file servers and CD files should be kept under lock and key. Redundant equipment (switches, routers, servers) also should be available as backup for the main network. *Fault tolerant* means the system has built-in features that allows it to recover from failure. Fault-tolerant hard disks are defined by a set of specifications known as Redundant Array of Inexpensive Disks, or RAID, which mirror resident disk drives.

SUCCESSFUL INSTALLATION

A successful network must be planned in advance. Here are some things to do.

- Conduct a survey of current technology and the constraints to be addressed up front.
- Document network requirements, including the number of computers in use, the required peripherals, the software in use, and the level of resource sharing required.
- Decide on the network operating system. This will determine the type of file server hardware and the transport protocols the system will support.
- Decide on the file server hardware platform. It means estimating the client traffic and how well certain technology will support the load. Any file server chosen should be supported by the network's operating system.
- Determine the physical environment and client support. User and company requirements dictate where and how file servers, routers, and switches are located and maintained.

MANAGERIAL FACTORS

The job of finding qualified staff to manage a network has become a prime consideration when planning an e-commerce system. It is no longer enough to simply wire the user to the Internet. Someone has to maintain an acceptable level of system availability; assure good response time; run the network at optimal capacity; route voice and data traffic around the clock; and enable managers, employees, and customers to communicate effectively regardless of time, distance, or location.

Not only has the job of the network manager become more complex, but the tools also have become more specialized. Today, tools help the network administrator ensure network performance by monitoring, analyzing, testing, diagnosing, and maintaining the network.

Figure 3.11 shows a typical network management system to support a centralized network. The key components are as follows.

- *The manager*—The network administrator manages the network via software loaded on a special workstation. The manager's main function is to monitor the network's printers, routers, switches, and other pieces of software and hardware. In a simple network, the manager uses a management protocol such as Simple Network Management Protocol (SNMP) to govern the way the manager communicates with the agent. It is a way of controlling network devices at the application layer.

agent: node or software that communicates with the manager on behalf of the node.

object: port or specific outlet on a managed node that the agent represents to the manager.

- *Managed nodes*—The manager monitors nodes or pieces of software called **agents** that communicate with the manager on behalf of the node, much the way a professional athlete's agent negotiates on behalf of the athlete.
- **Objects**—Ports on the managed node that the agent represents to the manager. Managers communicate to the agent requests about a specific port or that a port is to be disabled by a switch.

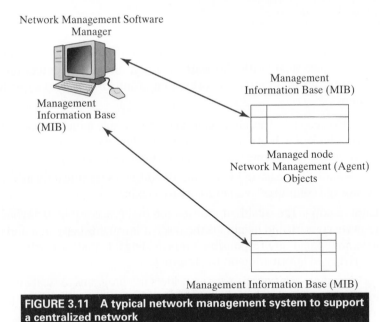

Network Management Software
Manager

Management
Information Base (MIB)

Management
Information Base
(MIB)

Managed node
Network Management (Agent)
Objects

Management Information Base (MIB)

FIGURE 3.11   A typical network management system to support a centralized network

Source: Based on Raymond Panko, *Business Data Networks and Telecommunications* (4th ed.), Upper Saddle River, NJ: Prentice Hall, 2003, p. 329.

Through SNMP, a manager can ask a file server agent about the status of an attachment like a printer and its readiness to print.

- **Management information base (MIB)—** another piece of software that defines the objects that can exist, based on the initial design of the database. An MIB on each managed node contains information about that node's objects. Sound confusing? It is, especially when you have to look at how data are stored, how they are accessed, and so on.

management information base (MIB): software that defines the objects that can exist, based on the initial design of the database.

- *Requests and responses—*an aspect of the network management system that uses SNMP to allow the manager and agents to work through pre-established cycles. A cycle begins when the manager sends a request. The agent sends a response that it has received the request, sends the requested data, or sends an error message. If an agent senses a condition that the manager should know about, it sends a message (called a **trap**) alerting the manager.

trap: message sent to the manager by an agent, alerting the manager to a special condition.

We have been building networks much larger than we can manage. When problems come up, it can take hours just to find the cause. What is needed are skilled technicians and highly trained specialists to monitor, diagnose, and fix the network to ensure reliability at all times. Companies must have policies to control the quality of service and security. We are entering an era of disciplined network management with an array of intelligent devices and new technology and a much faster and more reliable Internet.

E-COMMERCE ISSUES

Security management is a continuous and vigilant process in high-volume e-commerce. The key issues deal with firewall security, intrusion detection, and various security breaches in an internetworking environment. Several exposures are worth mentioning:

- Financial exposure—This factor can cause irreparable monetary damage to a corporation. Think of a disgruntled IT executive who sabotages the computer systems of the company after being laid off, causing millions in damages.

- IP exposure—The ease in identifying IP addresses significantly increases a networked computer's vulnerability to hacking.

- Legal security—The wealth of information that is accessible to anyone generates growing concern and heightens the risks of infringing copyright and defamation laws. Companies are responsible for providing adequate security for the protection of privileged information on the Internet.

- Packet sniffing—This occurs when outsiders use programs to steal information traveling through a company network. The unauthorized interception of this proprietary information can result in significant losses for the company.

- Firewalls—One approach to ensuring corporate information security is through firewalls. A *firewall* serves as an intermediary between an internal network and the Internet. It controls which packets can pass into the network. *Packet filter firewalls* check the fields of the IP packet and screen out entries by invalid source addresses or port numbers. *Application firewalls* are application specific and also are known as proxy firewalls. *Proxy firewalls* reduce IP exposure by intercepting outgoing packets and attaching their own IP address to it to conceal the client PC's IP address.

- IPSec—IP Security (IPSec) is a set of standards that allows virtual private networks (VPNs) to improve packet filtering and enable application-layer firewalls to have better means of host verification by using the IPSec authentication header in addition to the actual IP address (Interhack.net).

- Intrusion detection systems (IDS)—This security tool serves as a watchdog for unauthorized activities by first identifying suspicious activities, notifying the administrator, and then responding to the attack. IDSs often fall into two categories: network based, which inspect packets passing through the network, and host based, which monitor log files and data on individual computers. Each category has unique benefits and potential.

MANAGEMENT IMPLICATIONS

The area of Internet technology and networking continues to attract the best talent, with more job openings than there are qualified people to fill them. Choose any IT job, no matter what its title, and it is likely woven into the Web one way or another. Every firm wants to have faster and better technology than the competition. The demand for technical help makes it a candidate's job market. Most jobs are new, triggered by the continuing surge of e-commerce, especially business-to-consumer and now business-to-business.

Of the skills required in the Internet and e-commerce areas, technology alone is not enough. Most recruiters look for candidates with good project management skills, inter-personal communication skills, and business knowledge. Even college graduates with liberal arts and business background and good PC experience are attractive candidates.

Good, experienced network designers and people in TCP/IP are not easy to find. So where do IT recruiters find needed talent? After placement and recruiting firms, the second-best sources are Internet ads and Internet job sites. E-commerce companies and those developing business-to-business applications are in the lead. Many experi-enced Java programmers working on a contract basis earn at least $100 per hour. Any company in e-commerce with a focus on designing a network and Web site has a high demand for those who have technical skills, with a bachelor's degree in fine arts and knowledge of computer animation.

When all the necessary technical talent has been hired, a company must find ways to keep its IT employees. Regular training and the chance to work with the latest tech-nology seem to be the best motivators. Good benefit packages are important. Recognition for a job well done, pleasant working conditions, and a good working rela-tionship with IT staff also boost job satisfaction.

Here are some tips for retaining Internet and technical personnel.

- *Constructive and timely feedback*—One of the most important issues in managing and motivating technical people is consistent and constructive feedback on a day-to-day basis. This is especially true for new hires. Feedback is also important in helping per-sonnel develop new skills and advance to more challenging positions.

- *Recognition and appreciation of good, value-added work*—It is human nature that recog-nition is a reinforcer, especially when it is made in a timely manner. A simple thanks from the heart is what it often takes to restart a project that has been going nowhere.

- *Championing staff causes*—A champion in IT is someone who uses every opportunity to promote a project with those on higher organizational levels. Sometimes top management reluctantly approves a project, not knowing how it is going to turn out. An IT manager can keep top managers interested and reinforce the progress made by example, by scenarios, or by online displays of completed work.

- *Support of employee career goals*—Technical employees should not only have oppor-tunities to undergo training and improve their skills, but they should be able to utilize those skills. Technical people often are motivated more by opportunities for creativity than by money alone.

- *Match industry salary standards for in-house personnel*—Regardless of how well IT personnel are treated, it is still important to provide competitive salaries and attractive benefits to discourage defection to the competition. Many corpora-tions now offer sign-up bonuses, stock options, pleasant office surroundings, flextime, and other opportunities to ensure job satisfaction and loyalty to the organization. In the final analysis, it takes sensitivity, communication skills, timely feedback, and a genuine interest in people and their careers to make a department or a corporation successful.

Summary

1. A network is a connection between at least two computers for the purpose of sharing resources. There are three types of networks: local area networks (LANs), wide area networks (WANs), and metropolitan area networks (MANs). These networks can be peer-to-peer, client/server, or hybrid networks. Each has benefits and drawbacks.

2. Transmission lines and routers in the United States are owned by commercial organizations. To use the Internet, a computer must be connected to an Internet service provider. The ISP router connects the computer to the router of the other host computer on the Internet.

3. Internet host numbers are divided into two parts: the network part (first two numbers) and the local part (second two numbers). The four numbers are separated by dots. The initial bits of the IP address tell whether it is on a Class A, Class B, or Class C network, or whether it is a Class D multicast address.

4. Messages, invoicing, and other information transmission on the Internet are made possible by protocols, standards, and other software that transmits information via packets through a cable to its destination.

5. The OSI Reference Model is a seven-layer model that defines the basic network functions: application layer, presentation layer, session layer, transport layer, Internet layer, data link layer, and physical layer.

6. The standard for the transport layer is TCP, which is the most popular standard used on the Internet. It handles flow control, sequence assurance, and reliability and integrity issues.

7. To communicate over a line, you need a modem, which converts digital signals into analog form for transmission, and converts incoming analog signals into digital signals. To complete the transmission infrastructure, a hub is used to connect PCs to routers for transmission. A router is a piece of intelligent hardware that links the network into segments so users on different LAN segments can talk to one another.

8. Several factors need to be considered in designing a network: location, capacity, distance limitations, cost, potential growth, and security.

9. Several factors need to be considered in selecting network architecture: hardware requirements, software requirements, disaster recovery and fault-tolerance requirements, and corporate culture and organizational factors.

10. The main implication of networking for management is that firms need to have a work environment that technical people find conducive for long-term employment and one that promotes a career path for qualified employees.

Key Terms

- **agent** (p. 94)
- **client** (p. 73)
- **client/server network** (p. 73)
- **coaxial cable** (p. 89)
- **domain name** (p. 77)
- **Domain Naming Service (DNS)** (p. 82)
- **Ethernet** (p. 83)

- **extranet** (p. 85)
- **fiber-optic cable** (p. 87)
- **frame** (p. 83)
- **gateway** (p. 92)
- **host name** (p. 75)
- **hub** (p. 91)
- **Hypertext Markup Language (HTML)** (p. 81)

- **Hypertext Transfer Protocol (HTTP)** (p. 81)
- **Internet protocol (IP)** (p. 80)
- **intranet** (p. 85)
- **IP address** (p. 74)
- **Management Information Base (MIB)** (p. 95)
- **modem** (p. 91)

- **network** (p. 72)
- **Network Interface Card (NIC)** (p. 91)
- **node** (p. 71)
- **object** (p. 94)
- **OSI Reference Model** (p. 81)
- **packet** (p. 80)
- **peer-to-peer network** (p. 72)
- **point-to-point protocol (PPP)** (p. 83)

- **protocol** (p. 80)
- **router** (p. 75)
- **routing table** (p. 92)
- **server** (p. 73)
- **shielded twisted pair (STP)** (p. 87)
- **Simple Network Management Protocol (SNMP)** (p. 82)
- **switch** (p. 91)

- **TCP/IP** (p. 83)
- **Transmission Control Protocol (TCP)** (p. 82)
- **trap** (p. 95)
- **twisted-pair cable** (p. 87)
- **unshielded twisted pair (UTP)** (p. 87)
- **wireless data transmission technology** (p. 89)
- **zone name** (p. 77)

Test Your Understanding

1. What is a network? How does it differ from the Internet? Elaborate.
2. Distinguish between:
   a. Packets and IP addresses
   b. Protocols and TCP/IP
   c. Routers and hubs
3. In what way(s) are LANs, WANs, and MANs similar? Be specific.
4. Explain the function of a NIC card. Why is it needed in a PC or workstation?
5. Summarize the key benefits and drawbacks of peer-to-peer networks.
6. How does a peer-to-peer network differ from a client/server network?
7. Explain the role of the ISP in the Internet.
8. Does a 32-bit IP address tell you anything about the size of its network? Why?
9. In your own words, explain how computers communicate on the Internet.
10. Describe the types of cables used to link the network components.
11. More and more network installations employ fiber optics. Do you think this is the way to go? Explain.
12. What is unique about wireless transmission? Elaborate.
13. List and briefly explain the key components of a network.
14. What are the factors to consider in designing a network? Discuss.
15. Describe the key components of a typical network management system.
16. Which of the following describes a LAN and why?
    a. Connects networks across the globe
    b. A collection of computers residing within a small physical region
    c. Uses WAN to interconnect networks within a geographical region
17. What layer of the OSI Reference Model converts data into a generic format for networking transmission? Explain.
18. What layer of the OSI Reference Model manages flow control and error detection? Be specific.
19. Which protocol is considered a transport protocol—SNMP, TCP, or HTTP?
20. Of the three cable types, which is the most susceptible to cross talk: coaxial, fiber optic, or Category 5e unshielded twisted pair (UTP)?
21. Cost out an actual network installation and report your findings. Make sure you include labor costs.

Discussion Questions

1. Think about the network concept and the material covered in the chapter. What managerial implications can you draw that relate to a small- to medium-size organization like a regional bank?
2. A number of surveys have been conducted to determine the most wanted technical skills in 2005. Review the journals and surf the Internet. Write a three-page report reflecting new findings for 2005–2006.
3. You are a college graduate with a major in IT from a large university located in a metropolitan area. On your first consulting job, you are assigned to design a network for a small liberal arts college of five departments (science, business, religion, political science, and history) and 800 students in a town of 9,000 people. What aspects of your alma mater's networking applies to your new client? What aspects do not apply? Explain in detail. Sketch out a basic LAN for one department.
4. Is networking in a government agency any different from networking in a traditional business organization? Elaborate.
5. Netscape and Microsoft are battling over leadership in the Web browser market. Search the Internet to learn more about the offerings, strategies, and tactics of the two companies. Write a two-page report explaining why you think the competition will be good (or bad) for the consumer.
6. A company decides to start a networking operation that would allow it to sell various products on the Internet. What do you need to know before you recommend the network infrastructure that the company must install? Be specific.

Web Exercises

1. Which of these two statements is true about a server-based network? The server-based network can grow as an organization grows. One can implement centralized security to protect network resources.
2. Contact an Internet service provider (ISP) in your area and determine the procedure and cost of linking a company's intranet to the Internet.
3. Consider the class status of the following IP addresses and determine its unique feature:
   a. 11011101.01111100,00110010,00000111
   b. 01101101,11000101,01011001,00100010

CHAPTER 4

INTRANETS AND EXTRANETS

Learning Objectives

The focus of this chapter is on several learning objectives:

■ The concept, strategic significance, and technical infrastructure of intranets

■ How to plan for and install an intranet in the organization

■ The many issues, uses, and abuses of e-mail via a company's intranet

■ A company's extranet and how it links with its partners and vendors through SCM

IN A NUTSHELL

Using the Internet and Web technologies together as an enterprisewide information system is already common in business, industry, and government. Such systems are intranets. They are the internal information management systems and a powerful tool for client/server computing.

intranet: an organization-wide software and information distribution system that applies Internet technology to a closed network within the organization.

Intranet is the term for applying Internet technologies to serve the internal needs of an organization. More technically, it is a network connecting a set of clients using standard Internet protocols, especially TCP/IP and HTTP. Internet technologies are superior to conventional internal communication systems. The Web browser, for example, is a readily available and familiar access tool. Documents are handled easily, and multiple media can be supported as well. Mid- to large-size organizations are spending thousands of dollars just to keep their documents under control. Managers constantly share documents on inter- and intra-departmental levels. With various operating systems, network protocols, and application suites, trying to ensure homogeneity in managing documents can be a challenge. Intranets handle all these problems with ease.

groupware: programs or software that help people work together when they are located far from one another.

Groupware is software that helps people work together when they are located far from one another. It includes shared databases, e-mail handling, electronic meetings that allow participants to display and see others' information, and shared calendars. Groupware also includes document management, handling in-house form requests, and report filing. It seems logical to invest in an intranet that can perform locally (within the company) and link globally (via the Internet). Groupware applications on a company's intranet can help the organization do more for less.

Intranet technology operates with standards, protocols, languages, and tools that are easy to learn and to use. An intranet can be viewed as a tool that provides Internet-like capabilities at the internal organizational level. The user can simply point and click to access the available information. The drill is easy. Click on an icon, a button, or a link on the screen and go to different pages, and go forward or backward to find the information you want.

The following scenario is typical of what an intranet can do. Flameless Electric, the second-largest manufacturer of electric parts in Virginia, rolled out two major products in 2005. Its strategy used the Internet, an intranet, and an extranet. The Internet part was easy. The company's Web site displayed the products for customers to see and order. The company's intranet was accessible only by its 743 employees. Flameless's priority was to support its 112 sales reps statewide. The intranet supplied them with marketing and technical information about the products and an automated sales application that minimized paperwork, regardless of location or size of order.

extranet: an intranet with extensions that allow clearly identified customers or top suppliers to reach and access company-related technical and educational information.

The third part was Flameless's extranet. An **extranet** is an intranet with extensions that allow clearly identified customers or top suppliers to reach and access company-related technical and educational information. In Flameless's case, its extranet was accessible to 950 electricians and small electrical parts dealers via a special company Web page. An electrician, for example, enters an assigned password to access information about new products and special deals that are available to high-volume buyers. After seven months of use, Flameless's Net-based system was paying dividends. It cut down on phone calls and fax orders, and gave sales reps in the field immediate online support. It even improved shipment schedules and deliveries.

This is all well and good, but what did it cost Flameless to set all this up? The company hired a talented Webmaster on a full-time basis. The same person, along with a part-time IT person, was able to manage the entire operation. All design and implementation work was outsourced to a local consulting firm. For online extranet security, a firewall was installed in front of an Oracle database. The results were reduced costs, improved efficiency, and increased market penetration by sales reps, as well as direct customer access to the company's internal sales and marketing files.

In this chapter, we address three major issues: the role of the intranet in the company's technology-based architecture; the uses of extranets and how they relate to the intranet, the Internet, e-mail uses and abuses, as well as SCM and the value chain; and issues related to e-mail and communication traffic.

THE BASICS

WHAT IS AN INTRANET?

To engage in e-commerce and e-business, an organization needs an infrastructure that allows communications among employees, between employees and customers, and online connectivity with suppliers, vendors, and the sales force in the field. This environment makes it possible to promote the value chain and enforce SCM for everyday business. The technology is also a prerequisite for B2B commerce, which we cover in detail in Chapter 11.

Major organizations and companies as small as 15 employees are enjoying the benefits of working in an intranet environment. They have discovered a new way to deliver collaboration and coordination to employees around the clock. An intranet is simply an organization-wide software and information distribution system that applies Internet technology and standards to a closed network within the organization. It connects the various pieces of information and communications technologies in such a way that all the authorized resources of the organization are readily available to any authorized person who needs them, wherever and whenever they are needed. In the final analysis, it is a way of thinking about how people in a business work together.

Intranet operation is a communication system designed by technical staff. It is a network of people, not of wired machines. The focus is the message, not the media. Concentrating on the technology of the intranet is like a book author worrying about the presses and typesetting rather than the manuscript. Intranet systems often are run by technical people. When it comes to planning an intranet, users should worry about content, and technical staff should concentrate on the media—on how the script is delivered.

An intranet normally runs in a client/server environment and a local area network configuration. The Internet protocol (IP) connects the computers. This internal company network is separated from other networks by **firewalls,** which are a means of preventing unauthorized access to the company's internal data or leaks of sensitive company information.

firewall: a means of preventing unauthorized access to the company's internal data or leaks of sensitive company information.

Technically, the Internet and an intranet are the same, except that only selected people are allowed to connect to an intranet. An intranet uses TCP/IP as an Internet-derived communication protocol and user interface via Web browsers, e-mails, and so on. Intranets have grown by leaps and bounds among corporate users, which demonstrates the strength and potential of Internet networking. The complementary relationship between an intranet and the Internet is a significant contributor to the digital economy. In B2B e-commerce, for example, producer and seller information is readily accessible to suppliers, making it easy to share and disseminate information to the ultimate consumer.

STRATEGIC SIGNIFICANCE

For almost a decade, companies have been looking for cost-effective ways of distributing information throughout their organization. This has strategic significance in terms of competitive advantage—timely response to day-to-day demands on the business. An intranet assures better information faster. It provides many benefits and distinctive features. It links employees and managers around the clock and automates a lot of intraorganizational traffic. Today's communication systems are labor intensive, involving a stream of documents that are sent manually or by fax from one floor to another and from one building to another. Personal messages and memos also are carried in person or by fax, which takes time and causes numerous interruptions in a normal work process. Think of having the employee manual, employee pension plan, company newsletter all available on the company's intranet. It is a win-win setup, realizing savings in human resources and more. This is where an intranet begins to pay off.

A well-designed intranet makes it possible for a company to gain better access to its primary resource—the knowledge and experience of the decision makers who work within it. It is a creative and empowering tool for a company and the foundation for developing enterprisewide information systems. It is a model for internal information management and collaborative computing. Technically, intranets are portable and scalable, which means that a company can expand the system as it grows.

Using the intranet as part of a company's integrated environment means a wealth of information is available to employees, managers, and the company as a whole. It also means much easier integration of processes. For example, a company with field reps in remote locations has to manage continuous inflows and outflows of data from the field and integrate them into manufacturing, supply management, and delivery services. The cost of such a system based on an intranet is low. In this case, cost advantages and ease of access are unique benefits of an intranet.

APPLICATIONS

An intranet can provide several applications for strengthening the value chain of the business at low cost. Here are sample applications that rely on an intranet for efficient and effective productivity.

HUMAN RESOURCES. In human resources, employees can produce or reach information on an intranet. They can access company news, employee benefits, employee phone books, vacation schedules, cafeteria menus—any documents, software, or data that company managers want to provide. It is no longer necessary to call human resources or inquire by phone or in person about such information. For human resources, it means streamlining the recruitment process and keeping employees informed about the company. Employees can have immediate access to the latest information. They spend less time searching and are no longer overwhelmed by cumbersome manuals. The main human resources intranet applications and their benefits are as follows.

- Employee handbook—saves time printing and updating the handbook.
- Benefits information—human resources staff relieved from answering routine questions and enrolling employees in benefits programs.
- Employee surveys—all survey data are captured online, which saves time and paper.
- Internal/external recruiting—helps retain current employees and promotes wide dissemination of job information, which means a shortened recruiting cycle.
- Candidate screening—online screening of applications means faster resume handling.
- Organization charts—immediate access to and update of the company's organization chart.

- Newsletters—keep employees current on company events.
- Company calendar—keeps employees apprised of holidays and special events.

SALES AND MARKETING.   In sales and marketing, the sales staff uses an intranet to keep sales personnel and customers up to date on products, pricing, and sales trends. The intranet also is used to collect and integrate sales forecasts and monitor sales performance. The marketing staff keeps the sales department informed of marketing strategies, special promotions, and competitive information. Sales and marketing applications include:

- Product information—speeds the distribution of product data; sales representatives can obtain product availability and delivery dates quickly.
- Market research—instant access to a wealth of marketing information for product planning and forecasting.
- Prospecting—easy way to collect information about future customers quickly.
- Managing sales contacts—effective distribution of sales leads to appropriate salespersons in the field; ensures quick follow-up on profitable leads.
- Sales training—a ready forum for sales training, regardless of the location of trainees.

ACCOUNTING AND FINANCE.   In accounting and finance, an intranet facilitates a secure, central point for gathering financial and accounting data from multiple databases. It also generates consolidated statements to those who need them when they need them. In addition, intranets allow select business partners limited access to financial data to build an ongoing relationship as part of an extranet environment. The key accounting and financial applications are as follows.

- Financial reports—sensitive financial reports can be published on a secure-access intranet Web site.
- Expense reports—employees can e-mail expense reports on secure Web sites, reducing paperwork and delays in reimbursement.
- Accounts receivable/payable processing—faster collection of receivables and transmission of payables; allows fast access by customers and vendors to status information.
- Asset management—current assets can be placed online for review and update.
- Policies and procedures—corporate policies and procedures related to accounting and finance can be centralized for quick access by authorized personnel.
- Payroll—online submission of payroll data by managers and employees, including automated deposits and time sheets, promotes a high level of efficiency, regardless of the transaction or location.

MANUFACTURING AND OPERATIONS.   In manufacturing and operations, the main benefits of an intranet are maintaining effective inventory control, production scheduling, quality, and low operating cost. The quality assurance staff can update existing databases and maintain accurate quality statistics for management decision making. An intranet also provides a centralized facility for disseminating manufacturing information. It fosters collaboration between the production team and other functional teams within the firm, identifying product problems, improving inventory control, and the like. The key applications that are intranet-related are:

- Inventory control—reduces inventory costs by online tracking of raw material inventory, movements, expiration dates, and so on.
- Production schedules—key persons have instant access to products or parts for reordering or making just-in-time adjustments.
- Quality assurance—facilitates quality improvement quickly and reliably by allowing production personnel to obtain information that improves manufacturing quality and reduces costs.
- Part order/requisition system—allows customers and dealers to order products or parts quickly and in time to be of immediate use, cutting down on inventory and storage space.

Other uses of an intranet include the following.

- Real-time broadcasting of news, including medical information, from the county, the state, nationally, or from abroad.
- Document management to minimize unnecessary paperwork and waste of paper.
- Customized application modules like a travel or document library.
- Complete e-mail for interoffice and intraoffice communication.
- Internal company office circulars can be routed electronically.
- Bulletin board service.
- Real-time chat service that electronically logs all data for record keeping.
- Complete company staff, operations, and organizational chart directories.
- Channel for confidential exchange of data for electronic funds transfers (EFTs) and checks.
- A daily to-do list and assignments from a central desk to all connected desks.
- Foreign news and financial data broadcasting (running ticker) from direct feeds.

DOES EVERY COMPANY NEED AN INTRANET?

Not every organization has to have an intranet: The dividing line for intranet payback is 100 or more employees or more than one branch. An intranet can reduce phone bills, fax bills, and other charges. If nothing else, it will help branches work more closely together.

A company needs an intranet for the following reasons:

1. When it has a large pool of information to share among hundreds of employees. It is an effective way of cutting the cost of producing conventional multiple hard copies. It combats the problem of information overload. Intranets help individuals sort, filter, and store the mountain of information that otherwise comes across their desks.
2. Intranets are cheap, robust, and fast. Any employee with access to a TCP/IP can disseminate and publish information. Any information accessed is available in seconds rather than minutes or hours.

3. Intranets operate across platforms—Windows, UNIX, Mac. They are the easiest way to get people communicating.

4. Information is available 24/7 to all employees at the click of a mouse.

5. Information available on an intranet can be updated quickly, which keeps employees informed in a timely way.

THE TECHNICAL INFRASTRUCTURE

The trend in intranet design is to rely on the company's TCP/IP Internet infrastructure, utilizing Internet protocol suite technologies and newly developed client/server Web technologies. The client/server environment is user oriented and gives clients (users) great flexibility in the way they use data to make timely decisions.

CLIENT/SERVER BASICS

Intranets have multitier application architecture. The terms related to intranet design and implementation appear in Box 4.1. Anyone interested in understanding the basics of intranet architecture should be familiar with them. The client/server architecture on which intranets are based is a versatile, message-based, modular infrastructure intended to improve usability, flexibility, interoperability, and scalability as compared to centralized, mainframe, time-sharing computing. Within mainframe software architectures, all intelligence resides within the central host computer. Mainframes do not easily support graphic user interface (GUI) or access to multiple databases from geographically dispersed sites. As GUIs became popular, mainframes and terminal displays became less so. PCs are now being used in client/server architectures.

BOX 4.1

Intranet Design and Implementation Terms

1. Client: A requester of services (e.g., an employee or a manager).

2. Server: A machine or a PC that provides services, files, database information, and so on.

3. Interoperability: The ability of two or more systems to exchange information and to use the information that has been exchanged.

4. Scalability: The ease with which a system can be modified or expanded.

5. Graphic User Interface (GUI): A feature that can be used for developing complex user interfaces because it increases software development speed.

6. Client/Server Architecture: A model that introduces a database server to replace the file server. User queries can be answered directly. This architecture reduces network traffic by providing a query response rather than total file transfer. It also improves multiuser updating through a GUI front end to a shared database.

7. Remote Procedure Call (RPC): A client/server infrastructure that increases the interoperability, portability, and flexibility of an application by allowing the application to be distributed over multiple and different platforms. It also reduces the complexity of developing applications that span multiple operating systems and network protocols.

TYPES OF CLIENT/SERVER ARCHITECTURE

There are two types of client/server architecture for intranet design: two-tier architecture and three-tier architecture.

TWO-TIER ARCHITECTURE. The two-tier model is a good solution when an organization has between 12 and 100 users interacting on a LAN at the same time. It requires minimal operator intervention and is used frequently in non-complex, non-time-critical information processing systems. This model has three components.

1. User system interface (e.g., session, text input, dialog, display management)
2. Processing management (e.g., process development and process resource services)
3. Database management (e.g., data and file services). See Figure 4.1.

There are definite limitations associated with this model.

1. When the number of users exceeds 100, performance begins to deteriorate. This is because the server maintains a connection with each client even when no work is being done.
2. Implementation of processing management services using vendor proprietary database procedures restricts flexibility.
3. There is limited flexibility in moving (repartitioning) program functionality from one server to another without manually regenerating procedural code.

THREE-TIER ARCHITECTURE. The alternative to two-tier client/server architecture is three-tier client/server architecture. In this model, a *middle tier* is sandwiched between the user system interface client environment and the database management server environment. This middle tier manages distributed database integrity in a two-phase process. It provides access to resources based on names rather than locations and, therefore, improves scalability and flexibility as system components are added or moved. It also can perform queuing, application execution, and database staging. For example, if the middle tier provides queuing, the client can deliver its request to the middle layer and disengage because the middle tier will access the data and return the answer to the client. In addition to all of this, the middle layer adds scheduling and prioritization for work in progress. (See Figure 4.2.)

The third tier provides database management and is dedicated to data and file services that can be optimized without using any proprietary database management system languages.

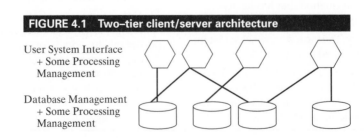

FIGURE 4.1 Two–tier client/server architecture

User System Interface
  + Some Processing
  Management

Database Management
  + Some Processing
  Management

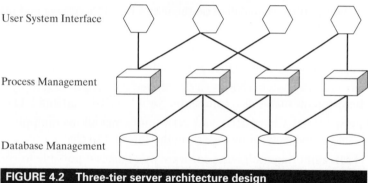

User System Interface

Process Management

Database Management

FIGURE 4.2   Three-tier server architecture design

Three-tier architecture is used in commercial distributed client/server environments, where shared resources like different databases and processing rules are required. It supports hundreds of users, making it easier to upgrade than the two-tier architecture. It also facilitates software development because each tier can be built and executed on a separate platform, making it easier to organize the implementation. Three-tier architecture also readily allows different tiers to be developed in different languages.

What is important is the ease of moving data from an old system to a three-tier architecture. It is low risk and cost-effective. Overall, the three-tier model improves performance for groups with a large number of users (in the thousands). It also improves flexibility, maintainability, reusability, and scalability, while hiding the complexity of distributed processing from the user. These features have made three-layer architecture a popular choice for intranet applications and Net-centric information systems. In the long run, it is better than the two-tier model.

ENABLING TECHNOLOGIES

An intranet infrastructure allows online communication between divisions and among employees within each division, and it provides an interface between any contact point within the organization and the Internet. This means that specified operating systems, dedicated servers, and communication links must be in place for the environment to be operational.

The technology involves protocols, standards, tools, and languages that are easy to use. As you read about the following technical building blocks, keep in mind that an intranet has Internetlike capabilities within a company's internal network.

Here are the key enabling technologies—the software cluster that must be acquired.

1. Server PC—the PC that stores all applications and Web pages. The user (client) downloads intranet information from the server PC for decision making.

2. Client PC—the employee's or user's PC that accesses the intranet information available on the server PC.

3. Web server—the cluster of software that manages and updates HTML files and allows online communication with other programs in the intranet infrastructure.

4. Browser—software installed on the user's PC for accessing and presenting HTML files on Web sites.

5. TCP/IP electronic mail—normally available in most organizations.

6. Graphic and multimedia files—files containing images and sound, respectively.

7. Network File System (NFS)—a distributed file system developed by Sun Microsystems that is also compatible with UNIX-based and DOS systems.

8. Internet Relay Chat (IRC)—a UNIX utility that allows multiple users to communicate interactively; allows users on the Internet to chat.

9. HTML authoring tools—the software that makes it possible to create pages in HTML.

10. Hypertext Markup Language (HTML)—the text that has links to other information. It is a programming language that manages and controls the way intranet information is displayed on the user's screen.

11. Portable electronic document (PED)—technology that addresses the shortcomings of HTML, while trying to maintain compatibility with it.

An intranet consists of a Web server running on an internal corporate network that manages intranet files and viewing tools, such as a browser running on a client PC; this allows the end user to access intranet information. The interface to the company's intranet will be the key to success. Browsers greatly simplify access to the company's computing resources and information by operating as the interface to available applications.

USING FIREWALLS

Intranets can be protected from unauthorized access via firewalls. As discussed in Chapter 3, a *firewall* is a hardware/software security system that can be programmed to prevent unauthorized access to a company's intranet or the Internet. Firewalls vary in complexity. Some permit all access that is not specifically forbidden (default commit), some forbid all access that is not specifically permitted (default forbid), and others permit only e-mail traffic.

proxy: a go-between agent that acts on behalf of another.

packet filter: device that checks each packet at the network level and stops any packet that might be a security risk.

Most firewalls are either proxies or packet filters. A **proxy** is a *go-between* agent that acts on behalf of another. Network proxies act on behalf of a company to transfer information to and from the Internet. Typically, a proxy receives a request from a user to connect to a site on the Internet. It first makes a decision as to whether the user is authorized to use the proxy before it decides on completing the connection. A **packet filter** checks each packet (small chunk of information) at the network level and stops any packets that might be a security risk.

Security, in general, is not easy to sell. It is hard to sell a fire extinguisher to someone who has never seen a fire. Intranet security, properly designed by knowledgeable users and administrators, can ensure that the system is run properly. One person, a "security czar," should be responsible for the entire intranet. In the case of a company with branches or remote sites, each location should be part of the total security umbrella. Like the Webmaster, the security czar should have a background in technology, communication skills, and knowledge of the company's practices and processes. Leadership attributes, foresight, and creativity are also important. (See Box 4.2.)

BOX 4.2

Intelligence Czar Has Tough Task

President Bush's nomination of diplomat John Negroponte to be the United States' first director of national intelligence, while not without problems, could ably fill a key gap in our nation's intelligence/security apparatus. The sooner his appointment is confirmed and Negroponte gets to work shoring up that apparatus, the better.

It's a plus that the London-born Negroponte, 65, the current U.S. ambassador to Iraq and former ambassador to the United Nations, is accustomed to handling super-tough tasks—such as helping persuade the UN Security Council to approve the use of force against Saddam Hussein. As intelligence czar, he would oversee the 15 agencies that collect and handle information vital to the national security.

In the past, many of those agencies have neglected or even refused to share and coordinate knowledge, with disastrous results. Many of those failings were well chronicled by the 9/11 Commission, which made the coordination of intelligence under a single director one of its key recommendations last year. Air Force Lt. General Michael Hayden, director of the super-snoop National Security Agency, was tapped to be Negroponte's deputy.

Negroponte, a former McGraw-Hill executive, is widely respected as a bright, creative figure whose considerable diplomatic skills will be put to the test dealing with 15 warring, turf-conscious federal agencies. He began his career with the U.S. Foreign Service in 1960 and speaks five languages fluently. His brother Nicholas is a noted futurist, technology author, and founder of MIT's Media Lab.

Source: Adapted from *The Enquirer,* February 18, 2005, 1ff. See also news.enquirer.com/apps/pbcs.d11/article?AID=/20050218/EDIT01/503180348.

PLANNING AN INTRANET

With complex technology, differing client demands, and heavy information traffic in a typical firm, a fair amount of planning is needed to design, implement, and maintain a corporate intranet. Planning is part of a five-step procedure that is explained briefly in the following sections.

PLAN AHEAD

The first step is to define the goal of an intranet and plan accordingly. A lot of the failures reported in the journals can be attributed to lack of preparation. "The competition has one, so why shouldn't we?" is not good enough for committing company resources to an intranet. It is important to determine who the primary users are, what content should be shared, and how the information will be accessed.

In principle, company information is there to be shared, and the larger the number of users is, the richer the information is. However, the designer should consider the risks of this information falling into the hands of the competition. Typically, the company has a license for only a certain number of users. Assigning passwords is a traditional way to help protect and limit access. In addition, each department should be evaluated to determine the type of information it needs. For example, the research and development department needs to know the pricing of a competitor's new products before developing a new design.

As part of planning, it is sometimes helpful to visit a firm that has been successful in installing an intranet site. Meeting with designers and users may bring up the problems and possible solutions. Seminars can be another source of information.

Once you have an idea of what an intranet can and cannot do, the next phase in planning is to outline the scope of the project. This means deciding on, among other things, the size of the intranet, how long it should take to install, the training involved, and the required financial and technical resources. The key is to map out the site well in advance. The map must account for every detail that contributes to a successful installation. "I forgot about that," after the site is underway can be costly.

PROVIDE JUSTIFICATION

In the process of planning an intranet, some homework should be done to justify the investment and ensure support from top management. The traditional approach to justification that makes sense to management is to do a return on investment analysis, comparing total costs with benefits. The human factor also must be considered: Planners need to map out strategies to acculturate employees to using the intranet once it becomes operational. Stories abound about companies that spend millions on intranet technology, only to learn that employees still feel more comfortable printing out their e-mail messages.

An effective strategy for selling upper management on the change is that an intranet can be modified to address changing needs. It can be demonstrated that hearing a president's quarterly report on the intranet is more effective than reading it. With an intranet, all it takes is one click on a button.

BUILD IN-HOUSE OR OUTSOURCE

After top management approves the master plan, the next step is to decide whether the technology should be built by the IT department or contracted to an outside firm. In deciding what to do, several factors must be considered.

- In-house resources—How available are they? How qualified are they?
- Cost—Which way is cheaper?
- Hardware and software—Do existing company networks support an intranet?
- Budget—Are adequate funds available to fully implement the proposed intranet?

Outsourcing has definite advantages. An outside firm dedicated to full-time intranet design has lots of specialists available. They are likely to be more efficient than in-house staff, who might better be used for other critical projects. Depending on the company's technology infrastructure, an outside firm might end up doing a better job, especially if the intranet site is to be hosted by the consulting firm.

In contrast to the benefits of outsourcing, limitations need to be considered. An outside firm will need more time to learn your business processes and requirements before beginning to design the site. Some sensitive information or files might be unnecessarily exposed to an outside firm. It is also likely that an outside firm will charge more for the work than it would cost to do it in-house, and additional costs may be incurred later when enhancements or upgrades have to be done.

The main advantage of building the intranet in-house is that in-house people are familiar with the company's goals, politics, and processes. Maintenance, upgrades, and enhancements will be easier to handle. With the basic infrastructure in place, future development can be done at a lower cost than if an outside contractor were used. Sensitive information also remains protected. On the negative side, lack of expertise in intranet design could cause all kinds of unexpected problems and delays.

FORM AN INTRANET TEAM

A company-wide project like an intranet requires a representative team from various divisions or departments to oversee the process from beginning to end. In addition to a representative from each department, one should be included from the IT department, as well as a consultant and a project coordinator. In the case of outsourcing, a representative from the contracted firm should set up an agenda with the company team and provide progress reports on a regular basis.

A tricky part of forming a team for this type of project is appointing people who have no political strings or hidden agendas that might affect the process adversely. For example, a representative from a large department might want to secure high-priority access for the department. This might mean compromising equal response time for smaller or remote departments.

The team normally consists of a representative from each department or division. When the team size increases beyond seven or eight members, it requires a chairperson with an agenda, predefined procedures, and subcommittees, all of which could make the whole process unwieldy.

BUILD AND TEST A PROTOTYPE

Before going all out to develop a corporate-wide intranet, it would be wise to build a piece of the site and allow users to test it. The feedback could be a timely contribution to the final system. One problem with prototypes is that when they work well, many users comment, "This is great. It is all I want." However, prototypes are only a representation of the system, not the system itself.

The champion is important to the prototype phase. A *champion* is a person in the organization (usually a respected manager or a senior person) who supports the project from the beginning, promotes it, and acts as an ambassador to explain to users how the system could do them a lot of good. Unfortunately, with complex projects that affect processes and people, more people will resist change than welcome it. A champion can do wonders to ensure the success of the new installation.

ENSURE EFFECTIVE MAINTENANCE

Keeping corporate information up to date and available around the clock is the most critical part of intranet operations. Poor maintenance means dated information, which quickly gives the impression that nothing new or different is going on in the company. E-mail will continue, but an intranet means more than just e-mail. Maintenance means making sure the intranet continues to operate based on the standards set in the design. An intranet can take more effort to update than to create. Included in maintenance is enhancement, which is the daily (sometimes hourly) upgrade of news, reports, and procedures.

Maintenance includes assigning a full-time person to be the site Webmaster. This person's main job is to keep in touch with management at all levels, gather and post news items, monitor the intranet traffic, and provide technical leadership. Communication skills, technical expertise, and ability to work with people are critical to a Webmaster's job.

E-MAIL AND THE INTRANET

Intranet and e-mail is a marriage made in cyber heaven. E-mail is what a company's intranet is best known for. It is the Net's killer app. Almost 90 percent of Net users report e-mail as the most frequently used online contact. It is a major communication platform in business and government. Scott McNealy, chief executive officer of Sun Microsystems, Inc., once commented: "You can take out every one of the 300 to 400 computer applications that we run our company on and we could continue—but if you took out our e-mail system, Sun would grind to an immediate halt."

Over 200 million inboxes are active worldwide. Frequent e-mailers already recognize that their inbox is as much a database of documents, appointments, and news as it is a place to store messages. With e-commerce volumes on the rise, this communication tool is becoming part of e-marketing and sales. It is a tool for bill presentation, customer feedback, shipping notices, and the like.

E-mail also is becoming smarter: It now can direct specific messages to defined folders and be a place to check voice, text, and fax messages. This is called content management or unified messaging services. Managing data and documents with e-mail is more efficient than dealing with the flood of paper (letters, faxes, and bills) we handle today. As e-mail becomes the standard for content dissemination of all kinds, it should attract more and more users and become as popular as the cell phone.

Intranets inherit Simple Mail Transport Protocol (SMTP) from the TCP/IP suite to operate e-mail. On top of SMTP, which enables plain text messaging, intranets rely on Multipurpose Internet Mail Extensions (MIME) to carry diverse content.

Inasmuch as e-mail is a great business tool, it is also a potential threat for employers. Threats include confidentiality breaches, legal liability, lost productivity, and damage to company reputation. Because of that, it is important for each firm to create an e-mail usage policy and make sure it is actually implemented.

In 2005, the *Washington Post* reported on the struggle in countries where e-mail is viewed as a threat to government control. For example, after sending a daily e-mail to 15,200 takers, the word *forbidden* appeared on reformer Ayman Abdul Nour's computer screen, barring him entry to his own Web site, www.all4syria.org. The same day, he collected the 1,700 e-mail addresses and dispatched his daily updated message. Two days later, the government blocked his e-mails from going through. This went on back and forth for weeks, even with new addresses and new Web sites. In the meantime, Nour's e-mail recipient list continued to grow. Finally, the censors gave up (Shahid 2005).

spamming: sending unwanted advertisements or literature through e-mail or the Internet.

SPAMMING AND APPROPRIATE E-MAIL USE

Spamming is sending unwanted advertisements or literature through e-mail or the Internet. The name comes from a Monty

Python comedy skit, where every item on a restaurant menu included Spam, regardless of how well it fit into the dish. This type of intrusion is similar to receiving a phone call from a telemarketer right in the middle of dinner. Spamming generates **flaming**—an angry response to a message or a call.

flaming: an angry response to an e-mail message or phone call.

Companies have been overwhelmed by e-mail traffic, and spam is out of control. It is the no. 1 complaint of most e-mail users. America Online says as much as 80 percent of incoming e-mail to its system is spam. E-mail may have become a valuable business tool, but users' inboxes are cluttered with unsolicited and virus-ridden messages, sales pitches, and irritating news that once were the talk around the water cooler. (See Box 4.3.) Companies also have been increasingly concerned about what is being sent out in e-mail, such as company secrets.

Many firms have learned that spot checks are no longer adequate. The trend is more toward systematic monitoring of e-mail traffic using content-monitoring software. Most such software scans messages for keywords. Messages that are

---

BOX 4.3

Employees Disciplined for Inappropriate Use of the Internet and E-Mail

A Longueuil-based aerospace company told several employees they had breached company policy. Some received disciplinary notices, some were suspended, and others lost their jobs. The company did state that it has a clear policy on how communications equipment should be used. The policy tries to ensure employees have a professional business environment, free of any inappropriate behavior.

The incident is another reminder that companies have clear guidelines for employees regarding computer and e-mail usage if they want to monitor how employees use the Internet and e-mail in the workplace. Many employers assume the right to set workplace rules grant them an unregulated right to monitor employees' computer usage provided that they disclose the practice.

Notice is a prerequisite to most forms of computer surveillance. However, notice alone is rarely sufficient to support the practice. The employer must analyze the employees' reasonable expectation of privacy to strike a balance with the employers' legitimate workplace concerns that support surveillance initiatives.

Six factors should be considered in the assessment of the reasonableness to regulate and implement a surveillance system in light of employee privacy issues. The six factors vary in importance depending on the circumstances:

- The target of the surveillance
- The purpose of the surveillance
- The prior use of alternatives to computer surveillance
- The type of technology used to conduct surveillance
- The adequacy of the notice provided to the target of the surveillance
- The protection of other privacy norms such as privacy administration, security, and data retention, once the surveillance data has been obtained.

Source: Hrinfodesk—Canadian Payroll and Employment Law, Sept. 2004. See also www.hrmguide.net/canada/law/inappropriate-use.htm.

suspect can be prevented from leaving the firm or forwarded to a company official in charge of reviewing them. The key problem is junk mail and inappropriate attachments that are a waste of employee time, whether they are sending or reading such mail.

More recently, new ways are becoming available to send an anonymous comment without your e-mail address giving you away. For example, www.theanonymousemail.com offers a $20 per year service, where no one can trace your e-mail back to you. The recipients can reply, but they cannot see who you are. In addition, sites such as www.myprivateline.com and www.anonymizer.com offer similar services.

By now, spamming is nearly impossible to eliminate, but solutions exist. One of the most widely used tools is Eudora.pro, which collects mail from different accounts and consolidates and manages all one's messages. First, the program asks you to pick a message as an example and specify certain rules. For example, you can set a rule to divert to a junk mail folder all messages not clearly marked to you. A filter also can be used to flag priority messages such as those coming from top management. You can even identify such messages by color (e.g., red for top priority, green for memo coming to you, yellow for junk mail, and so on).

A more recent approach to handling spammers is to give spammers a dose of their own medicine. Take the case of Scott Richter, a mass commercial e-mailer, who has become a frequent target of attackers known as antispammers. One of them is Mark Jones, a software engineer, who from his home at night tracks down spammers by tracing their complex routing code hidden in e-mail messages. After his three children go to bed Jones programs his personal computer to send a letter to a select number of alleged spammers downloaded from a Web site, slashdot.org. As he finishes the letter, he will have sent the message to each spammer 10,000 times.

Spammers are not easy to catch, to sue, or to collect damages from. Earthlink, a major Internet service provider, uses lawyers and private investigators to track senders of online junk. In a well-documented case, a so-called "Buffalo Spammer" kept harassing Earthlink customers for over three months, using 243 different accounts and dozens of telephones registered in other people's names. He sent 825 million spam e-mails and taunted Earthlink's investigators and other experts. Even when lawyers were trying to serve papers on him, the Buffalo Spammer continued to spam.

There are dozens of products to help block spam. Most search engines have taken the lead in this direction. Several techniques are in common:

- Blacklist the sender; obtain a spammer's address and block any e-mail from that address.
- Accept e-mail only from a list of approved addresses, called "whitelisting" the sender.
- Look for signs of spam—999, FREE, Get, Money, Lose, $$$, Earn, etc.
- Use antispam software, which analyzes new messages and determines how likely they are to be spam; examples are IronMail (www.ciphertrust.com), Authority (www.cloudmark.com), SpamKiller (www.networkassociates.com), and MailFrontier (www.mailfrontier.com).

There are guidelines as well. For example:

- Stop giving away your e-mail address, period.
- Do not "unsubscribe," because it simply confirms that your e-mail address is real and solid. If you do, it is likely that you'll get more, not less spam mail.
- Write to the Direct Marketing Association and credit bureaus.
- Contact your credit card companies, credit union, and mortgage companies and tell them not to release your name, address, and similar data.
- Contact all organizations you belong to, schools, magazines you subscribe to, airline frequent flyer programs, your long-distance telephone carrier, and just about anyone who sends you a bill.
- As a last resort, contact your phone company and change your listing in the phone book, or simply list your name with no address.

The question of what is inappropriate e-mail brings up the privacy issue. Companies have been wrestling with the issue of privacy versus liability for employees' e-mail activity. This concern was spurred by several well-known court cases where e-mail was produced as evidence.

The upshot of the privacy controversy is that firms must have a company policy that addresses privacy. At a minimum, such a policy should state in writing:

1. That the company's intranet and the networks that carry e-mail are company property, to be used for business purposes only. Any violators could be subject to disciplinary action or even dismissal. (See Box 4.4.)
2. A clear definition of what is and what is not appropriate use of e-mail. Examples should help.
3. A clear message to all employees that e-mail of any kind cannot be private and that all e-mail may be monitored at any time.

E-MAIL ETIQUETTE

When the secretary of the loan department of a commercial bank found her lunch taken from the staff refrigerator, she immediately sent an e-mail message to the 165 bank employees: "My lunch has disappeared from the refrigerator. Whoever took it, I hope you had a good lunch. Now, I am left with no lunch. No response necessary. Sandy." Within minutes, there were offers to take Sandy to lunch and a pizza was delivered anonymously to her desk. Early that afternoon, the senior vice president of the bank stopped by and gave her the first lesson in e-mail etiquette: "Don't send e-mail when you're angry. Choose your language, and although brevity is OK, don't discard manners."

Here is another episode: A Web designer asked a friend, another designer, to evaluate a client's homepage. The answer by e-mail was: "Your choices of purple for logo and triangle for buttons are ugly. I wouldn't mess with it. Your client is probably too dumb to notice it." Somehow, the client got a copy and was furious. It took the designer some explaining to continue on the project. He almost lost his job.

BOX 4.4

An Army of One and His 50 Fiancées

Here is a Ali Baba story that has gone electronic. While Col. Kassem Saleh was stationed in Afghanistan, he had plenty of support from back home. He could count on e-mails . . . from his women . . . more than 50 fiancées whom he met through Internet dating services. Now these women, recently clued in to his "chronic courting," want the Army to take action.

For years, Saleh met women through Web sites like www.tallpersonals.com, www.match.com, and www.christiansingles.com. What ensued were flowery e-mails . . . from his base in Afghanistan. "He wrote better than Yeats and wrote better than Shakespeare. He totally intoxicated you with feelings: 'Oh, baby, I want to tell you how much I miss you.' 'I can't wait to get home to you,'" Robin Solod, 43, told the *New York Times*. Solod read the news story on the Internet and tracked down Saleh's "fiancée" in Washington despite his denials that he and the woman were "just friends." Solod discovered that the two were indeed involved, an exposure that has deeply hurt the many women who thought they were soon headed down the aisle, according to the report.

According to some of the women, not even the sappy e-mails were unique. Saleh would reuse e-mails he received from his women and forward them to many others. In one e-mail message that the *New York Times* said Solod supplied, he wrote:

> You are my world, my life, my love and my universe. It's like my mother used to say to me in Arabic when I was a little boy. *Ya Yunni* (my eyes), *Ya hayatti* (my love), *Ya elbee* (my heart), and *Ya umree* (my life). She used to sing it to me so I would fall asleep in our one-bedroom apartment in the slums of Brooklyn.

"We are not a group of stupid, naïve women," Sarah Calder, 33, told the *Times*. "We are bright, intellectual, professional women. I can't tell you how much he wooed us with his words. He made us feel like goddesses, fairy princesses, Cinderellas. We had all found our Superman, our knight in shining armor."

Source: Adapted from www.msnbc.com/news/925113.asp?vts=061120031145&cp1=1.

Very simply, *etiquette* is a set of rules specifying what is appropriate. *Netiquette* is network etiquette or the etiquette of cyberspace, which has its own culture. You are bound to offend people without meaning to. To make matters worse, you might forget that you are interacting with other real people.

Sending an e-mail message to someone is one-to-one communication as if face-to-face: a dialog. As in a real-life exchange, common courtesies apply. In a business environment, where employees, officers, and executives exchange information with one another and with the outside world, it is important for each business to prescribe its own set of rules. Box 4.5 summarizes key user guidelines for one-to-one communication.

In terms of e-mail etiquette, here are some mistakes to avoid:

- Do not write when you're in a bad mood or angry. Simmer down and let things settle before you attempt to send.

- Read what you write carefully and stop the compulsion of clicking on the "send" button until you are sure of what you're sending.

- Do not use sarcasm in an attempt to be clever. E-mail was never designed to promote gags or ridicule.

BOX 4.5

Etiquette for One-to-One Communication

- Always assume that mail on the Internet is not secure. Never put in a mail message anything you would not put on a postcard.
- Be sure to respect the copyright on material that you reproduce.
- Never send chain letters via electronic mail. Chain letters are forbidden on the Internet. Your network privileges could be revoked.
- Do not send heated messages (flames) when you are provoked. It is prudent not to reply to flames.
- Be careful when addressing mail. There are addresses that may go to a group but the address looks like it is just one person.
- Sending mail overseas requires time to get a response due to the difference in time. Be patient, especially when you are sending an urgent message.
- Be especially careful with sarcasm. People from different cultures or upbringing have different ways of interpreting jokes, puns, or erotic humor.
- Use smileys to indicate tone of voice, but don't overdo it.

- Be brief but not overly terse. People don't respond well to long drawn-out messages. Plus, many people pay by the minute to use e-mail and that can be costly.
- Be sure to include a subject heading so the recipient will know what the message is about.
- For important messages, send a brief reply to tell the sender that you have it and that you will reply soon in more detail.
- Much of the etiquette in e-mail depends on how well you know the person. Norms experienced with a close person might not fly with new contacts across the globe.
- Know how large a message or a file you are sending. Do not send an attached file larger than 50 kilobytes. For a large file, cut the file into smaller chunks and send each as a separate message.
- Don't load people with large amounts of unsolicited information.
- When forwarding a message, make sure it does not somehow go to others included in the initial message.

Source: Adapted from www.dtcc.edu/cs/rfc1855.html.

- Stay away from using all uppercase. That is tantamount to yelling at the receiver. Exclamation marks are not welcome either. They are a sign of authoritarianism.
- Place the nature of the message in the subject line. It gives the receiver advance notice of the nature of the e-mail.
- Write short e-mails, normally less than two paragraphs. This author received a three-page e-mail from one senior, explaining in anger why his grade should be an A rather than an A−.
- Sending e-mail to the wrong person can be annoying and embarrassing. Think before you send.
- Watch your grammar, spelling, and vernacular. Words like "ain't" and double negatives like "I ain't saying nothin" show no class.
- Remember to send your attachment when you say you will. If you forget, your recipient might think you're growing senile.

BACK TO BLOGGING

Blogging is brought up in this chapter as a new form of mainstream, quirky, highly personal communication, like e-mail and cell phones (to be covered in Chapter 6). A blogger needs only a computer, an opinion, and Internet access to communicate. The opinions are open-ended for all repeat visitors to read, provide a rebuttal, and otherwise share in the two-way exchange of opinions 24/7 year round.

It seems that just about everybody is either celebrating blogs or worrying about them. Bloggers (in French, *blogeurs*) have come on like a cloud of locusts. Blogging in the 2000s is what Web sites were in the 1990s. Recently, we have begun to see video blogs (vblogs) and mobile blogs via search engines like Google and Yahoo!. More innovations are expected every day.

There are well over 10 million Weblogs worldwide as of October 2005 (Maney 2005), and more than 44 percent of Internet users had used the Internet to publish their thoughts, post pictures, share files, or respond to others. This is a shining example of shareability and exchange of information and knowledge by politicians, scholars, journalists, and plain common people. Bloggers have added depth to the way issues are discussed. For example, bloggers were the first to break the now infamous story of the Abu Ghraib prisoner abuse in Iraq in 2004. See www.rebeccablood.net and www.livejournal.com for a sample of a Weblog.

The term *weblog* was coined by Jorn Barger in December 1997. The shorter *blog* was coined by Peter Merholz in May 1999. After the attacks of September 11, 2001, many blogs that supported the United States war on terrorism quickly picked up readers due to the public's search to understand the events. A year later, "war bloggers" supported war in Iraq. Since 2003, bloggers have gained a worldwide reputation for breaking, shaping, or generating news stories.

Where do these bloggers come from? What motivates them to blog? In one recent study, blogging was found to be a global phenomenon. But certain regions have large numbers of bloggers, like California, New York, Michigan, and Florida, and countries like Canada, Russia, England, and Australia. Bloggers' interests are highly correlated with age (most are 16–24 years old). In 80 percent of the cases, expressions of friendship tended to be mutual; if Jay names Sandy as a friend, then Sandy names Jay as a friend. Friendship is clustered from commonalities (from the same block, company, snorkeling club, etc.). For further surfing and styles of bloggers and their respective bloggerspace, see www.bloggter.com, www.memepool.com, www.globeofblogs.com, www.metafilter.com, www.blogs.salon.com, www.blogtree.com, and Yahoo! blogs.

BLOGGING PRACTICES

Some bloggers post opinions several times a day; others once a month or less. Bloggers usually pour out their feelings with no letup, while others have difficulty saying much. (See Box 4.6.) For more information on the many types of blogs, see en.wikipedia.org/wiki/Blog.

In any case, there are four major motivators of blogging:

- Maintaining community forums
- Articulating ideas through writing
- Airing out pent-up emotions
- Documenting one's life

BOX 4.6

A Blogger's Comment

Katie, a graduate student, said she blogged to relate her life to others by telling her own personal story in close to real time. Even Evan, whose blog was primarily about scientific subjects, let his friends know of his whereabouts and sometimes to report a cold or other minor disturbance in his life. Arthur, a Stanford professor, and several others found blogging a superior alternative to mass e-mail: "I started blogging to communicate with friends and family, as well as for professional connections. It is easier than sending lots of e-mail. I'll just put it in my blog."

Lara, an undergraduate, wrote:

I've come to realize rather recently that I can't regret that I didn't form any romantic attachments [my phrases for such things are always overly formal to the point of stupidity, and I don't know why or what to use instead, but bear with me] because at the end of the day, a boyfriend would have taken away from all the awesome things that happened with people in the dorm, and all the great friendships that I formed and that will hopefully continue after this year (if you're reading this blog, you're most likely one of those people). Thinking back to the last couple of years, it is pretty obvious that I was really stifled by my insular, extremely time-consuming group of friends, and part of my discontent stemmed from a relative dearth of fun, casual relationships with interesting people. My friends are great, but they are also tightly knit to the point of being incestuous, and when I hang out with them it is difficult to maintain the time and energy necessary to play with other people.

Source: Adapted from Ravi Kumar, Jasmine Novak, Prabhakar Raghavan, and Andrew Tomkins, "Structure and Evolution of Blogspace." *Communications of the ACM,* December, 2004, 42–43.

Psychologists and psychiatrists would probably pick the third motivator as the main driver of blogging. Like travel viewed as an escape, so is blogging. It is a medium or an outlet for thoughts and feelings, with content often being emotional. Blogs help explore issues the contributor feels "obsessive" or "passionate" about. It is catharsis. It is a place to shout, to have fun, to expect listeners who care, and a stimulus for working through personal issues. It is a relief valve to get closure and peace.

To illustrate the point, think of the following episodes:

1. A Borland employee used the company's e-mail system to send confidential information to competitor Symantec, his new employer. The employee and recipient were both charged with trade secret theft.

2. Two employees (attorneys) of the United Kingdom law firm Norton Rose originated the "Claire Swire" e-mail, a sexually explicit e-mail that ended up being read by over 10 million people around the world.

3. A Gartner Group study showed 90 percent of e-mail users receive spam at least once a week and almost 50 percent get spammed more than six times a week. Personal e-mail causes network congestion since it is not only unnecessary but tends to be mailed to a large list of recipients.

4. E-mail records are increasingly used in lawsuits since they tend to contain important evidence. Worse still, the court could even confiscate your computers as evidence and the search might uncover some embarrassing evidence you never knew you were "safekeeping." (See www.email-policy.com.)

Finally, on the political scene, politicians and the Federal Election Commission (FEC) have to contend with hundreds of political blog sites and bloggers. For example, David Englin, a relative unknown, won a Democratic primary for a Northern Virginia House seat in 2005 (Cho 2005) by courting off-the-cuff Virginia bloggers. The FEC is now hearing bloggers bids to share media exemption (Faler 2005). Bloggers say they are bona fide journalists.

On the international scene, the 2005 race for Iran's next president was marked by campaign ads on blogs (Murphy 2005). The trend is growing widely throughout the world.

INSTANT MESSAGING

In our fast-paced e-world, sometimes the rapid response of e-mail is not fast enough. There is really no way of knowing if the person receiving your e-mail is online at that particular moment of e-mail arrival. Instant messaging (IM) is one alternative medium. You can type in messages that both you and your customer, vendor, or friend can see.

IM is an electronic communication system that involves immediate correspondence between two or more users who are all online simultaneously. It is sort of a conversation involving typing rather than speaking words. (See www.precisecyberfo rensics.com/glossary.html.) Here are some of the various features of IM.

- Sounds—play sounds for your counterpart
- Files—share information by sending files directly to your counterpart
- Talk—use the Internet instead of a phone to actually talk with another person
- Streaming content—real-time stock quotes and news in general
- Chat—create your own chat room with co-workers
- Instant messages—send notes or information back and forth with another person who is online

Major online services like America Online (AOL), Prodigy, and CompuServe were the main way that people could link and communicate with one another online. IM exploded on the Internet scene in November 1996, when Mirablis, a company founded by a group of Israeli programmers, introduced ICQ—a free IM utility that can be used by anyone.

EXTRANETS AND SCM

If a company Web site links two or more trading partners, it is referred to as an extranet: a B2B Intranet that lets limited, controlled business partners interact with the firm for all kinds of exchanges. (See Figure 4.3.) Intranets, extranets, and e-commerce have a lot in common. Intranets are localized within a firm and move data quicker than the more widely distributed extranets.

The use of Internet (primarily Web) protocols is common to connect business users. On an intranet, Web administrators prescribe access and policy for a defined group of users. On a B2B extranet, system designers at each participating company

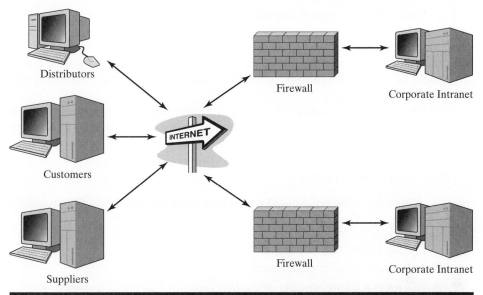

FIGURE 4.3   Basic extranet layout

must collaborate to make sure there is a common interface with the company they are dealing with. One participating business partner might be using Microsoft Explorer, and another might use Netscape Navigator 4.7. To collaborate via an extranet, the applications have to perform consistently on all platforms. The overall connectivity represents supply chain management, where allied businesses (manufacturer, supplier, retailer) are connected to expedite the business life cycle through integration, cooperation, and accommodation online.

Related to the extranet-SCM environment is Enterprise Resource Planning (ERP). An industry term, ERP is a software solution intended to meet the organization's goals of tightly integrating all functions of the business. This technology facilitates integration of company-wide information systems with the potential to go across companies. The increased complexity of businesses and the need to integrate all the functions within an organization led to using ERP.

Web-enabled ERP systems have an impact on SCM. The Internet allows linking the Web sites to back-end systems like ERP, offering connections to a host of external parties like vendors and suppliers. The Internet provides an interface between the ERP system and the supply-chain members, allowing an online flow of reliable information around the clock. Such an arrangement allows customers to configure their own products, get price information, and find out whether the product is in stock. This is made possible because the customer's request directly accesses the ERP system of the supplier.

Extranets are not a passing trend. They are already the backbone of the e-business future. The obvious benefits are faster time to market, customer loyalty, increased partner interaction, and improved processes. The easiest way to quantify return on investment for extranets is to identify a business unit within a company that might benefit from one. This means identifying a business goal (increasing revenue, improving the customer base, and so on) before deciding on feasibility, justification, and return on the investment.

Once a business goal has been established, the next step is to get together with the IT department to discuss feasibility. In a vertical industry like manufacturing, the focus is on improving operations through the existing supply chain, whereas in horizontal retail chains, the focus would be on improving revenue. Working with the IT group should bring technical and business information together for a master design of the company's extranet.

Understanding corporate business processes is the key to successful deployment of an extranet. By planning the deployment around a well-defined business plan, it is easier to prove how the technology is helping the bottom line.

KEY CONSIDERATIONS

When contemplating an extranet installation, here are some factors to consider:

1. Identify the user(s).
2. List the technology components.
3. Specify the security requirements.
4. Discuss the administration of the extranet.
5. Understand the functions of the extranet.

The users of an extranet are normally nonemployees—customers, suppliers, distributors, outsourcers, consultants, and vendors. They are categorized as an outside group with whom frequent contacts are made, and as business partners who yield high returns. In planning an extranet, questions should be raised early in the process regarding who will be included, how they will be prioritized, and what specific benefits (decreased inventory, increased revenue, and so on) will produce the best measurable improvements.

Eastman Kodak has expanded its use of extranets to cut costs and boost sales by sharing critical information with major business partners. Kodak has created extranet links to about 25 organizations, including dealers, contractors, joint-venture partners, and subsidiaries, and is adding new extranets at the rate of two per week. It's considering linking electronically to key suppliers and retail chains as well, says VP and CIO John Chiazza.

The extranets are being used mainly to exchange information. Kodak continues to rely on electronic data interchange for transactions, but the company is talking to some partners about the potential for conducting transactions over the extranets. "We've been involved in B2B e-commerce for many years as a user of classic EDI, but what has been emerging recently is more intimate interactions through the use of extranets, where we or our customers can reach into certain internal applications, so that, for example, we can learn how products are moving through their stores and do a better job planning for future orders from them," says Chiazza.

The extranets let authorized users at other companies "tunnel" under Kodak's firewall to access specific servers and even specific applications, Internet, intranet, extranets, and groupware users. Authorized outsiders can get past Kodak firewalls and run applications as they need to. Joint-venture partners have access to even more resources, such as intranets, databases, and mailboxes. Some of the networks give Kodak access to its partners' applications.

To ensure that only authorized users get under the firewall, Kodak uses an extranet management and security system that includes integrated VPN (virtual private network) services, as well as data encryption and authentication for security. Administrators can define privileges based on user identification, the method of authentication and encryption, the information resource being accessed, company affiliation, and day and time.

In assessing the technology components, the key point is to make sure that any technology meets open standards and can work with multiple technologies. Planners need to ask questions such as: How will the technology integrate with existing business partners' networks? Will it support all network protocols? Can the technology guarantee interoperability for business partners? Can the technology support all of the encryption and authentication methods for the type of interaction needed? Will the Internet be the only access path?

Security varies with the type of user, the sensitivity of the information transacted, and the communication lines used. Security questions deal with access control, authentication, and encryption. Access control relates to what users can and cannot access, what users can access and from which server(s), which accessible data are for display only, and which accessible data can be restricted to certain times of the day. In terms of authentication, decisions must be made regarding the level of authentication for each user, whether passwords and user names are adequate security, and how well other security measures complement the authentication. Is encryption required? If so, how strong should it be? What type of communication line or data should be encrypted?

The next item to consider is the administration of the extranet. Here, several questions must be raised: Does the company need to monitor all incoming traffic? Are staff skills adequate for handling the complexity of the extranet? How will the extranet fit in with the rest of the company's IT security? Although supporting every technology is not practical, knowing what to expect early in the planning phase undoubtedly will contribute to effective management.

Finally, usability should be discussed. An extranet must be usable to be attractive to customers and business partners. Like other issues, usability brings up several questions: How will users be authenticated? Will users need special training? Is client software required for allowing users to access the extranet? How will it be configured? Who will administer it?

In summary, installing an extranet brings up many issues involving different types of people in the organization. This is where planning becomes critical. Security and effective management make an extranet viable. Companies that have assessed these issues and weighed the risks and rewards stand to benefit significantly over the long run. As the saying goes, the focus is on the journey, not the short sprint.

EXTRANETS AND ERP

MANAGEMENT SUPPORT.   Extranets are changing how organizations share internal resources and interact with the outside business world. Built with technology and used by people, they can ensure lasting bonds between business partners and corporate members. The entire commitment should be viewed as a knowledge management asset rather than a mere networking expense to expedite business. This is where management support becomes a critical part of the installation.

Often a "champion"represents management support—someone who knows the organization's processes, goals, and politics, and who has technical experience and leadership qualities. This person is an advocate with the ability to build company-wide support. It is a demanding role, requiring a detail-oriented expert who can sell top management on the potential of the technology. The key to a champion's success is to demonstrate how an extranet can help the company meet its revenue goals. Specifically, a convincing argument should be made for how the extranet will generate revenue, how the technology will solve the business problems at hand, and how the work will get done through knowledge sharing via the extranet.

Think of a manufacturing organization with an e-business environment that allows its business partners, distributors, contractors, and suppliers to access extranet resources through a pre-established interface. Two of the applications could be an e-commerce storefront for suppliers or an enterprise resource planning application and a procurement system. The extranet can be used to manage all these applications and tie them into one integrated system for deriving real value from the company's entire range of business relationships. The extranet is bound to be the technical community that eventually will generate revenue and ensure competitive advantage.

MANAGEMENT IMPLICATIONS

Intranets are tools to manage corporate intelligence. They offer unique leverage and a competitive advantage at all levels of the organization. Among the key success factors are strong leadership, a focus on users, and effective management of the intranet. From a managerial viewpoint, change should be nurtured with care. This author spent seven weeks designing and implementing a $700,000 intranet site for a foreign central bank of 950 employees. After three months of training, coaching, selling, and demonstrating the uses of the new intranet, less than 20 percent of the employees made a habit of using the new system. The rest of the staff continued to deliver memos, documents, reports, and messages the old-fashioned way—in person.

Change is closely related to employee satisfaction, and the effect of the intranet on the way employees do their jobs is important. Those who are forced to use a new system will find a way to get back at the company. Gripe sites are available on the Internet where employees can state their dissatisfaction with their employer. For example, www.vault.com or www.brandstupid.com are gripe sites that accept such complaints. Competitors, disgruntled employees, whistle-blowers, or activists generally start these sites. Anyone with an ax to grind can smear the employer for the public to read. IT and company recruiters should review such sites and check what is posted about the company.

Another management implication is the strategy for recruiting qualified technical personnel. The trend used to be to offer significantly higher salaries than the industry average for technical personnel, but most organizations today look for applicants with stability, loyalty, and commitment to the work ethic. They offer bonuses based on performance rather than raises because they don't have to repeat them in later years.

Extranets are career enhancers for many IT professionals. Those who work on a successful extranet project usually end up having the biggest impact on their employer. In one case, a designer deployed an extranet with the goal of driving down costs. The system met the goal by automating processes, improving overall efficiency, and decentralizing functions for faster and better decision making. In addition to knowledge of the company's business processes, her skills included client/server technology, data communication and networking, and HTTP. She saw a way of securely linking customers, suppliers, and vendors to the corporate network. When the extranet was implemented, the company recognized the change in revenue, which translated into a hefty raise for the 23-year-old newcomer.

Summary

1. An intranet is a network connecting a set of company clients using standard Internet protocols, especially TCP/IP and HTTP. Intranets can handle all kinds of communication with ease.
2. An intranet offers several benefits. It links employees and managers around the clock; companies gain access to their primary resources; and it is the foundation for developing an enterprise-wide information system and a model for internal information management and collaborative computing. In addition, there are cost advantages and ease of access, plus portability and scalability.
3. The two types of client/server architecture for intranet design are two-tier architecture and three-tier architecture.
4. Intranets can be protected from unauthorized access via firewalls. In the case of a company with branches or remote sites, each location should be part of the total security umbrella of the intranet.
5. Planning an intranet is a six-step procedure: Define the goal, provide justification and management support, build an intranet in-house or outsource it, form an intranet team to oversee the process, build and test a prototype, and ensure effective maintenance.
6. E-mail is getting smarter: Now it can be used not just to store messages but to direct specific messages to folders and to check voice, text, and fax messages. This is called content management.
7. An alternative to e-mail is instant messaging, where people exchange ideas, information, and messages via typing the exchange online. This medium can be useful in situations where a response is expected to be immediate.
8. An extranet or company Web site links two or more trading partners. When contemplating an extranet installation, five key factors need to be considered: identifying the user, listing the technology components, specifying the security requirements, setting up the administration, and understanding the usability.
9. From the managerial perspective, intranets are tools to manage corporate intelligence. Among the key success factors are strong leadership, a focus on users, and effective management.

Key Terms

- **extranet** (p. 102)
- **firewall** (p. 103)
- **flaming** (p. 115)
- **groupware** (p. 102)
- **intranet** (p. 101)
- **packet filter** (p. 110)
- **proxy** (p. 110)
- **spamming** (p. 114)

Test Your Understanding

1. Is there a relationship between an intranet and groupware? Be specific.
2. Distinguish between the following:
   a. Intranet and extranet
   b. Two-tier and three-tier architecture
   c. Server PC and client PC
   d. Spamming and flaming
3. Explain briefly the function and purposes of a firewall.
4. What main benefits can one expect of an intranet installation?
5. In what way(s) can an intranet be useful in human resources? Explain in detail.
6. How is an intranet useful in manufacturing and operations?
7. In your own words, why does a company need an intranet?
8. Summarize the essence of client/server architecture.
9. Is there a relationship between RPC and GUI? Explain.
10. What would be some of the limitations of a two-tier architecture? Be specific.
11. "Browsers greatly simplify access to the company's computing resources and information." Do you agree? Explain.
12. In what way(s) do firewalls vary in complexity?
13. Summarize the key steps in planning an intranet.
14. What would be a deciding factor in whether to build an intranet in-house or to outsource it?
15. The chapter mentions that "intranet and e-mail is a marriage made in cyber heaven." Do you agree? Justify your answer.
16. List four key items that should be followed under e-mail etiquette.
17. Why is an extranet viewed as a B2B intranet? Explain.
18. Several factors should be considered when contemplating an extranet installation. Elaborate.
19. How is an extranet related to SCM? Explain.
20. Within the framework of the chapter material, what is your definition of a champion?

Discussion Questions

1. "Technically, there is no difference between the Internet and an intranet, except that only select people are allowed to connect to the intranet." Evaluate this statement in the light of the way intranets are designed.
2. Do you think an intranet environment is the best way to communicate within the firm? In answering this question, assess alternative modes of communication and report your findings in class.
3. If intranets offer so many good benefits, why do you think some companies resist having them? Is it the size of the firm? The nature of the product? The caliber of personnel? Discuss.
4. If you have a choice between two-tier and three-tier server architecture, which one would you consider? Which factors or criteria would you use in making your final decision? Be specific.
5. Within the framework of an intranet for a large business, what do you look for when considering a filter?

6. Would one be correct in thinking that more abuses than uses of e-mail occur in an intranet environment? Discuss.

7. Of the three applications mentioned in the chapter (human resources, accounting and finance, and manufacturing and operations), which application justifies the most frequent use of an extranet? Why?

8. How would one explain the relationship between an extranet and SCM? Look up projects.bus.1su.edu/independent_study/vdhing1erp and demonstrate the relationship between an extranet and ERP.

Web Exercises

1. Visit a large firm that has an intranet site. Identify the technology that operates the site.

2. Identify a large retailer in your area and determine whether it is ready to adopt an intranet and extranet. If the retailer already has one, interview the head of the IT division and learn about the technology in use. Report your findings to the class.

3. Design an intranet (on paper) for a small bank of 65 employees. Explain the details of the infrastructure to a local IT specialist. What did he or she find right and wrong with your design? Write a four-page report summarizing your experience.

CHAPTER 5

HOSTING YOUR WEB SITE

Learning Objectives

This chapter focuses on several learning objectives:

- ISPs and the services they offer
- How to choose an ISP
- How to register a domain name
- Role of application service providers
- How to select an ASP to suit your needs

IN A NUTSHELL

Before you complete the design of your Web site, you need to find a way to put it on the Internet. To support the exponential growth in commercial Internet traffic, an entirely new industry of **Internet service providers (ISPs)** has emerged. In 1969, only four hosting companies existed. In 1985, there were 1,960 companies; by 2005 there were more than 3,000 ISPs in the United States and more than 15,000 worldwide.

Internet service provider (ISP): a specialized company that connects customers with PCs and browsers to the Internet.

virtual hosting: a company with its own domain name, hosted by an ISP to conduct business via the Internet.

virtual domain: a company with its own domain name, hosted by an ISP to conduct business via the Internet.

domain name: a company's identifier in cyberspace.

For a fee, the ISP gives you a software package, a user name, a password, and an access phone number. Equipped with a modem, you can then log onto the Internet and browse the World Wide Web, send and receive e-mail, and download software packages or text files. Nearly every ISP today offers what is called **virtual hosting,** or a **virtual domain,** as well. This allows you to have your own **domain name,** such as www.yourcompany.com, rather than using your ISP's domain name with a subdirectory designating your site, such as www.isp.com/yourcompany/. More than half of today's *Fortune* 500 companies design and maintain their own Web sites, but more than one third of medium-size to small organizations turn to ISPs for many reasons:

- Companies often need a full-time staff and a Webmaster to handle day-to-day changes and enhancements to the site. In most cases, such specialization is not one of the company's core competencies.
- ISPs generally offer headache-free management of Web sites, operations, automated backup, and security.
- ISPs often have high-speed connectivity, multiple T1s, and even T3 lines to main Internet hubs. A T1 line transmits long-distance data at 1.5 megabits (million bits) per second. Large corporations employ a T3 line with the capability of transmitting 44.7 megabits per second. Smaller firms with limited resources have to settle for less.
- ISPs can handle real access and real physical security, from power supplies and air conditioning to network links.
- ISPs often have the latest technology for thousands of customers. Most organizations could not afford the constant costs associated with updating and upgrading the technology necessary to keep their Web sites current.

With a good ISP, things can go smoothly for a marketing campaign; with a poor ISP, many difficulties will arise. This chapter focuses on (1) what an ISP does, (2) what services to expect, (3) how to choose an ISP, and (4) how to choose and register a domain name.

HOW ISPs REALLY WORK

Why is so much attention given to hosting Web sites? Based on the author's years of consulting experience in e-commerce, most client organizations are anxious to go on the Internet without questioning the reliability of the ISP that can accommodate their Web site, like air travelers who negotiate the lowest price, regardless of the airline or "equipment" that will fly them to their destination. But there is more to deciding on an ISP than price. Technology, staffing, speed, and amount of congestion are all part of what determines price and continuity with an ISP. And changing ISPs when you are already into e-commerce can have an adverse effect on your business.

The more informed an organization becomes about an ISP's work, the easier it is to select one. For an initial investment of a few thousand dollars and a few thousand more per month, you can connect directly from your business to an Internet backbone and never see an ISP. You become the ISP. You will have to run your own e-mail, Web hosting, DNS (domain name server), and so on. The following is a rough guide regarding what it takes and how much it costs to host your own Web site.

1. **Hardware**—A Web server, communication gear, and a special router: $5,000 to $18,000 per year.
2. **Communications**—Typically a T1 or fractional T1 line: $8,000 to $12,000 per year.
3. **Staff**—At least a Webmaster, a Web designer, and a help desk: $45,000 to $80,000 per year.

The minimal operating cost can run between $60,000 to $120,000 per year for the first year and $50,000 to $100,000 each year thereafter. You also shoulder full responsibility for keeping the connection going 24 hours a day, 7 days a week. More on what it takes to start an ISP is found later in the chapter.

THE INFRASTRUCTURE

A reliable ISP involves more than the three items previously noted. ISPs are cheaper, more reliable, and provide services that are difficult to match with a corporate in-house equivalent. The average cost of a hosting service (ISP) runs between $1,200 and $5,000 per year. The service manages storage, tracks Web traffic, and maintains the Web server on a day-to-day basis around the clock. All hosts promise security and privacy for your data, but they cannot guarantee it. Some uncertainty also arises in Web hosting billing, including hidden charges and sudden "nickel and dime" increases. (A section on how to choose an ISP is included later in the chapter.)

For others to access your company Web site, it has to be stored on a Web server that is always connected to the Internet by a high-speed link. The infrastructure includes the following. (See Figure 5.1.)

1. Standby electric power as backup to keep the site available in the event of a blackout.

2. Redundant *fault-tolerant* servers to ensure that your Web site will continue in the event a hard drive or a server breaks down.

3. Redundant communications lines to keep your site active in the event a phone line or a router goes down.

4. One or more firewalls to protect your Web site from hackers or unauthorized access.

TYPES OF SERVICE PROVIDERS

There are five types of service providers.

1. The Internet service provider (ISP). An ISP is simply a specialized business that offers Internet access. ISPs like AOL offer Internet service to millions of

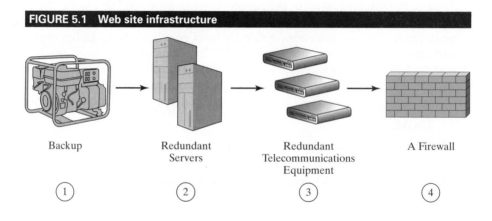

FIGURE 5.1   Web site infrastructure

Backup	Redundant Servers	Redundant Telecommunications Equipment	A Firewall
①	②	③	④

customers. They allow PC users to access the Internet via modems using a voice telephone network or directly via cables. An ISP provides an interface between the public phone system and Internet digital phone lines, which carry packets instead of voice conversations.

application service provider (ASP): a company that offers packaged software for lease online.

2. The **application service provider (ASP).** An ASP is an application renter. It offers packaged software for lease online, and generally focuses on high-end applications like databases and enterprise resource planning (ERP). These applications are expensive, take a lot of time to install, and are labor intensive to manage. Upgrades mean prolonged downtime and additional costs. Training also can be costly. ASPs allow small to midsize businesses to choose from a menu of applications without having to invest in the staffing or infrastructure to support them.

wireless application service provider (WASP): a company that offers untethered applications; hosting, developing, and managing applications are similar to that of an ASP.

3. The **wireless application service provider (WASP).** These service providers handle untethered applications; their responsibilities involve hosting, developing, and managing applications similar to that of an ASP. However, there is one real difference. WASP infrastructure requires integration between the Web and wireless networks. This means that WASPs have to deal with a wide range of hardware and mobile devices and wireless networking protocols. It makes the job more complex.

business service provider (BSP): an Internet service developer that rents only its own proprietary applications via the Web.

4. The **business service provider (BSP).** A BSP is an Internet service developer that rents only its own proprietary applications via the Web. Generally, the software is specific in function.

wholesale service provider (WSP): a service provider that packages a selection of BSP applications for distribution online.

5. The **wholesale service provider (WSP).** This is a new category of service provider that packages a selection of BSP applications for distribution online. These service providers generally cater to small to midsize businesses and can be an important addition to large IT operations. ISPs fall into one of three categories: the large wholesale access providers, the smaller Internet backbone providers, and the local ISPs.

Although it might seem that the number of smaller providers would decrease as a result of acquisitions by larger providers, just the opposite is taking place. Larger wholesale providers have been finding themselves the targets of consolidation and acquisition, while the ranks of the smaller providers have been growing and growing.

This trend is beginning to shift, though, with the emergence of firms such as OneMain.com, which is being formed as a conglomerate of several local ISPs. The idea behind the combination of these smaller firms is that the conglomerate will combine "local marketing, content, and customer service . . . with the cost savings associated with a large-scale enterprise and a common operating platform." This trend has brought big business into the world of smaller, often less experienced, local ISPs, which have survived thus far based on their local expertise and appeal. It puts larger participants on a local level and might bring about the faster demise of thousands of poorer performing local ISPs.

TYPES OF WEB HOSTING SERVICES

Web hosting: providing, managing, and maintaining hardware, software, content integrity, security, and reliable high-speed Internet connections.

There are four types of **Web hosting** services: dial-up access, developer's hosting, Web hosting only, and industrial-strength hosting. Thousands of local dial-up access providers handle Web page hosting for businesses. Developer's hosting usually involves hosting the Web pages of a business. This kind of hosting is usually customer focused, although at a high price. Some companies specialize in business Web site hosting. They allow no dial-up access but provide a wide variety of services to their customers. Finally, businesses with high-traffic sites find maximum reliability with the largest national industrial service providers, who supply coast-to-coast, 24-hour staffing and redundant connections to the Internet backbone at hefty prices.

PACKETS, ROUTERS, AND LINES

On the Net, information is sent and received in packets. A packet is small in size, usually just a few hundred bytes. When e-mail messages are sent, the TCP/IP layer breaks the message into tiny packets and writes the destination address on each packet to make sure it doesn't get lost. As a result, packets can be sent separately over the Net, like thousands of cars on a superhighway. Packets can even take a different route across the Net. From Washington, D.C., to San Francisco, for example, one packet of an e-mail message might go through Houston, but another might pass through Denver. They may arrive at their destination at different times and even out of sequence. The receiving computer rearranges them into a form just like the original message. (See Figure 5.2.)

In practical terms, assume a customer wants to send an e-mail message to a merchant somewhere in the United States. The Winsock program running on her PC splits her e-mail message into Net-sized packets. The packets are then sent through her modem, which converts them into analog signals across an ordinary voice telephone line to an ISP. A modem is needed to receive incoming messages and convert analog

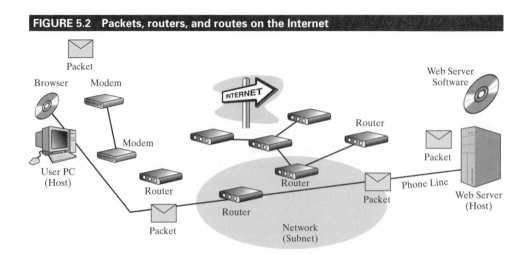

FIGURE 5.2   Packets, routers, and routes on the Internet

signals to digital and back. An ISP needs many lines to absorb the volume of data transmission coming from thousands of customers without delay.

Once the packets are received, the ISP needs to send them from its computer, with a dedicated connection, to some bigger ISP. Such a computer performs log-in procedures, authenticates customer IDs, and manages the traffic using special software. This is the primary function of an ISP.

There is one point worth noting about communication lines. Because conversion from analog to digital and vice versa introduces noise, it is the noise that limits certain modems to 33,600 bits per second. If the packets coming from the ISP to the phone lines could remain digital all the way to the customer, data could be sent at 56,000 (56K) bits per second from the ISP to the customer. The way to do this is for customers to get an **integrated services digital network (ISDN)** line from their phone company, so that the transmitted data will remain in digital format and transmission is possible at the 55K rate. The ISP also must connect to the phone system with a digital circuit like an ISDN line. We assume the customer is not too far from the phone office (around three miles) for 56K to work fast. The 55K digital modems are integrated into **access servers,** which combine a modem and a terminal server into a single integrated (and expensive) box. Many access servers like Sun Microsystems boxes handle up to 48 dial-up connections. Therefore, if the ISP has 4,800 customers and if 20 percent of the customers dial at the same time, the ISP will need approximately 10 access servers (48 × 0.20 = 9.60).

access server: a server that combines a modem and a terminal server into a single integrated box.

THE CONNECTION

As Figure 5.3 shows, when you dial into an ISP, you dial into a router owned by the ISP. The ISP also has a router connected to the larger ISP. This second router is the gateway to the Internet. For this connection and other services like an e-mail mailbox, customers pay a set monthly fee.

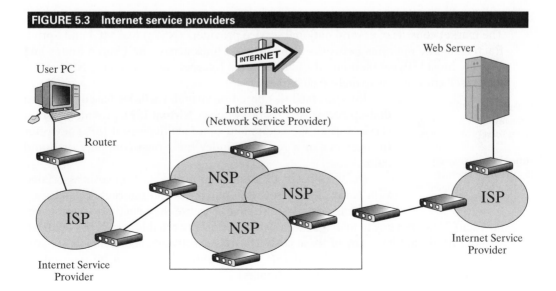

FIGURE 5.3   Internet service providers

TABLE 5.1 Selected connection types, features, and speeds (costs are estimates)

Connection Type	Theoretical Speed	Hardware	Connection Cost/Month	Provider Setup Cost	Provider Cost/Month
Regular phone line	33.6/56 Kbps	Modem	$25–40	$0–50	$15–30
Frame relay	56 Kbps to 1.544 Mbps	DSU/CSU	$200–4,500	$75–500	$40–400
T1 line	1.544 Mbps	T1 mux	$900–3,500	$500–3,000	$400–1,400
Direct PC	400 Kbps	Satellite dish	$10–130	$0–50	$15–30
Cable modems	10–30 Mbps inbound, 700 Kbps outbound	Cable modem, adaptor card	$35–45	Varies	None
T3 line	44.7 Mbps	T3 mux	$15,000–45,000	None (you are your own provider)	None (you are your own provider)

backbone: cluster of competing companies called network service providers.

The **backbone** of the Internet is a cluster of competing companies called network service providers (NSPs) that work together to provide total interconnection. To connect to an NSP, the ISP must pay the NSP a monthly fee. The money comes from fees collected from the ISP's subscribers. A portion of the fees goes to manage the ISP's internal operations and part to pay the NSP. Routers work together regardless of who owns them and how the charges are handled. They connect networks, filter bad packets, direct packets, and isolate traffic. See Table 5.1 for the main connection types and their features and speeds.

ISP STRUCTURE AND SERVICES

From a prospective customer's view, one important item to understand is bandwidth. The market consists of several national service providers (NSPs) like MCI and Sprint. Each company operates networks of high-speed lines across the United States and globally. Most ISPs get their initial T1 (1.54 Mbps) Internet "feed" from the NSPs. Then they resell connections to dial-up customers.

facilities-based ISP: a company that owns dial-up access servers or switches.

virtual ISP: a company that provides Internet service using equipment of a facilities-based ISP.

ISPs are facilities based or virtual. **Facilities-based ISPs** own dial-up access servers or switches. **Virtual ISPs** provide Internet services using the equipment of a facilities-based ISP. They offer the services of a real ISP under their own company or brand name.

Facilities-based ISPs have significant start-up costs associated with hardware and software purchases and Internet access leases. Operating costs are also high, because they need a technical support staff 24 hours a day to manage the network and ensure reliable service. By contrast, virtual ISPs do not have any of these costs. Hardware, software, and technical support are provided by the facilities-based ISP. Capital expenditures can be focused on marketing and sales to generate new customers.

Residential customers are the fastest-growing e-commerce users, with more and more households connecting to the Internet every day. Internet-connecting devices like handheld organizers, data-enabled mobile phones, and Web TV are attracting more business to e-merchants.

Commercial customers are established businesses surging toward e-commerce and e-business. These customers expect high-level, quality service, a dedicated connection, Web hosting, Web design, and reliable maintenance.

Public customers access the Internet via Internet Café or "Cyber" Café clubs, from motels, airports, and schools. The charges are somewhat higher than residential costs, depending on location and duration of the connection.

SERVICES

An ISP is expected to provide a variety of required and optional services—the expectations of any customer. The main services include the following.

Domain name server (DNS): a repository where the domain name for each ISP is stored.

- **Domain name server (DNS):** The DNS is where the domain name for each ISP is stored. It also identifies the mail server to be used for mail delivery from the Internet and stores information about any backup name and mail servers. ISPs must have at least one DNS server operating in their network, but two servers are common, each operating at opposing ends of the network.

- E-mail, the most commonly used service on the Internet. An ISP must dedicate a separate server for e-mail. The key issues to consider are mail storage capacity per user and the maximum size the server will allow. The depth of e-mail service the ISP chooses to offer customers is up to the ISP, but all consumers must have reliable e-mail access.

radius server: a network access server that authenticates a user's ID and password and triggers accounting to complete the customer's chargeable session.

- **Radius server:** A radius server is required to authenticate users and record accounting data for user authentication. A network access server forwards a request to the radius server's database to authenticate a user's ID and password combination. If the combination is valid, the request is accepted; otherwise, it is rejected and the connection is dropped. Authenticated connections trigger accounting, which is where IP addresses are returned to the dial-in client and a record is made of the start time of the session. When the session ends, accounting data and traffic statistics are transferred from the network access server to the accounting process to complete the customer's chargeable session.

The primary optional services include the following.

- World Wide Web server: This can be run on the same hardware as the DNS, e-mail, and radius systems. Nearly all ISPs offer Web access.

- File transfer protocol (FTP): An FTP is a widely accepted file transfer standard on the Internet. It usually is restricted to a select group or individual. It is a client/server application that accepts connections from clients trying to connect to its server. FTP servers can be run on most server machines on the ISP's local network and require careful configuration to ensure safety and security at all times.

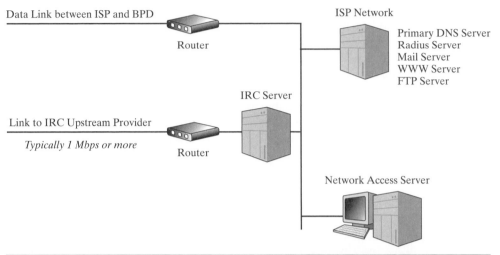

Data Link between ISP and BPD

Router

ISP Network

Primary DNS Server
Radius Server
Mail Server
WWW Server
FTP Server

IRC Server

Link to IRC Upstream Provider

Typically 1 Mbps or more

Router

Network Access Server

FIGURE 5.4   A typical ISP network with IRC services

Internet relay chat (IRC): a text-based chat service, where users connect to a local server as part of a larger network of IRC servers.

- **Internet relay chat (IRC):** This is a text-based chat service. Users connect to a local server as part of a much larger network of IRC servers. To install an IRC server, the ISP must apply to the administrator of the IRC network, which might require a minimum amount of Internet bandwidth dedicated for IRC services. The ISP has the option of establishing its own IRC server to provide local chat services. See Figure 5.4 for an ISP network with IRC services.

- News server: Internet Network News is becoming increasingly popular. Because there is so much data traffic for news, the cost for this type of service can be more than $100,000 a month. This is why many ISPs restrict the number of news groups they carry or offer a "suck" feed from another news server. A "suck" feed involves drawing news from an upstream news server upon request. This alternative is relatively inexpensive, simple, and can increase the functionality of an ISP because customers can access any news article over the Internet 24 hours a day.

- **HTTP proxy service**: A proxy server generates and manages a local store of Internet objects such as Web pages, images, or FTP files and delivers the objects

caching: Internet objects delivered by a proxy server when requested.

when requested (called **caching**). For example, when a Web page is requested, the proxy server examines its internal database to see if the page is stored in the cache. If the page is not found, the request is passed on to the Web site and the page is returned. HTTP proxy servers are best run on independent hardware. They serve to minimize data traffic control costs and speed up requests as more and more users join the ISP over time.

TECHNICAL SERVICES

In addition to these offerings, an ISP is equipped with the technical components for customer access to the Internet. The connection between the provider and the physical location is the local loop. The cost depends on the size of the pipeline and the distance (in air miles) from the provider and the local telephone company central office. A charge is assessed for the size of bandwidth required.

Several cable-based options are available. They include T1 and T3 lines, fiber-optic-based Internet access, and a number of servers.

A *T1 line* is a digital carrier line that transmits digital signals at 1.544 Mbps. This is the "raw" bandwidth needed for fast data and video transmission traffic on a 24-hour basis. It is also commonly used to connect LANs to the Internet. The line is split into 24 individual channels, each of which supports 65K bits per second. A T1 line can serve up to 3,500 subscribers at a minimum cost of $1,000 per month.

A *T3 line* transmits digital signals at 44.736 Mbps, which is equivalent to 28 T1 lines. A T3 line is split into 672 individual channels, each supporting 64 Kbps, and serves up to 100,000 subscribers. The lease cost starts at $18,000 per month.

Fiber-optic-based Internet access is usually reserved for businesses with large bandwidth requirements. The speed of fiber-optic networks is designated by optical carriers OC-3, OC-12, and OC-24. The main difference among the three types is speed. An OC-3 line serves up to a half million subscribers at 155 Mbps at costs upwards of $50,000 per month. An OC-12 line serves up to 2 million subscribers at 622.08 Mbps at costs upwards of $200,000 per month. An OC-24 line can support 10 million subscribers at 1.244 Gbps at costs starting at several hundred thousand dollars per month.

A minimum of two *servers* of each type are needed to launch a start-up ISP. They include DNS servers, e-mail servers, and radius servers. Optional servers may be considered for FTP, development and testing, registration, billing, tape, news, and proxy servers.

A *broadband connection* on the Internet means many times the speed of the old dial-up service via modems. Broadband communication can carry multiple messages simultaneously over the same medium (wire or fiber-optic cable). It also allows Internet transmission of text, video, images, or audio in virtual real time. Since it was first introduced in the late 1990s, over 20 million U.S. households have bought connections. The so-called broadband revolution now involves not only the three largest dial-up ISPs (AOL, MSN, EarthLink), but also cable and telephone companies that control the "last mile" of wires into the home.

Dial-up companies are trying hard to combat the surge of broadband by offering innovations like spam filters, parental controls, and pop-up advertising blockers. What favors cable companies, which sell two-thirds of the broadband in the U.S, however, is that ISPs are shut out of selling access to much of the market. As a result, cable companies sell broadband much cheaper than ISPs. See www.comparenow.net for the latest ISP prices and charges.

To attract customers, most ISPs use "accelerator" or special offers. For example, AOL offers new subscribers the first two months free, after which they charge $23.95 a month for unlimited access to the Internet. By contrast, EarthLink offers the first six months for half price ($10.95; the regular charge is $21.95) for unlimited access. Of course, subscribers are aware of the competition. What many do is to call the ISP looking for freebies. Knowing the cost of attracting customers, ISPs almost always offer a one-time repeat of the initial free offer to keep customers on the list.

There are three types of broadband available for home access:

1. *Cable* modems, first introduced in 1995. This is what launched the connection of Web users in North America to the Internet. Cable modems use fiber-optic and coaxial cable networks to provide Internet access at up to 10 megabits per second (Mbps).

2. *Digital subscriber line (DSL)* technology is an evolving competitor when it comes to home broadband access. Using intertwined copper wires originally intended for phone use, DSL is ideal for homes that are within four miles of a central office. Speeds are rated at 50 times faster than those reached by dial-up modems, although transmission quality declines as distance grows from the central office.

3. *Fiber-optic networks* offer the largest available bandwidth with speeds reaching 100 Mbps regardless of location. The main drawback is cost, although with recent developments in technologies, fiber optics for home use is becoming more affordable.

4. *Wireless technology* means universal availability as well as higher speeds than other technologies, except fiber-optics.

On top of these technical features are multiple routers and switches to make forwarding decisions for data packets within the network; firewalls to increase the network's security; cables, tools, test equipment, printers, equipment racks, furniture, shelving, and cold spares. It takes a lot of infrastructure to ensure online service on a regular basis.

CHOOSING AN ISP

Web sites are becoming the foundation for critical interaction with customers, partners, and suppliers. Site performance, reliability, and speed of network service are prerequisites for the viability and integrity of the site and the business itself. ISPs are increasing in number, size, and services. They range in size from the giants, like industry leader America Online (AOL), to thousands of tiny companies.

Some ISPs are local, and others are national and international, depending on their connection to the Internet backbone and the technology they use. Increasingly, companies that specialize in Web site hosting allow no dial-up access, which ensures that bandwidth (speed of connection to the Internet) is not compromised by competing traffic, such as customers accessing chat rooms. Ideally, a business putting up its Web site for the first time would want to look into industrial-strength Web hosting, where high nationwide traffic is handled quickly and responsibly, and where 24-hour staff and redundant connections to the Internet backbone are provided at competitive fees.

WHAT TO CONSIDER

Your ISP has become indispensable. As you spend more and more time surfing the Web, you become sensitive to e-mail, network brownouts, and fluctuations in performance—to say nothing of busy signals. The proliferation of big-name national ISPs with tempting access networks causes you to do some thinking.

There are special criteria to consider for implementing a selection process. Anyone who has done so knows that selecting a business partner from a long list of ISPs or application service providers (ASPs) is always a challenge. In most cases, the moment you decide to subscribe to one, you find a surge of membership and limited staff capabilities, resulting in gradual degradation of the speed and quality of service. Even if you buy network circuits from several top-tier IP networking providers, chances are your traffic will ride the same fiber cables from your data center to a telephone company's central office.

When an IP circuit provider sells bandwidth, it turns around and buys circuit capacity from a firm that has the fiber cables. This means a cut along the single cable from the tap that causes your IP provider's circuit to fail. To cushion this eventuality, make sure your vendor agrees to your requirements for dependability, reliability, and quality service before you sign any agreement. Additionally, specify not only vendor liability for failure to comply, but also recourse in quantitative terms. When you put your mind to it, you will see how important it is to take time to assess the caliber of the vendors before the final selection. See Table 5.1 for a summary.

SIZE OF THE PIPELINE OR BANDWIDTH.   High-speed T1 and T3 lines connect the ISP to the Internet backbone. A T1 line carries up to 1.5 Mbps (megabits per second), and a T3 line carries up to 45 Mbps. Smaller ISPs often have ISDN connections or *fractional* T1 connections. These connections (*network plumbing*) are what expedites or hampers the connection between the Web server and the Internet.

Depending on the volume of your Web site traffic, it might pay to have a T1 line that connects you directly to the Internet. The cost is high, but so are the charges via the ISP. It is no longer safe to assume that a Web site is made up of HTML documents using a few kilobytes. The increasingly media-rich content of Web sites requires high bandwidth to ensure speed and Web site readiness.

Network bandwidth growth is related to ISP growth. Bandwidth refers to the size of the *pipe* that feeds information across a network. In 1969, bandwidth was 9.6 kilobits per second (Kbps); in 1985, 56 Kbps; in 1990, 45 megabits per second (Mbps using T3 speed); in 1995, 155 Mbps; and in 2000, 2,048 Mbps.

Companies that sell Internet connections are struggling to survive the broadband competition. Cable and telephone companies that control "the last mile" of wire going to the homes make up about 90 percent of broadband connections (Angwin 2003). Dial-up services are enticing customers to keep their dial-up accounts by offering features such as spam filters and blockers for pop-up advertising. In contrast, broadband providers like America Online (AOL) are aggressively marketing exclusive access to magazine articles, videos, and music from Time Warner as a way to discourage customers from jumping ship.

The success of the dial-up services' broadband content focus will depend on how well the providers offer a subset of services at an affordable price—for instance, below $14 a month.

CONNECTION AVAILABILITY AND PERFORMANCE.   Connection availability and network performance are the most important criteria in evaluating an ISP. An ISP is viewed as a utility that should always be available. In terms of performance, the number of clients assigned to each of an ISP's computers and the space allotted on the computers are factors in ISP performance. Many successful ISPs use computers with fast Pentium processors to ensure performance. ISPs also assign a certain amount of server space on their computers for your Web site traffic.

Every business should consider how to manage media and downloads. In large businesses, for example, high-bandwidth media on the company's recruiting site is common. A popular fad on such job boards is interfacing with streaming video interviews with key officers who give you their view of their corporate philosophy, culture, and why a potential candidate should consider working there.

Including such features in a company Web site is not cheap. Videos use up a lot of bandwidth with frequent access. News and sports sites, which are media intensive, have similar needs. Those who visit these sites expect high resolution. In action-type videos such as earthquakes, the visitor expects to hear realistic sounds such as the howling winds and the thunderous rumble of the earth.

We also find a contrast when it comes to home improvement or technical equipment Web sites. To minimize customer service costs, commercial Web sites publish as much detail as the page or pages will allow. They may include huge documents (usually in PDF format), manuals, specifications, diagnostics, and appliances in high-resolution and color—in addition to the color of carpeting or tiles the appliances will go with. For this much density, end-to-end bandwidth is paramount. Five to 10 MB of ISP computer space is considered normal for most business Web sites. Yet e-mail, log files, and system programs can use up considerable space.

VIRTUAL HOSTING.   This feature allows you to have your own domain name, such as www.yourfirm.com, rather than using the ISP's domain name with a subdirectory designating your site (e.g., www.isp.com/yourfirm. isp.com/.) A business registers its own domain name for a nominal charge. It is a good investment should the business decide to switch ISPs at some time in the future. This means that any commitment to go with an ISP frees you from being locked into a long contract. Make sure when registering your domain name that your name is listed as the *administrative contact* with InterNIC (the domain name registration agency). This way, you're on your own and able to switch ISPs. You can see who is listed by checking your domain name at rs.internic.net/cgi-bin/whois.

E-MAIL ALIASES.   An ISP allows a certain number of e-mail addresses per account. Larger businesses might want to have multiple e-mail boxes at the Web-hosting ISP, which gives flexibility and independence, especially if the company has branches scattered all over the globe. Three to five addresses is a good number in a typical business environment.

STABILITY AND STAYING POWER.   The term *stability* refers to the longevity of the ISP's customer base. That is, how often do customers switch from one ISP to another? This is referred to in the industry as the **customer churn rate.** It is estimated that, on average, large ISPs can expect a monthly churn rate of approximately 4 percent. For a company the size of America Online (AOL), this amounts to thousands of customers per month. This movement of customers gives the smaller ISPs a chance to add to their own customer bases.

customer churn rate: how often customers switch from one ISP to another.

Staying power is the ISP's ability to continue to provide reliable service during downturns or during times when its business is not doing well. This has a lot to do with the ISP's cash flow and backup plans. The continuing mergers and acquisitions mania that has seized the industry provides even more reason for looking into the longevity of the ISP in question.

LOCAL ACCESS.   Is the phone number the ISP is providing you going to be free of long-distance charges? A local telephone number is always a safe bet, but an 800 number is not. Your monthly phone tolls could exceed the ISP fee, because the 800 numbers are not free. On the other hand, a local access number will not do much good if you are going to need the connection while traveling a lot. In any case, you need to know how many local access (also called **point of presence,** or **POP**) numbers an ISP has and how they are available for your use.

point of presence (POP): physical location on the premises of a local exchange carrier at which messages are transferred or linked to other carriers.

CUSTOMER SERVICE AND TECHNICAL SUPPORT.   *Support* is the key word in customer service. Whether you need to install a Web site or simply access the Internet, setting up your browser for a new ISP can range from straightforward to daunting, depending on your level of expertise.

If you're new to the Internet, you definitely should look for an ISP that will help you set up. Many offer free software that will automatically configure your computer to work with their service. Does your ISP have a 24-hour support line that you can call? Does it have the answers to your questions when you call? ISP customer service is key. Other questions to ask pertain to upgrades, customization, security, and scalability. For example, who decides when to upgrade? How much customization can the ISP do? What kind of security does it offer? Can the ISP's software and support staff handle your growth?

RELIABILITY.   The question of reliability is this: Does the ISP you are considering have the capability to handle all the customers it is taking on? If not, you can expect delays, busy signals while trying to log on, or slowdowns. Inquire about the ISP's call failure or call-success rates. How quickly you can go online depends on the time of the day. For example, mid evening is the busiest time on the Internet any day. By contrast, early risers have fewer problems logging on. For some reason, winter months attract heavier traffic. Other barometers of ISP reliability include network capacity and relationships with other ISPs.

PRICE.   Price is a major factor when choosing an ISP. Some ISPs offer free service or other seemingly great deals, but remember that the ISP is a *service,* not a *commodity*. These deals are not always the best for you or for your Web site. They might offer bare-bones access at no cost, but they come under attack for the heavy banner advertisement load that comes with the deal. See Table 5.2.

Prices vary with ISPs and the type of service. Most providers offer a fixed monthly flat rate with unlimited online time for about $20. A different algorithm is available for occasional users, and discounts might be offered for long-term commitments. Before signing on, most providers offer a free or low-cost trial membership so you can determine whether it is a provider you like.

TABLE 5.2   Factors in choosing an ISP
1. Bandwidth
2. Connection availability
3. Customer volume and traffic
4. Traffic volume during peak hours
5. Virtual hosting feature
6. Capacity of e-mail box
7. Stability and staying power
8. Customer churn rate
9. Free local address and access to the Internet
10. Customer service and local support
11. Price

QUESTIONS TO ASK

If you are serious about choosing the right ISP, here are important questions to ask.

INTERNET ACCESS

- Do you offer complete or partial access to the Internet?
- How do you connect to the Internet backbone?
- Does the Web site load quickly?
- Are you *really* sure the phone number is a local call?
- Is Internet access unlimited?
- Are you dialing straight into the ISP or are you dialing a remote terminal server that may be overloaded?
- Do you have a business address? Is the address a PO box or a rented mail drop?

FEATURES

- Do you offer any proprietary services such as chat lines or informational databases?
- How many mailboxes can be offered with my account? Any extra charges?
- Which e-mail utility do you offer? Can I attach through my e-mail account?
- Do you offer spam filters to help cut down on junk mail?
- What is the biggest attachment you can send in one e-mail?
- If you close the account, will the ISP forward e-mail to your new ISP for a while?
- Are Web logs available? Web usage reports?
- Does the ISP's Web site contain a mission statement?
- What are the limits on message size and total mailbox size?
- Does the ISP run e-mail through a virus scanner?
- How much Web space is included?
- Is there adequate information online to help resolve problems?

HARDWARE

- How many phone lines do you have?
- Which modem speeds are supported?
- Which leased line services are available?
- Do you offer ISDN? Which router do you use to support this?
- Do you use a full T1 line or better?
- What is the speed of connection to your regional provider?

SERVICE

- What kind of setup help do you offer?
- Can I see my account status online?
- Is there an 800 number I can call from out of town? How long are you on hold?
- How many help desk staff do you employ full-time?
- During what hours do you offer help desk support?
- How many subscribers do you have?
- Do you remove pages if you decide they have improper content?
- How are you permitted to update the pages?
- Does the ISP outsource its technical support?
- What connection types are listed under "Services"?

FEES

- Are any initial setup charges assessed?
- What is the monthly charge? What is included in the price?
- What is the charge to set up a Web page?
- If I go over my monthly allowance, how much is charged for additional time?
- In what increments of an hour do the charges accrue?
- Are you billed for the entire month if you sign up on the 28th?
- Is there a reconnect charge if the account is closed for nonpayment?
- What are the notice requirements if I decide to cancel?

MAJOR CONSUMER PROBLEMS WITH ISPs

Consumers face several problems when dealing with ISPs.

PAYING WITH A DEBIT CARD.   It is quick, easy, and convenient. But what many banks don't tell you is that your consumer rights are substantially weaker. Unlike credit card complaints that require your credit card company to reject all future charges from an ISP or to intervene in the event of charges in dispute, if you pay for your ISP service by debit card, the Federal Fair Credit Billing Act (FCBA) does not apply to your transaction or dispute settlement. In this case, you are essentially on your own. Your bank has no right to intervene and charge back items in dispute. It is up to you to resolve the dispute with the seller, as debit card transactions are treated like cash payments.

TECHNICAL SUPPORT THAT TURNS OUT NOT TO BE FREE. A common low monthly charge an ISP offers is based on keeping expenses at a minimum. The first thing they chop is technical support. Some of the free ISPs, for example, have no toll-free number, but offer technical support at hefty fees like $10 a call or $2 a minute, even if the problem is theirs. Another trick is boasting they are open 24/7, which means nothing more than capturing your complaint on tape and then addressing it during the next day or later. If this falls on Friday, you can expect things to drag on until Monday or sometime within their Monday–Friday schedule. So it does not hurt to check up front regarding this important service.

DIALING A NUMBER TO CONNECT TO THE ISP THAT IS NOT A LOCAL CALL. This is one of the most frustrating revelations customers face. Before signing up with a new ISP, make sure the phone number the ISP gives you to dial is a local phone call. If you have to dial "1" in order to connect to the ISP infrastructure, you can be sure it is a long distance call.

TROUBLE CANCELING AN ACCOUNT. This is a common problem with many of the lesser known ISPs. Read the Terms of Service (TOS) or Acceptable Use Policy (AUP) before signing up with any ISP. Make sure there are no setup fees when you join or cancellation fees when you sever ties.

IDENTITY THEFT AND THE PROBLEMS THAT ENSUE. Identity theft is a growing problem. It usually happens when you are coaxed to submit your personal information to a fake Web site. Hackers purposely misspell words like fake as "phake" and free as "phree." A phake ISP promises you a phree ISP account at ridiculously low prices (e.g., $4.50 per month). What you end up getting is limited hours, no Web space, and only one e-mail box with limited storage. Before long, you find that you don't have much space to store more than 20–50 messages. You then have to purchase extra storage at high charges.

Phake ISPs send many "warning" signals:

- The only contact with the ISP is via e-mail.
- The signup form is not on a secure setup.
- The Web pages are hosted on a free Web hosting service.
- The signup form asks for inappropriate information, such as place of birth, mother's maiden name, Social Security number, driver's license number, and home address.

RATING ISPs

Several agencies regularly rate ISPs and publish the results. ISPs are graded from A (excellent) to D (poor) on several criteria. The industry average is somewhere in the B range. The results are updated regularly and posted on Visual Network's Web site, www.visualnetworks.com.

Another ISP rating site worth reviewing is CNET, home.cnet.com/category/ 0-3765-7-285302.html?ex.ws.isp.ros.fd.gp.

To find an ISP, the most complete site, with more than 6,000 ISPs, is *The List: The Definitive ISP Buyer's Guide* at thelist.internet.com.

How do you balance all these criteria? Some quick questions over the phone should give you an idea of the basic philosophy, structure, and kind of service an ISP provides.

1. Find someone with experience who's been using the ISP for at least three months and ask how good they find the service.
2. Find out the number of users the ISP has in your area and the number of modems in use at the ISP. Pick one that has a ratio of about 20 users per modem.
3. Find out the pipe each ISP uses to the Internet (55K, T1, 10 Mbps, and so on) and, with the information collected so far, pick the ISP with the largest pipe.
4. What is the number of employees the ISP has and the range of services it offers? In general, the wider the base is, the more likely it is that your service levels will remain high.

TRENDS

A growing trend is toward no-fee and cut-rate Internet services that challenge existing ISPs like AOL. Giveaways such as Microsoft's Hotmail free e-mail service have caught on substantially worldwide. The largest free provider, NetZero Inc., has close to 2 million registered users and is growing. Others have begun offering no-cost Net access, as well.

The business of free ISPs is uncertain. With the heavy cost of supporting telecommunications networks and no monthly subscription revenue to cover costs, it is questionable how well or whether such companies can make up for the difference through advertising alone. Several free ISPs ran into trouble in 2000 and 2001. This is where the quality, reliability, speed, and integrity of a company's Web site should be weighed against those of the ISP under consideration. ISPs currently are following three basic trends in their attempts to lower customer churn rates: building a brand identity, providing broadband service, and focusing more on business users. To build brand identity, ISPs are giving customers personal Web sites to provide a personal connection between the customer and the ISP. Experience has shown that this increased loyalty translates into a lower churn rate.

Another approach to building brand loyalty centers on the ISP's Web site. To create customer dependency, an ISP can allow personalization for each customer from this Web site. It might want to include easy links to local weather forecasts (a popular use for the Internet) or stock quotes. Some ISPs also are beginning to experiment with offering proprietary services such as interactive gaming in order to build their brand identities.

In terms of broadband service, speed is what everyone wants. As customers continue to demand faster and faster access and download times, ISPs are beginning to look into broadband service, which is becoming available to more than 20 percent of home Internet connections.

Today, businesses are spending more time and funds on developing an Internet presence. This is important for ISPs because it allows them to expand into higher-profit services such as Web design, Web hosting, e-commerce support, and multiple e-mail accounts. By providing these services to corporate customers, an ISP will find itself with significantly lower customer churn in a segment of the industry that will be growing faster than the individual access segment. See www.witcapital.com.

ISP REQUIREMENTS

Once you decide on an ISP, you can expect a basic package of software and services. For online access, all you need is a reliable connection to the Internet. Changing an ISP, in this case, is simple, but for online marketing, you need an ISP that can do the following.

1. **Register your domain name.** You can register your domain name yourself, but it is more convenient to have an ISP do it, although it could cost you more. In either case, make sure the registration is legally in your name rather than the name of the ISP, which can charge you a hefty fee for full ownership later. (See discussion of domain names later in the chapter.)

2. **Capture and forward your e-mail.** Receiving and sending mail are important activities for an online merchant. The procedure is simple—your ISP receives your e-mail and routes it to you.

3. **Host your Web site.** Any ISP you choose should have the capability of hosting your Web site for a reasonable fee. To decide what is considered reasonable, check items like the basic rate, disk space charges, charges for hits, charges for number of visitors, fees for reporting statistical data, and fees for storing the Web site.

4. **Provide technical and managerial support.** This can be an extremely important service in terms of the availability of technical talent to help troubleshoot your Web site or to assist in upgrading, enhancing, or improving your presence on the Internet.

5. **Give on-the-road support.** Although not a mandatory feature, an ISP can allow access to your e-mail or other information through a local access number, regardless of location or time of day.

REGISTERING YOUR DOMAIN NAME

Internet domain names are everywhere. If you advertise and your advertisement does not remind potential customers of your products or services, the problem might not be in the advertisement, but more likely in a poorly chosen domain name. The trick is to choose a domain name that people will recognize and type easily and quickly. Care should also be taken to ensure the domain name is easily interpreted in different languages and cultures.

WHAT IS A DOMAIN NAME?

A domain name is a unique Internet address to represent a Web site. A domain name server (DNS) translates between the numeric Internet protocol (IP) address used by the computer and the English-like name identifier that users understand. For example,

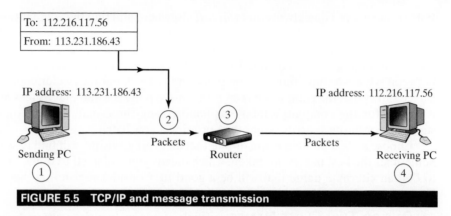

FIGURE 5.5   TCP/IP and message transmission

the numeric IP address 193.231.72.31 might be the address of an organization called Kroger, Inc. Users may enter www.kroger.com.

All Web access traffic and Web IP addresses operate at the Internet's TCP/IP layer. This layer is like a postal service that offers a set of rules called protocols for delivering messages between and among networks. Suppose you have a computer attached to the Internet via an ISP and you're assigned a unique physical address, called an IP address. To send a message to another computer on the Internet, four steps are involved, as shown in Figure 5.5.

1. The sending PC has a unique IP address that takes the form xxx.xxx.xxx.xxx, where each set of xxx's is between 0 and 255.

2. TCP breaks the message into specific bits called packets for easy transmission and handling. Each packet has the sender's IP address so it won't get lost in transit.

3. The IP packets are sent to their destination via a router that reads the destination address and sends it along the fastest available route. Like a traffic officer at an intersection after a football game, the router feeds traffic via several routes to minimize congestion and keep things moving. The sending computer does not have control over the route the message takes. It is up to the router to make an intelligent decision on the optimum path.

4. On the receiving end, TCP checks to make sure all packets are assembled correctly to present the message intact.

IMPORTANCE OF A DOMAIN NAME

Any real estate agent will tell you that the most important factor to consider in buying a house is "location, location, location." A domain name is the Web site's "house," the place where it handles its e-mail and other e-commerce transactions. The name will appear in newspaper ads, on business cards, and on company stationery. All employees will learn it, hopefully with pride. Every time a company advertises, it is effectively communicating its presence or location to the public at large. The company's Web URL should be easy to remember and should represent what the company is all about.

If it is remembered quickly, visitors will surf elsewhere and find the competition. It is as simple as that.

As noted before, make sure the domain name is officially in your name. You don't want visitors to go through your ISP to get to your Web site. There is a difference between www.isp.com/yourpoorcompany and www.diamondjeweler.com. The first choice shows that the company has an inexpensive presence and that its fees are low. It is as bad for the company's image as handwriting the e-mail address on existing stationery or business cards rather than printing a new batch.

Choose a good domain name or one that an average visitor will find easy to guess. Sometimes the best names are taken, which means you will need to think a bit harder to find an alternate name that will be a good fit. Consider registering the following kinds of domain names.

ONE OR TWO CLOSE NAMES. Think of one or two close alternative domain names for your company or names that visitors might think of. If available, register them as alternatives. The problem with so many alternative names is that look-alike Web addresses could funnel Web traffic to the wrong place. The Internet is awash in Web sites that trick people into visiting by using addresses that vary by one or more characters, a hyphen, and the like.

UNIQUE PRODUCT DOMAIN NAME. If a company has a product under development or a new product about to be released on the market, it is helpful to register a domain name that is the best fit for that product. Doing this should be part of strategic planning.

IDEAL COMPANY DOMAIN NAME. Think of the ideal representation of your company for a company domain name and then don't wait: Register it at once. Remember, though, the domain name is not a chance to rename the company or to be funny or interesting. The focus is on a name that is easy to guess. See Table 5.3 for a list of some of the most profitable American firms, their best domain names, and their most logical alternative names.

Take a look at the following URL—the address of the University of Virginia, and find the domain name in it: http://www.virginia.edu/schls.html. The URL has three major parts.

TABLE 5.3 Domain names, alternatives to names, and actual registered names

Company Name	Ideal Domain Name	Alternate Name	Actual Domain Name Registered
Bank of America	bankofamerica.com	bankamerica.com	bank-america.com, bofa.com
Coca-Cola	cocacola.com	coke.com	cocacola.com, coke.com
General Motors	gm.com	generalmotors.com	gm.com
Exxon	Exxon.com		exxon.com
IBM	ibm.com		ibm.com
Intel	intel.com		intel.com
Wal-Mart Stores	walmart.com	wal-mart.com	wal-mart.com

1. **http://**—Internet protocol (http or hypertext markup language) and separator (://).

2. **www.virginia.edu**—The domain name. www means World Wide Web; Virginia is the second-level domain; and .edu is the top-level domain.

3. **/schls.html**—A subdirectory of the file (/schls.html), which is the list of schools at the University of Virginia that will be retrieved.

However, reading a domain name is not that easy. It actually is read backwards. In this example, the address reads: I want the names of schools at the University of Virginia.

Here are the top-level domains.

.com Commercial organizations and businesses in general
.edu Educational institutions (colleges and universities)
.gov U.S. government agencies (nonmilitary)
.mil U.S. government military agencies
.net Companies that support the Internet
.org Organizations such as nonprofits
.uk, .ca, .sy, etc. Country codes formalized by an IOS (International Organization for Standardization) committee. For a complete list, visit the GeoCities Web site at **www.geocities.com.**

CHOOSING A DOMAIN NAME

In the world of the Internet, it is the *.com* at the end of the MyBusiness.com address that is the most desirable for Internet business. The *.net* domain is considered far less desirable. Unfortunately, the name that you most want might have been taken by someone else already. Domain-name speculators register domain names that come close to trademarked terms in the hope of reselling them at a huge markup.

The following procedure is suggested when choosing a domain name.

1. Jot down on a piece of paper all the possible domain names you can think of that fit your organization's image, products, or services. End each name with .com if it is a business, .edu if it is an educational institution, .org if it is a nonprofit organization, and so on.

2. Ask friends, peers, employees, and others who use the Web to suggest domain names for your company. Inasmuch as most people will guess at a name, some of the choices will be surprising.

3. Narrow the list to a few favorites. This should be based on the relevance of the names to your business and how easy it will be for Web visitors to guess the name.

4. Go to the InterNic Domain Services Web site, www.internic.net, and enter the domain name(s) you want to check for availability.

5. Enter all the domain names on your list. You might be lucky to find that 1 out of every 10 names entered is available.

6. For the available domain names, enter each name as a URL in your Web browser to see if the name is in active use. If not, then proceed with domain name registration.

When choosing a domain name, legal implications must be considered, especially concerning the issue of trademarks.

1. Determine if the proposed domain name infringes on trademarks. Trademark infringement is a problem not only with existing trademarks, but also with names similar enough to cause confusion for consumers.

2. Make sure the proposed domain name does not adversely affect any famous trademark. The federal Trademark Dilution Act prohibits weakening or tarnishing famous trademarks.

3. Once cleared of potential claims of infringement or dilution, the proposed domain name should be registered as a federal trademark with the U.S. Patent and Trademark Office.

4. Register the proposed domain name with InterNic or Network Solutions (NSI). This quasi-government agency assigns domain names in North America on a first-come, first-served basis.

5. Look for expanded top-level domain names and registries. The International AdHoc Committee (IAHC) was created by the Internet Society in 1997 to study revisions in the domain name system. Its proposed final plan will create the following eight new generic, top-level domains.

> **.arts** for entities emphasizing art, culture, and entertainment
> **.firm** for businesses and firms
> **.info** for providers of information services
> **.nom** for individuals
> **.per** and **.nom** for personal sites
> **.rec** for entities emphasizing recreation/entertainment sources
> **.store** for businesses offering goods
> **.web** for businesses emphasizing Web activities

REGISTERING A DOMAIN NAME

Once a domain name is selected, it should be registered to be active. Registering a domain name is as easy as filling out a Web-based form. There are two ways to register: on your own or through an ISP. On the surface, registering on your own seems simple. Go to the Network Solutions Web site, www.networksolutions.com, and follow the instructions online. You will pay a fee of $70 to register your domain, but your ISP cannot use the name until you contact them and inform them that you have registered. The ISP, in turn, will transfer the domain name to its DNS server for a transfer fee.

The problem with this approach is the headache for a first-time registrant. You have to make sure when you register that you have the registrant and the administrative and billing contact at Network Solutions. This is why the alternative of having an ISP do the job is preferable.

The ISP goes through a similar procedure, although it charges about $50 for processing in addition to the registration fee. However, the ISP must demonstrate responsibility for your online presence. Here are some pitfalls to keep in mind.

1. **Overcharging.** ISPs in general have their own algorithm of fees, including setup fees, transfer fees, monthly fees, special services fees, and so on. Shop around for

a reliable ISP with experience and a reputation for quality technical support at a reasonable charge.

2. **Domain name status.** The "don't ask, don't tell" concept applies in situations where, if you don't ask to make sure the domain name is registered in your name rather than in the name of the ISP, it is likely the ISP won't volunteer details. Make sure you own the exclusive right to your domain name.

3. **Backup.** When connection problems occur, does your ISP have another Internet connection for a backup? Surprisingly, many ISPs operate on a shoestring. Backup also has to do with how likely the ISP is to stay in business. Changing ISPs is neither pleasant nor convenient.

4. **Contractual language.** Before committing, read the agreement the ISP expects you to sign before your Web site is formally and legally on the Internet.

THREE FAQs

Here are three frequently asked questions about the domain name process that are worth considering.

1. What is involved in registering a domain name in .com, .net, or .org? To register a domain name, you need to provide the registrar of your choice with the contact and technical information that makes up the registration. The registrar stores the contact information and submits the technical information to a central directory called the registry. The registry, in turn, provides other computers linked to the Internet with the information to send you e-mail or to find your Web site. You also will have to enter a registration contact with the registrar that specifies the terms of your registration and how it will be maintained.

2. How long does a registration last? Can it be renewed? The original registration is for two years, renewable one year at a time. Since January 15, 2000, a registrar can offer initial and renewal registrations in one-year increments, with a total registration period not to exceed 10 years.

3. Can the registrar be changed after registering a domain name? Yes, but only after 60 days from the initial registration. Make sure to contact the new registrar before disconnecting from the current one.

For details on other FAQs, visit the InterNic Web site at www.internic.net/faqs/domain-names.html.

APPLICATION SERVICE PROVIDERS

The advent of the ASP industry spawned out of a desire to meet the changing needs of business of all sizes and structures quickly. Those who do not have the time, financial resources, or manpower to purchase and maintain their own software can now turn to other companies to do it for them. Currently, more than 500 ASP firms provide services to different businesses, large and small. Most of these firms belong to an organization called the ASP Industry Consortium—an advocacy group that sponsors continuing research on the ASP model and promotes the ASP industry around the world.

The consortium experienced 1,900 percent growth during its initial year of operation. More than $600 million has been spent on ASP services, and it is estimated that the market for ASPs will exceed $42 billion by 2006

Just what is an ASP? Here are some definitions:

- An organization that hosts software applications on its own servers within its own facilities. Customers access the application via private lines or the Internet. Also called a "commercial service provider." See www.windriver.com/news/glossary.html.

- An Internet service provider that also sells application software that runs behind the Web servers at the hosting service. ISPs provide minimal applications like e-mail and some file storage.

- Companies that sell, support, and manage applications that are hosted on the Internet on behalf of remote end users. See www.conxion.com/technology/glossary.htm.

- An extension of the ISP business offering Web-based applications as well as Internet access. Proposed for applications that are most useful when data is shared among a group of users, such as calendaring, or applications that are too expensive or infrequently used to be cost-effective for small companies, such as complex tax planning software. See www.techdis.ac.uk/PDA/glossary.htm.

With experience in time-sharing, outsourcing, and packaged software, going the ASP route is proving wise for many businesses. ASPs are companies that lease application software to customers via the Internet. They allow businesses to lease software on a monthly or yearly basis. The applications are hosted on the ASP's remote site, and the ASP also is responsible for updating and maintenance. In addition, the ASP provides technical support to its users. See www.netplusmarketing.com/resources_glos.cfm.

An application service package offers two unique service components.

- Web site hosting and delivery—physically storing software applications on centralized servers and then leasing them to other companies. The ASP provides the operating hardware and software to support a customer-developed Web site.

- Application technical support—providing end-to-end connectivity support.

Although many models would fit an ASP (e.g., airlines), most companies denote ASP as services provided through the Internet. Here is what an ASP offers. The ASP:

- Owns and operates a software application.
- Owns, operates, and maintains the servers that run the application.
- Employs the staff to maintain the application.
- Makes the application available to customers everywhere via the Internet, normally in a browser.
- Bills either on a per-use basis or on a monthly/annual fee basis. In many cases, the ASP can provide the service for free or even pay the customer.

Several benefits are distinct to an ASP.

- Outsourcing to an ASP lets the firm concentrate on its core competencies, strategic projects, generating revenues, and serving customers rather than on managing technology. ASP handles IT staffing, upgrades, and backups.

- With quicker access to the latest functionality and services, ASPs can keep their technical environment up-to-date as part of their agreement with the client. The ASP realizes this advantage by spreading the costs of creative solutions over many customers.

- ASPs also benefit from hiring highly skilled and talented staff that many small companies cannot afford or would not use full time.

- The low cost of entry and short setup time means an ASP can cut monthly costs of application ownership by as much as 50 percent.

- Internet bandwidth shifts to the ASP, which can provide this much speed at lower cost.

With these benefits come some concerns. The main concerns are as follows.

- Security and loss of control. The use of an ASP may raise fears about the safety of data. Because the provider hosts the application software, companies cannot be sure that confidential and critical information is not being viewed and used by outsiders.

- Reliability and quality of service. There is some debate about using the Internet as a medium for secure transfer of critical data. Viruses and hackers are rampant over the Internet, and it is not the best method of transferring certain data. There is also the question of the quality of service provided by inexperienced ASPs and their ability to deliver on their promises.

- Ambiguity. Another barrier to decision making is the difficulty of drawing up clear service-level agreements. There is no room for ambiguity when the client is totally dependent on the support of the ASP.

- ASP quality and financial stability. Not every ASP is the best for every organization. Because no standard form of pricing has been established, the client needs to decide whether it should be cost per transaction, database size required, or number of PCs.

- Standardization. ASPs discourage customization to keep costs down.

- Application performance. To counter this concern, top ASPs offer service-level agreements (SLAs) with performance guarantees and penalty clauses.

ASP INFRASTRUCTURE

A typical ASP model essentially hosts applications for the user on servers in a server farm. None of these servers is permanently allocated to a given customer. This means that allocation of applications is dynamically allocated to servers based on availability and capacity requirements.

With dependent relationships between the organization as a user and the ASP firm, the number one issue is security and reliability. Actually, it is *trust*. Lapses in this area can cause immediate customer dissatisfaction that is often difficult to repair. To ensure security and reliability, most ASPs rely on sophisticated backup of electric power through diesel generators, parallel hardware and software operation like tape backup, and redundant Internet service providers. Certification from ASP suppliers like Cisco Systems, for example, will improve the trust factor a great deal.

SHAKING HANDS IS NOT ENOUGH

service-level agreement (SLA): a contract between the user and the ASP vendor stating the vendor's commitments to ensure reliable delivery of information.

When it comes to the final selection, the relationship begins with a clearly written, well-defined **service-level agreement (SLA)** outlining the client's performance expectations. It is a contract that defines the technical support that an ASP will provide clients. Successful outsourcing of any application will require accountability, performance, and remediation to be spelled out and agreed upon by all parties.

In a business climate where the IT budget is scarce, the value of ASPs starts making sense. Hiring staff to build and implement internal systems is costly and time consuming. Many IT managers have been forced to take a harder look at ASPs. Even with some of the potential pitfalls, ASPs offer cost efficiency and implementation benefits. If a company does not have the funds to spend on a huge IT initiative, ASPs are increasingly becoming the only place to turn. Internet reliability and efficiency will first have to improve, but this is happening gradually. Carrier-class routers and switches are much more intelligent than before, with built-in quality-of-service features.

Working with an ASP is not straightforward, especially for high-volume business that derives much of its revenue from such a core application. To ensure viability and trust as an ongoing IT outsourcing organization, ASP firms offer service level agreements (SLAs).

Summary

1. Internet service providers (ISPs) are attractive to many companies for several reasons: specialized staff to manage Web sites, high-speed connectivity to main Internet hubs, real physical security from power outages, and the latest technology.

2. ISPs can belong to one of three categories: the large wholesale access provider, the smaller Internet backbone provider, and the local ISP. Larger wholesale providers have been the target of consolidation and acquisition, and smaller providers have been growing.

3. Hosting a Web site involves three major items: hardware, communications network, and qualified staff. Minimum operating costs can run from $60,000 to $120,000.

4. There are four types of service providers: ISPs, ASPs, BSPs, and WSPs.

5. The backbone of the Internet is the group of network service providers that

work together to provide total interconnection. ISPs connect to NSPs and pay a fee to do so.

6. Shopping for a Web-hosting ISP involves bandwidth, connection availability and performance, virtual hosting, number of e-mail addresses allowed per account, ISP stability and staying power, free local access, customer service and technical support, and ISP reliability and cost of service.

7. For online marketing, an ISP should be capable of registering your domain name, capturing and forwarding e-mail, hosting the Web site, technical and managerial support, and on-the-road support.

8. Your domain name is the "house" for your Web site, e-mail, and other e-commerce transactions. Make sure it is officially in your name. It should be easy to guess the name. Register a domain name that comes close to your product or company name.

9. The wireless application service provider (WASP) handles untethered applications, with responsibilities involving hosting, developing, and managing applications similar to that of an ASP. Mobile commerce is covered in more depth in Chapter 6.

10. ASPs are services provided through the Internet. They own and operate a software application, maintain the servers that run the application, employ the staff to maintain the application, and make the application available to customers everywhere via the Internet.

11. To consider becoming an ISP, it is important to consider the target market, the services to provide, the technical requirements, and the type of provider to be. Quality lines and bandwidth choice are extremely critical to a high-performance setup.

Key Terms

- **access server** (p. 135)
- **application service provider (ASP)** (p. 133)
- **backbone** (p. 136)
- **business service provider (BSP)** (p. 133)
- **caching** (p. 138)
- **customer churn rate** (p. 142)
- **domain name** (p. 130)
- **domain name server (DNS)** (p. 137)
- **facilities-based ISP** (p. 136)
- **HTTP proxy server** (p. 138)
- **Internet relay chat (IRC)** (p. 138)
- **Internet service provider (ISP)** (p. 130)
- **Integrated Services Digital Network (ISDN)** (p. 135)
- **point of presence (POP)** (p. 143)
- **radius server** (p. 137)
- **service-level agreement (SLA)** (p. 156)
- **virtual domain** (p. 130)
- **virtual hosting** (p. 130)
- **virtual ISP** (p. 136)
- **Web hosting** (p. 134)
- **wholesale service provider (WSP)** (p. 133)
- **wireless application service provider (WASP)** (p. 133)

Test Your Understanding

1. In what way has the World Wide Web brought back the old concept of time sharing? Explain.
2. What reasons drive medium-size to small organizations to Internet service providers?
3. Cite statistics that support the growing trend in commercial Internet traffic.
4. How do ISPs work? Give an example.
5. How much do you think it costs to host a Web site? Contact a local ISP and find out.
6. What infrastructure represents a typical ISP?
7. Explain briefly the various types of Web-hosting services.
8. List and briefly explain the five elements needed to be an ISP.
9. The backbone of the Internet is a cluster of competing companies called network service providers or NSPs. How do they work?
10. If you were looking for an ISP, how would you choose one? Be specific.
11. What is bandwidth? How does it affect Web site performance?
12. What is a domain name? Why would one need to be careful about choosing one?
13. How would a company with a new Web site choose and register a domain name? Be specific in terms of procedure.
14. Given what you now know about choosing a domain name, what procedure would you follow in choosing one?

Discussion Questions

1. When you contact an ISP to determine whether its services are appropriate for your new Web site, what questions would you ask or what type of information would you need to make up your mind?
2. Look up www.findanisp.com and determine the ratings of two local ISPs and one national ISP (e.g., AT&T). Elaborate on the fees, features, and ratings of each ISP.
3. Do you think free Web services will last? Discuss in detail.
4. The chapter talks about trends that ISPs are currently following to lower customer churn rates. Discuss.
5. Two businesses want the same domain name. How is the situation settled?
6. Newspapers, TV, and the media have made known the rivalry between Netscape and Microsoft for dominance in the Web browser market. Is this beneficial or harmful for the average consumer?
7. What is distinctive about the wireless application service provider?
8. Summarize the key services of an ISP. Which one is the most popular? Why?
9. Distinguish between facilities-based and virtual ISPs.
10. How would you explain the difference between T1 and T3 lines? What questions would you ask before choosing an ISP? Be specific.
11. How would ASPs work? Give an example.
12. What concerns would one consider in deciding on an ASP?

Web Exercises

1. Several domain name disputes arose in 2000 and 2001. Search the Netscape site for some of the domain name controversies. *Hint:* In the subject area, enter a subject such as *domain name disputes, domain name controversy,* and so on.
2. Choose a domain name and check it at the InterNic Web site, www.internic.net, to see if it is taken. If it has been taken, who has it?
3. Interview a local business with a Web site. Write a report showing the procedure the business followed to decide on its domain name and how the business registered it.

CHAPTER

MOBILE COMMERCE

The Business of Time

Learning Objectives

The focus of this chapter is on several learning objectives:

- The basic concept of wireless commerce
- The reasons for going wireless
- How wireless technology is employed
- Wireless security
- The role of cellular phones in wireless commerce
- Factors in designing a wireless local network
- The protocols for M-commerce architecture
- The dawn of wireless banking

IN A NUTSHELL

In today's society, it is rare to walk down the street without seeing people talking or checking their schedules on a mobile phone. Living life on the go, people are searching constantly for ways to keep in touch with anyone, anywhere, at any time. Wireless technology is all things to all people. From garage door openers to cellular phones, cordless keyboards to Blackberry devices, mobile connectivity is being driven by the acceptance of wireless devices.

In the business world, wireless technology is a necessity, and it is gaining ground everywhere. The cell phone is a tool of the smart-working elite—a way to squeeze more value-added time into long commutes, to check with clients, or to verify stock prices on the run. The new solution is wireless communication. The term *wireless* means transmitting signals over radio waves instead of wires. It also implies the growing area of microcomputer chip technology (see Box 6.1).

The emergence of wireless local area networks (WLAN) is a significant departure from wired networking (coaxial, twisted pair, fiber-optic cables) that has existed for decades. This new addition to e-commerce is becoming the backbone of mobile or **m-commerce.** Going wireless is like scuba diving wearing lightweight gear and not being linked by a long umbilical cord to a ship for air. It is data communication without physical attachments—microwave, radio wave, and infrared. It is a convenient alternative to network cabling connections and is quickly becoming the network of choice for an increasingly mobile workforce, due to the flexibility and freedom such technology offers.

Wireless LANs (WLANs) already have gained acceptance in a wide range of vertical markets, including the health care, retail, manufacturing, warehousing, and academic circles. The technology has increased the productivity of these industries through the usage of handheld terminals and mobile computers to transmit data in real time to centralized hosts. Because this technology is easily applicable to other industries, the worldwide wireless LAN market is expected to grow to $1.6 billion by 2005.

wireless LAN (WLAN): a standard for wireless networking.

Mobile phones are wireless. They are different from PCs. A connected PC is used to check e-mail or to shop on the Internet. It is not possible to tell when messages are checked or orders are placed. In contrast, consumers carry mobile phones wherever

---

BOX 6.1

How Tiny Swiss Cellphone Chips Helped Track Global Terror Web

The terrorism investigation code-named Mont Blanc began almost by accident in April 2002, when authorities intercepted a cellphone call that lasted less than a minute and involved not a single word of conversation. Investigators, suspicious that the call was a signal between terrorists, followed the trail first to one terror suspect, then to others, and eventually to terror cells on three continents.

What tied them together was a computer chip smaller than a fingernail. But before the investigation wound down in recent weeks, its global net caught dozens of suspected al Qaeda members and disrupted at least three planned attacks in Saudi Arabia and Indonesia, according to counterterrorism and intelligence officials in Europe and the United States.

For two years, investigators were able to track the conversations and movements of several al Qaeda leaders and dozens of operatives

after determining that the suspects favored a particular brand of cellphone chip. The chips carry prepaid minutes and allow phone use around the world. This chip is popular because people can buy it without having to give their name.

During the American bombing of Tora Bora in Afghanistan in December 2001, American authorities reported hearing Osama bin Laden speaking to his associates on a satellite phone. Since then, Mr. bin Laden has communicated with handwritten messages delivered by trusted couriers.

In 2002, the German authorities broke up a cell after monitoring calls by Abu Musab al-Zarqawi, who has been linked by some top American officials to al Qaeda, in which he could be heard ordering attacks on Jewish targets in Germany. Since then, investigators say, Mr. Zarqawi has been more cautious.

Source: Adapted from Don Van Natta and Desmond Butler, "How Tiny Swiss Cellphone Chips Helped Track Global Terror Web." *New York Times,* March 4, 2004, 1–3.

they go. It is kept on all the time, waiting for calls or ready to send messages. Yet doing business via the mobile phone continues to be a problem due to its limited interface and technical problems. An insufficient built-in security system is another problem. For end users, wireless networks are just as effective as wired systems. They have a transmission range of several hundred feet, allowing users to connect with the network from anywhere within most facilities and even from outside. In short, wireless networks are affordable, easy to install and operate, and eliminate the cost of cabling.

As wireless networks expand, m-commerce will follow. It is analogous to the growth of the Internet and the World Wide Web. The current growth of wireless and mobile networks has brought vast changes in mobile devices and user acceptance. According to one source, more than 350 million mobile devices are in use worldwide, 80 million of them in the United States.

Although wireless is the hottest computer topic today, it is also the least understood of the evolving technologies. In this chapter, we cover the essence of m-commerce: benefits and limitations, m-marketing, m-payments, languages, applications, security and legal issues, and emerging models for m-commerce. The goal is to provide a comprehensive coverage of this fast-emerging technology and its potential for enhancing trade, personalization, and customer service.

WHAT IS M-COMMERCE?

Imagine receiving an important e-mail while you're out to lunch or away on business, or checking your stock portfolio on the way to the airport. Or your pharmacy sends you a short note telling you that you're about to run out of your medication for diabetes and asks you if you want a refill. When you click "yes," the pharmacy knows it should have the medication ready so you can pick it up on the way home or have it delivered.

m-commerce: business transactions and payments conducted in a non-PC-based environment.

Although these seem like futuristic visions, they already can occur through m-commerce or mobile commerce. Until recently, *mobile data* referred to any nonmobile voice, such as a portable telephone, a pager, or even a garage door opener. Today's focus on services and applications on the mobile phone is what m-commerce is all about. Messages from one person to another are not m-commerce, but messages from an information service provider that are charged a rate constitute m-commerce.

M-commerce is the transmission of user data (e.g., e-mail, spreadsheet) without wires. It is also the management of the processes that handle the product or service needs of a consumer via a mobile phone, and the use of wireless devices to facilitate the sale of products and services, anytime, anywhere. This technology takes into account a viable relationship between a mobile phone and a person to generate a business opportunity that normally does not exist in traditional e-business.

M-commerce also refers to business transactions and payments conducted in a non-PC-based environment. These are carried out via radio-based wireless devices that can access data networks and conduct business-to-business and business-to-consumer transactions over wired, Web-based, e-commerce systems. The first thing to remember is that m-commerce is not about selling products or services on a mobile device. That is part of m-commerce but does not include the personal role played by a mobile phone.

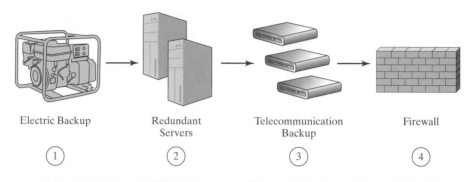

Electric Backup Redundant Servers Telecommunication Backup Firewall

(1) (2) (3) (4)

FIGURE 6.1   Business in the air

Source: Based on D. P. Hamilton, "Making the Connections," *Wall Street Journal*, December 11, 2000, R3.

Several categories of services comprise m-commerce:

- Information-based consumer services like searching the Web for restaurants or movies using a data-enabled cellular phone or sending e-mail.
- Transaction services, such as downloading and listening to digital music in a wireless setup, making purchases by using a cellular device and having the price added to the phone bill, or making "buy and sell" business transactions wirelessly.
- Location-centric, personalized services that anticipate your purchases based on your location and data stored in your "profile," by product, time of the year, and so on (see Figure 6.1.) This unsettling possibility means that companies can beam advertisements, coupons, and other electronic pitches at consumers depending on their location at the time. Related to this category is tethering employees to the office via wireless devices that can track their movements and communications. (See Box 6.2.)

In the mid-1990s, companies realized that going online was more than replicating static brochures in HTML format or developing interactive Web sites. Likewise, today, companies are beginning to realize that going wireless is more than reformatting HTML into Wireless Application Protocol (WAP) (to be explained later). The best way to understand the difference between the two technologies is to look at the physical size of a PC monitor (200 square inches) versus the display screen on a mobile device (approximately 10 square inches, which limits the amount of information shared). In terms of the bandwidth, the typical 9,400 bits per second (bps) is what a PC modem used several years ago. Finally, trying to enter text with a 12-key keyboard on a mobile phone can be frustrating.

Other differences exist, as well. Think of paying airtime for wireless Web use, but having to put up with banner ads and other distracting news without your permission. Once wireless becomes commonplace, trying to combat invasions of privacy or junk e-mail will become a challenge. Finally, although PC-oriented e-commerce employs HTML technology, m-commerce and the wireless Web use two distinct development languages: Wireless Mark-up Language (WML) and Handheld Device Mark-up Language (HDML). These languages, which require different browsers loaded on mobile phones, will be explained later in the chapter.

| BOX 6.2 |

Wireless Advertising

. . . Wireless advertising is real and here to stay. Whether it's the national advertiser promoting its brand, or the local merchant attempting to drive store traffic, wireless advertising provides convenience, efficiency, and customization. It enables consumers to access important information and take advantage of advertising promotions when and where they want them. A sample of potential avenues for wireless advertising include:

- Wireless yellow pages, where advertisements are placed within the "yellow page" content. For example, a consumer may be scrolling through the wireless yellow pages to find a listing of Italian restaurants. When the consumer receives the requested information about Italian restaurants, they also receive a series of embedded advertisements or promotions linked to that content.

- "Search-and-Pitch" channel, which dynamically targets and sends advertisements based on the search criteria entered by the consumer. For example, the consumer types in Italian cuisine and both content and appropriate ads are delivered to the device.

- Content-driven wireless advertising is similar to traditional Internet banner advertising, in that ad content is directly related to the content of the site being viewed by the consumer. For example, when a consumer accesses sports scores on their device, the accompanying advertisement may be from Nike or the local professional sports franchise.

To consumers and privacy advocates, wireless advertising can be considered an invasion, especially when considering the personal nature of the device itself. The fear is that everywhere you go and everything you do will be monitored—or that you'll be bombarded with advertising while you walk down the street. Today, wireless carriers simply do not possess the technical capabilities to track every single one of their subscribers all the time. In the future, this capability may become more technically feasible and cost effective. However, if the privacy issues are not addressed, then governments are sure to step forward with legislation.

Ultimately, consumers want to exert influence and choice over wireless advertising. They want to receive value-added information and direction on products and services. They want something dramatically different from what they receive in today's Internet advertising. Guidelines must be established. Targeted, permission-based advertisements must be the focus.

Source: Excerpted from Tim DePriest, "Wireless Advertising: Opportunities and Challenges," *Computerworld,* May 5, 2003, 42ff.

WHY WIRELESS?

The wireless Web is a technological frontier, open and growing. The technology already has taken off in Finland and Japan, where schoolchildren watch cartoon characters on their Web phones and businesspeople on the run participate in lotteries and pay for soda from vending machines using their personal digital assistants. Web phones in the future will be used to deliver information such as stock quotes and flight delays, and track supplies. According to an InfoWorld Wireless Survey of 500 readers, more than 95 percent currently use a cell phone and 69 percent use a standard pager. The projection for exponential use of Web-based phones is obvious. Another source estimates that the number of mobile telephone subscribers will exceed 1 billion in 2005 and will account for an annual value of $13 billion or 7 percent of all electronic commerce transactions.

Wireless technology means cutting the cord (cables) that forms today's computer network. Wireless networking makes it possible to connect two or more computers without the bulky cables, giving consumers the benefits of a network with little or no labor. Accessing events is easy, but knowing when important events will take place is totally different. By analogy, if a car crashes into a tree and no one sees it crash, did it make a sound? It must have. The same applies in day-to-day business. Just because consumers were not informed of a price change, it does not mean the change did not occur. It did. It means that time is a factor everyone is trying to minimize. We live in a dynamic business world where information changes by the minute, and value-added decision making is all about having the right information at the right time. Certain information must be delivered in real time, regardless of location.

The wireless initiative is launching a new battle against time. Compared to the Internet, which has demonstrated information availability *anytime,* wireless mobile technology makes such availability *anywhere.* When using the Internet, you are online (direct) with information as long as you are connected to the network. If you are not connected, you are out of luck. The problem is that users are committed to other activities and cannot be wired constantly to the Internet. Wireless technology frees users to be able to access any information anywhere, which brings up the time issue again. With wireless technology, information can be accessed as it happens. Employees can be empowered to make decisions faster, customers can ask questions more spontaneously, and business owners will be plugged in to their business, regardless of their location.

BRIEF HISTORY

Wireless communication traces its roots to the invention of the radio in 1895 by a young Italian named Guglielmo Marconi, age 21. He successfully transmitted radio waves without using wires. His first successful experiment was at a short distance, only about 330 feet between his home office and the end of the garden. By September 1895, Marconi had built equipment that transmitted electrical signals through the air. He placed a transmitter near his house and a receiver two miles away, with a hill between them. He instructed his servant standing by the receiver to fire his rifle the moment the signal was received. Marconi pushed the transmitter key three times and then heard a rifle shot. He proved that electromagnetic waves had traveled a distance and went over an obstacle (the hill). This was the beginning of wireless telegraphy.

Known as the true "grandfather of wireless communication," Marconi went on to win the 1909 Nobel Prize in physics for his contribution to the development of wireless telegraphy. Cellular planning continued during the mid-1940s, after World War II, but trial service did not begin until 1978, and it was not until 1984 that full deployment began in America (Farley 2003).

In the mid 1940s, two-way car radios were installed by police, government agencies, and utility companies to stay in touch. The problem was that such systems were not convenient to use. With only one central transmitter, one antenna, and car-mounted transmitters, transmission was not that powerful. The next step was to mount smaller receivers with antennas on top of buildings and on poles around the city to create "cells" or ranges of service areas. This was fine, except for the lack of available frequencies. At that time, the FCC gave priority to emergency services, government agencies, and the like. Capacity usage was only 250 users.

With much progress and advancement in mobile transmission by companies like AT&T and the Bell System, 1969 saw the introduction of a commercial cellular radio operation on trains running from New York City to Washington, D.C, using pay phones. Passengers could place phone calls on the train while it was traveling at 100 miles per hour.

In 1978, AT&T and Illinois Bell introduced analog-based cellular telephone services to the general public. Cellular traffic increased from 200,000 subscribers in 1985 to 1,600,000 in 1988. Growth lasted over the next decade before the introduction of digital cellular communication technology in 2000. Today, cellular deployment is global. There are well over 60 million cellular phone users, creating about $40 billion in annual revenues.

Digital cellular technology is described in terms of three generations:

- The first generation, known as 1G, operates in the 800–900 MHz (megahertz) frequency spectrum. With 832 frequencies available for transmission, there are 395 channels for voice traffic (each requiring two frequencies for cellular telephone conversation), and the remaining 21 channels (two frequencies per channel) are reserved for the control functions. Being analog and circuit-switching technology, 1G networks lock the channel for the caller and the recipient through the telephone company's switch. This proved to be inefficient, as well as vulnerable to interference, stemming from analog signals that require a modem to convert the signals from digital to analog and then back to digital. 1G phones had limited capabilities and relatively weak performance. Yet they were so popular, they attracted more than 1 million paying users by 1987.

- The second generation or 2G of cellular telephony started in the early 1990s and continues to date. Data transfer rate operates between 9.6 Kbps and 14.4 Kbps in the 800 MHz and 1.9 GHz frequencies. The unique feature of 2G is that it is digital, not analog transmission. This means the frequency spectrum is more efficient, the quality of voice transmission over long distance is better than analog, it offers better security because decoding digital transmission is more difficult, and digital transmission allows the use of smaller and less expensive individual transmitters and receivers. The main difficulty with 2G devices is lack of a universal system of wireless communication and lack of the bandwidth inherent in a circuit-switched network. A *circuit-switched network* consists of thousands of individual channels, called *circuits.* Each circuit accommodates one call. This is fine for voice communications with uninterrupted conversation with someone else. But for data transmission, circuit-switched networking is highly inefficient.

- The 2.5 generation is somewhere in the later stages of 2G, and getting to the third generation is not all that straightforward. The impetus for 2.5 networks is "always on" capability. It allows for the use of infrastructure and facilities on a per-transaction rather than per-minute-of-use basis. This has significant implications for mobile commerce and location-based services. See www.mobilein.com/2.5g.htm for more details. 2.5 networks are packet-switched instead of circuit-switched, which is a more efficient way of transmitting data. They operate at a maximum speed of 384 Kbps. Packet-switched design allows data transmission to be broken into smaller units or *packets,* and each packet is sent independently through the network to reach the destination. Prior to reaching the destination, the packets are assembled in the proper sequence for final delivery. Packet switching can also increase the amount of traffic from 3 to 5 times over that of circuit switching. It is an "always on" connection. The "always on" feature was a major factor that has made cable modems and DSL connections so popular over dial-up connections. See www.xlink.com/esp/wireless/cellular_networks/2.5g.htm for technical details.

- The third generation digital phone network, or 3G, marks the beginning of a uniform and global worldwide standard for cellular wireless communication. The standards set by the International Telecommunications Unions are 2 Mbps, which can handle streaming video, two-way voice over IP, and Internet traffic with high quality graphics and plug-ins for a wireless phone. The road to this type of technology is in its infancy. It promises fast transmission speeds of 144 Kbps for fast-moving mobile wireless devices, such as those built into automobiles and trains; 384 Kbps for pedestrian speeds, such as those built into wireless phones and PDAs; and 2 Mbps for stationary wireless devices. At that speed, you can easily download a 5MB file to a stationary 3G devices in 20 seconds. See Box 6.3. *3G* is a generic term that describes different "flavors" of wireless. For example, general packet radio service (GPRS) allows 115 Kbps (kilobits per second) wireless Internet and a 10-fold increase in data throughput (performance) rate (from 9.6–115 Kbps.) This means subscribers are always connected and always online. It is back compatible to 2G and circuit packet switched. It uses a combination of existing and evolved equipment and a data rate up to 2 Mbps (megabits per second).

- Future 4G technology is viewed as an extended 3G capacity by one order of magnitude. When operational (sometime in the next decade), it is expected to be entirely packet switched, with all network phases digital, and operate at a much higher bandwidth—up to 100 MBS.

BOX 6.3

One Step into 3G

The white-hot wireless technology known as 3G UMTS—short for Universal Mobile Telecommunications System—is finally making its U.S. debut. The high-speed Internet connection is fast enough to enable a customer to use a cell-phone, PDA, or laptop computer to receive streaming audio and video, create and share video clips, and much more.

Availability is limited. For now, AT&T Wireless is offering the service in just four cities: Detroit, Phoenix, San Francisco, and Seattle. For those enamored with the idea of harnessing the power of the Internet while on the go, 3G might be worth it. True 3G offers wireless transmission speeds up to eight times faster than conversational dial-up connections. At those speeds, the video and audio streams are Hollywood smooth—no herky-jerky feeds or scratchy sounds.

Source: Excerpted from Leslie Cauley, "AT&T Wireless Rolls Out Super-Speedy Internet Service." *USA Today,* July 21, 2004, 5B.

On the international scene, Japan, China, and Korea are working jointly to develop communications and other technologies for 4G cellular phones, with the goal of the technology's appearance on the market in 2010. One way to measure the success of the 2008 Olympic Games in Beijing is a plan to deploy a 4G mobile broadcasting network. Residents should be able to enjoy the games in vivid colors. See www.4g.co.uk/PR2004/Oct2004/2040.htm.

KEY BENEFITS

Given these differences, one wonders how the wireless Web benefits the consumer. The most obvious benefits are time and money, which give computing legs. It is the facilitator between the e-world and the real world. Think of being airborne at 32,000 feet over the Atlantic and being able to put the 8-hour flight to good use. You can do e-mail and maintain Web links at affordable rates. It is not necessary to wait out a connection with your business, customers, suppliers, and others. Employees can make decisions faster. Customers can ask more questions, and businesses can respond more accurately. Managers can control what happens at any time, because they are plugged into the heartbeat of the business. As a result one needs the *anywhere* functionality to stay competitive.

Consider the case of the U.S. army using mobile technology and a satellite link to track supplies during the 2003 war with Iraq. Sixty-four mobile units were used to scan information about combat and supply vehicles and send the data via a secure satellite link to an authorized central asset-tracking system. The equipment could be stationed virtually anywhere—roadsides or intersections—to scan vehicles in army columns and convoys as they approached (Songini 2003).

There is no question that mobility grants freedom of choice. Think of a situation where a consumer is on a lunch break and has limited time to shop. Instead of making several cell or phone calls to identify which store carries the belted leather briefcase for the right price, the consumer can use wireless (M) commerce to quickly check the selection at various stores and obtain the best price for the product in a matter of seconds. This benefit goes beyond products. Airlines, movie theaters, and even restaurants should soon begin to deliver special discounts for mobile users to generate store traffic.

Other benefits of m-commerce are productivity and flexibility in coordination. Mobile users tend to be more dynamic and manage time better. In terms of coordination, with mobile technology, you call to arrange a meeting, agree on a time and a place, and say, "I'll call you when I am one or two blocks from your office."

The number of two-way wireless messaging and cell phones for wireless Internet functions has skyrocketed everywhere. Today's emphasis is on applications that are location-centric. Location is a key ingredient for creating a personalized user experience for the wireless Internet. It allows users to pay bills, check their credit card balances, and bank over the wireless Internet. Just as the Internet has changed the way business is conducted, the wireless Web is expected to have similar or greater impact. According to the Gartner Group, within four years, 40 percent of all e-commerce will be conducted wirelessly.

LOCATION, LOCATION, LOCATION

Location is a critical factor in m-commerce. Knowledge of the consumer's location may be used to deliver timely and engaging content, product, and information. Managers of

---

BOX 6.4

Examples of Companies Making Progress on Location-Centric Commerce

Office Depot (www.officedepot.com)— This site is personalized by postal code. The site displays the product availability at the store that matches the customer's postal code. The customer can also order products and choose either to pick up the products at the local store or have them delivered.

Circuit City (www.circuitcity.com)—This site's store locator lets customers find all the stores in the vicinity of a given city or postal code. Customers can then select up to three stores to check for product availability.

Go2Online (www.go2online. com)—This mobile site allows users to search for directions and phone numbers for a variety of local establishments such as restaurants, shops, theatres, hospitals, police stations, and gas stations.

Autoweb (www.autoweb.com/)—In this site's used car section, users can look for a car from a particular manufacturer, with a certain price range, and within a certain distance from the user.

Ecompare (sprint2.ecompare wireless.com)—This mobile site allows users to compare the price of a particular product at one store with the same product at another store. This mobile site allows users to compare the price of that product with prices at other sites online.

---

physical stores would value technology that helps bring foot traffic to their location. The wireless channel for promotions can target promotion campaigns for their individual stores, whether they are hotels, movie theaters, or restaurants that have perishable items to sell.

Think of a restaurant that uses technology to attract local customers during a slow week. This would allow them to match prices, offer specials, or unload excess inventory. For example, a local theater can offer a 30 percent discount on tickets for a particular show. As the time of the show draws near, the discount can increase, right up to the beginning of the show. Box 6.4 shows examples of companies that have made progress on location-centric commerce.

SATELLITE HANDHELD DEVICE TRANSMITTER/RECEIVER CELLULAR SYSTEMS. Another benefit of **location-centricity** is in location tracking of products, services, and even people, which allows providers to focus more accurately on delivery times and improve customer service. For example, stores can track multiple trucks carrying a large amount of inventory and divert them to unload specific merchandise just in time for ready sale. This aspect saves time and minimizes inventory space. As shown in Figure 6.2, a handheld device works through a satellite-based wireless system to communicate with trucks that have onboard intertruck communication. Assembly plants, supermarkets, airlines, and other mass-transit corporations are candidates for location tracking systems.

In addition to mobile inventory management, another benefit of mobile commerce benefits the consumer. A consumer uses a mobile unit such as a Palm Pilot to access a database of particular products, the stores that sell them, and their

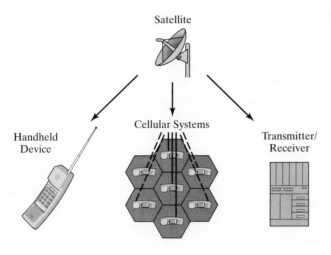

Satellite

Cellular Systems

Handheld
Device

Transmitter/
Receiver

FIGURE 6.2   Location
tracking of goods

Source: U. Varshney, R. J. Vetter,
and R. Kalakota, "Mobile
Commerce: A New Frontier,"
Computer, Oct. 2000, 32–38.

respective prices. Rather than going from one store to another, the customer sends
a signal (called a query) to the database that searches each vendor's inventory system and recommends the nearest location where the customer can purchase the
product. (See Figure 6.3.)

Location-centric services may be classified based on customer needs and type of
information to be delivered. The major drivers of demand are:

- "Where am I?" queries. The "where am I?" and "how do I get there?" questions
  are reflected in the availability of maps, driving directions, online directories,

FIGURE 6.3   Product location—a conceptual view

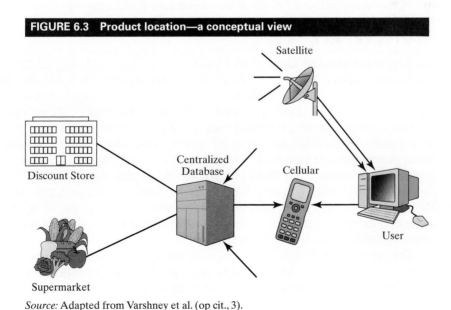

Satellite

Discount Store

Centralized
Database

Cellular

User

Supermarket

Source: Adapted from Varshney et al. (op cit., 3).

and yellow pages information. These types of queries are in high demand in dense urban areas like Tokyo, Beirut, Cairo, and Pittsburgh, where there are few street names, or where streets curve around in every direction. For example, in Tokyo, GPS capabilities allow users to find their way to destinations and alert their families or friends to their whereabouts in real time.

- Personalized information delivered at the time needed. This includes information about new products, special promotions, and special offers based on customer profiles available in existing databases or data warehouses.

- Niche consumer applications based on demands by individual consumers or business buyers. Examples are fish finders, soccer assistants, or people finders.

- Industrial applications such as tracking materials, products, and projects using innovative means (Rao and Minakakis 2003).

THE USABILITY FACTOR

Overall, the main benefits of m-commerce are convenience and flexibility with true anytime, anywhere access. There is also the advantage of efficiency for the store and the customer. The key service is mobility. The road map to wireless Web growth began in 1998 with the first release of a standard called **Wireless Application Protocol (WAP).** This standard was designed to deliver messages and data traffic to mobile phones within a geographical area. A year later, Japan introduced I-mode, which attracted 5 million users by year-end. More progress was made between 2000 and 2002, leading to the introduction of new third-generation (3G) networks that operate at more than 30 times the speed of earlier systems. Analysts forecast about 200 million users by late 2005. WAP is covered later in the chapter.

wireless application protocol (WAP): open, global, industry-wide mobile specifications for wireless network architecture; application environment and a set of communication protocols.

WI-FI IS THE KEY

The key to the growing surge of wireless Internet access is Wi-Fi (wireless fidelity), which represents a collection of related wireless technologies. It is an emerging industry standard that makes it possible for hardware firms to create wireless products that communicate with one another. It sends Web pages and phone calls via radio waves, bypassing the expense of cables and high-speed Internet service. In Iraq, for example, the rebuilding effort since the end of the war in 2003 could skip the build-out of traditional phone and cable networks altogether. Wi-Fi equipment makers such as Cisco Systems are implementing Wi-Fi in Iraq, which has already been proved in remote places such as Mount Everest, Indonesia, and Native American reservations. On Mount Everest, yaks carry Wi-Fi gear to a cybercafe that opened in April 2003 at the base camp at 17,000 feet. Climbers and support personnel use the technology for e-mail and phone calls round the clock.

The appeal of Wi-Fi is for home users as well as in business. For home users, going wireless means sharing a high-speed Internet connection with many computers without having to connect them by wires. The heart of a home wireless infrastructure is a device called an *access point*. The device plugs into a homeowner's Internet connection, which spreads Internet access to the rest of the house, up to 300 feet. Similarly, in a business, Wi-Fi makes the work environment more mobile and makes it easier to shift workspaces around within the firm. Likewise, business travelers at airports or airport lounges can access e-mail while waiting for flights (Wingfield 2003).

On the international scene, with speed a major challenge, a new version of the popular Wi-Fi standard (Wireless G) was introduced in 2003 that works with the older one (Wireless B) and is five times as fast. This development can now zip music files between computers and let laptop users surf the Web from coffee shops to airport stops at impressive speeds. The new product can stream a number of high-quality videos simultaneously, while the older standard could barely handle one stream under normal conditions.

Despite progress made on Wi-Fi, security remains a major concern. Hackers have been able to crack data-scrambling software that comes with most wireless hardware, making it easy to snoop on private exchanges transmitted through the air. (See Box 6.5.) While security is getting better in newer Wi-Fi products, it is still prudent to take certain steps to ensure security, privacy, and integrity of privileged data. The least that users can do is to make their networks a bit less visible to the outside world. It means adjusting the settings on the home network's access points—the antenna set up to link Wi-Fi–equipped wireless devices to the wired Internet connection. All access points let users create a unique name—called an SSID (service set identifier)—for their Wi-Fi networks. Users should create an SSID that is not totally obvious and change it on a regular basis.

Another form of protection involves creating the equivalent of an invite list for a Wi-Fi network. On an access point's setting, users can specify the machines permitted to connect to the Wi-Fi network. In networking language, it is known as MAC (media access control) address filtering. Of course, most Wi-Fi products have long relied on

---

BOX 6.5

Wi-Fi Vulnerable to Hackers

Here's how Army Lt. Col. Clifton H. Poole, who teaches classes here on wireless security at the National Defense University, gets his kicks on I-66. Several times a month, Poole turns on a laptop computer in his car as he commutes between his Reston home and the university campus at Fort McNair in southwest Washington. As he drives, a software program records the number of "hot spots," areas where wireless transmitters allow Internet access over the air. The results, Poole says, scare him.

After nearly two years of monitoring the same 23-mile route, Poole has watched the number of hot spots grow as the technology known as Wi-Fi has become the latest Big Internet Thing.

Setting up a home or business wireless network gives people freedom to jump onto the Internet without their computers being tethered to cables. The problem is that most of those networks are unprotected, vulnerable to hackers who could steal data, introduce viruses, launch spam, or attack other computers. The rough percentage of them that are unprotected remains above 60 percent.

Wi-Fi speaks to the Internet's powerful allure of an always-on connected world where it is possible to share things that might normally cost money. But like other popular applications, such as software for trading digital music over the Internet, Wi-Fi is bumping into the hard realities of economics and security.

Source: Adapted from *The Daily Progress,* August 1, 2003, B3.

encryption schemes called Wired Equivalent Privacy (WEP) to convert into gibberish all data transmitted back and forth between access points and wireless-equipped computers. Going through the protocol is not an easy task and requires some practice.

E-commerce continues to grow at phenomenal rates, although most of the development involves wired infrastructures. As wireless networks grow, m-commerce is bound to offer new avenues for growth and new opportunities in this emerging frontier. Plunging prices and easier deployment already are paying off. Even small companies can justify wireless systems once available only to giants such as United Parcel Service, Inc. Device makers continue to come out with smarter and smaller handhelds. As exemplified in Box 6.6, the wireless Web works in four major areas.

- Wireless work environments include offices that transmit data from a company's intranet to employees on the move. Several hospitals and family practice facilities have designed a wireless network for staff to check charts and patient data, which eliminates handwriting errors. In one case, the respiratory therapy group of one hospital cut staff by 20 percent, saving $1.5 million a year, and the group handled 13 percent more patients.

- Employees on the move help companies reach suppliers and improve customer service. Through a wireless network, service response time can be cut dramatically. Errors from the once-popular fax machine are all but gone.

- In a smart environment, wireless devices in a warehouse or a manufacturing facility can be programmed to automatically collect from neighboring computers data

---

BOX 6.6

Why Wireless?

Ten years ago, U.S. Fleet Services considered building a wireless network for its drivers, but soon decided against it. Customizing mobile devices and developing software was too hard, and the company didn't have computer systems robust enough to make it worth the hassle. Then, last year, U.S. Fleet revisited the technology—and this time it put the pedal to the metal. In hospitals, offices, and factories, a standard called Wi-Fi (aka 802.11b) that connects devices to wireless networks is simplifying installations.

This year, the number of employees using a Wi-Fi network are expected to more than double, to 12 million, according to Gartner Inc. Another boost: Tiny radios can now track parts in warehouses or alert techies when machines are on the blink. The biggest action is in reaching out to field personnel. In years past, Pepsi Bottling Group Inc.'s 700 soda fountain technicians spent too much time on the phone instead of time fixing the company's 1.3 million vending and fountain machines. Customers called in problems, then a call-center employee paged a technician, who would ring for details about the job. At the end of the day, repair workers would fax in forms detailing their visits—with results not available on Pepsi's intranet until five days later. That system is on its way to the trash heap.

The payoff? Pepsi answers calls 20 percent faster than it used to and has saved $7 million—meaning the project will pay for itself in just two years. "When we tried to figure out why customers switched to our competitors, part of the answer was customer service and equipment failure," said a senior vice president of Pepsi.

Source: Heather Green, "Winging into Wireless." *BusinessWeek,* February 18, 2002, EB9.

about workflow, status of inventory or parts availability, and so on. This means no more handwritten reports or bills and missed deliveries.

- Wireless devices open new shortcuts to stock trading, banking, and more. It is now possible to have direct access to and control over one's personal finances. Bankers, brokers, and others are pushing custom-tailored financial services by advances in communications and trading technologies.

KEY LIMITATIONS

No technology or system exists without limitations. One limitation is distance. For desktop computers, access points can reach up to 1,800 feet. For laptops, it is much shorter. Even though wireless signals go through walls and other barriers, they attenuate (weaken) en route. The network's range can be extended through repeaters that refresh the weak signal before sending it anew.

Speed is another limitation. The wireless network that uses the 802.11b standard runs at 11 megabits per second. This is one-ninth the speed of the wired network. This means it takes longer to send a large file by wireless. A third limitation of wireless technology is the security and privacy factors. As we shall explain later in the chapter, wireless security requires special technical safeguards to protect the integrity of e-mail and other data broadcast via radio waves. When wireless networks transmit data as radio signals, virtually anyone in the vicinity can tap into the data with the right software. To address this threat, every wireless product comes from the vendor equipped with built-in encryption.

There is also the question of privacy. The ability to track users is the number one privacy concern related to the growth of the wireless industry. Do you really want your cell phone to disclose to anyone where you are all the time? As explained in Box 6.6, consumers should be able to control who sees their location information. Yet, when consumers receive valuable services, they must be willing to give up their privacy.

With these obvious m-commerce limitations, there are other limitations and issues. Here is a brief list:

- The quality of service varies. Today's cell phone features are phenomenal, but the quality of service from the service providers continues to be a compromise.
- Even with the many useful services, it is difficult for the user to remember all the phone numbers, key words, or codes, especially with a small screen.
- Batteries have a poor record. It is rare that a cell phone battery runs more than five hours before recharging. Also, when you listen to music, you are simply shut off from using the phone.
- Mobility does not matter in situations where you don't need any information you left behind, especially when you are already overwhelmed with information at work.
- Connecting charges continue to be high, especially for long exchanges, downloads, or conversation.
- For information to reach certain destinations, a GPS in your car is not that useful. You will still have to ask for directions the old-fashioned way.
- People expect an immediate response when they leave a message on your mobile phone. This can be an utter nuisance, especially when you are trying to get away from work.

- There is no peace anymore in restaurants, cars, trains, or airplanes. Cell phones ring everywhere you go, which creates nothing but nuisance.
- There is poor implementation of many wireless networks, even in work/office environments.

CRITICAL SUCCESS FACTORS

For m-commerce to be successful, four factors are critical.

- Mobility: Most people consider their mobility critical to their lifestyle. Any m-service offered must take into account people's mobility and profile of usage if it is to benefit financially through m-sales and m-services.
- Personalization: This means identifying and following up on each customer's market segment and determining the best options. This is considered individualized service, similar to what customers would get in a reputable brick-and-mortar store.
- Global standardization: This critical success factor has two aspects. First, for m-commerce, customers want to continue moving around without having to change services or worry about taxation, legal rules, or other constraints that are unique to each country. Second, customers look for standardization in terms of one bill, one password, and one user interface. This will make it easier and quicker to transact business in a mobile environment.
- Customer profiling: This area of specialization addresses customer needs over a time period via certain behavior such as advertising, promotions, or special offers. This attempt takes into consideration personalization features, as well as customization.

When m-commerce was new business, the network was a major key success factor. Hearing quality and availability were the key concerns. Today's concentration is on customer satisfaction, which means paying greater attention to customer needs for services and quality. That is why customer control management is increasing in importance. This is also covered in Chapter 10.

HOW WIRELESS TECHNOLOGY IS EMPLOYED

BLUETOOTH

You just arrived home from attending a seminar. Your notebook and PDA are in your briefcase and your cellphone is tucked in your pocket. You take off your coat and try to relax. In the meantime your notebook locates the printer and instructs it to print your seminar notes. Your PDA contacts your desktop computer and ensures that your address book and calendar for tomorrow are all synchronized. All this happens while you're trying to take off your coat. Before you take your favorite snack from the refrigerator, your cellphone beeps to tell you that a hard copy of your notes is available. Your PDA also beeps to tell you that you have new e-mail.

Bluetooth: a universal, low-cost, wireless connection standard.

Welcome to a growing wireless connection standard. **Bluetooth** is a universal, low-cost, low-powered wireless technology that uses short-range radio frequency (RF) to hook up wireless connectivity among computers, scanners, and printers. It allows any Bluetooth-enabled device to communicate with other similar devices, regardless of manufacture. It is a type of wireless networking that allows electronic devices to communicate and share information without action from a user, wires, or cables. These devices include cell phones, Palm Pilots, computers, home appliances, headphones, and keyboards. Bluetooth communicates on a radio-frequency band of 2.45 gigahertz radio spectrum to wirelessly connect devices within 10 to 100 yards. Steps have been taken to prevent any interference with other systems. (See Figure 6.4.)

The concept was initially developed by Swedish mobile phone maker L. M. Ericsson in 1994 to make it possible for laptops to make calls over a mobile phone. Bluetooth is named after King Harald "Bluetooth" Blaatand II of Denmark (940–981 A.D.). He earned his nickname from the blueberries he ate that stained his teeth. Bluetooth unified Denmark and Norway during his reign. Ericsson hoped that the new standard would unite the telecommunications and computing industries, as well.

BLUETOOTH SIG.   In February 1998, Ericsson, IBM, Intel, Nokia, and Toshiba formed a Bluetooth Special Interest Group (SIG) to develop standards for the technology, hoping to expedite its development and final adoption. One of the SIG's goals is to gain global acceptance so that Bluetooth devices can be used anywhere in the world. Bluetooth is supported by over 2,500 hardware/software manufacturers who make up the SIG. It administers test facilities to ensure that various devices conform to the standards.

The SIG divides itself into two categories: Promoter members and associate companies work together like a board of directors to make decisions for the SIG. The associate companies are members of different work groups, and each has a charter outlining the work group's goals. For instance, the scope of the Car Profile working group is to ensure device interoperability in the car environment by wirelessly connecting portable and car-embedded devices using the technology defined in the Bluetooth specification (www.bluetooth.com/ sig/sig/sig.asp). Companies work within these work groups to develop standard devices for universal adoption by manufacturers.

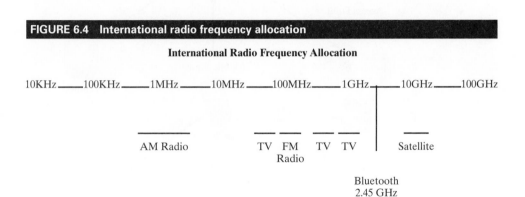

FIGURE 6.4   International radio frequency allocation

International Radio Frequency Allocation

10KHz —— 100KHz —— 1MHz —— 10MHz —— 100MHz —— 1GHz —— 10GHz —— 100GHz

AM Radio   TV FM TV TV │ Satellite
                     Radio

Bluetooth
2.45 GHz

MAIN CAPABILITIES.   Bluetooth uses short-range radio links to allow wireless communication between computers and all types of portable electronic devices, forming small, private networks. In one respect, it is an enabling technology. It creates a common language between various electronic devices that makes it possible for them to communicate and connect with one another.

The key Bluetooth features include low cost, low power consumption, low complexity, and robustness. As shown in Figure 6.5, Bluetooth-enabled laptops can communicate with palmtops and mobile phones to synchronize schedules and contacts. Bluetooth-enabled printers and mice can communicate without the tangle of serial port cables. Bluetooth also enables wireless access to LANs, the mobile phone network, and the Internet for a variety of portable handheld devices and home appliances. For example, a user with a cell phone can approach a vending machine that automatically links up with a wireless payment system, allowing the user to charge a vending machine purchase. The trick of the process is Bluetooth technology.

Bluetooth devices send out weak, 1-milliwatt signals with limited range to avoid interference. It is possible to have multiple devices in a room, because Bluetooth makes frequency overlapping unlikely with a technique called *spread-spectrum frequency hopping*. This "hopping" refers to a device changing regularly between the use of 79 randomly selected frequencies within an indicated range. With Bluetooth transmitting change frequencies 1,600 times per second, it is improbable that two would be operating on the exact same frequency at the same time.

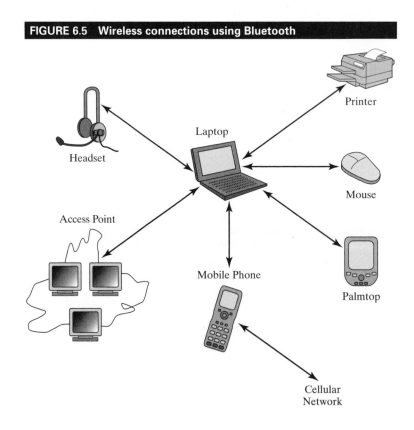

FIGURE 6.5   Wireless connections using Bluetooth

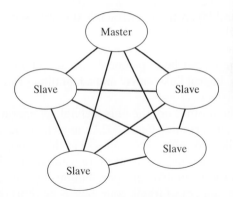

FIGURE 6.6   Two Bluetooth devices connected together create a network called a piconet. A single master device controls from one to seven slave devices.

PROTOCOL ARCHITECTURE.   Bluetooth SIG has released specifications for various Bluetooth architecture layers to speed the development of devices and applications. A primary layer, called the **radio layer,** forms the physical connection interface that oversees transmission within a small network called a piconet. A **piconet** is a group of devices connected to a common channel, identified with its unique hop sequence. (See Figure 6.6.) In addition, this layer specifies frequency, modulation scheme, and transmission power as a core protocol. (See Figure 6.7.)

radio layer: primary layer in Bluetooth architecture.

piconet: group of devices connected to a common channel, identified by its unique hop sequence.

baseband: second layer in Bluetooth architecture; converts the data into signals that the radio interprets and converts to a frequency of 2.4 GHz.

The second layer is the **baseband,** which with a radio and an antenna makes up the physical transmission component of a Bluetooth device. The baseband processor converts the data into signals that the radio interprets and converts to a frequency of 2.4 gigahertz. The signal is then transmitted through the air by the antenna and is received by the antenna of another Bluetooth device, which receives the data and processes it in the reverse order. The devices must be within 30 feet of each other, because radio signals suffer propagation (loss) effects at distances of greater length (www.darwinmag.com/learn/curve/column.html? ArticleID =12).

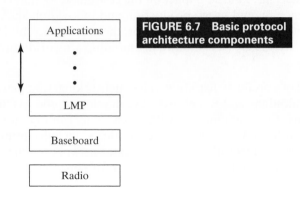

FIGURE 6.7   Basic protocol architecture components

link manager protocol (LMP): a Bluetooth layer that sets up ongoing link management with Bluetooth devices.

logical link control and adaptation protocol (L2CAP): layered over the baseband protocol and resides in the data link layer.

After the baseband layer, the next stack is the **link manager protocol (LMP).** This layer sets up ongoing link management with Bluetooth devices. This includes security features such as authentication and encryption. Upper layer protocols are adapted to the baseband layer via the **logical link control and adaptation protocol (L2CAP).** (See Figure 6.7.)

Unfortunately, Bluetooth is not the only technology operating within the 2.4-GHz region. HomeRF and 802.11, as well as the militaries of France, Spain, and Japan, transmit within this band, and officials wonder if the technologies will interfere with one another and cause errors. Bluetooth combats this problem through the use of frequency "hopping," which reduces the number of frame collisions using short data packets. Link Management Protocol (LMP) performs three important functions.

- Piconet management: A group of devices are connected to a common channel with a unique hop sequence. In this arrangement, an initiating device (master) and the receiving device (slave) are linked and detached by the LMP and can switch their roles, when necessary.

- Link configuration: The LMP ensures that the Bluetooth device does not operate below specified performance limits. If a device sits idle for a specified time period, the LMP minimizes power consumption by transferring the device to a "parked" state and also allows another device to join the piconet.

- Security functions: LMP controls various security functions in Bluetooth transmission. It monitors authentication of other devices trying to make a connection and manages the encryption keys used to establish secure links.

BLUETOOTH APPLICATIONS.   Application development is the responsibility of the individual work groups within the Bluetooth SIG. Current projects include car kits to allow for hands-free operation while driving, headsets to access devices stored away (cell phone in a purse), and synchronization software to keep schedule and contact data on personal devices up to date (www.ee.iitb.ernet.in/uma/~aman/bluetooth/tut2.html). In terms of distance, the range of each radio is 10 meters (30 feet), which can be extended to 100 meters with a special amplifier.

Although the technical aspects of the Bluetooth standard enable easy and efficient wireless communication between devices, the technology will be effective in everyday life only if the products have a true impact on the consumer. As the technology gains greater acceptance by end users, production and innovation should improve in kind. A study by Cahners In-Stat Group predicts up to 1.4 billion Bluetooth-enabled devices by 2005 (www.inquiry.com/pubs/infoworld/vol22/issues51/001218hnenable.asp).

PRODUCTS.   Most of today's products feature wireless networking. Companies such as 3Com, Socket Communications, and Brainboxes have developed products that enable computer components to communicate with each other automatically (www.Palowireless.com/bluetooth/products.asp). These products include printer modules that remotely connect computers within the personal area network to printers, and wireless networking devices that remotely connect computers to a broader network and to the Internet.

Bluetooth development is finding early success with wireless phones. Motorola, Ericsson, and Nokia have all developed Bluetooth-enabled phones that make the "wireless personal area network" more of a reality. For example, Motorola's Timeport 270 was designed to work with the Bluetooth Smart Module accessory and the Bluetooth PC card to allow all of a user's electronic devices to communicate seamlessly (www.beststuff.com/articles/737). Additionally, Motorola has developed a hands-free car kit for use with Bluetooth phones, which will make use of a wireless phone while driving much safer and more user friendly.

One factor that greatly limits the volume of Bluetooth devices is the technology itself. The technology has undergone significant changes in the past few years, making development much more difficult due to the lack of a stable platform for testing new products. The rapid development of application suites and the solidification of standards by the SIG should help counteract this problem.

The true potential of Bluetooth lies in applications that have yet to be developed. Bluetooth's ability to link multiple devices together holds limitless possibilities. For instance, Cambridge Consultants developed two Bluetooth products for day-to-day, less tech-savvy individuals. One device, called the "e-mail pen," enables users to read and write e-mail anywhere in their home without using a computer. The pen translates handwritten messages into computer text, which it then sends to the "pod" to create the e-mail and send it out over a phone line.

Another product is a car key to allow secure remote entry and possibly allow for fingerprint identification. It is capable of activating personal settings, displaying fuel status and mileage, generating diagnostic information, and much more (www.cambridgeconsultants.com).

SECURITY ISSUES. Even though each piconet link is encoded against eavesdropping and interference, security issues could stall Bluetooth development. One flaw could allow a hacker to obtain the encryption key to a device and "listen in" on communication between two devices or pretend to be a device and send false messages to the other party. Another issue is to allow unwanted individuals to track a device as it moves and eavesdrop on the other device's conversation. However, each case requires specialized skills on the intruder's part to succeed.

WIRELESS SECURITY CONCERNS

There are two basic concerns in wireless security.

- The transmitted message must be protected all the way to its destination host to ensure that it is delivered intact.
- The host system must verify or authenticate the user it is communicating with.

Without such a security move, the host system is left vulnerable to all kinds of wireless hacking.

Wireless security centers on wireless Ethernet networks using Wi-Fi (wireless fidelity) at speeds up to 11 million bits per second over 100 meters. As a wireless network standard, Wi-Fi is growing in popularity, especially in colleges and universities. It is ideal for frequent transmission of high-bandwidth files or for devices needing constant network or Internet connectivity (www.3com.com). (See Box 6.7.)

BOX 6.7

Why Wi-Fi Wants to Be Free

Wireless networks want to be free by providing hassle-free wireless bandwidth to homes, offices, and public spaces. Driven by the rapid drop in the cost of Wi-Fi hardware, no-fee wireless networks were popping up everywhere—in universities, offices, city parks, and homes. Dartmouth University's open network in New Hampshire alone boasted over 500 nodes covering many of the campus buildings and grounds.

Like the Internet a decade earlier, the idea of a "wireless cloud" spread from universities into the broader market. Once it reached homes and businesses, taking it outdoors was the next step. This would be the province of the free wireless movement. The most novel of the innovations in

this technology was the redeployment of Wi-Fi to provide connectivity not only indoors in homes and offices, but also outdoors in parks, porches, and plazas.

The spread of free wireless networks was rapid. Creating a hot spot was just a matter of installing a wireless base station, or access point, and advertising its presence through any of several means provided by the open wireless community. For larger areas or outdoor spaces such as parks and plazas, directional antennas and amplifiers could be used to sculpt a coverage zone using the meager 1 watt of power permitted by the FCC for unlicensed operators in the 2.4GHz band.

Adapted from Terry Schmidt and Anthony Townsend, "Why Wi-Fi Wants to Be Free," *Communications of the ACM*, May 2003, 47–52.

Wi-Fi equipment works like a cordless telephone. It invisibly extends a fast Internet connection up to 1,500 feet to any laptop or computer equipped with a wireless receiver. This makes it ideal for a business with officers to share the same stationary Internet connection, paying for only a single hookup.

Wired Equivalent Privacy (WEP): part of Wi-Fi security mechanism that makes it possible to encrypt messages before heading for their destination.

Other security standards exist, but most of today's wireless networks depend on the 80211b standard. Part of Wi-Fi is a security mechanism called **Wired Equivalent Privacy (WEP),** which makes it possible to encrypt messages before they head for their destination. Even then, concern still looms about the adequacy of security. An attacker can access a wireless network from outside the organization with no physical connection, which compromises the security infrastructure.

Briefly, WEP uses a secret key to encrypt messages transmitted between a mobile station and a base station connected to a wired network. The mobile station accepts each message after verifying its authenticity. A 40-bit key is standard but vulnerable to security threats. Even the latest 128-bit key is not fully secure. In 2001, Ian Goldberg, a Canadian cryptologist, broke WEP. However, it takes know-how and practical experience in cryptology to break down a seemingly secure standard.

SATELLITE TECHNOLOGY

repeater: a device that extends the distance of a physical link.

Most of today's "long-haul" data transmission is made possible via satellites circling Earth. A **repeater** in a satellite receives the signal representing the data and "repeats" the signal to another location—normally to an Earth station. A special frequency band is used to transmit to the satellite. The satellite regenerates the signal and transmits back to the Earth station at a different frequency band. Repeating a signal from one Earth station to another takes approximately 250 milliseconds.

To illustrate, a truck carrying fresh produce might be equipped with a satellite communication system to accept data from headquarters or from customers directly. One technology revolves around a smart wireless computer terminal installed in the steering wheel of the truck. Time-sensitive pickup orders, route alerts, or changes in the pickup schedule are transmitted from headquarters to the truck via satellite. The truck driver can make appropriate adjustments on the route without delay. (See Figure 6.8.)

2G DIGITAL CELLULAR TECHNOLOGY

Once the information is received by the online truck terminal, the driver drives to the address where the produce is available. The driver leaves the truck carrying a

personal digital assistant (PDA): handheld device that scans information and transmits it to a terminal in a vehicle via wireless digital cellular technology.

handheld device called a **personal digital assistant (PDA).** After the vendor fills out the shipping form (name of sender, type of produce in the box, and the grocer's name and address), the driver enters a preprinted tracking number into the PDA, which has a scanning facility and a keyboard. The PDA prints out a routing label and the driver pastes it onto the box before loading the box on the truck. The information stored in the PDA is transmitted instantly to the terminal in the truck via a cellular tower using wireless digital cellular technology.

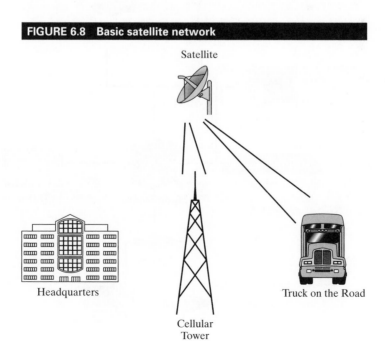

FIGURE 6.8 Basic satellite network

Satellite

Headquarters

Cellular Tower

Truck on the Road

PALM PILOT

PDAs are one of the fastest-selling consumer devices in history. Computer organizers originated in the 1990s, but they were too big, expensive, and complicated. In 1996, the original Palm Pilot was introduced, and it was a hit with consumers. It was small enough to fit in a shirt pocket, ran for weeks on AAA batteries, was easy to use, and could store a lot of information. The two types of PDAs are handheld computers and palm-sized computers. The major differences between the two are size and display.

No matter what type of PDA you have, they share the same major features. Both types store basic programs in a read-only memory (ROM) chip and are powered by batteries. Both have some type of LCD display screen that is used for output and input. The handheld computers have input devices that typically use a miniature keyboard, and the palm-sized computers use a touch screen in combination with a handwriting recognition program. This program allows the user to draw characters on the touch screen, and the software converts the characters to letters and numbers. Figure 6.9 sketches the parts of a PDA.

data synchronization: the communication between a PDA and a personal computer.

Palm Pilots function like cellular phones. The communication between a PDA and a personal computer is referred to as **data synchronization.** This is done mostly through a serial number

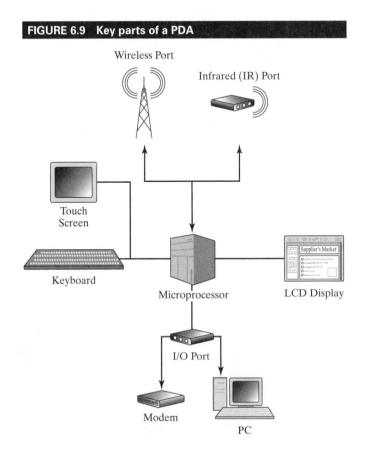

FIGURE 6.9   Key parts of a PDA

Wireless Port

Infrared (IR) Port

Touch Screen

Keyboard

Microprocessor

LCD Display

I/O Port

Modem

PC

connecting to an infrared light to beam information. These devices are all located in the microprocessor, which serves as the brain of the PDA. The microprocessor coordinates all of the PDA's functions according to programmed instructions stored in the operating system. To gain Internet access, the microprocessor also must connect to the **mobile telecommunications switching office (MTSO)** located in a certain cell site.

mobile telecommunications switching office (MTSO): cellular switch that places calls from land-based telephones to wireless customers.

CELLULAR PHONES

Wireless communications work around specific cells or geographic areas. When you are in a certain cell, you can access wireless communications. Cellular radio provides mobile telephone service by employing a network of cell sites distributed over a wide area. A cell site contains a radio transceiver and a base station controller, which manages, sends, and receives traffic from the mobiles in its geographical area to a cellular telephone switch. It also employs a tower and antennas and provides a link to the distant cellular switch, the mobile telecommunications switching office. This MTSO places calls from land-based telephones to wireless customers, switches calls between cells as mobiles travel across cell boundaries, and authenticates wireless customers before they make calls.

Briefly, here is how a cell phone works. When you power up the cell phone, it listens for a system identification code (SIC) on the control channel. The control channel is a special frequency that the phone and base station use to talk to each other about things like call setup and channel changing. If the phone cannot find any control channels to listen to, the user gets the annoying "Out of Range" or "No Service Found" display on the cell screen.

When the cell phone receives the SIC, the phone compares it to the SIC programmed into the phone. If the SICs match, the phone knows that the cell it is communicating with is part of its home system. Along with the SIC, the phone also transmits a registration request, and the MTSO keeps track of the phone's location in a database. This way, the MTSO knows which cell site you are in when it wants to ring your phone.

Once the MTSO gets a call, it tries to find you and your phone. It looks in the database to see which cell site you are in. The MTSO then picks up a frequency par that your phone will use in that cell to take the call. It communicates with your phone over the control channel to tell it which frequencies to use. When your phone and the tower switch to those frequencies, the call is connected.

As you move toward the edge of your cell site, your cell site's base station notes that your signal strength is diminishing. Meanwhile, the base station in the cell site you are moving toward sees your phone's signal strength increasing. The two base stations coordinate with each other through the MTSO. At that point, your phone gets a signal on a control channel telling it to change frequencies. This handoff switches your phone to the new cell. (See Figure 6.10.)

On the other hand, when the SIC on the control channel does not match the SIC programmed into the phone, the phone knows it is roaming. The MTSO of the cell site that you are roaming in contacts the MTSO of your home system, which then checks its database to confirm that the SIC of your cell phone is valid. Your home system verifies your phone to the local MTSO, which then tracks your phone as you move through the cell sites.

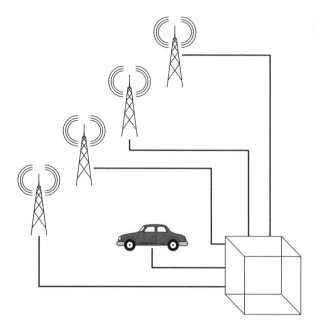

FIGURE 6.10   Signal passing from cell to cell during travel

Source: Adapted from Brain & Tyson, 2003, 1.

2G digital voice networks have earned respect since their introduction in 1990. The technology was updated in 1997 with a focus on improved speed and performance. The number of users of 2.5G standards reached 400 million worldwide in 2000. 3G voice and data technologies were introduced in 2001 and are expected to expand globally during the next two to three years. But despite their promise, 3G technologies have a way to go before wide adoption. The primary reason is that the mission-critical applications that sit in a corporate network use too much bandwidth to be accessed by wireless technology. These and other restrictions should be worked out in the near future.

WIRELESS LAN

The most common standard for wireless networking is the wireless local-area network (WLAN). WLAN has been growing steadily worldwide. In 2000, worldwide WLAN shipments were $1.10 billion; in 2002, $1.9 billion; and in 2004, $3 billion. Estimates of 2006 shipments are well over $3.85 billion (Redman 2004). The technology uses radio waves unbounded by the physical constraints of cabling and walls to connect laptops and other electronic devices to a LAN, using Ethernet connections over the air (Wexler 2004, 19). A WLAN is identical to a regular LAN, except that the devices are wireless. Each computer has a **wireless network interface card (WNIC)** with an antenna built into it. Signals from the WNIC are sent through radio waves to an **access point (AP).** The access point is bidirectional. It is designed to receive the signals and transmit them to the WNIC. (See Figure 6.11.)

wireless network interface card (WNIC): a card that interfaces between the wireless device and an access point for data or voice transmission and reception.

access point (AP): when a wireless station sends a frame to a server, an access point acts as a bridge that passes the frame over the wired LAN to the server.

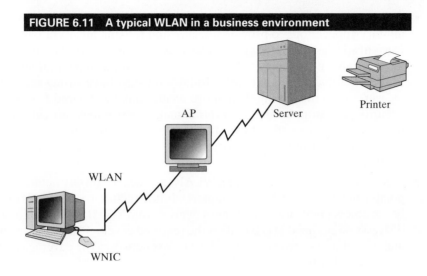

FIGURE 6.11 A typical WLAN in a business environment

WLAN design is flexible and is becoming cheaper to deploy. However, it only travels 150 feet. Most wireless LANs lack built-in security, leaving business networks open to potential hacking. Security can be strengthened by adding higher-level encryption, depending on the sensitivity of the information transmitted and the security requirements of the users. The problem today is that the security of a user name plus password is weak. It is too easy to figure out by hackers. In contrast, a strong password is difficult to deploy, needs to be frequently changed, is too long to remember, or has many "odd" characters. New algorithms should be available that will assure security and privacy of the communications transmitted.

FACTORS TO CONSIDER

For an organization to adopt wireless LAN technology, several factors must be considered.

- Range and coverage: The interaction between the airwaves and objects can affect how the energy propagates, which influences the coverage and range a particular wireless system achieves. Most WLANs use radio frequencies to allow the penetration of most indoor walls and objects. A typical WLAN infrastructure has a range of less than 100 feet to more than 300 feet. This coverage can be extended to allow roaming through the use of microcells.

- Throughput: The actual throughput or performance of a WLAN varies from system to system, but propagation effects significantly affect it and the type of WLAN technology implemented. The throughput of most commercial WLAN configurations is 1.6 Mbps and now more commonly 11 Mbps. These data rates provide enough throughput for most productivity applications such as e-mail exchanges, access to shared accessories (printers), Internet access, and the ability to access files and data from other users.

- Security and integrity: Wireless technology originally was developed for military applications to provide a secure and reliable means of communication. Current wireless technology provides connections that are far stronger and more reliable than cellular phone connections and with data integrity equal to or better than wired networks. Today's WLANs have strong security measures built in, making them more secure than most wired LANs. Security provisions such as encryption make it extremely difficult to gain unauthorized access to network traffic. In most WLAN configurations, individual nodes must be security enabled before they can access network traffic (Tuesday 2004, 42).

- Cost and scalability: The cost of a WLAN includes the infrastructure cost (access points) and user cost (WLAN adapters). Infrastructure cost depends on the number of access points used and ranges in price from $1,000 to $2,000. The number of access points needed is based on the required coverage area and the number and type of users participating in the wireless network. The coverage area is proportional to the square of the product range.

- User costs: These depend on the number of wireless LAN adapters (one per client device) and the cost of installing and maintaining a WLAN. Fortunately, WLANs are scalable and range from simple to complex systems. These networks can support a large number of nodes and large open areas by adding additional access points to increase or boost coverage.

- Standardization of WLANs: Widespread acceptance of wireless infrastructure depends on industry standardization to provide compatibility and reliability among vendors and manufacturers. In September 1999, IEEE ratified the 802.11b (High Rate) standard, which provides data rates of up to 11 Mbps. WLANs can now open new markets by achieving performance, availability, and throughput comparable to a wired Ethernet.

WIRELESS APPLICATION PROTOCOL

With our lives becoming more dependent on personal electronic devices, we consider Internet viewing options on cell phones and Palm Pilots of greater value today. Wireless Internet services are in high demand because the digital cellular network continues to be a rapidly growing market. To address the challenge, a group of cellular phone companies agreed that a universal standard was vital for positive wireless Internet implementation. This was especially the case because the HTML Internet standard is not efficient enough to allow communication via a wireless data network. As a result, they collaborated and created a wireless application protocol, better known as WAP.

WAP Forum: an industry association; develops the world standard for wireless information and telephony services on digital mobile phones and other wireless devices.

WAP is the basis for the mobile Internet. It is a result of the **WAP Forum**'s efforts to come up with industry-wide specifications for technology useful in developing applications and services unique to wireless communication networks. The objectives of the forum are to:

- Embrace existing standards and technology wherever possible.
- Create worldwide wireless protocol specifications that will work across differing wireless network architectures.
- Bring Internet content to digital cellular phones and other wireless terminals and devices.

With WAP, a sales representative can access data such as the status of a customer's recent order, review past buying history, assess current inventory, and look up a competitor's price list just before entering a meeting—well prepared to make the sale. Physicians use WAP to make efficient and effective use of their mobile phone to download current data about a patient and make decisions at a lower cost and improved care for the patient. On the opposite side of the exchange, customers now can see data about themselves on the business' computer system and make better and more informed decisions. A common application is in the airline industry, where customers can make reservations online, review their itinerary, find out their gate number, and learn when they should check in.

The WAP concept is straightforward. Cellular devices are connected permanently to a wireless network. By adding an Internet protocol layer to the network, these devices and millions of users can be connected permanently to the Internet without having to dial in. With this protocol, one is able to access the Internet and keep in touch with anyone, anywhere, anytime via a micro browser–equipped wireless phone. Imagine you are in a meeting with a customer who wants to know the balance of her account. You call up her account through a secure connection and find out that she has just become overdrawn. You alert her to use your cell phone to authorize an online transfer from her savings to checking accounts to cover the balance before the account is charged a penalty.

This type of interactive electronic exchange marks the dawn of the Mobile Internet Revolution. The world of information is available not just on our desktops but at our fingertips, and the possibilities are truly endless.

How WAP Works

When one accesses a Web site from a PC Web browser, the user requests data and the server sends that data in the form of HTML over an IP network (see Chapter 3). The Web browser converts the HTML data into text and graphics. In contrast, on a mobile device, a WAP browser performs the role of a PC Web browser. It requests data from a Web site via a WAP gateway that acts as a "go-between" for a Web browser and a Web server. It translates the Web Markup Language (WML) to or from HTML. A markup language is a way of adding information to content that tells the device receiving the content what to do with it. It specifies the format and presentation of text and the hierarchies of pages, and it links their pages.

Figure 6.12 is a schematic of the WAP model. The architecture follows the OSI layering model covered in Chapter 2. The protocol gateway converts user requests from the WAP protocol stack to the Web protocol stack (HTTP and TCP/IP). Encoders and decoders convert WAP content into compact encoded formats to reduce the size of data sent over the network. Here is a brief summary of the functions of each element of the stack.

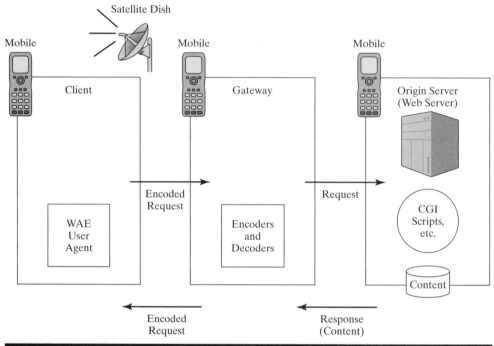

FIGURE 6.12 Schematic of the WAP model

wireless application environment (WAE): a WAP element that establishes an interoperable environment to allow operators and service providers to build applications and services for a large variety of wireless platforms.

wireless markup language (WML): based on XML, a markup language that has garnered enormous support due to its ability to describe data, unlike HTML, which is used to describe the display of data.

wireless session protocol (WSP): a WAP element that decides whether a network and a device will communicate back and forth or whether data will be transmitted straight from a network to the device.

- **Wireless application environment (WAE):** Based on a combination of Web and mobile telephony technologies, its job is to establish an interoperable environment to allow operators and service providers to build applications and services for a large variety of wireless platforms. It uses **wireless markup language (WML)** optimized for use in handheld mobile terminals. (See Figure 6.13.)

- **Wireless session protocol (WSP):** WSP is an application layer with a consistent interface for two session services: whether a network and a device will communicate back and forth (a connection-oriented session), or whether data will be transmitted straight from a network to the device (a connectionless session). If the session is connection oriented, the data will go directly to the next layer down, the Wireless Transaction Protocol (WTP) layer. Otherwise, the data will be transmitted to the Wireless Datagram Protocol (WDL) layer.

- **Wireless transaction protocol (WTP):** This layer serves to ensure that data flow from one location to another is efficiently based on a request/reply paradigm. WTP is

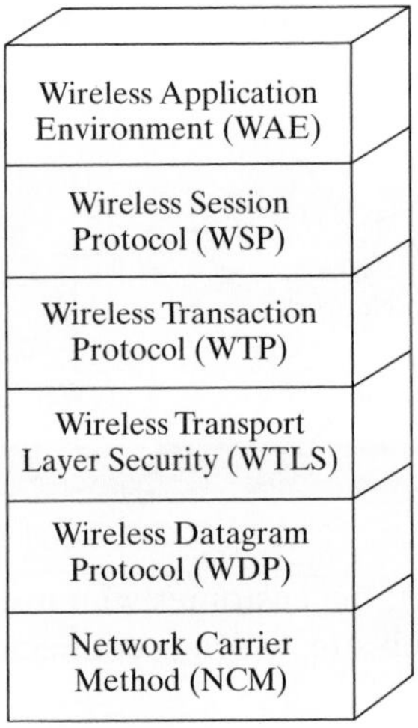

FIGURE 6.13 WAP protocol stack

| Wireless Application Environment (WAE) |
| Wireless Session Protocol (WSP) |
| Wireless Transaction Protocol (WTP) |
| Wireless Transport Layer Security (WTLS) |
| Wireless Datagram Protocol (WDP) |
| Network Carrier Method (NCM) |

wireless transaction protocol (WTP): a WAP layer that ensures that data flow from one location to another efficiently based on a request/reply paradigm.

wireless transport layer security (WTLS): a WAP element that gives security to the system via encryption, data integrity verification, and authentication between the user and the server.

wireless datagram protocol (WDP): a WAP feature that confirms easy adaptation to the WAP technology.

network carrier method (NCM): a technology that a wireless provider uses.

equivalent to the TCP layer of the TCP/IP OSI architecture and is responsible for packet segmentation, reassembly, and acknowledgement of packets.

- **Wireless transport layer security (WTLS):** WTLS gives security to the system through encryption, data integrity verification, and authentication between the user and the server. It also provides denial-of-service protection. The security aspect is important for providing secure connections for services such as e-commerce. To optimize security, dynamic key refreshing was developed to allow encryption keys to be updated on a regular basis during secure sessions.

- **Wireless datagram protocol (WDP):** WDP confirms easy adaptation to the WAP technology. It provides a common interface to the upper-layer protocols, and hence they function independently of the underlying wireless network.

- **Network carrier method (NCM):** Carriers are any technologies that a wireless provider uses. The information passed through the layers is received by WAP clients and relayed to the mini browser of the device. In m-commerce using WAP, the design idea underlying WAP is to use a gateway at the intersection of the wireless mobile network and the conventional wired network to conduct e-business. For example, when a customer places an order with an e-merchant, three parties are involved: the mobile service provider (MSP) that acts as a WAP gateway

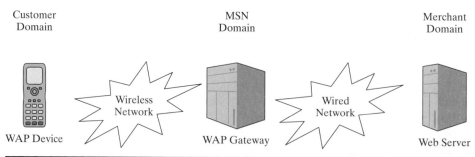

FIGURE 6.14   M-commerce: A typical WAP architecture

to connect between the wired and wireless Internet; the customer who uses a WAP-enabled cell phone; and the e-merchant's Web site, which is connected to the Internet (see Figure 6.14).

As can be seen, WAP bridges the gap between the desktop and the small-screen mobile device environments. The strength of WAP is that it is an open and free standard. Any manufacturer can produce WAP-enabled devices, and any Internet site can output WAP-readable Web pages. Currently, the most promise for WAP lies in its potential. Some of this potential for WAP-enabled phones is currently being realized in Europe, where users are able to buy books or CDs from Amazon.co.uk or Amazon.de. (www.cio.com/archive/071500/ wireless_content.html). WAP also helps standardize the applications that will proliferate using wireless communication technologies.

WAP BENEFITS

Most WAP benefits are reflected in wireless applications. The critical benefit of wireless applications is that they reduce the reaction time needed by mobile professionals. Greater mobility and instant access to critical information mean taking immediate action and dramatically increasing productivity from anywhere at any time.

Many WAP applications that are tailored for the business community are currently being developed. For example, some of these applications enable businesspeople to use their WAP devices to buy their own airline tickets and hotel reservations. Many experts believe that the first WAP applications designed specifically for businesses will come from enterprise software vendors that incorporate WAP functionality into their products. As long as the client handheld device has a WAP display, all of these applications are possible.

Experts envision WAP applications to capture micro payments, such as parking fees and vending machine payments. Other experts believe that WAP applications will link business transaction systems to other machines in the future. In this respect, handheld devices would act like smart devices that could interact with a central application system, such as vending machines, storage tanks, materials handling equipment, vehicles, and the like. Box 6.8 summarizes some of the known WAP applications in business.

WAP LIMITATIONS

- It is a challenge to explore the Web using a small keypad and without a mouse.
- The devices have limited memory.

BOX 6.8

Select WAP Applications

- Computer Sciences Corporation and Nokia are working with a Finnish fashion retailer who plans to send clothing offers direct to mobile telephones using a combination of cursors, touch-screen technology, and WAP to allow would-be shoppers to hot-link to order-entry pages on the Web.

- In Finland, children already play new versions of competitive games such as "Battleship" via the cellular networks. In the music world, Virgin Mobile in the UK offers to download the latest pop hits to customers in a daily offering.

- Scala has developed several WAP products for small- to medium-sized companies, which would allow, for example, a field sales force to access customer order information and stock availability details via a WAP handset.

- A key growth area for the technology will be business-to-workforce, with companies using WAP applications to reach employees at any time. Scala is currently working on time-sheet applications and techniques for entering and filing expense claims via the mobile phone.

- Nokia says applications that will benefit from WAP include customer care and provisioning, message notification and call management, e-mail, mapping and location services, weather and traffic alerts, sports and financial services, address book and directory services, and corporate intranet applications.

- A new Internet service called ePhysician helps doctors do their jobs. This technology runs on a standard Palm Pilot and allows the doctor to order prescriptions and lab tests, schedule appointments immediately, and verify drug interactions. Doctors can request prescriptions promptly and patients will have the medicine waiting for them when they arrive at the pharmacy. Another advantage is that providing this service to doctors reduces prescription errors by 55 percent, because miscommunication between doctors, pharmacists, and staff is common.

Source: Adapted from www.mobileinfo.com.

- There are questionable connections, making reliability uncertain.
- There is a period of high latency or delays before making the connections. Because most Web sites have detailed graphics and take time to load, handheld devices cannot load pages in a reasonable amount of time.

Yet, despite the limitations, there are good reasons why WAP should be used to implement mobile Web browsing.

- WAP already has earned wide acceptance from major players such as Motorola, Nokia, and Ericsson.
- WAP development and implementation are simple. Wireless Markup Language (WML) offers just about everything that a mobile Internet application needs. The programming part is also easy to learn and implement. WML is an integral part of WAP architecture.
- The WAP security algorithm works on lines similar to Web security. The key security measures include public key cryptography and digital certificates. They are adequate for almost any transaction using WAP.

SECURITY ISSUES

The emerging world of wireless connectivity presents multiple security threats to IT infrastructures. Even wireless Internet is under attack by hackers. In WLANs, there is something called the WAP gap—the small window of time between decrypting and encrypting when the information is vulnerable. However, the chances of a security breach are low. The most significant risk is to LANs. The 802.11 family of specifications used for wireless LANs relies on a protocol that has been broken. Without the proper security measures in place, a wireless LAN can be accessed by anyone with cheap equipment and hacking skills.

Serious weaknesses also have been found in the encryption system known as Wired Equivalent Privacy (WEP), which is built into the wireless networks. One research report described WEP's use of encryption as fundamentally unsound. However, this fundamental lack of security will not slow down the adoption of wireless technology. Consumers will still continue to purchase cell phones and Palm Pilots. Security professionals currently are focusing on limiting the gap between desired and achieved levels of control. They hope that within the next two years, wireless technology will be as secure as it can be.

LEGAL ISSUES

With the growth of wireless transmission, companies are beginning to consider the liability issues. For example, Smith Barney, an investment banking firm, has paid $500,000 to settle a lawsuit brought by the family of a motorcyclist who died after being hit by a car driven by one of its brokers, who was talking on the phone while driving. Because the broker was conducting business on the way to work, the jury concluded that his company was liable for damages.

Many more such cases are likely to come up as more employees travel on the job, contacting the home office and customers by cell phone while driving. Employers have been liable for decades, but the application of negligence doctrine to wireless transmission and m-commerce is still new in day-to-day business. Civil lawsuits against employers, however, continue. In the Smith Barney case, the broker served less than a year in a work-release program after pleading guilty to manslaughter. Legal issues are covered in greater depth in Chapter 12.

MOBILE BANKING

With next-generation mobile technology already at the front door, banking applications are part of day-to-day mobile payments and banking services. Today's user values mobile banking because of the inherent time and place independence and effort-saving qualities. In fact, improvement in mobile security has been viewed as the key driver for the growth of mobile commerce.

Personal mobile devices are capable of identifying the payer and confirming the transaction in a matter of seconds. For proximity, Bluetooth and micro-payments technologies have already been applied with an impressive degree of success. When it comes to macro-payments, such as Internet purchases, security requirements are higher, usually requiring secure lines or encryption techniques to transact business. Micro- and macro-payments and where they are used are summarized in Figure 6.15 (Mallat, et al. 2004).

It should be noted that most of these mobile billing and payment processes are in an early phase of development and have yet to reach critical mass. When the mobile

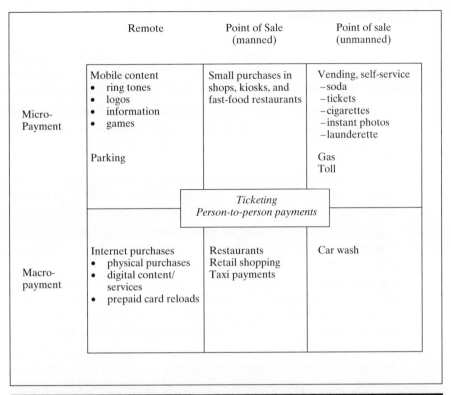

	Remote	Point of Sale (manned)	Point of sale (unmanned)
Micro-Payment	Mobile content • ring tones • logos • information • games Parking	Small purchases in shops, kiosks, and fast-food restaurants	Vending, self-service −soda −tickets −cigarettes −instant photos −launderette Gas Toll
	Ticketing *Person-to-person payments*		
Macro-payment	Internet purchases • physical purchases • digital content/ services • prepaid card reloads	Restaurants Retail shopping Taxi payments	Car wash

FIGURE 6.15   Mobile payments framework with examples

Source: Nina Mallat, Matti Rossi, and Kristiina Tuunainen, "Mobile Banking Services."
Communications of the ACM, May 2004, 43.

industry moves to a true 3G mobile networks, one can expect a surge in the number of users and the volume of the mobile traffic in mobile banking services. One reason is that mobile payments and funds transfers will become faster, easier, more convenient, and cheaper to use than what they are today.

DANCING TO THE TUNE

Music by cell phone is a relatively new trend for the increasingly mobile population. In Japan, cellular phones come equipped with music players, stereo speakers, and remote control to move through songs, adjust volume, and access additional fancy features. When a user passes by a speaker playing a favorite song, he or she simply has to aim a cell phone at the speaker. The phone recognizes the song, searches for it in the carrier's online music database, and offers it for sale. The price is high—$2.75–$3.60 per song.

In contrast, the U.S. version involves two steps—purchasing and downloading a song to a computer for use on an mp3 player at a cost of about a dollar per song. A 2004 Yankee Group survey found that Internet users' likelihood of downloading music from a licensed service declined 58 percent if the price was raised from $0.99 to $1.50—an indication of consumer sensitivity to price (Yuan 2005).

MANAGERIAL ISSUES

Adoption of any technology can be chaotic and traumatic. Designing technology for m-commerce requires a well-thought-out strategy that considers many different aspects of a business organization. The procedure for implementing wireless infrastructure is straightforward but requires careful and methodical steps. The key steps are as follows.

- Evaluate corporate needs. Survey employees or users to find the benefits a wireless network will provide for their jobs, their productivity, and their interpersonal relations. In other words, figure out how the corporate environment will be affected by the change.

- Evaluate the wireless needs. Find the best wireless technology that will meet corporate needs. Planning in advance can eliminate a number of unanticipated headaches later on, especially during testing, training, and deployment.

- Send out a request for proposal (RFP). This is a proposal in which wireless vendors are requested to bid on the project. Included in the RFP are the organization's specifications to be met by the vendor.

- Request a demo of the proposed wireless system. After evaluating all vendors' proposals, select the best two vendors based on criteria such as vendor reliability, quality of the product, customer support, price, and so on. Then ask each vendor to demonstrate a "lookalike" system before placing the order.

- Install and test the wireless system. Once you have decided on the top vendor, the system can be installed, and every component should be tested in line with every other component for integrity and reliability. Members of the company IT staff should be involved.

- Train employees. Prior to the final installation, employee training should be launched so that when the system is ready to use, company employees will be ready for the challenge. More importantly, members of the IT staff should be trained to maintain the infrastructure and ensure 24-hour service.

- Provide ongoing maintenance. Ongoing network maintenance and monitoring mean the IT staff never has to say "I'm sorry" when the system fails. All sorts of electric, hardware, software, and personnel backup are implied in this critical phase of system operation.

We can conclude that wireless technology in terms of hardware and software is all well and good when the wireless system operates effectively. The most important element in such an operation is the human staff that will address problems as they come up, the way they maintain and upgrade the system in line with changing corporate and employee needs, and how well they stay abreast of the technology to meet the demands of the wireless system they manage. Without the combined contributions and support of top management, the whole concept and adoption of wireless technology and m-commerce could be a bad experience.

Finally, the best practice to reduce support costs is to standardize wireless devices, predict wireless user problems to increase the efficiency of the help desk, and understand the limitations of wireless, such as transmitting data only for short distances as opposed to the speed and bandwidth requirements of company applications for today and down the road. In the final analysis, no m-commerce manager should promise more than what can be delivered. It is the only honest way of running a business—any business.

TRUST ISSUES

We have known for years that customers have an inherent resistance to sharing personal or private information with technology, especially Web sites, because they lack trust in the site. Gaining trust in mobile commerce can be a daunting task because of its unique features (Siau and Shen 2003). As a concept, trust is a psychological state involving confident positive expectation about another person's motive with respect to a given exchange or a relationship entailing risk. From a customer's view, trust in e-commerce is built on the Internet vendor's expertise and operational abilities. There is also goodwill trust involving trust in the Internet vendor's honesty. Until such trust is solidified based on security control, integrity, competence, as well as third-party recognition, legal framework, and experience in the field, customers will continue to have problems with trust that freely allows the exchange of personal information over the Internet. (See Figure 6.16.)

Gaining customer trust in m-commerce can be a daunting process, ranging from initial trust formation to continuous trust development. Mobile devices are ideal for wireless shopping, but their small screens, low-resolution displays, tiny multifunction keypads, and limited computational and battery power are major limitations. Limitations in bandwidth, connection stability, and function predictability are additional issues to consider (Siau and Shen 2003).

In order to enhance trust in mobile commerce, security must be designed into the entire mobile system. Encryption, digital certificates, and specialized private and public keys are among the measures that could help meet future security requirements in the mobile environment.

Finally, there are ways for companies to initiate customer trust in mobile commerce. They include:

FIGURE 6.16   Framework for building customer trust in mobile commerce

	Initial Trust Formation	Continuous Trust Development
Mobile Vendor	Familiarity Reputation Third-Party Recognition Attractive Rewards Information Quality	Site Quality Competence Integrity Privacy Policy Security Controls Open Communication Community Building
Mobile Technology	Feasibility	*Reliability* *Consistency*

Source: Adapted from Keng Siau, and Zixing Shen, "Building Customer Trust in Mobile Commerce." *Communications of the ACM,* April 2003, 93.

- Enhancing customer familiarity with the company and its business
- Building a vendor reputation that suggests certainty and less risk in doing business
- Providing attractive rewards such as free trials or gift cards to attract potential customers
- Maintaining company integrity on the basis that a mobile vendor's actions must match its promises
- Strengthening security controls via methods such as digital signatures and authorization functionality to relieve customer security concerns and enhance trust in wireless commerce
- Using external auditing to monitor operations

Regardless of the method(s) used, customer trust is crucial for the growth of mobile commerce. Building trust in general is a complex process of attitude, perception, practices, and policies. Only time can determine how likely or in what way customers are going to trust in the mobile environment.

IMPLICATIONS FOR MANAGEMENT

All indications point to the growing future of m-commerce. It will change business and consumer relationships, shift value chains, and create opportunities for healthy competition. Management should keep in mind, though, that the approach is long on technologies but short on standards. There are also other limitations. For example, how many consumers would be willing to pay a fee for accessing their checking balance or bank accounts? However, the time will come when mobile commerce and access to self-service functionality will become as common as the ATM. It will become an expected service rather than a distinct differentiator.

Mobile commerce opens doors to new ways of doing business. Mobile applications are becoming strategic parts of a company's technology base, rather than tools for tactical productivity gains. For example, location-based services will find a vacancy for you at the nearest hotel and will search for the best rate within your price range. Another way is in B2C, letting organizations more fully understand their customers' preferences. Mobile phones carried 24 hours a day are convenient personal channels for banking and instant communication from any location.

A third way mobile commerce will dominate is in mobile payments, mobile advertising, and other areas where they have a time-based and location-based value. Imagine your local electric company having to have a representative come and read your meter for billing. The information is copied or stored for at least one day before it is reported to headquarters for processing. Now imagine this information being sent directly to the company IT computer or server via a wireless network for instant update and billing. Bills can be transmitted directly to the customer's bank account for online payments by prior arrangement.

With all of these benefits and all of this potential, though, serious problems need to be addressed. With "push" advertising messages, special offers to mobile users, and so on, there is the potential to annoy rather than accommodate consumers with unwanted information, especially at the wrong time. They may react by switching off the device or filtering out messages based on source, content, and the like.

Here are three important issues that management must address.

- Consider the cultural and location-based issues that arise from introducing a mobile environment. A company with geographical locations must establish local expertise in each core location to address local demands or problems unique to the mobile practice.

- Prepare the company to offer mobile services at some point that will be strategically advantageous to the business, the product, or the manufacturing process. As mobile commerce matures, there is bound to be increasing customer demand to use mobile technology to competitive advantage.

- Experiment with the new m-technology and view the whole effort as an investment in tomorrow's way of doing business. Experimentation generates awareness and understanding of how best to put wireless communication to good and effective use.

The future of wireless lies in faster, more reliable methods of transferring data. Increased use of voice commands and audio improvements, as well as consolidation between devices, will be the next step in allowing easier communication. Secure connections also will prove to be more stable in this industry. Most importantly, speed and constant connectivity will play a vital role in the future of wireless communications.

There is no question that the future of wireless technologies lies in 3G, which is known as the next generation of wireless applications. This technology will include multimedia functions in addition to high-speed data transmission and system connections. 3G enables wireless networks to be connected at all times, compared to the old way of dialing into a network using circuit-switched communications. This generation of wireless has high speed with transmission rates up to 5 Mbps, has packet-based networks, and allows advanced roaming abilities (Dunne 2003). 3G will model the increased connectivity capabilities and improved reliability that we are looking for in the future of wireless technology.

Logic suggests that placing the Internet on mobile phones will create enormous business opportunities. Based on the experience to date, however, this has not yet happened. Mobile commerce still is struggling with the relatively slow Internet access speed. Faster networks are underway to correct the problem. Once successful, m-commerce will take on a different meaning. Some mobile devices will act as payment cards in stores. For example, a repair store won't give you an invoice after repairing an appliance. You will simply use your payment-enabled phone and the payment will be fully taken care of.

Overall, the risks in m-commerce still include merchant reliability, data integrity, user authentication, and dispute resolution between customer and merchant. These are not simple situations to resolve. There is hope that the payment card industry will solve these and other problems related to doing business via mobile.

Summary

1. M-commerce is the transmission of user data without wires. It also refers to business transactions and payments conducted in a non-PC-based environment. The main categories are information based, transaction services, and location-centric.

2. The wireless Web is a technological frontier, open and growing. It traces its roots to the invention of the radio back in 1894. Wireless networking makes it possible to connect two or more computers without the bulky cables, giving the benefits of a network with little

or no labor. The whole wireless initiative is launching a new battle against time. The focus is on *anytime*.

3. M-commerce offers several benefits: a facilitator between the e-world and the real world; easy and convenient shopping; and location-centricity to conduct business and tracking of products, services, and people. Overall, the main benefits are convenience, flexibility, and efficiency with anytime, anywhere access.

4. Wireless limitations address distance, speed, and security factors. Tracking users is the number one privacy concern.

5. In m-commerce, four critical success factors need to be monitored: mobility, personalization, global standardization, and customer profiling. Today's concentration is on customer satisfaction, paying greater attention to customer needs for services and quality.

6. A growing wireless connection standard, Bluetooth is a universal, low-cost wireless technology designed for short-range radio hookup for wireless connection among computers, scanners, and printers. In one respect, it is an enabling technology, creating a common language between various electronic devices that makes it possible for them to communicate and connect with one another. The key features include low cost, low power consumption, low complexity, and robustness.

7. The key layers of Bluetooth are the radio layer, baseband layer, and link manager protocol. The devices must be within 30 feet of each other, because radio signals suffer propagation effects at distances of greater length.

8. To have security in a wireless environment, the transmitted message must be protected all the way to its destination, and the host system must verify or authenticate the user it is communicating with. Wireless security employs wireless Ethernet networks using Wi-Fi at speeds up to 11 million bits per second over 100 meters. Other security standards include WEP, which makes it possible to encrypt messages before heading for their destination.

9. 2G digital cellular technology expedites vehicles in motion. Information is received by the online truck terminal, and the driver drives to the address where the pickup is available. A handheld device called a PDA captures the information related to that address. It prints a routing label that the driver can paste onto the box before loading the box onto the truck.

10. A cell site contains a radio transceiver and a base station controller, which manages, sends, and receives traffic from the mobiles in its geographical area to a cellular telephone switch. It employs a tower and antennas, and provides a link to the distant cellular switch called a mobile telecommunications switching office. This MTSO places calls from land-based telephones to wireless customers, switches calls between cells as mobiles travel across cell boundaries, and authenticates wireless customers before they make calls.

11. Once you move toward the edge of your cell site, your cell site's base station notes that your signal strength is diminishing. The base station in the cell site you are moving toward sees your phone's signal strength increasing. The two base stations coordinate with each other through the MTSO. At that point, your phone gets a signal on a control channel telling it to change frequencies. This handoff switches your phone to the new cell.

12. The most common standard for wireless networking is the wireless local area network, or WLAN. It is identical to a regular LAN, except that the devices are wireless. WLAN design is flexible and is becoming cheaper to deploy, but it travels only 150 feet.

13. For an organization to consider wireless LAN technology, it must consider range and coverage, throughput, security and integrity, cost and scalability, and standardization of WLANs. Related to WLAN is wireless application protocol, or WAP. It is the basis for the mobile Internet. The WAP concept is straightforward. This type of interactive electronic exchange marks the dawn of the mobile Internet revolution. The world of information is available not just on our desktops but at our fingertips, and the possibilities are truly endless.

14. Most WAP benefits are reflected in wireless applications, which reduce the reaction time of mobile professionals. Because of greater mobility and instant access to critical information, productivity can be increased dramatically from anywhere at any time. Experts envision WAP applications will be able to capture micro payments, such as parking fees and vending machine payments.

15. WAP has the limitations of low-power central processing units, small screens with questionable clarity, limited device memory, small keypads and no mouse, questionable connections for reliability, and high latency before making the connections.

16. With the growth of wireless transmission, companies are beginning to consider the liability issues, as well as managerial issues. To implement wireless infrastructure requires careful steps, which include evaluating corporate and wireless needs, sending out an RFP, requesting a demo of the proposed wireless system, installing and testing the system, training employees, and ensuring ongoing maintenance.

Key Terms

- **access point (AP)** (p. 184)
- **baseband** (p. 177)
- **Bluetooth** (p. 175)
- **data synchronization** (p. 182)
- **Link Manager Protocol (LMP)** (p. 178)
- **location-centricity** (p. 168)
- **logical link control and adaptation protocol (L2CAP)** (p. 178)
- **m-commerce** (p. 160)
- **mobile telecommunications switching office (MTSO)** (p. 183)
- **network carrier method (NCM)** (p. 189)
- **personal digital assistant (PDA)** (p. 181)
- **piconet** (p. 177)
- **radio layer** (p. 177)
- **repeater** (p. 180)
- **WAP Forum** (p. 186)
- **Wired Equivalent Privacy (WEP)** (p. 180)
- **Wireless Application Environment (WAE)** (p. 188)
- **Wireless Application Protocol (WAP)** (p. 170)
- **Wireless Datagram Protocol (WDP)** (p. 189)
- **wireless LAN (WLAN)** (p. 160)
- **Wireless Markup Language (WML)** (p. 188)
- **Wireless Network Interface Card (WNIC)** (p. 184)
- **Wireless Session Protocol (WSP)** (p. 188)
- **Wireless Transaction Protocol (WTP)** (p. 188)
- **Wireless Transport Layer Security (WTLS)** (p. 189)

Test Your Understanding

1. Define m-commerce in your own terms.
2. Briefly explain the main categories of m-commerce.
3. Explain the justification for introducing or adopting a wireless Web.
4. Summarize the key benefits and limitations of m-commerce.
5. What areas does a wireless Web work in?
6. When we talk about critical success factors of m-commerce, what do we mean?

7. Distinguish between:
   a. personalization and customization
   b. WLAN and WAE
   c. Wi-Fi and WEP

8. Explain briefly the main capabilities and limitations of Bluetooth.
9. Sketch the configuration of a piconet.
10. What is the difference between L2CAP and LMP?
11. What is a repeater? Illustrate.
12. What should an organization consider in deciding on wireless LAN technology?
13. Is there a difference between Bluetooth and WAP? Explain briefly.
14. In your own words, describe how WAP works.
15. Distinguish between:
    a. Bluetooth and piconet
    b. WTP and WTLS
    c. WDP and NCM

16. Briefly cite the key benefits and limitations of WAP.
17. What security issues are involved in WAP?
18. Summarize the legal and managerial issues in wireless transmission.
19. Exactly what differences do you find between 2.5G and 3G cellular technology? How is 4G likely to excel over its predecessors?

Discussion Questions

1. Go on the Internet and look up recent developments in the adoption of Bluetooth in banking. What were your findings?
2. If you were a consultant to a major firm interested in wireless transmission, what advice would you give the firm? How would you proceed before you recommend or do not recommend the technology? Be specific.
3. Security and privacy have been "drummed up" in virtually every area of the Internet and e-commerce. Do you think there are good reasons for this much sensitivity to these areas of concern? Discuss.
4. What is your opinion about companies funneling advertisements to your cell phone? Are there any benefits to you as a student? Can you think of any drawbacks? Write a three-page report explaining your thoughts.

Web Exercises

1. Search literature or the Web and address the features and capabilities of the latest Palm Pilot on the market.
2. Form a group of three to four and brainstorm the pros and cons of wireless transmission for a major bakery in your town. Write a two-page report summarizing your decisions.
3. Write a five-page report on the latest developments in wireless transmission for the academic area. For example, some schools already have installed wireless labs, and others have implemented a wireless environment for students to access their e-mail or authorized files.
4. Look up recent progress on 4G cellular technology and report any progress beyond what was covered in the chapter.

CHAPTER

BUILDING E-PRESENCE

Learning Objectives

The focus of this chapter is on several learning objectives:

- The main functions of a Web site
- The steps taken to build a Web site
- The importance of planning a Web site
- Factors in Web site structure
- Web design criteria
- What to consider before hiring a Web designer

IN A NUTSHELL

In the previous chapters, we discussed the role of the Internet, how to launch a business on the Web, and the technology that supports e-commerce. In this chapter, we focus on the critical component of e-commerce: the Web site as the interface between the e-merchant and the Web consumer. Remember that e-commerce is a unique way of doing business. It is available 24 hours a day, seven days a week, anywhere, and it is accessible to anyone. It allows a business not only to display products and services, but also to sell online.

Building a Web site is a major step toward doing business on the Internet. A Web site is the gateway to the Internet. Deciding how to design the site, what to include in it, how to organize its contents, and what security measures to incorporate are critical aspects of building an e-commerce infrastructure.

Take CDNow.com as an example. This e-merchant, a veteran in e-commerce, is the leading online music store. The Web site was launched in 1994 and averages 3 million visitors per day. Orders more than tripled in 2004 over 2002 during the holiday season. Reviewers praise the site for four attributes: straightforward navigation, sophisticated search functions, clearly displayed pricing and product descriptions, and customization features. Visitors can search easily for the item they want from the 500,000 items available on the site. Repeat customers can customize their visits with shortcuts to favorite artists, a wish list, and their current order status. The site has minimum graphics to

---

BOX 7.1

Criteria for a Workable Web Site

So you want a facelift for your Web site? We believe usability and creating a user friendly Web site are the most important issues. Unlike other Web design companies, we consider:

- A way to speed download time

- Adding a site map

- Making it easy for potential clients to get in touch with your company by making contact information accessible from every page on your site

- Link to home page from every other page

- Displaying products clearly

- Users to get their desired information in minimum clicks

- Design a Web site from user point of view and not the organization

- Use of technology like Flash, Java, or JavaScript

Source: www.anblik.com. Accessed 2/05.

---

ensure that it runs faster. CDNow is going global, with versions in different languages (German, Spanish, Portuguese, French, Italian, and Japanese) and alterations to accommodate the cultural, economic, and social constraints of the different regions in which it will do business. (See Box 7.1.)

Another aspect of Web site design is the match between what a business is trying to sell and the customers the site attracts. Most current Web sites fall short of meeting user needs. For example, buyers returned about 15 percent of all products bought online during the December 2004 holiday season, which is double the rate of returns of products bought at stores. Many customers found the return process tedious compared with going back to an actual store. A good Web site is flexible and intelligent enough to anticipate customer needs and accommodate them. For returns, something as simple as a downloadable return label would be a good start.

This chapter is about designing Web sites, from page design to stage or final display. We begin with the life cycle of design, then elaborate on planning and organizing the site, ways to build it, design tips and criteria, issues in site development, and how to evaluate site developers. In the next chapter, we focus on Web site maintenance and evaluation, site performance, traffic management, and Web staffing.

WHAT DOES A WEB SITE DO?

Think of a Web site as a storefront. It shows the name of the store, representative product displays, and special offers. The only difference is that a Web site is a virtual storefront, and the customers are cyber-customers. The emphasis is on speed, efficiency, good response time, and availability of procedures that expedite a sale.

A Web site is basically a series of pages with links to other pages or other sites. The pages contain text, banners (ads), graphics, and sometimes audio and video. The four key components of a site are the following.

homepage: the first page of a site; page that appears when one visits a URL address.

Web page: carrier of specific information reached by clicking a button on the homepage.

link: a connector that makes it possible to go to another Web page.

banner: a graphic display on a Web page, usually for advertising.

- Homepage: The **homepage** is the first page of a site that appears when one visits a URL address. It contains links that take the visitor to specific areas within the site and buttons to help the visitor navigate (get around) the site. It also contains general information about the e-merchant and its policies.

- Web page: A **Web page** is a carrier of specific information reached by clicking a button on the homepage. A Web page is related to a homepage as a series of paragraphs is related to a heading in a text chapter.

- Link: A **link** is a connector that makes it possible to go to another Web page on the site or on the Internet, or to go back to the homepage. A link has a specific title and directions for use.

- Banner: A **banner** is a graphic display on a Web page, usually used for advertising. The banner generally is linked to the advertiser's Web page.

A Web site has some special benefits over a brick-and-mortar storefront. Your site can help you:

1. Reach millions of customers quickly and reliably. In 2004, more than 230 million people worldwide were connected to the Internet, and more than 45 percent of them were well educated. These customers look for convenience, ease of finding services or products, and the ability to order directly from their computer.

2. Establish a presence in cyberspace. The entry-level goal of a new Internet business is presence. The new Web site displays "who we are" information, which may include office hours, location, a map showing how to get to the brick-and-mortar location, and perhaps featured products. Thousands of companies begin at this level before they turn the site into an interactive trading place.

3. Leverage advertising costs. Unlike radio, TV, or newspapers, where limited time or space is available at high cost, advertising on the Internet is cheaper, quicker, and limitless. Including a company's Internet address in a small print ad or a 30-second TV or radio spot should direct thousands of customers to the company's Web site to do business.

4. Reduce the cost of serving customers. A Web site can offer a variety of labor-saving services—application forms, information via links or e-mail, and order handling and shipment without human intervention. Answering frequently asked questions on a Web site cuts down on phone calls. Asking for feedback from customers via e-mail also can provide information while the experience is fresh in the customer's mind.

5. Promote public relations. A Web site on the Internet is like passing business cards to thousands of potential customers. It is like saying, "Here is what I do, what I am, and what I can do for you. You can reach me anytime, from anywhere, and I'll be available." The Web site also allows for the timely dissemination of information about a new product or a special sale.

6. Reach international markets and customers. The Internet is populated by millions of prospective customers all over the world. The main constraint is collecting payment for products and services.

7. Test-market new products or services. One or more Web pages can display changes in your product or service faster than you can feed a fax machine. In an increasingly time-sensitive environment where strategic thinking is critical, the time gap between manufacturing and retailing is becoming increasingly narrow.

THE BUILDING LIFE CYCLE–FROM PAGE TO STAGE

Site building is the science of figuring out what you as a site designer want the site to do and then creating a blueprint for the building process. The building life cycle is shown in Figure 7.1. Planning begins with developing the site's goals and collecting client opinions. The next step is to define the audience and the competition. The third step is the creative phase. The designer begins to build the site—forming a skeleton, picking the metaphors, and mapping out the navigation. The final step is the visual design.

PLAN THE SITE

The planning phase of site building is the foundation for great Web design. It is the blueprint for designing form, function, navigation, and interface. Planning is defining the site's goals in advance. Think of how many sites are on the Internet: Some are good,

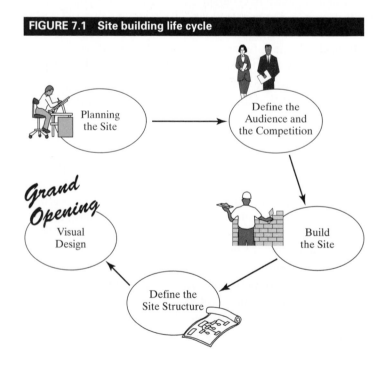

FIGURE 7.1   Site building life cycle

BOX 7.2

The Good, the Bad, and the Ugly

What makes a Web site "good" depends on your biases and criteria. Some resources that rate Web sites focus primarily on design. Others focus more on content, ease of use, uniqueness, currency, and organization, as well as general appeal. One of the top-rated subject guides that reviews Web sites, *McKinley's Magellan,* ranks sites by the following criteria:

- Depth: Is it comprehensive and up-to-date?
- Ease of exploration: Is it well organized and easy to navigate?
- Net appeal: Is it innovative? Does it appeal to the eye or the ear? Is it funny? Is it hot, hip, or cool? Is it thought provoking? Does it offer new technology or a new way of using technology?
- Content: Just how broad, deep, and amazingly thorough is the information? Are there good links? Good clips? Is the information accurate? Complete? Up-to-date?
- Presentation: Is the page beautiful? Colorful? Easy to use? Does it lead visitors through the information nicely? Does it use video, audio, and original graphics? Does it break new ground?
- Experience: Is this fun? Is it worth the time? Will we recommend it to friends? All things considered, does this site deliver the goods?

Good content, good organization, and ease of navigation are the top criteria for a good Web site.

Several things annoy visitors to a Web site:

- Blinking text and animation or other fancy tricks done just for the sake of showing off
- Broken links and dead-end paths
- Promises for functions, products, or contents that are not delivered via the site

Examples of "Good" Web Sites
www.yahoo.com (Yahoo)

www.bigbook.com (Big Book Online Yellow Pages)

www.parentsplace.com (Parents Place)

www.aetna.com/home.htm (Aetna Insurance Co.)

www.sun.com (Sun Microsystems)

www.disney.com (Disney)

www.nytimes.com (*New York Times*)

Examples of "Not So Good" Web Sites
www.pdxchamber.org (Portland Chamber of Commerce)

home.netscape.com (Netscape Home Page)

www.webpress.net/akc (American Kennel Club)

www.intel.com (Intel)

Source: www.tbchad.com/ipngweb.html, www.tbchad.com/gwebresp.html.

more are bad, and hundreds are ugly. Software is the main culprit. Sample good, bad, and ugly Web sites are represented in Box 7.2.

The overall objective of a customized Web site is to:

1. Speed up the interactive process

2. Reduce human intervention to a minimum

3. Save time

4. Make buying and selling through the site cost-effective

The aim of the planning stage is to provide for quick application development and deployment. Doing this means organizing the site—creating an efficient structure for the files and folders that make up the site. Ideally, the content should be finalized first.

Defining a site's goals involves two things: determining who will be involved in defining the goals and whether there is time or a need for formal definition. The scale of the Web site project is a major factor in deciding whether a formal process is necessary.

Another aspect of the planning phase is asking questions to decide on the site's mission, the short- and long-term goals of the site, who the intended audience is, and why people will want to visit the site. Once the questions are agreed on, they should be prioritized and passed on to involved personnel for conversion into goals. The hard part is to distill the final list into a master list of goals that are acceptable to all participants.

Part of planning is deciding on how the Web site will tie to inventory control, database lookup, personalization, and the like. Any tie-in should be part of the logical design that will make the connection operational. For example, visitors to www.sae.org, the Web site of the Society of Automotive Engineers (SAE International), can personalize their view of the 20,000+ page Web site, making it easier to find technical information about topics that are of interest to them. And because the majority of the Web site is drawn in real time from a database, visitors are provided with the latest technical information that SAE has to offer.

DEFINE THE AUDIENCE AND THE COMPETITION

In this phase, the key question is: How can you design a site if you don't know who will be visiting it? Determining your audience can pay handsome dividends. Defining the audience includes not just who the users are, but their goals and objectives, as well. The first step is to generate a list of intended audiences. If the list gets too long, divide it into categories.

Let's say a bank wants to put up a Web site to promote its services, with a focus on loans. Audience categories might be current brick-and-mortar customers, cyber-customers, young adults looking for auto loans, new commercial companies looking for commercial loans, contractors looking for lines of credit, and new homeowners looking for mortgage loans. Within the auto loan category, one can find people who need a car loan right away, those who need a car loan for the next season, and those who are just shopping. The audience list is ranked and agreed on before the final list is produced.

Another way of looking at defining the audience is to identify what prospective customers want. Here is what retail cyber-surfers look for when they shop online, according to research by BizRate.com, a firm that judges e-commerce Web sites using customer feedback (www.bizrate.com/ratings_guide/guide.xpml).

1. Competitive product prices
2. Well-designed product representation
3. Good product selection
4. Reliable shipping and handling
5. On-time delivery
6. Easy ordering
7. Valuable information about products

8. Posted privacy policy

9. User-friendly navigation tools

Any way you look at Web site design, the goal is to enhance site visitors' experience by escorting them quickly to the merchandise that best suits them. Speed and responsiveness are crucial. Remember the seven-second rule: If visitors wait more than eight seconds, they most likely click out and try the competition.

In addition to defining the audience, you need to create scenarios or design test cases of customers accessing the site for various reasons and see how well the site matches their needs. Another way of testing the site design is to select a representative set of users. Write up a scenario about each type of user to see how well the site will deliver what they're looking for. This exercise is part of defining the overall cyber-environment.

The second part of this step is competitive analysis. The idea is to be aware of what other sites are doing. Make a list of your competitors' Web sites, evaluate them, and see where your site needs work. Start with evaluation criteria such as personalization, consistency, and ease of navigation. (Web site evaluation is covered in detail in Chapter 8.) User experience, defining the audience, creating scenarios, and evaluating the competition are part of the *design document*—a prerequisite to moving ahead to the actual design.

BUILD SITE CONTENT

This phase pinpoints what the site will contain. The focus is this phase is on gathering the pieces for creating and organizing the structure of the site. The pieces represent the content. For example, if I were building a Web site for a bank, the homepage would contain basic information about each department (loans, customer service, trust, checking, and savings) as well as basic company information such as privacy policy, location, banking hours, and names of officers.

Here is what one company's boss suggested as a list of necessary items.

1. Company logo

2. A catalog of products, with pictures

3. A bio of the company, including a picture of the boss

4. A page of testimonials from loyal customers

5. A form for placing an online order

6. A counter showing that the site has received a high number of hits so far

To harness ideas about the prospective Web site, it is helpful to create a list of the content and functional requirements. Pass the list by key department heads or through a committee to make sure there is support and consensus before you proceed with the actual design. Another approach is to have each department create its own list of content and present the resulting integrated list for all to approve. You now have a **content inventory,** which can be used to launch the actual construction phase. Box 7.3 illustrates this process.

content inventory: a list of the company activities (contents) that make up the Web site.

When the content inventory list is final, determine the order of priority of each function or department. If the focus of the Web site is loans, then the loan function should be prominent. This ties into the goal of the site and the audience for which the

---

BOX 7.3

Sample Content Inventory for a Typical Commercial Bank

Homepage

1. Bank services
2. Personal deposit accounts
3. About loans
4. Trust and investment services
5. What's new?
6. Contact us

Bank Services

1. Automated teller machines (ATMs)
2. Basic commercial checking accounts
3. Certificates of deposit (CDs)
4. Foreign currency exchange
5. Money market accounts
6. Regular commercial checking accounts

Loan Department

1. Personal loans
2. Home equity line of credit
3. Commercial deposit accounts
4. Commercial loans
5. Money market checking

Trust and Investment Services

1. Investment management
2. Personal representative
3. Guardianship
4. Living trusts
5. Life insurance trusts
6. Escrow
7. Testamentary trusts
8. Trust services

---

site is being designed. After this step is completed, the designer needs to determine the feasibility of each function. For example, are technology and money available to buy or build the function? If money is limited, you may have to drop some functions in order to meet budget constraints and deadlines.

The result of this phase is a new addition to the design document, which could be labeled *content and functional requirements*. It should include a brief description of how the content inventory was gathered and finalized. This type of documentation will come in handy later on when you need to maintain the Web site if someone other than the original Web designer does the work.

DEFINE THE SITE STRUCTURE

In this phase, the focus is on creating a good site structure, exploring various metaphors to represent content items, defining the architectural blueprints, and deciding how the user will navigate the site. Once a **site structure** is created, everything else should fall into place. This step ensures easy site navigation and well-laid-out pages and templates. Think of the structure as a skeleton that holds the entire site together. It promotes order, discipline, organization, and trust.

site structure: an organized layout of a merchant's departments or functions that becomes the basis for the Web site.

Exploring metaphors as a way of trying to visualize the site's structure generates ideas and alternative ways of approaching site design. Metaphors can be organizational or visual. Organizational metaphors usually rely on the company's existing structure.

For example, if you are creating a bank Web site focused on loans, your metaphor could be a commercial bank where services are grouped logically by type (mortgage loans, commercial loans, bridge loans). Visual metaphors rely on graphic elements that fit the nature of the site. For example, if you were designing a Web site to sell music products and allow users to play music, you would include icons like "start," "pause," and "stop." This way, users don't have to learn anything new. Instead, they can rely on their experience with CD players.

Defining the architectural blueprint involves diagrams showing how elements of the site are grouped and how they relate to one another. Figure 7.2 illustrates architectural blueprints for our banking example. It is easy to understand the proposed design of the site and the order in which it is being planned. The client can see it and comment on it before it is adopted as the final blueprint.

In this phase, you also will define site navigation. How will visitors use the site? How will they get from one page to another? How do we make sure they don't end up on a competitor's site? Local navigation can take a number of forms. It can be a list of topics like the ones found on Yahoo! (www.yahoo.com). It can be a menu of choices such as those found on Bank of America's Web site. It also can be a list of related items such as loans, checking, and savings on a bank's Web site. For examples of Web site navigation, see this book's Web site, www.prenhall.com/awad. (Look up the Webmonkey site at www.webmonkey.com for information on navigating a multipart article via links to each section.)

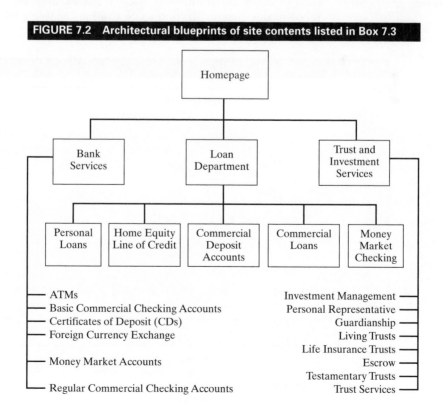

FIGURE 7.2   Architectural blueprints of site contents listed in Box 7.3

DEVELOP THE VISUAL DESIGN

The final phase of a site-building life cycle is developing the visual design. The goal is to give visitors a mental map of the Web site: where they are, where they have been, and how to proceed. The first step is to use a layout grid to show how well the icons, buttons, banners, and other elements fit together. Like the format of a letter, a layout grid is a template that shows the focus of every page. The company's brand should appear on each page to reinforce the company's image. An example of a layout grid is shown in Figure 7.3.

One way of getting started is to see how many page types can be generated from the site structure listing. Page style and form should be consistent throughout the site. Content is the critical part of a page, and that's where to start. Then add other elements like branding, advertising, navigation buttons, page titles, and headers and footers.

Another aspect of the design phase is establishing the look and feel of the site via page mock-ups. Mock-ups integrate the design sketches with the layout grids. Once completed, the visual design also is incorporated into the design document. The design document is now complete. It shows how to construct the site, add content, and revise the site after the site is up and running.

Web site design has, as its main goal, attracting and retaining visitors. Personalization is critical: The designer should tailor Web content directly to a specific user. Tracking the user's behavior on the site will help in doing this. Software on the site then can modify content to fit the needs of the particular user. With personalization, users can get information quickly and more reliably than on traditional sites. **Cookies** may be the most recognizable personalization tools. Cookies enable a Web site to greet a user by name.

cookie: bits of code that sit in a user's browser memory and identify the visitor to the Web site.

FIGURE 7.3 Layout grid

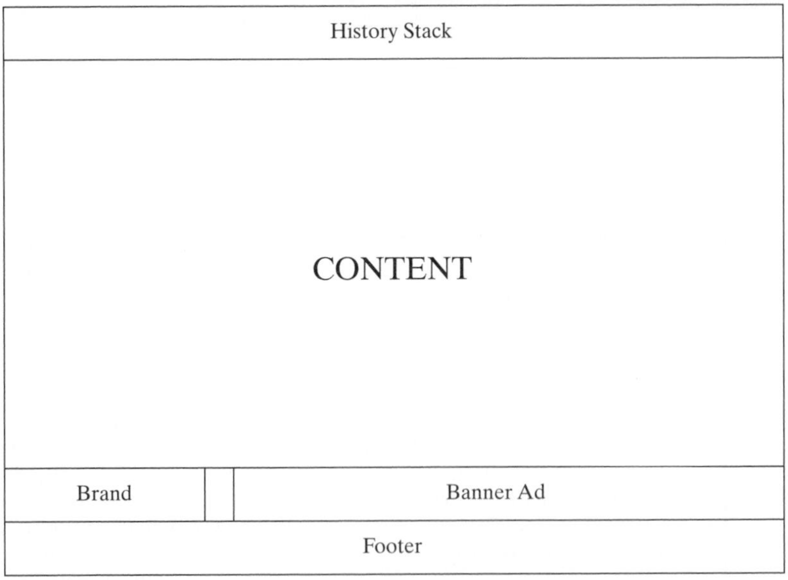

History Stack

CONTENT

Brand	Banner Ad

Footer

Source: Adapted from John Shiple, "Information Architecture Tutorial," *Webmonkey,* www.hotwired.com/webmonkey/98/28/index 4a_page2.html.

DESIGN LANGUAGES

The early years of Web site design began with Hypertext Markup Language (HTML). It is the first tool used to help in designing a Web site. The military as well as academic institutions were the first groups to use the Web. Their goal was simply to exchange information. Tim Berners-Lee created HTML as we know it today. In 1990, he imagined a simple hypertext language that could be used to transform documents onto the Web. Initially, it was used to indicate whether a paragraph was needed, a title was in place, or to describe the content of a Web site. Because HTML was also text based, anyone could master the language.

Inevitably, the demand for more stylized, highly colorful Web sites emerged. A graphical browser called Mosaic soon appeared. With it came increased demand from Web designers for color text, color background, pictures, different fonts, and so on. In response, a talented college student named Marc Andreessen added the tag <img> to his product, the Mosaic browser. The <img> tag inserts an image, image map, or animation into a Web page. A tag is an HTML code that identifies the contents of a Web page to a search engine index.

Andreessen eventually went to California and formed Netscape. Bill Gates, the chairman of the board and founder of Microsoft, saw the endless possibilities of Web design and began to add different tags to his browser, Internet Explorer. The <marquee>, <iframe>, and <bgsound> tags eventually were supported by Internet Explorer, which posed an interesting question. If the current trend continued down its intended path, Internet Explorer and Netscape would support two completely different versions of HTML 3.0, and there would be no way anybody could view all the sites the Web had to offer. Either the browsers would have to come together and form a single, compatible form of the current version of HTML, or Web surfers eventually would have to choose between browsers. Another solution would be for Web designers to create multiple versions of their Web sites. Such a solution would be prohibitive to provide.

Java became another popular language for designing Web sites. When John Gage of Sun Microsystems and Marc Andreessen of Netscape announced that their browser was going to be using Java exclusively, the language became a reality. Primitive applications of Java could no longer satisfy the public's need for bold, multimedia-enriched content. Out of this need rose the popularity of such technologically advanced utilities as Macromedia Flash and Shockwave, and next-generation languages like Extensible Markup Language (XML) and Vector Markup Language (VML). These advances increased visual pleasure exponentially without a comparably large increase in file size or loading time.

New-age languages have given designers more room for creativity and imagination. The offspring of Internet cornerstones HTML, XML, and VML integrate graphics with documents much better than earlier versions did. Because they are developed by software giant Microsoft, XML and VML figure to be a big part of Web design in the near future.

CONSTRUCTING YOUR WEB SITE

Like any brick-and-mortar site, a cyber-store needs a good location, a good look and feel, and a secure site to attract and engage customers. How should you build an ideal store? The range of choices is anywhere from having a Web-based service such as Yahoo! Store build a small-scale operation in a hurry, to enlisting the help of an Internet service provider to start small and grow, to doing it yourself with off-the-shelf software loaded on your own Web server.

STOREFRONT BUILDING SERVICE

A new class of dot.coms will help you build a customized online store quickly and cheaply. Most such Web-based services offer a Web catalog of up to 100 products and ensure the proper linkup to an online merchant account. The service includes giving your store a Web address, managing the Web traffic, and maintaining the store on its Web servers. The main drawback of this approach is the standardized nature, color scheme, and look of the site.

Services on the Internet allow you to build your own sites—and some of them are also free. For example, Bigstep.com provides an easy-to-build site environment, where you can sell as many products as you like. Getting a merchant account that will allow you to accept credit cards requires paying a nominal monthly fee plus a small fee per transaction. The downside is that Bigstep uses its logo on your site to advertise its presence. The logo links back to Bigstep's Web site (www.bigstep.com), which may compete with the products you sell. There is also the question of how well the ISP manages traffic spikes.

As summarized in CNN.com's experience in Box 7.4, having a traffic management strategy in place is important. Your options depend on budget and time frame. Since traffic spikes tax server load and network bandwidth, the IT manager should know which one is the weak link during heavy traffic. For example, you can have plenty of bandwidth, but not enough server power, and vice versa. Some vendors sell hardware that optimizes connections to reduce the servers' overhead and improve connection times by up to

---

BOX 7.4

Weathering a Crisis

On September 11, 2001, news-hungry users from around the world flocked to CNN.com for the latest headlines about the terrorist attacks in New York City and Washington, D.C. On an average day, the site serves about forty million page views. On September 11, that number climbed to more than 162.4 million page views, then to 337.4 million the following day.

Spikes like those called for drastic measures. "The first step we took was to slim down the page. We took off the graphics and the pictures and kept the most relevant information out there," says CNN.com spokeswoman Elizabeth Barry. At 10 a.m., she explains, the site's homepage consisted of the CNN logo, a single image of the World Trade Center, and minimal text.

But streamlined content wasn't enough. Without additional hardware, CNN.com could never have handled its increased load. Fortunately,

as part of AOL Time-Warner, CNN.com could borrow servers from its sister Web sites. Once engineers had increased the site's server capacity, the homepage regained much of its usual look, including links and multiple images. Webmasters kept advertisements off the site for several days, however, in order to free on-screen real estate for news content.

Even so, CNN.com did all it could to reduce the load on its servers by routing visitors to alternate information channels. "Another thing we did was to increase the number of breaking news emails that we sent out," Barry explains. "That way people who couldn't get to the site could still get the information they needed." By sending news to users who had subscribed to their email list, CNN could deliver news as it happened, while decreasing the load on its Web server from users looking for the latest news.

Source: www.savetz.com/articles/newarch_spikes.php.

20 percent. Good site design and proper configuration of your Web servers can ease the workload during traffic spikes. See www.savetz.com/articles/ newarch_spikes.php.

WEB-HOSTING SERVICE

By definition, Web hosting means placing an organization's Web page or Web site on a dedicated server that can be accessed via the Internet. (See www.e-formation.conz/ glossary.asp.) Think of the Web as a massive collection of Web sites, all hosted on computers called Web servers worldwide. The server where your Web site lies is called the Web host. So Web-hosting clients simply upload their Web sites to a dedicated Web server that the ISP maintains to ensure fast and continuous connection to the Internet. (See www.1stdomain.net/info/ glossary.html.)

Hundreds of organizations can help you build a presence on the Internet. They do it in a simple four-step process:

1. A Web host representative meets with you and explains the aspects of Web design, Web hosting, e-mail, and e-marketing. The session usually ends with a "not-to-exceed" price for the entire project.

2. The Web host begins to collect content from you to build a custom Web site. All graphic design and marketing material is done on the Web host's premises by specialists. Its programmers write the code and test the site for functionality, consistency, reliability, and scalability before it takes the next step.

3. Once the Web site passes the test, the firm begins to write the keywords and metatags and submits the Web site to leading search engines, Web directories, and industry sites.

4. A reputable Web host also supports maintenance and future enhancements in a yearly contract or a long-term agreement.

One advantage of enlisting an Internet service provider (ISP) to build and maintain your site is the support you get and the chance to grow your site as your e-business expands. An ISP is generally experienced in store-building technology that is more sophisticated what is available on sites like Bigstep. More and more ISPs license versions of their e-commerce software to help you build your own store. Other Web-hosting services such as Verio (www.veriostore.com) help you establish a merchant account and build shipping and sales tax calculations into the site. See this book's Web site, www.prenhall.com/awad, for some examples of these services.

DO IT YOURSELF

Setting up your own e-commerce Web site costs more; requires experience; and forces you to worry about security, management of Web traffic, and responding to technical and procedural details 24 hours a day. Costs are incurred for site development, hardware, bandwidth, and full-time Web administration. The main benefits are unlimited upgrades, customization, better control over performance, and potential for growth.

Over the long haul, this approach is worth the effort for a large business that is committed to online business. For a small business, it is usually cheaper and quicker to hire a Web designer to do the job, but a company employee also should be trained to become the Webmaster to maintain the site on a daily basis.

WEB NAVIGATION DESIGN

Designing successful Web navigation is an art and a science. The best way to approach Web design is to put yourself in the shoes of the prospective visitor. The merchant's goals and those of the user are often different. Profiling the user up front can help predict problems in the way the Web site will be navigated.

Take the bank example. A Web developer helps a commercial bank set up a Web site. In the early stages of discussion with upper management, the developer asks managers what they expect to get out of the site. What are their needs and concerns? In a few weeks, the designer creates a site that meets these needs. The bank is happy. However, when the site debuts on the Internet, e-mail includes comments from unhappy customers and new visitors. The number of hits is low, and visits to the site hardly go beyond the homepage. Four months later, the site is virtually abandoned. The bank management has the impression that the whole idea of being on the Internet is a bad joke.

In reality, no one stopped to consider the visitor's goals and how those goals differed from those of the bank. (See Table 7.1.) Conflicting goals and poor communication can spell doom for the site. When visitors can't achieve their goals, the bank eventually suffers the most in lost customers and substantial development costs. The Web developer, the bank, and select users should sit down and think through goals and expectations. Creating profiles and conceptualizing site design in terms of possible scenarios goes a long way toward avoiding such problems.

CREATING USER PROFILES

You are the vice president of operations of a medium-sized commercial bank near a major university. Your bank is best known for customer service and stability. So you develop an idea for a Web site that reflects this image. Think of the type of customer you attract and how unique your customer base is compared to the competition across the street. The area where your bank is located is competitive. Each competing bank has a Web site and is trying to attract new customers. What do people want from a bank like yours? What are their goals, besides opening a basic checking account? Some customer profiles can be helpful in answering these questions.

customer profile: brief study of the type of person who might visit your Web site.

Customer profiles are brief studies of the types of persons who might visit your site. Here are profiles of two customers who might represent part of your target audience.

TABLE 7.1 Goals	
Bank	*Visitor*
Wants to know more about customer	Wants to surf the site with privacy
Wants to generate revenue via the site	Wants to save money via the Internet
Coaches visitor to click first on loan button	Annoyed at having to start with loans
Rushes visitor to take a virtual tour of the bank	Irritated because other information is more important
Asks for personal information about banking needs	Feels personal information is none of the bank's business

GARY.   Gary is an assistant professor in his early thirties. He is recently divorced and has custody of his two children. Because of the divorce settlement, he is sensitive about his financial privacy. He has been living in a small community for more than two months and is interested in a bank that values customer service, located within a few miles of the university or his residence. In a couple of years, when he hopes to get tenure at the university, he plans to build a large home, replace his 1999 Toyota Corolla with a new Lexus, and open a trust fund for each of his children.

Since he moved to town, Gary has been trying various banks based on newspaper ads and recommendations from colleagues. He complains to associates that most banks are impersonal and have high charges for checking, use of the ATM, and overdrawn accounts. Gary is not sure about finding his ideal bank on the Internet, but he'd rather try that than ask more people the same questions.

MONIQUE.   Monique is a 22-year-old, fourth-year student at the same university. She is a member of a sorority. She comes from a close-knit family and has always valued personal contacts and attention. She heard about your bank's site from another student. Because she has one full year before she graduates, Monique hopes she can handle her personal and financial needs on the Web from the university computer lab. If she opens a checking and a savings account, the rest of her sorority could be attracted to do business with your bank. Monique worries that cookies and other snooping devices might invade her privacy, and that she might end up with a lot of junk mail. She is willing to try a Web site that looks conservative, presents a nice appearance, has value-added content, and might have a phone number that can be answered by a human voice.

The two profiles are not the same, but you can sense shared concerns that alert you to the patterns you should incorporate into the site. In this case, privacy, warmth, personal attention, and responsiveness should be central items in designing your bank's Web site. You also can predict that because of the university-oriented community, reasonable or low service charges to students might make a hit.

USING SCENARIOS

scenario: situation that helps you view the navigation process and the site as a point of entry.

Another way of conceptualizing prospective site users is through scenarios. A **scenario** helps you view the navigation process and the site as a point of entry. To illustrate, take Monique's user profile. How would she be likely to move through the site? What problems might she encounter? How would she handle such problems? When you add predictions or likely actions to a user profile, it becomes a scenario. For example, Monique is interested in accessing the bank's Web site. She's already got a browser on her PC, although she lacks confidence about navigating on the Internet. The first thing she looks for is easy-to-follow instructions, icons, or layouts to take her where she wants to go on the site. Because she is sensitive about privacy, the privacy statement button should be easy to access. Also, because she is more interested in information about opening a checking account, an icon that will take her to this function should be visible on the homepage.

If Monique cannot find these two key items on the homepage, she might lose interest and simply go elsewhere. This means that you need to build flexible navigation capabilities into your site if you want to attract Monique and her sorority sisters.

In Gary's case, the first thing he looks for is ease of navigation, a strong privacy statement, warm color that gives an impression of personalization and security, and trust.

Because he is sensitive about privacy, the privacy statement should be easily accessible from the homepage. Because he is interested in setting up a trust fund for each of his children, the homepage should have trust funds listed as one of the bank's specialties. Without these two features, Gary will likely click away to another bank's Web site.

What About Cultural Differences?

In designing Web sites for conducting business in different countries, the focus should go beyond just providing sites with different language versions. Sensitivity to and consideration for cultural concerns are critical in establishing an international presence.

One aspect of culture is color. As we shall see in Chapter 8, different colors mean different things to different people. For example, the color white represents purity in the United States, but the Japanese think white represents death. To the Chinese, a red background represents happiness; in the United States, red represents danger. The bottom line is that people in general learn patterns of seeing, sensing, and feeling from living within their social environment in the country of their birth. This means that people with different cultural backgrounds react differently to a globally generic Web site. In a Web site, unique features must allow the targeted consumer to feel at home. This includes the use of the native language, the country's national flag, or color as cues to attract a wider pool of visitors to the site.

Design a User-Friendly Site

A major conclusion drawn from profiles and scenarios is that you must design user-friendly Web sites. In fields such as Web architecture, a lot of effort is spent understanding user behavior and preferences. The same is true when assessing site navigation. The trick is to make your site as easy to learn and navigate as possible. Another trick is to anticipate problems. Remember what it was like the first time you accessed a Web site? I remember my first class in speech, when the instructor tried to help us design a framework for making a speech: Stand up, speak up, and shut up. The problem with this three-step process is that it lacks detail. A better framework would be: Walk to the podium, lay your notes on the lectern, greet the audience, present your speech, provide meaningful conclusions, end with a summary of sorts, recognize the applause, take your seat, and so on.

Providing guidance for Web site visitors is much the same. The easier it is for first-time visitors, the more likely they are to return. Remember, the stability, reliability, and security of a Web site is paramount. Sites that leverage the power of the Web in developing unique solutions to common problems will be way ahead of other sites in the same industry.

Design Guidelines

Several tips regarding Web site design are worth considering. Each idea can be as good as others, because design means integration of color, content, layout, speed, and the like. See Box 7.5 for a select list of Web design tips based on the author's experience. Remember, with no standard guidelines, it is rare that a Web site does everything right. No one even knows what that is. Luxury retailers have yet to learn that glitz is great, but not online.

Remember that no Web site is perfect. Some of the best sites continue to have problems like inconsistent graphics and outdated information, but with smart design, a less-is-more attitude may be all that is needed to drive up your company's Web traffic.

┌─────────────────────────┐
│   BOX 7.5   │
└─────────────────────────┘

Design Tips

1. Keep the site simple.

2. Web design involves problem solving. Clearly define the problem that needs to be solved.

3. Users come to your site for content. Give it to them fast and simple. Keep content current and structure it into simple hierarchies.

4. Transmission speed is an important aesthetic matter. You have 3 seconds to convince a user not to use the Back button. Something should be displayed on the screen immediately, and it better be interesting.

5. Everything on the screen should load in 30 seconds. The display should be fast.

6. Site performance is critical. Response time should not be longer than 8 seconds.

7. Site availability can make the difference between a one-time visitor and a loyal customer. Brownouts and outages cost time, money, and nowadays, a drop in stock valuation. The site should be available 24/7.

8. The organization fielding the e-business application needs to know what kind of traffic the site can handle. Victoria's Secret's experience was an example of successfully driving visitors to a site, and then not being able to serve them. The site attracted an unexpectedly high number of visitors, bringing its ability to display products to a virtual halt.

9. Make sure the company's name and logo are clear and visible on each Web page.

10. Be careful not to waste too much effort on bells and whistles. Keep graphics and other bandwidth-intensive design items to a minimum.

11. If you use animation, make sure it has a theme, story, or point. Otherwise, avoid gimmicky pages with animation that walks across the page.

12. Make it a habit to save your work periodically.

13. Remember to use color carefully. (Color is covered in detail in Chapter 8.)

14. If a visitor leaves the homepage to go elsewhere within the site, make sure he or she can easily return. Each page should have a link back to the homepage.

15. When designing a complex site, identify the decision makers, define the goals, and sketch a way for the design team to solve the design problems.

DESIGN CRITERIA

In designing Web sites, the primary goal is for visitors to experience the site as you intended them to. If the site presents information, or distributes or sells a product or service, the visitor must view the site as having credibility. Quality and reliability also must be assured. A Web site is a part of an e-business strategy that should be designed and managed effectively. Design criteria such as appearance and quality assurance, public exposure, consistency, scalability, security, performance, and navigation and interactivity are among the key factors to consider.

APPEARANCE AND QUALITY DESIGN

Is the site aesthetically pleasing? Most site developers agree that mixing text with graphics adds interest. Allowing text to flow around graphics or varying the margins also tends to make the content more attractive. The goal is to make the site easy to read, easy to navigate, and easy to understand. The attractiveness of a Web site has a lot to do with quality assurance. **Quality assurance (QA)** is a process used to check the readiness of a site before it is loaded on the Web. Visitors want to *trust* the site and be assured that it is reliable and has no glitches or blips, regardless of the frequency of access.

quality assurance (QA): a process used to check the readiness of a site before it is loaded on the Web.

style guide: a template designed to measure the materials used to build the Web site.

To live up to this level of quality, a Web developer must live up to a set of standards that will inspire trust in the site's visitors. These standards are established through a **style guide.**

To create a style guide, a Web developer pulls together all the existing information about the Web site design. The style guide includes corporate guidelines for maintaining the company image, such as how to use logos, slogans, and images; acceptable fonts; and so on. The goal is to provide the site with visual consistency. An extreme example of inconsistency in site design is using wild fonts for one page and conservative ones in the next page, without regard to how they blend with the content or the flow of messages.

PUBLIC EXPOSURE

E-business is public. Any mistakes, redundancies, misrepresentations, oversights, or unauthorized content or links are immediately displayed for the world to see. These problems all have legal, marketing, and public relations implications. The Web designer should verify that content as well as form are credible and reliable at all times.

Public exposure includes site availability—uninterrupted service 24 hours a day, seven days a week. The visitor in Saudi Arabia who just logged on to your site does not care if it is midnight in the U.S. To ensure availability, the networking and technology infrastructure must support this type of demand.

VIEWABILITY AND RESOLUTION

The key question here is whether the site is viewable in different browsers. The two major browsers are Netscape Communicator and MS Internet Explorer. Also, everyone uses different resolutions and screen sizes. Although a site will look best at a certain resolution, it should be viewable in 800 × 600 without a side-scroll and also be viewable in 1,024 × 768 and higher without the background tiling horribly.

CONSISTENCY

The fonts and font styles must be consistent so the Web site and contents will appear the same on all visitors' screens. Depending on the design tools used and the browser, a site might appear restricted on Netscape but not on Microsoft Explorer, or vice versa. To prevent this from happening, a Web designer programming in HTML needs to fine-tune the final draft of the site, or the site should advise the visitor as to the best browser to use before accessing the site. Fonts and font styles are a problem for most sites. A site should have not only a design theme, but a text theme as well. If you like Arial, stick to Arial for all your text, except your title and button graphics. The easiest way to ensure consistency is to make sure your site uses cascading style sheets.

SCALABILITY

scalability: potential for enhancement or upgrade.

Does the site provide a seamless growth path, and does it have the potential for enhancement or upgrading in the future? **Scalability** (ability to upgrade the site) is an important consideration for new Web sites because it is difficult to determine the number of future visitors. A Web site should be capable of being expanded as usage increases and as needs change. This means protection of the initial investment in site construction.

SECURITY

Protecting a site from hackers is a tricky business, especially when it comes to deciding on the security software, encryption algorithm, and methodology to ensure secure trading online. The site should show only what the visitor wants to see. Web sites where access security is critical should run on a dedicated secure server. In banking, passwords may be required to allow customers access to their bank accounts. E-security is covered in detail in Chapter 13.

PERFORMANCE

Security has a direct relationship to performance. The more security is embedded into a Web environment, the more a Web designer worries about performance. It is like catching a flight on a busy evening. The more checkpoints that must be passed before boarding a flight, the longer it take to board.

From the end user's view, performance is judged based on the answer to the question: How long does it take for the page to appear? Sites that are heavy on text often download instantly. Graphics take time and can bring downloading of the page to a halt. Most search engines have a 45-second timer: If the site takes longer than 45 seconds to download, it displays the message "can't find" or "can't access site."

NAVIGATION AND INTERACTIVITY

navigation: synonymous with "surfing"—how a visitor gets from one page in a Web site to another.

A Web site must be logically linked and allow visitors to get to another page that is of interest to them and then back to the homepage. Icons or buttons should be formatted and laid out to expedite **navigation.** Sometimes an explanation is given to describe the function of each icon and where it will take the visitor.

Think of navigation as a house with multiple entrances. The classic metaphor is that a house has only one entrance. In reality, there is a back door, a garage door, a dog door, or a window ajar on the second floor. Navigation must allow for a variety of access points, depending on the visitor's experience and needs.

Navigation and interactivity are closely related. Easily navigable sites promote interactivity. In banking, for example, a Web site may offer customers a variety of investment products described in a number of pages. After making a selection, customers click on a navigation bar to calculate the rate of return for that investment. Based on the results, they can change the investment decision and navigate accordingly. Customers also may be allowed to make investment decisions directly using funds in their checking or saving accounts.

A sample of what professionals in the field say about good Web site design is shown in Box 7.6. The bottom line is that the Web site must reach the intended audience and build an image of integrity, reliability, and quick accommodation around the clock. Sites like Web Site Garage can help you analyze your site. They provide the total file size and download time of the pages. For more examples of these sites, see this book's Web site. Another test is to select a sample from the competition. Find some sites you consider your competitors and see how they stack up in terms of file size and performance limits.

With the number of Web sites surging every day, Web site errors are driving off customers and causing huge losses in business. Some of the common failures include blank pages, wrong pages, and wrong items being presented. Losing business when a visitor tries in vain to complete transactions is like visiting a real store with the lights on but nobody at the cash register.

There are a number of things not recommended for a commercial Web site. Color should be kept simple, avoiding overuse of graphics. Do not make visitors look everywhere for e-mail, contact, or feedback links. Font size should not be so small that it strains the visitor's eyes. Musical plug-ins can be annoying, unless the visitor is in the music business.

One thing that works against navigation and customer focus is excessive Web advertisements. If you consider such a route, you can expect a clutter of advertisements pasted over, under, and next to the homepage you're looking at. These distractions can reduce the surfer's interest in what your Web site has to offer.

Ad blockers are now available to eliminate distraction. For example, Microsoft has added pop-up blocking features to Internet Explorer in its Windows XP to stamp out Web advertisements. Likewise, Opera, Mozilla, and Netscape give users a chance to block intrusive advertising while surfing the Web. Earthlink incorporated pop-up blocking tools in 2002, while Google has given people tools to suppress pop-ups via its popular search toolbar.

BOX 7.6

Professionals' Views of Good Web Sites

Lynn Siprelle:

- Content first,
- Organization second,
- Style third,
- "Cutting-edge" stuff last.

Tom Ricciardi:

- Easy to navigate—contains a site map
- Functional graphics, not just meaningless pictures
- Image maps are good if they serve a function relevant to the content or for navigation (but only if they load quickly).

- Text-only options are essential, especially for navigation and content.
- The page design and content should take into account that most users are working over slow modems.

Peyton Stafford:

- Keep to your purpose. If you are showing off your technical expertise, then go ahead and use technology that only you and your T-1 friends have. If you don't have to sell anything, don't worry about the public reading what you have to say. Better yet, throw in some quotations in classical Greek. But if you are trying to sell something for a client, keep things simple, fast, and easy. And hire or collaborate with a copywriter for the text.

- Don't like twirling globes, bounding bunnies, blinking words.
- Don't like "We're Cool."

Stanford Davis

- Help me solve a problem by providing useful content.
- Convey an air of professionalism through good layout, graphics, and copy.
- Work well on the Internet: Load quickly, fit the page, proper-looking color.
- Easy to understand
- Understanding conveyed through graphics, color, copy
- Fun, funny when appropriate. Humor, interest, entertainment are nice.

Mike Pritchard

- Effective use of graphics
- Easy to navigate
- Consistency to a degree—a good amount of common look and feel
- Minimal use of fancy tricks for the sake of it
- Don't make me wait too long before I can tell whether this site is valuable.
- Kept current
- Broken links, dead-end paths are bad.

Source: Excerpted from www.tbchad.com/gwebresp.html.

HIRING A WEB DESIGNER

Now that you're ready to do business on the Internet, you need a skilled designer to build the storefront and the Web site. You could teach yourself to build your own site if you have time and some knowledge; many Web sites offer tutorials and easy-to-follow procedures. For examples of such sites, go to this book's Web site, www.prenhall.com/awad. Another great site is www.hotwired.com, or www.webmonkey.com.

Unfortunately, although this approach might save you money, it is neither safe nor prudent for serious online business. If you want your site to attract visitors and beat the competition, and if you want a unique site and one that actually sells products online, you need to hire someone to build that site. In large site projects, a committee consisting of representatives from various departments works with the site developer to ensure the overall quality of the resulting site.

THE BUDGET

In addition to hiring costs, you need to budget for the costs of running a Web site, maintaining and upgrading the site, monthly hosting fees, and a dedicated Webmaster to keep the whole infrastructure on course. The challenge is to prepare a budget that incorporates all aspects of direct and indirect costs for a year and get top management approval so that as the site is being developed, the key decision makers can track its progress.

WHAT TO LOOK FOR IN A SITE DEVELOPER

A critical issue to consider in Web site design is the developer. That individual or company must not only have extensive Web design experience, but also be experienced with a variety of databases, security standards, and programming languages.

Competition for qualified Web developers has caused many companies to go out of their way to attract potential employees (e.g., Microsoft furnishes temps with cars and condos). Based on the surge of sites today, demand is growing faster than supply. It used to be that mainly high-tech firms hired Web employees. Now, almost every company from bank to bakery is looking for site developers to help them create a presence on the Internet.

What's the best way to find a Web designer? As a starting point, look at a site that you like and try to contact the Web designer who built it. Contact Web developers in the area and put together a short list to choose from. Look up their sites and draw up a list of the features you like and don't like. Find out what services the firms offer. Learn about logo design procedures, database development, animation, user testing, site hosting, language used in site design, and so on. Send out bids to a select few.

If you're having trouble deciding on the design shop, try visiting a few. Meet the designers, and check their competence and capabilities. Do you like working with them? Do they share your thoughts about what the proposed site should look like? Do they have what it takes to reach your visitors?

Many professionals often wonder why Web site projects fail. Here are some of the reasons for Web site project failure.

- Unrealistic deadlines. Web site designers agree to a completion date when they have no idea how to meet it. In trying to meet such an unrealistic deadline, the team pushes for an aggressive schedule to accelerate the work, only to encounter one error after another that delays the whole Web site project. To make up for lost time, testing begins to degenerate, which invariably causes problems after installation.

- Incompetent or inadequate staffing. When the project team is short-handed, lacks competency, or is under pressure to produce miracles, motivation is the first victim of such arrangements. For example, two designers working 14 hours a day to produce a Web site cannot be as reliable as two qualified designers working seven normal hours a day to do the same work. Tight deadlines have been known to burn two ends of the candle. See Box 7.7 for a partial résumé of a good professional Web designer.

- Poor quality design. When quality suffers, it is either because of incompetent staff or trying to meet unrealistic deadlines. In the latter case, quality reviews, inspections, and thorough testing take a back seat, especially when pressure comes from top management.

- Changing requirements of the client. This problem has been known for decades to cause delays in the completion and quality of Web site design. We have seen this problem in designing information systems since the 1960s. First, the client was not shown the product until after it was ready to use. The client complained, because they had no chance to see it sooner. Then a new approach was tried, making the client part of the design team. Still, the client who keeps making changes could drive the design team batty.

FILLING WEB POSITIONS

Because of the increasing demand for developing and maintaining Web sites, companies are creating full-time positions for this purpose. Hiring a Web development team means creating unique job descriptions. The employer needs to recognize this special talent with

---

BOX 7.7

Partial Résumé of a Professional Web Designer

Technical Experience

- Programming—HTML, Java Script, CGI, DHTML, CSS, SSI
- Design Applications—Macromedia, Dreamweaver, Adobe Photoshop; familiarity with Adobe GoLive, Microsoft FrontPAGE, Macromedia Flash
- Applications—Microsoft Office 2000, Adobe Acrobat Writer, FTP

Work Experience

- Design, develop, and implement new Web interfaces, graphics, and layouts
- Create, manage, and maintain company Internet and intranet sites, with key responsibility for creation of Web content
- In-depth experience applying graphic design principles to produce creative, innovative, and professional Web sites
- Cutting-edge technical knowledge of HTML programming
- Responsible for quality assurance of all Web design projects, including Web usability, accessibility, testing, and debugging
- Image creation, optimization, and manipulation
- Write, edit, and proofread a variety of documents; plan and prepare articles for online dissemination

- Advise clients on effective marketing techniques to increase Web site traffic
- Search engine optimization, including keyword research/selection, meta tagging, search engine submissions, position tracking
- Exceptionally well organized and detail-oriented
- Proven record of effectively managing multiple tasks without compromising quality
- Ability to meet deadlines
- Excellent planning and consulting skills

Education

- BA, 1999, Metropolitan State University, St. Paul, MN
- FastTrac, New Venture Program, 2003, University of St. Thomas, Minn., MN.

Professional Affiliations

- Association for Women in computing
- National Association of Women Business Owners
- Saint Croix Falls Chamber of Commerce
- Sales and Marketing Executives of Minneapolis, St. Paul

Source: Excerpted from www.glasspoole.com/resume.html.

---

a successful career path. In deciding on the right person for the job, the employer needs to realize that the most experienced candidate might not be the most qualified. The candidate needs to demonstrate the capacity to learn from experience and the ability to manage projects and communicate well. Capable employees with limited experience may see the job as an opportunity to learn and work harder at staying abreast of the technology.

Another way to attract Web talent is through an internship program. Interns get exposure and training, and generally leave with positive things to say about their experience with the firm. They might return at a later date and become permanent employees. In return, the company gets good public relations for the firm and good future employees.

Another path is in-house training of employees with potential for Web design work. This can be done through classroom meetings or presentations. A technical library with the latest technical and design-building information is also helpful. Classes that employees take at community colleges or universities are also positive moves. The company reaps the benefits of more highly trained employees with the potential to do Web design work.

ADA IS HERE!

So far, we have addressed e-commerce, Web design, and the Internet for the strong and the willing. People with disabilities have also been attracted to surfing the Internet and navigating the Web in a serious way. By one estimate, 50 percent of working people with disabilities now shop online.

Over 54 million people fall under the Americans with Disabilities Act (ADA), which guarantees certain benefits and protection. A sizable aging, affluent population is experiencing failing quality of life, physically and mentally. There are also an estimated 5.2 million American children and teenagers with disabilities on the way to becoming adult users of e-commerce. This suggests increasing the attractiveness of online shopping.

This demographic group may also experience failing vision and hearing loss that make it difficult to use Web sites with any degree of comfort unless customized technical assistance is provided. This awareness is beginning to make waves among the key players in e-commerce. The legal, business, and ethical dimensions of Web site accessibility for the disabled community generate several important starting points for understanding the e-business situation:

- ADA, passed by Congress in 1990, requires companies to adjust their physical environment to accommodate people with disabilities. ADA is already extending its influence into the Internet environment. The key question an organization now asks is: "What do we need to do to be ADA-compliant?" The Department of Justice has already expressed its opinion that ADA covers organizations that use the Internet to transact business, whether it is products, goods, services, or any mode of business exchange, and should be prepared to offer the mechanisms appropriate for people with disabilities (Loiacono 2004, 85).

- Public support for ADA is increasing everywhere. Lawsuits have been filed and lobbyists in Congress are active on behalf of passing laws that protect the rights of people with handicaps in the virtual environment. According to one source, the National Information Center for Children and Youth with Disability, Children with Disabilities, and the Association to Benefit Children are sending strong signals regarding the right of access to resources for children with disabilities. The same demands come from the American Association of Retired People (AARP).

- Public pressure is mounting in no uncertain way to bringing people with handicaps and senior citizens into the world of the Internet for a variety of reasons—entertainment, doing business, connecting to people anywhere, and so on.

All this means Web designers must look into ways of making sure the Web site is ADA-compliant. This means considering hearing, cognitive, and neurological disabilities, motor skills, and the like. See www.usdoj.gov/crt/ada/publicat.htm for details regarding this matter.

Any way you look at it, incorporating these adjustments in a Web site to provide Web accessibility to everyone, regardless of age or disabilities, is bound to be a daunting task. When Web designers begin work on a Web site, they assume that users possess certain capabilities to see, to hear, to interpret, and to use motor skills to navigate. But a synthesized voice that greets a user with "You've got mail!" might be meaningless to the hearing impaired. Likewise, animated graphics mean nothing to the blind.

As of early 2005, less than 20 percent of the *Fortune* 100 homepages are ADA-compliant. According to Loiacono, "college and university Web sites, which are federally mandated to comply with the ADA, are much more accessible than corporate homepages. In one study, almost three times the percentage of corporate homepages were found accessible" (Loiacono 2004, 86).

LEGAL CONSIDERATIONS

When mapping out a strategy for implementing the company Web site, one question that often comes up is, "Who owns the Web site?" Is it the company itself, the marketing department, the IT department, or some other department or entity all together? In most cases, whoever has the most compelling argument for dominance ends up being the owner. Technology specialists and corporate executives agree that ownership of a corporate Web site is often up for grabs. Each department vies for space or placement of department-specific content, especially graphics.

According to a 2004 report by Jupiter Research in New York, there is often little incentive for departments within a firm to work toward accommodating one another any more than as a mechanism for maximizing the overall effectiveness of the company's Web site as a corporate asset (Pratt 2004).

Another way to look at the ownership question is to identify Web funding sources by department. Using the 2004 Jupiter Research study, for example, various departments were responsible for different percentages of the total cost of the company Web site:

IT	29%
Marketing	26
Sales	13
Business lines	10
Customer service	9
Web budget	8
Other	5
	100%

In larger organizations, the prudent step to take is to form an entity focused only on the Web site's performance, with enough responsibility and authority to ensure maximum value of the Web site. To illustrate, Verizon instituted an e-commerce committee to develop strategies for the corporate Web site. It also initiated stakeholder forums so that various departments could comment on or react to proposed Web site changes. These initiatives turned out to be crucial in resolving inter- and intradepartmental conflicts in the interest of the firm (Pratt 2004, p. 32).

Overall, companies tend to put functionality to market first when it comes to its Web site and e-presence. More recently, security has been a top priority. A security team must rank as a critical stakeholder in the schema of Web design and Web upgrades. Collaboration, coordination, and regular cooperation of key players are necessary factors in running and maintaining a successful company Web site.

Internationally, the European Union is insisting that governments and the private sector must share in overseeing the Internet, creating a showdown with the United States on the future of Internet governance. Since its creation as a Pentagon project in 1960, the U.S. government has been the Internet's ultimate authority, rejecting calls for a UN body to take over in a September 2005 United Nations meeting in Geneva (White 2005).

Summary

1. Because a Web site is the gateway to doing business on the Internet and is the primary interface between a business and its prospective cyber-customers, deciding how to design the site, what to include in it, how to organize its contents, and what security measures to incorporate are the most critical aspects of building an e-commerce infrastructure.

2. The benefits of building a Web site for a business include reaching millions of customers quickly and reliably, establishing a presence on the Internet, leveraging advertising cost, reducing the costs of serving customers, and reaching international markets and customers.

3. Building a Web site includes the following steps: planning the site, defining the audience and the competition, building site content, defining the site structure, and visual design.

4. Defining the audience includes knowing who the users are as well as their goals and objectives. The assessment includes creating scenarios or design test cases.

5. In defining a site structure, the focus is on exploring various metaphors, defining the architectural blueprints, and deciding how the user will navigate the site.

6. There are several ways to build a Web site. One way is via storefront building services. Another way is to enlist a Web-hosting service that also maintains the site. The third way is to do it yourself, which requires experience in Web design, hardware and software, and Web administration.

7. Several design criteria should be considered: appearance, accuracy (because any mistakes are immediately displayed for the world to see), consistency, scalability, security, performance, navigation, and interactivity.

8. ADA-compliance is a new dimension in the Web designer's sphere of activities. Because of an aging population and the large number of people with handicaps, a typical Web site should be able to be accessed by people with disabilities as well as by those without disabilities. It is a matter of time and talent before we see this change universally implemented.

Key Terms

- **banner** (p. 203)
- **content inventory** (p. 207)
- **cookie** (p. 210)
- **customer profile** (p. 214)
- **homepage** (p. 203)
- **link** (p. 203)
- **navigation** (p. 219)
- **quality assurance (QA)** (p. 218)
- **scalability** (p. 219)
- **scenario** (p. 215)
- **site structure** (p. 208)
- **style guide** (p. 218)
- **Web page** (p. 203)

Test Your Understanding

1. Briefly summarize the benefits of having a Web site for e-commerce.
2. A Web site can offer a variety of labor-saving services. Do you agree? Give examples.
3. How does a Web site promote public relations?
4. Explain the major stages of building a Web site. Is one stage more important than all the others? Elaborate.
5. What goes into planning a Web site? Discuss.
6. What is involved in defining the audience and the competition? Be specific.
7. According to research by BizRate.com, what do retail cyber-surfers look for when they shop online? Explain.
8. What should one consider in building site content? Explain.
9. In what ways are architectural blueprints related to navigation?
10. How would you explain visual design in Web site development?
11. What is the difference in function between a storefront building service and a Web-hosting service?
12. What is involved in creating user profiles? Elaborate.
13. Is there a difference between performance and scalability? Explain.
14. If you were in a position to hire a Web designer, how would you proceed? What would you look for?
15. From a designer's point of view, how does ADA affect a company's final Web homepage?

Discussion Questions

1. Can one safely design a Web site without going through the planning phase? Discuss in detail.
2. In Web design, how much of the work can you do yourself without professional help?
3. What would you say if someone came to you and said, "Look, I know nothing about the Web, but my competitors are all on it. How about designing a Web site for my jewelry business in the next few days?" What questions would you ask?
4. How would you go about analyzing a small retail business that wants to launch itself on the Internet?
5. What might be some competitive strategies for an organization trying to launch a clothing business on the Web?
6. Select some of the better-known online travel agencies (priceline.com, cheaptickets.com, expedia.com), review their Web site features, and report your findings.
7. Check three search engines (e.g., Yahoo!, Excite, Hotbot). Compare and contrast their sites.
8. Explain how a shoe repair shop can take advantage of a Web presence for its business.

Web Exercise

A medium-size bank is in the process of installing a Web site that would allow it to interface with the larger global community on a full-time basis. The bank has 89 employees, $189 million in assets, 20,000 checking accounts, 11,000 customers, and intense competition from neighboring banks for marginal customers. The bank is customer oriented in the classical style of shaking hands and greeting people by name. The trend, however, is for the younger, computer-literate customers (such as students at a neighboring university) to want a different kind of customer service. The bank wants to be part of the Internet community and wants to grab the cyber-customer for information access, issuing small loans, and other services. You are the consultant. What questions or information would allow you to advise the bank on its readiness to make use of a Web site? What would you emphasize that the bank must do, and how would you sell any change to the bank's president? What type or level of planning is involved?

CHAPTER 8

WEB SITE EVALUATION AND USABILITY TESTING

Learning Objectives

The focus of this chapter is on several learning objectives:

- How color can affect a customer's perception of the company and its products
- The criteria used in evaluating Web sites
- The cookie and its many wonders
- What makes a Web site usable?
- Ideas about site content and managing Web traffic
- Role of the Web site administrator

IN A NUTSHELL

In the previous chapter, we discussed the basics of Web design—how to build a Web site, navigation design, and design criteria. It is tempting to think that the work is done once the site is designed and on the Web, but in a rapidly changing Web environment, day-to-day maintenance and evaluation are needed. Systematic evaluation of your Web site is like checking its pulse: It tells you if you're fulfilling the site's mission, suggests format or layout improvements, and makes sure the site evolves along with your company and the Web.

Web site evaluation means considering graphic identity, navigation quality, functionality, and content. Remember that a site built using solid design principles need not have lots of bells and whistles to grab a visitor's attention. The key is usability and performance.

Part of Web site evaluation is managing Web traffic. When the site was initially planned, the designer must have done some competitive research to determine the kinds of sites your competitors have. These sites should be revisited periodically to see what changes competitors have made and what changes your site needs. As you evaluate your site, think about how any changes might fit into what is already on the site. You need to keep the site user friendly, fresh, and cohesive.

ANATOMY OF A SITE

A Web page's design is basic to its ability to communicate information. The Web world is crowded with books on building "successful" Web sites, "killer" Web sites, "Web sites that work," and so on. Perhaps the best way to focus on building successful Web sites is to learn about how to build lame sites.

Based on common sense, lame sites:

- Keep customers clicking away to competitors' sites.
- Keep surfers wondering about the kind of product or service your company provides.
- Fail to update regularly, and lack anything new, innovative, or attractive to retain the surfer.
- Waste visitors' time by requiring them to fill out tedious forms, only to find out the Web site does not have much to offer.
- Use up the bulk of the homepage with ugly graphics that hardly represent anything about the firm or its products.

With these failures, a prudent Web site designer should always include mission and vision statements, and at least one way to reach someone within the firm—address, e-mail, contact phone, and so forth. This should easily be readable, accessible, and workable.

Impressive Web sites are not just another asset of large corporations. Some of the smallest firms have been known to build efficient and attractive Web sites that show professionalism and prominence. It is not uncommon to find large firms' Web sites looking unattractive and unprofessional in a number of ways. Web surfers continue to see company Web sites that have an abundance of mistakes, such as:

- Exclamation points and commas in the wrong places.
- Misspelled words—such mistakes show recklessness in Web site design.
- Usage errors such as *its* versus *it's, they're* versus *they are,* and *people* versus *people's.*
- Pages laden with text—long lines, narrow margins, and hard-to-read fonts.
- Promises of things that simply cannot be delivered. ValueAmerica.com set out to become a huge online retailer; it went bankrupt in less than six months in 1998. The company spent beyond any budget, had no way to return or reimburse customers for returned merchandise, while the owners allegedly withdrew company cash for personal means.
- Requiring visitors to install hardware or software.
- Attempting to run the e-business with no reliable or verifiable log to monitor traffic, number of hits, and so forth. This situation invariably threatens business existence.

The number one issue in Web site design is how it comes across to the visitor. Here are some questions to consider in evaluating a Web site:

- Are any elements placed incorrectly? Is the information accurate? Is it current?
- Are the topics covered? Does each topic show a minimum of bias?
- Is the information hierarchy properly arranged?
- Should the heads that relate to the page be enlarged?
- Should the fonts for the headings be made more readable?

See Table 8.1 for a sample of homepage standards.

TABLE 8.1   Example of financial institution homepage Standards

Factor	Standard	Page Position/Comments
Content		
About Us	Yes	Bottom
Careers	Yes	Bottom
Email hoax warning	No	
Privacy	Yes	Upper right
Product links	Yes	
Rates	Yes	
Security Center	Yes	Upper right
Site map	Yes	Upper right
Spanish language	Yes	Depends on design
Stock price (bank's)	No	
Functions		
Apply	Yes	Depends on design
Contact Us	Yes	Upper right
Find Us	Yes	Upper right
Help	Yes	Upper right
Log-in	Yes	Upper left/right
Search	Yes	Upper right
Design		
Alt-text	Yes	All graphic images
Banners/promos	1 or 2	No 3rd party logos
Color: background	White	
Color: text	Black & blue	
Copyright	Yes	Bottom
Download time (max)	20 secs	10–15 better (@56k)
FDIC/NCUA	Yes	Bottom
File size total	60K max	
Flyout menus	No	
Images (number)	15 max	

(Continued)

TABLE 8.1 Continued

Factor	Standard	Page Position/Comments
Links underlined	Yes	
Liquid layout	Yes	
Logo position	Top left	Clickable
Navigation: Main	Yes	Left or middle
Navigation: Sub	Yes	Upper right & bottom
Photos (number)	1 max	File size optimized
Server connection	1	
Tagline	Bank name + description	Less than 10 words (avoid "welcome")
Vertical scroll	No	800 × 600, 17"
Window title	Yes	Short description
Word count: main*	100 max	
Word count: total*	300 max	

Source: Online Banking Report, 10/03.

*"Word count main" excludes links. "Word count total" includes navigation terms and text in drop-downs.

In general, a Web site's anatomy is represented by three building blocks:

1. **Location! Location! Location!** A Web designer would be concerned with how to name the files, how and where the Web site should be created, and what title to give the first page. The Web site's identity is composed of its URL, the name of the homepage file, and the title of that page.

2. **Structure**—putting the site on paper. A Web site begins with preliminary sketches of the homepage and any other pages in the proposed site. Then a designer would list the links on each page and their logical grouping. The focus is on the essential content and interrelationships between content. There is nothing worse than a busy background and graphics.

3. **Page anatomy**—the details and samples of HTML coding. They include the elements of the design, the graphics, the links, the core HTML, and the various features that become part of the final design.

When all is said and done, you can submit your finished site for a possible award. To get an award, you want to make sure the site is finished, has quick loading time, no broken graphics, and no errors. Some of the award sites include www.awardsites.com, www.coolsiteoftheday.com, www.GoldenWebAward.com, and www.usatoday.com.

COLOR AND ITS PSYCHOLOGICAL EFFECTS

A site visitor has formed a first impression of your site within the first 8 seconds of clicking on. Appropriate design involves matching the demographics and content of expected visitors to appropriate colors, shapes, and typefaces. Like it or not, visitors to a Web site respond to visual cues on a psychological level. Educated Web designers have been taught to use color to tease, please, and attract and retain customers.

When was the last time you saw a Web site in black and white? For most of us, a rainbow of colors surrounds our lives. Most visual information is related to color. Colors convey messages that go beyond ethnic, racial, or gender boundaries. Color can sway thinking, change actions, and generate reactions. It can also irritate or soothe your eyes, or suppress your appetite. As a form of communication, it is irreplaceable: Red means "stop," green means "go," and yellow means "caution." Likewise, the color used for a Web site or a product causes powerful reactions.

Color is arguably the most important design element in a Web site. It expresses your site's values, goals, and personality. Many Web designers overlook the importance of color in the homepage and beyond. Web browsers can see only 256 colors. Even that number is limited, because Web browsers don't share the same 256-color pallet. They only share 216 common colors. This means that a designer has a 216-color scheme to consider. Realistically, far fewer colors are used in most Web sites.

There is one thing about color that you need to know—it is inherently unstable. Instability of color on the Web stems primarily from differences in gamma and the actual color space created by the operating system and monitor. Gamma is a measure of how compressed or expanded dark and light shades become in an image. Gamma is responsible for the brightness and darkness of an image. With operating systems designed around different standards of gamma, you can expect different shades of a given color. As one source suggested, the results are compared to "viewing an image through dark sunglasses." See www.colormatters.com/chameleon.html.

To promote color stability, most operating systems use filters to bring out a near stable color view. For example, an Apple computer's ColorSync does exactly that, which gives astounding results on a Mac monitor. So Web designers should treat the symbolism of color seriously. When color and form are combined, the symbolic power is bound to increase.

Before using color, ask yourself this question: What is the goal of the Web site? Entertain? Inform? Sell? The first consideration is to set up the Web site so that color appears immediately. If the purpose of the Web site is to inform, choose colors that are simple and not distracting. Choose colors that reflect your audience's values and cultural preferences. For example, if the site represents a community bank, then choose warm colors.

In deciding on color for a Web site, the first thing a Web designer should consider is whether the colors will strain the visitor's eyes. For example, yellow means "caution," but pure yellow will strain your eyes, because it is the first color your eye will fix on. Such color may be used for banners and advertisements to receive more attention, but it should be used sparingly along with red.

In contrast to bright colors, soft colors that represent appropriate settings are ideal. For example, in U.S. hospitals, nurses are usually dressed in light blue and pale pink. These are viewed as calming and soothing colors for the setting. Patients find it relaxing, which is a prerequisite for diagnosis and treatment. So, when choosing the colors for your site, you need to consider your audience. Colors and their psychological effects are listed in Table 8.2.

TABLE 8.2   Summary of major colors and their psychological effects

Color	Psychological Effects
Red	Red is the most emotionally intense color. It is the color of love. It creates attention, but tends to overtake other colors on the page. In clothing, the wearer of red appears heavier and gets noticed. It is not a good color in negotiations. Red cars are popular targets for carjackers. Red also can be viewed as power, energy, warmth, aggression, danger. Red with green is a symbol of Christmas. The recommendation is to use red as an accent, not as a background.
Blue	It is the color of the sky and the ocean—peaceful and calming. It creates an optical impression that objects are farther away than they really are. It is the second most favored color for business suits and is recommended for job interviews, because it symbolizes loyalty. It also represents trust, conservatism, stability, security, technology, order. Used in the United States by many banks to symbolize trust. Examples: www.Wachovia.com, www.bankofamerica.com.
Green	Nature, health, optimism, good luck. It is the color of money and has strong associations with finance and economic stability. But it is a mixed bag. It is linked with envy, sickness, and decaying food. It does not do well in a global market. Green is underused on the Web. Certain shades symbolize youthfulness and growth. Example: www.Firstunion.com.
Yellow	Cheerful sunny yellow is the first color the eye processes. It is an attention-getter and represents optimism, hope, and precious metals. Yellow is used for legal pads to enhance concentration. But people often lose their temper in yellow rooms. It is not an easy color for the eyes either, because it tends to be overpowering if overused.
Purple	Purple is a complex color and is the hardest color for the human eye to discriminate. Yet, it represents spirituality, mystery, intelligence, royalty, luxury, wealth, and sophistication. But it can be perceived to represent cruelty and arrogance. If purple is on the red side, the associations are more sensual. It is a rare color in nature.
Orange	Although orange represents energy, balance, warmth, and vitality, it is a color most detested by Americans. It signifies a product is inexpensive (outside of Halloween and St. Patrick's Day). The color has stronger appeal to Europeans and Latinos. Orange is best used when you are evoking a natural association like carrots.
Brown	Brown is the color of earth and is quite abundant in nature. It represents reliability, comfort, and endurance. Men more than women tend to prefer brown over other colors.
Gray	Intellect, futurism, modesty, sadness, decay. It is the easiest color for the eye to see.
White	Purity, cleanliness, precision, innocence, sterility, death. It reproduces freshness and is quite popular at luxury Web sites

(Continued)

TABLE 8.2 Continued	
Color	*Psychological Effects*
	that cater to the upper middle, because it gives the sense of "pristineness." "Pages with a white background print the quickest and are therefore employed when a company thinks users may need to print pages on a regular basis."
Black	Power, sexuality, sophistication, death, mystery, fear, unhappiness, elegance. It signifies death and mourning in many Western cultures. It is definitely not a good background color for printing. The color is used often at fashion Web sites, because it makes people appear thinner. Some fashion experts say women wearing black send a message of submission to men. Black works well as background for many photo shots. www.infoplease.com/spot/colors1.html.

Source: Adapted from Color Voodoo Web site at www.colorvoodoo.com.

COLOR AND CULTURAL, AGE, GENDER, AND CLASS DIFFERENCES

With the Internet being global, Web site colors take on different cultural hues. They obtain symbolism through cultural references in the culture one grows up in. For example, in Asia, white is the color of funerals, while in the West, it is the color of weddings. In China, a green hat symbolizes that a man's wife is cheating on him. The trick is to use a color that is acceptable to various cultures, while simultaneously representing the product or service. Most global firms load their unique Web site on a server in the country where it will be viewed. See Box 8.1 for examples of the relationship between color and culture.

If one is designing for a worldwide audience, blue is probably the most globally accessible color. It is a winner in almost every culture, regardless of its audience, goal, or location. Someone speculated that "there's nothing on the planet that exists in isolation except the sky—that stands alone" www.webtechniques.com/archives/2000/09/desi. In most religions, the deity is above. In contrast, pink is a vague color. For example, for an East Indian audience, East Indian men view pink as a feminine color; in countries like Japan, pastels are popular with both sexes. Purple is quite unsafe for a global environment. It is a symbol of death and crucifixion in Catholic Europe. In some Middle Eastern cultures, it signifies prostitution. Euro Disney made the mistake of using purple for signs, which visitors found "morbid."

Related to cultural differences are also age, class, and gender differences. Web sites intended for young children favor brighter, more solid colors, while those for adults tend to use more subdued colors. In terms of gender differences, in many cultures men are attracted to cooler colors like blue and green, while women prefer warmer colors like orange and red. When it comes to class differences, marketing research in the U.S. suggests that working-class people tend to prefer colors with basic names like blue, red, green, and so on. In contrast, more highly educated classes tend to prefer colors with names like taupe, azure, and so forth. According to one source, this is the reason why Wal-Mart's store logo is red (webdesign.about.com/od/color/a/aa07204.htm).

BOX 8.1

Color and Culture

What makes Red Square red? Any visitor to Moscow can see that the venerable square is predominantly gray, notwithstanding the blood-red crenellated wall that surrounds the Kremlin. The red in Red Square is a particularly striking example of the way color can shed light on how different cultures see the world. Where English-speakers might associate red with danger or rage, in Russia it is linked to the word for beauty.

Red (*hong*) also carries positive associations in China, where it connotes happiness and is used on festive occasions. A Chinese bride is more likely to wear red than white, flaunting her joy the way a traditional whiteclad Western bride flaunts her alleged virginity. White, in fact, is most definitely out on Chinese wedding days. It is the color of mourning. And in France, a bride won't be wearing white if hers is a *mariage blanc* (white marriage), that is, a marriage of convenience for reasons like obtaining working papers.

In France, meanwhile, when someone's seriously frightened, he'll say he has *une peur bleue* (he's scared blue). If he's got the blues, on the other hand, get out the bug spray—he'll tell you he's got *le cafard* (the cockroach). Red hair in France is not *rouge* but *roux,* and to call *une rousse* (a redheaded woman) *une rouge*—"a Red"—could produce an unpleasant reaction. Blond, of course, is easier—the French gave the world the word—but the line between *blond* and *châtain clair* (light brown) is not that easily discernible, even to the French.

Source: Excerpted from Meg Bortin, "When Colors Take on Different Cultural Hues," *International Herald Tribune,* September 28–29, 2002, 9.

GEOMETRIC SHAPES AND GENDER DIFFERENCES

In addition to color and its effects on various visitors, geometric shapes also mean different things to different sexes. As summarized in Table 8.3, men tend to associate a circle with femininity and rate it low in preference. Women, on the other hand, view a circle as "tender, loving, warm" and rate it high in preference. For men, a square is associated with being "solid, predictable, sure," while women view it to mean "brittle, hard, and abrasive." Men prefer blue to red; women prefer red to blue. Men prefer orange to yellow, where women prefer yellow to orange (www.coolhomepages.com/cda/color). Finally, a triangle means "powerful, exciting" to men, but "threatening and dangerous" to women. (See www.gmarketing.com/tactics/weekly_29.html.)

THE COLOR BLIND AND THOSE WITH IMPAIRED VISION

Partial sight, congenital color deficits, and aging all produce problems in perception that reduce the visual effectiveness of certain color and color combinations. Color perception problems are widespread. Color deficiency can occur in any population, economic class, or ethnic group. As many as one man in twelve has color perception problems—less so for women. For some Web sites, this means an awful lot of traffic with questionable results. Most color-blind people have red-green perception deficiency. The defect is always with one color or the other.

So, what should a Web designer do to address the problem? First, any designer should be aware of the problem. Second, he or she should understand how color deficiency works

TABLE 8.3 Consumer association with key shapes (by gender)				
Consumer	*Visibility*	*Retention*	*Preference*	*Association*
Circle—male	high	high	low	feminine, weak
Circle—female	high	high	high	tender, loving, warm
Square—male	low	low	high	solid, predictable
Square—female	low	low	low	brittle, hard, abrasive
Triangle—male	high	high	low	mysterious, powerful
Triangle—female	high	high	low	forceful, danger

so as to minimize the side effects of color to visitors with color deficiency. According to various color experts, black on white is the safest. White on black is reasonably safe, but other colors on black are questionable. Any text on any mixed-color background is inviting trouble. Of all colors, blue is safer across the board than any other color. Blue on black is terrible, but combining blue and black is OK as long as it is not used for fine details (see www.firelily.com/opinions/color.html).

Most color-blind people see black and white well. They also see shades of yellow and blue accurately. Most of them even see dimmer shades of yellow, such as gold and olive. The important thing is to keep colors bright so visitors can tell them apart easily.

SITE EVALUATION CRITERIA

In evaluating Web sites, several criteria can be used. The following criteria are not listed in order of importance: All are considered important for site evaluation.

- Color: Color and general layout have a definite psychological impact on site visitors. An ideal layout is one with minimal text on a page and lots of white space. The Web site should be easy to navigate, with navigation bars on each page. Pictures should be chosen and placed carefully, not just scattered throughout the site.

- Shape: Shape is an extremely powerful (but overlooked) tool. It can motivate consumers, inspire visitors, and make a visit to the Web site enjoyable. A circle represents connection, community, wholeness, endurance, and safety. It refers to feminine features like warmth, comfort, and love. Rectangles represent order, logic, and security. Triangles represent energy, power, balance, law, and science. A circle and triangle in combination can result in an energetic, dynamic impression. A circle and a rectangle can convey warmth and security. Check the FedEx logo (www.fedex.com) as an example.

- Type: Type should be appropriate and used carefully. For example, a serif typeface (like Times Roman) expresses organization and intelligence. It is also elegant and conservative. Sans serif faces like Helvetica and Arial are warm and friendly type styles. They are excellent choices for screen fonts because they are clear and easy to read. Decorative fonts are best used for titles and display; they should not be used for body type.

- Content: Companies new to the Web think that once they put up a site, people will flock to visit it. This is far from the truth. Studies have found that users don't want to scroll up and down the page looking for information. This means that Web sites should provide valuable, timely information—not lots of text. Popular sites include updated information, interactivity, fun, and freebies. Well-organized, edited, and timely original content set in an attractive and consistent format are traits of great Web sites.

- Services offered: What unique services does the site offer? It is not enough for a bank to simply list its services. It must provide some detail on those services, along with contact information in case of questions or a need to follow up.

- Primary focus: Every Web site should have a primary focus. Take Oakley, Inc., maker of designer sunglasses, for example. The company's main focus is making glasses, yet it also produces shoes and watches. It is the same with banks. All banks have a primary focus, whether it is home equity loans, auto loans, or CDs. They also might offer personal checking accounts or savings and investment plans, but these may not be their primary focus.

- Ancillaries: In Web design, it is important to have links to **ancillaries** that do unique things for the visitor. For example, one banking ancillary is to evaluate current mortgage loans or help answer questions such as whether the visitor qualifies for an auto loan. These ancillaries have been known to attract customers who want more services or advice that is freely available.

ancillary: supportive services or features of a product.

- Site classification: Web sites also can be evaluated based on five categories: category 1 (mere presence) to category 5 (multimedia, interactivity). Category 1 sites offer the bare essentials such as hours, location, directions to the company, and a list of services; these sites are purely informational. Category 2 sites offer more detailed information (forms, applications) and options that allow visitors to send in data for services like loan applications on a bank site. Category 3 sites involve greater inter-action and use video and color to guide the visitor to primary buttons, links, or ser-vices. Category 4 sites use multimedia as well as workflow tools, and begin to show personalization. Category 5 sites are highly customized and offer advanced services that stretch across the Internet. They also coach the visitor in making decisions, ordering products or services, and using electronic cash to consummate transactions.

- Professionalism: This criterion considers how professional the site looks to a visitor. It includes neatness, spelling, and grammar.

- Speed: The critical question here is how long it takes the visitor to click from one page to the next. A page that takes more than 8 seconds to come up rates low. Pages that come up within 1 second are considered fast (see Box 8.2).

- Consistency: This criterion looks at how similar Web pages are in layout and design. If the site doesn't have a theme, it will not attract many visitors.

- Personalization: Sites that are high on personalization use cookies, which keep track of repeat visitors and their preferences, and respond to them as though the interface is one-on-one. Sites that have no personalization also have no log-in screens and little interactivity with the user as an individual.

BOX 8.2

A Quick Loading Site

Do you want your site to load quickly? If you are trying to run a business or offer people important information, this can be very important. Remember that not everyone has a T1, cable modem, or ISDN connection to the Internet. So, as Web designers we must see to it that our sites load as quickly as possible without losing anything important.

Let's start with the obvious bandwidth hogs: images and other media. My suggestion here is to take out every form of multimedia embedded in your front page except for images. Sure, a background song can be nice, but these sound files can take up a great deal of bandwidth, especially if the sound is a .wav file. Videos can be even more taxing (1MB or more at times) and should probably be avoided unless absolutely necessary. As a surfer, if I have to wait more than 10 seconds for something like this to load, I'm tempted to hit "Stop" or

"Back." So if you use these, keep the file sizes small (probably 30–40K or less would be OK). Better yet, save them for a later page.

Your images will be your next big worry. These can also get quite large, so caution is necessary when dealing with images. If you have an image that is 600 × 600 pixels, your page could take forever to load. One trick you can use is to define the width and height in all of your image tags. This way, the browser knows how much space the image will use on the page, and will not have to adjust everything once the image starts loading. It will save a little time, and will also keep the page from jumping when an image loads.

Finally, be sure your front page is as short as possible as well. A longer page can take a long time to load, even if it is all text. Put extra information on another page and use a link for people to go view it. You will save a little extra time, and maybe reduce clutter a little bit.

Source: Excerpted from www.pageresource.com/zine/ quick.htm.

- Security: Sites with firewalls and digital certificates, as well as SSL for information and transaction processing, would rate high on the security scale. (SSL is a protocol for transmitting private information over the Internet.)
- Scalability: This criterion is related to how easily a site can be updated. A site high on **scalability** has a simple structure, uses frames and Extensible Markup Language (XML), and has a design that lends itself to easy maintenance.

scalability: how easily a Web site can be updated.

SAMPLE EVALUATIONS

To illustrate the extremes in Web site evaluation, let's look at two Web sites. The first is www.mediterraneanbakeryanddeli.net. It is a good example of how putting little thought into implementation can compromise a Web site. First, the light blue and dark gray colors are unappealing. Beyond that, they do not promote a feeling of being invited. The opening page is text intense, although the owner's picture represents a small, private business. If I were a visitor, I would not spend much time accessing such a homepage every time I logged on. When you click on six of the nine options, you face graphics unrelated to the product.

The site is a category 2, which offers detailed information about products with text and some graphics. Among the complete list of products and recipes that might be of interest to customers, it offers no links to the outside world.

The other extreme of Web site design is the Wachovia Bank site, www.wachovia.com, which is an excellent site. Not only is it full of information and useful ancillaries, but it also is well organized and easy to navigate. The company uses dark blue, light blue, and beige as the primary colors. The color scheme helps organize a wealth of information. In addition to good use of color, the site employs slightly rounded, rectangular tabs to aid navigation and organization.

BOX 8.3

Statements That Represent a Good Web Site

Impressions on first entry   YES   NO

- The URL/domain name is appropriate and meaningful.
- The surfer sees something meaningful within 8 seconds.
- The site name and product/purpose come up instantly.
- The first page is less than 20 K, and images are kept small.
- Text is visible while graphics are loaded.
- Graphics are named with useful text content.

The homepage is exciting, interesting, attention grabbing   YES   NO

- There is useful information on the homepage.
- The homepage looks good, and has a clean, uncluttered look.
- Important information is "above the fold" (top 600 × 300).
- Not distracted by excessive animation or flash.

The homepage contains the key facts   YES   NO

- Name of organization (preferably in H1 text heading).
- Shows business, products, where based.
- Style appropriate for target audience.
- Shows the sort of information available in the site.
- Shows name, address, telephone, fax, e-mail.

- Title is meaningful.
- META statements are correct.
- If frames are used, correct text links and METAs are provided.

Shopping Experience   YES   NO

- Friendly and quick route to buy.
- Secure handling of credit card information.
- Order acknowledged with delivery date stated.
- Order tracking provided.
- Delivery reliable.
- Returns policy stated.
- Certificates obtained from trade bodies.
- Privacy of data statement.
- Appropriate use of cookies.

The following is a list of the remaining headings in the paper. For details regarding the "ticks" under each heading, e-mail the author at waller@waller.co.uk:

- Back office support.
- Links are clear and meaningful.
- The whole site has a structure.
- All the pages obey the same rules.
- Long Web pages have their own structure.
- All Web pages have a reference.
- Useful external links are provided.
- The Web site achieves its purpose.
- Browser compatibility and accessibility.

Source: Excerpted from Richard Waller, "60 Ticks for a Good Web Site," *Website Creation, Training and Consultancy,* West Sussex, UK, April 24, 2001, 1–4.

Concise frames with Java script pop-up menus provide viewers with subjects they can then investigate at increasing levels of depth and complexity without being overwhelmed with too much plain text and too many numbers. The site focuses on personal finance (all types of lending, investing, and typical banking services), as well as corporate services (accessing capital, managing risk, enhancing productivity). The site does a good job of demonstrating the company's overall focus on providing total solutions for personal and corporate banking.

Wachovia's Web site falls within the category 4 classification, because customers can apply for loans and services and conduct various business transactions through the site. The site gives an extremely professional impression, with an easy-to-follow layout and presentation of services in addition to consistent use of toolbars and organization schemes. These factors all contribute to quick navigation and convenient exchange of information.

No apparent personalization exists on the Wachovia site, but it does let customers log in. The bank is able to compile a database of customer preferences and transaction behaviors so that it may someday take advantage of cross-selling services. Crucial to this endeavor is the clear presentation of privacy and security policies. Secure connections are made whenever any kind of personal information is transferred to and from the company. Although the Web site is complex, with an extensive number of services, the organization should mean improvements can be made with minimal difficulty.

Web sites are evaluated in various ways, using all kinds of criteria. The problem to date is lack of guidelines or standards with which to evaluate Web sites. Several "ticks for a good Web site" are summarized in Box 8.3. The important point to remember is that a Web site is evaluated best by coordinating preset criteria that are unique to the nature of the firm, its products, its audiences, and its mission. Cultural factors continue to be important.

GETTING PERSONAL

In designing a Web site, the question that lurks in the back of a developer's mind is: Are we getting the most out of the Web site? Web personalization allows users to get more information about themselves and their interests, although it could mean giving up some privacy. For example, visitors to www.sae.org, the Web site of the Society of Automotive Engineers, can personalize their view of the Web site, which makes it easier to find technical materials that are of special interest to them. Because the Web site is in real time from a database, visitors can count on the latest technical information offered by SAE. The idea is to tailor Web content directly to a specific user by having the user provide information to the Web site either directly or through tracking devices on the site. The software can then modify the content to the needs of the user. This is not a simple process and does not guarantee success (see Box 8.4).

Web personalization is not technology. It is a strategy, a marketing tool, and an art. It is visitor-oriented rather than product-oriented. It is the ability of Web visitors to customize the content and layout of their own portal Web page. Personalization of the visitor's experience makes his or her time on your site more productive and engaging. Properly implemented, it should deliver a visitor experience that is quick to inform and relevant to what the visitor is looking for. Personalization tries to treat all customers as unique. Users can get more information on the Internet faster because the Web site already knows their interests and needs.

BOX 8.4

The Privacy Dilemma

Personalization is only as good as the data it is based on: The more you have and the better it is, the more relevant the personalized interaction. The problem is privacy concerns have customers increasingly shy about sharing. This, coupled with legislative handcuffs such as the "do not call" initiative, means businesses have to figure out ways to maximize each interaction with a customer and then securely develop the relationship.

"Companies have to avoid the 'marketing gone wild' mentality, as every interaction is a reflection on brand," says analyst Elana Anderson at Forrester Research Inc. She recommends that they focus on building customer relationships based on proactive service, leveraging personalization technologies on inbound channels to maximize the interaction when a customer makes contact. "It's the reason marketing should own the contact center; if messages are done right, they are service-oriented instead of the hard sell," she says.

For its part, Schwan Food makes it a policy not to collect data it won't use, both to streamline operations and because the company doesn't want to intimidate customers. According to Gartner, Inc. analyst Adam Sarner, privacy legislation can actually be a boon to personalization initiatives—at least in the case of "explicit" personalization, in which a company collects data with the customer's permission, with the promise that it will use the data to only make relevant contact. Every company should have user profiles that allow customers to set preferences: when they want to be contacted, how often and about what. That is explicit personalization and it can be extremely powerful. While the sit-down nature of the Web offers the best interface for creating user profiles, the data should be populated across databases that touch every relevant contact point—whether it be through e-mail or call center or at point of sale. The trick is not just leave it on the Web but make it part of the complete user profile.

Source: Excerpted from Kym Gilhooly, "The Privacy Dilemma." *Computerworld,* August 16, 2004, 24.

Common content features provided by the portals include news, weather, sports, TV and movie listings, maps, people finders, yellow pages, favorite links, and the like. Many even offer an address book and a calendar. To create a personalized page, you simply choose a link on portal's homepage (for example, www.yahoo.com). Then you are asked for registration information (user ID, password, name, e-mail address, Zip code, gender, birth date, etc.). Once entered, you are presented with a page on which to select content for your personalized page. If you approve the page, it becomes "My" followed by the portal name (e.g., "My Yahoo"). The page is set to display every time you sign onto the Internet, creating your own homepage.

It is important to note the difference between personalization and customization. With customization, the focus is on direct user control. For example, the user decides to click between options (e.g., headlines from CNN, the *New York Times,* the *Wall Street Journal,* from a specific portal) and enters the stock symbol that he or she wants to track. Personalization is driven by artificial software that tries to serve up individualized pages to the user based on a model of that user's needs (past habits, preferences, and so on). Personalization of a Web site assumes that the computer infrastructure can address the user's needs. With users having different preferences at different times, personalization is not all that perfect. In any case, attempts have been made to use artificial intelligence to match the product with users' needs.

Personalization requires more than a software package or a tool and mining a Web site's data. The e-company's technical Web staff extracts, combines, and evaluates data taken from multiple sources and integrates the results into custom-facing channels before personalization becomes operational. It is costly and highly technical (see Figure 8.1). It also requires knowledge of the product, human behavior, and marketing strategies.

When it comes to personalization and content management, the trend is more toward specialized software packages than proprietary in-house software. For example, the proprietary system that Intercontinental Hotels Group (IHG) developed in 1998 lacked flexibility. To make changes on the Web site, changes had to be made in the company's master reservation system—a formidable task. This made the system inefficient in keeping up with the booming e-commerce portion of the company's business.

FIGURE 8.1   Components of personalization

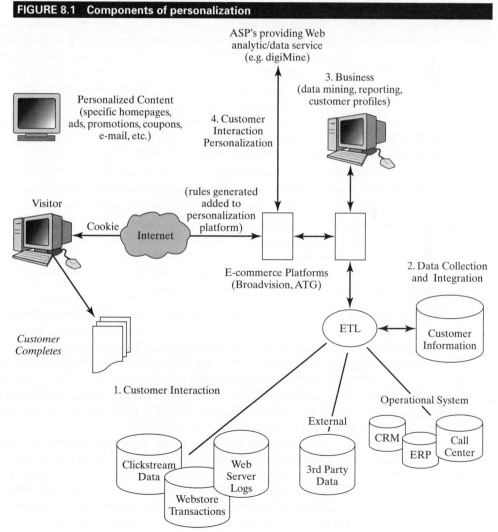

Source: Adapted from Curt Hall, "The Personalization Equation," *Software Magazine,* April 1, 2001, 27.

To correct this problem, IHG moved into commercial software, which included a personalization server. The result was significant. The new system generated more than $200 million in increased annual transaction revenues. IHG's traffic grew from 10 percent in 2001 to more than 40 percent in 2004, and the number of site changes increased from 300 per year to over 11,000 in 2004 (Bailor 2005, p. 57).

Figure 8.1 shows the processes required to operationalize Web personalization. It also specifies the components and hardware that support the processes. The four key steps are:

- Customer interaction: Visitors interact with the Web site and gradually provide information that profiles the visitor in terms of shopping preferences, likes, dislikes, and so on. In many cases, the site requests visitors to fill out a form stating their preferences.

- Data collection and integration: This process activates primarily ETL (extraction, transformation, loading) unique to each e-merchant's goal. Some companies might only want to capture Web site visitors' clickstream data, try to make sense out of customer interests, and make proper enhancements or changes to the Web site. Other companies want to go deeper into customer analysis, bringing certain data from multiple databases and storing it on a customer information repository. **Clickstream** refers to lines of code stored in a file every time a surfer views a Web page. Clickstream data make it possible for a company to track surfers as they navigate through the company's Web site—the pages they click on, how long they stay on each page, the ads viewed, and so on.

  clickstream: lines of code stored in a file every time a surfer views a Web page.

- Business intelligence: Company analysts rely on artificial intelligence packages and other techniques to figure out customer preferences based on the data collected in the customer information data warehouse or repository.

- Customer interaction personalization: In this process, the results of business intelligence help in generating personalization rules, which are integrated into the e-merchant's Web site personalization engine. The rules serve to target surfers with specific content based on preestablished behavioral profiles in the customer information repository or data warehouse.

Because our focus is on e-commerce, personalization should be customer-centric in that it should be looked at from the consumer's viewpoint and driven by Internet users themselves. An example of user-driven personalization is my.yahoo.com, where anyone can create a personal profile of the information resources that he or she wants to see displayed on the homepage when connecting to the Yahoo! site. The Web server tailors the displayed content around the specifications of each user's profile. This type of personalization is used for filtering content rather than for the one-to-one e-marketing of products via the Internet.

inference-based personalization: a technique that tracks a Web user's behavior, identifies other people with similar behavior, and uses those people to recommend products.

For e-business applications, a popular technique called **inference-based personalization** tracks a Web user's behavior, identifies other people with similar behavior, and uses those people to recommend products to the surfer. For example, the well-known Amazon.com waits for customers to commit to a product (e.g., book), and then the customer is shown a list of other products purchased by people who purchased the same book.

INTELLIGENT PERSONALIZED AGENTS

Another approach in the rapid evolution of interactive Internet services to improve consumer-supplier relationships is through *intelligent personalized agents*. This approach plays the role of virtual assistant for users. A software system, called *chatterbot* (chat robot), "learns" about users' habits, interests, and preferences to construct a user profile. Developing a user profile this way has distinctive advantages:

- A Web site that considers user preferences can suggest products that the user might be looking for, turning surfers into buyers.
- Users no longer need to insert information about their tastes or preferences, building customer trust and confidence.
- Every time the customer interacts with the Web site, the chatterbot collects new information, which updates the customer's profile. All of this has implications for improved usability of the Web site.

The following is a scenario between a chatterbox (we call it Brenda), and a user named Tyler.

Brenda: Hello, and welcome to my horse-trading Web site. It is nice to see you found www.horsetraderbrenda.com. My name is Brenda and I am your personal assistant for this site. What is your name?

User: My name is Tyler. I hope you don't get too personal with me. I am happily married.

Brenda: Nice to meet you on this beautiful evening, Tyler. What can I do for you?

User: I am looking to buy an Arabian horse that is less than 5 years old.

Brenda: This is the right place to be, then! I have several horses to choose from. Are you looking for a horse for a specific function?

User: Yes. When are you going to stop asking questions?

Brenda: Sorry, but what do you want to buy an Arabian horse for?

User: Breeding.

Brenda: I shall check to see which horse has potential for breeding.

Brenda finds 17 horses for future breeding and displays them on the Web site, each with a brief history of the horse, its lineage, and so forth. If the user is not looking for an Arabian horse for breeding, he can scroll down the list and refine the choice.

APPROACHES TO WEB PERSONALIZATION

Five general approaches can be taken in Web personalization. Each approach is adopted for a reason.

- Cookies: **Cookies** are probably the most recognizable personalization tools. They are bits of code or a text file that sits in a user's Internet browser memory and identifies that person to a Web site when they return. In a way, a cookie allows the site to greet the user by name. It is also a way to communicate information about you to Web sites that you visit. An example is Yahoo! Inc.'s My Yahoo! pages. Technically, a cookie is a message

cookie: information about a Web site visit deposited in the visitor's browser.

a Web server sends to a Web browser. The browser stores the message in a text file. The message is returned to the server every time the browser requests a page from that server.

- Collaborative filtering software: **Collaborative filtering software** keeps track of users' movements across the Web to interpret their interests. It views their habits, from how long they stay on a page to the pages they choose while on the Web site. The software compares the information about one user's behavior against data gathered about other customers with similar interests. The result is a recommendation to the customer. A good example is Amazon.com's "Customers who bought this book also bought . . ." feature.

- Check-box: In **check-box personalization,** a user-controlled process, a visitor chooses specific interests on a checklist so the site can display the requested information. The approach is less obvious than cookies.

- **Rule-based personalization:** Users are divided into segments based on business rules that generate certain types of information from a user's profile. For example, BroadVision (www.broadvision.com) asks visitors to fill out a form to determine the type of product or information it can provide. The information on the form becomes the visitor's profile, which is stored in the database by user segment (community, income, sex, age, and so on). The decision to give personalized information is based on business rules. The database looks up the visitor's profile and triggers a business rule to fit the profile. For example, if the person lives in California, then deliver travel information about California; if the person's income is greater than $100,000 per year, then send information about first-class airfare to Bermuda and product information about Hartman luggage.

- Neural networks: This software uses statistical probability algorithms to deliver personalization based on movements such as a visitor's actions. One thing unique about this technology is that it "learns" from customer behavior on the site and continues to adjust to his or her preferences, changing needs, and the like.

WHAT'S THE BIG FUSS OVER COOKIES?

When it comes to monitoring Web site traffic, it is impossible to differentiate among visits to a site unless the server can somehow mark a visitor. To do this, the Web site deposits a piece of information in the visitor's browser called a cookie. It's like a claim check at the dry cleaner. You drop off a suit or shirts and get a claim check. When you return with the claim check, you get your clothes back. A site uses cookies to personalize information, to help with online sales/service as on Amazon.com, or to track popular links or demographics as on DoubleClick.

Technically, a cookie is an HTTP header with a text-only string placed in the browser's memory. The string contains the domain, path, how long it is valid, and the value of a variable that the Web site sets. If the user spends more time at the site than the lifetime of this variable, the string is saved to file for future reference.

Several myths about cookies continue to bother the layperson. Among the popular ones are the following.

- Cookies clog the hard disk. **Transient cookies**—cookies that contain information about the user that the Web server can access until the browser is closed—occupy no hard drive space. In contrast, **persistent cookies**—cookies that contain information that the Web server retains on the hard drive of the user's computer—carry with them an expiration date and remain on the hard disk until the date expires. Transient cookies lack expiration dates and last only for the duration of the session.

transient cookies: cookies that contain information about the user that the Web server can access until the browser is closed— occupy no hard drive space.

persistent cookies: cookies that contain information that the Web server retains on the hard drive of the user's computer, carrying an expiration date and remaining on the hard disk until the date expires.

- Cookies can put a virus on my computer. Because cookies are always stored as data in text format instead of an executable format, they cannot do anything hostile. Even then, a virus would not be able to spread automatically until the user opened the file. According to www.cookiecentral.com, making a cookie that could spread a virus would be virtually impossible.

- Cookies give companies access to my personal file. Cookies can store any information the user provides to a Web site. Unfortunately, depending on the ethics standards of each company, whatever personal information is offered to a company's Web site may be spread, but laws limit the details that can be released. Legal and ethical issues are covered in Chapter 12.

- Disabling cookies in my browser will prevent any Web sites from gathering information about me. According to a U.S. government report, the data that cookies collect also can be recorded in a Web server's log files. Cookies just make it easier (content.techweb.com/wire/story/TWB19980316S0015).

The original purpose of cookies was to save users' time. This has continued to be one of the major benefits of this technology. Disabling certain cookies might disable the service that identifies you as a member. For example, the author has a free portfolio account on www.quicken.com. To access the account, Quicken asks for the user ID and password, which have been stored in advance (a cookie on my PC). Deleting the cookie in cache memory prompts Quicken to ask you for the same information, as if you're a new entrant.

There are other benefits, as well. A case can be made that the consumer is actually the winner, because cookies can help reduce the distance from consumers to the product(s) they seek, since cookies automatically provide access to goods consumers might be interested in. If used properly, marketing information contained within cookies is a quick and convenient means of keeping site content fresh and up to date. (See www.cookiecentral.com/faq.)

If one is looking for limitations or cause for concern, cookies utilize space on a client's hard drive for a Web site's purposes. They do so without permission to use space or capture the information. The strongest argument against cookies is that they threaten our privacy as Internet users. They know which Web browser you are using, which operating system you are running, and even your IP address. They also track which Web site you came from and which Web site you are going to, without your permission. In most cases, you are not revealing your information to just one Web site but to multiple sites. A marketing company can track your movements on all pages containing its advertisements. They can follow only which pages you are looking at and for how long, but not what you do within those pages as the host site can. What makes this whole business disconcerting is that companies share information and combine it into one large database and, many times, sell it to telemarketers, who then attempt to push their products to you in the middle of your dinner. Laws have been instituted to bar such practices during certain hours, but the whole idea is another nuisance to cope with.

DELETING AND REJECTING COOKIES

Cookies can be deleted or rejected at will. To do so, you need to first close your browser, because cookies are held in memory until you close your browser. If a cookie is deleted with the browser open, it will make a new file when you close it and you won't be able to get rid of it. Remember that if you delete a cookie, you start from scratch with the site that once recognized you through the cookie. Instead of deleting all cookies, you probably should open the cookies folder and delete the ones from servers that you don't want to keep.

Netscape and Microsoft Internet Explorer provide features that can alert you every time a cookie is being added to the browser. For example, Netscape 4.7 allows an alert before accepting the cookies feature to be set. Through the Edit/Preferences/Advanced menu, a user has the following choices: (1) accept all cookies, (2) accept only cookies that are sent back to the originating server, (3) disable cookies, or (4) warn me before accepting a cookie.

In Microsoft Internet Explorer, cookies can be disabled by using the Tools/Internet Options/Security menu. Microsoft saves cookies in the Temporary Internet Files folder, which takes up approximately 2 percent of the hard drive. Netscape limits the total cookie count to 300. (The average size of a cookie is from 50 to 150 bytes.)

PRIVACY CONCERNS

Are cookies a threat to privacy? The sad truth is that you are as anonymous as you want to be. Revealing any information through the Web makes it public information, except for the safeguards available to the user in the PC browser. Some companies abuse the information they receive from visitors, resulting in that most hated product of Internet commerce—**spam.** Because of spam, people are becoming increasingly skeptical about what happens to the information they provide to certain Web sites.

spam: online or e-mail equivalent of junk mail.

Recent high-profile breaches of Web users' privacy have raised public concern about data collection through cookies and other techniques. Many companies are revisiting their privacy policy statements because the privacy issue has become so explosive. For example, the privacy statement on Intuit's popular Quicken.com Web site makes it clear that customers have the option of not accepting cookies used to gather information and that the company "will not willfully disclose customer data without their permission."

Despite the publicity regarding the privacy issue, Web sites continue to collect an unprecedented volume of data about customers. Oracle built a data warehouse for Amazon.com that holds up to 3 terabytes (billions) of customer sales data. The warehouse has the capability of scaling up 1,000 times to 3 petabytes (trillions) in 5 years.

Some companies are reevaluating their reliance on cookies as a way to collect customer data, but unless an alternative is adopted, lawsuits will continue to be filed. In 2000, Yahoo.com and Broadcast.com were the targets of a $50 billion lawsuit in Texas, where the use of cookies is considered a violation of the state's antistalking law.

WHAT MAKES A WEB SITE USABLE?

The term *usability* has been used with different meanings in different situations. Usability refers to a set of independent quality attributes like performance, satisfaction, ease of navigation, and learnability. For the end user, it means an application that allows the user to perform the expected tasks more efficiently. For managers, it is a major decision factor for selecting a product. For the software developer, usability is viewed in terms of the integral attributes of a system that affect user performance and productivity.

What good is a Web site if no one can use it effectively? On the Internet, it is survival of the easiest. If visitors cannot find what they're looking for, they can't buy it. The sad truth about doing business on the Web is that most Web sites rebuff more than 70 percent of the customers who visit them, which means passing up millions of dollars in potential sales. A lost customer is lost for good. The cost of flipping to another Web site is so low, it does not make sense to go back to a site that failed once or twice. In Web design language, this is called **churning.** It is a basic measure of visitor dissatisfaction with online products or bad interface design.

churning: basic measure of visitor dissatisfaction with a site.

The key to attracting customers back to one's Web site includes high-quality content, ease of use, quick downloads, and frequent updating. The fact is that searching for information can be an experience. It can be a good experience when users find what they're looking for quickly and painlessly. This is what usability is all about. It can be a bad experience when the information is elusive. It does not matter whether the user is a novice or an expert: No amount of information can overcome a poorly designed Web site.

The goal of effective Web site design, then, is to give users good experience that will turn them into frequent and loyal customers. The main difference between a person's behavior in a physical store and on the Web is related to **switching costs.** In a physical store, a customer goes to the store, finds the merchandise, and begins the purchase with a salesperson. In this case, switching costs are high. Once we find a product, most of us will go ahead and deal with a rude salesperson rather than go to another store and possibly encounter the same behavior. In contrast, switching costs on the Internet are low. If visitors do not find what they are looking for, the competition is only a mouse click away.

switching costs: the time it takes a visitor to switch from one Web site to another.

Studies of user behavior on the Web have found low tolerance for inefficient designs or slow sites. People simply do not want to wait or learn how to navigate a cluttered site. Most Web sites are tough to use. Usability studies consistently find less than 50 percent of Web sites usable. Bloated graphics, cluttered text, and minimal useful information leave little for visitors to work with, so they go elsewhere and are unlikely to return.

When you visit Canon's Web site, the site makes no mention of and displays no interest in selling printers. Its homepage has a link to "products" that requires you to click on a specified country before it allows you to go any further. Then, you click on "office product"; then on "printers" on the left task bar; then choose whether you want network printers, non-network printers, or office printers. You click on "office printers," which finally brings up the page that shows Canon's ink-jet printers. The descriptions are brief and the frustration continues.

Finally, on the Epson site, you have a list of Epson America Inc.'s printers, with a short, easy-to-understand description, in two clicks. One more click on any of the printers and you get a list of features and technical information to help you make a decision. In the meantime, the whole process from Hewlett-Packard to Epson took close to 15 minutes. You click on Amazon.com as a last resort. All you have to do is enter "ink-jet printer" in the search window on the top-left corner (first thing the human eye sees) and voila! You have a list of all the ink-jet printers that you can choose from. This time, you have access to all the information you need in one click. It is quick, accurate, and reliable.

USABILITY GUIDELINES

Designers strive to make a Web site as inviting and easy to navigate as possible, but for one reason or another, many forget to follow some basic guidelines (see Box 8.5). In checking for usability, a number of questions need to be addressed (see Box 8.6).

If you forget everything else, remember the three most important criteria for successful Web sites: conciseness, scanability, and objectivity. Meeting them results in a well-written, easily navigable, pleasantly interactive, distinctive, and thoroughly tested Web site.

Access the following Web sites and see how well they address usability:

CNN (www.cnn.com): A high volume of information displayed on the surface; all stories are available in a clear format.

eBay (www.ebay.com): This site provides a unique feature: It gives the visitor the impression that the site's purpose is strictly buying and selling.

BOX 8.5

Tips for Web Shopability

- Show the full product cost as soon as possible.
- Explain why you need to collect personal information.
- Use opt-in rather than opt-out policies to give the shopper more control over data sharing.
- Don't overemphasize promotional products.
- Cross-reference products.
- Ensure that images are big and show features that are important to buyers.

- Put the search box on every page.
- Make "All" the search list default (so it searches the whole site).
- Avoid jargon and clever or made-up names.
- Have the customer select options before the product goes in the shopping cart.
- Expect users to hit the Enter key when filling out forms.
- Offer a toll-free number for placing phone orders.

Source: Sami Lais, "How to Stop Web Shopper Flight." www.computerworld.com/managementtopics/ ebus/story/0,10801,71990,00.ht.

BOX 8.6

Usability Checklist

- **Is the site engaging?** That is, do visitors enjoy the experience? Do they feel in control of the site tour?

- **Is the site efficient?** Is response time fast enough to keep visitors on the site? Does the site make it easy for visitors to understand what each page is about?

- **Is the site supportive?** When visitors make a mistake, is it easy for them to undo their mistake? Does it offer help, advice, or directions when necessary?

- **Is the site consistent and reliable?** Does the site respond consistently throughout a visitor's tour?

- **Decide on a writing style and stick to it.** For example, don't use a variety of forms for the same term, like *e-commerce, E-commerce, ecommerce,* and *EC.* Consistency is critical. Do a walkthrough with someone else to edit all pages before posting. At least run a spell check. Remember that errors erode visitor confidence.

- **Give visitors what they're looking for.** Give visitors a reason to visit. For example, if you're selling office supplies, show visitors how to purchase them. The site should be designed to reflect what visitors want to buy rather than what the merchant wants to sell.

- **Identify your business.** When the homepage comes up on a visitor's screen, it should show your business in a unique light. This is called **branding.** Take time to create your own brand.

- **Keep the big picture in mind.** Good design should result in a usable and easily navigable site. Designers, marketers, and technical people should work together to come up with a site that results in a positive user experience.

- **Make the site easy to navigate.** Like good software, an effective Web site should not need a tutorial or a user's manual. A visitor who gets lost in the middle of the site will most likely leave out of frustration. Remember the 8-second rule.

- **Focus on content before graphics.** Content should be useful and usable. Good content should guide, educate, sell, and make a hit with the visitor. Graphics and animation are no substitute for content. Use fewer words, because it is *painful* to read online. Users read 25 percent more slowly online than in print because of the poor resolution of most monitors.

- **Make your text scanable.** According to Nielsen's research, 79 percent of Web users scan rather than read. Only 21 percent read word for word. When visitors were presented with a scanable version of a site, their performance improved by 47 percent. To improve scanability, consider bold text, large type, highlighted text, captions, graphics, content lists, and bulleted lists.

- **Be careful about flashy marketing language.** Present information without boasting and minimize any subjective claims. Hype is not attractive in Internet marketing. People do not appreciate being misled. If users do not like what they see or read, they'll click to another site.

- **Encourage visitor feedback.** The Web site should incorporate an opportunity for visitors to offer praise, criticism, suggestions, and the like. Make it easy for them to reach you via the Web, by phone, fax, or e-mail.

- **Test, test, and test again.** Remember the two levels of testing: First, see if the Web site is technically right; then see if the site is right in the eyes of the visitor. Simply analyzing site logs (records of how many hits each page got, the paths users took through the site, and so on) is not a reliable way to test the Web site. The site should be tested on people.

Fidelity Investments (www.fidelity.com): This site gives visitors the impression that the information they want is easy to find. The material is displayed in a clear and concise format.

Disney (www.disney.com): Visitors know why they went to the site but tend to get lost easily.

MSNBC (www.msnbc.com): This news agency presents essentially the same stories as CNN, but the way the site is designed forces users to work around ads, which often makes it irritating to navigate.

Perhaps the most critical factor in keeping customer loyalty is fostering trust through Web site design. Customers must believe that an e-merchant will follow through on an order, protect the privacy of the e-customer, and assure end-to-end transaction integrity. For online stores, trust means profits, especially when most of the traffic is generated by repeat customers. Also, more and more people complain about the download time, not because of the 8-second rule per se, but because they are having trouble completing a task. This means that designers must develop navigation efficiency and clear content together.

RELIABILITY TESTING

The Internet's increasing role as a medium for commerce has placed new emphasis on **reliability.** Reliability is related to usability. If the scanners at a local grocery store go down, the cashiers will be hard pressed to do business—but they can still manage. If the Web server of a store like Best Buy crashes, the whole operation stops. For a Web administrator, the core of reliability is availability. For example, 98 percent reliability per year means the Web site is not available roughly seven days out of the year.

The three components to Web availability are system availability, network availability, and application availability. A system might be available, but if the network is down, the system is not available and, therefore, not usable. If the system is up and running, but not the application, the system is still down.

To ensure Web site reliability and usability, these ideas are worth noting.

- Provide system backup. The system that supports the Web site should be coupled to a second system that can take over in the event the first system fails.

- Install a disk-mirroring feature. This device allows you to add or replace hardware while the system is in operation.

- Ensure that the system hardware is fault-tolerant. Have a specially designed operating system that keeps the Web site or any application running, even when the central processing unit (CPU) goes down. The goal is to eliminate unplanned or unexpected shutdowns.

- Be sure applications are self-contained. If the Web server uses other applications such as Domain Name Server (DNS) or e-mail, provide a dedicated server for those jobs.

- Be sure there is adequate hard disk space. Enough hard disk space must be available to handle unexpected surges in Web traffic.

- Buy everything from a single vendor. Unless the company is adept at buying hardware and technology from various vendors, reliability, integrity, and maintainability of the total system are best served by buying everything from a single vendor.

USER TESTING

The churning problem is best corrected early in the process by simply asking prospective visitors or customers what they want before finishing the design. Once the design is complete, user testing is crucial before loading the site on the Internet. To test, invite people who will most likely be using the product. Try to eliminate bias by selecting users who have no preconceived notion about the product. For example, if you're building a site for Sears, don't invite people who work for Wal-Mart.

Once the sample has been determined, the next step is to decide what to look for during the test. This type of testing is not a matter of statistics. It is tempting to think that if 6 out of 10 users say they like the company logo on the homepage, that 60 percent of the potential audience likes the logo. Unfortunately, this is not necessarily true because Web site evaluation is essentially subjective. It depends on the visitor's perception of appearance, color, layout, navigation, and so on.

In most cases, you do not need statistics to tell if something is not working well. If every user testing the site finds it difficult to locate certain buttons, there is a good chance that the wider audience will have the same difficulty. The bottom line is not to take test users' choices literally. It is better to look for trends in the way the site is succeeding or failing to reach users.

In conducting user testing, remember that your subjects are not the most reliable source of information, especially for subjective items like color, format, or page integration. It is still critical that the designer present the site with a description and an explanation of the layout. Then if you place the site in front of users and let them try it (review it, place orders), their reactions can give you a good sense of the underlying patterns in their responses.

What should be done after a bug is found? Any bugs should be relayed and assigned to developers who can fix them. After the problem is resolved, fixes should be retested and decisions made to check that fixes did not create problems elsewhere. A number of commercial problem-tracking/management software tools are available that can do the work.

WEB TESTING TOOLS

Available on the market are automated Web testing tools designed to verify and validate several areas related to Web performance in real time. Web administrators can test Web applications for the integrity of text placement, hyperlinks, and pop-up windows. The Web site testing tools essentially emulate the end-user viewpoint firsthand. These are generally organized into several categories, depending on the type of testing your Web site should undergo. The tools range from load and performance test tools, to Java test tools, to Web site management tools and log analysis tools. See www.softwareqatest.com/qatweb1.html for a detailed listing.

Most of the automated Web testing tools look into the interactions among HTML pages, TCP/IP communications, Internet connections, firewalls, applications that run in Web pages (Javascript, plug-in applications, etc.), and applications that run on the server side like database interfaces and logging applications. The end result is that testing for Web sites can become a major effort. Other considerations might include:

- Expected loads on the server and the kind of performance required under such loads
- Downtime for the server

- The kinds of security (firewalls, encryptions, passwords, etc.) required
- The connection speeds the target audience will be using and whether they are within the organization or Internet-wide

A detailed list of considerations is available on www.softwareqatest.com/qatfaq2. html.

MANAGING IMAGES AND COLOR

A company can optimize its Web site in a number of ways. The main areas include images and color, speed, format, layout, and links. Images are appropriate when they are in the right location and are the right size. Experience has shown that bigger images are not always better. Unattractive images can be a serious problem. In one consulting job, the client wanted a large picture of the bank on the homepage. When the site was loaded on the ISP's Web server and launched on the Internet, it took 45 seconds to download and the result was simply ugly. After receiving quite a few complaints from site visitors, there was a quick retreat to the drawing board. The large image was replaced with a much smaller one.

In terms of color and contrast, the key question is: Do the colors you pick work well with the goal(s) of your site? The main point for the Web designer is to be smart about the colors. It is not a good idea to think in terms of favorite or least favorite colors. Just make sure the color supports your message and presents your story in the best light. Most Web site designers agree that dark text on light background is most appropriate. The trick is to have enough contrast between text and background.

READABILITY TESTING

Readability is more than just contrast. As we discussed earlier in the chapter, font type and size, color of background, length of line, and layout of text, when combined with graphics, are all important contributors to readability. White type on a black background is readable, but light gray type on black is easier on the eye. The safest combination is black type on a white background. It might not be the flashiest combination, but it is safe. The larger the type is, the more readable the text is, but the longer the line is, the more difficult it is to read. Long lines and narrow margins just don't work well.

IMAGES: GIFs VERSUS JPEGs

It is inevitable that some images or graphics will appear on your Web pages. Adding graphics is a little complicated, but it is easier when you understand the basics. The best method is to put the graphic in a separate file and then reference that file in your Web page so the browser retrieves the graphic and displays it on the page.

To optimize the page, you need to decide whether a given image ought to be in a GIF or a JPEG format. Either format can be used. The main difference between the two is the compression technique. The **GIF** format is perfect for smaller graphics that should look crisp and bright, like simple company logos, icons, small buttons, and navigation bars or images with large page areas of solid color. Using GIFs for large pictures often leads to huge file sizes and long download times.

JPEG is a popular bit-mapped graphics format ideal for scanned photographs. JPEGs can display thousands of colors and can be compressed into smaller file sizes than GIFs. They're ideal for scanned photographs or multicolor images because they handle true color well. One problem with JPEGs is that they do not handle large areas of solid color or sharp edges well. Some older browsers do not handle JPEGs at all. In contrast, all graphic browsers handle the GIF format.

CACHES

Images that repeat throughout a Web site, such as logos or navigation bars, do not need to download again and again. Netscape and Microsoft Explorer set aside a memory **cache** to store recently used images in RAM and on the hard disk by default. Once the images are stored, a browser recognizes the file name and pulls the image straight from the cache rather than downloading it. This makes images appear to download faster and gives a performance boost to the Web site.

How It Works.   A memory cache works using the following steps:

1. A user requests a Web page.
2. The user's browser checks the cache to see if the request is in. If it is in, then no more is necessary; otherwise, the browser asks the local server.
3. The server checks the cache to make sure the page is not stored there. If it is in, then it serves the browser.
4. The server requests the page from the Internet.
5. The server checks the location of the request and refers it to the closest distribution server.
6. The distribution server delivers the request to the local server.
7. The request is delivered to the local server.
8. The local server sends it to the original requesting user. The browser caches the object.

How Many Links?

As part of site navigation, links and cross-links are inevitable. The critical question is, how many? The more links that appear on a page, the less likely it is that any link will be read. Visitors tend to tune out and just read the text. Also, links can take up as much as half of a page's HTML and, like logos, images, and icons that reside in a cache, they are downloaded repeatedly with every page. Minimizing the links will help speed up site performance.

The Role of the Web Server

It is not just the links, images, color, or format that can affect the performance of a Web site. It is also the speed of the servers and the network connection. Review the status of your ISP's Web server, the bandwidth used, the Web sites it hosts, and the nature of the Web traffic the ISP handles. If you are hosting your own Web site, revisit the server software to ensure that it is tuned for speed. In the meantime, test your site against the competition to see how well it fares in terms of speed and overall performance.

SITE CONTENT AND TRAFFIC MANAGEMENT

Now that you have a Web site in operation, the next step is to learn how to manage its content and traffic.

CONTENT MANAGEMENT

Web content management is the process of collecting, assembling, publishing, and removing content from a Web site. The focus is on version control, content security, and visitor approval. Web content management differs from Web site management, which focuses on easy navigation, availability, performance, scalability, and security. Web content management makes sure a site eliminates waste and clutter. Stuff gets tucked away on a Web site until a visitor hits it and finds dated, irrelevant, or incorrect material. Managing content means promoting the reliability and integrity of the site.

WEB TRAFFIC MANAGEMENT

In terms of traffic management, the idea is to monitor the volume of business coming into the site and interpret its impact on sales, productivity, and inventory turnover. This is based on the philosophy that speed thrills. Never let your visitors get lost. Purge outdated content and never let your visitors see dead links, which sap your credibility. The most common tool for this kind of management is usage statistics reports generated for the client by the ISP. A sample report is shown in Figure 8.2. The report contains a monthly physical count and graphic representation of the total hits (per hour, per day), total pages, total visits, total kilobytes, and usage by country.

One important point to make in reviewing such reports is to be cautious regarding the reliability of the numbers. For example, many reports specify the total time the user spends on your Web site but cannot tell you whether the user was lost for 10 minutes on the credit-card verification screen before clicking away in frustration.

How quickly visitors browse a Web site is another statistic many tools measure. This measure is often falsely associated with speed. In practice, the speed with which visitors move around the site has little to do with their usage patterns. In one study, Spool found that visitors rated the Amazon.com site faster than About.com (Spool, 2003 1). Paradoxically, Amazon.com's pages took an average of 36 seconds to download over a 56-bit modem, but About.com's pages were downloaded successfully in 8 seconds. His conclusion from watching how users traversed the site is that "speed equals ease of information retrieval." To improve the perception of how fast your site loads, take visitors more quickly to the information they're looking for.

THE WEB SITE ADMINISTRATOR

On the Web, success is measured in terms of increased traffic, which can quickly slow down a site. The resulting performance drop can discourage visitors and cause problems in attracting repeat customers. Rising traffic is not the only problem site

FIGURE 8.2   Usage statistics report

Summary by Month

| Month | Daily Avg | | | | Monthly Totals | | | | |
	Hits	Files	Pages	Visits	Sites	KBytes	Visits	Pages	Files	Hits
Aug 2005	25450	17287	2309	562	4006	1530602	10680	43872	328466	483553
July 2005	29584	20037	2468	593	6509	3030926	18384	76529	621159	917117
Jun 2005	30441	20754	2451	606	10069	3045612	18195	73558	622643	913247
May 2005	34391	22466	2600	612	7383	3505548	18986	80609	696468	1066141
Apr 2005	33610	23727	2318	631	8024	3607861	18938	69564	711819	1008305
Mar 2005	23301	20240	972	376	6814	3004429	11283	29167	607202	699058
Feb 2005	25868	22418	978	369	8256	2914490	9977	26412	605293	698457
Jan 2005	19660	16810	780	298	5649	2505802	9254	24190	521114	609487
Dec 2004	31053	26320	1220	432	7626	3864926	12989	36626	789620	931609
Nov 2004	38725	32868	1345	483	9132	4407387	14510	40355	986066	1161757
Oct 2004	38246	30385	1615	543	10023	4207947	16855	50089	941944	1185653
Sep 2004	30555	20279	2023	538	6743	2774905	16141	60710	608382	916654
Totals						**38400435**	**176192**	**611681**	**8040176**	**10591038**

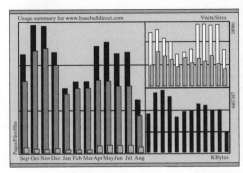

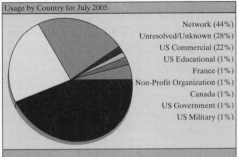

Top 30 of 55 Total Countries

#	Hits		Files		KBytes		Country
1	400251	43.64%	288229	46.40%	1371281	45.24%	Network
2	257525	28.08%	135056	21.74%	524388	17.30%	Unresolved/Unknown
3	201363	21.96%	151252	24.35%	887054	29.27%	US Commercial
4	11961	1.30%	10211	1.64%	57281	1.89%	US Educational
5	6639	0.72%	3616	0.58%	13708	0.45%	France
6	6329	0.69%	5091	0.82%	26717	0.88%	Non-Profit Organization
7	5821	0.63%	4812	0.77%	23075	0.76%	Canada
8	5127	0.56%	4368	0.70%	23175	0.76%	US Government
9	5119	0.56%	3850	0.62%	19507	0.64%	US Military
10	3152	0.34%	2794	0.45%	16633	0.55%	Australia
11	3112	0.34%	2885	0.46%	12671	0.42%	United States
12	1749	0.19%	1523	0.25%	9995	0.33%	Italy
13	1413	0.15%	1139	0.18%	7083	0.23%	Netherlands
14	1291	0.14%	1125	0.18%	7083	0.23%	Germany
15	1018	0.11%	953	0.15%	4741	0.16%	Mexico
16	929	0.10%	734	0.12%	4252	0.14%	Japan
17	503	0.05%	500	0.08%	2331	0.08%	United Kingdom
18	442	0.05%	442	0.07%	2389	0.08%	Dominican Republic
19	320	0.03%	314	0.05%	1280	0.04%	New Zealand (Aotearoa)
20	315	0.03%	302	0.05%	2486	0.08%	Switzerland
21	230	0.03%	217	0.03%	921	0.03%	Peru
22	221	0.02%	219	0.04%	1082	0.04%	Portugal
23	187	0.02%	185	0.03%	701	0.02%	Denmark
24	185	0.02%	114	0.02%	462	0.02%	Spain
25	163	0.02%	163	0.03%	691	0.02%	Brazil
26	161	0.02%	161	0.03%	585	0.02%	Norway
27	159	0.02%	159	0.03%	634	0.02%	Finland
28	124	0.01%	123	0.02%	455	0.02%	Hungary
29	113	0.01%	110	0.02%	591	0.02%	Sweden
30	103	0.01%	105	0.02%	472	0.02%	South Africa

Source: www.baseballdirect.com

designers face. Site technology and infrastructure are also becoming increasingly complex. They involve front-end Web servers, middle-tier application servers, back-end databases, and a number of special-purpose servers. The result is increasing stress for the Web site administrator.

Successful site administrators understand the business value of fast performance. They also understand that they must be proactive and correct situations that can affect the speed with which content is delivered to the site visitor. The situations range from Internet congestion at the ISP to sluggish database performance on the Web site's end. Web site administrators have to evaluate the architecture and figure out which problems they have enough control over to correct and which ones have to be addressed through outside sources or services.

As Figure 8.3 shows, several aspects of a company's Web architecture are the responsibility of the Web site administrator.

- Database server: The administrator's main concern is efficient use of the database server and how well the database can scale up to meet rising traffic. A lot of sites rely on client/server technology that is not designed to handle thousands of simultaneous users. The upgrade can be expensive and difficult to do. Some database managers are now opting to distribute their databases over several low-cost machines to support the Web site.

- Application server(s): The main concern with application servers is having sufficient power and good-quality components. Servers should not be overloaded. Jobs such as sending automatic e-mail to many destinations do not have to be done in real time. A batch approach could save CPU time and leave real time for end-user traffic.

FIGURE 8.3   Main elements of Web architecture

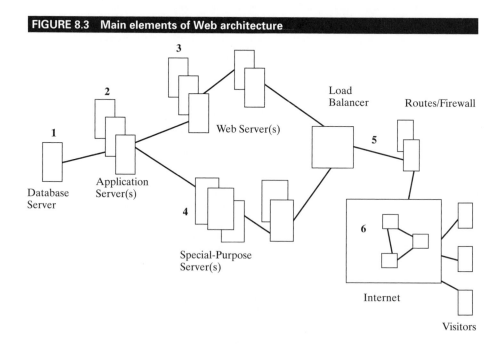

- Web server(s): The main problem here is not having enough servers to accommodate high-volume simultaneous users. Low-cost servers can be added to ease the handling of the total traffic generated by the Web site.

- Special-purpose servers for encryption, security checks, and so on: The main concern for the Web site administrator is CPU-intensive encryption slowing down special-purpose servers. Also of concern is the importance of monitoring the server-to-server switching infrastructure to ensure the viability, continuity, stability, and integrity of the entire technology-based environment.

- Internet bandwidth: Bandwidth is the Web site's connection to the rest of the world. The main question is whether there is enough bandwidth to expedite the Web traffic for the site. In the past, site managers had to decide how much bandwidth to have; today every Web site can be provided with a co-location service to be assured of adequate Internet connectivity. Once connected, your site can bank on additional bandwidth in seconds to accommodate a sudden increase in site traffic.

- Internet performance status: The administrator's main concern is how badly backbone congestion, distance, and the many hops affect traffic performance. Most site managers measure site performance from the inside out: They track how long the system takes to handle content and requests during peak periods. This approach does not reveal anything about the user's experience because the traffic could be on different ISP infrastructures connected to the Internet at different times and speeds and using PCs with different capabilities. The new alternative is using specialized services that regularly check URLs from different points or locations around the Internet. The resulting statistics help site managers determine how badly their sites are suffering from performance problems.

With good control over all these technology-based elements, site managers should have a grip on the performance and integrity of the Web site. Other than financial problems and budgets, one other problem should be addressed—people. Technology that must function round the clock requires experienced, highly trained people to manage it. With more and more visitors entering the Internet, the demand for site use and site management will continue to increase. The increase in demand for technical people poses serious challenges for the site manager. Ensuring an adequate staff requires planning, professional recruiting, and attractive financial packages to retain qualified help.

Summary

1. Web site evaluation means considering graphic identity, navigation quality, functionality, and content. It also includes managing Web traffic.
2. Appropriate site design means matching the demographics and content of a Web site to appropriate colors, shapes, and typefaces.
3. Several criteria have been established for evaluating Web sites: use of color, layout, minimal text, timely information, unique service, speed of performance, consistency in design, protection from invasion and hackers, and scalability.
4. There are four general approaches to Web personalization: cookies,

collaborative-filtering software, check-box personalization, and rule-based personalization.

5. Cookies are the primary means of tracking visitors and personalizing the site experience for the repeat visitor.

6. A Web site should be as inviting and easy to navigate as possible. In checking for usability, a number of questions need to be addressed: Is the site engaging? Is it efficient? Is it supportive? Is it consistent and reliable? Reliability testing means checking for availability: What percentage of the time is the site available?

7. In user testing, the first step is to determine the sample of users and then decide what to look for during the test. It is important to remember that people in general are not the most reli-

able source of judgment, especially for subjective items like color, format, or page integration.

8. Web content management means collecting, assembling, publishing, and removing content from a Web site. Without Web content management, the site will have serious problems from waste and clutter.

9. In terms of traffic management, the idea is to monitor the volume of business coming into the Web site and interpret its impact on sales, productivity, and inventory turnover. The most common tool is usage statistics reports generated for the client by the ISP.

10. Web site management involves good control over the technology-based elements of the site to maintain a high level of site performance and integrity.

Key Terms

- **ancillaries** (p. 238)
- **branding** (p. 251)
- **cache** (p. 255)
- **check-box personalization** (p. 246)
- **churning** (p. 249)
- **clickstream** (p. 244)
- **collaborative filtering software** (p. 246)
- **cookie** (p. 245)
- **GIF** (p. 254)
- **inference-based personalization** (p. 244)
- **JPEG (Joint Photographic Experts Group)** (p. 255)
- **persistent cookies** (p. 247)
- **reliability** (p. 252)
- **scalability** (p. 239)
- **spam** (p. 248)
- **switching cost** (p. 249)
- **transient cookies** (p. 247)
- **Web content management** (p. 256)

Test Your Understanding

1. What are some key questions to consider in evaluating a Web site? Explain.
2. How does color have an impact on the site visitor? Be specific.
3. List and briefly elaborate on the criteria for Web site evaluation.
4. Distinguish between: page content and personalization; category 1 and category 5 Web sites; personalization and scalability; cookies and collaborative-filtering software; check-box personalization and user-based personalization.
5. Elaborate on the general approaches to Web personalization.
6. In what way is a cookie considered a personalization tool? Explain.
7. What makes a Web site usable?
8. The main difference between a person's behavior in a physical store and that on the Web is switching costs. Do you agree? What is switching cost? Explain.

9. If you were to recommend a set of guidelines for effective usability testing, what would you include?
10. What is the difference between (a) reliability and user testing, and (b) reliability and readability testing?
11. What is involved in Web content management?
12. What is involved in Web traffic management?
13. What is the role of the Web site administrator?

Discussion Questions

1. Is Web site design an art or a science? Explain.
2. In your own words, what would you say are the two most important measures of a Web site's performance?
3. How does the Internet keep track of a person's preferences between browsing sessions? Are there security restrictions that a browser could impose that would force a change in the way information about users is recorded?
4. If you were consulting a first-time client whose main products are perishables (fruits, vegetables, and so on), what Web site features would you recommend? How much emphasis would you place on the concept of usability?
5. Color and graphics are important in Web site design. How do you know how many graphics or what type of color to incorporate in a Web site? Be specific.
6. If you were asked to test a new Web site for usability, how would you proceed? Elaborate.
7. It has been said, "Graphic design neither helps nor hurts." Do you agree? Discuss.
8. There is a lot of discussion about navigation and content being inseparable. Do you agree? Expound.

Web Exercises

1. Evaluate the following sites:
   - www.statefarm.com—State Farm Insurance
   - www.wachovia.com—Wachovia Bank
   - www.fedex.com—FedEx

   a. Evaluate each site in terms of color scheme and the profile of the organization as perceived by the visitor.
   b. Does each site follow the use of proper color for psychological effect or impact? What changes would you make? Why?
   c. Is there a relationship between color and how conservative an organization is? Elaborate.

2. Team assignment: Review the bank site assigned to your team by number.
   1. www.bankofamerica.com, Bank of America
   2. www.fnbsm.com, First First National Bank of South Miami, Florida
   3. www.banknd.com, Bank of North Dakota
   4. www.fmtulsa.com, F & M Bank, Tulsa, Oklahoma
   5. www.countynationalbank.com, County National Bank, Hillsdale, Michigan

6. www.mortgagesfbhp.com, First National Bank of Highland Park, Illinois
7. www.kawvalleybank.com, Kaw Valley State Bank, Topeka, Kansas

a. What is the size of the bank (large, medium, small)?
b. What is the category of the site?

   Category 1: Homepage, who we are, and so on
   Category 2: Electronic catalog, data collection
   Category 3: Interactive, business transactions
   Category 4: Multimedia, workflow/BPR integrated
   Category 5: Delivery platform expansion, individualization

c. In what language is the Web site written? (Hint: Right click on the screen and select Source view.)
d. Does the site accommodate a shopping cart? Security features? Tally the number of hits per hour.
e. When you bring up the homepage, what is displayed first, second, and so on?
f. Is the site business-to-consumer, business-to-business, or both? Why? How do you explain this?
g. How well designed is the site? How user friendly is it? Elaborate.

3. Choose a business or social group and design a Web site for it. For example, you might choose a small jewelry store, your sorority or fraternity, or a personal site for your friends or family.

a. What did you set out to do? Exactly what is the title or topic of the project? What benefit do you foresee in taking on this topic? Justify your choice.
b. How did you proceed? That is, what steps did you take to do the work? For example, if you were assessing shopping carts, did you first begin setting criteria as a step for the evaluation? How did you choose or decide on the product? How was the work organized and executed?
c. What did you end up with? What results did you get? How reliable were the results? That is, how did you test the Web site? What do the results mean for the client, for the business, for business in general, for the industry, and so on?
d. What problems (if any) did you encounter while on step 3b? How did you correct them? What do you conclude from the results of your work? Be specific and complete.

CHAPTER 9

INTERNET MARKETING

Learning Objectives

The focus of this chapter is on several learning objectives:

- The many offerings of online shopping
- Various ways to do Internet marketing
- The steps to take in launching a marketing campaign
- How to attract and track customers on the Internet
- The importance of customer service
- The basics of CRM and how it contributes to adding value to e-commerce

IN A NUTSHELL

The Internet will transform every organization in the world. It will create winners and losers, and force corporations to rethink strategies and directions. In the Internet world, companies either evolve or are eliminated. As Lou Gerstner of IBM said, "We're not selling a Web server or a 3-D engine for your PC. We're selling ways for companies to make money."

The Internet offers a high degree of interaction and affords consumers unprecedented benefits, from convenience to bargain prices. Shopping is as easy as searching the Web. Selling on the Internet affects two key areas of e-commerce: business-to-consumer (B2C) and business-to-business (B2B). Both areas involve connecting people and processes to suppliers, customers, and business partners. The connection is the Internet, or the Information Superhighway, and the process is reaching people to consummate a transaction or to deliver a product. Online marketing is direct marketing. It is securing transactions, paying for business services in a secure way, automating the sales force, and having the proper network to finalize a sale.

The bottom line is reaching people, making money, growing with technology, and improving the corporate core process. For example, Chrysler reduced operating costs by $1 billion per year by collaborating with suppliers electronically. The state of

Connecticut reduced the number of delinquent taxpayers by 30 percent by publishing the names of delinquents on the Internet.

Marketing is "the art of the possible." It is the process of planning and implementing the conception, pricing, advertising, and distribution of goods and services to meet the demands of the market for which the product or service is intended. When it comes to reaching people online, the opportunities are virtually unlimited.

It is important to know that online marketing is about business, not just technology. The goal is leveraging an existing investment, starting simple and growing fast, anticipating where you're going with the product, understanding what is unique about the product, attracting and promoting a repeat customer base, and keeping the lines of communication with the customer or supplier open and operational around the clock. Internet marketing is unique in its approach, process, and protocols, but everything must work together in the interest of the corporation, its customers, and its suppliers. This chapter covers online marketing: It sets guidelines and clarifies the rules of the process.

One of the areas covered in this chapter is the role of personalization in online marketing. Marketing on the Internet is unique because it is personal. It is not enough for e-commerce to be fast and cheap. An online business must know its customers, their habits, behaviors, and potential. Almost everything the customer does on a Web site can be used for a profile. Unless the customer is studied and tracked carefully, it will be difficult for the business to know what to offer in the way of products and how such offerings will lead to growth and profitability, but this kind of tracking often raises ethical and legal issues. These are covered in Chapter 12.

THE PROS AND CONS OF ONLINE SHOPPING

The Internet is a meeting place where shoppers and buyers conduct business. The number of shoppers and the volume of business continue to surge. Study after study points to the exponential growth of online shopping. For the online merchant, it is important to understand why people shop, the pros and cons of online shopping for the customer, and the business justification for doing business on the Internet.

THE PROS OF ONLINE SHOPPING

From the consumer's viewpoint, the Web as a whole is empowering, because consumers can opt to click away to the competition any time they wish. The Web is about choice, and the options are endless. Three factors make online shopping attractive.

1. Choice: Consumers in general enjoy having choices before they decide whether to buy or what price they are willing to pay for a product.
2. Vast selection: Online, products can be displayed, reviewed, and compared at no cost in time or funds. This feature makes online shopping much more efficient than having to visit store after store.
3. Quick comparison: Consumers can quickly compare products in terms of price, quality, shipping terms, and so on before making a final choice.

Online shopping boils down to a supply of information. By offering extensive product information, online merchants can help people make the best choice. What does all this mean? Strong evidence suggests that online shopping has inherent advantages that will attract consumers to the Web (even if prices are slightly higher than those of brick-and-mortar stores), due to the availability of information and the speed of information access. Less legwork is needed for shopping on the Internet.

THE CONS OF ONLINE SHOPPING

With all the good features of online shopping come a few drawbacks: Certain buying decisions require information that can best be found in traditional brick-and-mortar stores. For example, when buying personal items like perfume or clothing, the consumer needs to see, feel, smell, or test. Products that require in-store help continue to be bought at traditional stores. For example, Lowe's Home Improvement Warehouse, whose employees advise consumers about products and tools and how to use them, would not do as well on the Web as Barnes & Noble, which sells books with virtually no in-store help. Certain other products do not sell well on the Web because of delivery problems. For example, large items like lumber, fencing, or furniture are best sold in local stores.

Unfortunately, most Web sites do not provide a consumer experience that feels like real *shopping*. Instead, consumers continue to search on their own, which is not the goal. Worse, the tools available on the Web site to help the user reach the right product are inflexible. They generally are designed without any consideration of how real consumers approach shopping. Yet brick-and-mortar stores aren't perfect, when one thinks of parking, obnoxious salespeople, waiting in line to check out, and so on. A shopper can walk out of one store, but going to another store to check a price is another hassle. (See Box 9.1.)

JUSTIFYING AN INTERNET BUSINESS

The first question a merchant should ask before plunging into Internet marketing is this: Is the Internet right for my business? To answer this question, you need two pieces of information: a clear picture of the business and an understanding of the forces that might threaten its survival.

Several reasons can be given for going on the Internet.

1. **Establish presence.** Many companies provide just basic information (general company information, name, history, location, shopping hours, and so on), products for sale, today's specials, methods of payment, special discounts or offers, and the like. Their Web sites have basic links, are simple to navigate, and can be quite responsive. A comment page usually has an e-mail button that the surfer clicks to send a message. The overall goal is to tell customers why they should do business with you.

2. **Serve customers.** In marketing, one of the first things to do is make customers aware that you're available to serve them. Many brick-and-mortar stores use online marketing to attract new customers. The level of service offered depends on the type of business and the product. For example, making a form available to prequalify for a loan would be considered entry-level Internet marketing for a bank. The consumer fills out the form online and clicks on the "submit" button to send it via e-mail to the loan department for processing. It is quick, safe, and saves having to drive to the bank.

BOX 9.1

Brick and Mortar versus Online Shopping

Here is an area of e-commerce design that could exceed the capabilities of real people in physical stores in terms of speed, accessibility, and comprehensiveness. In reality, search is one of the most common, and one of the least successful, ways that users look for things on the Web. Customers can't ask to speak to search's manager, although we've often seen users go to outside search engines such as Google when they have no success using a site's own search engine.

Tell customers what you don't have. A salesperson in a brick-and-mortar store generally tells you if the store doesn't carry what you're looking for. Search engines, on the other hand, often tell you nothing in this situation. When a search returns no hits, users struggle to understand what it means. Does the site not have the item? Is it called something else? Did you misspell the name? Think of the horror of a salesperson staring dumbly as you repeatedly ask for an item using different names, vocal inflections, anything to get your point across.

People like to comparison shop. Without comparison tools on Web sites, users must drill down to get information on a product, grasp the most important details, and either remember them or print them out, back up, find another item, and start the process again. Often users can't remember key features of one product once they've gotten to another, so they're forced to compare based only on what they do remember.

Filtering through the good and the bad can overwhelm them if they don't get any help from the Web site. In physical stores, good salespeople listen to what a customer is looking for, and then point the customer to a selection of stock that meets the criteria, Similarly, when you have a large number of products or a lot of content on your Web site, you need to provide ways for your customer to narrow down the choices. We saw an interesting behavior in our study. No matter how Web sites displayed their product listings, users stopped looking at product listings after two or three pages. This means that if you have a large number of products, you need to help your customers narrow down the list to fit on two or three pages. We use the term *winnowing,* which originally meant "separating the wheat from the chaff," to refer to this process.

Source: Excerpted from Jakob Nielsen and Marie Tahir, "Building Sites with Depth," *Web Techniques,* February 2001, 46ff.

---

3. **Heighten public awareness.** Anyone who accesses a company Web site and learns about the company and what it has to offer is a potential customer. No alternative marketing medium can do the same job this quickly or this well.

4. **Share time-sensitive information.** When it comes to timing and availability of information, the Web has no equal. For example, a quarterly earnings statement, merger news, or the name of the grand-prize winner can be made available in a matter of seconds for the world to know. Also related to this feature is the availability of color, graphics, video, and audio to go with news releases, interviews, or special announcements. No brochure can do this as well.

5. **Sell goods.** This attraction carries high priority in Internet marketing, but before getting serious about selling, it is important to consider the other features listed previously. That is, before online customers begin to order, they need to know about the business.

6. **Answer important questions.** Every day organizations spend time and money trying to address customer queries, most of which are repeat questions. Among the roles of the Web site is to compile frequently asked questions (FAQs) that customers can access. This will remove another time-consuming task from the company's staff.

7. **Stay in touch with field personnel.** The sales force occasionally needs information from the home office about a product, a procedure, or a special situation. Using the Web to provide such information is the most efficient and effective way to do business from afar.

8. **Market at the international level.** With a Web page, a company can reach international customers just as easily and quickly as it can reach the customer next door. In fact, many companies have learned that before going on the Web, they must have a plan in place to handle the surge of orders.

9. **Serve the local market.** Local or global, Web access is everything. A local restaurant, a movie theater, or an auto repair shop can benefit from Web marketing. No matter where the business is located, the customer should be able to access it on the Web.

10. **Market specialized products.** Specialized products or services, from baseball caps to flying lessons, are ideal for Internet marketing. For example, how about a briefcase made of African ostrich skin for $1,100? (See www.africa-exotic.com/clothing.htm.) With millions of surfers on the Web, the smallest interest group could turn out to be a sizable number of customers for the product.

11. **Reach the youth market.** The "under 25" surfer is fast becoming a formidable segment of the Web market. With offerings from athletic products to specialized international tours, start-up firms catering to that market segment are reaping dividends.

Someone summarized the justification for entering online marketing by suggesting that if you answer "yes" to your business being local and dependent on face-to-face customer contact, chances are the Internet is not for you. On the other hand, if you have an unusual product and the product can be shipped by mail, then you should seriously consider Internet marketing.

INTERNET MARKETING TECHNIQUES

The Internet allows for a continuum of marketing techniques ranging from strictly passive to aggressive. The passive tack comes down to viewing the Web as a variation on television and the visitor as a variation on the TV viewer. Take **banner** ads. With sound, animation, and other techniques, these messages try to get a visitor to quit surfing long enough to read or click on them. Banner ads are covered later in the chapter.

banner: advertising with links to a merchant's Web site.

Passive Internet marketing is called **pull marketing,** because it requires the user to pull the information from the site. The user must actively seek out the site. Currently, most people access Web site content by pulling. Each time a user clicks a link, the browser sends a request to the Web server (a pull) asking for a specific page. The browser downloads the page and displays it on the user's screen. (See Figure 9.1.)

pull marketing: passive Internet marketing, where the user takes the initiative requesting specific information from the Web site.

PULL TO PUSH CONTINUUM

PASSIVE	MODERATELY	MODERATELY	AGGRESSIVE
Providers of information (mere presence) advertising	Site registered with many search engines Specialized services to users requesting information Specialized e-mail to users requesting periodic information	Off-line advertising Banner advertising Targeted e-mail to past customers	Spam mail Chain mail

FIGURE 9.1   Range of Internet marketing techniques and applications

Source: Adapted from P. Greenstein, *E-commerce.* New York: McGraw-Hill, 2000, 368.

push technology: the Web site "pushes" the information at the customer, irrespective of his or her interest.

In aggressive Internet marketing, the Web site seeks out potential customers. This is called **push technology,** because the Web site "pushes" the information at consumers, irrespective of their interest. The Web server does not wait until the consumer requests a page. When the content the consumer has signed up for is ready, the server delivers (pushes) it automatically to the consumer's PC so it can be read, reviewed, or watched. As shown in Figure 9.1, most Internet marketing techniques fall somewhere in between these extremes. Table 9.1 shows examples of pull and push activities. Not all products translate well online and, therefore, may not need anything beyond the passive-type site.

Registering with search engines and directories is one way of trying to attract visitors. Getting information about specialized services to users who request it usually is done by e-mail. This is a way to attract visitors to a site that requires action by the Web site and the visitor. Interested visitors usually sign up for the service. Because the visitor requests the information, this type of Internet marketing is more pulled than pushed by the customer via the Web site.

Off-line advertising, such as on radio or television or in magazines and newspapers, although expensive, is necessary to promote a Web site. This is more push than

TABLE 9.1   Examples of push and pull technology

Pull Technology	*Push Technology*
You turn on your computer and begin to read the electronic newspaper personalized around your favorite subjects or headlines.	You receive a note from Barnes & Noble that your spouse's favorite novel has just arrived. You click on the bookseller's Web site and order a copy.
Around 9:30 A.M., a window pops up from your stock brokerage house displaying the ticker tape of NYSE and NASDAQ stocks.	You are alerted by your brokerage house that the two stocks you want to sell have just been rated "strong buy" by Merrill Lynch.
Before you go home, a news flash from your airline reminds you to be at the gate one hour early because the flight is booked solid.	Amazon.com sends you an e-mail reminding you that the impact wrench you hesitated to order on June 3 is now on sale, plus a $20 coupon if your total order within the next 10 days is $100 or more.

pull marketing. Web sites don't just attract business the moment they are on the Internet. It takes repetitive ads locally and nationally, which means a hefty budget and a professional marketing effort.

Online banner advertising is a service offered (for a fee) by Internet marketing firms that install advertising banners on popular Web sites (like search engines) with links to a merchant's Web site. This is more costly than other methods, but it is also more effective in attracting visitors.

I'LL BE SPAMMED

Targeted e-mail to past customers is **aggressive marketing** because past visitors do not expect further contacts with the online merchant. This method is effective, because it discontinues the advertisements if past visitors do not return to the site within a designated time period. *Cookies* are used to identify and track customer responses to e-mail advertisements.

aggressive marketing: a marketing technique where the Web site seeks out potential customers; push technology.

The most aggressive (and abusive) Internet marketing technique is spamming. **Spamming** is sending out millions of e-mails to recipients who never asked for them. E-mails are sent to individuals and organizations that have never visited the merchant's Web site. Addresses are purchased, swapped with other businesses, or obtained via software robots that scan the Web and collect addresses from Web sites, Web pages, mailing lists, and other public sources. Spamming is the online equivalent of junk mail.

spamming: sending out millions of e-mails to recipients who never asked for them.

E-mail has been proven as a unique medium for direct marketing. It offers a low-cost means to target individuals round the clock. The problem is with junk mail—unsolicited bulk commercial e-mail. According to one source, spam accounts for 60 percent of all Internet e-mail or 76 billion messages, requiring 10 petabytes (10,000 trillion bytes) of storage (Sipior et al., 2004).

One of the most objectionable aspects of spam is invasion of privacy. This has become especially critical with location-based marketers sending direct mobile spam, with a message based on location and personal characteristics. What makes spamming difficult to stop are the incentives that tempt recipients to read messages. Even then, many spams are scams. As a result, the Federal Trade Commission (FTC) set up an e-mail address (uce@ftc.gov) to which customers may forward spam for further investigation.

Spamming is costing corporations millions each year to fight unwanted messages. The cost includes personnel time spent reading and deleting spam messages, implementing blocking software, or recovering from spam volume that often slows down servers and even blocks the entire bandwidth. The risk of corporate liability for employee claims of a hostile work environment do not help matters much.

The key question is how to combat spam. The first line of defense is simply not to publish your e-mail address. AOL and other search engines are taking aggressive action to block and tackle spammers at all levels. As far as the laws are concerned, not much has been done, because of the free speech protection of the First Amendment to the Constitution. Numerous spamming bills have been enacted since 1997, such as the Controlling the Assault of Non-Solicited Pornography and Marketing Act of 2003 and the CAN-SPAM Act in January 2004. The latter act applies to wireless spam and required the FTC to disseminate rules within nine months to protect consumers from unwanted mobile spam. (See Box 9.2.)

BOX 9.2

Fighting Spam

A New York-based online jewelry retailer blasted an e-mail to customers with the subject line "Hot Summer Styles." Even though the intended recipients had asked to receive mailings from the company, some 300,000 of them never saw it. The word *hot* apparently triggered filters that blocked the message from being delivered.

Online retailer eBags sends out about 8 million electronic messages per month to customers who opt to receive its mailings. A year ago, 22 percent of the recipients made purchases as a direct result of those messages. Now the conversion percentage is 13.2 percent. One conclusion is that e-mail is no longer the primary growth driver. It now ranks behind affiliate marketing, off-line catalogs, and search technology on the priority list.

Spam is to blame. Mike Frazzini, vice president of technology at eBags, estimated that at least 30 percent of the company's e-mail is being blocked or filtered, although he acknowledged that it's tough to quantify.

Source: Excerpted from Carol Sliwa, "Electronic Retailers Hurt by Spam Flood." *Computerworld,* August 18, 2003, 10.

POP-UP ADVERTISING

The increasing need for getting consumers to pay attention to online products and services has led to the well-known, annoying pop-up: an advertisement that "pops up" in a new browser window regardless of the user's wish to open such a new window. (See Box 9.3.)

Pop-up messages are among the most common forms of online marketing and are another example of push marketing. But they have been viewed as the most frustrating

---

BOX 9.3

Pop-Ups Work

Advertising.com concluded that pop-ups, for all the fuss they generate, are the best creative format for generating consumer conversions. Heavy pop-up advertisers like Orbitz have long said their pop-ups work well in generating conversions.

While spam is the runaway favorite for top villain of Internet marketing, pop-ups consistently rank not far behind. IVillage, which banished pop-up ads from its site in August 2002, reported that 92.5 percent of its users tabbed them as their least favorite part of the site experience.

EarthLink and AOL have dueled over which is tougher on pop-up ads, with EarthLink going so far as to run an ad campaign lambasting AOL's pop-up policy. Advertising.com, which serves pop-up ads for clients, cited a Dynamic Logic study from 2001 that found consumers accepting of pop-up ads so long as they were infrequent, regarding the unit with the same mild irritation with which they regard direct mail.

Advertising.com's study found that all ads lose their effectiveness when impression levels rise, with one to five impressions generating the best revenue return.

Source: Excerpted from Brian Morrissey, "Pop-up Ads." itmanagement.earthweb.com/ecom/print.php/2213861.

feature on the Web. Pop-ups are an effective form of advertisement because they are relatively cheap and can be tailored to individual consumers. These new pop-ups have quickly spread throughout the Internet. Unfortunately, there are no standards on which to judge their usage. There are well over 12 billion pop-up advertisements on the Internet; 10 billion of which are from 63 of the 2,208 firms using pop-up advertisements.

A new technique for pop-up ads is called "kick-through" advertising. Users are directed to another Web site as soon as they move the cursor across the pop-up ad. The novelty requires no clicking. Companies attribute a lot of their online success to the "kick-through" technique. The most recent technique, called "mouse trapping," becomes active when a user decides to close a particular online application. That site initiates a program that sends a barrage of smaller pop-up windows to the user. The user is often more concerned with closing windows than with actually looking at the messages being displayed.

Among the largest companies to capitalize on the easy mass production of pop-up ads are travel sites such as Orbitz.com, Expedia.com, and Travelocity.com. Orbitz.com, for example, created over 700 million pop-up impressions in 2004, second only to X10 Wireless, which created more than one billion pop-up impressions the same year.

Pop-up ads are among the most controversial forms of online marketing. From the surfer's view, in addition to slowing down the human side of Internet use, pop-ups can sometimes slow down software on surfers' computers by the creation of another window and by crowding the World Wide Web with excess packets and bundles of information. If this is left unchecked, in time the Internet could become considerably slower due to the presence of these unwanted ads.

From the ISP's view, pop-up ads are a major source of revenue. After receiving numerous consumer complaints, some ISPs have made adjustments to the onslaught of this form of advertising by simply eliminating or regulating pop-up ads. One such ISP is EarthLink, which in 2003 began providing its 5 million users with free pop-up blocking software. In doing so, ISPs could charge their clients a monthly fee for eliminating such online interruptions.

The adverse impact of pop-up ads was so pronounced in 2003 that some computer programmers have taken the time to create programs with the sole purpose of eliminating pop-ups. One example of anti-pop-up software can be found at www.intermute.com, which also includes programs to eliminate spam-mail.

Are there ethical implications to pop-up ads? Many Internet users, including this author, feel that pop-up ads are intrusive and even violate privacy issues as well. Some advertising agencies have become so invasive that they place a shortcut icon to the company's Web site on users' desktops without their consent. From the cyber world to the real world, this is tantamount to a firm intruding into a home and placing its number on speed dial without the permission of the household. It is obvious that some regulation is long overdue, but who should be responsible for this regulation? No single person or agency owns the Internet or its content, so regulating it will prove to be a daunting task.

PERMISSION MARKETING

Successful Internet advertising depends on consumers viewing the ads. Adware companies know their industry faces big challenges, including lawsuits alleging the violation of third party sites' copyrights, proposed legislation banning adware, and questionable transparency to the user typical of spyware. Spamming and e-mail marketing are intrusion marketing. They are a mere nuisance and do nothing but alienate the customer. Alternative approaches to Internet marketing had to be developed.

permission marketing:
marketers ask permission before they send advertisements to prospective customers, requiring that people first "opt in" rather than "opt out" after the ads have been sent.

Internet advertising approaches recently developed by two Israeli-based marketing firms offer Internet marketers a more direct channel on which to deliver their sales messages. These methods adopt a long-traditional one-to-one marketing form to the Internet. Called opt-in or **permission marketing,** it simply means obtaining the customer's consent to receive information from a company. The company sends the advertisements that the customers are interested in and, therefore, can develop a strong relationship with its customers. (See www.marketing.org.nz/emarket_dictionary.php.)

Here is how permission marketing works. Consumers opt in for the marketing service through an Internet merchant with whom there is already a sales relationship. This is done through a form or a survey that the customer fills out at some point in the relationship. The merchant then begins to deliver targeted banner ads in the consumer's browser when surfing the Internet. When consumers see a message in a banner ad, they already know the message fits their interests. In one respect, the process elevates the traditional ad banner space to a personal messaging opportunity. (See www.ecommer cetimes.com/story/38113.html.)

Typically, a consumer empowers a marketer to send promotional messages in certain interest categories. The marketer then matches advertising messages with the interests of consumers. Permission marketing helps marketers to provide relevant promotional messages. See www.yesmail.com as an example of a permission marketing firm.

One motivation for this approach has been the failure of the direct mail approach of sending unsolicited promotional messages via e-mail or spam. The psychology behind permission marketing is that individuals recognize that letting companies provide information is in their self-interest. As a result, there is ready participation in an exchange of information for a promise of better service in the future. Customers realize that this is an incentive-compatible (win-win) program. (See www.ascusc.org/jcmc/vol6/issue2/krishnamurthy.html.)

THE E-CYCLE OF INTERNET MARKETING

Like any business venture, Internet marketing follows a life cycle that begins with planning, followed by the four P's: product, pricing, place (distribution or delivery), and promotion. (Customer personalization is unique to marketing on the Internet and is discussed later in the chapter.) (See Figure 9.2.)

THE BUSINESS PLAN

business plan: a written document that identifies a merchant's business goals and how to achieve them.

Whether you are an experienced business owner or a start-up organization, the basic steps for starting an online business are the same. The first is a business plan. A **business plan** is a written document that identifies your business goals and how you will achieve them. It can be as simple as laying out the things you want to do and matching

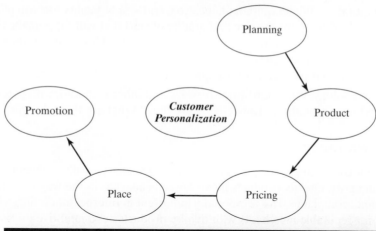

FIGURE 9.2   The e-cycle of Internet marketing

them against other products on the market, the competition, the constraints, and the cash flow requirements. In virtually every case where an online business failed, it was either because of poor planning or poor management. A business plan is critical for an Internet business.

For a small business, it is a good idea to check with the local Small Business Administration office; call the national toll-free number (1-800-697-4636), or visit its Web site, www.sbaonline.sba.gov. The SBA has generic business plans and can help you make your own. For a large business, planning is more elaborate and can take weeks and months to complete. A committee of experienced staff usually looks at the entire life cycle of the business, does simulations to see how well a Web site operates using sophisticated software, and matches all the alternatives against set goals before generating the master plan. Elaborate planning involves attorneys, accountants, and strategists, in addition to business owners and managers.

The content of a business plan varies with the type and size of the business, but generally includes the following elements.

vision: perception or insight into what can happen or take place in the future.

1. Mission: What is your business is trying to achieve? Missions are related to the **vision** of the owners, which is also considered.

2. Product: What are you selling? What makes it unique?

3. Competition: Who are your competitors? How well established are they? Analyze their Web sites and review the unique features they offer customers.

4. Target audience: Are prospective customers likely to use the Internet at work or at home? Do they use e-mail? News groups? AOL?

5. Marketing: How do you plan to reach your customers? What advertising media do you plan to use?

6. Sales plan: What sales methods (telemarketing, agents) do you plan to employ? What about distribution channels, pricing, and fulfillment processes?

7. Operation: What equipment, location, and size of facility are you planning to start with? What about the size and quality of staff that will support the operation? Who are your suppliers? How reliable are they? How many of them are on the Internet? What experience do they have? Do they deal with your competitors? What about customer service and support? How will customers reach you?

8. Technology: What hardware/software and other technology do you need? Which ISPs are available? How reliable are they? What are their charges?

THE PRODUCT

When it comes to product, the emphasis is on viability, quality, reliability, dependability, and integrity. Quality products mean fewer headaches in the way of returns, repairs, or customer complaints. This is especially important in Internet marketing, where customers look for reputable merchants with quality products at competitive prices. Products may be physical goods or services. Physical goods are tangible, like grocery items, shirts, and automobiles. Service products are the work performed by professionals like doctors, certified public accountants, and travel agents, along with information like real-time stock quotations. Identifying the unique features of either type is critical in Internet marketing.

PRICING

Once the product is identified, the next step is to decide how much to charge. Web-based pricing strategies differ with the merchant, the market, and the type of customer. For example, ParenthoodWeb.com (www.parenthood.com) offers a free service for visitors in order to develop a community. It is devoted to offering families and those about to become parents Web sites that are most likely to be of interest. Other sites, like those of airlines, use frequent purchase plans to reinforce customer loyalty and encourage repeat purchase, or Web-only specials to encourage online purchase. In online auctions, an auction item starts at an attractive minimum price, allowing purchasers to bid up the price. Another approach is that of www.priceline. com, which asks customers to offer a price that they would be willing to pay to purchase a ticket, stay at a favorite hotel, rent a car, and so on. In this case, Priceline's pricing process *is* its product.

PLACE

Electronic commerce facilitates the exchange of information between businesses and delivery companies to ensure prompt delivery of physical goods to customers. More and more companies align their fulfillment phase with delivery companies like Federal Express so that direct deliveries are made to the customer from the supplier, bypassing the need to stock many items in a warehouse.

The Internet itself can be viewed as a delivery channel for digital products. Thousands of software packages and applications can be ordered online and downloaded directly onto the customer's PC. Some Internet merchants deliver online news services and stock trading services electronically. This is a new distribution channel for sellers of digital products that is cheap, fast, and effective. The only drawback is the possibility of tapping or theft of digital data.

PROMOTION

Internet marketing is about promoting a product to get the attention of prospective customers. Internet marketing follows the AIDA (attention, interest, desire, and action) guidelines for direct mail marketing. The first goal is to get the *attention* of the prospective visitor. Web site quality, ease of navigation, and personalization are important, because attention is the entry point or the front of the marketing process. Good graphics, attractive banners, and proper use of color are essential to draw visitors to the Web site. A brief search of the Internet would undoubtedly yield good, bad, and ugly Web sites. Box 9.4 lists good sites and sites *not* worth seeing.

Banners are the most popular type of Internet ads. They continue to be the staple of Web advertising. They are to the Internet what 30-second commercials are to television. A banner is a rectangular graphic strip placed horizontally across the top of a Web page. Some flash and others blink. They are an example of push marketing. The idea is to attract the consumer to click on the banner as an entry point to the Web pages to follow. However, consumers quickly became click resistant, and less than 0.5 percent of customers clicks through them. Banner ads are also the most controversial. Critics view them as window dressing that can easily be tuned out by surfers. Supporters say that banners are cheap and fit the traditional ad agency formula. Leading Web marketers think that enough banners will create a footprint—a reminder of the product or service that is available. (See Box 9.5.)

The use of banners is not as easy as it may seem, as click-throughs hover below 1 percent. A *click through* is every time a user clicks on the banner and goes to the advertiser's site. There are numerous ways to make banners useful for awareness or advertising. Banners should be small and fast loading. If animation is used, it should be action in horizontal movements, because evolution has trained the human eye to be very alert to such motions for survival. A banner text should also be used wisely by using the largest size font possible and a simple readable font like Courier or Times New Roman. Business marketers should test their banners by getting a number of different designs and trying them in different ad networks. This way, they can learn where customers are and what makes them respond best.

In any case, once the site gets the visitor's attention, the next step is to create *interest* in the product(s) displayed. The display is like bait. Quick response time and ease of navigation make a difference in how quickly a visitor is guided through the choice of products. Information creates interest in a site. Web pages have to be updated constantly and provide excitement to keep visitors interested.

The interest phase should lead to the next step—building a *desire* for action. Interactivity through navigation generates a desire to continue or to click away. In most cases, the visitor clicks back and forth, reviewing and assessing every product before making a decision. That decision is the *action*—placing the order or the sale. This is as easily done as filling out an online form. Once it is completed, the visitor clicks on a button to e-mail the form to the company for processing. When the form is received, the company initiates the fulfillment phase of the marketing process.

Promoting a product requires a persistent online presence. Many off-line brands do not always translate to the Web. One strategy is to combine online and off-line marketing in a consistent, continuous way. Messages across multiple media should work together.

BOX 9.4

Examples of the Best and Worst Web Sites

THE BEST

- **CNET.com** has technology everywhere, from your cubicle to your car. The site covers comparison shopping, hardware reviews, and free software downloads.

- **Shutterfly.com** is more of a digital darkroom. The site specializes in preparing and printing users' digital images at reasonable prices.

- **ESPN.com** is home to all things sport, from pitches to pucks and from Red Grange to Secretariat.

- **NationalGeographic.com** covers the world online, discovered from your desk.

- **Evite.com** is a party planner. It sends e-mail invitations to your friends, family, and others, and then waits for a response. It coordinates various aspects of party planning, including car-pooling, who is bringing what, and so forth.

- **Amazon.com** is an e-tailer selling everything from cookbooks to DVD recorders. The site allows users to see what other people are buying, where they work and live, and other information. Its motto is "Where technology meets business."

- **ZDNet.com** is rated the best site for keeping up with the ever-changing world of computer technology.

- **EBay.com** carries the logo "You want it, someone's got it." Millions of items are for sale daily, with a sophisticated feedback system to check out comments about sellers.

- **CNN.com** is one of the best-known sites for up-to-the minute worldwide news and in-depth reporting about sports, show business, politics, food, and more.

- **E-Trade.com** offers all the services of investing, from day-to-day trading to long-term security.

See www.web100.com for more of the best Web sites.

THE WORST

- The online clothing retailer modestapparelchristianclothinglydia ofpurpledressescustomsewing.com has a 62-character domain name; that fact alone makes business difficult. Look it up to make your own assessment. What do you think?

- The now-defunct site titled "Hello my future girlfriend" can still be viewed here: www.2 atoms.com/comedy/worstoftheweb/ blount.htm. It is a classic example of a laughably ineffective use of Web space. The site was active for two years, and became something of a cult phenomenon on the Web.

- Web surfers can actually hunt live animals at www.live-shot.com. For less than $95, visitors can sign up to kill the animal of their choice with the click of a mouse. Using a webcam and Internet connection, hunters from thousands of miles away can shoot animals by controlling the position of a rifle using their computers. Rifles are mounted in a structure on a fenced-in ranch in Rocksprings, Texas. Hunters see the gun's sight on their computer screens. They guide the mouse to train the rifle on the target. One click operates the trigger and the rest is history.

See www.worstoftheweb.com for more examples of bad sites (low quality, most severe, and furthest from the standard), and www. whoisjesus-really.com/english/default.htm for one of the worst.

BOX 9.5

New Format Brand Ads

There are different approaches to designing Web ads. The ones worth noting are the skyscrapers, bulky boxes, buttons and big impressions, pop-up ads, and e-mail.

SKYSCRAPERS

Banners represent a lot of the real estate on a Web page. So perhaps it isn't surprising that one of the latest offshoots is known as the "skyscraper." It is simply a tall, skinny banner ad, and it can take up even more space than the pioneering top-of-the-screen rectangles. Because a typical personal computer monitor is wider than it is high, a skyscraper ad can perch on either side of the screen without infringing too much on the page itself. But text in vertical ads is harder to read. And if an ad sits too far off to the side, a viewer may never even scan it.

BULKY BOXES

On the News.com Web site of San Francisco's Cnet Networks Inc., banner ads are about the size of a CD case and sit smack in the middle of the page. Instead of being taken to another site, readers who click on the ad get more information without having to leave the page. News stories wrap right around the ad box. This makes the ad a lot harder to ignore. But the reader's eye has to track around it in order to see the content.

BUTTONS AND "BIG IMPRESSIONS"

Not all banners are so aggressive. Walt Disney Co.'s Web sites, including ESPN.com and ABC.com, now run business-card-size banners on the upper-right-hand corner of the page. Disney calls this format "the Big Impression." The nice part about this design is because the Disney ads sit off to the right side, they aren't interfering with other material on the screen and can remain there for a long time. Yet, because the ads are off in a corner on the right side, they might get overlooked. After all, people read from left to right.

POP-UP ADS

Some ads don't hesitate to get in your face. So-called pop-up ads appear in a second window that pops up on the screen while a Web page is loading. These speedy connections allow for what online ad types call "rich media" ads, which use animation, sound, and streaming video. Banner ads can include rich media and are getting livelier these days, but flashy content is found more often in the pop-up ads. These lively ads are more intrusive and memorable because they pop up and have to be clicked on to be gotten rid of. They are used primarily as a brand-building tool by automakers, consumer-products companies, and movie studios. Yet many people banish the box from their screens even before they see the ad. They can be incredibly annoying, precisely because they are so intrusive. They often slow down the loading of the site you are trying to view.

E-MAIL

Because recipients have to subscribe to receive e-mail, marketers are guaranteed a highly targeted audience. Response rates can run as high as 5 percent to 15 percent. The positive part is that e-mail marketing has proved to be a cost-efficient way to acquire new customers. There are no postage fees and no hassle of pickup and delivery. But, as e-mail surges, so will the clutter in customers' inboxes. The challenge will be to retain high response rates and low "unsubscribe" rates.

Source: From Jennifer Rewick, "Choices, Choices," *Wall Street Journal,* April 23, 2001, R12.

With surfers ignoring online marketing, advertisers are trying creative new approaches. Among the changes are the following.

- Smarter ads, with Web sites using improved tracking software to decide which demographic category surfers fit into, their likes, dislikes, and so on. From there, the ads the surfers see do a better job of matching their interests. Some of the ads even ask surfers to recommend products they might like.

- Forcing ads to appear smack in the center of the monitor before the surfer's eyes. Some companies have devised huge, animated mega-banners that dominate a Web page. Some even keep reappearing on other pages within the Web site even after the site is shut down.

- Advertisers creating their own "information-heavy" Web sites, on the basis that it is easier to get surfers to read or listen to a sales ad if offered free content in the bargain.

PERSONALIZATION

The fifth P in e-marketing is **personalization.** The technology combines two P's— promotion and product—so customers receive personalized information or visit a home-page customized for them (for example, a customer's favorite stock quotes displayed on his or her screen). The role of personalization in e-commerce has been on the increase. The personalization software provides the one-to-one recommendation of products and services and direct access to personally relevant news, and it collects information about user interests for customer relationship management (CRM) activities. Three main ideas make up the personalized presentation of information.

personalization: a technique that combines product and promotion for customers to receive information customized to their needs.

- Technically detailed descriptions are presented to the level of the user's knowledge.
- Product presentations are customized to suit the user's interests.
- The user's expectations are met regarding the amount of relevant information.

IMPORTANT PERSONALIZATION RULES. Online personalization is a new field, and its practice is a new art. Based on experience in the field, common practices have been established for this area of specialization. Several rules are worth noting.

- **Prevent resistance to personalization.** Customers do not like to fill out forms or participate in surveys about themselves or about product preferences. Use subtle ways to draw them in little by little.

- **Consider any source of information.** The sources include data warehouses, databases, and data mining performed on data warehouses.

- **State preferences of users through forms or similar procedures.**

- **Focus on privacy in every way possible.** Customers do not mind sharing personal information if they can be sure they trust you. The last thing you can afford to do is share their information or sell it.

- **Make an effort to learn from every move.** Infer from customers' action or inaction. Study it and mine it for future use. A satisfied customer is best shown the moves that worked last time.

- **Jump-start a personalization relationship by posing the user a set of questions.**

- **Sell the goodness of personalization.** This can be done after you start asking surfers what they need. Then demonstrate how your personalized environment can meet their needs.

- **Make life easier for users to tell you what they want and what they hate.** Provide an optional, brief questionnaire that customers can respond to "on the fly" whenever they feel in the mood.

- **Make sure there is no delay in a personalization environment.** Nothing is worse for the user than to encounter unnecessary or unwarranted delays, especially when they know the interface is personalized.

In most personalized interfaces, a bit of *artificial intelligence* is incorporated into Internet marketing. For example, if you visit Hallmark's Web site, its database can store information about your visit so that it can provide personalized, free service such as sending you a message about forthcoming birthdays of family members. Amazon.com does something similar. After your first visit, the homepage greets you by name automatically brings up your credit card number to verify, and while you're still deliberating on a book, brings up information about the book you're considering from people you know or from reviewers.

This is true personalization. It crosses promotion and product and enhances both in the process.

MARKETING IMPLICATIONS

A power shift has occurred from the merchant to the consumer in terms of accessing and controlling information that leads to a buy–no buy decision. The consumer has acquired additional power that today is called *knowledge.* At the core of this knowledge is the information at one's fingertips 24/7. At any time, from anywhere, the consumer can access any information on virtually any topic. Consumers are now actively participating in jobs that were once the domain of the marketer. In the past, consumers were limited to purchase and consumption. Today, they can design the product they want from their own homes. Technology is changing the marketing game and altering the way marketers do business with consumers.

Another marketing implication behind the power shift is the unique Internet marketing strategy that today's online merchant must adopt. Such a strategy follows common-sense rules like these.

1. Content: Don't bore your customers with unnecessary content or detail. Make the site simple and get to the point.
2. Dynamic and attractive sites: Make your Web site attractive using technology that personalizes information to fit the visitor's profile.
3. Brands: A merchant's Web site should be his or her most important brand. From the banner to the buttons, links, graphics, text, audio, and video, the site becomes the storefront of the business.
4. Get to the point: Conciseness, clarity, and ease of navigation are important criteria to keep in mind for a Web site. Customers do not like clutter. They have a low tolerance for reading a lot of text. Information should be in short paragraphs, spread over several pages.

5. Promotion: Don't expect customers to line up for your Web site just because you have one. Promote your site everywhere—local newspapers, radio program, mass mailings, and so on.

6. Online events: Events such as a new product offering or a two-day discount on hot items create customer awareness, especially when they are presented on the site's homepage.

7. Free giveaways: This can be a great reinforcer for loyal customers. Amazon.com has a program that evaluates the frequency of customer traffic and recommends a series of enticing giveaways for customers who suddenly stop placing orders.

8. Consistency: The Web site's pages should have consistency in layout and overall flow. Content also should be distributed consistently across pages in an easy-to-follow format.

HOW TO MARKET PRESENCE

Millions of Web sites are on the Internet. You are a newcomer. How do you market your presence? How quickly does your Web site begin to get hits? How do you promote your Web site elsewhere on the Web? A marketing colleague once commented: "When you find something that works, don't fix it!" It is obvious that Web site promotion takes planning to draw attention, interest, and interested visitors. Visitors won't come unless they know where to find you and why they might want to visit. For ideas on how to generate traffic, check www.submit-it.com. The goal is not just to get the greatest number of hits; it is to generate business and increase profits.

PROMOTING YOUR SITE ON YOUR SITE

Self-promotion begins with your domain name. Most domain names are company names that remind the visitor about the product (e.g., IBM), the founder, or something that will encourage a click to that site. One way to increase the number of hits is to encourage repeat visits. Over time, visitors begin to sense stability, reliability, and availability of products and service.

Many first-time merchants arrange with a software developer to distribute its browser with the logo (trademark, trade name, company name, seal) in it whenever a visitor boots up the software. This type of promotion can be mailed to existing customers with an invitation to visit your site with giveaways or special prizes to the nth visitor. Other ways include bartering an ad exchange, accepting paid advertising, recruiting sponsors, or negotiating reciprocal links. For example, a bank that receives a query through its Web site about a loan that it cannot handle has a button on its homepage that will link the customer directly to a designated bank for follow-up. If the latter bank issues the loan, the initiating bank earns a commission or a flat fee, based on a prior arrangement.

Note that raw hit rate alone does not tell you (1) how many computers visited the site, (2) feedback from users by e-mail, (3) number of times a specific file was accessed, (4) number of repeat visitors from the same address, (5) how long users spent on the site, (6) addresses from which calls were made, or (7) frequency of requesting whole pages. Most ISPs can provide this information so that hit rates can be evaluated properly.

Updating site content is important in attracting return visitors. Every time something new is added, repeat the announcement via your site, e-mail, or other sources that have worked well for your business. A "what's new" button on each page is an effective way to expedite traffic.

Another area worth considering is sharing with visitors any awards or recognition from the media your business has received. In other words, "toot your own horn." This goes beyond putting out a local press release. It is a testimonial to your viability and should bring repeat visitors.

What about promotional giveaways, contests, and games? The whole idea behind these marketing tools is to remind visitors that you are there. They can be enticed by reminding them of future promotions and the dates when they are offered. Visitors need a reason to come back. Use your mailing list to remind visitors when a new game will be available online and when they can see if they have won in a drawing. This momentum can get visitors to broadcast the news to others who might look up your site.

PROMOTING YOUR SITE ON THE WEB

search engine: a program that uses a logic search to find sites based on a combination of keywords.

directory: an organized listing with specific categories such as yellow and white pages in a telephone directory.

spider: a program that explores the Web, collects keyword information, and stores it on a huge database.

Search engines and directories are the most frequently used vehicles to locate sites on the Web. A **search engine** uses a logic search to find the site you want based on a combination of keywords. A **directory,** like the traditional telephone directory, is an organized listing with specific categories such as yellow and white pages. Sometimes hundreds of matches are found in response to a search on a particular topic. Some search engines list the top 10 sites, with a probability (e.g., 85 percent) that it is the site you're looking for.

Keep in mind that the best search engine can look up no more than 35 to 40 percent of the hundreds of millions of Web pages. Lycos, for example, uses a robot called a **spider.** This is a program that explores the Web, collects keyword information, and stores it on a huge database. In contrast, the well-known search engine Yahoo! requires you to submit information to include in its database.

Regardless of where your site is included, it must stand out from other sites. You want your site to top the list, because most surfers click only on the top three or four sites before they click away. Choice of keywords makes a difference. For example, one commercial bank coded 42 keywords into its homepage (*commercial, small loan, personalized, prompt service, people oriented, independent, student loan, low interest rate,* etc.) Brainstorming among staff for the best keywords is a great idea.

More than 25 major directories and search engines can be found on the Web. Some of the more popular ones are listed in Table 9.2. The registration procedure is simple. Fill out an online form including your name, URL address, and a brief description. In the case of one Miami bank, the paragraph was: "Customer-oriented, full-service bank highly rated for quality service, security, and solvency. The Bank offers Dade County residents automated services, lobby and branch facilities for prompt, courteous service. Annual statement available." Many search engines limit the number of keywords you can include. Some sites allow only a single URL address, a single description, and a single keyword. Other sites allow several pages as long as the description, URL, and keywords are different.

TABLE 9.2 Search engines and directories	
encarta.msn.com	Encyclopedia entries
newslink.org/mag.html	Magazine articles
newslink.org	Newspaper articles
www.barnesandnoble.com	Copyrighted books in print
thomas.loc.gov	Federal (U.S.) legislation
www.healthcentral.com/home/home.cfm	Medical information
www.searchmil.com	Military information
www.yahooligans.com	Material appropriate for children
www.clrn.org/home	Children's software

Should you submit your address to search engines and directories before launching the site? In most cases, a new online business should ensure that the site's design is flawless before launching. Many things can go awry, especially the quality of the graphics. One client organization spent more than a year before it agreed on its Web site's content, layout, colors, and so on. Then the president decided that he'd better get the site loaded on the Internet overnight. He did. A few days later, a customer called to tell the president what a shoddy picture she had on her screen and how long it took to appear. The site also included typos and other errors that no one caught during the final meeting of the company's Web committee.

PROMOTING YOUR SITE ON THE INTERNET

The most common way to promote a Web site is to use e-mail to contact registered customers and remind them of new content on the site. Smaller businesses and first-time online merchants can use an automatic service that allows visitors to request e-mail when site changes take place.

Another way to advertise your Web site is through news groups and mailing lists. News groups can be used to test the viability of your site. A mailing list discussion allows site presence, leaving your URL address virtually everywhere. Check out some of the more often-accessed topical news groups for details. Most news groups allow only new or revised Web site addresses. Other news groups (regional, event oriented, or industry specific) might be appropriate for your type of business or product. Usually, most of their addresses end in ".announce." A list of news groups can be found on List (www.list.com). On any of these sites, a photo, video, or a sound file in addition to your announcement or press release would add value.

A relatively new way of reaching customers on the Internet is what is referred to as mobile marketing (M-marketing). Wireless advertising is real and here to stay. With location-based technology proliferating, advertising to wireless devices is on the rise. Wireless advertising provides efficiency, customization, and convenience. It makes it possible for consumers to take advantage of advertising sales when and where they may be.

One potential avenue for wireless advertising is via wireless yellow pages. In this design, ads are placed within the "yellow page" content. For example, a user can scan through wireless yellow pages to locate a Chinese restaurant. Once the user receives the requested information, the content comes with special promotions or discounts linked to that content.

As we gain experience with M-marketing, we will realize that advertisers, consumers, and service providers benefit. Advertisers increase sales opportunities by reaching more targeted consumers. The wireless consumer saves time and money by receiving the right ad at the right time. It is also a highly personalized experience for the consumer. To the seller of advertising space, it means additional revenue stream and value-added promotion to subscribers.

ATTRACTING CUSTOMERS TO YOUR SITE

E-commerce is booming. Online merchants are selling everything from yachts to diapers. How does one lonely Web site attract customers in a vast Internet? In many cases, it takes effective marketing and a hefty budget. However, between off-line and online TV ads, radio spots, and online banner ads, sooner or later your site will become known and visitors will begin to come.

GENERAL GUIDELINES

Attracting customers to your site involves the following.

1. *Keep the site content current so visitors continue to return for news.* After a site was on the Web for several months, one merchant was reluctant to make changes. His argument was that because mere presence was the goal, it was not worth the expense of updating. As a result, the number of hits and volume of business began to dwindle. So much for this merchant's online business.

2. *Offer free information or products.* Like it or not, customers tend to swarm toward sites that have something to offer. Giveaways like mouse pads are a low-cost attraction. Once visitors register, greeting them by name the next time they visit is a great reinforcer. When they order things, they should not have to reenter information given in previous visits.

3. *Implement a cross-selling strategy* designed to assist the visitor to make a final decision. For example, in online bookshops like Amazon.com, the customer is presented with other books by the same author or on the same topic that other customers have bought after buying that particular book. This marketing technique applies to other online businesses, as well.

profiling/personalization: Web site technology that anticipates the needs of the customer based on past purchases.

4. *Ensure easy and quick navigation* and incorporate technology that anticipates the needs of the customer based on past purchases. This is called customer **profiling** or **personalization.** The Web site should be designed so that any piece of information can be accessed with no more than three clicks.

5. *Introduce event marketing.* Special events on an online merchant's Web site attract new customers and encourage repeat visitors. One day Victoria's Secret broadcast its fashion show live on the Internet. Real Player was used to transport the streaming media. More than 250,000 copies of the software were downloaded per hour on the day of the event. The idea was a great success, but unfortunately, the technology was not designed for real-time media. As a result, the server crashed.

6. *Enlist affiliates.* Web site owners can be affiliates of an online merchant by advertising the merchant's products for a fee. Amazon.com has about 260,000 such affiliates, who earn between 5 percent and 15 percent commission for any sales on their sites. The added exposure is free.

7. *Try out viral marketing as a tool for getting noticed.* To secure their business, you need to earn customers' trust. What better way to do so than to be referred to them by a friend?

Viral marketing encourages people to pass along a marketing message that spreads quickly, when you allow the consumer to promote your business. It is sending a message via e-mail and making it so compelling that recipients want to pass it to everyone they know, like a virus—spreading by "infection." Referrals invariably lead to profits.

Viral marketing is cheap. You can reach a huge audience and can build your reputation. You can also combine it with other marketing methods. Yet it has drawbacks. Like banner ads, the problem is its potential to explode in volume to the point where it would be like spam. To date, most viral campaigns have targeted high school and college students, going directly to their campus e-mail. This, in itself, raises privacy concerns. (See Box 9.6.)

How do you generate referrals from your Web site? First, you allow visitors to send a link to a page on your site to a friend. You allow the visitor to recommend a product on your site to a friend, offering him or her 10 percent off. Next, you allow your e-mail

---

BOX 9.6

Why I Don't Entirely Hate Online Viral Marketing

Over the weekend, I did a segment about online viral marketing on public radio's *Weekend America.* Although most of us think of advertising as *predominantly evil* (or if forgiving, *necessarily evil*), an interesting contradiction arises out of viral marketing—it's both detestable and fascinating at the same time. In that sense, viral marketing introduces complex issues about how we relate to media, how we want to believe in fantasy, and how we still cling to the notion of authenticity. Sometimes it is strangely addicting (Subservient Chicken), and other times it is like watching your parents dance to Outcast (Raging Cow).

Following are links to some online viral marketing campaigns.

Subservient Chicken—Burger King. www. subservientchicken.com. Although it wasn't the first, it seemed to kick off the trend. It also created spin-offs, including Crystal Clear's *Ask Crystal Show* and *Subservient President.*

Chicken Fight—Burger King. www.chicken fight.com. Trying to follow up the buzz behind Subservient Chicken, this was a game with a boxing bout between two chickens. It was pretty dumb.

Raging Cow—Dr. Pepper. http://blog. ragingcow.com. Dr. Pepper enlisted six blogging teens to promote the product Raging Cow, a new milk-based drink. The strange thing is that the bloggers aren't paid, yet they enjoy talking about the product—a clear precursor to *the persuaders.*

Source: Excerpted from www.fimoculous.com/archive/post-783.cfm, March 5, 2005.

message to be reprinted in and linked from other Web sites. Third, you offer visitors something they will want to share with their friends from your site, for free (a game, a utility, etc.). Once implemented, the process mushrooms in a geometric sense into a mass following. See www.brillianceweb.com/betterwebdesign/tips_60.aspx.

The guidelines address the criticality of managing content quality. Message management to e-marketing organizations is what total quality manufacturing is to the industrial community. The focus is on improving the value of the message and the quality of writing. With major e-organizations, it means a set of strategic principles to apply content quality, the actual development process, and an implementation process to leverage the strategic principles. A summary of the message management life cycle is covered in Box 9.7.

CULTURAL DIFFERENCES

Cultural differences play a definite role in what the Web site displays and how marketing comes across to the local customer. Take the case of Kellogg's highly successful British TV ad featuring a child wearing a Kellogg's T-shirt displaying the vitamins and the iron in the product. The ad was banned in the Netherlands because advertising vitamins and iron content is considered a claim to medical benefits, which is forbidden. The same ad was disallowed in France because French law forbids using children for product endorsements.

One issue to consider is local habits and how online marketing should adapt to them. For example, an American hotel could offer a reservation service that allows pets, because it is common for Americans to take pets on trips. However, if the pages are translated into Arabic, it would not make sense to have a pet option, because it is unlikely that Arab visitors would travel with pets, let alone to an American hotel.

BOX 9.7

Managing Web Site Content

Last year, Web content came of age as more and more organizations recognized it as an asset, and not just some commodity. Gratefully, more and more organizations have begun to put content first, technology second. However, there is a lot to do. Managing a Web site can be a frustrating experience. But it's definitely worth persevering, because we are making progress.

Slow change can sometimes be the best change of all. Content is a form of communication, and communication is fundamental to what an organization does. Changing how we communicate is thus a profound change.

Managers who put content first, technology second will have a great 2005. Managers who think like editors will have a great 2005. Managers who put the reader first will have a great 2005.

Interest in Web content as a genuine asset grew and grew in 2004. I now see organizations investing in quality content, and seeing quality results from that investment. More and more organizations have promoted or hired professional editors. In those organizations where the Web is working, the put-it-upper is being replaced by the editor. That is where the future of Web content management is.

Source: Excerpted from Gerry McGovern, "Web Content Management: Coming of Age in 2004." www.marketingprofs.com/5/mcgovern33.asp, January 11, 2005.

A company that observes local habits is Amazon.com, which is Amazon.de in Germany. The online bookseller uses a German domain name, the site is in German, the books are German, and the people who run the business are Germans who know the culture and how to conduct business in Germany.

A company that plans to expand into foreign countries must get to know the local customs, habits, and behaviors. Visit local Web sites and see how they do business. This includes Web site design: use of color, banners, size and type of links, and so on. If you plan to do business over a long period, consider hiring local talent to handle customer service. One source of information about cultural differences is the National Forum on People's Differences (www.yforum. com). It offers answers and solutions to a variety of situations unique to different cultures. This can be a good starting point for planning an online venture.

PREDICTING BUYING BEHAVIOR

Consumers worldwide can shop online day and night, year-round. With projections that the Internet will generate sales in excess of $600 billion, online merchants may wonder how to market on the Net. The key question is, what factors influence online shopping? Various sources agree on the following directions and trends in e-commerce:

1. The online population is younger, more educated, and wealthier than the overall U.S. population.
2. Most online consumers are white, and more than 40 percent reported spending more than 20 hours per week browsing on the Web from home.
3. The most regular use for the Internet is for work and at work.
4. The Internet is used regularly at home to read news and for entertainment.

There is no question that Web consumers shop online or use online services to save time. The Web site should make it convenient to buy items (like the one-click-to-purchase approach at Amazon.com), and the checkout process should be smooth and flawless. Customers are increasingly valuing time savings over cost savings; that may be the key benefit offered by successful online stores.

The e-merchant should be careful to predict buying behavior when introducing a new product. For example, in February 2005, Kraft Corporation introduced on its Web site a fruity-flavored Trolli Road Kill Gummi Candy in shapes of partly flattened snakes, chickens, and squirrels. The company thought it was so funny and so innovative that it would take the children-focused market by surprise.

It certainly did. The New Jersey Society for the Prevention of Cruelty to Animals viewed the product as one that fosters cruelty toward animals and was considering petition drives and boycotts to remove the candy from the market before Kraft pulled the animated advertisement from Trolli's Web site (www.cnn.com/2005/US/02/25/ roadkill. candy.ap/index.html).

PERSONALIZATION

Imagine looking up a Web site that sells books. It welcomes you. It is no coincidence that it lists the last two books you bought. The site proceeds to make you special offers on a book you have been thinking about buying. You're so taken by the offerings that you click on the submit key. Two days later, the book arrives. Your VISA or MasterCard has already taken care of the payment. This type of marketing (also called one-to-one marketing, profiling, or personalization) is the wave of the future, because it addresses individual needs. The idea is to gather information about consumers and send the right message at the right time.

The first step in personalization is identification. Information technology is used to identify a customer. Digital certificates also can be used to authenticate a customer because they contain information about the user, usually stored in the browser or in a smart card. After identification, the server looks up the user's personal record in the database to determine his or her buying pattern and presents attractive products, information, or services to the customer. This type of automated assistance promotes differentiation, which means customers are treated on a personal basis. The merchant's system addresses the needs of every single customer in a unique way. Digital techniques make it easy to track customers, store their information in the database, and create special offers on the Web site.

The World Wide Web is not a mass medium. It is a personal medium. Unlike television, newspaper, or radio, which deliver to a mass audience, the Web is delivered continuously and is experienced differently by each visitor to the site. Personalizing the experience of each customer—giving a customized view of your content or product offerings—is done by enticing customers to give you information about themselves and their habits. The information is then run through a database for analysis and profiling. The transformation process is not cheap, but it is easily justified when it works. It can lock in a repeat customer and promote long-term customer relationships.

There are three ways to add personalization to a Web site: keywords, collaborative filtering, or rule-based personalization. In *keyword-based* personalization (see www.my.yahoo.com), users are presented with a set of categories of information on the Web site. After they register and click on categories, they are offered information within these categories for future sign-ups for products or services. This is a straightforward approach to delivering a personal experience without much expense. To deliver information from a keyword-based system, users' names and passwords are matched to a list of keywords they entered on previous visits. The data linked to these keywords are drawn instantly through a format that embeds HTML codes for headings and other details.

In *collaborative filtering* (e.g., www.netperceptions.com), the input of many users is compared before the program comes up with a recommendation to the visitor. The process begins with a user database like that of a keyword-based system, but with extensive demographic information (age, sex, education, economic status, and so on) and detailed user preferences that are then matched against other user preferences in the database. The preferences also can be matched against the demographic data before the final recommendation is displayed. This approach is more expensive and requires a lot of information from many people to make recommendations reliable. The software alone can run upwards of $50,000.

In *rule-based* personalization (see www.multilogic.com, www.kodakpicture network.com, and www.broadvision.com), the system matches user input to a set of rules about user behavior. If you input that you are a retiree and would like to travel in a country where accommodations are cheap, the Web site might suggest Armenia or Uzbekistan for starters. Like collaborative filtering, however, this software is expensive. It takes time and know-how to set up and maintain. The rules used to generate recommendations are more valid and reliable the more information is collected from people.

In collaborative filtering, user preferences are first aggregated and then queried to produce the answers. In rule-based personalization, large volumes of data have to be captured before the program comes up with the rules that are later used to generate the recommendations.

MOBILE AGENTS.   Early online retailers saw advanced technology as the silver bullet and believed that once the e-business was built, customers would flock to it. Today's dot.com survivors learned to focus on basics, such as attracting customers to the site and making them satisfied. The current push is to integrate Web site activities and brick-and-mortar operations. There is also a continuing drive toward wireless and Web site personalization.

Part of the trend is the dawn of mobile agents and artificial intelligence (AI) software. *Mobile agents* are autonomous, intelligent programs that move through a network, searching for and interacting with services on the user's behalf. AI mimics real-life consumer behavior by tracking patterns of movements and the like.

Mobile agents are likened to touring members of the agent clan, with the ability to "pack their bags and move on." They are not only autonomous, but adaptive (learn), goal oriented, collaborative, flexible, and proactive. These mobile agents are beginning to change the shape of e-commerce and e-business, with new concerns regarding who really owns information.

As can be seen, mobile agents are beginning to make changes in the e-world. The key question is whether mobile agents are partners or predators. EBay made headlines in 1999 when it won a court case against third-party predatory search agents or intelligent agents that would access the auction site, search for items that address a customer's query, and notify the customer about prices and other attributes unique to the query. This is a process performed by *shopbots*—intelligent agents that aggregate information from various databases and recommend the product and the store that has the best price.

EBay's response suggested that agents are predators, not partners. Despite the court ruling, third-party companies are still evaluating the legality of eBay's stand. In any case, intelligent agents fall into many categories and carry out numerous problem-solving tasks such as planning, negotiation, diagnosis, and the like. As mentioned earlier, they answer and screen e-mail messages, act as a secretary screening phone calls, and even provide recommendations to the "boss" about how efficiently he or she is running the show.

TRACKING CUSTOMERS

From an e-marketing point of view, attracting visitors to a Web site is just the first step. The next is to track their movements to ensure that as many visitors as possible are converted into purchasers and repeat customers. For this reason, e-marketers need quick insight into the activities that affect the Web site—who is visiting the site, the number of page hits, number of visitors, number and type of purchases, how visitors behaved, and how to reinforce or influence consumer behavior. Customer tracking is the future of Web marketing. It allows marketers to gain important information about customers including demographic profiles and likely future purchases.

Certain procedures, benefits, and issues are related to this ever-growing need to manage customer needs and expectations. From all indications, tracking customers with ads in mind is growing rapidly via wireless. To illustrate, when sports retailer GearDirect.com sent out wireless ads to 1,000 customers, it resulted in a 50 percent increase in visits to its Web site. Some even visited its store. Cost and limited cell phone screens continue to be a constraint. For more details, see www.aef.com/06/news/data/2001/1719.

GATHERING WEB DATA

There are three main ways of collecting data on Web site visitors: log files, forms, and cookies. Each is briefly explained in the following paragraphs.

log files: files on the Web server that keep track of domain types, time of access, keywords used, and search engines used.

LOG FILES.   **Log files** are files on the Web server that keep track of domain types, time of access, keywords used, and search engines used. The keywords, for example, tell the merchant what visitors were looking for when they came to the Web site.

FORMS.   Registration and purchase forms are the two most effective ways of gathering Web site visitor information. They capture customer-provided personal information (name, address, birth date, sex, zip code, e-mail address, and so on). Web retailers place links and contests on the Web site homepage to capture visitor preferences via forms. The more interaction there is with customers, the more information there is that can be gathered about their tastes and preferences.

COOKIES.   As noted in Chapter 8, a **cookie** is a small piece of information that is sent to the visitor's browser when the visitor accesses a particular site. When it arrives, the browser saves it to the hard disk. When the visitor returns to that site, some of the stored

cookie: a small piece of information that is sent to the visitor's browser when the visitor accesses a particular site.

information will be sent back to the merchant's Web server along with the new request. Cookies are standard components for tracking visitor activities on most Web sites. They tell retailers who is a first-time visitor and where repeat visitors have been within the Web site. In general, cookies are harmless. Some cookies have expiration dates, and when that date comes, the visitor's browser simply erases it from the hard drive. Cookies with an expiration date generally are referred to as *persistent cookies*. Cookies that will last as long as the browser stays open are referred to as *session cookies*. When the browser is closed, session cookies simply disappear.

Any way you look at it, cookies make a lot of people uncomfortable. They invade people's privacy. Unlike e-mail, cookies are hidden from the visitor's view. They allow the merchant to recognize individual users instead of just machines. There are, however, a number of things that a cookie cannot tell anyone—whether more than one person uses the same computer to view a Web site; whether one person uses more than one computer to visit a Web site; and the person's name, age, and the country from which he or she is accessing the Web site.

CLICKSTREAM DATA ANALYSIS

clickstream data: Web site visitors' clicks, which leave footprints representing their behavior.

When visitors go on a site, their clicks leave *footprints*. This type of information is called **clickstream data.** It includes any measure that helps observers learn how visitors navigate a site and why.

Today, nearly every Web site collects and evaluates clickstream data in one form or another. The data can be used to learn how to design better customer-friendly sites, where to spend Internet advertising dollars, how to run successful e-marketing campaigns, and even how to personalize Web pages.

Clickstream data can pinpoint a host of customer behaviors. Online retailers began analyzing clickstream data to figure out why customers might leave the site prematurely and abandon their shopping carts. These data are then compared with similar data from other carts to determine the following.

1. Whether the products in the abandoned cart were high-profit or loss-leader items
2. The value of the products in the abandoned shopping carts
3. The volume of products in the abandoned carts
4. The number of different product types in the abandoned carts
5. The average and total value of the products in the abandoned carts compared to those that cleared the checkout process

Customer satisfaction is the most sensitive and gratifying goal for an online retailer. Treating the customer differently based on these findings is bound to improve customer satisfaction. Software packages help retailers analyze clickstream data to help them do just that. Unlike most Web server log analysis packages that overwhelm you with voluminous amounts of trivial data with little marketing information, ClickTracks focuses on visitor patterns *directly on the pages of your Web site*. This is a new approach to log file analysis that makes it easier for anyone to understand visitor behavior at a glance. Where visitors click, how long they stay on each page, and when they leave the site is immediately apparent. ClickTracks provides an easy way to understand the actions performed by visitors when they reach your Web site. Visitors can be separated into groups based on whatever marketing program generated the referral and then displays results for each group. Visitors are "tagged" based on a common attribute like the referring domain. Tagged visitors are then highlighted graphically through the site, no matter how far they click.

Based on a number of studies, the common data to track include the following.

1. Where a visitor first landed on the site
2. How the visitor got to the site (typing in a URL address vs. a subject name, clicking on a banner ad, and so on)
3. The number and sequence of pages viewed
4. The number and cost of each product purchased
5. The length of time the visitor stayed on each page and on the entire site
6. The total cost of each visit
7. The point on the site where the visitor clicked away

These are only guidelines, because the key is to decide what specific information an e-merchant considers important to the marketing business plan. An example of clickstream products is DoubleClick. It combines data on Web surfers—such as IP address, operating system, and sites visited—with off-line data—such as name, address, and a customer's purchase history taken from the separate databases—to target customers with impressive precision. From a marketer's viewpoint, the process is attractive. Its technology can tell where customers have been on the Internet and where they are going. If the Web can be used as a surveillance device, then the marketing opportunities are virtually endless.

THE RELIABILITY OF E-INTELLIGENCE

It is clear that e-marketing means more than just putting up an attractive Web site. The goal is to identify and retain repeat customers, especially for high-margin products. This requires e-intelligence or information that helps merchants understand who their customers are and what entices them to buy. This is where artificial intelligence is used to mine the Web to answer people's questions. (See Box 9.8.)

Clickstream analysis tools alone do not elicit much behavioral information about Web site visitors. We need to know the following.

1. What Web site content most often gets people to buy online?
2. Why do people abandon their shopping carts and click away?
3. How do e-sales compare to those on other channels?

Finally, one should be careful how much of the data collected are reliable. Different log analysis tools produce different results. Industry measurement standards are lacking. Log analysis software vendors have their own definitions of how to handle open visits, errors, search engines, and the like. Questions still arise about how to identify a unique visitor or how to count visitors. Is it by cookie? By IP address? To make things worse, the data-gathering software often comes with bugs that distort the accuracy and reliability of the statistics generated from traffic analysis.

ROLE OF THE SHOPBOT

Since online shopping began, the quest has been on to help customers find the best price. Even though online shopping is quicker than bricks-and-mortar shopping, customers still don't want to spend too much time surfing sites to buy a particular item. For this reason, shopping **bots** were created, whose software searches several sites and will tell you what each site charges for the same item and where the best buy is located. Bots are a bargain hunter's dream. The consumer decides on an item, sets a price, and sends a bot into cyberspace on a search mission; the result is finding the consumer's favorite item at the best available price.

bot: short for robot; also called a shopping agent.

Bots have been part of Web technology since the beginning of Web business. Historically, bot technology first appeared in the form of spiders and crawlers that search engines still use to locate Web sites. More recently, the technology has become more intelligent. Bots sit on Web servers. First, they try to learn your preferences and specific needs, and then they go to work for you. It is like telling the bot, "Hey, I am looking for a 2001 BMW 325i convertible with less than 30,000 miles, and I want to spend no more than $5,000, period."

Are bots a threat to e-merchants' tenuous foothold in a shifting digital market-place? Turning off a shopping bot could deprive a merchant of an important visitor—the bot that could recommend the merchant's product. Because more than

---

BOX 9.8

The Business Case for E-Intelligence

E-intelligence systems provide internal business users, trading partners, and corporate clients with rapid and easy access to the e-business information, applications, and services they need to compete effectively and satisfy customer needs. They offer a significant number of business benefits to organizations in exploiting the power of the Internet.

1. They integrate e-business operations into the traditional business environment, enabling end users to obtain a complete view of all corporate business operations and business information

2. They help business users make informed decisions based on accurate and consistent e-business information that is collected and integrated from the organization's e-business applications.

3. They assist e-business applications in profiling and segmenting e-business customers to personalize the actual Web pages displayed, and the products and services offered to the customer, through the Web interface.

4. They extend the business intelligence environment outside of the corporate firewall to trading partners.

5. They extend the business intelligence environment outside of the corporate firewall to key corporate clients.

6. They link together e-business applications with business intelligence and collaborate processing applications, allowing both internal and external users to seamlessly move between different systems.

In terms of e-intelligence requirements, they include:

1. 1-to-1 e-marketing analysis applications that customize and personalize the information, applications, services, and products offered to consumers and clients via the Internet.

2. Channel and cross-channel analysis and campaign applications that measure and analyze the success of the Internet as a sales, marketing, and services channel.

3. Supply chain analysis applications that enable the organization to work with trading partners to optimize the product supply chain to match the demand for products sold through the Internet.

4. A simple and integrated e-intelligence Web interface that provides secure and managed access by internal and external Web users and applications to the organization's business information, applications, and services.

5. Demand-driven business intelligence gathering and analysis, and real-time decisions and recommendations as consumers and clients interact with e-business systems via the Internet.

Source: Excerpted from Colin J. White, "Leveraging the Power of the Web Using E-Intelligence." Database Associates, Inc., 1–15.

---

80 percent of online shoppers comparison shop before they buy, search-and-comparison tools like bots are the perfect way to bargain hunt. Bots also give equal airtime to large and small Web sites. This helps the consumer as well as the merchant. They force retailers of every size to keep their prices competitive, which helps the consumer. Merchants complain that bots consume bandwidth on the merchant's site, and that can be a big problem. Each hit from a shopping bot is like one user, and the requests can run into the thousands at once, often overloading sites and slowing traffic for other users.

Today's newer bots are more intelligent and more efficient. They store information on a site's thousands of products in a local cache (storage) and refresh them only every three days, rather than every 10 seconds as older bots did. They gather data about a merchant responsibly, search during off hours, and give merchants the option to release direct data regarding product prices rather than spidering their way through the sites with each request. They also compare customer service, delivery options, warranties, and the like. In the end, e-merchants that give the customer a satisfying experience will prevail over those with simply the lowest price.

CUSTOMER SERVICE

For all the positive and promising things that e-commerce provides, it continues to suffer from the nature of its business: the automation that removes the human contact between buyer and merchant. Impersonal business has rarely been a plus with the consumer. Therefore, anything that can be done to improve the contact between the seller and the buying public will build bridges of confidence that can have a lasting effect on the business. In the final analysis, it is customer support and customer service that will pay dividends.

DON'T ANNOY THE CUSTOMER

Consumers face the never-ending problem of trying to buy a product at the lowest price and with the best customer support—good warranties, quick response to repairs, minimum wait time at the phone, replacement of defective products within days, and the like. Unfortunately, merchants must make a minimum profit if customer support is to survive. The author remembers several consulting situations where negotiations with the vendor reached a point where one vendor commented, "I don't mind selling you our system at near cost, but that leaves me nothing to support the product or, in fact, the business." In every transaction (off-line or online) where quality of customer service is a given, the price is usually not the lowest or the best.

Regardless of the combination of price and customer service, rule number one in Internet marketing is, "Don't annoy the customer." There must be improved logistics to keep the customer happy. From the time the order is placed to the time the product is delivered, a mechanism should be in place to keep the customer informed about the status of the order, where it is in transit, and whether it is being shipped on schedule. There must be minimum wait time over the phone. According to a survey of 10,000 computer owners, the average time spent on hold, waiting for technical support, is 17 minutes. Staffing phone help lines during that year cost software companies worldwide about $11 billion of the nearly $18 billion spent on support services.

Regardless of the reasons or the procedures followed in e-commerce, botched logistics can spell disaster. Order taking is the easy part; fulfillment is where the merchant promotes or destroys customer satisfaction. Among the 10 reasons why e-shoppers come back to a merchant's Web site are level and quality of customer service and on-time delivery. Seasoned e-retailers know they need a good system for order fulfillment and delivery. (See Box 9.9). In most online shopping, when a customer initiates an order, it triggers an automated process that sends the order from the merchant's Web site to a distributor via electronic data interchange (EDI) or over the Internet. The merchant

---

BOX 9.9

I Ordered That?

For Internet shoppers, it is the question that derails many trips to the virtual checkout line: "What if I don't like it when it gets here?" To encourage more people to click the "buy" button, a growing number of online retailers from ToysRUs.com to NeimanMarcus.com are making it considerably easier to return purchases. Some companies will come right to your door to pick up rejects. In major cities, Office Depot will have its delivery trucks swing by your house to pick up stuff you want to send back.

The looser policies are coming at a time when the explosive growth in online sales is slowing down. So companies are beginning to focus more on retaining their existing customers by rolling out service improvements like easier returns. Some stores save free returns as a perk for big spenders. For example, Gap Inc.'s BananaRepublic.com promises free returns to customers with the store's highest-level credit-card account. (Anyone who spends over $800 a year on the card is eligible.) It is also offering free returns on its petite line of clothing, in a bid to entice shoppers who might be particularly worried about fit.

A snapshot of return policies at online retailers:

www.Zappos.com (shoes)—Lets you return unworn shoes for 60 days for any reason. They pay for reverse shipping.

www.crutchfield.com (electronics)—Pays for return shipping and offers a money-back guarantee on anything returned within 30 days. No restocking fees.

www.OfficeDepot.com—In major cities, Office Depot delivery trucks will swing by your house and pick up packages you want to send back. They accept returns for 30 days.

www.amazon.com—Accepts returns on most items for 30 days. Pays return shipping costs only if the return is due to their error.

www.Gap.com—You can return unwashed, unworn items by mail or in a retail store for 14 days.

Source: Excerpted from Jane Spencer, "I Ordered That? Web Retailers Make It Easier to Return Goods." *Wall Street Journal*, September 4, 2003, D1ff.

---

updates the customer by e-mail on the status of the order, how long it will take, and when the order should arrive. More and more merchants now give customers the procedure for tracking the status of their orders online.

SALESPEOPLE AND INTERNET MARKETING

One of the critical side effects of Internet marketing is the role of the salesperson accustomed to controlling the information the customer receives. All of a sudden, the customer has that information over the Internet. In industries like real estate and insurance, which are salesperson heavy, resistance to new technology continues. For example, Nationwide Insurance, which is planning to get its 15,000 agents to use the Web through a Siebel System 99 customer relationship management suite, is already getting resistance from the initial users. Understandably, most agents come from the "old school," but the firm has no choice. Traditional systems can no longer distribute leads to agents effectively, and the firm has to cut operating costs to remain competitive.

Many other companies are trying to convince their sales staffs that using the Web to improve efficiency does not mean eliminating the human touch or replacing the sales force. Take the case of Oracle Corporation and its attempt to automate sales processes. Oracle's automated Web-based software installation encountered similar resistance. Its sales force is now being used as educators and in customer support.

To date, no matter how much automation technology provides in direct marketing, customers will still rely on human salespeople before making complex purchases. Even at the highest level of e-commerce, the need for live sales help continues. E-commerce today is eliminating administrative sales work, letting human salespeople focus on providing value to customers. Companies must find a way to forge a balance between e-commerce operations and sales force operations. Personalization tools can be made available for salespeople to check on their progress, their commissions, and their standing in the sales department at their convenience.

T-COMMERCE IS HERE

The household TV remote control is fast becoming the next tool for e-retailing. It is the technology that will let you buy without leaving your sofa. T-commerce is similar to the simple process of ordering a cable pay-per-view or video-on-demand (VOD) movie, users will be able to press a button on the remote to select a product, scroll through to decide on size, color, shipping address, and payment. T-commerce requires satellite TV or digital cable service (Grant 2005, 1B).

Imagine *American Idol* contestants wearing Neiman Marcus outfits that viewers see, want, and buy while watching the show. Obviously, cable and satellite providers' participation are prerequisites to interactive T-commerce methodology.

Inasmuch as it promises ease and convenience of e-shopping, some question the potential of T-commerce. The current market is limited to 50 million households. According to the National Cable and Telecommunications Association, about 25 million U.S. cable subscribers pay an average of $10 per month for digital service, which can be a limitation if the charges are not reduced. T-commerce retailers will also have to work harder to ensure shopper privacy and security of the interactive exchange (Gates 2005, 5A).

CUSTOMER RELATIONSHIP MANAGEMENT AND E-VALUE

Since the early 1990s, globalization has become part of everyday business. In this context, e-marketing was one of the first to realize the need for a relationship schema for attracting and retaining business. Called *relationship marketing* (RM), the approach emphasizes relationships with all stakeholders, networks, and interactions—all interlinked with the customer in mind. See Figure 9.3.

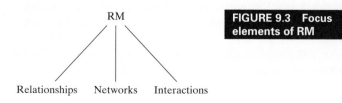

FIGURE 9.3   Focus elements of RM

From RM evolved today's buzzword, CRM, or *customer relationship management*. There are many views and definitions of CRM. The simplest view is that CRM is an information system that combines methodologies, software, and the Internet to help an organization establish stronger customer relations with customers. It also involves using human resources and information technology to gain insight into customer behaviors and their values.

CRM offers a key strength in connecting information about customers, marketing, sales, and market trends. An organization might collect data about customers in a way that gives a clear and complete customer profile for management, the sales force, and customers themselves to match customer needs with product roll-outs, special offerings, and customers' purchase history.

MAIN GOALS AND INSIGHTS

CRM does not happen by simply installing CRM software. If it works as planned, an organization should first decide on the customer information it is looking for and what it intends to do with that information. In any case, CRM is expected to achieve several worthwhile goals:

- Better customer service and customer revenues
- More efficient call center
- Faster closing of deals by sales staff
- More effective cross selling of products
- Simplified market and sales processes
- Discovering new customers and personalizing relationships to improve profitability and customer satisfaction

Building strong relationships begins with understanding customers. Here is some insight into achieving customer satisfaction:

1. It is a process of customer identification, customer attraction, customer retention, and customer development.
2. The intersection of company capabilities and its goods and services is the surest way of ensuring customer satisfaction.
3. It involves carefully collected and intelligently mined data, customer analysis, and insight-driven interaction for reliable results.

See Figure 9.4.

The overall goal of CRM is to identify what truly matters for the customer. In one respect, it is building a learning relationship with customers. First, one *notices* what customers are doing. Second, *remember* what customers have done over time. Third, *learn* from what is remembered. Fourth, *act* on what has been learned. See Figure 9.5.

In a B2B environment, CRM is more about relationships than customers. Establishing bonds, trust, and loyalty between businesses ensures a successful CRM installation and is a definite contribution to the profitability of both firms.

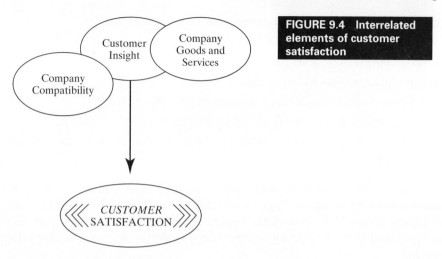

FIGURE 9.4   Interrelated elements of customer satisfaction

E-CRM INDICATORS AND CHALLENGES

Electronic CRM means applying CRM processes to business on the Internet. In most cases, customer relations are inherently more dynamic or interactive. Kiwilogic (www.kiwilogic.com) and Vividence (www.vividence.com) are examples of e-CRM solutions providers.

When you look up a merchant's Web site, what indicators or features are CRM? The most noticeable ones include:

- Complaining ability—allowing customers to communicate with the seller regarding delayed or missed orders, a poor product, and so on
- Privacy policy—especially a policy that clarifies support for privacy, ensuring privacy by not selling customer lists to advertisers, and the technology or procedures followed to provide private and secure customer shopping
- Online product information—to give customers the information needed before placing an order, including product highlights and product preview
- Site maps—showing a hierarchical representation of the Web site
- E-mail—as a medium for customers to contact merchants for specific arrangements, filing complaints, or questioning contractual conditions

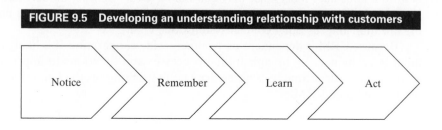

FIGURE 9.5   Developing an understanding relationship with customers

Notice → Remember → Learn → Act

- About us—company history, mission, who's who, and so forth
- Mailing list—offer to receive information by mail
- FAQ—answers to frequently asked questions
- Toll-free number—as a contact channel
- Track order status—especially important in tracking an order
- Site customization—customer ability to filter content
- Find branch location—help a customer find the nearest store or branch to his or her location

It should be obvious that these indicators can only help customers stay long enough on the Web site to place an order rather than click away. Despite these dedicated efforts, there are challenges. The top ones are dedicating financial and human resources, resistance to policy changes, conflicting organizational priorities, and justifying the return on investment.

Another challenge has to do with the nature of the world we live in. In a perfect world, data from every conceivable source would pour into a database or a data warehouse dedicated to CRM operations. From that point, data marts would access subsets of the warehouse data and work with one of many CRM applications. But in an imperfect world, integrating data into a usable data warehouse invites all kinds of CRM problems, especially when dealing with CRM analytical applications.

To avoid these problems, CRM project teams must ensure a stellar mix of technical specialists and business savvy—business knowledge and ability to communicate with users. Too often, business people and technical persons specify two different languages and need an interpreter. While it is easy to find top-notch technologists with specialized CRM software tools, familiarity with the nature of the business continues to be critical. The team must understand the underlying assumptions behind the model being used.

FROM MARKETING TO MANAGEMENT

There is an inherent "disconnect" between marketing and consumer perceptions of this endeavor. Consumers see many of a company's efforts as trivial. In fact, some customers feel penalized for their loyalty by the way they are taken for granted. The problem is that most organizations continue to follow a rigid product-management perspective.

What is needed is a move away from customer relationship marketing to CRM. In addition, interfaces must exist between noncustomer contact models like ERP—an integrated approach to data communication between departments and between the organization and customer contact systems. See Figure 9.6.

Because CRM is dependent on company-wide cooperation, it is likely that investment in reengineering organizational processes and functions to improve planning among various departments is necessary. Figure 9.6 brings us the four critical processes for an integrated CRM.

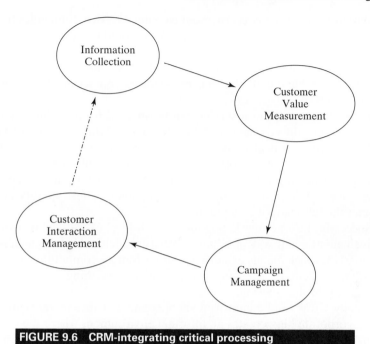

FIGURE 9.6   CRM-integrating critical processing

MANAGEMENT IMPLICATIONS

An important implication for management is return on investment. With the huge investment that most of today's successful Web sites have made, it is important to look into tools that can analyze what visitors have done and predict what they will do. These tools also should be capable of providing insight into where customers are coming from and how they behave on the Web site. This means continuous analysis and handling data about thousands of visitors interactively. With online, real-time solutions, e-businesses can react in time to stay alive and to grow.

It seems clear that the future of the Internet and e-commerce lies in customer tracking and personalization. As technology continues to surpass its own limits, available marketing techniques will evolve to become ever more dynamic. E-marketing has come to incorporate new aspects based on the nature of Internet consumerism. For starters, as consumer options continue to extend beyond a brick-and-mortar atmosphere, the marketplace has been forced to expand. Many firms have evolved with the business environment and have taken advantage of Internet marketing's ability to reduce total costs and time, while boosting the volume of sales.

Communication has also evolved since the days of "snail mail." Internet marketing allows firms to communicate with customers around the clock, whether it be through pop-ups, banners, or e-mail, by increasing the intensity and velocity of contact. Additionally, because the Internet facilitates consumer accessibility to products (reducing travel, time, etc.), Internet marketing allows business to capitalize on the *convenience revolution.*

With the increasing concern about customer service, companies that have gone all out to solidify a successful future on the Web should reconsider their approach to customer support. Software is available that businesses can use to manage all aspects of customer encounters. Software can handle field service and dispatch technicians, and call centers can handle all channels of customer contact including voice and self-service via a Web site.

E-commerce without e-service can be suicidal for a business. When a customer order goes awry, the customer won't come back. Talking to your customers is not only good for business, it is also good for name recognition. It is healthy for your brand. Trusty phrases like "Thank you" and "We apologize" still work in most cases. The only taxing part is dealing with events beyond your control. Then you have to handle customer complaints on a case-by-case basis. This is where quality customer service becomes the lubricant of e-commerce.

Successful Internet marketing means high-level executive involvement and thinking fresh about a new way of selling, advertising, delivering merchandise, and knowing your market, which means exploring your customers, competition, and supply sources. It also means defining, selecting, and prioritizing the things it takes to implement the company's e-business vision.

Finally, CRM can be improved via blogging. Because markets are mere conversations, a corporate blog creates an informal environment where the public can provide feedback about a product of treatment. One way to activate a corporate blog is to run up an idea up the pole and see what kind of response you get. Do people comment? What do they say? Do they link to your post? How long do they stay? Steady blogging also improves your search engine ranking.

Summary

1. Marketing is the process of planning and implementing the conception, pricing, advertising, and distribution of goods and services to meet the demands of the market. Online marketing is about business, not just technology. The approach, the process, and the protocols in Internet marketing are unique and must work together for the merchant, the customer, and the supplier.

2. Three factors make online shopping attractive: quick sorting through choices, vast selection of products, and quick comparison of products.

3. Online shopping has some drawbacks: Certain products like tools are still best bought through brick-and-mortar stores; bulky products like lumber do not sell well on the Internet; and certain buying decisions require experiential information.

4. The Internet provides a continuum of marketing techniques, from passive (pull) techniques where visitors seek out merchants, to aggressive (push) techniques where the Web site seeks out the customer.

5. Internet marketing is made up of an e-cycle that begins with planning followed by the four P's: product, pricing, place, and promotion. Personalization is a unique e-marketing feature.

6. One marketing implication behind the power shift from merchant to consumer is a unique marketing strategy that follows rules that make sense. They include simple content, dynamic sites,

conciseness and ease of navigation, effective promotion of the Web site, free giveaways, and consistency.

7. To promote a site on the Web, it must be available to search engines and directories. The site must stand out from other sites. Choice of keywords makes a difference.

8. Attracting customers to a site involves keeping site content current, offering free information or products, implementing cross-selling strategies to assist visitors in making a final decision, quick and easy navigation, introducing event marketing, and enlisting affiliates.

9. The first step in personalization is customer identification. The three ways to add personalization to a Web site are keywords, collaborative filtering, and rule-based personalization. The three ways of collecting data on Web site visitors are log files, forms, and cookies.

10. Successful Internet marketing means high-level executive involvement, thinking about a new way of selling and delivering merchandise, and finding what it takes to implement the company's e-business vision. The test of successful e-marketing is customer service and customer satisfaction.

Key Terms

- **aggressive marketing** (p. 269)
- **banner** (p. 267)
- **bot** (p. 291)
- **business plan** (p. 272)
- **clickstream data** (p. 289)
- **cookie** (p. 289)
- **directory** (p. 281)
- **log files** (p. 289)
- **passive marketing** (p. 267)
- **permission marketing** (p. 272)
- **personalization** (p. 278)
- **profiling** (p. 283)
- **pull marketing** (p. 267)
- **push technology** (p. 268)
- **search engine** (p. 281)
- **spamming** (p. 269)
- **spider** (p. 281)
- **vision** (p. 273)

Test Your Understanding

1. Marketing is "the art of the possible." Do you agree? Explain.
2. From the consumer's view, what makes online shopping attractive? What are some of the drawbacks?
3. How would a merchant justify going on the Internet? Elaborate.
4. What is spam? How does it differ from viral marketing?
5. In what respect is customer personalization unique to Internet marketing? Be specific.
6. What are the phases that make up the e-cycle of Internet marketing?
7. What are banners? In what way are they controversial?
8. Define personalization. Give an example of your own.
9. What is involved in attracting customers to a Web site? Explain briefly.
10. How is customer tracking carried out? Of the ways covered in the chapter, which one is the most common?

Discussion Questions

1. Do you think e-businesses are more concerned about presence than brick-and-mortar businesses? Why?
2. From a marketing view, what Web design mistakes do first-time e-firms make?

3. In what way(s) is promoting a product on the Web different from using mass media (TV, radio, newspaper, and so on) and word of mouth? Explain.
4. How can passive and aggressive (pull/push) ads work together for a given firm? Discuss.
5. What managerial implications can one draw regarding Internet marketing?

Web Exercises

1. As a network administrator of Shenanigan's, a retailer of children's products, you have seen the business expand from one specialty store in a downtown location to 11 stores throughout the Commonwealth of Virginia. The company hired a marketing research firm that found that most of its customers are females between 23 and 30 years of age who are avid users of the Internet. These customers would not mind ordering children's products (clothing, toys, and so on) on the Web.

    a. Design a business plan that can be used as a step for Shenanigan's to go on the Internet. In the plan, make sure to consider the elements covered in the chapter.
    b. Write a memo to Shenanigan's CEO, explaining things like customer tracking, banner advertising, and the like, that relate to the recommended site.

2. Interview a senior manager of a company that uses electronic marketing or e-commerce about his or her experience in this area of operation. Is the company making money? How costly has the building and maintenance of the electronic system been? What performance criteria does he or she use to determine success or poor performance? Write a short news release to your college newspaper to report your findings.
3. Go on the Internet and evaluate three companies that have recently announced their first Web site. How much e-marketing is there? How effective do you predict it will be?
4. Access two business Web sites and review their homepages. Evaluate the goals of the sites. Are they primarily used for advertising new products? General awareness? Special product sales? Career opportunities? How much overall e-marketing does each Web site offer?
5. Look up the following Web site and evaluate the uses and issues related to banner ads: Doubleclick.net (www.doubleclick.com).

CHAPTER 10

WEB PORTALS
AND WEB SERVICES

Learning Objectives

The focus of this chapter is on several learning objectives:

- The concept of a Web portal
- How portals transform a business
- The main techniques and functionalities of an enterprise portal
- Knowledge portals and their uses
- Web services and portals
- Who is building and sponsoring enterprise portals
- How to select a portal product

IN A NUTSHELL

One of the most important contributions of the Internet is information access via Web portals. Companies are fast learning that certain information or applications can become available more quickly and reliably via portals. Portals are among the leading success stories of e-business. They are the most powerful tools that help achieve communication goals. An e-commerce solution employs a portal for capturing information wherever it exists (in documents, managers' minds, databases, and historical data). Another important tool is a user interface that makes information available to a larger community of employees and knowledge workers. By providing an integrated framework for linking together people, processes, and information, portals play a central role in simplifying managerial complexity, increasing operational productivity, and adding value to a company's business operations.

content management: also referred to as content management system (CMS); a system used to manage the content of a Web site.

personalization: software system that allows an Internet site to provide the user with a Web page that reflects the interests, needs, and actions of the user.

Portals can be valuable tools for enhancing business processes. They employ distribution channels such as the Internet, intranets, and extranets that allow companies to take advantage of information lying dormant in their databases. Portals evolved from pure information providers to sophisticated interfaces containing knowledge management features such as **content management** for knowledge categorization, collaboration tools for knowledge sharing, and **personalization** capabilities to facilitate the search function. Box 10.1 is a summary of one area where portals have been useful.

THE BASICS

WHAT ARE PORTALS?

"Content is king" is the traditional credo of media firms on the Web. The goal of companies in portal services centers on content, helping people find a needle in a haystack, that is, achieve a particular task taking place in a complex setting. A **portal** gives access to relevant information, knowledge, and human assets delivered in a highly personalized manner. It is a Web site featuring common services as a starting point. It can refer to virtually any type of Internet entry point. Examples are corporate Web pages, Yahoo!, and state portals for renewing driver's licenses.

portal: a Web page that offers links to other Web sites. Portals can be broad or narrow, specific or general.

vertical portal: electronic exchanges that combine upstream and downstream e-commerce activities of specialized products and/or services.

A portal is a complex piece of software that delivers functionality and information coming almost exclusively from outside the portal. It provides coherent delivery and integration across the content sources. It also ensures a secure and reliable interface to participants in a business process and collaborates with users through the integration of external Web-based applications or internal back-office systems. Such a site is a frequent gateway to the Web (Web portal) or a niche topic (a **vertical portal**).

Portals are considered virtual workplaces for the following functions:

- Promoting knowledge sharing among different categories of end users such as customers, partners, and employees
- Providing access to structured data that are stored in data warehouses, database systems, and transactional systems
- Organizing unstructured data such as electronic documents, paper documents, lessons learned, stories, and the like
- Offering varieties such as portals on intranets, customer-facing information portals, supplier-facing information portals, and enterprise portals

Portals are emerging as the most promising tool for simplifying the access to data stored in various application systems, facilitating collaboration among employees, and assisting the company in reaching its customers. Other benefits include reduced cost, better quality, keeping pace with technology, improved customer satisfaction, and attracting skilled staff.

<table>
<tr><td align="center">BOX 10.1</td></tr>
</table>

Role of Portals in the Insurance Industry

While Web portals have been around for a while, the trend now is toward ones specifically designed to meet the demands of an industry, and insurance is among those adopting this **knowledge management** (KM) strategy. Although insurers face the same basic needs as any organization — customer service, human resources, and accounting — the industry also has some distinctive **workflow** requirements that can be met through a tailored Web portal.

For example, a claim that has come in for processing might take one route if the dollar amount is under a certain figure, and another route if the claim is above a certain figure. An application must be reviewed by a number of people in the organization before it is approved, and the group of people reviewing an application might vary, depending on the type of insurance the applicant is seeking and the level of documentation required.

knowledge management: the process of gathering and making use of a firm's collective experience wherever it resides.

workflow: order in which work is performed.

The need for more effective communication and improved service spurred Humana (humana.com) to look for a Web-based KM system. Louisville, Kentucky-based Humana launched a Web-based community "hub" for doctors, patients, employers, and insurance brokers called Emphesys. The insurer deployed technology from InSystems. Electronic certificate delivery provides a dramatic reduction in the time it takes to put benefit plan information in customers' hands, as well as improved efficiency and customer satisfaction.

Certificate revision is also paperless. With InSystems' Calligo, new versions can be generated, delivered, and maintained in the repository without having to reissue everything on paper. If a state mandates a change, for example, the system can generate and deliver the revised document electronically, as well as highlight the differences for customers to see. The potential to do changes and put the documents in the hands of the insured quickly is a tremendous benefit and enhances company relationships with customers.

Source: Excerpted from Kim A. Zimmerman, "Portals Help Insurers and Their Customers," *KM World,* September 2002, 23.

From a business perspective, portals provide the company's employees with task-relevant information. They also can supply partners and customers with knowledge quickly. The goal of such a portal is the transparent enterprise, reducing the complexity of reaching needed information. For example, Hewlett-Packard has an employee portal on the Internet that lets an employee quickly look up a colleague's phone number, track product information, file expenses, book travel arrangements, and get daily updates on what is going on within the firm, all by clicking the mouse. Everything is right there on the portal. It is the best way to create a sense of community among employees and save on costs.

Portal disadvantages include the following:

- Difficulty integrating with other applications
- Organizational and financial costs
- Culture shock
- The need for additional investment in technology

- The difficulty of retaining skilled staff
- Uncertainty of benefits
- Expense of technology
- Unprepared suppliers
- Incompatibility with existing IT infrastructure (Pickering 2002)

EVOLUTION OF PORTALS

The original purpose of a portal was to consolidate a company's disparate data and allow ready access to that data. Web portals were mere search engines for news, e-mail, maps, stock quotes, shopping, and the like. They employed simple search technology for locating information on the Web applied to HTML documents. The first Web portals were online services such as AOL. They provided access to the Web and were one-stop destinations for advertisers and marketers, offering a variety of choices and options. Advertising formats included banners and buttons, text links, and multiformat sponsorships.

The next phase transformed today's portals to navigation sites; this describes the functions available at sites such as Quicken, MSN, and Yahoo!. Such portals categorize personal interests into groups (e.g., news, sports, finance, education, science, and others).

PORTAL CATEGORIES

A portal may focus either on many subjects (a **horizontal portal** like Yahoo! or MSN) or a specific subject (a vertical portal like WebMD). Portals also can be enterprise or Internet public portals. To facilitate access to a large accumulation of information, portals evolved to include advanced search capabilities and taxonomies. With an emphasis on information, they were called information portals. The evolution of the portal concept is shown in Figure 10.1.

horizontal portal: electronic exchange that focuses on many subjects (e.g., Yahoo!).

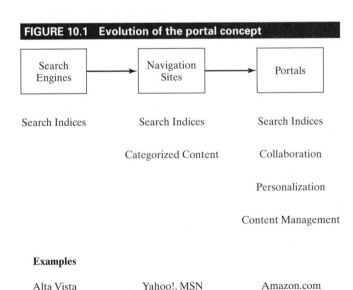

FIGURE 10.1   Evolution of the portal concept

Search Engines	→	Navigation Sites	→	Portals

Search Indices   Search Indices   Search Indices

                           Categorized Content   Collaboration

                                                       Personalization

                                                       Content Management

Examples

Alta Vista   Yahoo!. MSN   Amazon.com

ENTERPRISE INFORMATION PORTALS.   These portals provide the next step in the portal technology evolution. In November 1998, Christopher Shilakes and Julie Tylman of Merrill Lynch's Enterprise Software team introduced the concept of the **enterprise information portal.** The concept was described as "applications that enable companies to unlock internally and externally stored information and provide users a single gateway to personalized information needed to make informed business decisions." They are an amalgamation of software applications that integrate, manage, analyze, and distribute information across and outside an enterprise (including business intelligence, content management, data warehouse and data mart, and data management applications).

> **enterprise information portal:** a portal that ties together multiple, hetero-geneous internal repositories and applications, as well as external content sources and services, into a single browser-based view that is individualized to a particular user's task or role.

Companies are becoming more aware of the potential value of information lying dormant in various repositories. Integration and consolidation are important goals of enterprise portals. Applications are integrated by combining, standardizing, analyzing, and distributing relevant information and knowledge to the end user—customers, employees, or partners. (See Box 10.2.)

A step forward in enterprise portal services (EPS) is globalizing a company's portal site. It is a process of positioning a company's people, processes, and technologies to communicate and operate in the world marketplace. This is quite a challenge, considering the cultural, language, and ethnic differences within U.S. firms. It is the direction more and more international firms take in an effort to capitalize on international revenue and knowledge-sharing opportunities.

KNOWLEDGE PORTALS.   We have learned quickly that successful companies in the twenty-first century will be those who do quality work in the way they capture, store, and leverage what their employees know. It is important, then, not to focus solely on technology, because the large number of unsuccessful knowledge management projects was unable to deploy technological potentials to establish long-term solutions for efficient knowledge transfer or skill management.

Today's trend is to build applications that combine the search, analysis, and dissemination of information through knowledge portals. In **knowledge portals,** the focus is less on information content and more on improving knowledge worker productivity. The knowledge portal is a key component in knowledge management architecture and the central piece that allows producers and users of knowledge to interact. It provides a variety of information on various topics and can be customized to meet a user's individual needs online. Two types of interface are provided:

> **knowledge portal:** a Web page or a facility that offers a single, uniform point from which all of an enterprise's data sources can be accessed.

- Knowledge producer interface allows the knowledge worker to gather, analyze, and collaborate with peers or colleagues to generate new knowledge.
- Knowledge consumer interface facilitates the dissemination of knowledge across the enterprise. A key feature is a sophisticated personalization facility that takes into account the consumer profile before providing customized results.

Historically, portals started as Web-based applications, providing a single point of access to distribute online information like documents stemming from a search

---

BOX 10.2

The Emerging Next Generation Portals

The first generation portal strove to make sense of government for the external customer—it served as a thin "lid" stretched to cover multiple government stovepipes. The next generation portal provides a new interaction point for government's key stakeholders:

- Citizens—anticipates constituent needs and delivers content, services, and transactions on their terms

- Businesses—reduces the cost in time and resources to establish, operate, and manage a fully compliant business

- Government employee—provides one-stop access to people, applications, and content from across organizations to save valuable time and support key processes and customer service

- Government entities—combines services from multiple organizations to provide integrated delivery to the end customer and to create effective interagency process.

The next generation portal infrastructure goes beyond a single Web site—it positions underlying content and systems to create multiple Web portals for specific categories of stakeholders. It also creates specialized Web portals for various types of channels—such as the interactive voice response (IVR) and mobile device portals—to extend government's ability to serve customers on their terms.

The list below presents the digital government portal value proposition as it relates to the six essential factors of the Value Measuring Methodology, a framework presented by the Social Security Administration and the General Services Administration:

- Strategic/political value—leadership representation of elected officials; highly visible, constituent-focused improvements near term

- Direct customer value—simple navigation to cross-agency information and services; personalized services

- Government financial value—minimize total costs, achieve economies of scale, and provide end-to-end architecture

- Social/public value—transparency and accountability, consistent security/privacy

- Government operational/foundation value—increase employee effectiveness/productivity, accelerate deployment of new online services

- Risk—reduce deployment risk of new online services, decrease IT risk through common infrastructure, enhance security

Specialized portals include ones for homeland security, health and human services partnership, business, voice, and authentication portals; each with its own unique benefits, services, and customization.

Source: Excerpted from Mark Youman and Matthew Thompson, "Know-how," *AMS,* 2004.

---

and links to specialized Web sites. They quickly evolved to include advanced search capabilities and organizing schemes like taxonomies. Because of their emphasis on information, they were called information portals or first-generation portals. Yahoo! was one of the first and continues to be one of the most popular information portals on the Internet.

Information portals used by knowledge workers are referred to as knowledge portals, to distinguish the unique role a knowledge worker plays in analyzing and evaluating

knowledge worker: a person who transforms business and personal experience into knowledge through capturing, assessing, applying, sharing, and disseminating it within the organization to solve specific problems or to create value.

information for problem solving. A **knowledge worker** is a person who transforms business and personal experience into knowledge through capturing, assessing, applying, sharing, and disseminating it within the organization to solve specific problems or to create value.

Knowledge portals provide a flexible knowledge climate to a potentially large number of users. The goal is not only to provide a library-like pool of information, but to actively support the user in complex problem solving at the time needed in the format requested. Companies will have the ability to build technology around knowledge requirements (not the other way around), customize desktop access around individual requirements, make better decisions as a result of quick access to crucial information, and maximize speed, efficiency, accuracy, and flexibility of knowledge transfer. (See www.amanet.org/books/ catalog/0814407080.htm.)

KEY CHARACTERISTICS

Enterprise knowledge portals distinguish knowledge from information. They provide a facility for producing knowledge from data and information. They also provide a better basis for making decisions than do other portals.

enterprise knowledge portal: an electronic doorway into a knowledge management system.

Gaining knowledge means competitive advantage over those with mere information. A summary of the key characteristics of enterprise information and enterprise knowledge portals is shown in Table 10.1.

To illustrate, take the case of the army knowledge online portal. The objective of this portal is to transform the army into a networked organization that leverages its intellectual capital to better organize, train, equip, and maintain a strategic land combat force. More specifically, the army needs quick access to its enterprise information at a low cost, and it must be able to use information technology to leverage army-wide innovation in services, processes, and knowledge creation.

TABLE 10.1   Knowledge portals versus information portals

Enterprise Information Portals	*Enterprise Knowledge Portals*
• Use both "push" and "pull" technologies to transmit information to users through a standardized, Web-based interface. • Integrate disparate applications including content management, business intelligence, data warehouse/data mart, data management, and other data external to these applications into a single system that can "share, manage, and maintain information from one central user interface." • Access external and internal sources of data and information and support a bi-directional exchange of information with these sources.	• Goal-directed toward knowledge production, knowledge acquisition, knowledge transmission, and knowledge management. • Focus on enterprise business processes (e.g., sales, marketing, and risk management). • Provide, produce, and manage information about the validity of the information it supplies. • Include all EIP functionalities.

Source: J., Firestone, "Enterprise Knowledge Portals," White Paper 8, www.dkms.com. Accessed March 2003.

Among the key features of the army knowledge online portal are the following:

- User-customizable messages on the Web page
- Directory search
- Knowledge channels
- Powerful search engine
- Acquisition knowledge center
- Officer career announcement and management knowledge center
- Calendar and frequently asked questions (FAQs)
- Career contact points

TYPES OF CONTENT

Depending on the intended target group, there are several types of content a knowledge portal provides. Briefly, these groups include the following:

- Employees—education, skills, experiences, know-how
- Customers—company information, competitors, projects, contacts
- Competitors—products, company information, services, best practices
- Projects—documents, lessons learned, news and views
- Solutions—FAQs, case studies, methodologies, impact
- Technology—news, reports, vendors, trends and directions

The key functions of a knowledge portal are summarized in Table 10.2. They include process support, document management, teamwork, and personalization. The latter function transcends the entire portal, while others are specialized or needed only in special areas of a portal platform. Process support and teamwork are the most important features of a knowledge portal. Discussion groups and e-mail are the most common communication function. The most typical document management features are search and version control, while personalization offers a wide variety of functions that enable users to customize their personal working environment based on their preferences.

TABLE 10.2   Functions of a knowledge portal

Personalization	*Active Process Support*	*Teamwork*	*Document Management*
• Personal inbox	• Checklists	• Video conferencing	• Subscribe to contents
• Customizing	• To do list	• Audio conferencing	• Versions control
• News push	• Project management	• Discussion groups	• Access control
• User manager	• Push	• E-mail	• Search (navigation)
• Scheduling	• Workflow	• Find experts	• Document sharing
• Profile matches		• Message boards	• Append/modify/delete
• History		• Chat rooms	• Content rating
• Replication		• Meeting planner	• Office integration
• Personal favorites			
• Save queries			

Source: Christoph M., Jansen, Volker Bach, and Hubert Osterle, "Knowledge Portals: Using the Internet to Enable Business Transformation." *www.isoc.org/inet2000/cdproceedings/7d/7d_2.htm.*

Here is a sample scenario involving a consultant engaging in the initial steps with a customer.

- Customer contacts knowledge worker (consultant) informing her of interest in building a management system based on customer's products and services. Consultant *schedules a meeting* with customer and technical staff to look into their needs and requirements.

- Consultant relies on the portal to *find documents* about the customer. She looks into the "Engagement Life Cycle" option, *navigates* down this feature, *downloads* the relevant documents to her workstation, *modifies her workload* by adding the customer and the nature of the problem to her schedule, and *requests additional input* from external Internet sources that address the problem at hand.

- Consultant explores help from company experts who are familiar with customer's problem. The portal *retrieves resumes* of selected experts.

- Consultant develops a project plan or *template* that identify the major phases of the project. The template specifies gathering information; creating approaches to solving the problem; eliciting information about competitive products, skills, or technology; resulting in a statement of work as a strategic planning document.

- Consultant sends e-mail to the customer with a proposed *meeting schedule* in person, via telephone, or videoconferencing, knowing the time when the customer might be available.

- Consultant *drafts a presentation* that covers the customer's needs, the consultant's company products and services, and a *master plan* with a notification to all colleagues in the company to read, review, and react, with a deadline.

The entire process listed above is what knowledge work is all about. Knowledge workers are problem solvers. They make use of existing information by the way they analyze and synthesize information and exchange knowledge with resident experts. They retrofit the resulting analysis to the problem at hand and end up with a prescribed procedure that essentially produces a solution to the problem. The relevance of portals is twofold: Solutions contain useful information that can become part of a knowledge portal, and as portals evolve into more broad-based knowledge workplaces, they become increasingly interwoven with other tools that support analysis and project implementation.

SEARCH ENGINES

As mentioned earlier, portals were mere search engines. To distinguish between the two, it would be useful to briefly cover the functions and role of search engines in e-commerce. E-merchants depend on search engines as sources for large volumes of Web traffic. **Search engines** are like yellow pages for online businesses. Many search engines have been created, and they vary in database size, navigation format, and collection method. Engines can collect Web site data by employing a traditional crawler, a human editor, or a paid subscriber.

search engines: software agents whose task is to find information by looking at keywords or by following certain guidelines or rules.

Crawlers are computer-automated programs that scour the Internet for Web links. These links are added to a database and categorized by keywords and relevancy for future reference. The human method also employs Web surfing to find links to be added to a database, but subject to human analysis. Search engines that operate by paid subscribers will add a Web site to their database with the understanding that they will be paid for each Web surfer who clicks on a link to the business's Web site. Webmasters who understand and can take advantage of each type of search engine will be more successful in gaining exposure.

Historically, search engines were first implemented in small units that searched only one site or at most a handful, but their usefulness was soon recognized as the Internet grew. Various methods were used, from searching the titles of Web pages to counting the number of keywords that showed up on the page. As the technology of indexing Web pages matured, one search engine—Google—rose in prominence above all others.

Most of Google's success is attributed to its unique way of ranking pages. PageRank is an algorithm that assumes that the more links a page has, the better it is. The page with the most links to it from relevant outside sites gets the highest ranking; the more pages that are linked to those linking pages, the better. The algorithm considers every link from an outside page as a vote of confidence in that particular page by the linking page.

Search terms are then determined by content and links instead of a simple word count. Domain names and the text of a hyperlink are important determinants of ranking and keywords. Googlebot, the crawler program, is fast, efficient, and objective in its categorization of Web pages. As a result, in October 2004, it had more than 3,988,542 Web pages indexed, and 36 million surfers have searched on Google. (See www.google.com.)

Getting listed in this massive directory is not a problem, but getting a good ranking is a different story. Because Google ranks mainly by recording the number of links that go to a Web page, any prospective Webmaster has to be able to spread the word about its Web site, especially among relevant sites. This might mean cooperating and trading links with a powerful competitor or first getting listed with specific directories.

Site content and relevance are integral parts of automated search engines. Consolidation of themes can help with the overall keyword searches that are so popular now. Crawlers use a combination of URL text, titles, keyword densities, metatags, and descriptions to extrapolate an overall theme for a Web site. If one is selling paper clips, it would help to have a large selection of different types of paper clips and to have relevant information and facts about paper clips.

To illustrate, when searching for "money," CNN's Financial News Web page shows up as the top site. More than 150 Web sites link to CNN, including AOL, CompuServ, *AsiaWeek, TIME,* and the *Wall Street Journal.* The second-ranked Web page, Smartmoney.com, has more than 800 Web pages linked to it, but they are relatively obscure listings or directories. Furthermore, the 100th-ranking Web site, Moneynet.co.uk, is a bank in the United Kingdom that focuses on loans and mortgages. It has more than 120 linked pages but clearly does not have the breadth of coverage on the subject of money. As this example shows, the PageRank and content algorithms operate in a clear and logical manner.

It should be noted that no search engine is free of drawbacks. Yahoo! is the largest directory, but it gave up on maintaining its human-edited monstrosity in favor of simply reshuffling results from Google and Dmoz. Likewise, although Google dominates the Web, its reach is still limited. For marketers interested in promoting their items, the best plan of action is to thoroughly test and streamline the site based on set criteria. Exposure can be gained by simply joining forums, small directories, e-mail lists, and the like. Then the Webmaster can submit not only the main site, but a few major subcategories within the Web site, as well. It is also good practice to submit the URLs of referring sites in order to increase rankings.

After the site is more or less optimized and has a somewhat mature feel, it is time for submissions to human-edited directories. Because the chances of rejection are high and the backlogs are extremely large, it is best to optimize the site as much as possible before attempting admission. At this point, one should know what keywords and terms are most popular, and most of the editor-distracting errors should have been smoothed over, thus increasing the chances of success when the editor comes around.

THE BUSINESS CHALLENGE

Today's organization is evolving from a product- to a customer-centric organization. At the same time, there is inherent pressure to optimize the performance of operational processes to reduce costs and enhance quality. Customer-centric systems allow companies to understand and predict customer behavior and offer the right product at the right time, while commercializing products at the lowest price.

PORTALS AND BUSINESS TRANSFORMATION

The challenge stems from two fundamental aspects underlying the current computing environment. First, the explosion in the volume of key business information already captured in electronic documents has left many organizations losing their grip on information as they transform into new systems and process upgrades. Second, the speed with which quantity and content are growing means rigorous internal discipline to mine and integrate the sources of enterprise knowledge.

Consider the pressures faced by today's typical organization.

- Shorter time to market: New products and services have to be conceived, developed, and delivered in months or even weeks.

- Knowledge worker turnover: When a pivotal person leaves, the pain is felt widely and quickly. Organizations that do not tap into their employees' minds and take advantage of the knowledge within will fall behind quickly.

- More demanding customers and investors: For virtually every organization, customers want to pay less while investors want more value from their investment. That means all the resources to which an organization can lay claim, including its intellectual resources, must be managed for the best results.

Today, more companies realize that they must develop strategies and processes designed to best utilize intellectual resources at strategic and operational levels. Ten years ago, companies began using groupware (e.g., e-mail, discussion forums, document libraries) for coordinating activities. Now, they are inundated with new tools for communicating, sharing knowledge, and interacting electronically. They are deploying next-generation information and application platforms (e.g., enterprise portals) and real-time tools (e.g., instant messaging, Web conferencing, streaming audio/video), but struggling to manage process engineering across partners and suppliers as another aspect of collaboration.

Today's organizations are looking for solutions to support new e-business models. As a result, the demand for tools to negotiate, plan, decide, and collaborate more effectively has increased dramatically. Unfortunately, most organizations meet collaboration requirements on a piecemeal basis, fulfilling requests as they emerge from business units or partners without an overall strategic plan. "The result is a hodgepodge of overlapping and redundant technologies" (see www.metagroup.com/cgi-bin/inetcgi/commerce/productDetails.jsp?oid=29277).

MARKET POTENTIAL

Knowledge portals have emerged as a key tool for supporting the knowledge workplace. There is no doubt that portals are big business. More than 85 percent of organizations plan to invest in portals during the next five years, with a median expenditure of $500,000. As the world becomes more networked, these estimates are bound to climb. Portals can provide easier, unified access to business information and better communications among customers and employees. See Box 10.3 for sample pressures facing portals.

BOX 10.3

The Role of Portals in Facing Business Pressures

- Business Integration vs. Information Integration or Application Integration: Integrating information and applications are first steps to support business integration. A portal can support application and information integration, but the weakness at this point can be a lack of providing business context, or meaning, to the information. Business integration is the integration and translation through the metadata layer of information and applications to provide context.

- Process Integration: In addition to providing context, the portal solution should support process integration. Process integration includes work flow, categorization, and taxonomy services. These services provide the foundation for context. Information with work flow, categorization, and taxonomy equals context.

- Application and Information Integration: This is a strict reference to source systems from which information is generated. It also includes the data administration layers, such as cleansing, transformation, and extraction.

- Enterprise Metadata Repository: Metadata are vital as the mechanism for context. The repository should not include every piece of information that exists, only the information that will be utilized to provide meaning. The repository then becomes the "single version of understanding," not just the "single version of the truth."

Source: Excerpted from Robert Bolds, "Enterprise Information Portals: Portals in Puberty, Best Practices in Enterprise Portals," *KMWorld*, May 2004, 13.

The portal market is comprised of several infrastructure components: content management, business intelligence, data warehouses and data mines, and data management.

ENTERPRISE PORTAL TECHNOLOGIES

KEY FUNCTIONALITIES

The main goal of a portal is to provide a single point of access to all information sources. Hence, portals must be the ultimate tools for universal integration of all enterprise applications. At the same time, because organizational staff members have different information needs and knowledge uses, portals have to deliver a personalized interface. Given the complexity of this challenge, portals must include the following seven functionalities.

1. **Gathering.** Documents created by knowledge workers are stored in a variety of locations (e.g., files on individual desktops, Web sites on the network, databases on servers, and so on). In order to be accessible, data and documents need to be captured in a common repository.

2. **Categorization.** This functionality profiles the information in the repository and organizes it in meaningful ways for navigation and searching. Portals are expected to support categorization at all levels, including the employee, partners, and customers. They also should support categorizations in various dimensions, including the process, product, and service dimensions.

3. **Distribution.** Portals must help individuals acquire knowledge, either through an active mechanism (search interface) or a passive mechanism (push). This functionality supports the distribution of structured and unstructured information in the form of electronic or paper documents.

4. **Collaboration.** Collaboration is achieved through messaging, work flow, discussion databases, and so on. This functionality expands the role of portals from passive information provider to an interface for all types of organizational interactions.

5. **Publish.** The goal of this functionality is to publish information to a broader audience, including individuals outside the organization.

6. **Personalization.** A key component of the portal architecture is to allow individuals to enhance their productivity. Personalization is becoming a necessity for successful portals, due to the proliferation of information available through the portal. To take advantage of this functionality, knowledge workers must be able to manage and prioritize the delivery of information on a task function or an interest basis.

7. **Search/Navigate.** This functionality provides tools for identifying and accessing specific information. The knowledge worker can either browse or submit a query.

Common Features	Business Benefits
Search	Quick access to hidden information to **facilitate business processes**
Categorization	Ability to organize information assets by business process, group, or job category thus **promoting access to relevant information**
Query, Reporting, and Analysis	**Better decision support** as well as information dissemination and sharing
Integration of Information and Applications	Ability to access through a single interface, all applications and information required for **increased job throughout**
Publish and Subscribe	Maturation of business processes by collaborating with others, sharing information, and **improving business performance**
Personalization	Arranging the interface to meet an individual's needs and desires for **increased job productivity**

FIGURE 10.2   Portal features and their corresponding benefits

Figure 10.2 illustrates the most common features and business benefits of portals. Figure 10.3 sketches the Microsoft portal architecture. Briefly, the key components are the following.

- The knowledge management platform offers a typical, but extended, three-layered architecture that allows a company to build a flexible, powerful, and scalable knowledge management solution.
- The knowledge desktop layer consists of familiar productivity tools, such as Microsoft Office, and integrates tightly with the knowledge services layer.
- The knowledge services layer provides important knowledge management services such as collaboration, document management, and search and deliver functionality, with modules for tracking, work flow, and data analysis.
- The system layer is a foundation that includes administration, security, and directories for managing the knowledge management platform. All services run on the system layer and benefit from the integrated communication services that connect with external solutions, platforms, and partners.

COLLABORATION

Collaboration is a fundamental starting point for e-business transformation. The goal of the collaboration tool is to support information sharing. It means two or more people working together in a coordinated manner over time and space using electronic devices. In a well-designed collaborative environment, knowledge flow can be captured easily in e-mail, stored in document and discussion databases, and be available in a knowledge management system for later use.

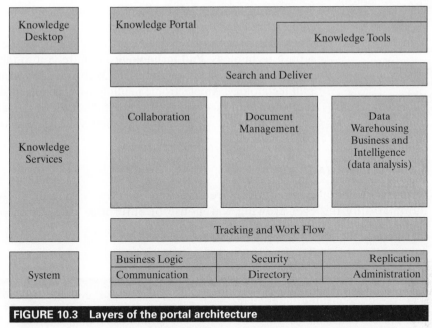

FIGURE 10.3   Layers of the portal architecture

Source: Jerry Honeycutt, "Knowledge Management Strategies," *Microsoft,* 2000, 167.

asynchronous collaboration: human-to-human interactions via computer subsystems having no time or space constraints.

synchronous collaboration: computer-based, human-to-human interaction that occurs immediately (within 5 seconds) using audio, video, or data technologies.

Collaboration is distinguished by whether it is synchronous or asynchronous. **Asynchronous collaboration** is human-to-human interactions via computer subsystems having no time or space constraints. Queries, responses, or access can occur at any time and in any place. In contrast, **synchronous collaboration** is computer-based, human-to-human interaction that occurs immediately (within five seconds). It can use audio, video, or data technologies. Figure 10.4 summarizes the requirements for successful collaboration. Table 10.3 shows the technologies available to perform asynchronous and synchronous collaboration.

FIGURE 10.4   Requirements for successful collaboration tools

1. E-mail systems that support collaborative services such as shared calendars, task lists, contact lists, and team-based discussions
2. Web browser for browsing and presenting the documents to the user
3. Simple search functionalities such as file services integrated with the operating system or search services integrated with an application (e.g., e-mail, discussions)
4. Collaboration services with a multipurpose database for capturing the collaborative data
5. Web services for providing the access layer to documented knowledge
6. Indexing services for full-text search of documents
7. Well-organized central-storage locations such as file, Web servers, and documents databases

Source: Jerry Honeycutt, "Knowledge Management Strategies," *Microsoft,* 2000, 176.

push technology:
technology that places information in a place where it is difficult to avoid seeing it.

pull technology:
technology that requires one to take specific actions to retrieve information.

Another important distinction is whether to use push or pull technology. **Push technology** places information in a place where it is difficult to avoid seeing it. E-mail is a classic example of a push technology. **Pull technologies** require you to take specific actions to retrieve information. The Web is a good example of a pull technology. An electronic mailing list that uses push technology of e-mail is extremely powerful as a collaborative tool, because it requires little learning or behavioral change on the part of the user.

CONTENT MANAGEMENT

Content management requires directory and indexing capabilities to manage automatically the ever-growing warehouse of enterprise data. This component

---

TABLE 10.3   Advantages and disadvantages of synchronous and asynchronous collaboration tools

Synchronous Collaboration	*Asynchronous Collaboration*
Teleconferencing	**Electronic Mailing Lists**
Used extensively by senior management and staff, conference telephone calls represent an effective (if relatively expensive) collaboration technology used for a number of years and represent an extremely cost-effective collaboration technology.	Lists have been in use for a number of years and represent an extremely cost-effective collaboration technology.
Advantages: personal, immediate feedback	*Advantages:* cheap
Disadvantages: expensive, often doesn't work well across time zones.	*Disadvantages:* limited communication medium
Computer Video/Teleconferencing	**Web-Based Discussion Forums**
Computer-based **teleconferencing** and video-conferencing are rapidly evolving technologies that have tremendous potential for distributed organizations.	A number of different online discussion forum applications are in use.
	Advantages: same as electronic mailing lists except requires slightly faster Internet connection
Online Chat Forum	*Disadvantages:* cultural resistance
Such forums allow multiple users to communicate simultaneously by typing messages on a computer screen.	**Lotus Notes**
	Lotus Notes is a comprehensive collaboration tool that includes e-mail and groupware
	Advantages: comprehensive collaborative solution employing state-of-the-art technologies for communication, document management, and work flow.
	Disadvantages: expensive to deploy when compared with other collaboration technologies.

addresses the problem of searching for knowledge in all information sources in the enterprise. This knowledge includes structured and unstructured internal information objects such as office documents, collaborative data, Management Information Systems (MISs), Enterprise Resource Planning (ERP) systems, and experts, as well as information from outside sources. This component ensures that knowledge assets get into the knowledge management information base. This new complexity is handled by building sophisticated knowledge management taxonomy based on **metadata** (data that describe other data). Metadata are needed to define types of information.

metadata: data about data, such as indices or summaries.

Another issue handled by content management is the way documents are analyzed, stored, and categorized. Once the documents have been gathered, they must be analyzed so that their content is available for subsequent business queries, retrieval, and use by the end user. As documents enter the portal system, they are stored for later retrieval and display. Systems typically analyze the document content and store the results of that analysis so that subsequent use of the documents will be more effective and efficient.

As the number of management documents grows, it becomes increasingly important to gather similar documents into smaller groups and to name the groups. This operation is called *categorizing*. All automatic categorizing methods use features to determine when two documents are similar enough to be put into the same cluster.

Because document collection is not static, portals must provide some form of taxonomy maintenance. As new documents are added, they also must be added to the taxonomy. As the clusters grow, and the conceptual content of the new documents changes over time, it might become necessary to subdivide clusters or to move documents from one cluster to another. A portal administration, using the taxonomy editor, can monitor and implement these suggestions, in general, and can periodically assess the health and appropriateness of the current taxonomy and document assignments within it.

In the publishing process, several things should be considered concerning the e-commerce taxonomy. Although tagging documents with metadata is important for the quality of content in the stage of document publishing, it is a burden to submit information if tagging the metadata is a time-consuming process. This is where the **Extensible Markup Language (XML)** comes in. See Box 10.4 for a brief description of XML.

Extensible Markup Language (XML): a specification developed by the W3C designed especially for Web documents.

INTELLIGENT AGENTS

Intelligent agents are tools that can be applied in numerous ways in the context of enterprise portals. As a tool, intelligent agents are still in their infancy. Most applications are experimental and have not yet reached the efficient commercial stage. However, there is no doubt that they will play a crucial role in all aspects of enterprise portals, especially in intelligent searches and in filtering the right documents according to some criteria.

intelligent agents: programs used extensively on the Web that perform tasks such as retrieving and delivering information and automating repetitive tasks.

BOX 10.4

XML: The Basics

XML was created to structure, store, and to send information. In contrast, HTML was designed to display data and to focus on how data looks. As a markup language, XML is a complement to HTML, not a replacement for HTML. It is a cross-platform, software and hardware independent tool for transmitting information. This makes it much easier to create data that different applications can work with. It also makes it easier to expand or upgrade a system to new operating systems, servers, applications, and new browsers.

With XML, your data is stored outside your HTML. When HTML is used to display data, the data is stored inside your HTML. With XML, data can be stored in separate XML files. This way you can concentrate on using HTML for data layout and display, and be sure that changes in the underlying data will not require any changes to your HTML.

In the real world, computer systems and databases contain data in incompatible formats. One of the most time-consuming challenges for developers has been to exchange data between such systems over the Internet. Converting the data to XML can greatly reduce this complexity and create data that can be read by many different types of applications.

Expect to see a lot about XML and B2B via the Internet. XML is going to be the main language for exchanging financial information between businesses over the Internet. A lot of interesting B2B applications are already available.

The syntax rules of XML are very simple and very strict. The rules are very easy to learn and very ease to use. Because of this, creating software that can read and manipulate XML is very easy. XML documents use a self-describing and simple syntax. For example,

```
<?xml version=1.0" encoding="ISO-8859-1"?>
<note>
<to>Tove</to>
<from>Jani</from>
<heading>Reminder</heading>
<body>Don't forget me this weekend!</body>
</note>
```

The first line is the XML declaration; it defines the XML version and the character encoding used in the document. The next line describes the root element of the document (like it was saying: "this document is a note"): The next four lines describe four child elements of the root (to, from, heading, and body); the last line defines the end of the root element.

Remember that all XML elements must have a closing tag, which are case sensitive. The elements must be properly nested. All XML documents must have a root element. Attribute values must always be quoted and the white space in your document is not truncated.

There is a lot more to XML. For a tutorial, see www.w3schools.com/xml/xml_whatis.asp.

Source: Excerpted from www.w3schools.com/xml/xml_whatis.asp.

Consider the relationship between companies and their customers. As these relationships are becoming more complex, organizations need more information and advice on what the relationships mean and how to exploit them. Intelligent agent technology offers some interesting options for addressing such needs.

Customers are known to set certain priorities when purchasing products and services. Intelligent agents master individual customers or customer groups' demand priorities by learning from experience with them, and can quantitatively and qualitatively analyze those priorities. Agents are software entities that are able to execute a wide range of functional tasks (such as searching, comparing, learning, negotiating, and collaborating) in an autonomous, proactive, social, and adaptive manner. The term *intelligent* in this context means only that we are dealing with entities that are able to adjust their behavior to the environment. In other words, they are able to learn from previous situations and replicate the behavior of the customer if we want to predict that customer's purchasing pattern.

Customers require a vast range of services that intelligent agents can address. Some of these services might include the following.

- Customized customer assistance with online services: news filtering, messaging, scheduling, making arrangements for gatherings, ordering, and so on

- Customer profiling, including inferring information about customer behavior based on business experiences with the particular customer

- Integrating profiles of customers into a group of marketing activities

- Predicting customer requirements

- Negotiating prices and payment schedules

- Executing financial transactions on the customer's behalf

These examples represent a spectrum of applications from the somewhat modest, low-level news-filtering applications to the more advanced and complicated customer relationship management applications that focus on predicting customer requirements. The main point is that an intelligent agent is an intermediary between the enterprise and its customers, and a source of effective, utilitarian information encountered at different virtual destinations.

In terms of the future, the emphasis is on collaborative technologies to create communities of practice, advanced human computer interaction to enhance performance, and intelligent agents to automate the search function.

WEB SERVICES AND PORTALS

A major goal of software vendors is to employ Web services for seamless integration of applications into portal software. To explore this possibility, the difference between the business perspective and the technology perspective of Web services needs to be clarified. The business perspective centers on delivering software as a utility or a service, like electricity or telephone service, over the Web. Today's Web technology is capable of providing the platform for delivering software as a utility. In contrast, the technology perspective uses specifications that will allow software system functions to be executed by other programs over the Internet, an intranet, or an extranet, regardless of location. (See Box 10.5.)

Unlike regular services that are intangible assets, Web-based delivery channels provide evidence of service. For example, a ski resort has used Web cams to provide tangible evidence of current snow conditions (see www.vail.snow.com/m.mtncams.asp). Also, unlike services provided by people that are often inconsistent and fraught with errors, Web services are electronically based and provided on a machine-to-machine basis, ensuring minimal variations in quality from one customer to the next.

BOX 10.5

Academic Gets Creative with Web Services

A Web service can help you catch a bus. Or test an electronic circuit from a dorm room. Or even take English writing tests in a new way. These creative uses of Web services—a method for connecting software systems over the Internet—at the Massachusetts Institute of Technology (MIT) stand in stark contrast to the more mundane, workaday uses of Web services at corporations. But these applications suggest that Web services may be an important link in realizing the vision of broad access to information originally promised by the Web browser.

For Microsoft's $25 million investment in MIT's project is far from purely altruistic. On top of gaining more credibility in the academic research world, Microsoft is garnering valuable insights into how it should design future software. Although iCampus is specifically focused on using technology to improve teaching, Microsoft said the lessons it is learning can be applied to business, particularly to Microsoft's primary customer: the information worker. The university's experiments with Web services, col-laboration, security, Tablet PCs and visualization tools will translate directly back into Microsoft's product planning cycle, according to Randy Hinrichs, group research manager of learning science and technology at Microsoft.

The iCampus/MIT Online Assessment Tool (iMoat) application, which is already in use at MIT and other universities, is a replacement for freshman-placement writing exams. Students register to take a test and are sent reading material via e-mail. Three days later they submit an essay. A teacher uses the same iMoat application to grade the exam on a PC.

Rather than asking students to use pen and paper to write on a subject unprepared, iMoat was meant to give students a more realistic setting for composing essays—that is, writing on a PC after some preparation, said Leslie Perelman, the principal investigator of iMoat. The Web services-based system is also less costly than sending dozens of professional graders to a hotel to read through thousands of exams, and it can be more competitive with machine scoring systems, he said.

Source: Excerpted from Martin LaMonica, "Academia Gets Creative with Web Services." news.com.com/ 2102-7345_3-5096702.html?tag=st_util_print.

WHAT TO EXPECT

Technology is the enabler of Web service. **Web services** are essentially business services, composed of standards that allow different platforms, operating systems, and languages to exchange information or carry out a business process together. They make it easier for people to construct and integrate applications via the Web. The whole concept is a *customer-centric* concept. It is based on reducing costs through automation and increased efficiency and placing emphasis on maximizing revenue by improving customer relationships. (See Figure 10.5.)

Adopting Web services is expected to improve the way a company conducts electronic transactions with trading partners (e.g., shipping, ordering supplies, billing, etc.) and the way information moves through the supply chain. (See Box 10.6.)

Web service technology is a simple packaging technology accessible over the Internet that does not require any technology tied to a vendor's platform. It makes it possible to have portal connectivity. This means that applications and content, external information, and trading partner applications can be brought together in seamless integration. For example, a company may employ the assistance of a Web service to

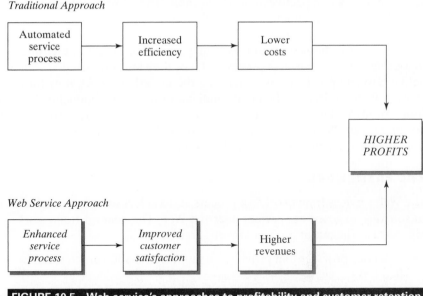

FIGURE 10.5   Web service's approaches to profitability and customer retention

---

BOX 10.6

Surfing at the Bus Stop

A Web services project spearheaded by MIT graduate students, called Shuttle Track, is a system that lets students find out where shuttle buses are located as they drive along their routes. Rather than stand waiting in the cold New England winter weather hoping they haven't missed the last bus home, students can use their PCs or Web-enabled handheld devices to check where the bus is.

The application uses GPS tracking equipment and cellular modems attached below bus seats to transmit location information to a central server in MIT's transportation office. The application stores information in an XML-based Web services data format, which allows people with many different devices to check bus locations. Using Web services formats to store and publish data, the application can distribute scheduling information in a variety of formats, including plain text or graphics.

Source: Adapted from Martin LaMonica, "Academic Gets Creative with Web Services," news.com.com/ 2102-7345_3-5096702.html?tagg=st_util_print.

---

streamline its employees' travel arrangements, another Web service to bill its customers, a Web service for procurement, and so forth. Web services must also be able to communicate with one another to solve specific problems.

Many of today's so-called Web services have yet to make use of Web service technology. Instead, they adhere to the business definition of a Web service. What makes the situation more confusing is that portal vendors tend to use the business and technology perspectives interchangeably. The components delivered by portals (called portlets) are sometimes called Web services.

Using Web services to connect to content is an encouraging first step. The next step is to provide functionality within existing portals that can allow multiple Web services to assemble unique business processes. Once they are completed, it should be easy to define business processes by generating the underlying work flow for each business process. Web services can be great candidates for such functionality. Every indication from portal vendors suggests that Web services have a constructive future within the portal software. Web services will make it possible for portals to connect multiple functions together in a predefined complex business process.

THE FRAMEWORK

The Web services framework is a process and a select set of protocols for connecting to software exposed as services over the Web. The general framework is shown in Figure 10.6. The major aspects to Web services are:

- A service provider that provides an interface for software that can perform specified tasks
- A client that invokes a software service to provide business solution or service
- A repository that manages the service

Service providers place their services with the repository. Clients request the services placed in the repository by the service provider.

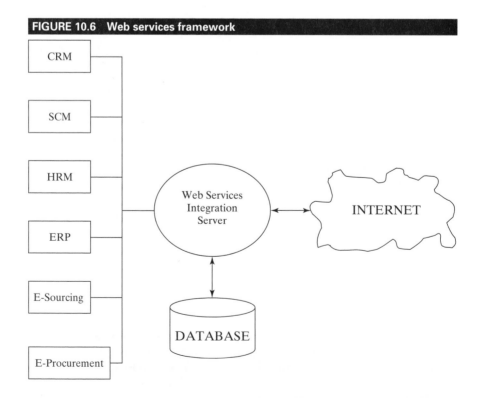

FIGURE 10.6 Web services framework

Business processes are becoming increasingly complex, global, and intertwined between and among different organizations. Pressure to reduce costs drives the increasing need for better information and higher productivity round the clock. Globalization has also increased competition, which has prompted shorter time-to-market. Web services are "electronic offerings for rent." They made it possible for an organization to instantly connect and interoperate with divisions, partners, customers, and suppliers to complete tasks, solve problems, or conduct transactions 24/7 year round.

Web services are mobile and interactive. Consider the case of a traveler driving to the airport to catch a flight. He or she can be automatically rerouted, rescheduled for a later flight, and have the next set of meetings or appointments rescheduled when interlinked e-services using GPS systems identify a traffic jam on the way to the airport. All this happens on behalf of the traveler well ahead of the impending traffic jam. Prior to this scenario, a traveler's e-service might have submitted the travel request to several different airline reservation e-services that compete for the customer's business. With Web services, the customer has many more choices.

Standing in the way of interoperability are inconsistent platforms, different languages, and Internet protocols. Web services overcome these barriers and render information business-to-business (B2B), to a customer service portal or a logistics provider's wireless device. They reduce cycle times and managerial costs by providing procurement/order tracking, invoice billing, receiving, and payment in the most efficient way possible. They also promise improved collaboration with customers, suppliers, partners, and authorized outsiders.

In conclusion, Web services demonstrate that the traditional e-commerce approach based on goods and e-transactions has largely failed. E-merchants that survived the meltdown of 2000 quickly learned to adopt the Web services approach—moving away from cost reduction per se, to learning more about customers and building long-term customer relationships and retention. In this way, profitability is based more on revenue expansion than cost reduction.

It should be noted that Web services are more about successful business strategy than about technology. They are proving to be a great implementer of effective strategies. The focus is on collaboration, cooperation, and coordination of activities and processes among people, partners, and their ultimate success.

MOBILE WEB SERVICES

The wireless approach to Web services attempts to enable new business opportunities in the mobile space and deliver integrated services across wireless networks. Mobile Web services use XML-based Web services architecture to expose mobile network services to the broadest audience of developers and software users. Developers can begin to integrate mobile network services such as messaging, location, authentication, and billing into their PC-based applications. This should enhance business opportunities to promote further applications and enable solutions that work seamlessly across mobile environments. It means more flexibility in how applications create value for customers worldwide.

In contrast, customers can see benefits from mobile wireless networks. When these networks are finally available, they can experience the flexibility of using their preferred device or the mode of communication that is best suited to their needs.

IMPLICATIONS FOR MANAGEMENT

WHO IS BUILDING ENTERPRISE PORTALS?

META Group conducted a survey of 350 organizations (respondent organizations had at least 500 employees) to find out how widely enterprise portals are being deployed, how the portals are utilized, and which services and vendor organizations are used for portal deployment. More than 80 percent of the respondents knew the term *portal,* and one in three currently either have a portal installed or have one in the development stage. Large organizations (more than 10,000 employees) have a significantly higher portal installation rate.

IMPLEMENTATION ISSUES

Although technology issues can be categorized in many different ways, the codification versus collaboration paradigm also provides a particularly useful structure for understanding current trends in information technology. For globally distributed organizations (i.e., most international development organizations) that

bandwidth: how fast a network connection is; a fast connection allows the user to view images and videos, and interact with remote sites as if they were a local computer.

rely on the Internet as a medium for the sharing of knowledge, the issue of **bandwidth** is fundamental. At this point in the evolution of the Internet, bandwidth is a chief constraining factor for many applications. The determination of an organization's overall KM strategy will provide guidance for the implementation of appropriate technology.

BANDWIDTH

Current trends point toward a steady decrease in the cost of Internet access. The rapid and pervasive spread of Internet communication coupled with the evolution of faster and cheaper technology is resulting in improved access to the Internet at lower costs. This trend has been slowest in Africa. However, even there, Internet access is spreading rapidly and is becoming much less expensive, especially in capital cities.

Given the importance of collaboration and the creation of communities of practice as a method for knowledge sharing, it is worth investigating the costs of a significant increase in bandwidth for regional offices that could support (1) desktop videoconferencing, (2) Internet telephony, (3) improved access to information systems based at headquarters, (4) other collaborative tools, and (5) access to more sophisticated information resources.

Most of the technological tools now available tend to help dissemination of know-how but offer less assistance for knowledge use. Tools that assist in knowledge creation are even less well developed, although collaborative work spaces offer promising opportunities. Such work spaces enable participation, across time and distance, in project design or knowledge-base development, so that those most knowledgeable about development problems—the people who are dealing with them on a day-to-day basis—can actively contribute to their solutions. Some of the more user-friendly technologies are the traditional ones: face-to-face discussions, the telephone, electronic mail, and paper-based tools such as flip charts. Among the issues that need to be considered in providing information technology for knowledge-sharing programs are the following:

- Responsiveness to user needs: Continuous efforts must be made to ensure that the information technology in use meets the varied and changing needs of users.

- Content structure: In large systems, classification and cataloging become important so that items can be found easily and retrieved quickly.

- Content quality requirements: Standards for admitting new content into the system need to be established and met to ensure operational relevance and high value.

- Integration with existing systems: Because most knowledge-sharing programs aim at embedding knowledge sharing in the work of staff as seamlessly as possible, it is key to integrate knowledge-related technology with preexisting technology choices.

- Scalability: Solutions that seem to work well in small groups (e.g., HTML Web sites) might not be appropriate for extrapolation organization-wide or on a global basis.

- Hardware-software compatibility: This is important to ensure that choices are made that are compatible with the bandwidth and computing capacity available to users.

- Synchronization of technology with the capabilities of the user: Such synchronization is important in order to take full advantage of the potential of the tools, particularly where the technology skills of users differ widely.

PLANNING AND DEVELOPING AN ENTERPRISE PORTAL

Creating an enterprise portal vendor shortlist can save time and effort typically devoted to large-scale market scans. Once a portal vendor shortlist has been created, each vendor should be evaluated through the use of test cases that test key business functionality, based on architectural fit, vendor viability, and product features. This is all based on advanced planning and development of a portal. The three key steps are:

- **Identify the sore points in the business that a portal can help address.** Related to this step is developing a set of metrics that enable the firm to measure the return on the investment in the portal on a continuing basis. With that comes the critical requirement of defining the business goals and requirements of the portal project and the potential risks that may arise from the project.

- **Identify the portal users and their role in the firm,** the type of decisions they make, and the business content of their job. With that information, you can begin to develop a prototype that gives an inkling of what the proposed portal will do and how it should go about doing the work for users at large.

- **Select, install, and incorporate portal technology and associated hardware.** The most important aspect of this step is adequate and certified user training on the various products making up the portal.

Summary

1. A portal is a secure, Web-based interface that provides a single point of integration for and access to information, applications, and services for all people involved in the enterprise including employees, partners, suppliers, and customers.

2. Born with search engines such as Yahoo! and Alta Vista, portals have made their way into enterprises, bringing together not only information from the Internet, but in-house data as well. These portals, which are known as enterprise knowledge portals (EKPs), aim to offer a single, uniform point from which all of an enterprise's data sources can be accessed.

3. The term *data sources* encompasses structured data (databases, Lotus Notes, and so on) and unstructured data (e-mails, files, archives, and so on), but also includes the data resulting from specific processes and enterprise applications (ERP and CRM tools, and so on). Today, the enterprise intelligence portal (EIP) market is thriving, and many vendors are betting big on portals' well-founded ability to fulfill enterprise needs.

4. Content management in the EKP context requires directory and indexing capabilities to manage automatically the ever-growing store of structured and unstructured data residing in data warehouses, Web sites, ERP systems, legacy applications, and so on. Using metadata to define types of information, good content management can serve as the backbone for a system of corporate decision making where business intelligence tools mine data and report findings back to key role players in the enterprise. Content management also can involve going outside the enterprise; employing crawlers that find pertinent data via the Internet; incorporating it into existing systems; indexing it; and delivering it to appropriate analysts, knowledge workers, or decision makers.

5. The collaborative functionality of EKPs can range from tracking e-mail to developing workplace communities. Some EKPs might allow workers in different parts of the world to create virtual meeting rooms where they can conference by chat, voice, or video communication.

Key Terms

- **asynchronous collaboration** (p. 317)
- **bandwidth** (p. 326)
- **content management** (p. 304)
- **enterprise information portal** (p. 307)
- **enterprise knowledge portal** (p. 309)
- **Extensible Markup Language (XML)** (p. 319)
- **horizontal portal** (p. 306)
- **intelligent agents** (p. 319)
- **knowledge management (KM)** (p. 305)
- **knowledge portal** (p. 307)
- **knowledge worker** (p. 309)
- **metadata** (p. 319)
- **personalization** (p. 304)
- **portal** (p. 304)
- **pull technology** (p. 318)
- **push technology** (p. 318)
- **search engine** (p. 311)
- **synchronous collaboration** (p. 317)
- **teleconferencing** (p. 318)
- **vertical portal** (p. 304)
- **Web services** (p. 322)
- **workflow** (p. 305)

Test Your Understanding

1. Why are portals needed? How are portals similar to the concept of data warehouses and data marts?
2. What are the advantages and disadvantages of having your portal on the Internet instead of an Intranet?
3. List the differences between knowledge and information portals. Discuss the benefits of each.
4. Discuss the strategic and technological fit required for an organization to implement a portal.
5. Discuss the advantages and disadvantages of purchasing a portal from a vendor. Make sure you explore vendor Web sites such as Viador (www.viador.com/) and Autonomy (www.autonomy.com/).
6. Discuss the differences between static and dynamic portals. When would you use each one?
7. Discuss how you can use content management to sort knowledge from external and internal sources. Illustrate with examples.
8. Discuss the implementation issues that can arise from implementing a portal. Focus on technology, management, corporate strategy, and end users.
9. Give examples and uses of portals for the following: B2B, B2C, B2G, C2C, and C2G.
10. List the number of possible ways a portal can be made accessible, given current technological trends. Focus on five of these technologies and discuss their strengths and weaknesses (Hint: Web browsers, cell phones, info kiosks, and so on).

Discussion Questions

1. In the past, companies used electronic data interchange (EDI) to communicate with suppliers and customers. Discuss how portals can be used to replace the functions of EDI. Give examples.
2. An audit firm needs to develop a system that allows auditors and public accountants to search accounting standards, share knowledge, communicate, and share Word and Excel files between the head office and clients' sites. As a consultant, you have been asked to recommend such a system. What would you suggest?
3. A hardware retailer wishes to offer real-time support to customers via the Internet. Suggest how a knowledge portal equipped with chat and CRM can be used to accomplish this. What additional support can the hardware retailer offer? What information from the portal can be given to the manufacturer?
4. A multinational conglomerate has a centralized human resources department in Cleveland, Ohio. The human resources director wants to launch a new set of multilingual policies to all employees, according to their function, category, and grade. The HR director also wants to have employees interact and give feedback on the policies. Suggest a computerized solution to this.
5. Discuss how synergy between different strategic business units can be harnessed and utilized by knowledge portals.

6. Discuss how portals can offer a solution to the centralized versus decentralized information dilemma. What forms of knowledge can be collected centrally, and what should be left decentralized? Why?

7. How can personalized portals use data-mining techniques? Suggest how knowledge management and data mining can be integrated on a portal and give supporting examples.

Web Exercises

1. 1NCR, www.ncr.com

   Challenge: Establish e-learning portals for customers and partners to help those audiences succeed with their NCR products and to generate new revenue for NCR.

   Strategy: Use THINQ e-learning solutions to launch and track courses and provide community features—such as chatrooms and message boards—around the courses.

   Results: NCR has extended nearly 4,000 online and classroom courses to more than 2,000 registered users and is meeting its e-learning revenue goals.

NCR Turns to THINQ to Power Customer and Partner E-Learning Portals

NCR has come a long way in the 117 years since it introduced the first mechanical cash register, but the $6 billion company's tremendous success still hinges on the individual customer relationship. Today, NCR helps companies harness the vast amount of customer information they collect at the sales counter, over the phone, at the ATM, and on the Internet. With this information, businesses can satisfy each customer's unique needs, often automatically, and transform customer transactions into rich customer relationships.

From the dawn of the cash register through NCR's leadership in data warehousing, the company's offerings have always been sophisticated. Accordingly, it has always been important for NCR to help customers learn how to reap the full potential of their NCR hardware and software. It is also important for NCR partners to completely understand the company's products so they succeed in selling and implementing them.

NCR has traditionally offered classroom training for customers and partners to achieve these goals. Recently the company started offering courses over the Internet. These classes combine the incisive content of NCR's classroom training programs with the reach and efficiency of the worldwide network, letting students anywhere in the world take a class any time they can access a Web browser. In addition to helping customers and partners succeed, this e-learning program also generates new revenue for NCR.

NCR evaluated a number of e-learning tools for the job of powering its two customer and partner e-learning portals. One portal is the Teradata Education Network (TEN), an e-learning Web site for the company's data warehousing customers. The other is the external NCR University (NCRU), which extends award-winning NCR employee e-learning to partners. After a rigorous review, NCR selected THINQ to build and power the portals, which offer customers and partners Web-based, self-paced training, course tracking, employee-learning reporting, live virtual classes, hosted educational chats, a reference library, message boards, and instructor-led courseware registration.

"Employee training is important, but it just scratches the surface of e-learning's potential," said Janet Perdzock, program manager, Global Learning Operations of NCR. "These initiatives improve our customers' and partners' businesses, enrich our relationships with those audiences and generate significant new revenue for us. THINQ provides a bridge to our courses, content, and other back-end systems and is a key ingredient in our success."

NCR chose THINQ over other e-learning vendors because of THINQ's long experience in the learning industry, its integrated product, reputation, flexibility, affordability and ability to interoperate with NCR's existing infrastructure. THINQ's satisfied customers also tipped NCR's decision.

The NCRU portal for partners went live in July 2001 and offers 3,600 courses, including 859 NCR proprietary Web-based training courses, NETg information technology courses, NETg desktop computing courses, multilanguage courses; CDs, books, tapes and classroom courses; all filtered based on each company's profile. Since the launch, NCRU has signed up 766 users at 49 companies who have completed 375 courses. They can create individual learning plans, register online, and view their entire training histories. Counting users who registered for a previous "interim" site prior to July 2001, the NCRU portal for customers and partners has 1,528 authorized users.

NCR's Teradata Education Network learning environment went live March 30, 2001 to its membership-based Learning Community. Teradata Education Network is exceeding all projections with more than 1,300 members, more than 1,000 user sessions every week, and more than 660 course completions in the first six months. One-third of all Teradata companies have an associate who is a member of TEN, and TEN is on track to meet its revenue goal for 2001. A 13-month membership to the site comes in many shapes and sizes, depending on the customer's need. An individual membership can cost as little as $895, and a corporate membership can cost as little as $6,795. Not only do members receive access to the learning community, but they also are provided with access to over 50 Teradata courses. Members get into message boards, access white papers, take virtual classroom courses, and review recorded virtual classroom presentations.

Unlike most online training programs, Teradata Education Network allows students from around the globe to communicate with other students and make direct contact with instructors. One of the most powerful aspects of the network is the access to knowledgeable Teradata professionals worldwide, giving students a chance to stay current in an ever-changing market. In the future, NCR plans more curriculum mapping/skill-building capabilities and additional, customized portals for specific customers or partners. It also plans thorough profiling of individual users and corporations to better meet their e-learning needs.

"Customers were asking for an alternate way to train without leaving the office that would supplement their classroom learning," said Adam Zaller, program manager, e-learning, Teradata Customer Education. "Our customers say the Teradata Education Network learning community is like having 'Partners,' our annual user conference, 365 days a year. It's a community of customers helping each other, a revenue stream for the company, and a great way to help our technology solve critical business problems in the real world. Our customers and our prospects are now a lot more aware of education and what we have to offer. We anticipate usage to continue to grow, revenue to expand, and the program to eventually cover the globe."

Questions

1. Discuss the advantages of Teradata as a learning option. What advantages does it give over conventional learning in terms of content delivery, convenience, growth opportunities, and so on?

2. Discuss the possible disadvantage of having a purely electronic learning solution. How can the human element be incorporated?

3. Suggest ways in which NCR can incorporate curriculum mapping/skill-building capabilities and customized portals for specific customers or partners, as mentioned in the case.

4. Suggest ways in which Teradata can be used to train some of its divisions and departments. Can Teradata also be used to train line, middle, and upper management? If so how can they go about this, and what content can they use?

CHAPTER 11

BUSINESS-TO-BUSINESS E-COMMERCE

Learning Objectives

The focus of this chapter is on several learning objectives:

- The meaning, benefits, and opportunities in B2B
- B2B building blocks and their relationship to supply chain management
- Key B2B models and their main functions
- EDI as a B2B tool
- Role of leadership in B2B as an ongoing concern

IN A NUTSHELL

It should be obvious by now that the Internet is changing the face of the worldwide economy. The nature of business competition is changing in a fundamental way. The greatest impact is on business-to-business (B2B) commerce because of its effect on the way companies form strategic alliances and supplier relationships. The increased volume and speed of the business-to-consumer (B2C) e-commerce surge and the promise of supply chain efficiencies is driving B2B demand in companies that have to reduce operating and handling costs while accelerating the supply-chain process. Companies that take advantage of B2B efficiency stand to become market leaders in their industries. The savings they realize from supply-chain costs can be passed along in improved IT operation and, ultimately, to B2B clients.

The differences between B2C and B2B e-commerce are far greater than those between retail and wholesale purchasing. From a business viewpoint, it means savings behind the scenes, ready and convenient alliances with suppliers, meeting cost-cutting objectives while delivering goods and services on a just-in-time basis, and fine-tuning complex procurement collaboration, timely delivery collaboration, and electronic payment systems within the alliance.

In one respect, B2B is collaborative commerce. Companies forge long-term alliances while reducing the cost of doing business. Collaborative commerce requires that information such as product pricing, inventory, and shipping status be shared among business partners. One user of collaborative commerce is Ensco Inc., a company that hauls hazardous chemical wastes from manufacturing plants. Each plant requires Ensco to keep it briefed on the disposal process, because the plants have legal responsibility for the disposal of waste material. Ensco's system shares this information with all of its customers—information that was not available before.

The B2B market is estimated to be more than 10 times larger than the B2C market. Web-based B2B companies profit in a number of ways. They can help other companies set up sites where goods or services can be sold. They can act as brokers at auctions and get a percentage of each sale. They can earn revenues by allowing companies to advertise on their Web sites. The search engine Yahoo! has entered the B2B business, hoping to ride the wave of success.

Yahoo! provides users with access to a rich collection of online resources, including forums and shopping services. It offers auctions and a B2B facility where companies can find products of all varieties for their businesses.

This chapter focuses on the concept and mechanics of B2B, how it differs from B2C, the pros and cons of this emerging strategy, the technology supporting B2B, and implications for the integration of B2B and B2C for the enhancement and profitability of the business process.

WHAT IS B2B E-COMMERCE?

Historically, business has always been about exchange. Back in the days of barter, a seller exchanged an item with a buyer for a different item. In one remote Syrian village in the 1940s, for example, the only cobbler made a new pair of shoes for two dozen eggs if the soles were made from car tire rubber or 10 kilos of wheat if the soles were made from cow leather. When money is introduced to represent economic value, it eliminates barter.

Supply chains have existed since business was organized to deliver goods and services to the customer. The silk route between India, China, and west Asia and the English and Dutch East India companies are early examples of global supply chains. However, the concepts of competitive advantage and supply-chain management (SCM) are relatively new. There are reasons for the emerging events.

- Today's customer has become more cost conscious and value conscious and demands quality products in a timely manner.
- The maturation of information technology and networks makes it possible to design a supply chain to meet customer demand.
- The global dimension, involving distance, costs, time, variety, and uncertainty, makes it almost mandatory that the long supply chains be managed efficiently around the clock.

In today's digital world, money is exchanged by the invisible transfer of funds between businesses via computers, regardless of distance or location. E-business uses the same process. Companies continue to form business relationships. The unique contribution of B2B e-commerce is in the way these relationships are established and maintained. They are established for the mutual benefit of all parties. When hundreds of businesses are connected, the Web eliminates distance and creates a market where price and time are the main constraints.

As can be seen, B2B activities are critical to any enterprise, regardless of size, volume of sale, or type of product. A company almost certainly has relationships with other businesses. The nature of the relationship is both operational and strategic. The operational activities of a B2B process support those relationships based on strategy. The software helps track operational activities that are moved through the B2B information pipeline.

Defining B2B

The literature provides a number of definitions of B2B. *E-commerce* refers to alternative ways of executing transactions or activities between buyers and sellers. It is the exchange of products, services, or information between them. **B2B** implies that both sellers and buyers are business organizations. With or without the Internet, commerce between business and consumer (**B2C**) is different from commerce among businesses. B2B involves complex procurement, manufacturing, and planning collaboration; complex payment terms; and round-the-clock performance agreements. The goal is to improve a firm's processes by optimizing the transfer of goods, services, and information between buyers and suppliers in the value chain.

B2B: alternative ways of executing transactions between buyers and sellers that are business organizations; a network of independent organizations and long-term trading partners.

B2C: alternative ways of executing transactions between buyers and sellers in which the buyers are individual consumers.

E-business is not information technology, and information technology is distinctly separate from e-business, although they are intertwined with each other. With today's increasing emphasis on "just-in-time" processing, e-business cannot survive without technology. It is considered the backbone of the supply chain that keeps businesses operating together. This involves ease of product return, timeliness of delivery, product availability, product information, and Web site navigation. A proposed list of technologies that qualify for satisfying B2B processing needs includes the following.

- Messaging products for facilitating secure, reliable data movement between trading partners.
- Work flow and process flow products for implementing conversational logic.
- Trading partner management products for helping identify where the data need to go and how they should get there.
- Directories for assisting businesses in locating other businesses that provide a particular service or product.

Traditional B2B e-commerce involves negotiations and contractual commitments between long-term trading partners (suppliers, manufacturers). The nature of the commitment is clearly defined and highly repetitive. It is about buying and selling commodities such as paper, plastics, and even cows. Ben Zaitz traded in his farm boots and acquired a laptop to develop the Cattle Offerings Worldwide (COW) Web site at a time when the idea of using the Web to trade cows was unheard of. After the concept caught on, the site attracted 40,000 visitors per month and held in excess of $2 million worth of auctions of livestock and commodities.

B2B is more than a mechanism for taking orders online. It is a network of independent organizations involved in a business area or an industry such as chemicals, plastics, automotive, or construction. It is also a new way to view products, production, and pricing. It is delivering customized services and goods, and managing inventory for business partners. This means extending the supply chain so companies will be able to respond on a minute-by-minute basis.

It all boils down to the concept of exchange. For example, Alliant Food Service Inc. had long followed the traditional way of handling food distribution. Distributors controlled how suppliers funneled products to restaurants and other businesses. Now, through its Web site (AlliantLink.com), Alliant lets users such as restaurants and hotels order goods without using catalogs, faxes, or phones. Infomediaries play a critical role in the way that managed information flows to support the business processes required in the e-marketplace. They bring together buyers and vendors by facilitating transactions.

In addition to direct communication and speed, the efficiency factor must be considered. In the case of Alliant, the company ships about 1 million cases of food and supplies per day. Under the traditional method, the process offered many opportunities for errors. Now the company is using the Web and wireless technology to reduce errors by more than 60 percent. For example, when orders were entered by fax and phone, an average of three ordering errors occurred per 1,000 cases of food shipped. Ordering directly via the company's Web site cut the error rate to less than two errors per 1,000 cases. Similar error reductions also appeared in handling out-of-stock queries, delivery returns, and inventory mis-picks.

The traditional approaches to communication (phone, fax, face to face, and mail) are being replaced by Web-based models—auctions and exchanges. In geographically dispersed markets, buyers who cannot find the right suppliers end up paying more or settle for inferior products. With B2B e-commerce, supply-chain participants are directly connected. For example, marex.com, a marine exchange, links boat builders, dealers, and yacht brokers who buy and sell wholesale.

Figure 11.1 presents the following specific elements of B2B.

1. **Buying company.** Focus on procurement in terms of reduced purchase prices and cycle time. The buying company announces a request for purchase of a certain product on its Web site, and the participating suppliers in the B2B network send their bids.

2. **Selling company.** Focus on marketing and sales. The seller attracts the buying organization to its Web site for business. Each seller has its unique catalog, pricing policy, and discount schedule.

3. **Intermediating service provider.** Focus on ensuring order fulfillment. Such a service provider mediates between the buying company and the supplier (seller), usually for parts and unique products. For example, GM plays the role of intermediary between its dealers and the hundreds of suppliers that provide spare parts.

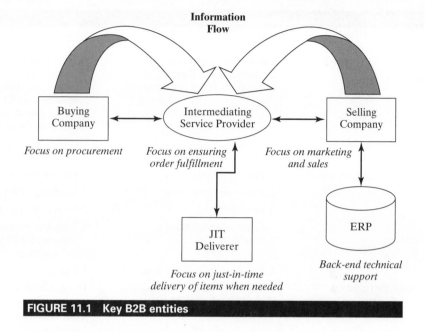

FIGURE 11.1   Key B2B entities

4. **JIT deliverer.** Focus on just-in-time delivery. This phase of B2B is critical because ensuring delivery of items just when they are needed means savings in time and money.

5. **Web-based platform.** Focus on the Internet, intranets, and extranets. An intranet connects islands of information on separate computers within the firm. An extranet is a dedicated network between business partners on the Internet. (Intranets and extranets were covered in detail in Chapter 4.)

6. **B2B Tools.** Focus on **electronic data interchange (EDI)** and software agents. EDI is the electronic exchange of business documents like bills, orders, and shipping notices between business partners. EDI is designed to convert proprietary data into a format that can be transmitted electronically. (EDI is covered in more detail later in the chapter.)

electronic data interchange (EDI): electronic exchange of business documents such as bills, orders, and shipping notices between business partners.

7. **Back-end technical support.** Focus on enterprise resource planning (ERP). Integrating B2B with technical infrastructure such as ERP, database management systems, and intranet data flow means keeping most information traffic on the supplier's servers.

B2B vs. B2C

Table 11.1 summarizes the key differences between B2B and B2C. Essentially, the following characteristics differentiate them.

1. **The connection mechanism.** In B2C, the connection mechanism is consumer-to-system. In B2B, one business uses a Web browser to interact with a Web server application of another business.

TABLE 11.1   Contrast between B2C and B2B

	B2C	B2B
Type of connection	**Consumer-to-system—** Consumers use their PC browser to order products via the merchant's Web site	**Business-to-business—** Representatives of a business use their company's Web browser to order products or to inquire via another business's (e.g., supplier) Web site
Type of relationship	1. Placing orders 2. Executing payments 3. Fulfilling orders 4. Browsing merchant's catalog 5. Sending feedback e-mail	1. Online procurement 2. Tracking order status 3. Executing payments 4. Managing promotions, returns, catalog information 5. Fulfilling orders
Nature of control	Unidirectional—relationship defined by the merchant	Ranges from unidirectional to peer-to-peer (mutual agreement) among businesses
Level or nature of needs-based segmentation	**Moderate to low**	**More focused than B2C** (e.g., Boeing buys only aircraft parts, not garden tractor or automobile parts)
Sales complexity	**Moderate**	**Complex**

2. **Type of relationship.** The relationship in B2C mainly involves placing orders and executing payments. In B2B, the relationship focuses on online procurement, order fulfillment, and work-in-process tracking for high-volume transactions.

3. **Nature of control.** The control mechanism in B2C is unidirectional. The seller controls the relationship with the consumer. In B2B, control ranges from one-sided control to peer-to-peer setups, depending on the nature of the relationship between the two businesses.

4. **Nature of needs-based segmentation.** Needs-based segmentation is more focused in B2B than in B2C, which tends to drive down costs and procurement. For example, GE developed a Web-based TPN (trading process network) that allows suppliers to bid on component contracts. This $1 billion per year business reduces procurement time by half and processing costs by at least one third.

5. **Sales complexity.** The level of sales complexity is higher in B2B than B2C. Many products are purchased as parts for other products, making the relationship more like a partnership. Bigger purchases mean bigger discounts, and prices are nearly always negotiable. Large businesses also use sophisticated computer systems to exchange invoices with suppliers, whose Web sites must be integrated to do business.

ADVANTAGES AND DISADVANTAGES OF B2B

B2B e-commerce is e-commerce between businesses. It is a worldwide bazaar where one can buy anything, from paper clips to oil tankers. The goal is to save money on purchases that are negotiated instantly. Suppliers use the purchaser's Web site to respond to bids and sell excess inventory. Replacing a purchasing bureaucracy with online links means savings, improved efficiency in ordering material, many fewer errors, and a just-in-time environment that minimizes inventory sitting in the warehouse.

Electronic alliances with distributors, suppliers, resellers, and other partners generate information for businesses regarding customers, products, suppliers, transportation, inventory, competitors, supply-chain alliances, and marketing and sales. Businesses have access to customers' sales history; product sales history; terms and discounts; product offerings and availability; and promotions, sales, and marketing information. They also can get shipping costs and terms, shipping schedules, inventory locations, carrying charges, and response time for inventory replenishment. They can learn about roles and responsibilities in supply-chain alliances and available partners, along with competitors' products and market share.

There are also drawbacks. B2B sites were exploding in number in early 2000. Hundreds were launched to support major buyers in the automotive, chemicals, pharmaceutical, retailing, and other industries, with the goal of getting supplies more cheaply and quickly. Yet, as with any other new process, there have been major obstacles. Despite the hype, B2B has been slow to catch on. E-business does not fit every business.

One problem with B2B is possible antitrust violations resulting from doing this type of business. For example, owners of major e-markets may conceivably shut out smaller, competing exchanges. The electronic open-bid process itself might lead to questionable price signaling. Here is one scenario: Buyer A wants to buy 100,000 linear feet of lumber for a housing project. It posts a proposal at an online exchange. One supplier bids on the project, and competing suppliers see the bid and undercut it. This process continues until Buyer A accepts the lowest bid. Meanwhile, Buyer B and other suppliers watch the process and have a good idea of how the bidding takes place. See Box 11.1.

This part of the process was once done more discreetly using paper, phone, and face-to-face meetings. Price signaling may be smart business, but it is being questioned as a violation of antitrust laws. During a two-day workshop on exchanges, FTC officials and legal experts said the key to avoiding antitrust problems is to allow an open Web exchange and keep the prices and trade secrets of all suppliers in the B2B system confidential. There should also be confidential bidding and restrictions on competitors' access to competitively sensitive information.

To date, no one has figured out a formula that will ensure success in B2B commerce. Most Web exchanges charge a small percentage of each transaction as a fee for doing business. To make money, billions of dollars in transactions must be handled each month, which is not easy. One reason is the competition. Also, companies as well as suppliers that dominate a specific niche are building their own exchanges tailored to their products and industry.

BOX 11.1

No Trust, No Business

Most B2Bs aim to reduce industry expenses by as much as 15 percent. The savings are realized through reduced transaction costs, volume-related economies of scale, improved inventory management, and/or facilitated bidding by a broad spectrum of buyers and sellers.

For all of its benefits, B2B can raise issues of antitrust liability. A B2B exchange exists to bring competitors together and thus it has the potential to diminish competition. Both the Department of Justice (DOJ) and the Federal Trade Commission (FTC) have already opened investigations of certain B2B exchanges. Although government officials, as well as legal commentators, have identified the potential benefits and problems with these arrangements, no clear guidance has been forthcoming as to the government's enforcement intentions in this area.

A B2B formed by a group of competitors for the purpose of collective action directed by the controlling participants will have to be espe-

cially sensitive with respect to its compliance with the antitrust laws. The concern is that a group of buyers could work to depress the price of a product or service through what is known as monopsony power (power wielded in a market where there exists only one buyer).

Direct or indirect exclusion from participation in a B2B, versus open access, may also raise antitrust concerns in cases where the B2B dominates the marketplace for a product or a group of products, or if the B2B is owned or controlled by competitors of would-be participants.

Antitrust concerns need not deter businesses from the promise of increased efficiencies and savings that legitimate B2Bs offer. With the current uncertainty surrounding the antitrust issues, however, the prudent manager will add antitrust counsel to the planning team at an early stage. By clearly articulating the goals for the exchange and showing some flexibility in its structure and operation, management should find little impediment in the antitrust laws.

Source: Excerpted from Richard E. Donovan, flabusinessinsight.com/Articles/Features/B2B.htm.

SUPPLY-CHAIN MANAGEMENT AND B2B

Supply-chain management (SCM) refers to overseeing materials, information, and finances as they move in a process from supplier to manufacturer to wholesaler to retailer to consumer. It involves coordinating and integrating these flows within and among companies. The ultimate goal is to reduce inventory on the assumption that products are available when needed. As a solution, sophisticated SCM systems with Web interfaces are competing with Web-based application service providers (ASP) who promise to provide part or all of the SCM service for companies who rent their service.

supply-chain management: the process of moving goods from the customer's order through raw materials, supply, production, and distribution of products to the end user.

There are two main types of SCM systems: planning applications that use advanced algorithms to decide on the best way to fill an order and execution applications that track the physical status of goods, management of materials, and financial information involving all companies involved.

The classic model of company vs. company is giving way to supply chain vs. supply chain. Success is now measured by assembling a team of companies that can rise above

---

BOX 11.2

Supply Chain vs. Supply Chain

There are two business stories to tell about the potency of supply chain in e-commerce—the tortuous experiences of Nike Inc. and Cisco Systems Inc. when they ran into trouble with their supply chain. In Nike's case, the crisis came in May 2001, when the company announced that the sales for the preceding quarter were $100 million lower than expected because of confusion in its supply chain. This loss was soon eclipsed by Cisco's announcement that it was writing down $2.2 billion in unusable inventory due to problems in its supply chain. It was the largest inventory write-off in the history of business.

The day Nike announced the breakdown in its chain, the company's stock dropped 20 percent, an amount so staggering that it makes the $100 million loss seem like pocket change. The total drop over the 12-month period was a whopping 18.5 percent with an estimated loss in shareholder value averaging more than $350 million.

Source: Increasing Role of Supply Chain. Excerpted from David A. Taylor, "Supply Chain vs. Supply Chain." *Computerworld,* November 10, 2003, 44–45.

---

the win/lose negotiations of conventional trading relationships. It means working together to deliver the best products at the most attractive price. In a way, it is an admission fee to be a member of the increasingly popular game of supply-chain competition. It is no longer an exciting opportunity. It is a survival skill. See Box 11.2.

In terms of relationships between businesses, B2B can best be explained using the supply-chain process. The **supply chain** represents all the events associated with the flow and transformation of goods from the raw material stage to the end-user customer. It is the process of moving goods from the customer's order through raw materials, parts supplier, production, wholesaler, and retailer to the end user. This process includes order generation, order taking, status feedback, and timely delivery of goods and services. Traditionally, many of these processes have been done with paper transactions such as purchase orders and invoices requiring verification and signatures. B2B is beginning to replace these time-consuming activities.

B2B SUPPLY-CHAIN COLLABORATION

A B2B supply chain requires collaboration among a group of manufacturers, retailers, and suppliers using the Internet to exchange business information and work jointly at forecasting demand for their products, developing production schedules, and controlling inventory flow. There are many benefits: reduced inventory, higher sales, improved ability to customize products for different business buyers, and reduced production costs. The main challenge is establishing trust among partners to share sensitive business information and upgrading business applications that will advance collaboration. Partners also have to agree on a common standard for exchanging information and transactions. See Box 11.3 for an illustration of supply chain collaboration.

BOX 11.3

An Example of Supply-Chain Collaboration

Let's look at consumer packaged goods as an example of collaboration. If there are two companies that have made supply chain a household word, they are Wal-Mart and Procter & Gamble. Before these two companies started collaborating back in the '80s, retailers shared very little information with manufacturers. But then the two giants built a software system that hooked P&G up to Wal-Mart's distribution centers. When P&G's products run low at the distribution centers, the system sends an automatic alert to P&G to ship more products. In some cases, the system goes all the way to the individual Wal-Mart store. It lets P&G monitor the shelves through real-time satellite link-ups that send messages to the factory whenever a P&G item swoops past a scanner at the register.

With this kind of minute-to-minute information, P&G knows when to make, ship, and display more products at the Wal-Mart stores. No need to keep products piled up in warehouses awaiting Wal-Mart's call. Invoicing and payments happen automatically too. The system saves P&G so much in time, reduced inventory and lower order-processing costs that it can afford to give Wal-Mart "low, everyday prices" without putting itself out of business.

Cisco Systems, which makes equipment to hook up to the Internet, is also famous for its supply chain collaboration. Cisco has a network of component suppliers, distributors, and contract manufacturers that are linked through Cisco's extranet to form a virtual, just-in-time supply chain. When a customer orders a typical Cisco product—for example, a router that directs Internet traffic over a company network—through Cisco's Web site, the order triggers a flurry of messages to contract manufacturers of printed circuit board assemblies. Distributors, meanwhile, are alerted to supply the generic components of the router, such as a power supply. Cisco's contract manufacturers, some of whom make subassemblies like the router chassis and others who assemble the finished product, already know what's coming down the order pipe because they've logged on to Cisco's extranet and linked into Cisco's own manufacturing execution systems.

There you have it. No warehouses, no inventory, no paper invoices, just a very nosy software program that monitors Cisco's supply chain automatically, in real time, everywhere, simultaneously. If there is a weakness to these collaborative systems, it is that they haven't been tested in tough times—until recently. Cisco's network was designed to handle the company's huge growth. Cisco and its network were caught completely off guard by the 2000 tumble in the economy. It took a while to turn all the spigots off in its complex network when demand for its products plummeted and Cisco and its supply chain partners got stuck with a lot of excess inventory—as did most other big manufacturers in high technology. Cisco was forced to take a hard look at its supply-chain planning capability. It was found that SCM software is much better at managing growth than it is at monitoring a decline and correcting it.

Source: Excerpted from www.cio.com/research/scm/edit/012202_scm.html.

SUPPLY-CHAIN ELEMENTS

Several elements make supply-chain management a collaborative endeavor.

- Production: A decision is made on the products to create at a specific plant, the supplier(s) that will service the plants, and how goods will find their way to the ultimate customer.

- Inventory: To keep the supply chain in operational order, each link in the chain must keep a certain inventory of raw material, parts, and partially manufactured products as a hedge against uncertainties. This way, in the event of a momentary delay in any of the links, the process continues uninterrupted.

- Location: It is critical that production facilities, warehousing points, and initiation points are known in advance. Once known and assured, the supply chain as a process begins to operate reliably around the clock.

- Transportation: This step simply determines how materials, parts, and products logistically get from one point in the supply chain to another. Deciding on how to ship often is a trade-off between shipping cost and timing of availability. High-priority parts that are sorely needed will likely be shipped by air rather than rail or truck.

The connectivity of these elements, linking sales to trading and trading to purchasing (e-procurement), along with logistics, marketing, planning, government, and financial institutions all operating in real time, gives you an idea about the complexity of SCM in a B2B environment. See Figure 11.2.

Another way of looking at SCM is in terms of a life-cycle process:

- Plan—The strategic portion of SCM. A big portion of planning is developing metrics to monitor the SCM to ensure efficient quality and value to the customer.

- Source—Select the suppliers who will produce or deliver the goods or services. This step includes setting pricing, deciding how payment will be made upon delivery, and establishing metrics for improving relationships with suppliers.

FIGURE 11.2 Supply chain management—an example

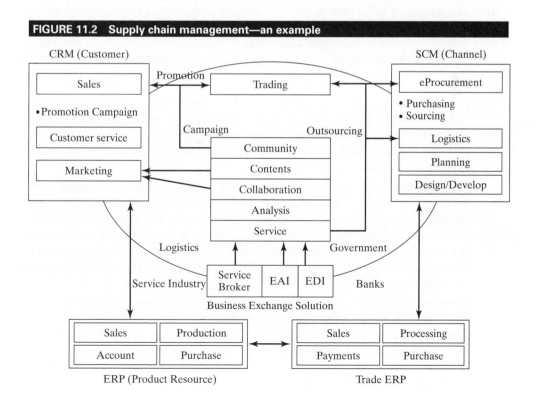

- Make—The production phase, where B2B schedules the procedures for production, inspection, and preparation for just-in-time delivery.
- Deliver—This step covers the overall logistics related to coordinating customer orders with a network of warehouses that have the product, picking carriers to deliver the order to customers, and creating the infrastructure that invoices the customer and secures payments.
- Return—The serious part of SCM, developing a network for receiving defective products back from customers and dealing with customers' complaints.

Knowledge management (KM) has become a critical element in the supply-chain system. KM is the process of capturing and making use of a firm's collective expertise anywhere in the business—on paper, in documents, in databases (called *explicit knowledge*), or in people's heads (called *tacit knowledge*). In the supply chain, knowledge management provides the ability to manage decision points and areas where human expertise is required. The new focus of a supply chain is *collaboration, coordination,* and *cooperation* of all parties involved so that organizational processes, technology, and experienced people assure the necessary integration for the good of the chain. The emphasis on collaboration involves all partners from the supplier to the retailer. Box 11.4 describes the relationship between knowledge management and the supply chain.

B2B Building Blocks

B2B e-commerce operates on a technology-based e-business platform. Functions that are typical to B2C, such as personalization and content management, are also relevant to B2B architecture. An e-business platform for B2B services consists of five key components: the application server infrastructure, the B2B integration server, the personalization software, the content management facility, and the e-commerce package.

1. The application server: The function of this component is to develop, manage, and execute B2B services and traffic for high-performance, nonstop service. The application server manages connections and applications, makes services available during upgrades, detects dead connections, monitors security, and ensures a fault-tolerant B2B environment.

2. The B2B integration server: Because so many systems and protocols must work together to support B2B e-commerce, the integration server joins company, external, and application data or documents for quick, reliable, secure service. For example, a purchase order is acknowledged as an incoming document. The integration server then directs the document handler to forward it to an order desk. Once the system processes the order, the document handler queries the inventory database before it schedules a shipping date.

3. The personalization software: The personalization feature in B2B is similar to that in B2C. It makes it possible for a company with multiple buyers (called partners) to display or provide only the content that is unique to the partner. The software takes into consideration factors like stored partner profile, purchasing behavior, and user privileges. The goal is to allow a tightly focused B2B interface and interaction with each partner.

BOX 11.4

Knowledge Management and the Supply Chain

Without an efficient knowledge management model in place, information that is critical to the current, ongoing, and future success of the supply chain may be jeopardized. Without information, no supply chain would be able to function successfully or competitively.

Consider the value potential between explicit information and tacit knowledge:

- Explicit supply management information is data, reports, and procedures retained within an information system.

- Tacit supply management knowledge is deeper experience, expertise, and know-how of the organization. This knowledge is undocumented and exists in the minds of employees. A retiring senior supply management executive demonstrates how to analyze various reports to forecast the next year's inventory. If he does not share his knowledge, what he knows goes out the door.

Private exchanges are becoming the most effective way to share and use knowledge throughout the supply chain. Originally, online auctions were expected to accomplish this task. However, what occurred in the online auction environment was more "electronic transacting" than knowledge sharing.

To achieve knowledge sharing success, supply management organizations and their suppliers have to adapt to current conditions and prepare for inevitable changes in the near future. Trust is a valuable component that is necessary for supply management organizations to proceed into the knowledge creation process. Also, without a trusting, collaborative supply manager/supplier relationship, it would be nearly impossible to succeed in the knowledge creation phase of the information supply chain.

By recognizing and adapting to change, supply managers are setting themselves on the right path for implementing knowledge management into their organizations and supply chains. Supply managers themselves can lead their organization in the behaviors necessary to implement a successful knowledge management model.

Source: Excerpted from J. Yuva, "Knowledge Management: The Supply Chain Nerve Center." *Inside Supply Management,* July 2002, 34–43.

---

4. The content management facility: This special facility is the deliverable of B2B e-commerce. Comprehensive content management supports a workflow process that facilitates B2B content review and approval. The content manager's main responsibility is to ensure that the content reaches the designated user or online system. It also taps the personalization software to serve the content to the appropriate user, whether another server or an online system.

5. The e-commerce package: This set of programs plays a role similar to that of the one it plays in B2C. It includes customer service and product management, a storefront for direct delivery, a shopping cart, and order-fulfillment modules.

To do its job, the e-business platform must run on open standards. This means that when companies integrate with buyers and suppliers, the B2B architecture must run on any hardware or any operating system. Security is also a serious issue. The security protocol might need to cover an entire application, parts of an application, or even specific components of an application.

Quality of service is an important consideration. As in traditional business, highly valued and long-term business partners get special treatment. Once they log in and are verified, the B2B system diverts them to a premium-level server, but other partners are routed to the regular server. Quality of service also might improve when partners increase their business.

Finally, for e-business to achieve maximum efficiency, its infrastructure must meet several criteria.

- The technology must accommodate evolving needs. This implies flexibility and adaptability.

- Performance must be ensured in terms of rich and superior user experience.

- The infrastructure must be reliable and available 24 hours a day, year round. The cost of downtime can be staggering in terms of lost business.

- The infrastructure must have *scalability,* which means how well the current system can be upgraded to standards that can accommodate change and growth in e-business.

- Because e-business means global business, it must be technically capable of reaching as many as 550 million Web surfers over more than 12,000 ISP networks covering hundreds of countries each hour of the year.

- The system must be easy to use and consistent. Sometimes this is achieved by leveraging the capabilities of a reliable third-party vendor to pick up the slack.

- The system must be secure and protected from cyber-fraud, denial-of-service attacks, viruses, and the like.

To keep track of supply-chain operations, special tools are available. Referred to as supply-chain event management (SCEM), such software lets users analyze, monitor, and control functions in the supply chain. As illustrated in Figure 11.3, a retailer sends an order to a supplier for 500 cans of driveway sealer. When the order is processed, the supply warehouse finds out it is short 150 cans. The shortage is fed back to the supply-chain server attached to an SCEM system. SCEM automatically orders the 350 cans from an alternative supplier, who ships the cans directly to the retailer's warehouse. In this case, SCEM acts as a watchdog.

B2B Integration Challenges

B2B integration has been subject to many interpretations. Some technology people view it as mere electronic data interchange (EDI). Others see it as an application integration extended outside a business organization. A third view sees it as putting a Web front end on applications so that suppliers, customers, and business buyers can share information for making deals. Each interpretation makes sense but misses the fundamental meaning of B2B integration.

B2B integration means spanning independent businesses, each with its own set of applications and users. Some applications are enterprise resource planning (ERP) packages heavy on integrating a company's total applications; others are traditional systems running on a mainframe. In each firm, transactions are processed differently. Orders, production scheduling, and other internal processing also are handled differently. B2B integration means interacting with these heterogeneous systems without being tied to one specific system technology.

There are other challenges as well. If the buyer is not providing a prompt and reliable stream of information to the supplier, the vendor is unlikely to produce the

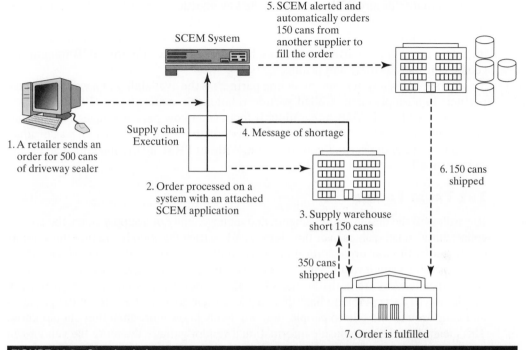

5. SCEM alerted and automatically orders 150 cans from another supplier to fill the order

SCEM System

1. A retailer sends an order for 500 cans of driveway sealer

Supply chain Execution

4. Message of shortage

2. Order processed on a system with an attached SCEM application

3. Supply warehouse short 150 cans

6. 150 cans shipped

350 cans shipped

7. Order is fulfilled

FIGURE 11.3   Supply-chain event management

Source: Adapted from Marc L. Songini, "Policing the Supply Chain," *Computerworld*, April 30, 2001, 55.

necessary goods in a prompt and consistent manner. Suppliers also have other companies they cater to. Larger, more profitable clients are going to get first attention even if that has a negative effect on one buyer's lead times. When a SCM system is not flexible enough to deal with these problems, it can prevent the buyer from gaining competitive advantage in the market.

To get around the near independence of suppliers, buyers need to rely on alternatives. One option is to choose suppliers whose cycle times are more in line with the needs of the buyer's business. Of course, the other alternative is to make an effort to improve the flow of information to the supplier. That alone could be the cure to ensuring a smooth cycle time.

Standardization has been an ongoing issue. One problem with standards such as TCP/IP, HTTP, and EDI is that they take time and effort to develop. Business conditions among partners also change, and many businesses find it necessary and attractive to form an agreement before standards are available. In most cases, the cost of developing standards is justified when there is high-volume demand or use. Standards are ideal for products and interactions that are stable over a long period of time, but finding candidates is neither easy nor predictable.

The criteria used for B2B integration, then, depends on how close a relationship an organization wants to establish with another, how much agreement is required between them, how complex the integration must be, and whether it threatens their autonomy.

Eventually, for any B2B agreement, the key question is whether a B2B agreement specifies an exchange protocol. Are agreements industry-wide, national, or international? Are they agreed upon in advance or on an ad hoc basis? All these issues, including managing e-business alliances, have to be resolved before B2B integration can be considered stable and lasting.

Embedded in any agreement among partners is the availability of a way to manage partners in a supply chain. Called partner relationship management (PRM), this system is a new phase in B2B integration. It focuses on how partners engage each other on a regular basis. For example, we could have collaborative processes such as product design that are under serious consideration. Without PRM, no organization can expect to have an effective value chain.

THE TRUST FACTOR

Regardless of the design, arrangements, and manageability of a supply chain, the core of collaborative relationships over time is trust. A key trust question is whether the vendors connected with your organization are trusted allies or corporate spies. Much can be known about a vendor relationship by the level and quality of experience over time. One view is that vendors are in the business to make money. They will do whatever they can that is ethically acceptable to help them achieve their goals. If they are on the premises and hang around and talk to people, they will likely know more than they should know. This means that the more inside information a vendor gathers, the more the vendor can use that information to advantage, especially during negotiations. See Box 11.5.

Every vendor wants to know three things: company budget, the area where critical operations have the highest priority, and who in the organization makes the final decisions. Any of these factors could circumvent the procurement process. (See Box 11.5 for the pros and cons of a trusting relationship.) Ethical or not, vendors should be handled with care. The happy medium is to share with vendors only whatever is relevant to business. Employees should be selective in terms of what they may or may not share

---

BOX 11.5

Trust Factors in SCM

Trust is a critical factor fostering commitment among supply chain partners. The presence of trust improves measurably the chance of successful supply chain performance. A lack of trust often results in inefficient and ineffective performance as the transaction costs (verification, inspections and certifications of their trading partners) mount.

Information sharing reduces the level of behavioral uncertainty, which, in turn, improves the level of trust. A partner's reputation in the market has a strong positive impact on the trust-building process, whereas a partner's perceived conflict creates a strong negative impact on trust. The level of commitment is strongly related to the level of trust.

The bottom line is that trust needs to be supported by a measurement system that motivates all the parties to do what is good for the chain as a whole. The measurements need to contain both time and money.

Source: Excerpted from Brig Sarma, "Trust Factors in SCM." *Supply Chain Management Forum,* June 29, 2004. See www.managementlogs.com/2004/06/trust-factors-in-scm.html.

with a vendor. A security protocol also should be established on every project. One does not perform security checks at 37,000 feet. It is done before takeoff.

With B2B relationships on the Internet, trust takes on a unique meaning. For example, how do you know you're dealing with a legitimate and trustworthy business? Also, how do you know electronic exchange is secure and that your trading partner on the other end is who he says he is? Concerns of trust have kept many organizations away from B2B trade. B2B buyers worry that they won't receive the right merchandise, the right quality, and at the right price from a certified vendor in the right quantity and time. The same feeling goes for the seller. Sellers often worry about getting paid on time and extending credit to questionable buyers.

TRUST ELEMENTS.   One way of looking at trust in the supply chain is to break it into key elements. They are competence, goodwill, and vulnerability to failure. In the SCM, competence is the ability of the parties in the chain to meet commitments. It is also the ability of people to work with people and transact business based on facts and trustworthy procedures. For a procurement manager, it means visiting a supplier and seeing that the supplier has the facilities and expertise to carry out the contract.

In contrast, goodwill is a cognitive and affect-based trust that assures you the vendor means well and stands by his or her reputation. Vulnerability is choosing a course of action even if such action has a probability of failure greater than 50 percent. It means that trust is a risk relationship that increases the vulnerability of the one(s) being trusted.

WHAT IF THE CHAIN SNAPS?   With so many suppliers, vendors, retailers, financial institutions, and intermediaries making up the supply chain, what happens when one of the links snaps or is temporarily inactive? For example, UPS Logistics Group was caught unprepared and braced for a supply-chain disaster following the September 11, 2001 terrorist attacks. It found itself without a key distribution center that kept critical repair parts flowing to customers. That center was destroyed only 150 yards away from the World Trade Center. An alternative UPS LG service parts hub in Manhattan was written off because of safety concerns after the terrorist attacks. A third alternative hub could not be reached, because the roads were closed. This is an example of a situation in which a company is truly in a crisis mode.

One of the aftereffects of the September 11, 2001, terrorist attacks has been a growing awareness of the need for disaster planning so that the chain can keep operating. Without such a plan, the mere announcement of a disruption in production or shipment could be costly. According to a Georgia Institute of Technology study, after such an announcement, the company's stock price can fall an average of 8.62 percent on the day of the announcement and can drop as much as 20 percent within 6 months.

disaster planning: taking specific steps to ensure the flow of products and services during a disaster.

Disaster planning means taking specific steps to ensure the flow of products and services during a disaster. The first step is to work with the highest-risk customers and collaborate on a contingency plan to suit their needs in the event of a disaster. Pricing should be stable during such a disruption, and alternative inventory sources should be identified and guaranteed without any costs of delivery. Finally, it is important to empower employees on supply-chain disruptions and how to communicate effectively to minimize unnecessary delays.

B2B MODELS

Several models have been established for B2B e-commerce based on who controls the marketplace: buyer, supplier, or intermediary. Each model is explained in the following sections.

BUYER-ORIENTED B2B

buyer-oriented B2B: a buyer purchases thousands of products and uses the Internet to open a marketplace and a Web site for suppliers to do the bidding.

In the **buyer-oriented B2B** model, a buyer like General Motors that normally purchases hundreds of thousands of products each month uses the Internet by opening a marketplace on its own server and opening the window for suppliers to do the bidding. As shown in Figure 11.4, the buyer loads products via a catalog or a directory, with specific requests regarding make, model, size, price, and so on. Outside suppliers access the catalog, decide what product they want to bid on, send the information to the buyer, and hope to be the lowest bidder.

SUPPLIER-ORIENTED B2B

supplier-oriented B2B: a supplier invites individual consumers and business customers to order products via its electronic market store.

The **supplier-oriented B2B** model is close in design to the B2C model. A manufacturer or a supplier invites individual consumers as well as business customers to order products via its electronic store. (See Figure 11.5.)

Well-known examples of supplier-oriented B2Bs are Dell and Cisco. Dell's sales to business buyers represent 90 percent of its computer sales. Likewise, in 2004, Cisco sold more than $34 billion worth of routers, switches, and other networking devices to businesses via the company's Web site.

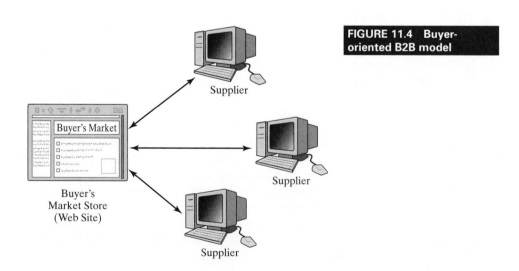

FIGURE 11.4   Buyer-oriented B2B model

Supplier

Buyer's Market

Supplier

Buyer's
Market Store
(Web Site)

Supplier

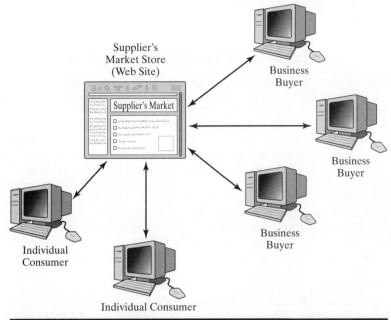

Supplier's
Market Store
(Web Site)

Supplier's Market

Business
Buyer

Business
Buyer

Business
Buyer

Individual
Consumer

Individual Consumer

FIGURE 11.5   Supplier-oriented B2B model

ELECTRONIC AUCTIONS

One of the Internet's unique features is bringing together people with narrow interests who are geographically dispersed. Web auctions can cater to such groups by providing an auction site.

In an auction, a seller offers a product or an item for sale. This is called "putting an item up for bid" because the seller does not put a price on the item. Interested buyers get information about the item and offer bids—prices they are willing to pay. An auctioneer, who handles the whole process, keeps the auction going until the bids are closed.

electronic auction: auctions carried out on electronic Web sites such as eBay.

A unique version of supplier-oriented architecture is the **electronic auction.** The Internet is booming with all kinds of auctions from eBay to hundreds of smaller imitators with questionable reputations. There have been reports of fraud, where purchasers got less than they bargained for from auction sites. In some cases, the product was misrepresented, and in others the product was never delivered.

There are various mechanisms for ensuring the integrity of online auctions. The most common form is a feedback forum, which is a distinctive feature of eBay. Once a transaction is completed, the successful buyer and seller are requested to record feedback about each other. The feedback profile is open to all users, unless they choose not to allow it. Feedback is an efficient way to protect security and fairness in online auctions. Feedback extortion is always a possibility, however. (See Box 11.6.)

Other mechanisms to handle improper trading behavior are buying an insurance program or installing an escrow program. An insurance program protects buyers who send

---

BOX 11.6

Questionable Integrity of Auction Sites

Joan Spingelt, an elementary school teacher, got less than she bargained for in her first purchase from auction site eBay. She bought a Palm Pilot V Personal Digital Assistant from Tec Computers to organize her addresses and schedules. The company never sent her the unit. Instead, she says she received excuses—and soon no replies at all to her e-mails.

The Federal Trade Commission filed charges related to auction fraud against the company. In all, some $90,000 in goods ordered from the company were never delivered. Ms. Spingelt will likely receive only about $40 from the settlement, her first return on that $361 money order she mailed 3 years ago.

Law-enforcement agencies have the power to elicit information from money-wire services and credit card companies—something the defrauded consumer cannot do alone. Still, most law-enforcement agencies don't yet have experienced Internet investigators, and many don't investigate frauds if only a small amount is lost. Florida's Department of Law Enforcement will only probe cases of fraud involving $50,000 or more, although the agency's Computer Crime Center recently lowered the floor to $10,000 in cases of suspected Internet fraud.

And if scammers are tracked down, victims often won't receive full restitution. Suing probably won't help much, either. The best thing to do is probably to hire a professional. Experts emphasize that you should not take the law into your own hands with any information you might dig up. Give it to the professionals investigating your case.

Source: Excerpted from Carl Bialik, "Getting Your Money Back," *Wall Street Journal,* September 16, 2002, R7.

money in good faith to the seller but do not receive the goods or service. An escrow program accepts payment from the buyer through a third party that holds the funds until the buyer inspects the purchased item and decides whether to accept or reject it.

Electronic auctions can be of three basic types: forward auctions, reverse auctions, and Internet exchanges. Each has unique features and promises.

forward auction: an auction where a seller entertains bids from buyers; an auction used to liquidate merchandise.

FORWARD AUCTIONS.   A **forward auction** generally is used to liquidate merchandise. One seller entertains bids from many buyers. This seller-controlled model allows the seller to post products or services it wants to sell via its auction Web site. Buyers view the offer and submit competing bids. Sometimes, buyers can see other buyers' bids and respond to them. Sometimes the auction is *blind,* and bids are sealed from competing buyers. After the expiration date, the seller reviews the bids and selects the highest one. Payment and fulfillment are handled through normal electronic channels. (See Figure 11.6.)

Forward auctions are used most often for surplus merchandise, last year's models, and so on. They are ideal in situations where supply and demand are unpredictable and a time factor is pushing the seller to unload the merchandise. Sellers have more control than in traditional liquidation sales.

reverse auction: an auction used to solicit bids; the lowest bidder wins.

REVERSE AUCTIONS.   A **reverse auction** generally is used to solicit bids, and the lowest bidder wins. It is buyer controlled: Buyers post the goods they want to buy, and sellers compete to

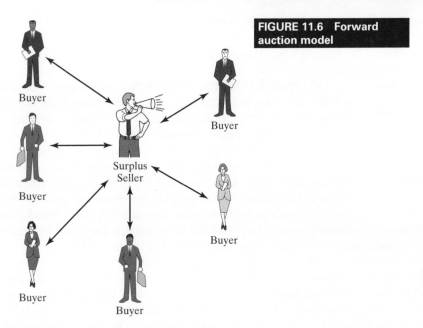

FIGURE 11.6   Forward auction model

provide them. The buyer pits suppliers against one another in a bidding war. The buyer reviews the bids and considers factors such as the location of the seller, cost of delivery, and whether the seller can deliver on time. When the auction expires, the lowest bidder is selected. The buyer produces the money, and the seller ships the goods. (See Figure 11.7.)

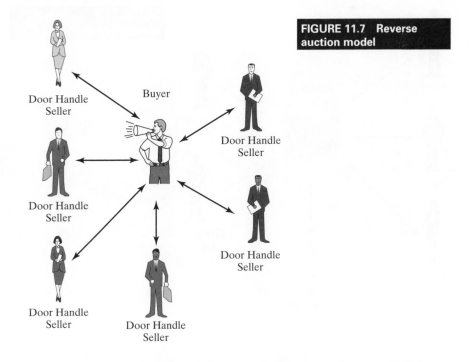

FIGURE 11.7   Reverse auction model

Reverse auctions are typical of large corporate purchases; for example, GM buying rearview mirrors or John Deere buying mower blades. This model tends to drive down prices and expand the buyer's zone of choice among suppliers.

Internet exchange auction: an electronic auction involving many buyers and sellers who trade bids and offers until an agreement is reached to exchange product for payment. A third party often operates the exchange.

INTERNET EXCHANGE AUCTIONS.   An **Internet exchange auction** involves many buyers and sellers who trade bids and offers until an agreement is reached to exchange product for payment. A third party operates the exchange. All kinds of companies, trading products from airplanes to livestock, are included. A company first places a bid to buy or sell a product. Buyers and sellers work interactively with the bids and offers. When a deal is made, it is a match between a buyer and a seller on variables such as price, volume, and delivery costs. Third parties often help in the exchange process. They have the responsibility for credit verification, quality assurance, and prompt delivery of the goods. (See Figure 11.8.)

One issue involved in this model is exchange ownership. There are three kinds of ownership. One manufacturer or broker can set up the exchange and run it; a third-party intermediary can set it up and promise to run it fairly; or several industry leaders can put it together so no one dominates and all can benefit. Visionaries have been touting the concept of linked exchanges that form a "true network economy." One concept is to combine competing exchanges into one, similar to the exchanges operated by General Motors and Ford. Another concept is wiring different exchanges so that the B2B part includes many similar markets connected by bridges. Either way, many more connections will exist than we have today, which eventually will contribute to the reshaping of today's economy.

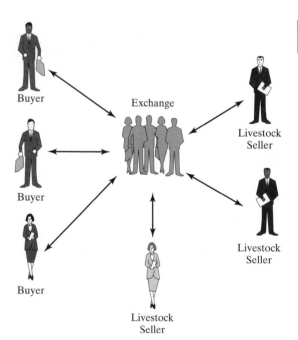

FIGURE 11.8   Internet exchange model

Buyer

Buyer

Buyer

Exchange

Livestock Seller

Livestock Seller

Livestock Seller

INTERMEDIARY-ORIENTED B2B

The **intermediary-oriented B2B** setup revolves around an electronic intermediary company that establishes an exchange market where buyers and sellers can make deals. (See Figure 11.9.) Typical of this type of exchange are intermediary malls like www.Grainger.com and Procure.net, a large industrial distributor that handles maintenance, repair, and operations (MRO) purchases. This Web site has an electronic catalog containing more than 100,000 products and 30 seller sites, and it averages more than 60,000 hits per day.

intermediary-oriented B2B: an intermediary company establishes an exchange market where buyers and sellers can make deals.

MRO is where most B2B product sales take place. Every industry has its own MRO needs. Quantities purchased range from one to 1 million units. The more a business buyer buys, the more savings it realizes on purchases. Companies that succeed in an MRO business specialize in a specific industry to minimize potential competitors and offer customers information vital to their business growth and success.

informediary: a firm that facilitates the transformation of the traditional industrial economy to a new, information-based economy.

With the likely surge of B2B and B2C through the decade, a major segment of the revenue is likely to be claimed by a new breed of company referred to as the information intermediary. Informediaries facilitate the transformation of the traditional industrial economy to a new information-based economy. According to Grover et al. (2002), **informediaries** are companies whose main job is to match the needs of a large consumer base and a large supplier base, requiring the analysis of an enormous amount of information. (See Figure 11.10.)

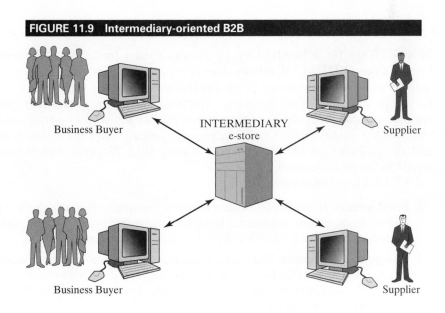

FIGURE 11.9   Intermediary-oriented B2B

Business Buyer   INTERMEDIARY e-store   Supplier

Business Buyer   Supplier

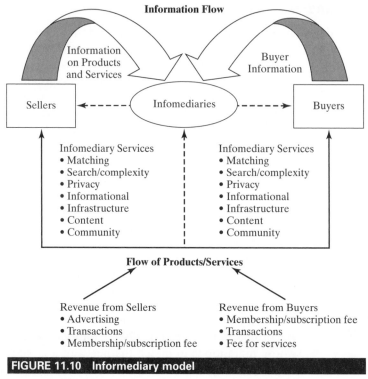

FIGURE 11.10 Informediary model

Source: Adapted from Varun Grover and James Teng, "E-Commerce and the Information Market," *Communications of the ACM,* April 2001, 81.

B2B TOOLS–EDI

Most B2B traffic is handled by a communication tool called electronic data interchange (EDI). EDI allows one computer system to communicate with another computer system using a standardized electronic form. It is a computer-to-computer transfer of business information among businesses that use a specific standard format. The information exchanged could be transaction data, requests for quotes (RFQ), order acknowledgments, shipping status or schedule, and so on. This type of data represents more than 75 percent of the total EDI traffic between businesses.

EDI has four components.

1. **Interbusiness.** Transmission of data between businesses. Because there is little standardization, most companies using EDI use a third-party service provider or value-added network (VAN) as a communications intermediary.

2. **Computer-to-computer.** Data communication from one computer to another. This means providing online links between a buyer's and a seller's business applications, with no human intervention at the receiving end. Delivery to the receiver is by electronic transactions.

3. **Standard transactions.** Electronic versions of standard business forms. In EDI, a computer program processes all data. EDI is designed to allow the receiver to handle a standard business transaction (e.g., bill a customer) in machine-readable (not human-readable) form between trading partners' computers.

4. **Standard format.** Transactions must be transmitted in a predefined form.

HOW EDI WORKS

Prior to EDI, purchase orders, acknowledgments, invoices, and purchase order changes depended on communication between trading partners for limited hours each day, using phone or fax. Today, computers enhance communication between trading partners, regardless of time, place, or distance. Figure 11.11 shows the general configuration of information flow without EDI. A request for a product is sent to purchasing for action. The purchasing department places a purchase order, which is sent to the seller via regular mail or by fax. A copy of the purchase order is sent to the finance department for payment upon receipt of the product. On the seller's part, the purchase order goes to the sales department, which fills the order through manufacturing or the warehouse. The product then is sent to shipping, which delivers it to the buyer's receiving department. Once received, it goes to the warehouse. This triggers payment of the invoice by the finance department.

As you can see, the process is labor intensive and promotes delays and waste throughout the entire purchase cycle. The alternative is EDI. (See Figure 11.12.) With EDI, a buyer makes a decision to order a product. The buyer's EDI computer generates the purchase order transaction in its purchasing application (the same step it took in the traditional method; see Figure 11.11). The purchase order transaction is

FIGURE 11.11   Traditional information flow between buyer and seller

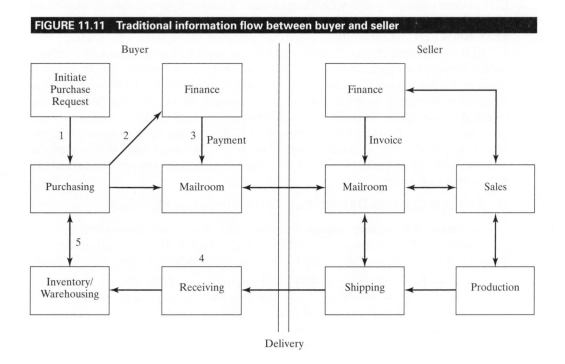

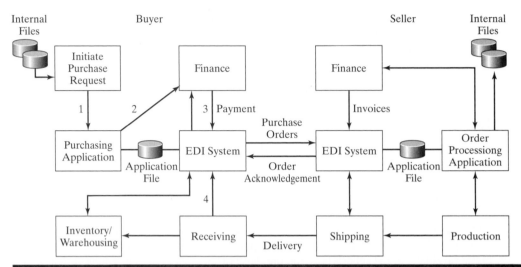

FIGURE 11.12 **Information flow between buyer and seller with EDI**

transmitted directly to the seller's EDI system in machine-readable EDI standard generated by the buyer's EDI system.

The seller's EDI system sends an acknowledgment notice to the buyer's EDI system after it passes the order information to the receiving order entry application for processing. The processing is handled like any incoming purchase order. The seller's EDI system communicates with the company's network to activate shipping and billing. It also generates shipping confirmation to the seller and a copy to the buyer. The buyer's EDI system sends an electronic payment to the seller's computer.

EDI is a fast and efficient way of handling business transactions such as purchase orders, shipping notices, invoices, and other documents. All communications occur through the interactive EDI servers of the buyer and the seller. EDI contributes to competitive advantage in the way it expedites transactions, information flow, and payments. It speeds up the business exchange between buyer and seller as well as between seller and seller. The latter benefit is unique to B2B e-commerce. Well-known retailers like Wal-Mart, Proctor & Gamble, and Levi Strauss could not have been successful without the quick response, fast product delivery, speed, data integrity, and standardization that EDI offers.

ADVANTAGES AND DRAWBACKS. EDI has three tangible benefits.

1. **Cost reduction and time savings.** By eliminating unnecessary paperwork, information flow becomes more efficient. The seller's EDI computer sending acknowledgments and electronic billing eliminates the paper invoice, for example.

2. **Improved B2B problem resolution.** EDI responds quickly to business inquiries and transfers of documents with an automatic audit trail to ensure accuracy and consistency. This improves trading partner relationships. In most cases, partners cooperate on how to set up EDI and its various applications. The result is improvement in information sharing and cooperation between trading partners.

3. **Accuracy with integrity.** Eliminating data entry means improved accuracy in the way data are processed. This contributes to the integrity and reliability of the business process. The receipt of more accurate and complete business transactions through EDI improves information processing in the affected application. For example, the receipt of an EDI purchase order invariably improves the accuracy of the order entry application of the seller.

Despite the benefits, EDI has definite drawbacks.

1. EDI has yet to catch on as the perfect solution to information flow or for doing business. With millions of businesses in the United States, fewer than 200,000 have adopted EDI. EDI is expensive and requires a heavy investment to launch and maintain the technology.
2. EDI is point to point. Every contact requires special hardware and software.
3. EDI requires expensive VAN networking to operate at peak efficiency. Only high-volume, large trading partners can afford this investment.
4. As a system, EDI is not easy to use, learn, or implement.

JUSTIFYING EDI

Under what conditions could a business justify implementing EDI? We know that EDI is a candidate if the business situation is paper intensive, people intensive, and requires fast information processing or delivery of goods.

1. **Volume of data.** Companies that handle a large volume of data on a regular basis find EDI a welcome relief. Also, if the nature of the information stored (such as a catalog) is large but requires frequent access, the business can use EDI. It will eliminate the manual handling of the catalog, along with the error rate in updating it.
2. **Frequency of document transmission and reception.** Because of high installation and maintenance expense, EDI is justified when documents are sent and received frequently.
3. **Content sensitivity.** Information contained in documents involving international contracts or orders make the content highly sensitive for accuracy.
4. **Time sensitivity.** EDI can ensure quick delivery, provided the firm's internal information processing procedures are also quick and accurate.

In doing the rating, it is important to evaluate the overall results rather than each criterion alone. For example, inventory queries are short in content (mostly product number, quantity, and a descriptor), but might be high in frequency. Think of the long term and use realistic criteria along with the experience of the business to make the final commitment to go with EDI.

One alternative is to opt for Web-based EDI. As an open communication channel and publicly accessible network, the Internet can bring online B2B trading to virtually every organization. It can cut communication costs in half and complement or replace existing EDI applications. Web browsers and search engines are also user friendly and require little training. (See Figure 11.13.)

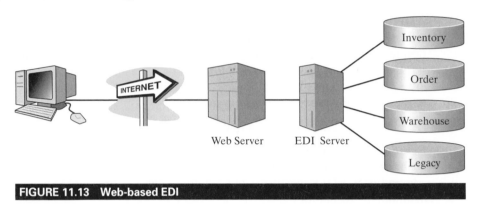

Web Server   EDI Server

FIGURE 11.13   Web-based EDI

FINANCIAL EDI

This specialized EDI centers on the electronic transmission of payments between a payee and a payer via their respective banks. Financial EDI is part of B2B because it allows businesses to replace the labor-intensive activities of collecting, disbursing, and processing payments with an electronic system. It also improves the certainty of payment flows between trading partners' bank accounts. By prior protocol, a payee's bank can electronically credit the payee's account, and the payer's bank can debit the payer's account on the scheduled day of payment.

Two main types of noncash payment procedures are presently in use for B2B payments: bank checks and electronic funds transfer (EFT). Checks are used worldwide; they are instruments of payment by which payees collect funds from payers. The life cycle of check processing is an established routine. If payee and payer have an account with the same bank, the bank's check processing system simply debits the payer's account and credits the payee's account by the same amount. This is done instantly via a teller, and the process is called *on us* check processing. If payee and payer have accounts in separate banks, the procedure is more complicated.

The payer mails a check to the payee, drawn on Bank A. The payee deposits the check in his or her account at Bank B. Upon receipt, Bank B sends the check to the IT department, where the amount of the check is entered on the bottom-right corner of the check using magnetic ink character recognition (MICR). This process uses special ink that can be read easily and accurately by a check sorter/reader. The check is read by an electronic sorter/reader, which recognizes that the check is drawn on Bank A. It is stacked in a special pocket for clearance later.

In the evening, the *not on us* checks are processed through an automated clearinghouse (ACH)—a computerized system that clears checks drawn on other banks. ACH notifies the payer's bank electronically to verify the payer's account and the amount drawn against the account. If the payer's bank says the account against which the check is drawn is invalid, closed, or overdrawn, ACH returns the check to the payee's bank marked "insufficient funds," "account closed," and so on. If the payer's bank acknowledges the account and the amount as valid, ACH instantly processes a debit to the payer's account and a credit to the payee's account. This transaction, plus millions of others, is processed in a matter of minutes and hours.

EFT is the transfer of credit between banks, where payments flow electronically from the payer's bank to the payee's bank. Banks settle their payments either by having accounts with one another, through the Federal Reserve's system called FedWire, or through the Clearing House Interbank Payments System (CHIPS). FedWire is a Federal Reserve board system and the largest funds transfer system in the United States. It is used by banks to transfer funds from one bank to another. CHIPS is a huge operation, processing more than 90 percent of all international dollar transfers. With the Federal Reserve guaranteeing Fedwire funds, transfers cannot be revoked once the receiving bank is notified that its account has been credited by a reserve bank.

EFT is one of the earliest examples of online payment systems in banking. Although funds transfers account for a small portion of the total noncash payments, they account for more than 85 percent of the value of all noncash payments. EFT is used when a high priority is placed on timeliness and certainty of payment. For lower-priority payments, ACH is usually the alternative mode of payment processing.

Unlike EFT, ACH processes a high volume of relatively small-value payments for settlement in less than two days. The two primary ACH services are:

1. Preauthorized credits, for example, a university depositing payroll in faculty/staff's respective banks.
2. Preauthorized debits, such as bill payment.

To provide these services, banks have shared ACH systems with other bank systems, such as FedWire and CHIPS.

In conclusion, one can view EDI and SCM systems as fostering closer relationships between the companies within a supply chain, but it tends to be a one-way relationship. EDI is a way for a company to place orders with suppliers. The supplier's ability to produce the components is taken as a given. SCM goes a step further—it controls stock in multiple warehouses for fast moving consumer goods (FMCG) manufacturers. With this role, it attempts to maintain the required stock levels, while deciding how and from where to fulfill each customer order.

ROLE OF LEADERSHIP

From all evidence, e-business is maturing. Business strategies contribute to e-business strategies, which require a long-term commitment to product development; innovation; and effective execution of products, services, and information with partners and others alike. To do all this requires a high order of discipline and close adherence to business and communication fundamentals. The so-called Net-ready leaders must have a set of qualities, skills, and experience to see e-business navigate as part of the supply chain and ensure strength in the value chain.

To create traction in B2B, each e-business in the chain must develop traction around leadership, management, and technology. This means leaders who can empower rather than delegate and sell goodness of fit rather than impose. Cisco, Dell, Amazon, and Charles Schwab are names that consistently appear on any list of leading e-businesses. According to one source, they are successful not because of cool technology, but because they use technology to achieve business objectives.

MANAGEMENT IMPLICATIONS

B2B e-commerce is creating an opportunity for the greatest change in corporate efficiency and performance since the invention of the telephone. The technology riding on the Web enables unprecedented improvement in the buyer/seller relationship. It is affecting all kinds of information flows. (See Box 11.7.)

BOX 11.7

E-Commerce Trends: Managing E-Commerce Alliances — A Checklist

TEN SUCCESSFUL FACTORS IN DEVELOPING YOUR PARTNERSHIP

1. **Are you socializing enough?** When you want to attract partnering attention from firms much larger than your own, do everything you can to reach them on a personal level. When you start, be willing to take on any job, no matter how awful.

2. **Are you compatible?** Partners need to have compatible business practices in order to effectively sell and deliver solutions. That single-mindedness covers everything from employing a common engagement methodology to agreeing on the same technical definitions.

3. **Are you flexible?** Partnerships can't afford to be bureaucratic, given the fast pace of e-commerce and the rapid evolution of business models.

4. **Have you put someone in charge?** Establish one partner as the project leader. Usually, whoever lands the customer should be the one to run the show, because the deliverables are a continuation of the sales cycle.

5. **Are you managing project transitions?** You could have e-anarchy on your hands without a clear road map of each partner's roles and responsibilities. That includes managing the handoffs that occur when one phase of a project melds into another.

6. **Have you decided on a billing method?** Most customers would rather have a single bill than multiple invoices. Figure out who is going to do the deed (the prime contractor is the likely choice).

7. **Are you electronically linked?** Electronic links between business systems can further ease the administration burden. Some partners also have opted to create a common repository for software code. Just be sure to protect your intellectual property.

8. **Have you minimized partner overlap?** Minimize the overlap between your skills and services, and those of your partners. Choose partners whose specialties are outside your own where you're unlikely to step on each other's toes. It also cuts down on employee raiding.

9. **Are you maintaining a healthy skepticism?** Don't trust your partners unquestioningly. When push comes to shove, a larger partner may choose you as the scapegoat. Document everything to ward against this. And keep in close communication to ensure that everyone's expectations are understood and met.

10. **Have you considered unlikely sources?** These days, even companies that have traditionally ignored the channel are looking for partners. VA Linux, for example, sells most of its products via the Web. But the company also sells to Web integrators and will need to partner as it grows its own service offerings.

Source: See ecnow.com/top10checklist.htm and www.infomatika.com/consulting-top10.asp.

As we have seen, there are supplier-oriented B2B, buyer-oriented B2B, and third-party intermediary B2B models. The goal is to line up partners, work with them, and allow them to compete for the lowest price to help the buyer improve profitability. The power of the buyer is putting pressure on the suppliers to be more customer oriented and to demonstrate value-added deals for competing buyers. With intelligent agent software, customized and personalized information is now available to attract and retain suppliers around the clock.

The changes in B2B e-commerce are so intense that technology has become a mere enabler, not a solution. The real issue is managerial—how to handle privacy, taxation, and security, and how to make the Web safe for its participants. On the human side, as complex and timely as B2B is, IT talent is the critical component that makes this technology reliable.

Compensation is a major issue and always will be a high priority. Employees know what they are worth and what the competition is paying. Beyond compensation are intrinsic factors that promote a professional's career, including utilization of abilities, creativity, security, good working conditions, competent supervision, autonomy, independence, and recognition. These elements are all part of the package that employees feel is job related. Job loyalty does not come cheap: Employers must look at the elements that enrich employees' professional life and add benefit to the business, from flexible work hours to taking a Spanish course.

Finally, IT employees should be involved in the decision process, especially in projects that affect their jobs. Taking ownership of one's career is attractive to any employee. Assuming a proactive role in deciding what one wants to do is also a strong motivator. In 1999, Allstate went all out to sell its policies via direct call centers and its Web site. It offered a series of job opportunities for employees to consider. Allstate.com is "our biggest-priority, number one project with a number one focus," according to a senior official. Apparently, it's an attraction for prospective employees who want to know what the company is looking for. In the end, success, profitability, and growth become joint ventures between the business and those who run it. No better combination is available to handle B2B e-commerce.

Summary

1. B2B involves complex procurement, manufacturing, planning collaboration, payment terms, and round-the-clock performance agreements. In one sense, B2B is collaborative commerce. Companies forge a long-term alliance and reduce the cost of doing business.

2. B2B and B2C have distinctive characteristics: In B2C, the connection mechanism is person to person; in B2B, it is the Web browser of a business interacting with a Web server application of another business. In B2C, the business is placing orders; in B2B, it is online procurement and order fulfillment. In B2C, the control mechanism is unidirectional; in B2B, control ranges from one-sided control to peer-to-peer setups.

3. Among the advantages of B2B are suppliers using the purchaser's Web site to respond online to bids and sell excess inventory. B2B also allows business firms to form electronic alliances with distributors, suppliers, resellers, and other partners. On the other hand, most of the B2B Web exchanges have yet to

make money. The question of antitrust violations resulting from alliance types of business also arises.

4. B2B is part of the supply-chain process. Supply-chain collaboration involves a group of manufacturers, retailers, and suppliers using the Internet to exchange business information, develop production schedules, and control inventory flow.

5. Among the models in B2B e-commerce are buyer-oriented B2B, supplier-oriented B2B, the electronic auction, and intermediary-oriented B2B.

6. B2B integration is about coordinating information among partners and their information system infrastructure. One solution to B2B integration is via a Web site. Another is to extract information from a partner's application and convert it into a format for transmission via EDI, file transfer protocol, e-mail, or HTTP. A third approach is for two companies to use common technology to coordinate data exchange.

7. Most B2B traffic is handled by EDI, which is computer-to-computer transfer of business information between two businesses that use a specific standard format. A specialized area of EDI centers around the electronic transmission of payments between a payee and a payer via their respective banks. The three main types of noncash payment procedures in use today for B2B payments are bank checks, EFT, and ACH.

Key Terms

- **B2B** (p. 335)
- **B2C** (p. 335)
- **buyer-oriented B2B** (p. 350)
- **disaster planning** (p. 349)
- **electronic auction** (p. 351)
- **electronic data interchange (EDI)** (p. 337)
- **forward auction** (p. 352)
- **infomediary** (p. 355)
- **intermediary-oriented B2B** (p. 355)
- **Internet exchange auction** (p. 354)
- **reverse auction** (p. 352)
- **supplier-oriented B2B** (p. 350)
- **supply chain** (p. 341)
- **supply-chain management** (p. 340)

Test Your Understanding

1. What is B2B e-commerce? What makes it so unique?
2. In what way is B2B considered collaborative commerce? Elaborate.
3. B2B is more than taking orders online. Do you agree? Explain.
4. Compare and contrast B2B and B2C e-commerce.
5. Cite the pros and cons of B2B e-commerce. Do you think the advantages exceed the drawbacks? Justify your answer.
6. What is price signaling? Give an example of your own.
7. What red flags could run B2B exchanges into antitrust trouble? Explain.
8. Identify the distinctive characteristics and give an example of each of the following electronic auctions:
   a. Forward auction
   b. Reverse auction
   c. Internet exchange auction

9. In what way is the application server different from the B2B integration server? Be specific.

10. What management implications can one consider for B2B e-commerce?

Discussion Questions

1. With all the activities and developments in B2B e-commerce, address the implications for a career in e-business.

2. B2B has been changing rapidly during the past decade. Review the literature (via the Internet) and cite five factors in the B2B sector that have contributed to key changes.

3. Locate a major organization in your area and conduct an interview to elicit the following information:

   a. The type of e-business environment available
   b. The level of sophistication of business-to-business technology
   c. The return on the investment

4. Work with your team and discuss B2B integration challenges in detail. Specifically, identify the concept of B2B integration and the various solutions to B2B integration.

Web Exercises

1. Go to www.fedex.com and investigate the type of support available to customers (e.g., checking the status of deliveries).

2. Go to www.dell.com and evaluate the site from the business buyer's perspective. Is there a procedure that would allow ordering in the supplier-oriented marketplaces?

3. Access www.ibm.com and evaluate the services offered. For a first-time business on the Internet, which service would you recommend the new e-merchant consider? Why?

4. What can one foresee beyond B2B e-commerce? Surf the Internet and address new events or developments in the area.

5. Surf the Internet and choose a software agent application or package. Write a 300-word report summarizing its features, where it would best be used, and the technology required for optimum performance.

CHAPTER 12

E-CORE VALUES

ETHICAL, LEGAL, TAXATION, AND INTERNATIONAL ISSUES

Learning Objectives

The focus of this chapter is on several learning objectives:

■ Ethical issues and how to improve the ethical climate in e-commerce

■ Legal issues in terms of liability, warranties, copyrights, trademarks, and trade names

■ Taxation issues, legal disputes, and domain name disputes

■ Encryption laws and what they mean

■ International issues, especially with regard to intellectual property and developing countries

IN A NUTSHELL

An international airline's Web site cost the company a $14,000 fine. It advertised an attractive fare for seats that were never available, a violation of U.S. airline regulations. Customer complaints poured in, which triggered the fine by the U.S. Department of Transportation. When it comes to the legal implications of Internet business fraud, the Department of Transportation is one of many government watchdogs that include the FBI, the Federal Communications Commission (FCC), and the Federal Trade Commission (FTC), among others. Even the U.S. Postal Service has an interest in Net fraud, especially in the areas of vacations, prizes, or rigged contests by fictitious Web merchants.

In approaching this topic, it is important to note that corruption is virtually everywhere. It is embedded in many cultures, regardless of geography, race, or color. It takes the form of discrimination, inequity, and injustice. The computer does not need ethics; it is the user who does. Computers are tools that allow people to communicate, to run a business, or to delegate the mundane part of work. Child pornography or money laundering are not computer problems; they are the result of people deciding between goodness and evil or between honesty and corruption.

The legal, moral, and ethical implications of the Internet are attracting a lot of attention among industries and governments around the world. There are international implications, as well. Diverting one's income to an overseas bank account to evade taxes is considered illegal. Peddling child pornography over the Internet is immoral. An employee submitting an inflated expense report is unethical. *Ethics* deals with honesty, trustworthiness, and fairness. *Legal* means "abiding by established laws for certain acts."

Law enforcers from Canada, the United Kingdom, and other countries are loosely organized in terms of monitoring and enforcing the punishment of illegal acts. This is especially critical since the establishment of the U.S. Patriot Act following the tragic events of September 11, 2001. The rapid development of communications technology and the heavy use of the Internet for business present many challenges for the law everywhere. There is no doubt the Internet has promoted fast, cheap, and out of control tax evasion and privacy issues that are causing a nightmare for the law. As long as there have been borders, people crossed them in search of the most advantageous legal environment. The borderless Internet is pushing the matter that much quicker.

Here is a case in point: A professional front man provides "sovereign services," saying he will put your business or personal affairs in the best mix of global jurisdictions to keep the authorities at bay. Such services involve exploiting differing rules in different jurisdictions—for a profit. Over time, all this border hopping could lead to a showdown between businesses and the forces of control at all levels. It is an open question whether more than 200 governments can coordinate such traffic. In any case, given today's open electronic borders, the possibilities look limitless. As one attorney remarked, "It's difficult to arrest an electron."

Taxation, especially sales tax, is another hot issue. No single place owns the Internet, but every state and country tries to control it. Norbert Elbert of Hackensack, New Jersey, was sentenced to two years in prison for child pornography, convicted by a federal court in Tucson, Arizona. Elbert has never been to Arizona, but a federal investigator in Arizona was able to retrieve the evidence from Elbert's computer in New Jersey via the Internet. Elbert had violated a new Arizona law against pornography. This means that today an e-business can easily break the law anywhere. Copyright and trademark laws differ from one country to another. Even sending an encrypted message to someone in a country where encryption is prohibited could cause a legal nightmare.

Like all business, e-commerce operates in a legal environment. Some traditional laws apply, but other laws must be developed to address the unique way business is conducted in a borderless world. This chapter addresses various practical legal, ethical, and privacy issues for Internet commerce. It covers the primary issues faced by law enforcement agencies, businesses, and consumers—privacy rights, tax policies, Net tort law, and liability.

When we look at the Internet as global, involving a multitude of different cultures and governments that cannot agree on most things, the issues of legal, moral, and ethical environments become truly daunting. Despite these differences, legal disputes and case law are beginning to surface. The author is not an attorney, and the text does not replace attorneys' opinions or state the law. It is merely an overview of the problems, processes, and implications of this important subject and how they affect business and the consumer.

ETHICAL ISSUES

IT professionals and those in disciplines such as medicine and law subscribe to codes of ethics that govern the way they behave with clients, customers, and the public at large. Trust is linked to the expectation that a professional will behave ethically. This is essential in business because society depends on fairness and good judgment. Businesspeople are expected to tell the truth and warn customers when a fault is discovered in a product.

The inclusion of ethics in e-commerce is the current challenge confronting U.S. organizations. It is easy to see how businesses have become accustomed to lower standards of ethics and a rising insensitivity to IT glitches. Consider an IT conference that offered tutorials on how to act without morality, how to leave decency behind, and how to seize the future by the throat and make it cough up money—all for a fee of $2,340 for each tutorial. How about the well-known case of Microsoft versus the U.S. Justice Department? Late in 1999 a key Microsoft executive provided a misleading demonstration of Windows 98 before a federal judge. Or what about America Online releasing Version 5.0 without alerting users that it interfered with Internet service providers and disabled competing software?

This type of arrogance attests to the increasing tendency of IT software developers to show a smug disregard for problems affecting businesses and consumers alike. As technology advances, users and developers have a responsibility to consider the ethical implications that may arise.

DEFINITION

Ethics is not easy to define, but to discuss ethical issues we need a common definition. **Ethics** is one or all of the following: fairness, justice, equity, honesty, trustworthiness, and equality. Stealing, cheating, lying, or backing out on one's word all describe a lack of ethics. Something is ethical when a person feels it is innately right, which is a subjective judgment. For example, the Biblical phrase "thou shalt not steal" is a belief held by most people, but a parent who steals a loaf of bread to feed four starving children may be forgiven for this behavior.

ethics: justice, equity, honesty, trustworthiness, equality, fairness; a subjective feeling of being innately right.

An unethical act is not the same as an immoral or an illegal act, although one may lead to the other. (See Box 12.1.)

1. Cheating on a federal income tax return is more *illegal* than immoral, although it is implicitly unethical.

2. Cheating on a friend is more *immoral* than illegal, although it is tacitly unethical.

3. Sending a padded bill to a client is *unethical* and possibly illegal.

Incidents such as these are related to value systems, beliefs, and culture. More specifically, several factors influence ethical judgment. As Table 12.1 shows, they are individual (family, associates), community, societal (social norms), professional (code of ethics), belief system (religious or personal), and legal. Laws often are created to combat unethical acts that threaten a society's survival. They also are used to reinforce existing systems of ethics. Codes of ethics also create a strong sense

---

| BOX 12.1 |

The Saga of a Yacht

During a board of directors meeting of a commercial bank, the first agenda item was a review of the Statement of Condition (expenses, revenues, and so on) of the bank for the previous month. John, a new member of the board, noticed a line item under "entertainment" for $12,000. He thought to himself, "Here's a local bank of 140 employees. What kind of entertainment is going on at the bank or by the bank to add up to this much expense?"

Out of curiosity, he raised the question at the meeting: "Mr. Chairman, I'd like to know a little about the entertainment expense item. Could this be from the Christmas party, reflected as a January expense?" The bank's president, sitting next to John, replied: "Well, as you know, John, the bank incurs all kinds of entertainment expenses. Why don't you stop by my office after the meeting and I'd be happy to explain it some more. Mr. Chairman, I move that we take the next item on the agenda as listed. . . "

After the board meeting, the president explained, "Listen, John, the entertainment item is the bank's monthly contribution to the chairman's entertainment of customers and officers of the bank. A chairman has certain privileges." John then asked, "How long has this been going on?" The president, his face turning red with irritation, said: "I really don't want to elaborate further on this. Remember, you are new on the board. I wouldn't advise asking the chairman about it. I'd let it go. The bank is making enough money. The chairman's family has 78 percent equity in the bank. What more explanation do you want? How about lunch today at the country club where I play golf? This is all tax-deductible."

John later discovered that the monthly charge of $12,000 was a dockage fee for the chairman's 140-foot yacht. As a board member, John had the responsibility of reviewing the integrity of the information reported and how funds were used. This type of expense is questionable, especially when, for the past six years, there had been no bank-related entertainment aboard the vessel. John is now in a quandary about whether he should stay on the board or resign.

TABLE 12.1   Factors influencing ethical decision making

Factor	Description
Individual	Significant others; peer group. What does mom or my close friends say?
Belief system	Religious values and beliefs from one's spiritual or religious environment. What does one's church/religion say?
Societal	Social/cultural values. What does society say should be done?
Professional	Codes of conduct and professional expectations. What does my profession say?
Personal values	One's internalized values and experience. What do I say?
Characteristics of the person	Gender, age, education, experience, etc.
Awareness of consequences	Association of behavior with outcomes
Ethical issue (scenario)	Issues related to privacy, ownership, trust, etc.

Source: Excerpted from Jennifer Kreie, and Paul Cronan, "How Men and Women View Ethics." *Communications of the ACM,* September 1998, 70–76.

code of ethics: a declaration of the principles and beliefs that govern how employees of a corporation or an association are expected to behave.

of professionalism. A **code of ethics** is a declaration of the principles and beliefs that govern how employees of a corporation or an association are expected to behave.

To illustrate, take the case of a loan advisor function built into the Web site of a commercial bank that uses 17 criteria to determine whether an applicant qualifies for a loan. For several years, the bank has been criticized by state auditors for not granting enough loans to minorities or to people living in minority districts. A review of the software package revealed that most loans favor applicants who are white and married rather than single, separated, or divorced.

When the discriminating rules were pointed out, the Web designer said: "I work for the vice president of mortgage loans. Why don't you talk with him?" The vice president replied, "I follow the requirements of the board of directors." When the president was questioned, he said, "I don't deal with this type of investigation. I know the bank is in compliance."

A more recent finding that questions ethics points to companies that make money with employees' life insurance when they die. Hundreds of banks take out insurance policies on employees with the company as the beneficiary. Some have received as much as 15 percent of their net income from the tax-free interest they get from premiums they pay on the policies. The ethical question is whether the bank should notify the employee's spouse or parent about the practice. Should the bank share in the proceeds when the employee dies?

One of the problems with ethics in business is that many firms overlook ethics issues. From 1988 to 1993, Arthur Andersen LLP (now Accenture), one of the Big Five U.S. accounting firms, invited 10 well-known ethicists and spent $5 million developing an ethics program. The real ethics question is, how did this firm end up being convicted of obstructing justice through corrupt auditing in the Enron fiasco?

Have you ever been ensnarled on a Web page that won't let you go back or get out, or one that somehow diverted you to a pornographic Web site? On the Web, dirty tricks are everywhere. One of the most annoying aspects of Web surfing is that you do not always go where you want, and if you do end up in a place you did not want to go to, it is not always easy to get out. The ethical question centers on whether it is ethical or moral to trap people in one spot, especially if it is a pornographic site.

Ethical issues also have moral implications. Take the case of Colonel Kassem Saleh who was stationed in Afghanistan during the war against the Taliban. He could count on e-mails from his women—more than 50 fiancées whom he met via Internet dating services. His scheme fell apart in May 2003 when a local Washington television station broadcast a story about a woman who was engaged to a "Saleh." Before too long, other women who thought they were Saleh's fiancées called the television station (*Times* Report 2003).

WHAT IS COMPUTER ETHICS?

Computer ethics has many faces and is interpreted depending on people's involvement in computers, information flow, or networking integrity. There is no doubt that the information revolution has altered many aspects of life, whether it is banking, employment, medical care, or national defense. As a result it has begun to affect community and family

TABLE 12.2	Brief history of computer ethics
Decade	*Event*
1940s–1950s	Norbert Wiener created a new field of research called cybernetics—the science of information feedback. It helped him draw significant insightful ethical conclusions about information technology.
1960s	Donn Parker of SRI International examined unethical and illegal uses of computers by computer professionals. He published ACM's first Code of Professional Conduct, which was officially adopted by ACM in 1973.
1970s	Walter Maner of Bowling Green State University coined the term *computer ethics* to refer to a field of inquiry dealing with ethical problems aggravated, transformed, or created by computer technology.
1980s	Ethical and social consequences of information technology, invasion of privacy, computer crime, and major lawsuits were becoming public issues.
1990s	The beginning of a second generation of computer ethics—elaborating the conceptual foundation while at the same time developing the frameworks within which practical action can occur.

life, education, freedom, and democracy. In its broadest sense, *computer ethics* is that branch of applied ethics that looks at the social and ethical impact of information technology. Table 12.2 summarizes the historical developments leading to today's use of computer ethics. From the 1940s to 1960s, there was no discipline called computer ethics. The 1970s and 1980s were years during which most of the work on computer ethics took place.

Is there a place for ethics on the Internet? One source suggested that ethics per se means acceptance that the Internet is not a value-free zone or something apart from civil society. With that in mind, we endeavor to apply the law that we have evolved for the physical space to the world of cyberspace to cover problems like child pornography, libel, copyright, and consumer protection. Yet, trying to apply a sense of ethics to cyberspace, we need to decide how we apply up to 170 separate and different legal systems to the Internet. Also, how does an organization based in one country peddle its products, services, and culture customized to various countries and various cultures? See Box 12.2.

Example topics in computer ethics include computer crime, privacy, intellectual property, globalization, and computers in the workplace. With viruses and hackers everywhere, it is important to include security in computer ethics. The problem is not physical security but logical security, which includes privacy, integrity, and unimpaired service. Intellectual property rights are a controversial area of computer ethics. The problem is illegal and unethical piracy and copying of software. Global information ethics addresses the establishment of mutually agreed standards of conduct and efforts to defend human values in a global context. Finally, computers in the workplace involve issues of safety and health, jobs eliminated by computers, and deskilling of workers by turning them into button pushers.

MAJOR THREATS TO ETHICS

Ethics in e-commerce is more openly discussed as a serious concern today than ever in the past, because the threats have steadily increased. Today's e-businesses face

---

BOX 12.2

A Case in Global Ethics Compliance

Legal action was brought in April 2000 by the French organization, International League against Racism and Anti-Semitism, and the French Jewish students organization, charging that the American company was in breach of French law for allowing French users to access the company's American site where Nazi memorabilia was being auctioned, since the sale of such items in France is illegal. The French judge found in an order talking of "an ethical and moral imperative" that the company was guilty, ordered it to block access by French users to the relevant part of the American site, and threatened fines for noncompliance of 100,000 francs ($13,300) a day.

Six months later, Yahoo! announced that it would no longer permit the sale of Nazi memorabilia on its American site, thereby removing access not just to French Internet users but all users. Undoubtedly, it was the views of Yahoo! users around the globe that persuaded the company to make such a policy reversal.

Source: Excerpted from www.rogerdarlington.co.uk/Internetethics.html.

---

ethical dilemmas of dimensions not imagined 10 years ago. The main threats are the following.

1. Faster computers and more advanced networks
2. Sophisticated global telecommunications
3. Massive distributed databases
4. Ease of access to information and knowledge bases
5. Transparency of software
6. The idea that captured information can be used as a competitive weapon

Technological advances have resulted in the need to reevaluate ethical standards and their implications for privacy, confidentiality, and integrity. Software copyright infringement, unauthorized e-mail access, and the sale of competitive data are serious issues. High-speed, low-cost data transmission is raising new questions about property rights, piracy, and plagiarism. All of this is forcing a reevaluation of the e-merchant's code of ethics.

FAKING A HARD DAY

Ethics is having a hard time with white-collar slackers who get help from e-mail and Internet technology. Think of a manager lingering over coffee and a doughnut late at night. He could actually open windows and work with documents on his screen via the hand-held phone, giving every impression to those around him that he is somewhere around at this late hour.

Spencer (2003) reports that the tactics are not new, but the tools are. Think of the old trick of leaving a jacket on the back of the desk chair or keeping the lights on to show presence. The new options allow people to operate the office computer by remote control. One feature in Microsoft Outlook allows e-mail to be sent at any specific time, day or night. Another option in this program allows the system to send e-mail at the designated time during your absence. Is this considered ethical?

IMPROVING THE ETHICAL CLIMATE

E-businesses can take a number of steps to improve ethical behavior in their IT departments, which is where Web sites are updated and programs are written.

1. To promote ethical behavior throughout the organization, top managers should act as role models.

2. The company should establish a code of ethics that takes into consideration the state of technology (intranets, extranets, local area and wide area networks, and so on). Goals should be realistic, achievable, and agreed upon by all employees. Each organizational level should create its own customized ethics program, using the company's code of ethics as a framework.

3. Unethical behavior should be dealt with promptly according to criteria and procedures set in advance.

4. The company should set up and support a strong ethics training program for all new employees and reinforce the training on a regular basis.

5. The company should motivate employees to focus on honesty, integrity, fairness, and justice as goals that are just as important as money or the bottom line.

Codes of conduct are informal codes of online behavior developed by the online community and specific communities, like "netiquette." One of the most frequently referenced guides on netiquette is Arlene H. Rinaldi's "The Net User Guidelines and Netiquette" (www.fau.edu/rinaldi/net/index.html). Included in the guide are 10 commandments of Internet conduct from the Computer Ethics Institute:

1. Thou shall not use a computer to harm other people.
2. Thou shall not interfere with other people's computer work.
3. Thou shall not snoop around in other people's files.
4. Thou shall not use a computer to steal.
5. Thou shall not use a computer to bear false witness.
6. Thou shall not use or copy software for which you have not paid.
7. Thou shall not use other people's computer resources without authorization.
8. Thou shall not appropriate other people's intellectual output.
9. Thou shall think about the social consequences of the program you write.
10. Thou shall use a computer in ways that show consideration and respect.

Once the code of ethics has been agreed upon, the next step is to decide who is going to lead the ethics movement. Organizations have used a *bottom-up* approach to inculcate ethics behavior at the employee level or a *top-down* approach on the basis that company attitudes start with the CEO. By personal acts, decisions, and overall behavior, the top corporate officer sets the tone for the kind of image the company will have.

With today's heavy use of the Internet by company employees, an ethics question is: What should a company do about employees who spend much of their time on non-productive or non-business-related Internet browsing? Is it ethical for a company to track employee e-mail? Is it ethical for one business to get the lowdown on a rival? Any of these issues is a threat to ethics, because they involve privacy.

Employees are expected to devote eight honest hours of service on the job. When they spend non-business-related time on the Internet, it is viewed as cheating the employer. There is also the liability problem, because any business transacted on the Internet makes the company liable. Because the business owns the Internet line and the equipment, the employer is entitled to determine when, for how long, and for what reason the Internet can be in use. This was the case when a brokerage firm's agent hit a pedestrian while using a cell phone to do business with a company client.

Ever since e-mail began in the mid-1990s, companies have questioned whether they should scan employee e-mail or monitor the traffic that is leaving or coming into the company files. Companies are stepping up measures to police it, especially as they realize they can be held legally responsible. Like the telephone, using e-mail for limited personal business is acceptable, but some controls must be in place.

Managers can have problems in controlling unproductive Internet surfing. The ideal approach is to limit cyberslouching, while at the same time not offend employees. Ultimately, the best way to conduct electronic monitoring is a combination of feedback and control monitoring. For example, one company monitors all Internet usage and logs all traffic. Logs are reviewed only at the request of the human resources department to investigate an employee productivity problem.

Electronic monitoring for pornography and sexual harassment has increased in recent years among most firms. For example, in one case at a premiere institution, an IT specialist was fired on the spot when caught exchanging information about child pornography after having been given one written warning. The employee manual clearly stated such an exchange would result in immediate dismissal.

In terms of one business "spying" on another, whether it is legal or ethical depends on the procedure followed. A company crosses the line if it anonymously coaxes proprietary information from an unsuspecting competitor. The alternative is to use legitimate Web sites to gather useful information.

Electronic monitoring of outgoing e-mail that contains sensitive information is also on the increase and costing companies big time. For example, in 2004, Goldman Sachs paid $2 million to settle federal regulators' charges that its employees improperly offered securities via e-mail to institutional customers in 2000. During 2004, an employee of America Online used company e-mail to steal 92 million screen names of subscribers.

Employees might be surprised to learn that their e-mail is monitored. But companies have the right to do so, because they own the e-mail accounts. Ethically, employers should use the technology only when necessary. People should accept the idea that e-mail at work is just for work.

Business ethics is closely tied to corporate culture and values, which means that a code of ethics should represent all that the company stands for. The code should be all-encompassing and stable over time. It does not make sense, for example, to change the code for every new situation that comes up.

What about codes of ethics? Codes of ethics notices and privacy policy notices on the Web site can be problematic. They may be hard to find, use vague and unspecific language, or fail to provide a contact address or a procedure for dealing with complaints. They also may not state the site's commitment to data security or have clear access requirements.

An honest workplace, where managers and employees are held accountable for their behavior, is the best environment in which to promote ethical corporate behavior.

self-assessment: a question-and-answer procedure that allows individuals to appraise and understand their personal knowledge about a particular topic.

To keep the ethical climate healthy, an organization must stress regular self-assessment and encourage open debate within the workplace. **Self-assessment** is a question-and-answer procedure that allows individuals to appraise and understand their personal knowledge about a particular topic. In the case of ethics, it is not an exercise to satisfy others. The goal is to think about ethics and adjust one's behavior accordingly. It should be an educational experience for the participant.

One self-assessment procedure asks a participant to assess a scenario and judge whether an ethics issue is involved. The response is recorded on a special form and later compared to the judgment of a panel of experts. The following is an example.

Company XYZ has developed the software for a computerized voting machine. Company ABC, which manufactures the machine, has persuaded several cities and states to purchase it. On the strength of these orders, ABC is planning a major purchase from XYZ. XYZ software engineer Smith is visiting ABC one day and learns that problems in the construction of the machine mean that 1 in 10 is likely to miscount soon after installation. Smith reports this to her superior, who informs her that it is ABC's problem. Smith does nothing further.

Question: *Is an ethics issue involved?*
Opinion: Participants nearly unanimously agreed that doing nothing further would be unethical. Use of inaccurate voting machines could invalidate elections and potentially harm the general public. Responsible (ethical) behavior and good business practice are not inconsistent. The software engineer should pursue the matter further.

THE PRIVACY FACTOR

Privacy is a basic American value. It is also one of the most pressing concerns of computer users today and an issue that is inadequately addressed in e-commerce. Cyberspace, originally intended for scientists, is now dominated by marketers seeking information—the lifeblood of e-business. What makes information so valuable is that most of it is gathered discreetly. E-companies are taking advantage of their ability to obtain information without the customer's knowledge or permission. Such private information is being documented, sold, and used to promote e-business. E-businesses have an ethical responsibility to inform users what information is being captured and how it is being used. See Box 12.3.

The thought of being watched is unsettling. Hidden video cameras, phone taps, and surveillance bugs are all examples of technologies that are considered to be unethical (and sometimes illegal), because they allow data to be collected about individuals without their knowledge. Web sites have been developed whose only business is selling information about people who visit their sites. Some businesses use game sites to attract children and then gather personal information from them.

BOX 12.3

Sample Ethical Principles

As Hi-Ethics members, we are dedicated to providing Internet health services that reflect high quality and ethical standards, health information that is trustworthy and up-to-date, and empowering consumers to distinguish online health services that follow ethical principles from those that do not. With these goals in mind, we adopt the following ethical principles:

- Positive commitment to use security procedures to protect personal information from misuse

- Provide procedures for consumers to review their personal information that we maintain

- Safeguard consumer privacy in relationship with third parties

- Clearly state who owns any health Web site we operate

- Comply with existing federal and state laws regarding any promotions, rebates, and free or discounted offers on our health Web sites

- Ensure authorship and accountability of any information we display on our Web sites

- Design Internet health services to enable professionals to adhere to professional ethical principles in the online Internet environment

- Make it easy for consumers to provide us with feedback or comments concerning our health Web sites.

Source: Excerpted from www.hiethics.com/Principles/index.asp.

The Online Personal Privacy Act, enacted in 2002, creates uniform laws across the United States relating to Internet privacy. The bill covers two types of information: sensitive and nonsensitive. Sensitive information is "any financial, medical, ethnic identification, religious affiliation, sexual orientation, or political data." Companies must seek the consent of users they are collecting sensitive information about through a procedure called "opt in." Companies also must allow users to "opt out" of any data collection of nonsensitive material. They must inform users how their information will be used and who will have access to it. The Federal Trade Commission (FTC), the state's attorney general, and the user can sue companies that release sensitive information in federal court.

Related to the ethical/privacy dilemma is the story of the reservist who was killed in Iraq and who left Internet material that his family wanted. The reservist's only means of communicating with the outside world was through a computer. Several times a week, the 20-year-old combat engineer would log on, send out a batch of e-mails, and update a Web site with pictures of his adventures. When he was killed in an enemy ambush, his parents wanted to know how they could acquire and preserve their digital memories. Citing privacy, the firm withheld his e-mail from his survivors (Cha 2005).

A new federal law created a new precedent, in which federal authorities may monitor Internet users. The Patriot Act, passed in response to the terrorist acts of September 11, 2001, gives federal authorities the right to tap into what you are doing on the Internet and your e-mail. Also, Internet service providers must make themselves more susceptible to wiretaps by the federal government. This act drew many concerns from civil libertarians, in that the surveillance powers give law enforcement agents too much leeway to collect private information on people who are on the periphery of investigations.

When Internet online services get personal, privacy tends to take a hit. Hot in pursuit of Google's launch of "My Search History," which allows users to store past searches, Yahoo! brought up a similar service. The most serious privacy concern is using such services on public computers. You have to log in to use them. If you forget to log off properly, the next person could access your past searches. What if a pedophile were visiting a pornographic site or a cheating spouse were active on dating sites? Can his or her searches be subpoenaed?

The FTC has identified the following five principles of privacy protection, which are widely recognized in the United States, Canada, and Europe.

1. Notice: Consumers have the right to be told in advance about any personal information being gathered.

2. Choice: Consumers should have the final say regarding the use of personal information, other than the processing of such information.

3. Access: Consumers should be able to access and correct any personal information captured in files or databases anywhere.

4. Security/integrity: Consumers' personal information should be processed, stored, and transmitted in a secure way so as to assure integrity at all times.

5. Enforcement: The courts should back consumers if any of the aforementioned principles are violated.

Three categories of concern arise regarding information privacy. The first involves the electronic data that businesses store about consumers. Who owns such data? The second is the security of electronic data transmission. Encryption has been promoted as a secure way to transmit data over the Internet. The third concern is the unauthorized reading of personal files. Public key architecture (PKI) and other technologies are used to control unauthorized access.

The FTC has been watching a number of e-commerce companies closely, such as Amazon.com. In the past, the FTC has sided with businesses, favoring self-regulation over legislation, but because the public is worried about surrendering personal data online, the likelihood of government intervention to protect the consumer is on the rise. Watchdog groups such as Junkbusters, the Electronic Frontier Foundation, Privacy International, and the Online Privacy Alliance are pushing for government oversight to protect the public. E-merchants, on the other hand, continue to prefer self-restraint to legislation.

With Net privacy in its infancy, sites including the following have been established that serve as building blocks for the next generation of privacy protection.

- www.spybot.com—This site helps scan your computer to advise you whether it is vulnerable to hidden programs that lurk in the background.

- www.privacy.org—This site offers a collection of Net privacy articles derived from top news organizations.

- www.junkbusters.com—A great site for assisting consumers in their fight against unsolicited advertising practices, from spam and junk mail to cookies and the like.

- www.freedom.net—This is an Internet privacy software package designed to protect your personal information. It can block junk mail and stop online tracking. The package sells for less than $50 per copy.

- www.epic.org—This site contains a massive collection of news, links to software, guidelines, and a report on the privacy policies of the top 100 U.S. firms.

The privacy factor hit auction sites like eBay and Yahoo! Auctions. The key to eBay's success is trust among buyers, sellers, and the company that facilitates the auctions. eBay displays its TRUSTe-approved privacy statement, which clearly outlines how it protects users' privacy (see www.ebay.com). Yahoo! identifies clearly what the seller is allowed to sell and cannot sell. A summary list is shown in Box 12.4.

THE PROFESSIONAL ETHICIST

As the Internet has dominated e-commerce, e-business, and society in general, ethics in the use of technology to protect one's privacy has generated a new breed of professional ethicists to help firms navigate the moral gray areas of the Web. More and more firms are hiring people with integrity; who are well grounded academically; and who practice ethics, morality, and objectivity in problem solving.

Ethics consultants perform a number of important functions. They hold workshops and meetings, and advise executives on setting ethical guidelines for the day-to-day operation of their firm. They conduct surveys and talk to employees to figure out where the ethical loopholes are and how to correct them. The idea usually works for most firms, but it is not a guarantee that the company will become ethical in attitude or

---

BOX 12.4

A Sample List of Prohibited Auction Items

You are not allowed to sell:

- Trade-sensitive goods such as bootlegs, CD-ROMs, or demo copies of software

- Counterfeit goods, such as fake brand name goods

- Items subject to embargo, such as Cuban cigars

- Hate materials like KKK patches or swastika flags

- Illegal drugs like cocaine, heroin, and anabolic steroids

- Prescription drugs and medical devices, like Viagra or Prozac

- Body parts and body fluids like urine, blood, or organs

- Stolen products like stolen art or lock-picking devices

- Fireworks and hazardous materials like bombs, grenades, or dynamite

- Government IDs like birth certificates, passports, or driver's licenses

- Police items like badges or sirens

- Gambling items like lottery or sweepstakes tickets

- Services like massage or legal services

- Weapons and accessories like switchblades, ammunition, or rifle scopes

Source: Excerpted from help.yahoo.com/help/auct/asell/asell-21.html.

practice. As mentioned before, Arthur Andersen's $5 million investment in an ethics program did not deter it from the audit scandal with Enron. Whether an ethics program works depends largely on the commitment and support of top management, and honest maintenance of ethics on a daily basis.

A typical ethicist holds a graduate degree in the humanities, psychology, behavioral science, communications, or human resources. The ethicist holds values designed to put integrity, trust, and honesty into corporations, especially in terms of their relationships with employees, the community, and local government. Communication skills, training, and facilitating skills are critical. Business knowledge and basic legal understanding are helpful.

Some of the ethical core values to consider include putting funds and resources back in the community, striving to play the business game in a way that is a win-win endeavor, treating employees to enrich the feeling of belonging, providing recognition, and giving a share of the company wealth to those who have added value to the firm's productivity. Ethics consultants can earn as much as $9,000 per day at corporations or close to $200,000 as full-time specialists.

IS THERE A CPO IN THE HOUSE?

Since 2000, U.S. companies have faced heavy responsibilities stemming from privacy-related regulations, including the Health Insurance Portability and Accountability Act (HIPAA), the Gramm-Leach-Bliley Act, the Sarbanes-Oxley Act, and the Fair Credit Reporting Act. The explosion of privacy regulations, along with limited resources, has made it clear that legal compliance is the number one priority in running an online business. The response has been to make a chief privacy officer (CPO) a compliance job. An example of compliance-driven privacy measures is the HIPAA mandate that any health-care related business, especially major hospital chains, install a privacy officer on a full-time basis.

As a result, the roster of CPOs is growing. For example, in 2001, at least 100 businesses employed CPOs. In 2003, the two largest CPO organizations merged to form the International Association of Privacy Professionals, claiming over 1,000 members. In 2004, the estimated number of U.S. CPOs is well over 2,000 (Ulfelder 2004). The number is expected to grow as privacy compliance becomes a reality in virtually every business, here and abroad.

What makes the compliance issue more imposing is the increasing targeting of big business by privacy advocates pushing large enterprises to refrain from voluntarily giving sensitive data about customers to the government. The American Civil Liberties Union is leading a "no-spy pledge campaign" that is beginning to take root. Privacy activists hope to stem the volume of data that the government collects on the average citizen. This will pose a problem when it comes to the goals of the Homeland Security Administration and the Patriot Act, whose charge is to protect the country from terrorist attacks and the Internet from money laundering.

THE MORAL FACTOR

The Internet generated a moral dilemma arising as computer technology impacts American citizens' privacy, values, and practice of democracy. It has contributed to the availability of products and services that threaten morality everywhere—in schools, in the home, in business, and in society in general. The Computer Decency Act (CDA) has changed much with respect to Internet access. Yet, tons of Web sites devoted explicitly to adult pornography continue to flood the Internet. They have yet to be removed or banned because of our concerns for free speech. Pornography carries with it viruses, spyware, adware, and hard-to-erase cookies that send information about the user's pornographic habits and compulsions. Pornography also threatens the moral fabric of every business, regardless of size or location. If left unchecked, it often backfires in the way of harassment and costly lawsuits.

Take the case of Chevron, which allowed a newsgroup that contained pornographic images of women to be carried on its systems. Some employees used such images as the default background screen saver on their monitors at work. Offended employees charged that such vulgarity created a hostile environment, fostered by the company that facilitated such environment. The court agreed and fined the company $2 million for sexual harassment.

Child pornography is a different threat to morality and is not protected by free speech. It is out and out immoral and illegal. Companies that care to stay away from such illicit trade must have a clear-cut set of principles, procedures, and penalties regarding child pornography. A case in point is when one of the senior staff members of the Internet Technology Center at a university was caught trading child pornography on the university network. What caught this individual red-handed was the heavy traffic his terminal generated. It was traced to the terminal with all the URL addresses pointing to child pornography and beyond. The dean of the business school where he was working called the university police, who impounded the terminal and escorted him to the payroll department for his last paycheck.

LEGAL ISSUES

Every legitimate business, whether it is brick-and-mortar or click-and-mortar, operates in a legal environment. Contracts, taxation, and copyrights are among the legal issues that all face. Many of the legal questions that arise from e-commerce are not settled, but new laws can change the rules and plug loopholes. In an age of prolific litigation, online shoppers and e-merchants should be aware of the legal ramifications of e-commerce. Consider the following situations.

1. Via its Web site, a large computer firm sells a server to a client, with proper configuration, ready to go. When the server is installed, the user discovers that the configuration is faulty and the server, as it stands, is worthless. The company operates in Europe, and the cost of shipping the unit for repairs would be prohibitive. It also would bring the user's business to a standstill.

2. A customized computer system used by an architect incorrectly determines the stress requirements of a new multimillion-dollar public building. Unknown to the architect, the software, acquired via the Internet, had definite bugs. As a result, the completed structure soon collapses, killing or injuring dozens of people.

3. A radiation machine bought over the Internet by a young doctor calculates the dosage for the treatment of cancer patients. Two years after hundreds of people were treated, four die due to radiation overdose. The problem was faulty programming. The e-merchant denies responsibility.

4. Software has been used recently by online services to divert online sales commissions that would otherwise be paid to small Web merchants by big sites like Amazon.com and eToys. This "stealware" is considered legal, because the users agree to the diversion. The diversion involved is estimated to be in the hundreds of thousands of dollars and probably will continue, either because most users are unaware that the software is operating on their computers or because it might be too costly to contest.

Each of these cases is real. Who is liable in such situations and for what reasons?

The Question of Liability

When a product is bought over the Internet and found to be defective, liability becomes an issue. The blame may fall on the merchant or the vendor that shipped the merchandise. Depending on how the warranty is worded, liability could fall on the manufacturer. Tort and contract laws present challenging questions for organizations and the legal community. If a product produces the wrong solution, which causes injury to others, the resulting damage often leads to litigation. Each entity involved in the process (e-merchant, vendor, shipper, and manufacturer) is potentially vulnerable to legal action.

product liability: a tort that makes a manufacturer liable if its product has a defective condition that makes it unreasonably dangerous to the user or consumer.

strict liability: a seller is liable for any defective or hazardous products that unduly threaten a user's safety.

The nature of the Internet and technology have not yet reached a point where new legal remedies are required for e-commerce. The old, familiar liability issues are still applicable. Tort law and **product liability** are the two major (and often overlapping) areas of concern, with the issue of warranties falling under the first area, and **strict liability** and negligence falling under the second.

One area that is attracting attention in m-commerce is doing business by cell phone. The use of two-way pagers, mobile phones, and other m-tools now means that business can be conducted anywhere, but it might make companies liable if employees using these gadgets are involved in accidents, such as car accidents.

Take the case of Smith Barney, an investment banking brokerage firm that paid $500,000 to settle litigation brought by the family of a motorcyclist killed in Pennsylvania by one of its brokers who was conducting business on the phone while driving. Yet, in Minnesota, where a psychiatric nurse crashed into another car when she reached for her cell phone while driving home, the jury concluded that answering the call was not part of her job.

Employers have been and will continue to be found liable for negligence, but the application of the negligence doctrine to today's technological society is relatively new. The Virginia lawsuit against Cooley Godward (the employer of the attorney who ran over a 15-year-old girl in the summer of 2000) helped set something of a precedent in this fuzzy area. The driver, lawyer Jane Wagner, pleaded guilty to a felony and has completed a one-year work-release program, according to her lawyer.

tort: a wrongful act subject to civil action.

tort law: a special area of law focused on remedying wrongs between parties.

Tort Law on the Internet

Torts are wrongful acts subject to civil action. **Tort law** is a special area of law focused on remedying wrongs between parties. In e-commerce, it can mean settling contract problems between the e-merchant and the ISP. ISPs have yet to be regulated by any federal or state agency. That is why each ISP can decide on prices, quality, speed, reliability, and the like. Internet tort cases already have been brought against businesses and clients. Most of the cases relate to fraud, negligence, false advertising, misrepresentation, and trademark violations.

fraud: the intent to deceive.

Fraud is the intent to deceive. It is knowing a material fact about a product, but covering it up in a sale. This applies to the e-merchant as well as to the consumer. For example, if a customer gives an unauthorized or stolen credit card number over the Internet, that customer would be committing fraud. If a merchant advertises a product on a Web site and makes false claims about what it will do, the merchant can be liable for fraud. In many countries, watchdog organizations and government agencies watch closely for Internet fraud.

negligence: failing to take a certain action, which in turn causes injury or material loss to another.

Negligence is failing to take a certain action, which causes injury or material loss to another. A farmer who buys infected chicks on the Internet, which cause the deaths of other chickens, can sue the merchant for gross negligence.

false advertising: advertising the availability of a product or a service when no such thing is available.

False advertising is simply advertising the availability of a product or a service when, in fact, no such thing is available.

misrepresentation: a tort area that tags to fraud.

Misrepresentation is another tort area. Like false advertising in intent, claiming that a product will perform certain functions when in fact it cannot is misrepresenting the product. Likewise, salespersons who fail to disclose the negative aspects of a product when they know all along about such weaknesses would be subject to prosecution.

Related to this is a report from April 14, 2003 on MSN.com, "Does Pfc. Jessica Lynch Own the Movie Rights to Her Life?" Jessica Lynch is the American POW rescued during the Iraqi war in 2003. NBC is planning to make a movie about her life. In one respect, legal sources suggest that facts about particular people are not exclusively owned by anyone and copyright law (explained later) only protects creative expression, not facts. Yet, the so-called "disclosure of private facts" tort or right of privacy allows people to block publication of certain intimate facts about their life. Ms. Lynch might be able to sue if NBC gets certain facts wrong or if an error in the TV movie harms her reputation.

WARRANTIES

Uniform Commercial Code (UCC): a law drafted by the National Conference of Commissioners on Uniform State Laws, which governs commercial transactions.

The **Uniform Commercial Code (UCC)** is the foundation of commercial contract law in all states except Louisiana. It contains provisions for computer contracts in the form of warranties. A **warranty** is an assurance made by the seller about the goods sold. An additional safeguard is the federal Magnuson-Moss Consumer Product Warranty Act, enacted in 1975, which clarifies the issues relating to warranty information disclosure requirements and regulates the limitation of implied warranties. Both the UCC and the warranty act identify the various types of warranties (express and implied) and serve as references for further information on the subject.

warranty: an assurance made by the seller about the goods sold.

express warranty: a warranty offered orally or in writing by the maker of the product.

implied warranty: a warranty that arises automatically from the fact that a sale has been made and the assumption that the product will do what it is supposed to do.

disclaimer: evidence of the seller's intention to protect the business from unwanted liability.

There are two types of warranties. An **express warranty** is offered orally or in writing by the maker of the product and is usually part of the sale. The buyer purchases the goods in part because of a statement by the seller with respect to the quality, capacity, or some other characteristic of the package. An express warranty need not be a specific statement. It may be found in the seller's conduct.

An **implied warranty** arises automatically from the fact that a sale has been made and the assumption that the product will do what it is supposed to do. For example, a Web site should be fit for the ordinary purposes for which it is used. This implied warranty of *merchantability* indicates that the Web site should do what it is expected to do. The other aspect of implied warranty is one of *fitness*. A knowledge base should be fit for the particular use intended by the buyer. Violation of this warranty is probably not common among Web designers or software developers, although it might be more common among companies that do customized programming.

Disclaimers and warranties are closely related. A **disclaimer** is evidence of the seller's intention to protect the business from unwanted liability. Many software packages are labeled "as is," meaning they are sold without warranty of any kind regarding performance or accuracy. Other disclaimers go so far as to state that neither the developer, retailer, nor anyone affiliated with the developer is liable for damages even if the developer has been forewarned of the possibility of such damages.

Even though disclaimers are clearly stated, their legal status is fuzzy. The main issue centers on whether the software in question is a product or a service. In either case, the courts are inclined to include warranty disclaimers for final judgment. Express warranty disclaimers are effective, provided they are conspicuously placed and in writing.

A Web customer can reasonably look toward warranties as protection if damage is caused through the use of a product purchased through a company's Web site. Showing a reason why a warranty exclusion should not be accepted is difficult. In fact, two states have enacted *shrink-wrap* laws, which hold that all warranties made or disclaimed on the license found inside the shrink-wrapping are legal and final. Cases involving warranties also require that the user shows who is at fault and why, which is a difficult task.

out-of-bounds error: an error that occurs because either the software did not have the expertise to address the particular problem or the designer improperly condensed the technology.

nontrivial error: an error that triggers other areas in the software to malfunction and is difficult to correct.

DESIGNER'S LIABILITY.   In Web design or software development, the designer is often responsible for system accuracy and reliability. A variety of errors may become embedded in the system: Some are nontrivial and others are out-of-bounds errors. An **out-of-bounds error** is one that occurs either because the software did not have the expertise to address the particular problem or the designer improperly condensed the technology. A **nontrivial error** is one that triggers other areas in the software to malfunction and is difficult to correct. This type of error has a large financial impact on the e-business, especially if the product is mass marketed. The consequence is decommissioning the system or facing litigation.

Because designers rely on their experience to develop the product or software, when a malfunction occurs, designers are vulnerable to charges of personal liability under the doctrine of *respondent superior* (an employer-employee relationship). If the designer is an employee of the organization that sells the software, the employing company is involved in the negligence action. In the end, the company is responsible for certifying the system before it is released for public use. See Box 12.5.

USER'S LIABILITY. Even end users of the product are not immune from lawsuits. They are directly responsible for proper use of the product. Users' refusal to comply with the product directions will increasingly come into question. By not properly utilizing an available resource, users could be negligent by omission (what is called *passive negligence*). For example, the use of an intelligent system in medical diagnosis could place the responsibility for utilizing the system on the user as an *affirmative duty*.

COPYRIGHTS, TRADEMARKS, AND TRADE NAMES

The area of Internet copyright and trademark violations falls under intellectual property law. **Intellectual property** includes software, books, music, videos, trademarks, copyrights, and Web pages. Controversy is growing over who owns the intellectual property of domain names, programming, and Web sites. Even the HTML coding of the Web site is in question. More on intellectual property is covered later in the chapter.

intellectual property: includes software, books, music, videos, trademarks, copyrights, and Web pages.

BOX 12.5

Legal Issues of Web Design

1. Web designers own their knowledge of the work if no prior agreement was established.

2. A pre-employment contract or intellectual property agreement can limit the Web designer's liability for the Web site.

3. If a Web designer builds the Web site and a problem arises with the site, the Web designer is subject to charges of personal liability under the doctrine of *respondent superior.* If the Web designer is an employee of an organization, the organization also is involved in the negligence action.

4. If a Web site is a product, proving negligence is unnecessary to hold the developer liable. The UCC allows developers to limit liability for defective work via a disclaimer of warranties in the contract. For these liabilities, the loss falls on the developer, regardless of fault, as a cost of doing business.

5. If a Web site is a service, the contract law of the state applies, rather than the UCC.

6. Courts tend to be reluctant to exclude warranty disclaimers or attempts by the software house to avoid their applications as unconscionable (corrupt).

7. Cases involving warranties require that the user show who is at fault and why.

8. The software in question should be considered a product under UCC rules for warranties to be relevant or for the tort theory of strict liability to apply.

copyright: ownership of an original work created by an author.

copyright law: a law that gives the author or creator of a tangible product the right to exclude others from using the finished work.

Copyright is ownership of an original work created by an author. It is a form of intellectual property protection that covers the look, feel, and content of printed media like articles and textbooks, as well as software programs and software packages. It was the spread of the printing press that provoked the need for a copyright law. **Copyright law** gives the author or creator of a *tangible* product the right to prevent others from using the finished work. That is why authors and publishers place a copyright notice on the back of the title page. Copyright protection applies immediately upon creation of the manuscript.

Several kinds of works are protected—literary, musical, dramatic, pictorial, graphic, and sculptural works; Web sites; sound recordings; and architectural works. Computer programs and most compilations can be registered as literary works. Several categories of material are not eligible for copyright protection. For example, works consisting entirely of information considered common property and containing no original authorship are not copyrighted. Familiar symbols or designs, or mere listings of ingredients or contents are also not copyrighted.

A copyright is good for the life of its author plus an additional 70 years after the author's death. In the case of a joint authorship, the term lasts for 70 years after the last surviving author's death. Specific conditions and laws also protect people from copying someone else's work without permission. For example, a writer can quote up to 250 words without permission, provided recognition is given to the author of the quoted work. The same procedure applies to copying material on other people's Web pages. Beyond that, users need permission from the copyright holder to quote or to copy. A magazine that once copied only 300 words of ex-President Gerald Ford's 200,000-word autobiography was found guilty of copyright violation.

The Digital Millennium Copyright Act (DMCA) approved by Congress in 1998 extends copyright law to digital content. It is intended to protect "the technological locks that content owners can put on any type of copyrighted content to prevent circumvention."

In information technology, a database or a directory and the way it is organized are considered a compilation and are copyrightable. A compilation's copyright protects all components within it. An original compilation of names and addresses that are now in public domain is also copyrightable. The same applies for logos and trademarks. Copyright protection on the Internet has its own set of limitations. By international agreement, only an expression can be copyrighted, but not facts. The biggest problem on the Web is not the text content, but images and programs. Because JPEG images are so easy to download, cut, and paste on any Web page, images are not easy to protect.

TRADEMARK.   A word, a picture, or an image that identifies a product or service is intellectual property and is protected by a **trademark.** It is "registration of a company's trade name so that others cannot use it." It is also a word or a symbol that distinguishes a good from other goods in the market. It is useful in establishing alliances because the marks of one firm may complement another, just as products of the two companies may be complementary. Co-branding agreements reinforce joint marketing programs. With the Internet, trademarks can be a powerful marketing tool. It is common to see Web sites on which marks of different, distinct

trademark: registration of a company's trade name so that others cannot use it; a word or a symbol that distinguishes a good from other goods in the market.

┌─────────────────────────────────┐
│   BOX 12.6   │
└─────────────────────────────────┘

Intel Inside

An American manufacturer of microprocessors, Intel Inc., produced successive generations of "X86" microchips (the 8086, 286, 386, and 486). However, Intel did not take trademark protection for its numbering system. As a result, its competitors such as AMD, Chips and Technologies, and Cyrix also used the X86 name for their own processors. Realizing its mistake, Intel in 1991 started encouraging computer manufacturers like IBM, Compaq, Gateway, and Dell to put the "Intel Inside™" logo in their computer advertisements and on their packages. The incentive to computer companies was a cooperative advertisement allowance paid by Intel that amounted to 3 percent of the company's purchase of Intel's processors (5 percent when the logo is put on the packaging).

The campaign resulted in more than 90,000 pages of advertisements in an eighteen-month period, with a potential $10 billion exposure. The recognition of the Intel brand among business end-users went up from 46 percent to 80 percent. After a full year of the Intel Inside campaign, Intel's worldwide sales went up by 63 percent in 1992. Prominent display of the Intel Inside logo by the leading computer manufacturers has influenced consumers to think that Intel's microprocessor must be very good.

Source: Chiranjeev Kohli and Mrugank Thakork, "Branding Consumer Goods: Insights from Theory and Practice," *Journal of Consumer Marketing*, Spring 1997, 12–13.

companies combine to demonstrate to the viewer the complementary nature of products. Strategic use of a trademark to cement alliances is shown in Box 12.6.

Trade secret theft is a serious problem, especially with the growing outsourcing of software development to Asian countries like India. Because overseas court systems and laws are not as strong as in the U.S., the odds of intellectual property theft are likely to be higher. Lower software development costs have triggered a surge of U.S. software work to regions of the world with high piracy rates. In China, for example, the software piracy rate is 92 percent, followed by India's 73 percent, compared to 22 percent in the U.S.

Trademark liability is well known among most firms. ISPs receive immunity from defamation and other tort claims committed on their hosted sites through the federal Communications Decency Act (CDA). However, this protection does not include trademark infringement. When it comes to litigation, suing ISPs for trademark infringement is a tricky route to take. Take the case of fashion company Gucci's American subsidiary suing Hall & Associates, the owners of www.goldhaus.com, claiming that the online jewelry retailer infringed on Gucci's registered trademark. According to court documents, Gucci America twice warned Mindspring, the Atlanta-based ISP, that Hall & Associate's www.goldhaus.com was using Gucci trademarks illegally. Mindspring asserted that it was not liable for its client's infringement, because it is immune by the CDA. The court denied Mindspring's defense, because it found that the ISP contributed to trademark infringement by knowingly keeping the client on board.

Who owns a trademark (or a copyright) is often a contractual matter. Trademark protection is a maze of federal and state laws that have to be reviewed carefully before securing protection. Some trademarks might be registered in one state but not in others, and some states have individual laws covering trademarks. An example of the difference between a copyright and a trademark is shown in Box 12.7.

BOX 12.7

An Example of Copyright and Trademark Language

Welcome to Amazon.com. Amazon.com and its affiliates provide their services to you subject to the following notices, terms, and conditions. In addition, when you use any Amazon.com service (e.g., Friends & Favorites, e-Cards and Auctions), you will be subject to the rules, guidelines, policies, terms, and conditions applicable to such service.

COPYRIGHT

All content included on this site, such as text, graphics, logos, button icons, images, audio clips, and software, is the property of Amazon.com or its content suppliers and protected by U.S. and international copyright laws. The compilation (meaning the collection, arrangement, and assembly) of all content on this site is the exclusive property of Amazon.com and protected by U.S. and international copyright laws. All software used on this site is the property of Amazon.com or its software suppliers and protected by U.S. and international copyright laws. The content and software on this site may be used as a shopping, selling, and e-card resource. Any other use, including the reproduction, modification, distribution, transmission, republication, display, or performance, of the content on this site is strictly prohibited.

TRADEMARKS

AMAZON.COM; AMAZON.COM BOOKS; EARTH'S BIGGEST BOOKSTORE; IF IT'S IN PRINT, IT'S IN STOCK; and 1-CLICK are registered trademarks of Amazon.com, Inc., in the United States and other countries. PURCHASE CIRCLES, SHOP THE WEB, ONE-CLICK SHOPPING, AMAZON.COM ASSOCIATES, AMAZON.COM MUSIC, AMAZON.COM VIDEO, AMAZON.COM TOYS, AMAZON.COM ELECTRONICS, AMAZON.COM e-CARDS, AMAZON._COM AUCTIONS, zSHOPS, CUSTOMER BUZZ, AMAZON.CO.UK, AMAZON.DE, BID-CLICK, GIFT-CLICK, AMAZON.COM

ANYWHERE, AMAZON.COM OUTLET, BACK TO BASICS, BACK TO BASICS TOYS, NEW FOR YOU, and other Amazon.com graphics, logos, and service names are trademarks of Amazon.com, Inc. Amazon.com's trademarks may not be used in connection with any product or service that is not Amazon. com's, in any manner that is likely to cause confusion among customers, or in any manner that disparages or discredits Amazon.com. All other trademarks not owned by Amazon.com or its affiliates that appear on this site are the property of their respective owners, who may or may not be affiliated with, connected to, or sponsored by Amazon.com or its affiliates.

USE OF SITE

This site or any portion of this site may not be reproduced, duplicated, copied, sold, resold, or otherwise exploited for any commercial purpose that is not expressly permitted by Amazon.com. Amazon.com and its affiliates reserve the right to refuse service, terminate accounts, and/or cancel orders in its discretion, including, without limitation, if Amazon.com believes that customer conduct violates applicable law or is harmful to the interests of Amazon.com and its affiliates.

COPYRIGHT COMPLAINTS.

Amazon.com and its affiliates respect the intellectual property of others. If you believe that your work has been copied in a way that constitutes copyright infringement, please follow our Notice and Procedure for Making Claims of Copyright Infringement.

DISCLAIMER

This site is provided by Amazon.com on an "as is" basis. Amazon.com makes no representations or warranties of any kind, express or implied, as to the operation of the site or the information, content, materials, or products included on this site. To the full extent permissible by applicable law, Amazon.com disclaims all warranties, express or implied, including, but not limited to, implied warranties of merchantability and fitness for a particular purpose. Amazon.com will not be liable for any damages of any kind arising from the use of this site, including, but not limited to direct, indirect, incidental, punitive, and consequential damages.

If a company hires an outside firm to develop its Web site, the contract should clearly give the company all intellectual property rights. The Web designer's contract is a "work made for hire." If the design is done in-house, the employment contract also should make clear that any creative work performed by employees belongs to the company. For a $30 fee, anyone can copyright his or her work with the Library of Congress. Its Web site address is www.loc.gov/copyright.

TAXATION ISSUES

One of the most controversial issues facing e-commerce and global tax authorities is taxation, especially sales tax. In every state, a business enterprise is required to pay taxes and collect taxes. In brick-and-mortar businesses, computers or electronic machines compute and account for taxes to comply with local, state, and federal tax laws.

On the Internet, tax collection is not so easy. What is collected depends on the location of the e-merchant's business, the location of the buyer, the types of goods for sale, and so on. Each state and county has different sales taxes and different jurisdictions. For example, cough drops are taxable in Massachusetts but not in Maryland, while in Ohio a gift basket of fruit is not taxed, although a crystal dish filled with candy is. Cloth diapers in Wisconsin are tax-exempt, but not disposable ones. The rules for taxation also differ by country.

To make the problem worse, quantifying the lost tax dollars has been difficult. States have had trouble collecting sales tax even for off-line purchases. If tax authorities are struggling with these tax issues, how will they deal with taxation via m-commerce? All indicators suggest that sales-tax revenue loss is projected to increase exponentially unless something is done to collect it.

INTERNET TAX FREEDOM ACT.   To date, the most important bill passed by the U.S. Congress regarding Internet taxation is the Internet Tax Freedom Act (ITFA), written into law on October 21, 1998. The act established the following.

- A three-year moratorium on special, multiple, or discriminatory taxes on the Internet that would be imposed by any state or local governments. Any goods or services sold over the Internet cannot be subject to new or special taxes that apply exclusively to Internet transactions.
- An advisory committee to explore different issues relating to Internet taxes, government Internet policy, and its effects on e-commerce.
- The federal government is barred from taxing the Internet or any transaction that takes place through it.

Despite all this, many issues remain unsolved. For example, what would be taxed? Who would set a tax rate? Who would collect any taxes from the Internet? Would the collected taxes end up being used by local governments to compensate for lost sales tax? Who would regulate the system, and how would such a regulatory agency do so? How will a tax affect the profitability of e-commerce? Would such a tax affect consumers' purchasing habits on the Internet?

In April 2000, the advisory commission sent a formal report to Congress and recommended a moratorium barring special or discriminatory Internet taxes for another five years (till 2006). The Internet Nondiscrimination Act of 2000, passed in May 2000 by the House of Representatives, extended the Internet tax moratorium set forth in the ITFA for five years. The commission also recommended permanently banning taxes charged on Internet access.

LEGAL DISPUTES ON THE INTERNET

In B2C, several kinds of disputes have legal implications.

1. The customer pays for the merchandise, but the e-merchant fails to deliver.
2. The customer pays in full but receives either the wrong merchandise or a partial order.
3. The customer does not like the product, but the e-merchant has no procedure for accepting returned merchandise.
4. The customer does not like the product, but the e-merchant refuses to accept returned merchandise or give a credit to settle the dispute.
5. The e-merchant delivers, but the customer does not admit that he or she ever received the merchandise.
6. The e-merchant delivers, but the customer refuses to pay. The customer's child ordered the product using a parent's VISA card without authorization.
7. The customer receives the merchandise, but it arrives damaged. The carrier denies responsibility, the e-merchant claims it is the carrier's responsibility, and the vendor is located overseas with no customer service number.
8. The customer receives the merchandise, but it does not operate properly. The e-merchant asks the customer to ship the product to the manufacturer at the customer's expense. The manufacturer has no in-house service center.

In terms of recourse, a lot depends on the laws protecting buyers in the state in which they reside. It also depends on where the e-merchant operates. Legal costs often exceed the value of the contested merchandise, which leaves the customer with no choice but to abandon the product. Where the Web server or the business is located determines the rights of the customer to recover. Unfortunately, it is not always clear where the server is located, especially when the e-merchant has multiple Web servers in different countries. What makes the situation more difficult is the fact that no legal restrictions apply regarding where the top-level domain (e.g., ".uk") can be used and where it cannot be used. About the only thing that counts is the country where the e-merchant is located. That location determines the jurisdiction on the Internet.

One legal issue that has surfaced relates to products that are available in one country but are restricted in the country from which the customer is ordering. For example,

Amazon.com was criticized by Germany's Simon Wiesenthal Center for selling books like *Mein Kampf,* which are banned in Germany. Although Amazon.com's German subsidiary does not offer these books on its Web site, the U.S. Web site does. If the product is confiscated in Germany, what recourse does the customer have to recover the product?

jurisdiction: the legitimate scope of government power.

This matter boils down to the legal issue of **jurisdiction,** or the legitimate scope of government power. A court must have jurisdiction over the litigants and the claims before it entertains a lawsuit.

In the context of Internet commerce, this issue erupts when a dispute arises between businesses from different states. For example, is a customer in Chicago required to travel to California to defend against a firm that is suing him for breaking a sales agreement? Except in criminal cases, state and federal laws limit a court's jurisdiction over a defendant from another state. This means that e-commerce and ensuring security and integrity in e-business are still clouded by such legal issues.

Related to the issue of jurisdiction at the international level, in a landmark decision for defamation law, Australia's high court in 2002 ruled that a Melbourne businessman can sue a U.S. publishing company (Dow-Jones & Co.) in Australia over an article published in the United States and distributed on the Internet. According to legal experts, the decision could have wide-ranging implications for how information is disseminated on the Internet.

The final legal dispute relates to bots. Are bots legal? A shopbot is a software package that roams the various Web sites, accesses information related to a specific product, and produces the location of the seller or store that will sell the product at the lowest price.

The legality of the practice depends on the way one looks at the process. On the one hand, a Web site should be open to all surfers—customers and competitors—like a general brick-and-mortar store. On the other hand, how much business is this practice taking away from the Web sites visited?

WEB LINKING AND DOMAIN NAME DISPUTES

hyperlink: text or image whose address can be linked to another Web page for reference.

The infrastructure of the Internet is designed around **hyperlinks**—text or image whose address can be linked to another Web page for reference. When you click on the link, it automatically goes to the attached location and the designated Web page. This jumping from one site to another raises legal issues that include the following points.

1. Referencing a linked site without permission from the site owner
2. Retrieving or downloading information from a linked site without referencing or permission
3. Unauthorized use of a company's registered trademarks
4. Adding a Web program to a company's Web site without permission

Inappropriately referencing a Web site is not a clear-cut issue; it depends on the intent of the referencing. For example, one bank's Web site advertised online automobile loans. When a visitor entered the amount she would like to borrow (in this case, it was $47,000 for a Mercedes), the Web site asked her to click on the referral button, giving the impression that her application would get special attention. She ended up on the Web site of a large bank in another state that specializes in jumbo auto loans. The visitor was unhappy about this runaround and promptly clicked away from both sites.

One New Jersey bank Web site had this note on its homepage: "Want to compute your mortgage rate on a house? Click here." The software package that did the mortgage calculation was registered to a Chicago bank. The networking algorithm detected unauthorized use of the package by the New Jersey bank Web site and promptly sued for damages. The case was settled out of court, and the New Jersey bank had to delete the referral to the mortgage calculator.

Domain name disputes have existed since business hit the Internet. In 1992, the U.S. government contracted with Network Solutions, Inc. (NSI), which also goes by the name InterNIC, to manage the top-level domains. Initially, domain names were assigned on a first-come, first-served basis, but this caused companies and individuals to register domain names for which they had no use and hold them for future sale at exorbitant prices. Since 1995, the policy has changed so that domain names are still issued on a first-come, first-served basis, but applicants are reminded in writing that such issuance does not duplicate or replace the legal right of another party, such as one with a registered trademark, to use the name.

The low-cost registration fee of $70 for two years of registration has caused several individuals to register and hold known names hostage for big money. One poacher registered for 200 domain names, including his former employer's, but he kept losing cases filed against him by firms defending their right to use their trademark name. The general rule to resolve domain name disputes is to compare the date the claimant of a dispute first used a trademark or the effective date of a validated trademark registration. If the registered holder appears to have infringed on the registered trademark owner, then NSI assigns the registered holder a new domain name. The court is the only other avenue for seeking relief.

Here are some guidelines regarding domain names and trademarks.

1. Find out whether the proposed domain name infringes on any trademarks. The fact that someone registers for a domain name does not in itself give the owner the legal right to use it.

2. Secure federal trademark registration of the proposed domain name. Once the name clears against possible claims of infringement, it should be registered as a trademark with the U.S. Patent and Trademark Office.

3. Register the proposed domain name with InterNIC (Internet Network Information Center), the agency that represents the U.S. government in assigning domain names.

4. In the event of a poached domain name, bring a lawsuit to force InterNIC to reassign the name to the original owner—the owner of the same name or trademark.

5. Get permission before linking to other Web sites.

ENCRYPTION LAWS

Encryption is not a pleasant word to use in certain countries. Some Middle Eastern countries, for example, prohibit any form of encryption for business or personal use within the country or across the border. Encryption poses a threat to the powers of many governments, but because of the impressive surge of traffic on the Internet, awareness of security has increased significantly within governments worldwide. In 1999, France abandoned its policy of disallowing encryption for message transmission.

Cryptography has had its share of attention over the past decade. Among the issues are these: What can be exported and what cannot be exported? How safe is the computer from Internet crime? In the United States, there tends to be a difference of opinion on encryption between federal agencies like the FBI and big business. Secure electronic payments require secure lines.

The belief is that encryption makes lines more secure. In 1997, the FBI made a strong pitch before a U.S. Senate panel on the need for stricter control over digital encryption products. Cases have already come up in which criminals and terrorists have relied on encryption to evade the law. The debate continues with no definitive end in sight. More on encryption is covered in Chapter 13.

ONLINE GAMBLING

One of the fastest growing online businesses is online gambling. The scope of this business is so enormous that some experts claim it is the single most important factor in the growth of e-commerce. The French online casinos have been in full swing for several years. The increase in high-speed Internet connections within France contributed to a surge in popularity of the online casino business. One country that bucks the trend is Spain. It has one of the lowest rates of online gambling in Europe despite the availability of high-speed Internet.

In the U.S., online gambling continues to be illegal. The Justice Department position is that advertising of Internet gambling is an illegal activity. Anyone promoting it could be charged with aiding and abetting. The law violated is the Interstate Telephone Act of 1964 and the federal Wire Wager Act of 1961.

The April 2005 launching of www.pokerRoom.com, however, highlights the fast growth of online gambling. The U.S market is the world's largest, yet the government remains adamantly against Web wagering. The irony is that the government has not shown the will to bust individual bettors. There is also the problem, for U.S regulators, of enforcing the prohibition because major Internet gambling sites work from sites outside the U.S. in countries where Internet gambling is legal—for example, Antigua. The resistance is fear of heavy social costs. If online gambling is allowed, there is the chance of a growing venue for problem gamblers to feed their addiction.

INTERNATIONAL ISSUES

With the Internet cutting across countries around the globe, a number of international questions have arisen recently regarding controls of Web site contents and e-commerce in general. Two major questions come up when reviewing the international scene: What right does any one country have to determine the materials that should be available on the Internet? Can a country regulate an entity in cyberspace, but not on the soil of that country?

To address these questions, let's take the issue between France and Yahoo!. Yahoo!'s legal counsel believes that because Yahoo! is a U.S. company, subject to regulation by the United States, it would violate domestic freedom of speech laws if the company were to block French users from accessing these materials. To extrapolate on Yahoo!'s position, it seems that if a French citizen could come to the United States to purchase contraband that is illegal in France, then that same citizen should be able to buy it over the Internet. Assuming that buying over the Internet is analogous to buying in person, it would be up to France to regulate which physical objects enter its borders. This idea would hold regardless of where the goods originated.

As predicted, the issue between France, Yahoo!, and the United States is not that simple. Yahoo! seems to be skipping the crucial second question—where the transaction takes place. Yahoo! is assuming that the transaction must be taking place in the United States—a position that is not necessarily the case. Yahoo! wants the United States to step in and apply its laws to protect the company from international regulation, but it does not attempt to determine where the electronic transaction takes place. Without this information, it is impossible to apply an appropriate law based on current trade agreements or treaties with France. Nothing applies until the jurisdiction is determined.

A similar problem faced the German high courts, but it was dealt with on a domestic level. Germany prohibits certain material from being viewed on the Internet and ruled that German ISPs were not to host any Web sites that published "restricted materials." Any German ISP that did not comply would be subject to prosecution. One can conclude that because no existing international laws apply to Internet commerce, legislation is best left up to individual countries and their ISPs.

Another important issue has to do with different laws in many countries. In an uncertain legal climate surrounding e-commerce, an online business often opts to let go of some customers in certain countries rather than be vulnerable to possible libel or product liabilities in those countries. Years of litigation have failed to establish international legal standards to protect the rights of sellers and buyers on the Internet and prevent unauthorized copying of software or digitized products. Many online merchants today refuse to sell beyond their immediate home countries.

Here is a summary of some of the major international rules—passed or pending—that relate to the Internet:

- The World Intellectual Property Organization (WIPO) succeeded in two treaties to adapt copyright rules for e-commerce. Not only do the treaties cover physical copies and broadcasting, but books, songs, and films distributed online as well. Forty-one countries also committed to outlawing cyber-piracy of CDs and DVDs and hacking into online music and film subscription services. The ratification went into effect in 2002. See wipo.int/treaties/ip/wct/index.html and wipo.int/treaties/ip/wppt/index.html.

- The European Union's Electronic Commerce Directive gave online business firms assurance in 2000 that they would have to comply with laws only where they are based, not in any other country in the Union.

- The Digital Millennium Copyright Act of 1998 adapted U.S. legislation to the WIPO treaties. See copyright.gov/legislation/dmca.pdf.

- The European Union's Rome II Directive hopes to allow consumers to sue e-businesses in their home country. Online business firms are concerned they will have to comply with 15 different laws on product liability and defamation.

- The Hague Convention on International Jurisdiction and Foreign Judgments in Civil and Commercial Matters is a draft treaty in 1992 designed to set global standards for defamation, copyright, and libel on the Internet. The idea is that if one wins a judgment in one country, it will be enforced in other countries.

ISSUES FOR DEVELOPING COUNTRIES

We spoke in Chapter 1 of the digital divide and how Internet access is available in some countries and not in others. Although the Internet is global, developing countries have yet to benefit equally from e-commerce, e-mail, and other services provided by the Internet. The sorely missing item is telecommunications and networking at affordable prices. A number of governments and intergovernmental organizations have taken steps to establish a global framework for electronic commerce. The high-priority areas are customs, taxation, and market access. The goal is to have governments avoid placing undue restrictions on electronic commerce in order to avoid competitive distortions.

The taxation of electronic commerce in virtual goods like information and services and physical goods is a complex issue. The position of the U.S is that no new taxes should be imposed on electronic commerce. Access to technology may be a main issue for the growth of e-commerce in developing countries. There are questions of investment, expertise, government policies, market access, and the like. A developing country that supports e-commerce and with a political climate conducive to investment is likely to attract foreign investment in areas related to information technology. As of this writing, developing countries have no say. Most of the fast-emerging technologies reside in the private-sector laboratories of North America, essentially in the U.S.

Any way one looks at it, the Internet is a product of the U.S. public sector (academia and defense). It was built on a single Internet protocol standard and is predominantly American in the number of sites, number of servers, and the resulting e-commerce transacted on them. It is also American in content, language, and culture, with no ownership for the traffic that runs on leased telecommunication lines nationwide and globally. Not only is this infrastructure capital intensive, but it is on the technological edge of emerging potential that requires a strong financial base. This is what developing countries do not have, which is an obvious handicap for adopting e-commerce.

INTELLECTUAL PROPERTY

The scientist Albert Einstein once said, "Imagination is more important than knowledge." Intellectual property is based on the power of imagination, which is a source of personal, cultural, and economic advancement. It has been the imagination of the world's creators that made it possible for humanity to advance to today's levels of technological marvels.

Intellectual property describes the ideas, inventions, technologies, music, and literature that are intangible when created and are converted into tangible products for market consumption. Intellectual property means "ownership." Ownership is important, because potential economic gain is an incentive to innovate.

Remember that the power of imagination applied to create products or solve practical problems is not the exclusive province of any nation, people, or race. Box 12.8 gives a short list of some of the inventions that changed the course of history.

Basically, some people do not respect the rights of others. The reasons vary from greed, ruthless criminal intent, or lack of awareness all the way to innocent mistake. The

BOX 12.8

Inventions That Changed the Course of History

Inventor	Country	Invention
Conrad Gesner	Switzerland	Pencil, around 1560
Samuel Morse	U.S.A.	Telegraph, 1840
Alfred Nobel	Sweden	Dynamite, 1863
Alexander Graham Bell	United Kingdom	Telephone, 1876
Orville and Wilbur Wright	U.S.A.	Airplane, 1903
Vladimir Zworykin	Russian Federation	Electronic TV, 1929
Gertrude Elion	U.S.A.	Immune system drug to fight cancer and AIDS, 1956
James Russel	U.S.A.	Compact disc, 1965

Source: Kamil Idris, *Intellectual Property: A Power Tool for Economic Growth*, World Intellectual Property Organization, 2003, Ch. 1.

scale of disrespect varies from copying a protected work in one's home to large-scale commercial criminal enterprises that produce hundreds of thousands of illegal copies. One case in point is this author's visit to a premiere Middle Eastern university to teach an e-commerce course, using this publication. The class enrolled 41 undergraduate students. The university bookstore ordered 45 copies. Only one copy was sold. Every other student came to class with a photocopy of the text (cover to cover) duplicated by a photo copier across the campus for a mere $6 a copy.

Typical affected products include computer software, music, luxury goods, sportswear, perfumes, toys, auto and aircraft components, and pharmaceuticals. Because of the high profit potential and low risk, organized criminal organizations are deeply involved in counterfeiting and piracy. Profits are then used to fund other criminal activities as well as the criminal enforcement infrastructure. This in turn, contaminates the banking industry through money laundering and the like.

The social and economic consequences can be devastating. Counterfeiting of medicine and airplane and auto parts has a tragic impact on the health and safety of the public and cheats creators and legal marketers of billions of dollars each year. Developing countries account for the largest portion of such sales. According to some estimates, up to 70 percent of all medicine sold in some African countries is counterfeit and produced ill effects, including death. Think of counterfeit paracetamol syrup that cost the lives of 109 children in Nigeria or the one million counterfeit birth control pills distributed to unsuspecting women that resulted in unwanted pregnancies and irregular bleeding. Providing such products via the Internet is not going to solve the problem.

IN RETROSPECT

No question, e-commerce has revolutionized the business world by expanding the market worldwide. Its economic influence has been considerable, resulting in political, legal, and social implications. While e-commerce is a global concept, political and social barriers continue to impede effective online transactions and potential for growth. One of the barriers is security. As inherently insecure the World Wide Web is, the Internet has enabled a new type of crime: Computer crime—a social ill. With that came money laundering, hijacking accounts, viruses, spam, spyware, adware, and pirating intellectual property.

The independence of the Internet makes accountability virtually impossible. What is socially and ethically acceptable in one country might be illegal in another. For example, Australia levies severe penalties on advertising cigarettes, while it is legal in countries like the United States. If a cigarette company uses the World Wide Web to advertise its cigarette products, it may reach an Australian audience without actually breaking any Australian laws.

Countries enforce their own laws regarding computer crimes, but these laws have no effect outside those countries. New laws should be established to combat online crimes like online gambling and money laundering via the Internet.

MANAGEMENT IMPLICATIONS

One conclusion from our discussion of legal and ethical issues is that the legal rules that define the Internet are yet to be clarified. The questions that constantly come up before various technical, academic, and government groups dealing with cyberspace are these: What rules should be instituted to govern the Internet? Who will make and enforce those rules? What shape should copyright protection take in the Web—a world of costless, instantaneous, and undetectable copying?

Communication networks are essentially defined by a set of rules—the network protocols that specify the characteristics of the messages to be transmitted, the medium through which they can travel, and how the messages are routed through the medium to their destination. Because the Internet is a set of relationships among networks, network protocols may be viewed as part of the "law of cyberspace."

Keep in mind that the Internet is not a physical object, but a set of protocols that has been adopted by a large number of networks to make the transfer of information among them possible. Physical location and physical boundaries are irrelevant, which means that the legal implications will continue to be a problem. Each country has to police its own portion of the Internet traffic and use its jurisdiction to enforce its laws.

Another area of concern is the long-range effect of Internet patents, especially those held by e-companies like Amazon.com that cover fundamental online business practices. Patents have become something that no company can comfortably ignore.

So far, e-commerce has forced companies to differentiate themselves on the basis of what is unique and unavailable to competitors—knowledge, business methods, and the skills to implement the methods. A company's competitive advantage no longer stems from its market position, but from difficult-to-duplicate intellectual assets and how it deploys them. Take the example of Dell Computer. Its success comes not so much from the technological superiority of its products (most of its computer components are off-the-shelf components), but from its build-to-order, direct sale approach. To protect this advantage, Dell secured 42 patents that cover its customer ordering system as well as its business methods.

Regardless of laws that might ensure integrity and protection for consumers and merchants, the ultimate goal in doing business on the Internet is to promote standards that everyone can accept or adopt. Those who do business on the Internet have a responsibility to monitor their employees' behavior and the traffic that their Web site generates to ensure a stable, lasting, and satisfactory relationship with clients, vendors, visitors, and distributors. Without such a commitment, the business could easily fail.

Finally, management must focus on legal and consumer protection issues surrounding B2C e-commerce. Ethics may be tangential to running a business, but lack of ethics could mean serious erosion of the company's customer base. That very problem sealed Value America's fate: It went bankrupt. In addition, ethics means different things in different countries. Companies need to develop a code of ethics tailored to each country or region in which they operate. Finally, the privacy issue continues to haunt the e-consumer. With Web sites amassing vast amounts of information about their visitors, pressure is mounting for new laws. As Congress considers the legal route, new software, designed to give consumers control over how much protection they want from the e-merchant, is appearing. The stakes are high. Information about consumer activities has become necessary for the survival of the e-merchant. Yet there is a consumer outcry about invasion of privacy.

Microsoft is working on a software package named Privacy for Protection Preferences (P3P) that lets consumers decide how much protection they want. When visitors look up a Web site, their Web browsers automatically load the P3P-encoded privacy policy and compare it with the visitor's preferences. If the site does not match, the browser blocks the transmission of personal information. As a result, the visitor may not have access to certain features offered by the e-merchant's Web site. On the surface, P3P functions only if the Web site makes its privacy policy "talk" in P3P's special language. It could be some time before either new laws or reliable software can address the sensitive issue of the consumer's right to privacy.

On the wireless end, the privacy of consumer location data is a key issue facing banks, airlines, and retailers as they send advertising to wireless users. The sanctity of location data is a business's responsibility, especially for wireless carriers. In the final analysis, consumers should be given an option to start services and to stop them.

Summary

1. Legal and ethical implications of the Internet are attracting attention in industries and governments around the world. Taxation and sales tax are hot issues. Legal disputes and case law are beginning to surface quickly.

2. The question of ethics in e-commerce is the current challenge confronting U.S. organizations. Ethics is fairness, justice, equity, honesty, trustworthiness, and equality. An unethical act is not the same as an immoral or an illegal act, although one may lead to or imply the other.

3. There are several threats to ethics: faster computers and advanced networks, massive distributed databases, ease of access to information, transparency of software, and the view that captured information can be used as a competitive weapon.

4. Privacy is a basic American value. To formalize what constitutes privacy, five widely recognized principles of privacy protection are worth remembering: notice, choice, access, security/integrity, and enforcement. There are three

categories of concern: collection of electronic data by businesses about consumers, security of electronic data transmission, and unauthorized reading of personal files.

5. Many of the legal questions that arise in e-commerce are not settled due to lack of specific laws or legal guidelines. Situations involving products that produce the wrong solution, causing injury to others, fall under laws of strict liability or negligence. The basis of liability involves product liability and tort law. If an e-merchant advertises false or wrong products or a customer gives an unauthorized credit card over the Internet, he or she is liable for fraud. Fraud, negligence, false advertising, and misrepresentation are bases for litigation.

6. Internet copyright and trademark violations fall under intellectual property law. Copyright law gives the author of a tangible product the right to exclude others from using the finished work.

7. The question of whether a Web site is a product or a service elicits varied opinions. If a Web site is a product, proving negligence is unnecessary to hold the developer liable. If a Web site is a service, the contract law of the state in question would apply.

8. On the Internet, tax collection is not easy, depending on the location of the e-merchant's business, the location of the buyer, the types of goods for sale, and so on. Those who support taxing Internet commerce include many state officials who are concerned that taxing online shopping could put online merchants at a disadvantage.

9. Regardless of the laws that might assure integrity and protection for consumers and merchants, the ultimate goal of doing business on the Internet is to promote ethics through standards that everyone can accept or adopt. Management must focus on legal and consumer protection issues surrounding B2C e-commerce.

Key Terms

- code of ethics (p. 370)
- copyright (p. 385)
- copyright law (p. 385)
- disclaimer (p. 383)
- ethics (p. 368)
- express warranty (p. 383)
- false advertising (p. 382)
- fraud (p. 382)
- hyperlink (p. 391)

- implied warranty (p. 383)
- intellectual property (p. 384)
- jurisdiction (p. 390)
- misrepresentation (p. 382)
- negligence (p. 382)
- nontrivial error (p. 383)
- out-of-bounds error (p. 383)
- product liability (p. 381)

- self-assessment (p. 375)
- strict liability (p. 381)
- tort (p. 381)
- tort law (p. 381)
- trademark (p. 385)
- Uniform Commercial Code (UCC) (p. 382)
- warranty (p. 382)

Test Your Understanding

1. Why are legal and ethical implications attracting attention around the world?
2. Give an example of an unethical act that is not necessarily illegal.
3. Elaborate on some of the ethical issues surrounding the Internet. What single issue do you consider the most important? Why?
4. How can a company improve the climate for ethical behavior on the job?
5. The FTC identified five principles of privacy protection. Explain each briefly.
6. What is tort law on the Internet? What makes it so unique?
7. How is fraud different from misrepresentation? Be specific.

8. Distinguish between trademarks and copyrights.
9. What exactly is intellectual property law? Give an example.
10. Is a Web site a product or a service? Justify your answer.
11. Briefly explain the Uniform Commercial Code.
12. Give examples of your own of disputes on the Internet that have legal implications.

Discussion Questions

1. Why do you think companies adopt a code of ethics? Do they apply what they advertise?
2. The Internal Revenue Service acquires demographic data about taxpaying citizens in an effort to elicit relationships to their tax returns. In your opinion, is this effort an unethical act? An illegal act? An immoral act? Discuss.
3. Shoppers at a national retail chain are asked for their Zip codes as part of the check-out process. This information is used to figure out the pattern of business coming from various regions in the community. As a result, the store decides on the prod-ucts, prices, specials, and so on to maximize sales volume. Shoppers are not told why Zip codes are solicited. Is the store's action ethical? How does it compare to the use of cookies in Web shopping?
4. E-commerce has generated much controversy regarding privacy. Why do you think this has happened?
5. Taxing Web shoppers has been a controversial subject for several years. Should Web shopping be taxed in the same way as brick-and-mortar shopping? Discuss this mat-ter using recent evidence.

Web Exercises

1. An ongoing debate is taking place regarding taxing e-shoppers. Look up informa-tion on the Internet about the Internet Tax Freedom Act. Learn about it and write a report arguing against it.
2. Review the Medical Board of California Web site (www.medbd.ca.gov), where California reports data about doctors, disciplinary actions by hospitals, court cases and judgments against doctors, and so on. Do you think the information invades doctors' right to privacy? What about the consumer? Do consumers have the right to learn about doctors' records before they commit their bodies for diagnosis, surgery, and so on?
3. Evaluate five Web sites of your choice. Review their respective privacy policies. What did you find common in all policies? What was unique in each policy? What important clauses were missing, if any?
4. Go to the Federal Trade Commission Web site (www.ftc.gov) or other Web sites and investigate types of scams on the Internet. Present your findings in class.
5. Visit the Cyberlaw Web site (www.cyberlaw.com) and learn about what you can and cannot represent on your Web site before you break the copyright law. Report your findings in class.
6. Go the Zelerate Web site (www.consumers.com). What services does this site offer? Write a two-page report.
7. Look up a Web site that explains how to prevent unsolicited e-mail. Summarize your findings for the class.

8. Zoro, Inc. is a new entrant to the e-commerce market, with an existing store in Pittsburgh. The company is known for delivering custom-designed sportswear over the Internet, which has allowed it to establish a niche in the market with a unique product that is the envy of the competition. The sales manager was looking for a way to access customers quickly so the company can sell the custom-designed concept and build a reliable customer base. He learned about a new startup company with a similar market base. He convinced the CEO to purchase the customer database of the new firm; the price amounts to 75 percent of Zoro's annual advertising budget.

   The newly purchased list generated a 10 percent increase in new customers in the first week. But the flood of complaints starting coming from people wanting to be taken off the list and wanting to know how they got on the list in the first place. When Zoro contacted the company it purchased the customer database from, it learned that the company went bankrupt and all its assets had been sold. When the customer database was sampled for reliability, it was found that none of the customers on the list ever gave permission to have their personal information used for marketing or sales purposes. The customer database was essentially gathered through an illegal tracking mechanism with no trace for prosecution.

   a. Should Zoro continue to use the list, especially when it is experiencing a strong surge in the number of custom-designed orders?
   b. Is Zoro ethically responsible for continued use of the customer database, knowing that the defunct company had in fact defrauded it? Explain.
   c. Would you say this is a case of losing privacy? Security? Fraud? Criminal act?

CHAPTER 13

E-SECURITY AND THE USA PATRIOT ACT

Learning Objectives

The focus of this chapter is on several learning objectives:

- What is involved in designing for security
- The many faces of viruses and other contaminants on the Internet
- How to build a secure system and recover from disaster
- How biometrics contributes to security
- The makeup of the USA Patriot Act and its contribution to security via the Internet

IN A NUTSHELL

There is no question e-commerce is here to stay. The most critical phase of e-transactions is ensuring the security of e-payments and the privacy of the information that executes the payment process. Transaction contents can be read, modified, or made up by anyone with sufficient experience or tenacity. Because of spyware, adware, viruses, worms, and other malicious threats, today's increasing focus is on security and privacy in cyberspace.

Call it the e-commerce paradox: E-commerce firms must be open to sharing information with customers and vendors, but closed to hackers and intruders. Creating a security culture and procedure that straddles this fine line can make the difference between success and failure. When it comes to e-commerce integrity, security is the bottom line for everything a business must accomplish.

Internet security is not about protecting hardware or the physical environment. It is about protecting information. The risks inherent in e-commerce can be harnessed only through appropriate security measures and business and legal procedures that ensure the integrity and reliability of Internet transactions. Solving the security problem makes the Web storefront a reality.

The field of electronic security focuses on designing measures that can enforce security policies, especially when a malicious attack occurs. Security in e-commerce generally employs procedures such as authentication, ensuring confidentiality, and the use of cryptography to communicate over open systems. In this chapter, our focus is on electronic security, security design, server security issues and procedures, and how to achieve application security. The name of the game is security—security management, security update, and security maintenance. Without a regular program that monitors the status and integrity of the security of a Web site, unanticipated problems can occur. (Encryption, which is part of security, is covered in Chapter 14.)

Built by academics when everyone who accessed the Internet was assumed to be a "good guy," today's Internet is infected with all kinds of security threats, buckling under the weight of over a billion users worldwide. When you consider this chapter's coverage of hackers, spammers, spyware, phishing, and identity theft, it seems futile to trust the "highway" that once carried your e-mail messages with security and ease. The many layers of security, from firewalls to anti-spyware software, eat up computer performance cycles and are quickly bringing the Internet to a virtual halt.

SECURITY IN CYBERSPACE

The electronic system that supports e-commerce is susceptible to abuse and failure in many ways.

- Fraud, resulting in direct financial loss. Funds might be transferred from one account to another, or financial records might simply be destroyed.

- Theft of confidential, proprietary, technological, or marketing information belonging to the firm or to the customer. An intruder may disclose such information to a third party, resulting in damage to a key customer, a client, or the firm itself.

- Disruption of service, resulting in major losses to the business or inconvenience to the customer.

- Loss of customer confidence stemming from illegal intrusions into customer files or company business, dishonesty, human mistakes, or network failures.

Although e-commerce is surging by leaps and bounds, a variety of hurdles remain to the widespread acceptance of the technology and the entire process of shopping on the Internet. The recent growth of the Internet has focused worldwide attention on the growing problem of privacy, security, and the potential for fraud and deception unless security standards are implemented properly. For all parties to trade electronically, a way of verifying identities and establishing trust must be created.

Someone once said, "Network security is the most important thing on the planet," yet the first time it hinders performance, security is relaxed. The massive volume of traffic on the Internet and the staggering amount of personal, commercial, governmental, and military information in the networking infrastructures worldwide pose monumental risks. The missing step in most cases is a plan that considers the security of the network as a whole.

WHY THE INTERNET IS DIFFERENT

In traditional ways of doing business, merchants expect to be paid with real money. When they accept credit, they require personal signatures on credit forms. When they lock up at the end of the day, the alarm is set or the guards take over for the night, and the police come in case of a break-in.

Practical and legal differences exist between traditional store- and paper-based commerce and computer-based commerce. Signed documents have inherent security attributes that are lacking in computer-based files. Table 13.1 summarizes the differences. Some of the security attributes include the ink embedded in the paper fiber, the biometrics of signatures (pressure, slant, shape, and so on), unique letterhead, changes or deletions in the document, and the like. Computer-based messages are represented by a string of bits that reside in computer memory, using measured fractional volts that distinguish between zeros and ones. Computer-based records can be modified quickly and without detection. Sometimes all it takes to corrupt a record is a few simple keystrokes. One of the problems of security engineering is that subverted systems often function normally.

Unlike the traditional 10:00 A.M. to 6:00 P.M. store hours, an online store is open 24 hours a day, 7 days a week. It is unattended, except for the technology that performs the shopping and payment processes and the voice of customer service on an 800 number.

Remember, we're allowing anyone, anywhere, anytime to use these connected computers as long as they have the password that gives them access to the public network. As mentioned earlier, the Internet is the largest interconnected data network infrastructure in the world, with no central control and, therefore, not much security. Because of this and the lack of standards, the Internet gives thieves and hackers the opportunity to cause all kinds of problems.

Without good security, computer fraud is virtually untraceable. To make things worse, communications over the Internet seem impersonal and distant. Some people with little knowledge crank up enough courage to defraud a merchant, deface a Web site, or corrupt a database—feats they would not think of trying if they were dealing with a merchant face to face in a local store. The lack of laws punishing the intruder or protecting the innocent makes things worse. The legal system relies on physical evidence such as a canceled check, a person's original signature, place

---

TABLE 13.1   Paper-based versus electronic commerce attributes

Paper-Based Commerce	*Electronic Commerce*
Signed paper documents	Digital signature
Person to person	Electronic via Web site
Physical payment system	Electronic payment system
Merchant and customer are face to face	No face-to-face contact
Easy detectability of modifications	Detectability is difficult
Easy negotiability of documents	Negotiable documents require special security protocol

of residence, and similar details to determine whether the plaintiff has a case. What on the Internet substitutes for such evidence? Digital signatures identify the individual (signature) in the same way that DNA identifies the missing person at the crime scene.

CONCEPTUALIZING SECURITY

Any way we look at security, it means addressing risk and protection from the unknown. Risk is a matter of degree. For example, banks require greater security than stores because of the risk of losing millions of dollars in nontraceable cash. The biggest risk in e-commerce is fraudulent credit card usage and the mishandling of personal e-mail information. Security concerns are about network and transaction security. Lack of transaction security has made many customers leery of making payments over the Internet. Network security means that lines and networks are protected from the threat of unauthorized third-party access to data and information.

The first issue in security is identifying the principals. They are people, processes, machines, and keys that transact (send, receive, access, update, delete) information via databases, computers, and networks. Security concerns generally involve the following issues.

- Confidentiality: Knowing who can read data and ensuring that information in the network remains private. This is done via encryption. (See Chapter 14.)

- Authentication: Making sure that message senders or principals are who they say they are.

- Integrity: Making sure that information is not accidentally or maliciously altered or corrupted in transit.

- Access control: Restricting the use of a resource to authorized principals.

- Nonrepudiation: Ensuring that principals cannot deny that they sent the message.

- Firewalls: A filter between corporate networks and the Internet to secure corporate information and files from intruders, but that allows access to authorized principals.

E-commerce began with electronic data interchange (EDI) in the early 1980s, when banks and businesses electronically transferred funds and made payments to one another. It was interbusiness trading in many industries—manufacturing, retailing, automotive, and government—and security was an add-on expense. The network was a controlled digital infrastructure. With the advent of business-to-consumer e-commerce and the Internet in the 1990s, information security became paramount. Several factors are driving this change: global trading far beyond the scope of EDI, which was confined to U.S. industries, and online, real-time trading. With trading partners around the world, the reasons are obvious for exercising prudence through effective security measures to keep businesses out of foreign courts. Online, real-time trading means a limited amount of time for consumer and merchant to investigate each other. To delay online transactions, as was the case with delayed EDI business, defeats the whole purpose of real-time business. The availability of reliable security packages leaves no excuse for not ensuring information security in e-commerce, regardless of the size and type of business. This is especially true in transacting e-payments.

Changes in attitudes toward security have opened the door to serious considera-tion of security technology. In e-commerce, security can make or break a business; it already has become a strategic asset. It is the best way to protect information flow, ensure integrity, and reinforce customer confidence.

The time has come to get serious about secure electronic commerce. The technical part involves the use of cryptography and digital signatures to ensure the reliability of transactions over insecure networks.

THE PRIVACY FACTOR

Can you imagine being followed in a shopping mall by a survey taker trying to record every store you visited, the products you bought, or the conversation you carried on? From cell phones to ATM withdrawals and credit card use, the everyday activities of most Americans are monitored and documented for a variety of questionable uses and without authorization. After a while, the right to be left alone addresses issues related to privacy, confidentiality, and freedom from abuse.

The lack of **privacy** has been more of a problem with the Internet than it has with any other medium invented to date. Incredible amounts of infor-mation are collected and stored every day, and no one knows what is done with it. It is getting to the point where in 10 years, the aver-age person will be unable to run for public office unless he's been living in a monastery. Today, an array of sophisticated new tools is beginning to make a difference. Biometrics is covered in detail later in the chapter. (See Box 13.1.)

privacy: the ability to control who may see certain information and on what terms.

Every time the issue of security surfaces, privacy is involved. A secure Web site implies a site that ensures the privacy and confidentiality of the visitor's transactions. This means a Web site should post the vendor's privacy policy for the consumer to evaluate.

Most people's fears with respect to the sharing of personal information in buying online can be handled through education. Companies should review the information by-products that result from a product purchase, observe good information-handling practices, and disclose privacy policies to give customers a reason to trust them.

In the absence of regulatory protection, experts urge privacy-sensitive surfers to take basic steps to protect their privacy while online.

- Send anonymous e-mail through remailers, which reduces the chance of the e-mail being read by hackers who might be monitoring Web traffic from sites like Microsoft's Hotmail. An example of a remailer is www.gilc.org/speech/anonymous/remailer.html. Through such a site, the message bounces through a number of computers that forward it on, making it virtually untraceable.

- Improve security through your Web browser. One feature is to deactivate or block cookies. You also can set it to alert you when a site is trying to embed a cookie on your machine. The downside is that you might have difficulty visiting popular sites that require installing cookies on your PC.

- Use a secondary free e-mail service like Microsoft's Hotmail to prevent your main e-mail account (personal or business) from receiving spam.

BOX 13.1

Biometric Passports Set to Take Flight

The State Department's Office of Passport Policy, Planning, and Advisory Services recently announced that it is ready to begin issuing biometric passports. These passports feature an RFID chip to bring about more secure entry into and exit from the United States. RFID stands for radio frequency identification chip equipped with miniature antennae. It stores data for transmission to nearby receivers. Critics say the technology puts your personal privacy at stake. The agency plans to issue the first passport carrying an RFID chip by mid-2005.

The chip includes all the personal data found on the information page of today's passports. It also contains a biometric component—a digital facial image. The RFID chip will contain a chip identification number and a digital signature (a series of numbers assigned to the chip when the passport is issued). The two numbers will be stored in a central government database along with the personal information contained on the information page.

Under the new system you'll have one year from when your information changes to apply for a new passport free of charge. That is the key, as the price of passports will go up to cover the cost of the new technology. Congress has authorized a $12 surcharge to all new passports, which brings the cost of new 10-year passports from $85 to $97.

One of the primary concerns with using RFID chips in the new passports is that the chips can be read from a distance. It means someone with the proper equipment could access the data on your passport if they are physically close enough. How close is in question. The State Department will require all chip readers to be electronically shielded so that electronic signals sending and receiving information will not be transmitted beyond the reader. Each passport will contain an anti-skimming feature designed to prevent identity thieves from activating and reading the chip from a distance.

Source: Excerpted from Erin Biba, "Biometric Passports Set to Take Flight." *Technology—PC World,* March 21, 2005.

- Stay away from filling out any form or questionnaire online. This is especially the case when the form is asking for personal information such as address, age, annual income, and so on. Investigate the site and see how much you trust them with such information.

- Consider using privacy software to give your files or PC contents some privacy. For example, Anonymizer@anonuymous.com offers a pay service that encrypts the content and address of the Web sites you visit to shield you from employers and other prying eyes. Software called Window Washer (www.webroot.com) washes off (erases) all files, cookies, temporary Internet files, and other garbage that might have resided on your hard disk. A special feature of the software, called "bleach," goes over the erased material repeatedly to "bleach" your disk clean, depending on the number of times you set the feature.

- Install a firewall program to protect your computer from hackers. It can filter specific information leaving your computer or information coming into your computer. One example of a firewall is Internet Security Systems Inc. The software sells for about $40.

E-companies that take privacy seriously hire a full-time chief privacy officer as a first line of defense. Such a person would be expected to have a fundamental commitment to morality. A privacy officer looks at privacy as a human right that involves the global information infrastructure for most international firms. Once a chief privacy officer is aboard, that person's job includes a number of functions, from setting up a privacy committee to conducting privacy reviews of all products and services regularly and consistently.

In addition to addressing the privacy factor, such an officer could also be in charge of the growing problem of security breaches of the company's trade secrets and yet-to-be released products. He or she can in fact be in charge of the hackers, spammers, and any "espionage" that threatens the privacy and security of the firm. See Box 13.2.

THE WOES OF THE "OLE" PASSWORD

The password has been used for decades to protect files from unauthorized use. Password security is an essential form of user authentication on the Internet and anywhere within the organization. Unfortunately, with today's hackers and technocrats, the system of user name and password works less and less. A South Korean security analyst used a stolen password from a rival to make a $22 million illegal trade; a Kinko's facility was found to have keystroke-capture software that sent over 450 user names and passwords to a thief who later used them for bank fraud.

BOX 13.2

Here Comes the Espionage Officer

SSF Imported Auto Parts works out of a nondescript building just off the main retail drag in South San Francisco, California. In a space half the size of a football field sit rows of metal shelves filled with brake discs, alternators, water pumps, and other components for Audi, Mercedes-Benz, Porsche, Saab, and Volvo cars. Workers in blue shirts move briskly about picking and packing parts for delivery overnight to repair shops and dealerships around the country.

SSF's computer systems were repeatedly broken into over seven months starting in early 2001. An FBI agent who investigated the incident said he believed large portions of SSF's electronic catalog of 20,000 car parts were copied, so rivals could build a better catalog. The culprits? The chief technology officer, chief executive officer, and a computer consultant for a rival. The trio became criminals when they accessed SSF's computers without authorization and illegally trafficked in SSF computer passwords.

This is one of the most flagrant violations of trust when the people you trust to defend your networks turn around and execute something that could put your organization at such significant liability. Not only are corporate technologists usually well-versed in the latest electronic intrusion tools and hacking techniques, but they also know where to look for valuable information once they have gained access to a system. The danger becomes more apparent in a country where the main value-added component of operations is ideas about how to design, create, and market products that actually get built elsewhere.

Source: Excerpted from John McCormick and Deborah Gage, "Wanted: Chief Espionage Officer." *Baseline,* December 2004, 33–35.

It is becoming obvious that if a hacker gains access to a poorly defended file server and those passwords are stolen, they can in turn be used to gain access to a more secure corporate system. The so-called domino effect results, with no end to the ever-escalating threat to company's information infrastructure.

So what alternative schemes are available to ensure security, privacy, and integrity of data and files in e-commerce? One alternative is to resort to public-key encryption (PKE), where the user is authenticated by the private key to encrypt a message to the server. The private key is stored on a client computer or smart card, eliminating the need for the user to memorize the code. The server verifies the code by decrypting certain information sent by the client (versus comparing to a password file), eliminating any storage of passwords on the server side. A separate chapter on encryption follows this chapter.

Another alternative to passwords is biometrics, which represents data about the user's physiology (scanning an eye, fingertip, face, patterns in voices, handwriting, or motions, etc.) while signing a document. This form can be seen as another form of password, generated by the interaction of the user and a scanning device. While convenient, the pattern is vulnerable to network analyzers. It cannot be changed once stolen or lost. This limits the use of biometrics to situations where network and biometric capture devices are secure.

This new class of fingerprint security system is relatively inexpensive and can protect your top-secret electronic files by recording your fingerprint on a small sensor attached by a USB line to your computer. Anyone trying to open the files must place a finger on the sensor. In the least, it can reduce the incentive for hackers to break into corporate networks, because it is a lot harder to steal a finger than a password.

A third alternative is via smart cards that can store a password to perform complex encryption on the card. Better than that is a new scheme, "two-factor solutions," which combine a pass phrase with a keychain token that continually generates unique passwords used only once per transaction or log-in to a network. In this scheme, the user enters a secret PIN and presses a button on the token to generate a unique one-time password. He or she then enters that password into the PC. Subsequent log-ins require generating new passwords (Fisher 2004).

One can see that there is no silver bullet solution to user authentication. There are ideas, however, to improve security systems:

- Limit the number of times a password can be repeated in accessing a sensitive system.
- Train employees, customers, and the general public in more advanced methods like biometrics, PKE, and smart cards and be prepared to use such technology when it becomes available.
- Ensure that systems designers and systems analysts are well versed in security issues and security procedures as part of every future application.
- Review and evaluate the strength of the current password schemes used by customers and employees alike.

IDENTITY THEFT AND PHEAR OF PHISHING

As mentioned in an earlier chapter, identity theft has become a real nuisance. It is a crime and, like a disease that goes into remission, it flares up again and again when least expected.

An example of attempted identity theft might be something like an e-mail this author received in October 2005:

> *JP Morgan Chase is constantly working to ensure security by regularly screening the accounts in our system. We recently reviewed your account, and we need more information to help us provide you with secure service. Until we can collect this information, your access to sensitive account features will be limited. We would like to restore your access as soon as possible, and we apologize for the inconvenience. Your case ID is PCUI-410-320-3334. Please confirm your identity here: [hyperlink] Restore My Online Banking and complete the "Steps to Remove Limitations." Completing all of the checklist items will automatically restore your account access.*

This author has never had dealings with the alleged bank directly or indirectly. An unsuccessful attempt was made to verify the information with the bank.

As described in Box 13.3, ID theft has already become a societal and governmental concern. For years, the traditional cause of ID theft has been thieves rifling mailboxes, snatching purses or diving into trashcans for discarded bank statements or credit card receipts. More recently, ID theft has gone electronic. We have seen the onslaught of phishing—sending bogus e-mails that mimic those of legitimate businesses, asking for lost or outdated personal information. It is no longer losing IDs one by one; that is too slow for today's identity thieves. Criminals are getting hold of a massive amount of consumers' personal information at an estimated annual cost of $53 billion. ID theft covers five major areas: credit card fraud, phone or utilities fraud, bank fraud, employment-related fraud, government documents/benefits fraud, and loan fraud (Levy & Stone 2005).

BOX 13.3

ID-Theft Victims Fight for Years to Fix Mess

Since falling victim to identity theft four years ago, John Harrison has been having nightmares. The man who misused his personal information not only obtained credit using Harrison's name, he also opened checking accounts and wrote more than 125 bad checks as Harrison, some of them on government installations.

Recent disclosures by consumer-data collection companies including ChoicePoint and LexisNexis as well as Bank of America that sensitive information about millions of consumers was compromised have fueled concerns that many more people could be victimized like Harrison.

In January, for example, a Springfield, Ill., police officer made a routine traffic stop of a 79-year-old woman, an identity-theft victim. The officer ran the motorist's name through the state's criminal database, which turned up a warrant for writing bad checks. It was the identity thief, however, who wrote the checks. The poor old lady was hauled off to the police station, even though the identity theft took place in 1996 and she had reported it to state law-enforcement officials.

You really don't have any control over what these other people do or don't do. With ID theft, you are not bleeding . . . you haven't lost an arm or a leg. It is real difficult for people to see your loss or your damage.

Source: Excerpted from Frank James, "ID-Theft Victims Fight for Years to Fix Mess." *Chicago Tribune Online Edition,* March 20, 2005.

Viruses and worms carrying Trojan horse code are powering massive ID theft rings. At sites like www.mega-oem.biz and www.atlantictrustbank.com, users are presented with a chance to buy popular software at attractive discounts. What the sites will do is steal your ID and make it available to the highest bidder. ID theft and spyware are beginning to get the attention of government regulators, and various actions and lawsuits are currently under way to combat the threat to citizens' privacy. For example, based on an October 2005 report, the Federal Trade Commission is working to shut down Odysseus Marketing, which is allegedly downloading spyware onto Internet users' computers. Final action in the case is still pending.

Today's thieves are using wireless devices to impersonate legitimate Internet access points with the intent to steal credit card numbers and other privileged information. The unfortunate thing is that anyone equipped with a wireless laptop and software widely available on the Internet can broadcast a radio signal and intrude onto the data on the hard disk by remote. They view the information sought within several hundred feet of the hot spot.

The recent surge in the so-called "evil-twin" attacks parallels phishing scams—fraudulent e-mail messages that mimic those sent by banks and credit services. They trick customers into divulging personal information (like the example mentioned earlier in the chapter). Wi-Fi—the standard of wireless communications—sends Web pages via radio waves. Hot spots are areas within the range of a Wi-Fi antenna. Even though it is a bit slow in sprouting, phishing has alerted business systems that are heavily dependent on wireless communications.

- Phishing is a relatively recent phenomenon, having appeared within the past two years. It is becoming an effective tool with online criminals. The Gramm-Leach-Bliley Act requires all financial institutions to protect nonpublic personal information through security controls and restriction on access to data.
- The VISA USA Cardholder Information Security Program requires that personal information related to the cardholder be encrypted in the company database.
- The Sarbanes-Oxley Act requires executives and auditors to vouch for the effectiveness of internal controls over financial reporting (Newman 2004).

Online thieves are luring an increasing number of Internet banking customers to fake Web sites to fleece them of their personal bank account information. In 2003 alone, over 1.9 million people reported their checking accounts were breached, accounting for $2.4 billion in fraud. Over 57 million people received phishing e-mail during the same time. The problem is that banks are not reporting all attacks because of fear of undermining consumer confidence in online banking (Glanz 2004).

Phishing has several characteristics:

- Trojan horses are installed on vulnerable machines to gather data.
- They "harvest" user names and passwords to distribute to attackers.
- Users' PCs are compromised without their knowledge.
- Software vulnerabilities force PCs to download code.

What is more alarming is the recent finding that criminals are cooperating with crackers and virus writers to swap ideas and illicit schemes. The joint schemes are smart and well polished. They even collaborate by sharing codes. Users who click on a fraudulent site are rerouted across other sites that load Trojan horses onto the user's PC (Fisher 2004). They also prompt you to give your user names and passwords. In doing so, thieves bring in quite a haul.

What should you do when your ID is electronically stolen? At the top end, there are companies (e.g., Gavin de Becker & Associates of California) and private investigators that will track down records and fix ID theft. There are Web sites such as www.privacyrights.org that offer fact sheets on how to protect your privacy. A third alternative is to carry insurance. For example, in 2004, Allstate Corporation began offering ID theft insurance in Texas and a few other states as a $30 rider on homeowner policies. Through an affiliate risk-consulting company, all paperwork and legwork is included under the policy.

Victims of ID theft have been known to find no quick fix to clearing their names. In a nationwide survey of 1097 ID theft victims released in July 2005, nearly one third said they have been unable to repair their wrecked credit or restore their identities to good standing a year after their personal information was stolen. Most victims spent an average of 81 hours trying to resolve their cases (Swartz 2005, IB). The survey's findings underscore the financial toll and nuisance of ID theft. The typical victim is in his/her 40s, white, married, college educated, with an average income between $50,000 and $75,000.

Here are some basic guidelines for protecting yourself from identity theft:

- Protect your social security number by supplying it when absolutely necessary.
- Check your credit reports at least once a year. Check your statements for unexplained charges or unusual withdrawals from your bank accounts.
- Be careful whom you talk to on the telephone—telemarketers, ISP employees, or even members of government agencies could all be disguised criminals.
- Use shredders to get rid of your statements or receipts. When using ATMs, never leave your receipts behind.
- If you carry a laptop around, use "strong" passwords (combination of upper and lowercase characters, symbols, numbers, etc.). Don't use the last four digits of your social security number, birthdate, or your mother's maiden name.
- Remove your mail from your mailbox promptly, especially while on vacation. Thieves could make a habit of following the mail carrier for rifling through your mail.
- Place a fraud alert on your credit reports by calling Equifax (888-766-0008) or Experian (888-EXPERIAN).

File a report with local police if any of your personal information is stolen or lost. Keep a copy for dealing with creditors later.

DESIGNING FOR SECURITY

Hacking, netspionage, cracking, viruses, global worms, employees with malicious intent, cyberterrorism, internal theft—these are just some of the security challenges today's organizations face. Hackers and malicious code writers are automating the

Internet shell game that ensures they stay one step ahead of the laws and security officers. See Box 13.4. While various attempts have been made to "cut and paste" security, attempts to secure data based on a plan have failed miserably. Technology without strategy can actually leave the organization more vulnerable.

For information security design, the key question is: How do you know that the design will be secure? The answer lies in an effective design that should be part of the business-to-consumer installation from the beginning. Adding security mechanisms as an afterthought can be costly and ineffective. The design process begins with a chief security officer and involves five major steps: (1) assessing the security needs of the firm, (2) establishing a good policy, (3) fulfilling Web security needs, (4) structuring the security environment, and (5) monitoring the system. (See Figure 13.1.)

ASSESS SECURITY NEEDS

A chief security officer is in charge of overseeing the entire security setup for the firm. He or she should be well versed in the technology as well as the nature of the business. The person must also be able to pinpoint which security breaches threaten the company's business and how well the company is in compliance with various laws and regulations.

Common sense tells us it is prudent to look for security vulnerability before it is too late. The cheapest and most effective way to fix problems is while they are in

---

BOX 13.4

The Kuwaiti Hacker Group

On March 8, 2004, a Russian source reported to F-Secure analysts the existence of a Trojan horse created by Q8See called Slacke. But what made Slacke unique was the extraordinary lengths to which its authors went to hide their tracks and the mystery that remains about the group's intent.

First, the work downloaded code from a Web site hosted in São Tomé and Príncipe, a small island nation located off the Atlantic coast of Africa. Analysis by F-Secure, however, showed that the domain rights for the Web site had been sold to a company in Sweden. But registration information listed the company name as JordanChat and the location as Irbid, Jordan. The contact name was TeR0r.

As thousands of infected computers downloaded the malicious code from the Web server

in São Tomé and Príncipe, they were then linked to an Internet Relay Chat system operated by CNN in Atlanta. Once logged into CNN's IRC server, the systems connected to an IRC channel in Mexico called Noticias. And when Hypponen and his analysts studied the channel, they were astonished at what they saw. There were 20,000 clients just sitting on the channel doing nothing. They looked like people, but they were bots—programs that perform repetitive, automated functions.

According to Hypponen, three Kuwaiti users, presumably members of Q8See, were sitting on the channel and sending commands to the bots to scan various ranges of IP addresses. And while CNN eventually shut down the chat server, nobody knows for sure what the hackers were doing.

Source: Excerpted from Dan Verton, "Organized Crime Invades Cyberspace." *Computerworld,* August 30, 2004, 19ff.

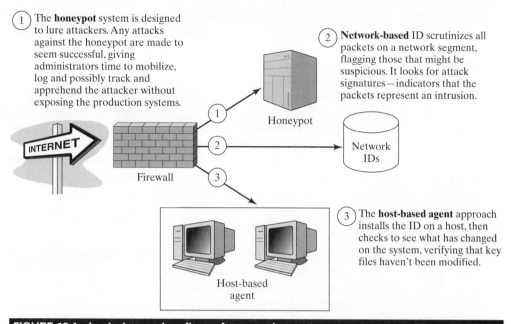

① The **honeypot** system is designed to lure attackers. Any attacks against the honeypot are made to seem successful, giving administrators time to mobilize, log and possibly track and apprehend the attacker without exposing the production systems.

② **Network-based** ID scrutinizes all packets on a network segment, flagging those that might be suspicious. It looks for attack signatures—indicators that the packets represent an intrusion.

③ The **host-based agent** approach installs the ID on a host, then checks to see what has changed on the system, verifying that key files haven't been modified.

FIGURE 13.1   Logical procedure flow—An example

development. As shown in Figure 13.2, a system assessment life cycle begins with the development of a new system using security best practices. Then the system should be tested to detect unforeseen security flaws before it is released for implementation. Finally, a running system should be monitored and maintained at all times.

ADOPT A SECURITY POLICY THAT MAKES SENSE

One of the serious mistakes companies make when it comes to security is failing to establish good security policies and ensure that they are followed. Policies should cover the threats that attack confidentiality, integrity, and privacy. Unfortunately, policies are easier to write than to enforce. The worst thing to do is just to replace the

FIGURE 13.2   The security assessment life cycle

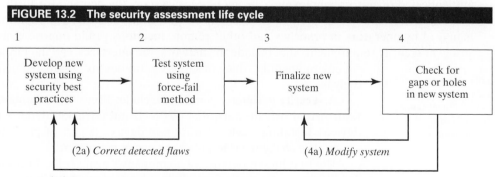

Source: Adapted from Timothy Dycke, "A Vulnerability Scan Plan," *eWeek LABS,* May 20, 2002, 43.

components or procedures that need to be replaced—enough to keep the company security intact. For example, replacing a router because of upgraded technology does not do much good, unless one reviews the volume of traffic or incidents of unauthorized access. The entire e-commerce infrastructure should be reevaluated and proper security software upgraded with long-term goals in mind.

Security policies should cover the entire e-commerce system including the merchant's local area networks, hardware, software, firewalls, protocols, standards, databases, and the staff directly involved in the e-commerce process. The policies should spell out Internet security practices, the nature and level of risks, the level of protection, and the procedure to follow to react to threats and recover from failure. Above all, policies must have the blessing of top management if they are to have a chance of succeeding.

CONSIDER WEB SECURITY NEEDS

The second design consideration is for the company to list top vulnerabilities and take a close look at critical applications to decide risk levels. The amount of security a Web merchant needs depends on the sensitivity of its data and the demand for it. For example, if your site collects credit card numbers for access, you'd want the highest security possible for the Web server, the network, and the Web site. You would want to consult with your Web administrator or an outside security consultant to see what options are available and how to put them to good use.

DESIGN THE SECURITY ENVIRONMENT

The design begins with sketching out the stepping-stones—the sequence and parameters in the security network based on the security policy and requirements of the e-commerce system. Physical security design looks at PCs, local area networks, operating systems, firewalls, security protocols, other networks, physical location and layout, bandwidth, security protocols of the ISP, and the cables that connect the merchant to the Internet Service Provider. See Box 13.5.

How much security goes into a system depends on how much risk the company is willing to take, the security policy it is willing to adopt, and the present state of security practices in the workplace. For example, if an e-application is run by certified and authenticated operators, employing a strong physical system, the demand for further authentication and access control should not be that high. The same application managed by operators in branches and other remote locations would impose more stringent security requirements that include the network, the interfaces, and the physical environment in which business operations are conducted on a daily basis.

security perimeter: security boundary that includes firewalls, authentication, VPNs, and intrusion detection devices.

A **security perimeter** generally includes firewalls, authentication, virtual private networks (VPNs), and intrusion detection devices. Installing such software and devices is part of physical design. The challenge is to police the entire perimeter.

firewall: a system that enforces an access control policy between two networks.

The first line of defense of a company's e-site is the **firewall.** Traditionally, firewalls included a host of applications and services such as file transfer protocol (FTP) support. Today's

---

BOX 13.5

Trusted Operating Systems

The National Security Agency's SELinux, which makes Linux into a trusted operating system, is particularly good for systems hosting Web-facing services that must be exposed to potential attacks over the Internet to serve their functions. This trusted software demonstrates how mandatory access controls could be integrated into a mainstream operating system and is becoming a core operating system component.

Administrators can install it on pretty much any Linux distribution and it is a good fit for server setups. Yet drafting effective application security profiles is a complicated task. Changing a system's behavior from a scheme that grants broad swaths of permissions to one that requires specific clearance for every action is not a simple process.

SELinux is a set of kernel patches and utilities that boost the security of the Linux system on which it is enabled by providing for the enforcement of mandatory access control policies. For example, we could configure a Web server to serve read-only pages, delegating the rights needed to generate or modify the pages to a separate role.

Policies define the interaction between types and roles to determine a machine's access controls. Writing such policies is an involved business, and it's possible to write conflicting policies. The first step to creating a new policy is to run an application with SELinux set to permissive mode. A utility called audit2-allow scans the auditing messages that an application triggers when run under SELinux in permissive mode and creates a policy that would enable the application to run properly in enforcing mode. From here, an administrator can review and further tailor the policy.

Source: Excerpted from Jason Brooks, "In Operating Systems We Trust." *eWeek,* September 6, 2004, 43–46.

---

special-purpose firewall appliances hone in on security-related functions. This is a better approach because it reduces the chance of misconfiguration. The less there is to configure, the less chance there is that things can go wrong. (Firewalls are covered later in the chapter.)

authentication: the process of deciding the identity of a user attempting to access a system.

Another technology protecting the perimeter is **authentication.** Under the old EDI system, both sender and receiver had to sign up for the service with the value-added network (VAN) provider and agree on the format to be used before transactions were carried out. On the Internet, you don't know whom you are dealing with. To grant authentication, a hardware token generates a unique password every so many seconds. The password must match that on a central server that is synchronized with the token, and VPNs provide encryption for data transmitted across the wire, but companies must still worry about sensitive data stored in databases, such as credit card numbers and consumer profiles that have been searched over time.

AUTHORIZE AND MONITOR THE SECURITY SYSTEM

Once the perimeter is secure and only authorized users are allowed access to the e-commerce site, the next step is to install a system that generates authorization to different users to handle different jobs. Most companies adopt a policy that denies access to all except those who are explicitly allowed. This policy, along with good security design, should keep a site reasonably secure. However, in situations where customers are routinely placing big-ticket orders, the security system should provide strong authentication for such orders and an audit trail. You must be able to prove that customer A at company X did, in fact, place an order on May 3 for $113,000 worth of diamonds. This is called nonrepudiation, and it is covered in the next chapter. Security design steps are shown in Figure 13.3.

monitoring: capturing processing details, verifying that e-commerce is operating within the security policy, and verifying that attacks have been unsuccessful.

These functions require that the security system be monitored via feedback mechanisms to ensure that the entire system is working properly. **Monitoring** means capturing processing details for evidence, verifying that e-commerce is operating within the security policy, and verifying that attacks have been unsuccessful. This system does not replace the human guard who checks the doors, makes the rounds on each floor, and makes sure badges and IDs are valid at all times. The guard and the electronic security system complement each other to keep an e-commerce site reliable at all times.

RAISE AWARENESS OF POSSIBLE INTRUSIONS

With today's firms relying more and more on the Internet, they face an ever-growing spectrum of threats, which means an increase in protection against cyber-risks far beyond what traditional property and casualty insurance policies cover. Denial-of-service attacks already have targeted businesses such as Amazon.com, Buy.com, CNN.com, eBay, and E-Trade. Attackers have even tried to slow down the entire Internet.

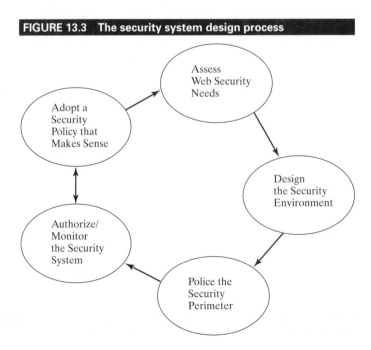

FIGURE 13.3 The security system design process

User organizations and ISPs can ensure that traffic exiting an organization's site or entering an ISP's network from a site carries a source address consistent with the set of addresses for that site. This would allow tracing of attack traffic to the site from which it emanated, substantially assisting in the process of locating and isolating attack traffic sources.

Dial-up users are the source of some attacks, so stopping spoofing by these users is also an important step. ISPs, universities, libraries, and others that serve dial-up users should ensure that proper filters are in place to prevent dial-up connections from using spoofed addresses. Network equipment vendors should ensure that no-IP-spoofing is a user setting and the default setting on their dial-up equipment.

HOW MUCH RISK CAN YOU AFFORD?

CIOs and other top management officials often ask two questions regarding their company's security and how it relates to e-commerce: How secure are we? How much will it cost to secure our e-system? Other questions arise as well: How secure do we need to be? What are we doing to monitor and improve security? What monitors do we have that tell us whether we've been hit and how hard? The level of security can be determined by the specific threats inherent in the system's design.

Another way of addressing the risk factor is to estimate the pain threshold your company and the attacker are willing to tolerate. In this case, the network administrator needs to know what is being protected, its value to the company, and its value to outsiders. The statements "When you have nothing, you have nothing to lose" and "There is not that much that they can steal" do not apply in network and Internet security. The goal of security strategies, methods, and procedures is to raise the threshold of pain an attacker must endure to access and cause damage to a system.

One of the key questions in designing a security policy is the level of protection required against the risks the merchant is willing to assume. It is like deciding whether to put cash in a savings account with 100 percent security (up to $100,000) or invest in stocks that could go up or down in value. In any case, security risks address the adversaries that could wreck an e-commerce business. Professional attackers might view a site as a challenge and work day and night until they crack it. A casual attacker might just try hard enough to be a nuisance. In looking at security risks, the focus is on the determined attacker's intentions and resources.

KINDS OF THREATS OR CRIMES

Organized virus- and work-writing activity has been surging in the open, with nothing to slow it down. It is powering an underground economy specializing in ID theft and spam. Signs of the underground economy include:

- Credit card databases bought and sold
- Hacked servers bought and sold
- Distributed denial-of-service attack networks bought and sold
- Windows machines infected with viruses, then turned into proxies or attack networks

The July 2004 outbreak of MyDoom.M was a reminder that spammers are now resorting to sophisticated threats, mixing spam, virus, and denial-of-service attacks. During that month alone, a marketing research firm reported more than 16 million directory harvest attacks, where spammers were trying to hijack a company's entire e-mail directory. See Box 13.6.

Before promoting security, you must know what you are trying to prevent. Web merchants must consider three kinds of threats or crimes.

1. *Those that are physically related.* For example, a hacker might attempt to steal or damage inventory. Other examples include stolen credit card records, stolen computer hardware or software, and sheer vandalism. An attacker, often by guessing passwords, might succeed in gaining access to another user's account. The attacker might even be capable of drumming up unauthorized features such as discount coupons or specials in an effort to get merchandise free of charge.

2. *Those that are order related.* For example, a customer might attempt to use an invalid or a stolen credit card or claim no merchandise was received on a good credit card. Children might use their parents' credit card without permission. Insiders can do a lot to infect an order because they have access to sensitive systems and information. All it takes is a disgruntled or greedy employee to disrupt or divert an order to his or her advantage.

3. *Those that are electronically related.* A hacker might try to *sniff* e-mail information or attempt to steal credit card numbers and use them illegally at a later date.

BOX 13.6

MyDoom and Its Venom

The latest version of the MyDoom e-mail virus, MyDoom.M fooled tens of thousands of computer-savvy workers into triggering a disruption that knocked Internet search sites Google, Yahoo!, Lycos, and AltaVista offline for several hours Monday. It lured office workers facing stuffed post-weekend in-boxes into opening a folder presumably holding details about an undeliverable message. That action sent copies of the virus to all e-mail addresses on the victim's hard drive.

The deluge knocked Google offline as it is trying to look its best for an initial public offering. In May, the Sasser Internet work, created by a German teenager, knocked down computer systems in transportation companies, banks, and hospitals. Last August, the MSBlaster worm blasted business networks, exacerbating a massive power outage that darkened the northeast USA.

Like MyDoom's author, those hackers sought to amass infected PCs and turn them into zombies to help spread other viruses. Wider collateral damage occurred by accident. If somebody [tried] to do really bad things on purpose, this proves it is very possible.

The latest virus underscores growing concern about the changing nature of hack attacks. Viruses used to destroy data. Now viruses are designed to filch data or take it hostage.

Source: Excerpted from Byron Acohido, and Jon Swartz, "MyDoom.M Virus Slams Search Sites." *USA Today,* July 27, 2004, 1B.

sniffer: a person or a program that uses the Internet to record information that transmits through a router from its source to its destination.

A **sniffer** (also called a cracker or a cyber-punk) might vandalize a site by replacing files, deleting files, or attempting to intercept and decode communications between the merchant and customers. Crackers often use off-the-shelf attack software from technical magazines with little knowledge or experience in its use or potential. Another example of an electronically related attack is damaging, defacing, or destroying a Web site and infecting the entire business-to-consumer interface with malicious software called a virus. (More will be presented on viruses later in the chapter.)

Other potential groups of attackers or criminals can threaten the e-commerce environment. How about payments from legitimate user accounts being diverted to an unauthorized person's account? Payment could go to the wrong party, with the real buyer completely unaware of what is happening. What about attackers creating a look-alike Web site to draw unsuspecting users?

Finally, some intruders attack the Web site a little at a time so that it is difficult to detect the continued drain on the system. For example, an attacker who succeeded in accumulating a large number of credit card numbers might opt to use one credit card at a time at small businesses, for small purchases, or during a time when traffic is heavy, without arousing any suspicion.

CLIENT AND SERVER SECURITY THREATS

Two types of security threats affect a company's Internet client-server environment: attacks on client computers—all the PCs attached to the local area server—and attacks on the server(s) itself. In either case, we need to know the types of attacks, how an attacker breaks in, and what the attacker does once in the system.

CLIENT COMPUTER ATTACKS.   The literature on security and survey specialists in the security business indicates that three main reasons explain why client computers are attacked.

1. **Sheer nuisance.** This includes unsolicited mail, displays of advertisements on the Web site, or anonymous messages that are disruptive and potentially destructive. No malice is involved, but the mere inflow of this type of garbage causes irritation and loads up the person's PC hard disk.

2. **Deliberate corruption of files.** It's no secret that viruses can cause all kinds of problems with data integrity. Melissa, WORM, and hundreds of other viruses since the early 1990s show how vulnerable the PC is in an e-commerce environment. Protecting against a deliberate invasion of files means backing up files regularly so that a copy is available for updating or restoring what may have been lost.

3. **Rifling stored information.** This is a direct attack on the client computer—the PC attached to the server. In this case, vital information such as a file of credit card numbers, a school's file of student transcripts, or the mental health history of psychiatric patients is the target. Think of a situation where a program or a virus enters your PC, steals information, and transmits it through e-mail to the public at large. This kind of attack clearly has legal implications, which was covered in Chapter 12.

The next question is: How are client computers attacked? There are three ways.

1. **Physical attacks.** The first line of attack is through unattended computers during business hours, computers not logged off at night, or computers with easy-to-break passwords. Client computers should never be left unattended without appropriate security checks.

2. **Viruses.** Anyone who has used a Web e-mail service knows the potency of a virus. Hackers and crackers have little difficulty propagating Trojan horses or e-mail viruses. The good news is that new intrusion-detection systems and firewalls have done a lot to block security breaches and identify the sources of unauthorized access.

3. **Computer-to-computer attacks.** With client computers linked via the server, it is not uncommon for one computer to export or publish information to others in the network. In a corporate environment, where security protocols and procedures are lax, the adage "a chain is as strong as the weakest link" applies. One disgruntled employee can spam or **spoof** the entire network.

spoof: an imposter; someone who pretends to be someone else or representing a Web site as authentic when it is a fake.

SERVER SECURITY THREATS.   In e-commerce, the execution software on the client side or the server side poses real threats to the security of all transactions. When security measures are weak, the adage "in the presence of obstacles, the path of least resistance is always the path of choice" applies. Good design is important for software quality. It is also important to think of security not as an add-on piece of software, but as part of the security system from the beginning.

All the reasons for attacking client computers apply to attacking servers as well, except that an attack on a server affects all the computers attached to it. The impact can be astronomical in terms of disruption of service, loss of information in transit, and the integrity of the files. Furthermore, because servers store security credentials for client computer users, it is all the more necessary to incorporate cryptographic schemes to protect such information from attack.

How are server attacks launched? Attacks range from those with limited objectives, such as access to a specific file or application, to access to a major application with the intent of running it like a legitimate user. The worst are **denial-of-service (DOS)** attacks, where users are bombarded with hundreds or thousands of messages that clog the Internet site so nothing can get in or out.

denial of service (DOS): attack by a third party that prevents authorized users from accessing the infrastructure.

The first step in an attack is to log in by guessing at a password. Unfortunately, the typical password is someone's street number, the last four digits of a Social Security number, a telephone number, or something similar. An attacker also might latch onto the client-server traffic using a sniffer virus and catch passwords as they whiz by. Unattended terminals are ready targets for attackers wanting to take over a network connection. Once user privileges are compromised, the attacker will have access to all kinds of files, applications, and the like. The attacker will have no difficulty embedding viruses, transferring files to computers located anywhere in the world, or simply rendering the terminal inoperable. Three years after the high-profile hits, DOS attacks are still a threat.

DOS attacks are hard to characterize, because what they have in common is their end effect, not the means by which they are carried out. Some DOS attacks flood a network with traffic or modify a router's configuration. One of the main reasons why DOS attacks are so hard to fend off is that on the surface, they appear like ordinary Web site traffic. The difference, though, is their intent, along with the volume, frequency, and source of the traffic.

Protecting e-mail is another aspect of server protection. Sending e-mail is a part of every workday. So is e-mail abuse. It is not only e-mail servers, but also the connections between servers that must be protected. Devices such as S/MIME and SMTP over Secure Sockets Layer (SSL) are employed to combat attackers. S/MIME ensures that a message is encrypted and digitally signed by the client and then by the Web server it is leaving. SMTP SSL is installed between two e-mail servers to make sure all e-mail packets are encrypted. These devices are covered in detail in the next chapter.

HACKERS

In early February 2000, a historic surge of attacks left "Top Gun" Web sites like AOL and Yahoo! few options for defense. Imagine a prankster arranging for thousands of people around the world to dial your home number continuously for hours at a time. This, in effect, is what happened to the Web sites of eBay, E*Trade Group, and Yahoo!. They fell victim to what is commonly known in the Internet security business as a denial-of-service attack. As the name implies, the attack does not intend to harm anyone or any file, as is the case with viruses. Its aim is to prevent the Internet from performing its vital function of linking people and technology. These attacks take advantage of the Internet's open nature, and there is no surefire way to defend against them until after they're underway.

It is worth noting that it does no good to worry about hackers and hacker attacks if departing company officials are free to leave with sensitive programs and data. In one incident in early 2005, one executive's employment contract included a clause that allowed her to keep her laptop. The problem was that no one bothered to erase company information on such a machine. This included e-mail correspondence, product prices, merger or acquisition information, and the like. Later on, when a court inquiry came up about the company's merger process, the executive in question refused to release her laptop to make a copy of the content and belatedly erase company-related information.

Related to this problem is the infamous 9/11 attacks, where criminals were trained to fly inside "the system" and allowed to board U.S. aircraft. That episode created the USA Patriot Act by Congress a month later. Despite the war on terror, however, the Internet continues to be a hacker's haven.

Denial-of-service falls under cyberterrorism—unlawful attacks and threats of attacks against computers, networks, and the information stored in them when done to intimidate or coerce a company or a government in furtherance of political or social objectives. Denial-of-service attacks against Yahoo!, CNN, eBay, and other e-commerce Web sites are estimated to have caused over $1 billion in losses in 2004. It also shook the confidence of business and individuals in e-commerce.

To activate a denial of service, the hacker breaks into a large number of less-secure computers and servers connected to a high-bandwidth network, usually corporate or government. The attacker installs stealth programs that are hard to spot and serve as electronic soldiers, lying undetected on the hijacked computers, waiting to attack a Web site. In and of itself, this stealth program does not harm a Web site, but because the program duplicates itself thousands of times, the hacker can create unimaginable congestion in network traffic.

From a remote location, the hacker (called a remote hacker) specifies a target network such as eBay or Yahoo! and activates the planted programs with a brief command via the Internet to a number of computers. The command triggers the computers to start flooding target sites with bogus requests for information. This is when the attack begins. The victim's network is overwhelmed. The source of the deluge of network traffic has been intentionally masked, making the attack hard to trace. Legitimate users encounter the equivalent of a constant busy signal and are denied access to the site. (See Figure 13.4.)

There are several ways a hacker carries out his or her trade:

- Social engineering. This approach tricks a person into revealing his or her password. Sometimes, this is carried out via a company executive's unsuspecting relatives to get access to sensitive information.

- Shoulder surfing. In this method, the hacker looks over an employee's shoulder while he or she types in a password.

- Dumpster diving. A hacker simply waits for a company's trash to be dumped in a container on a public street or in an alley and looks through it for sensitive information. The attempt is legal, unless there is a "no trespassing" sign.

- Whacking (wireless hacking). All a hacker needs to have is the right kind of radio within the range of a wireless transmission zone. Once tapped into a wireless network, the hacker easily accesses anything on both the wired and wireless networks, unless the data is sent unencrypted.

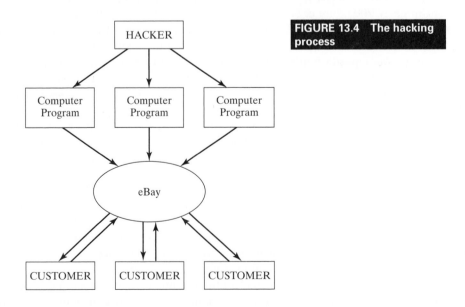

FIGURE 13.4 The hacking process

Hackers and ethics do not mix. What is the remedy? First, site operators track a flood of information to a specific computer. Once they detect the source, they block any further requests from that computer. This is difficult when many computers are involved. To protect your computer against hackers, perform an online security checkup or install a firewall on your computer workstation. If you are running a commercial site, commercial firewall software with intruder tracking is available from various vendors.

intrusion detection: sensing when a system is being used without authorization.

Intrusion detection is sensing when a system is being used without authorization. An intrusion-detection system is designed to monitor company systems and network activities. Using information collected from these activities, it notifies the authorities when it identifies a likely intrusion. (See Figure 13.1.)

Another way of fighting hackers is to hire one who works at foiling the efforts of the troublemakers. Under certain conditions, it is better to hire burglars than cops. Hackers have a better understanding of technology infrastructure than a typical IT manager. Ethical or reformed hackers normally hire themselves out to break into a client's computer network with the client's consent in an effort to patch up security holes.

More recently, cyber-forensic investigations have been employed to combat cyber-criminals. In many cases, large businesses use cyber-investigators to set up alarms and traps to watch and catch intruders and criminals within their networks.

The trend is for more and more government agencies and private businesses to look toward the work of the benign or reformed hacker. For example, since the tragic September 11, 2001 attack, chronic security concerns led Uncle Sam to deputize the country's hackers in the summer of 2003 to help fight the war on terrorism. The White House cybersecurity adviser encouraged hackers in an address to the annual Black Hat convention of hackers in Las Vegas that summer to probe popular computer programs and share any weaknesses they found with the software developers for tightening security. A White House official also suggested the government would look into legal protection for benign hackers.

In the final analysis, no single entity is responsible for the interconnected computers, servers, routers, switches, and fiber-optic cables that make up cyberspace. This means every Internet stakeholder must follow strict guidelines for cybersecurity. In February 2003, President George W. Bush released the 76-page final draft of *The National Strategy to Secure Cyberspace*. The policy statement calls for the creation of an emergency response system against cyberattacks and a reduction in the nation's vulnerability to such threats. Five major initiatives are involved:

- Create a cyberspace surety response system
- Establish a threat and vulnerability reduction program
- Improve security training and awareness
- Secure the government's own systems
- Work internationally to solve security issues (U.S. Dept. of Homeland Security).

THE VIRUS: COMPUTER ENEMY NUMBER ONE

The most serious attack on a client computer or a server in an Internet environment is the **virus.** By their nature, viruses tend to mystify the average user. A virus is a malicious code that replicates itself and can be used to disrupt the information infrastructure. They can infect a number of different portions of the computer's operating and file system.

virus: a malicious code that replicates itself and disrupts the information infrastructure.

Viruses commonly compromise system integrity, circumvent security capabilities, and cause adverse operation by taking advantage of the information system or the network. They incorporate themselves into computer networks, files, and other executable objects, and replicate whenever those programs are executed or those infected diskettes are accessed. The replicates are not always exact and are often capable of spreading further in many different ways, including through e-mail attachments. Fortunately, 95 percent of viruses do not contain destructive codes that harm the system. They do no more than copy themselves and execute trivial codes that activate a beeping sound, display a message box, or simply do nothing. See Table 13.2 for a brief summary of viruses.

Despite the most valiant efforts to detect and eliminate it, exposure to malicious code will always be a problem. Virus developers are creative and are constantly inventing new viruses for all kinds of occasions. Therefore, no network is immune. In the near future, companies will need to deal with stealthy viruses carrying more destructive payloads. Surreptitious worms are expected to spread more slowly but in a harder to detect "contagion" fashion.

TYPES OF VIRUSES

The most common way of classifying a virus is by the way that it infects the system. These categories include file viruses, boot viruses, macro viruses, stealth viruses, fast and slow infectors, armored viruses, multipartite viruses (infect different kinds of files by going into the master boot record and then going into memory), tunneling viruses, and camouflage viruses.

A file virus is one that attacks executable files; a boot virus attacks the boot sectors of the hard drive and the diskettes. It does not infect the hard drive simply through someone using the disk, but if the user forgets to take the disk out of the drive and reboots the computer, the virus copies itself to the boot sector of the hard drive. Once there, it will infect any floppy diskette used on the computer. A macro virus exploits the macro commands in software applications such as Microsoft Word.

Today, 80 percent of all viruses are macro viruses. They are growing in popularity due to the increasing number of people connecting to the Internet, downloading high-volume files, or executing Usenet groups.

Macro viruses are written in a macro language used in Microsoft applications such as Office Suite. It is easier to write a program that infects data files such as Word documents and Excel spreadsheets than it is to write a program that affects executable files. With data files exchanged more often than executable files, the virus spreads rapidly. Embedded into the data files and well disguised, the virus can run anywhere Microsoft applications are present. The platform-independent nature of the virus makes it more potent.

TABLE 13.2   A brief summary of viruses

Year	Virus	Comments
1970s	Hipboot	Worked very much like later boot sector virus
1981	Elk Cloner	Displayed a little rhyme on the screen ("It will get on all your disks; it will infiltrate your chips; yes it's Cloner! It will stick to you like glue; it will modify RAM too; send in the Cloner!")
1986	Brain, PC-Write Trojan, Virdem	Brain infected the boot sector of a floppy disk Virdem was the first file virus
1988	MacMag and Internet Worm	First Macintosh virus
1989	AIDS Trojan	Famous for holding data hostage
1991	Tequila	First polymorphic virus came from Switzerland
1992	Michelangelo, DAME, and VCL	Michelangelo caused a worldwide alert with claims of massive damage predicted, but little happened
1995	Year of the hacker	Hackers attacked Griffith Air Force Base, Goddard Space Flight Center, and Jet Propulsion Lab
1996	Boza, Laroux, Staog	Boza was first virus designed for Windows 95 files; Laroux was first Excel macro virus; Staog was first Linux virus
1999	Melissa, Corner, and Bubbleboy	Melissa was first Word macro virus and worm to use Outlook Express address book to send itself to others via e-mail
2000	Love Letter, Timofonica, Liberty, Streams, and Pirus	First major distributed denial of service attacks shut down major sites like Yahoo!, Amazon.com, and others; Love Letter worm became the fastest spreading work, shutting down e-mail systems around the world
2001	Gnuman, Winux, Windows/Linux Virus, Nimba	Gnuman was first to attack a peer-to-peer communications system
2002	Donut, SQLSpider, Benjamin, Scalper	Donut was first worm directed at .NET services
2003	Slammer, Sobig, Lovgate, Blaster	Slammer exploited vulnerabilities in Microsoft's SQL 2000 servers, hit on Super Bowl weekend
2004	Trojan.Xombe, Bizex, Witty, Bofra/Iframe	Trojan.Xombe posed as a message from Microsoft Windows phishing for personal information
2005	Bropia, Troj/BankAsh	Bropia Worm targets MSN Messenger for spreading; Troj/BankAsh is first Trojan horse to attack the new Microsoft anti-spyware product

SPYWARE AND ADWARE

A relatively new uninvited, unwanted, annoying, stealthful, exploitative, and potentially privacy-threatening intruder called **spyware** is software that users unknowingly install onto a computer that sets up shop without the user's knowledge or permission. Once in residence, it could be used for myriad reasons, like collecting information about users' computer habits. Spyware is usually installed in conjunction with the installation of another software package, such as a shareware application or even a commercially purchased package such as Turbo Tax.

spyware: software the user unknowingly installs through an e-mail attachment or downloading an infected file that could be used for illicit reasons.

adware: software that sneaks into a user's hard disk installed by Internet advertising companies to promote pop-up ads and release information for advertisers on the outside.

Adware is software that sneaks into your hard disk and lurks in the background, allowing pop-up ads and releasing information for outsiders without authorization. Here is how it works:

- The user accepts free software that comes with pop-up ads. Gator's adware program sneaks in with the free software on the user's hard drive.
- Adware tracks the Web pages the user visits and sends a report to Gator.
- Gator analyzes the data and sends ads targeted to the user. It keeps track of the user's response.

In general, viruses infect system sectors, files, macros, disk clusters, batch files, and source code. Many of these viruses are never spotted except in the laboratory. When they infect a computer unintentionally and spread, the virus is said to be "in the wild."

While viruses are malicious, they are often obvious. Users know they have a virus, usually when it is too late, but spyware can sneak past antivirus software and firewalls. A virus destroys data; spyware steals it.

It may first appear as a new button on your desktop, or a new menu item to be selected. Once spyware is in the system, it will always be running in the background, randomly scanning hard drives, monitoring keystrokes, spying on chat applications, reading cookies, or changing a home page. The program sends the information back to the "home base" where the software creators can use the information as they please, usually for marketing purposes or to sell.

More specifically, here is what spyware does:

- Allows the hijacking of your computer for unauthorized use
- Collaborates with a hacker to steal your files
- Attacks third-party computers in denial-of-service (DOS) attacks that expose them to legal liability
- Profiles your surfing habits (what sites you access, graphics you download, purchases you make, etc.) and releases them to a third party for future spam or pop-up junk.
- Monitors every keystroke you type, your e-mail traffic, passwords, bank information, perhaps giving the information to a blackmailer.
- Changes your computer settings and sets a default URL address that you cannot remove. Even if you did remove it, many spyware programs have a feature that will automatically reinstall them.

Before you know it, your computer is slowing down, and the job that once took 2 minutes to complete now takes 7 minutes—a huge productivity sinkhole. The Web page that you once accessed directly now takes you to Web sites you have never seen before. You eventually reach a point where you encounter total system degradation.

As you can imagine, the rampant invasion of spyware into homes and businesses comes at a large cost to the user, the corporate world, and the networked economy with far-reaching legal and financial consequences. To use this author as an example, he gets an average of 25 spam e-mails a day, and spends anywhere from 2 to 20 minutes clearing the inbox. This amounts to 40 days a year—a total waste of time and energy. Transferred to a corporate environment, the cost in employee time, performance, and unnecessary consumption of PC storage is virtually unquantifiable.

Users are apathetic about the threat spyware represents to their efficiency, privacy, and data security. Imagine the havoc spyware wreaks in computer cycle time and the way it hogs computer resources in noticeable ways (see www.iamnotageek.com/a/359 -p1.php). Even installing anti-spyware software sucks up machine time, causing costly delays. It becomes obvious that spyware is a high price for users to pay for freeware.

POSSIBLE SOLUTIONS.   Inasmuch as spyware intrusion is more difficult than the regular virus, there are ways to prevent or protect users from spyware's rapidly growing threat. The most obvious way is to avoid downloading it in the first place. One way to do so is to go to a Web site such as www.spychecker.com, which has a searchable database of software titles that include spyware. Another way is to install a special firewall such as ZoneAlarm (www.zonelabs.com), a free program that prevents spyware programs from "phoning home," blocking its ability to report back to the home base about the user's Internet usage.

Another free program at www.lavasoft.de/software/adaware scans memory, hard drives, and registry for adware programs much the same way a virus scan works. When it is done with the scan, it presents a list of all found files and the user has the option of deleting or keeping the culprit files.

Other tips to stop spyware are:

- Enforce strict user Web policies on surfing and downloading activities.
- Install a desktop firewall on every laptop and desktop.
- Do not give users administrator privileges.
- Configure an e-mail gateway to block all executable e-mail attachments.
- Ensure desktop antivirus software signatures are up to date.
- Use commercial antispyware software to detect and remove existing spyware programs (Mitchell 2004).
- Enforce the usage of higher security settings in Internet browsers to prevent sites that cause spyware infection.
- Use pop-up blockers that lead to Web sites of low trustworthiness.
- Educate your employees and staff about spyware threats by creating an active outreach with groups and organizations, including the Consortium of Anti-Spyware Technology (COAST).

Finally, we should remember that adware, sneakware, snoopware, web bugs, key loggers, spybots, or malware are all terms for spyware. The law is catching up with this malicious act, but not fast enough. The CAN-SPAM Act passed late in 2003 has had no noticeable impact on the volume of spam traveling the Internet. See Box 13.7. A similar bill passed by the Senate in October 2003 prohibits messages that peddle financial scams, fraudulent body-enhancement products, and pornography. Cybercriminals and hackers have been inventing ways to bypass filters and firewalls, mainly through flaws in applications open to the Internet. Overconfidence and a series of missteps open the door for viruses through the corporate defenses. When that happens, reinfected desktops that were once cleaned compound the problem with increased negligence. As someone commented, "It is like bailing water from the Titanic."

In terms of security and compliance, more and more regulations are making organizations accountable for information management practices. For example, the following statutes have already taken hold on compliance:

- The Gramm-Leach-Bliley Act requires all financial institutions to protect nonpublic personal information through security controls and restriction on access to data.

- The VISA USA Cardholder Information Security Program requires that personal information related to the cardholder be encrypted in the company database.

- The Sarbanes-Oxley Act requires executives and auditors to vouch for the effectiveness of internal controls over financial reporting (Newman 2004).

- The Basel II Capital Accords, developed by a committee of 10 countries including the U.S., specify how internationally active banks report on cash and credit risks to protect against losses resulting from internal or external causes. Full compliance is required by the end of 2006.

BOX 13.7

Keeping Up with CAN-SPAM Act

CAN-SPAM stands for Controlling the Assault of Non-Solicited Pornography and Marketing Act of 2003. It took effect January 1. It permits damages of up to $2 million against companies that violate the provisions of the law. According to this act, e-mail must meet five basic requirements to avoid being labeled "unsolicited commercial" e-mail:

- The e-mail message must have correct header information.

- The message must have an accurate subject line.

- The message must contain a functioning return e-mail address.

- Senders must not send e-mail more than 10 business days after receiving a request to be removed from a mailing list.

- Commercial e-mail must contain a clear identification that the message is an advertisement, must contain a conspicuous notice of opportunity to decline further e-mail, and must display the physical postal address of the sender.

This means IT departments must work to ensure that database systems storing customer information are maintained in such a way that unsubscribe requests are processed quickly.

The amount of spam delivered since the act took effect January 1 is virtually the same as before. One reason is that spammers are getting smarter and have been feverishly trying to advance spamming around the law.

Source: Excerpted from Cameron Sturdevant, "Keeping Up with CAN-SPAM Act." e*Week*, February 2, 2004, 43.

VIRUS CHARACTERISTICS

In terms of characteristics, viruses can be classified as fast, slow, and stealth. Fast viruses spread quickly. Although it is just as easy to clean a computer hard disk with 1,000 infected files as one with 10 files, the possibility of a fast infector in computer memory causes a big headache. If a virus is located in memory and the antivirus program opens the files to scan them, the fast virus will invade and infect these files easily. Slow viruses are as dangerous as fast viruses because users are less likely to detect and destroy them. A slow virus is replicated only when a particular action is executed, such as copying diskettes. Stealth viruses appeared in 1986; the first was called Brain. All stealth viruses are memory resident and are capable of manipulating their execution in order to disguise their presence.

Another way of categorizing viruses is according to destructive capability, severity of the damage done to the host, or how long it takes to destroy and fix the damaged host. We arbitrarily divide the damage scale into six groups, ranging from trivial damage to unlimited damage, as shown in Table 13.3.

PROTECTION AGAINST VIRUSES

With the growing popularity of the Internet and e-commerce, e-mail, and the increasing number of advanced viruses, it is difficult for a system to stay pure. The best protection is to know how to locate viruses and how to recover quickly by establishing and implementing a set of prevention practices and policies. The two available approaches are antivirus software and firewalls. (Firewalls are explained later in the chapter.)

TABLE 13.3 Levels of virus damage

Scale of Damage	Characteristic
Trivial Damage	Done by file virus.
	Takes seconds to remove and fix the host computer. *Example:* File virus that makes speaker beep on 18th of each month.
Minor Damage	Small amount of damage.
	Virus is removed easily; host fixed by reinstalling the corrupted application(s). *Example:* Jerusalem virus that deletes (on Friday the 13th) any program that has run after the virus has gone memory resident.
	Virus either formats, scrambles, or overwrites hard disk. Host can be recovered by reinstalling the backup version. *Example:* Michelangelo. Virus hits hard drive and backups.
Moderate Damage	Virus discovered after days or weeks. *Example:* Dark Avenger overwritten on a random sector on the hard disk with the phrase "Eddie lives . . . somewhere in time" message. Virus makes gradual and progressive changes to hard disk and backups.
Major Damage	User is oblivious to whether the data are infected because the changes are not obvious.
Severe Damage	Virus that allows a third party (usually the designer) to enter a secure system. *Example:* Cheeba creates a new user with
Unlimited Damage	maximum privileges with a fixed user name and password in the system. Anyone with this user name and password can log on to the system.

Here are several steps for putting an antivirus strategy in place.

- Establish a set of simple enforceable rules for others to follow. These might include statements like: Any incoming disk must be checked for viruses. Do not borrow applications or files from people you do not know.

- Educate and train users on how to check for viruses on a disk; provide a better understanding of viruses and their causes. Users are often told as little as possible because security departments see them as "inherently insecure." Users should be taught how to construct usable and secure passwords. They also should be given feedback during the password construction process to assist them in choosing secure passwords and to increase their awareness of system security.

- Inform users of the existing and potential threats to the company's systems and the sensitivity of information they contain. Users should be given guidance as to which systems are sensitive and why.

- Periodically update the latest antivirus software. Some companies have reached the point of performing updates daily.

Despite these measures, the war between virus creators and antivirus software developers is escalating. Most virus creators today are endlessly inventive, and viruses mutate too quickly for even the best system to detect them all. Some viruses are capable of updating themselves in order to penetrate the most up-to-date antivirus program.

Many researchers are predicting the emergence of a new e-mail virus, this time not as an attachment, but as e-mail itself. Because many of the latest e-mail readers display e-mails as an HTML page, they provide an excellent place for JavaScript viruses to hide. Some viruses will even target the antivirus software, creating more confusion and vulnerability. The speed with which malicious codes propagate is increasing as well. The time between discovery of a new virus and the moment it went wild averaged about six to nine months just few years ago. Today, it is almost instantaneous.

PROTECTION AGAINST FRAUD

Another area under the banner of security is fraud or scams. Each year, fraud bleeds companies to the tune of hundreds of billions worldwide. Fraud is a deliberate act of deceiving illegally in order to make money or obtain goods. The immoral aspect of fraud is that the individuals involved are unscrupulous. They often employ illegal and always immoral or unfair means to cheat the target organization.

Fraud management means keeping an eye on the unusual or out-of-the-ordinary invoices, happenings, or even behavior of those with whom the organization is dealing financially. Fraud management involves a number of activities including generating profiles of users; fraud detection, prevention, and avoidance; monitoring customer dissatisfaction; risk analysis; monitoring computer and networking security; maintaining billing and accounting integrity; and cooperating with law-enforcement agencies. In addition to enormous volumes of data, any changes in the behavior of users and employees must be monitored and adjusted accordingly.

With these vulnerabilities in mind, an organization can take several steps to prevent e-commerce fraud.

- Be aware of corporate critical assets and who might be after them.
- Investigate common attacks and electronic-fraud schemes that could be used against the company's critical assets.
- Install strong encryption such as public key infrastructure (PKI).
- Develop a program for evidence collection (called forensics) via committed investigators.
- Ensure maintenance of strong and reliable transaction, network, and Internet service provider logs.
- Conduct penetration testing to judge the integrity of existing security.
- Investigate the availability of cyber-fraud insurance to provide coverage for potential losses.

SECURITY PROTECTION AND RECOVERY

What are e-commerce firms doing to improve security? Unfortunately, most firms don't know the state of their security until an auditor or a consultant alerts them to the gaps. The combination of lack of knowledge and lack of accountability results in vulnerability and easy attacks. Automated detection software is now available to help a firm determine whether its system has been compromised.

Good tools are not enough, however. One way to ensure basic control is to train system and network administrators in security assessment and administration. More and more security breaches originate from within the organization. Vulnerability from within can be costly, despite federal laws such as the Economic Espionage Act. Each firm must identify theft, control its vital data, apprehend the criminal, and ensure punishment.

There are common-sense precautionary security steps company employees can take:

- Install proper firewall(s) to protect data.
- Ensure that your network is configured properly.
- Protect your most sensitive data through encryption.
- Maintain and update all antivirus programs on your PC or terminal.
- Restrict access to your files by "need to know."
- Assign unique IDs to authorized personnel and track all IDs on a daily basis.
- Ensure that your system administrator has contemporary security skills.
- Enforce and update company information security policy. Inform employees of any changes.

BASIC INTERNET SECURITY PRACTICES

PASSWORDS.   Choosing a password is the first basic principle in security. How often have you heard of people writing down their passwords or hanging them right on the top of the monitor frame? How often have you known someone to choose the easiest password to remember and then lend it to a friend or an associate to let the other person act on their behalf? The majority of hackers access client computers because of easy passwords (last name, last four digits of one's Social Security number, car's license plate number, dog's name, and so on).

One of the reasons hackers can break into a network so easily is that many system administrators never bother to change the standard, vendor-supplied passwords that come with the software. Hackers have lists of such vendors. The first password they try is GUEST. Other popular words are ADMIN, SYSADM, VISITOR, and the ever-popular PASSWORD. If these do not work, then they'll try site-specific names such as company name, e-mail addresses, and birthdates. Microsoft has a one-page write-up on creating passwords. (See www.microsoft.com/security.)

Here are the basics.

- Include at least one capital letter and one lowercase letter in the password.

- Mix numbers with letters. Short passwords won't do anymore.

- Stay away from passwords that are anywhere near your birthday, your last name, spouse's name, too obvious a name, too well-known a name, or too common a name.

- No dictionary names—hackers have dictionaries.

- Change your password often, because a hacker on the prowl eventually will crack any password. Like the army, you'd want to change passwords depending on the sensitivity of the information or site you're trying to protect.

- Disable an employee's password the moment that person leaves.

Web site owners should consult a security expert, especially if they're new at the business of issuing or assigning passwords. If you're running your Web site for the first time, review the security section of the appropriate manual, follow a procedure that makes sense, and be wary of any security software that does not have vendor backup in the way of a help desk, 800-number availability, and a good set of references that you can check prior to installation. If you're working with an ISP, review its security measures, listen to the recommendations, and assess its procedures in the event of a site attack. Someone within the firm (a Webmaster, an IT person, or a security specialist) should be in charge of the security protocols of the e-commerce environment around the clock.

ENCRYPTION. **Encryption** is part of the basics of Web site security. This is the encoding of messages in traffic between the time when the consumer places an order and enters personal and credit card information and the time when the merchant's network processes the order. Many ISPs have special servers to provide for secure order forms. Encryption applies to a company's server, as well as to its e-mail traffic.

encryption: the coding of messages in traffic between computers.

Encrypting e-mail is easy. Most companies start by using an S/MIME compatible e-mail client, such as products from Microsoft, Netscape, or Eudora, and installing a *certificate* from a certificate authority. Although many customers send credit card information through standard, unencrypted e-mail, they should be offered the option of sending encrypted e-mail. Encryption is so important that we use the next chapter to discuss methodology and implementation details.

WATCH FOR THE CREDIT CARD THIEF

Credit card thieves are not difficult to catch if you know what to look for. Here are some basic warning signs.

- A customer placing a large order without regard to size, style, or price
- A first-time customer who places a large order and wants it shipped overnight
- A single customer placing orders using different e-mail addresses
- A customer living in one state who places an order to be shipped to a different address, using a credit card issued by a bank located somewhere else
- An international customer who places a huge order and wants it shipped by air overnight
- A customer who insists on calling you or who prefers to communicate only by e-mail
- A customer who places multiple orders on the same day and demands that they be shipped separately to the same address
- A minor using a parent's credit card to place a large order

There is no question credit card fraud affects a merchant's cost. Allowing a stolen credit card to be used at one's store is like getting arrested for drunken driving. It is a lose-lose situation. The merchant loses the merchandise (the license) and the money (the fine), and customers pay more for merchandise (higher car insurance rates). Customers must be told how to protect their credit cards and be informed of the security measures the merchant has installed to ensure their privacy.

Considering the way the banking industry handled the 2003 theft of more than 8 million credit card account numbers, those most at risk of incurring losses are consumers (identity theft) and merchants that accept "card-not-present" transactions. The card associations' policies continue to be adverse to publicizing credit card thefts in any way, do not require card issuers to notify affected card owners unless they ask, and do not share a list of affected account numbers with merchants.

In a world where credit cards are floating around for identify theft or fraud, there is a moral obligation to disclose such compromises to cardholders and merchants as soon as fraud is disclosed.

FIREWALLS AND SECURITY

If Billy the Kid were alive today, he probably would break into corporate networks and databases before he'd think of robbing a bank. It is more lucrative and less dangerous. Network outlaws, disgruntled employees, hackers, thieves, and the like are all threats to e-commerce business. One of the most effective ways of combating adversaries is building *firewalls*—software and hardware tools that define, control, and limit access to networks and computers linked to the networks of an organization. Firewalls shield an organization's networks from exposure when connecting to the Internet or to untrusted networks, and prevent hackers from gaining access to corporate data.

Firewalls can be used to protect a corporation's network in a number of ways. Most firewalls are configured to protect against unauthenticated log-ins from the outside world, preventing unauthorized users from logging into machines on the company's network. Firewalls also can be employed to block all unsecured access to the internal network, while also limiting users on the inside to connecting only to acceptable external sites. Finally, a firewall can be designed to separate groups within an organization. For example, the human resources department might place their network behind a firewall to safeguard confidential payroll and personnel information from the rest of the firm.

The firewall must ensure (1) data integrity, so no one can change data from outside; (2) authentication, which guarantees that senders are who they claim to be; and (3) confidentiality, so sensitive data or messages are masked from intruding eyes.

One category of firewalls, called **cyberwalls,** is a reliable addition in firewall technology. Although they are software based, they are more characteristic of hardware technologies. Think of cyberwalls as the software version of a firewall appliance. A firewall appliance is generally one piece of hardware that is no larger than a small desktop PC, which quickly plugs into a small firm's existing network infrastructure between the firm's Internet access device (router, DSL modem, modem) and the firm's first hub or switch.

cyberwall: all-in-one software package to improve security for the entire private network of an organization.

Cyberwalls are an all-in-one software package. They are developed with the understanding that the end goal is to improve security for the entire private network. Therefore, they should be the preference with shared networks among users, and virtual private networks among customers and suppliers. Unlike traditional software firewalls, which require many software packages to handle a network's border security, cyberwalls can protect applications, networks, and systems on the whole LAN. They provide this level of security by residing at the interconnection of the internal networks, the application and database servers, the client machines, and the perimeter.

HOW DOES A FIREWALL WORK? A firewall is a software system that enforces an access control policy between two networks. It detects intruders, blocks them from entry, keeps track of what they do and where they originate, notifies the system administrator of mischievous acts, and produces a report.

How this is done varies, but most firewalls do one of two things: block traffic (called default deny) or permit traffic (called default permit). In either case, the focus is on access control. Default deny blocks all traffic except that explicitly allowed by the firewall administrator. Only the necessary traffic is specified to make it across. Default permit allows all traffic except the traffic that is explicitly blocked by the firewall administrator. Default permit requires continuous update of a list of explicitly blocked traffic every time there is a change in protocol or new applications. Default deny does not have such requirements.

WHY WOULD YOU WANT A FIREWALL? The Internet is permeated with those who take pleasure in the electronic equivalent of writing on other people's business property, tearing into files, corrupting records, degrading e-commerce traffic, or simply bringing a business to its knees. The firewall's primary goal is to keep such people out and away from the company's e-commerce infrastructure. It provides real security and often plays a key role as a security blanket for company management.

A firewall protects against the following situations.

- E-mail services that are known to be problems
- Unauthorized interactive log-ins from the outside world
- Undesirable material such as pornographic images, movies, or literature
- Unauthorized sensitive information leaving the company

When they work well, firewalls can act as an effective phone tap and tracing tool. They provide administrators with summaries of the kind and amount of traffic that passed through the firewall, how many attempts were made to break into the company's network, and so on.

In contrast, a firewall cannot prevent the following.

- Attacks that do not go through the firewall; for example, exporting data to the outside via magnetic tape or a diskette.

- Weak security policies or no policy at all. In this case, no firewall can do much good. As someone said, "It's silly to build a six-foot-thick steel door when you live in a wooden house."

- Traitors or disgruntled employees within the organization. All an attacker needs is a helpful employee who can be fooled into giving access to the company network.

- Data-driven attacks in which something is mailed to an internal host that proceeds to execute it.

DESIGN AND IMPLEMENTATION ISSUES.   A number of design issues should be addressed by the firewall designer. The first is policy. How does the company want to operate the system? That is, is the firewall to be default deny or default permit? Firewall design is done under the larger umbrella of a clearly defined network security access policy.

The second design issue is the level of monitoring and control the organization wants. Once the risk level is agreed upon, a checklist is drafted of what should be monitored, permitted, denied, and so forth.

The third design issue is financial and administrative. A complete firewall product can run from almost zero cost to upwards of $100,000. A lot depends on the outcome of the first two design issues and the long-term management view regarding firewall security. Good and effective administrative practices in managing firewall breaches can make the difference between real security and security that is full of holes.

The fourth design issue is whether the company wants internal firewalls installed. Some companies separate the research and development network from other networks within the firm. Internal firewalls are important to limit access to company resources: If one network is infiltrated by an attacker, other networks are left uncontaminated.

The International Computer Security Association (ICSA) identifies specific features that should be considered in firewall design. The primary ones are as follows.

- Security policy: A strong security policy should dictate the firewall design, not the other way around.

- Deny capability: Every firewall should be able to support "default deny." It should not have to be programmed to do the task.

- Filtering ability: A firewall design should allow filtering techniques (deny, permit) for each host system within the organization. Filtering ability also should be flexible to filter on as many attributes as necessary. These attributes include IP source and destination addresses, source and destination TCP ports, and user-friendly inbound and outbound interfaces.

- Scalability: A firewall design should be flexible enough to respond to the network's changing environment.

- Authentication: A firewall design should do a good job of screening users for specific applications and allow deny/permit privileges to be individualized.

- Recognizing dangerous services: A good firewall should be able to identify potentially dangerous services and disable them in time to minimize damage.

- Effective audit logs: A good firewall system should log ongoing traffic and suspicious activities, and produce reports in an easy-to-read format. This feature also implies good documentation of the design and implementation process.

MANAGED FIREWALL SERVICES.   Many firms do not have the technical experience to design their own firewall systems; they use managers of firewall services. ISPs and long-distance carriers tend to be the main suppliers of such services. They set up firewalls at their data headquarters or on customer premises. Either way, they monitor customer security remotely through their network operations center. (See Figure 13.5.) Unfortunately, not all providers do a secure enough job.

The question for the typical firm is whether providers of managed firewall services are cheaper and more reliable than doing the job in-house. Much depends on factors such as available technical talent, recurring and nonrecurring costs, and payback.

FIGURE 13.5   Corporate networks and firewalls

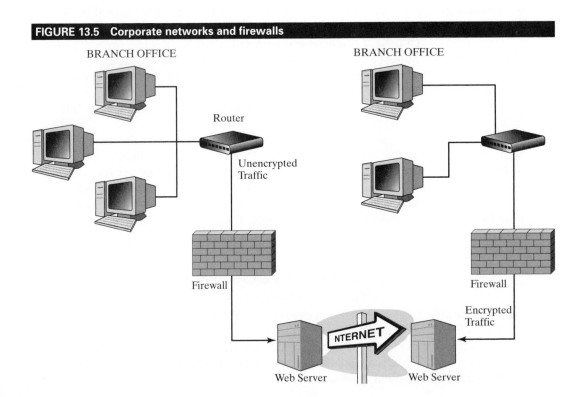

RECOVERY FROM ATTACK

Security prevention and detection gets most of the attention, yet recovery is equally important in defending a Web site. Regardless of the protection measures, not all attacks can be averted. In e-commerce, the merchant must anticipate and block possible means of attack. The security system must detect intrusion, respond in a way that limits damage, maintain the system's availability, and ensure full recovery without delay. Assuming prevention measures are in place, the cycle of recovery includes the following.

- Attack detection and vulnerability assessment: The business monitors symptoms of a software or file problem and senses that an attack may be in progress. Special analytical tools are available to gather, diagnose, and determine whether an attack has been launched and the type of attack.

- Damage assessment: Once an attack is verified, the business should estimate the extent of the damage, such as corrupted data or failed software functions.

- Correction and recovery: In this phase, the business must decide on the procedure to correct the damage and reestablish normal system functions. It should minimize risk by making it harder to crack into an existing system. HotStart, WarmStart, or ColdStart are recovery methods. HotStart is primarily a forward error recovery procedure: The attacker introduces an integrity attack to a limited part of a specific site that can be detected and contained in time by the existing security system. The system, in turn, uses an uncorrupted copy of the system to replace the corrupted portion, with no noticeable delay to the user. WarmStart involves an integrity attack that prompts automated recovery from confined damage. Some system operations can be trusted while the repair is underway. ColdStart is appropriate for severe attacks, where the goal is to bring the system back up as quickly as possible.

- Vigilance and corrective feedback: Once the system is up and running, the business should decide on the improvements to be made in the current security system and ensure no recurrence in the future.

The sad thing about all this effort is that as companies build defenses and fight intrusion, spammers continue to fight back. As Congress and high-tech companies fight to stop junk e-mail, spammers grow more aggressive and creative. For example, spammers hire hackers to break through spam defenses. They have been known to forge names and addresses, including recipients' names in the mail to confound filters. They also launch viruses that dismantle defenses.

ROLE OF BIOMETRICS SECURITY

Biometrics is the science and technology of quantifying and statistically scrutinizing biological data. It generally refers to technologies used for identifying people based on behavior or physical characteristics, primarily for authentication purposes, such as retinas, irises, voice patterns, fingerprints, and hand measurements. Research shows that body scanners, facial pattern systems, and other biometric systems are well poised as replacements for computer passwords in the future.

biometrics: science and technology of quantifying and statistically scrutinizing biological data.

The concept of biometrics is not new. As early as the fourteenth century, the Chinese implemented the fingerprint biometric as a mode of signature. Throughout the 1890s, detectives were charged with the responsibility of identifying those criminals with existing arrest histories. Detectives had to use their photographic memories to identify criminals until the late 1800s. This changed in 1883, when Alphonse Bertillon came up with a biometric system called Bertillonage, which was a method of bodily measurement deployed by police worldwide. This system quickly faded after the discovery of two indistinguishable individuals with the same names. The replacement for Bertilonnage was fingerprinting, which in essence was the ultimate tool utilized by police.

It was not until 1968 that biometrics was applied in the United States. Studies show that the United States was a late adopter of this security technique. (See www.preci sebiometrics.com/match/nr3/frontline.asp; accessed June 2003.) Many organizations were unaware of the benefits that biometrics have over PKI. Those who knew the technology could not afford to invest in it because of its high cost. In 1968, a biometrics application cost about $20,000. Today, the cost is about $1,700. It is expected that the cost eventually will drop to less than $300. (See www.banking.com/aba/cover_0197.htm; accessed June 2003.)

Currently, PKI facilitates the secure transmission of data over third-party networks. As mentioned earlier, PKI consists of an infrastructure and a set of procedures that manage the distribution, storage, and revocation of public keys, private keys, and digital certificates. It sets up a process of authentication to verify the identity of the sender. Further, it ensures that the sender cannot disown its message through nonrepudiation.

This seems all well and good, until examining some of the loopholes that make PKI weak as a form of security. When it comes to authentication, a potential risk exists in that the private key of an individual may be misused, misplaced, or stolen. If the private key is protected with only a PIN number, a felon may easily discover the PIN of another person simply through observation. If the private key is stored within the hard drive of a workstation, a felon could tap into the hard drive and quickly make a copy of the key. Also, in transactions over a third-party network, a felon could simply pretend to be another person and intentionally destroy that person's account and reputation.

Biometrics can enhance authentication considerably. In using a private key for encryption and decryption, biometrics significantly enhances the level of confidence that another user won't be able to access the same private key. Within a network setting, a biometric device would ensure that the person who encrypted that data would be the only one who could decrypt and have access to it. A recent biometric application is a federal plan for border control.

Applying biometric technology on a smart card also would increase the level of confidence in the security. By placing the private key directly on a smart card, the risks of a felon stealing the private key from the hard drive of a workstation would be eliminated. The user would have the advantage of mobility with the smart card, being able to travel with the identification as if it were a regular physical key. If the smart card were lost or stolen, a person other than the original user would not be able to gain access to the private key or any other information owned by the original user. The smart card would respond only to the unique characteristics of the person engrained within its private key.

FORMS OF BIOMETRICS

Biometrics falls under two categories: physiological and behavioral. Under the physiological category are fingerprint verification, iris analysis, facial analysis, and hand geometry-vein patterns. The behavioral category consists of speech analysis, handwritten signature verification, and keystroke analysis. Table 13.4 summarizes the categories and key application areas. Table 13.5 addresses the benefits and drawbacks of biometrics.

TABLE 13.4 Types of biometrics and select application areas		
Forms of Biometrics		*Application Areas*
Physiological		
Fingerprint Verification	Government agencies	Banking
	Identity authentication	Information security
	Airport traffic security	Police department
	ID of missing children	Welfare and unemployment benefit recipients
	Medical and insurance industry	Immigration/naturalization services
Iris Analysis	Correctional facilities	
	Department of motor vehicles	
Facial Analysis	Banking	Telephone companies
	Airport security	Hospitals/health care institutions
	Building security	Drivers licenses
	Welfare agencies	Police authorities
	Computer facilities	Voter registration processes
	Credit card companies	
Behavioral		
Speech Analysis	Antitheft system for vehicles and doors	Passport control
	PC and computer network access control	Prison pay phones
		Pharmacy
	Door entrance systems	Aerospace company
	Hospitals (access to nursery)	Fraud control in prisons
	Universities (access to labs, student unions)	
	Air force in-air communications (pilot identity)	
	Telephone networks	
Handwritten Signature Verification	Banking	Internal Revenue Service
	Post office	Social Medicare
	Home shopping	Welfare

TABLE 13.5 Benefits and drawbacks of biometric devices

Types of Biometrics	Key Benefits	Major Drawbacks
Physiological		
Fingerprint Verification	Nonintrusive	Wear and tear of fingers
	Low level of error rates	Perception of invasion of privacy
	Fraud-deterrent documentation capabilities	
Iris Analysis	Low error incidence (highly accurate)	Infrared iris scanning perceived as intrusive
	Reliable	Portability issues arise with laptop users
		Video cameras make employees feel like they are being spied on
Facial Analysis	Can recognize when user leaves PC	Constant camera surveillance may intimidate user
	Nonintrusive can be used with low light or no light	
	No vulnerability to disguises	
	Greater accuracy, speed, reliability than fingerprinting	
	Easy to use	
	Versatile with respect to usability (videoconferencing and security)	
Behavioral		
Speech Analysis	Voice serves as unique identifier	Hard for computer system to analyze voice characteristics
	Public acceptable	Change in voice depends on emotional state
	Suitable for hands-free environments	Acceptability issue
	Less vulnerable to unauthorized access	Highly complex
		System lacks differentiation capability between real and prerecorded voices
Handwritten Signature Verification	Fast and easy to use	Lower levels of performance and reliability
	Any pen that produces fine lines can be used	Possible issues with portability for laptop users
	Easily integrated into existing equipment	

Source: Heinzdell Conate, and Maria Hart, "Biometric Security: Retina Scan," unpublished research paper, University of Virginia, April 22, 2002, 19–20.

OUTLOOK

Biometric technology has greatly solved the problems of forgotten passwords and stolen IDs. As more and more electronic transactions are carried out, the need to secure private and sensitive information related to these transactions will grow. An array of biometric devices has gotten a foothold in the mainstream security arena from iris scanners to voice recognition technology. It is important to note that competition does not exist between biometric technologies. It is not a race of which biometric technology will surpass the others. Iris scanning will become most popular and reliable for high-security operations. Other biometric technologies are expected to be coupled with passwords. Furthermore, some analysts believe that the way in which passwords are typed might become a biometric solution, or perhaps the very action of typing will become a password in itself.

With all of these developments, it is predicted that biometric fraud will become more sophisticated as personal computers, financial networks, passports, and even border crossings make more use of the technology. To ensure security, IBM researchers produced a biometric device that reduces an image to a "template" of "minutiae points" in the form of a loop in a fingerprint or the position of an eye. These points are then transformed into a numeric string by a mathematical formula and stored for later analysis. Such mathematical templates are then converted to altered images, so that if hackers should crack a biometric database, they could steal only the distortion rather than the original face or fingerprint (Associated Press 2005). See Figure 13.6.

When considering biometric technologies for future use, management does need to implement a cost-effective system appropriate for their particular circumstance. It is important for each business to analyze its needs and determine which system works best in the given environment. Currently, fingerprint identification devices lead the way in terms of cost and reliability. The reason is the one-in-a-billion chance that two people will have the same fingerprint. Law enforcement and other agencies rely on the expensive and expansive fingerprint identification systems, and inexpensive and smaller machines are now making their way into computer-based companies and financial organizations. Today, biometric systems also are being adopted at an increasing pace for controlling access to restricted facilities such as airports and laboratories.

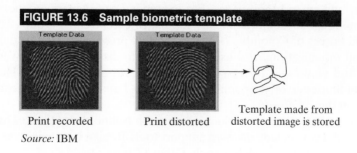

FIGURE 13.6   Sample biometric template

Print recorded   Print distorted   Template made from distorted image is stored

Source: IBM

HOW TO SECURE YOUR SYSTEM

A number of steps can be taken to make a system secure. Turn off unneeded or unnecessary services. On Unix environments, services that are not in great demand can be disabled easily. In peer-to-peer sharing, make sure the machines linked to the Internet share no files. Any shared files should be password protected. Install a firewall between your network and the Internet such that the firewall will allow outgoing connections from the network to the Internet but forbid incoming connections, except a selected set of services (default deny). For a basic network-Internet environment, an inexpensive router provides simple firewall filtering and other firewall functions.

Monitor and know your system. Most network administrators never realize their systems have been attacked. Successful attacks leave traces. If you review logs, they can alert you to follow a procedure to prevent attacks from recurring. Automated log analyzers can be used to flag suspicious activities.

One way of knowing your system is to stay on top of basic features that keep it secure. For example, install and run a virus-checking package. If your system gets hacked and has to be rebuilt, make sure you have the methodology to rebuild quickly with minimum delays.

SECURITY AND TERRORISM

We live in an age of terror and growing fear. Spam, viruses, denial of service, intellectual property theft, transactional fraud, and national security espionage are already at all-time highs. What is adding fuel is Internet misuse by terrorists. Like it or not, the Internet has become a forum for terrorist groups to spread their hate and to communicate with one another and with sympathizers. The Internet has become the mule for spreading fear and laundering money. Terrorists use the Internet to electronically funnel funds to their cells worldwide. Attacking computer networks earned them the title of "cyberterrorists."

Recent fears of terrorism have prompted the *National Strategy to Secure Cyberspace*. The five initiatives, overseen by the Department of Homeland Security, were passed by Congress in 2002. A selected list of foreign terrorist organizations is shown in Table 13.6.

The State Department has over 30 foreign terrorist organizations on its black list. Most of them maintain Web sites, using encrypted e-mail messages to plan attacks and spread their cause. For example, Latin American guerrilla movements are among the most electronically sophisticated extremist groups. The revolutionary Armed Forces of Colombia (FARC) conduct press inquiries through e-mail. Islamic militant organizations also use the Internet to disseminate anti-Western, anti-Israel news and views and to raise funds. In fact, organizations like Hezbollah (a pro-Iranian Shiite terrorist organization in South Lebanon) sell publications about their cause on their Web site.

To combat terrorism, various information technology (IT) tools have already been employed. They include decision support tools, foreign language tools, pattern analysis tools, and predictive modeling tools. Other IT tools include:

TABLE 13.6   A sample of U.S. labeled terrorist organizations

Organization	URL	Language
Al-Gama'a al-Islamiyya (Islamic Group)	www.azzam.com	English
Al-Qaeda	www.alneda.com	Arabic
Hamas	www.palestine-info.com/hamas	Arabic, English
Harakat ul-Mujahidin (HUM)	www.ummah.net.pk/harakat	Arabic, English
Hezbollah	www.hezbollah.org	Arabic, English
Kahane Chai (Kach)	www.kahane.org	English
Kurdistan Workers Party (PKK)	www.pkk.org/index.html	Kurdish
Liberation Tigers of Tamil Eelam	www.eelamweb.com	English
National Liberation Army (ELN), Colombia	www.eln-voces.com	Spanish
Palestine Islamic Jihad (PIJ)	www.entifada.net	Arabic
Popular Front for the Liberation of Palestine (PFLP)	www.pflp-pal.org/main.html	English
Revolutionary Armed Forces of Colombia (FARC)	www.farc-ep.org	English, Spanish, Portuguese, Italian, German, Russian
United Self-Defense Forces of Colombia	colombia-libre.org/colombialibre/pp.asp	Spanish

Other Organizations	Home
Tupac Amaru	Peru
Shining Path	Peru
Hizbut-Tahrir	UK
Jerusalem Battalion (offshoot of PIJ)	West Bank
Republic of Texas	Texas
Ohio Unorganized Militia	Ohio
Anti-Defamation League	New York

- Biometrics—Identify human terrorists via fingerprint, face, gait, iris, voice.
- Event detection and notification—Monitor simple and complex events and notify users.
- Categorization and clustering—Use artificial intelligence, machine learning, pattern recognition, and statistical analysis to extract meaning and cluster documents with similar contents.

- Knowledge management—Use semantic Web and related technologies to make explicit (expose via Web services) an analyst's tacit understanding of a problem.

- Publishing—Generate concise, accurate summaries of recent newsworthy items.

- Visualization—Provide graphical display, time-based charts, and built-in drill-down tools to help investigators discover and visualize networks of inter-related information. (Popp, et al. 2004)

SECURITY AND THE USA PATRIOT ACT

Just six weeks after the tragic September 11, 2001 terrorist attacks on the World Trade Center and the Pentagon, a jittery Congress passed the USA Patriot Act. The act confers vast powers on the executive branch. It expands government law enforcement agencies' surveillance and investigative authority in the United States, especially with regard to the Internet. Such authority interferes with fundamental constitutional protections of individual liberty and privacy. This is especially the case when intercepting information transmitted over the Internet and other high-speed technology.

The hastily drafted and far-reaching legislation spans 342 pages and was passed with virtually no public hearings or debate. The USA Patriot Act is a clumsy title, which means "**U**niting and **S**trengthening **A**merica by **P**roviding **A**ppropriate **T**ools **R**equired to **I**ntercept and **O**bscure **T**errorism **A**ct of 2001" (www.epic.org/privacy/terrorism/usapatriot.) The act is a compromise version of the Anti-Terrorism Act of 2001 (ATA), intended to strengthen the nation's defense against terrorism. It sacrifices political freedom in the name of national security. The essence of ATA was to monitor private communications and access personal information. It also included the so-called "sunset provision" that provides an automatic expiration date for several sections of the act, unless renewed by Congress.

The USA Patriot Act brought major changes to U.S. law and the Internet, including several amendments:

- Wiretap Statute (Title III): Allows law enforcement authorities to perform interception of voice or data content.

- Electronic Communications Privacy Act (ECPA): This law determines government access to one's stored e-mail and other electronic communications. All a government agency has to do to obtain a court order is to certify with the court the need to initiate surveillance that is relevant to an ongoing criminal investigation.

- Foreign Intelligence Surveillance Act (FISA): This act allows the government to conduct electronic surveillance against any person based on probable cause.

There is no question these major acts have had implications for online privacy. The USA Patriot Act authorizes a "trap and trace" device to capture incoming phone numbers placed to a specific phone line, which allows the recording of all computer routing and signaling information. The government can also capture the incoming electronic impulses that identify the originating number, routing, addressing, and signaling information that identify the source, a wire, or electronic communication. This covers e-mail, Web surfing, and other forms of electronic communications. Doing so means the government is now able to gain access to personal financial information without any suspicion of wrongdoing.

Related to online security is Internet casinos that have become an attractive bet for criminals needing to launder their ill-gotten gains, because of the increasing difficulties in tracking cyber transactions. Online gambling is a cover for money laundering over the Internet. Other organized crime groups known for money laundering include:

- Columbian Cali Cartel—perfected money laundering mechanisms and flood Western Europe and the Americas with hundreds of tons of cocaine each year.
- Hell's Angels—extend their illicit business (amphetamines and LSD) into prostitution, extortion, and theft, much of it by e-mail.
- Nigerians—have used the Internet, regular mail, and e-mail to flood the world with over 400 scams. Nigeria has been labeled the world's capital of scam.
- Italian gangs, especially the Sicilian Mafia—active in fraud and drugs. They have been known to own and operate legitimate businesses, which are then used for money laundering and other illicit acts.
- Indian and Pakistani gangs—deal in heroin from Pakistan and Afghanistan and are quite good at credit card fraud and major thefts in the subcontinent.
- Russian Mafia—heavily involved in drugs, car theft, immigration, and prostitution in Belgium, the Netherlands, Germany, and neighboring countries. They are heavy users of establishing fake accounts, transferring funds into and out of such accounts—all via the Internet.
- Turkish gangs—deal heavily in drug trafficking across Middle Eastern and former Soviet Union borders. It is estimated that over 80 percent of its illicit business now is carried out encrypted over the Internet. (See Chapter 12 on online gambling.)

MONEY LAUNDERING AND THE INTERNET

More powerful than the high-speed boats or jets that transport illicit money to the drug cartels or terrorists is the electronic use of legitimate commercial banks to move illicit dollars in a chain fashion, wherein they eventually reach their destination intact. Money laundering is any act of concealing or disguising the identity of illegally obtained proceeds so that they appear to have originated from legitimate sources. Illegal money is put through a cycle of transactions—"washed"—so that it comes out the other end (destination) as legal, or clean money (see www.laundryman.u-net.com/page1hist.html).

Money laundering involves two stages:

1. Cash paid into banks and used to buy high-value goods, property, etc.
2. A few days following the initial transaction, cash is wire transferred overseas, to be received "clean" by the same party or a representative.

A complex web of transfers makes tracing original source funds virtually impossible. To illustrate, here is a summary of Saddam Hussein's oil scam:

- A company intends to buy oil from Iraq.
- Instead of a direct payment, it acquires oil from a Saddam-controlled brokerage company outside Iraq, in Russia or Switzerland.

- The broker forwards 95 percent of the money to the Iraq Oil Ministry and keeps the remaining 5 percent as a kickback to Saddam. The 5 percent, in turn, is deposited electronically in smaller amounts to various accounts in Eastern European and Middle Eastern banks under Saddam's family members and relatives via shell companies controlled by Saddam's agents. A shell company is a "front" organization in countries like Luxembourg, Panama, and Lichtenstein.

- Once deposited, the 5 percent is converted to cash or gold, which went directly to Saddam in Baghdad.

It is important to understand that money laundering is global. Money gets wired electronically via private lines and over the Internet anywhere under pseudonyms or false accounts around the clock. Soon after Congress created the USA Patriot Act, special-purpose technology was developed to combat money laundering worldwide. Progress is slow, but it is beginning to show results.

IMPLICATIONS FOR MANAGEMENT

Right now, the Internet is running amok. It is becoming an increasingly filtered channel of communication. The material in this chapter should send a warning to management about the growing threat of attacks on the company's information infrastructure. Computer security vulnerabilities have shot up as more people start to use the Internet. Based on a 2005 Carnegie Melon University CERT Coordination Center Study, there were 945 million Internet users worldwide compared to 400 million in 2000. Likewise, 3,780,000 vulnerabilities were reported in 2004 compared to 1 million in 2000. All of this adds up to one conclusion—knowing the enemy is the first requirement for shaping an information security defense system. Security must also be the priority when it comes to the next generation of the Internet (Cha 2005, A1).

Despite these warnings, information security continues to be deemphasized or ignored by management at all levels of the organization. The result is vulnerable systems with easy breaches from within and from outside the firm. To correct this situation, those responsible must begin with an understanding of the threats facing the information system and examine the vulnerabilities in a methodical and timely fashion. Once identified, vulnerabilities or threats should be prioritized and action taken immediately.

Changes in the identification of threats, the growing advancement of technologies, and the identification of new threats continue to shift the organizational security focus. Based on various studies conducted since 2000, the five major threats facing today's organization are deliberate software attacks, technical software failures, human error or failure, deliberate acts of trespass, and deliberate acts of vandalism. The number one threat continues to be malicious code.

Any serious profile should begin with a valid security policy, which is then translated into an effective security plan with a focus on prevention, detection, and correction of threats. Additionally, each firm should implement an employee security education and awareness program. Such programs should be geared to instilling the importance of security and protection of information throughout the firm. With the support of employees and an established company security policy, there is not much more a security officer can do but wait and handle events as they occur.

Summary

1. The electronic system that supports e-commerce can fail due to fraud, theft of confidential information, disruption of service, or loss of customer confidence. Internet security is about protecting information.

2. Paper-based commerce involves signed paper documents, person-to-person interaction, physical payment systems, and easily negotiable documents of title. In contrast, electronic commerce involves digital signatures, electronic payment systems, no face-to-face interaction, difficult-to-detect modifications, and negotiable documents requiring special security protocols.

3. Several reasons account for the recent emphasis on information security: Global trading; online, real-time trading; availability of reliable security packages; and changes in attitude toward security.

4. Designing for e-security involves five steps: adopting a security policy that makes sense, considering Web security needs, designing the security environment, policing the security perimeter, and authorizing and monitoring the security system.

5. Web merchants must consider three kinds of threats: those that are physically related, those that are order related, and those that are electronically related.

6. No network is completely immune from viruses. A virus is classified by the way it infects the system. Examples are a file virus, a boot virus, and a macrovirus. In terms of characteristics, a virus may be a fast virus, a slow virus, or a stealth virus.

7. To install an antivirus strategy, you need to establish enforceable rules, educate users in how to check for viruses, and periodically update the latest antivirus software.

8. A firewall is a software system that detects intruders, blocks them from entry, and keeps track of what they do and where they originated. Most firewalls either block unwanted traffic (default deny) or permit only wanted traffic (default permit). In either case, the focus is on access control.

9. Hackers, spammers, spyware, phishing, and identity theft have already infected the Internet, and are on the verge of bringing it to a virtual halt. This means the Internet that was created by academics must be reinvented, reborn, and redesigned with better security and far improved privacy for business and private traffic.

10. Spyware and identify theft are beginning to get the attention of government regulators, who are now trying to enact laws to eradicate these unyielding menaces from continuing to wreak havoc with business and private Internet traffic.

11. Guidelines have been publicized in various technical magazines and newspapers about how users can protect themselves from identity theft. The guidelines in the chapter are a general summary.

12. When it comes to the use of Internet for illicit acts, money laundering is a major activity that continues to get worse. The USA Patriot Act was designed to combat laundered money that is funneled to terrorists worldwide.

Key Terms

- **adware** (p. 426)
- **authentication** (p. 415)
- **biometrics** (p. 437)
- **cyberwall** (p. 434)
- **denial of service (DOS)** (p. 420)
- **encryption** (p. 432)
- **firewall** (p. 414)
- **intrusion detection** (p. 423)

- **monitoring** (p. 416)
- **privacy** (p. 405)
- **security perimeter** (p. 414)

- **sniffer** (p. 419)
- **spoof** (p. 420)
- **spyware** (p. 426)

- **virus** (p. 424)

Test Your Understanding

1. The electronic system that supports e-commerce is susceptible to abuse and failure in many ways. Do you agree with this statement?
2. In what way is the Internet different from the traditional ways of doing business?
3. Elaborate on the security design process. What steps are involved? How does each step contribute to effective security?
4. What threats or crimes must Web merchants consider? Why? Be specific.
5. How are client computers attacked? Explain briefly.
6. How are server attacks launched? Give an example.
7. What is a virus? How does a company know its computers or files have a virus?
8. List some of the basics of choosing a password.
9. What are the design and implementation issues that should be addressed by a firewall design?
10. The ICSA identifies specific features that should be considered in firewall design. Explain each feature briefly.

Discussion Questions

1. How would a business decide how much risk it can afford?
2. Given the momentum in Internet business, is there a reason to worry about security in cyberspace? Why?
3. Suppose your e-commerce server is under attack from at least one malicious source. What types of threats are possible? How would you recommend handling such threats?

Web Exercises

1. Work with another classmate and set up an interview with a local e-merchant to address the security schemes embedded in its business-to-consumer business. Report your findings in class.
2. Assume you have been asked to serve as a consultant for a local grocer interested in launching an online business on the Internet. Develop a security plan that can be incorporated as part of the technical infrastructure.
3. MasterCard, Visa, and American Express are interested in the SET protocol for securing credit card transactions. Contact one of the agencies and find out the latest in security protocol and how well SET is being supported.
4. Review three Web sites on the Internet: one large e-business Web site (e.g., Dell.com), a large bank Web site (e.g., Bankofamerica.com), and a portal Web site (e.g., Yahoo.com). Review each site's security measures. How do they compare? What is unique about each site's security protocol? Write a 300-word report for class.

CHAPTER 14

ENCRYPTION

A MATTER OF TRUST

Learning Objectives

The focus of this chapter is on several learning objectives:

- Understanding the basic algorithm used in encryption
- Issues in public-key cryptography
- Tools used for authentication and trust
- Brief coverage of the main Internet security protocols and standards
- Implications and future of encryption in e-commerce

IN A NUTSHELL

Ensuring the security of electronic data is a serious business. The transmission of purchase information, credit card numbers, and other transaction information must be secure to give consumers and merchants the confidence they need to do business over the Internet. One way to have secure transmissions is to use cryptography to **encrypt** or encode data so it can be read only by the parties to the transaction.

encrypt (encipher): transform a plaintext into ciphertext.

In Greek, *cryptography* means "secret writing," which is the science of communication over untrusted communication channels. **Encryption** is a cryptographic technique that encodes data so it cannot be read without a key. The ancient Egyptians developed hieroglyphics to disguise their messages (www.computerworld.com). Julius Caesar used an alphabetical code to communicate with his field commanders. Technology has progressed significantly since ancient times, and now we have a number of sophisticated encryption tools.

encryption: a mathematical procedure that scrambles data so that it is extremely difficult for anyone other than authorized recipients to recover the original message.

Without encryption, e-commerce is nearly impossible. When shopping online or doing Internet banking, encryption makes payments or transmittal of financial information safe. Encryption is important in protecting burglar alarms, cash machines, postal meters, automated teller machines (ATMs), electronic funds transfers, trade secrets, health records, personnel files, and credit card transactions on the Net. It is also essential for national security. Because good encryption is so valuable, the U.S. government has developed stringent rules for cryptography. Organizations such as the National Security Council, the National Computer Security Center, and the National Institute of Standards and Technology work to control the use of encryption and to prevent it from becoming a threat to society.

In this chapter, we cover the basic principles of cryptography, why it is essential, and how it is used in e-commerce transactions. Remember that payment systems (Chapter 15) and security measures (Chapter 13) rely on encryption. We also look at the future. Currently, encryption protocols use mainly public-key infrastructure (PKI) software. The future of encryption, however, lies in elliptic-curve cryptography and eventually in quantum computers. Quantum computing is far ahead of anything we are familiar with today and will make any current cryptography obsolete.

WHAT IS ENCRYPTION?

Encryption is a way to transform a message so that only the sender and recipient can read, see, or understand it. The mechanism is based on the use of mathematical procedures to scramble data so that it is extremely difficult for anyone other than authorized recipients to recover the original message (**plaintext or cleartext**). The formula or algorithm converts the intended data (credit card number, Social Security number, medical record, and so on) into an encoded message using a key to decode or decipher the message. A **key** is a series of electronic signals stored on the PC's hard disk or transmitted as blips of data over transmission lines. A special key decrypts the message back to its original state.

plaintext (cleartext): the message that is being protected.

key: a series of electronic signals stored on a PC's hard disk or transmitted as blips of data over transmission lines.

If someone scrambles information before it is transmitted, eavesdroppers cannot read what was written, unless they take pains to crack the code. The good news is that it took years before the United States allowed the use of encryption. The government focused not on the benefits, but the dangers—the fear that terrorists, child pornographers, or drug dealers would be able to promote their businesses using cryptography. (See Box 14.1.) Yet, even with today's increasing use of cryptography, millions of medical records, credit card databases, and other repositories continue to be vulnerable.

Think of a cryptographic algorithm as the lock on a home's front door. Most door locks have a spindle containing four pins, and each pin can be set in 1 of 10 positions. When you insert the right key, it sets the pins in a configuration that matches

---

BOX 14.1

Encryption and Terrorism

The destruction of the World Trade Center and the attack on the Pentagon come at a delicate time in the evolution of the technologies of surveillance and privacy. In the aftermath of September 11, 2001, our attitude toward these tools may well take a turn that has profound implications for the way individuals are monitored and tracked, for decades to come.

Did encryption empower these terrorists? And would restricting crypto have given the authorities a chance to stop these acts? The answer is quite possibly yes. We do know that Osama bin Laden, who has been invoked as a suspect, was a sophisticated consumer of crypto technology. In the recent trial over the bombing of the Libyan embassy, prosecutors introduced evidence that bin Laden had mobile satellite phones that used strong crypto. Even if bin Laden was not behind it, the acts show a degree of organization that indicates the terrorists were smart enough to scramble their communications to make them more difficult, if not impossible, to understand. If not for encryption, notes former USAF Colonel Marc Enger (now working for security firm Digital Defense) "they could have used steganography [hiding messages between the pixels of a digital image] or Web anonymizers [which cloak the origin of messages]."

Source: Excerpted from Steven Levy, "Did Encryption Empower These Terrorists?" *Newsweek Web Exclusive,* www.msnbc.com/news/627390.asp?0si=. Accessed June 2003.

---

the teeth in the key. When both align correctly, the door opens. With 104 or 10,000 possible keys, a burglar potentially has to try all these possibilities before being able to break in. Imagine an improved lock with 100 million (108) possible keys. Unfortunately, when the going gets tough, the burglar might use brute force and attack via the window or side door, or by forcing entry at gunpoint. The same thing happens with encryption. Hackers first use generic software that has been tried on low-security PCs and if that does not work, they physically enter one combination after another until they succeed at breaking into the PC or decrypting the message(s) they're after. With the right experience, they usually succeed one way or the other.

Today's powerful PCs and cryptographic algorithms make it possible for anyone to use authentication and encryption. How do you know whether your browser is encrypting your information? One way to tell when you purchase an item online using Netscape's browser is this: If the picture of a lock in the lower left-hand corner is in the *locked* position with a glow around it, you're most likely using encryption. Another way is to look at the Internet address you are visiting. If it starts with *https*, the "s" means secure—you're using a secure server that has encryption.

Encryption has had a long history of improvement, dating back to the early 1970s when an effort was made to learn how to create new tools of privacy. As summarized in Box 14.2, the most recent event was in 1999, when Al Gore, former vice president of the United States, signed off on regulations allowing the export of strong crypto.

BOX 14.2

Brief History of Encryption Growth

1971: Below the National Security Administration's (NSA) radar, math vagabond Whit Diffie begins crisscrossing the country to learn how to create new tools of privacy.

1974: Berkeley undergrad Ralph Merkle finds a way that two people can communicate secretly without prearrangements. His teacher suggests he write about something more sensible.

1976: Diffie and Martin Hellman publish "New Directions in Cryptography," introducing the public-key concept that enables large-scale privacy and e-commerce.

1977: Three MIT professors — Ron **R**ivest, Adi **S**hamir, and Len **A**dleman — create RSA, an elegant implementation of public key.

1979: NSA goes public to warn people about the spread of crypto not under its control.

1983: RSA Data Security is founded, the first company to commercialize public-key crypto.

1986: Lotus Development Corp. licenses RSA for its planned Notes software, then fights NSA for export clearance.

1991: Phil Zimmermann gives away PGP, a strong encryption program. To Fed dismay, it becomes a global favorite.

1993: Clinton administration endorses the ill-fated Clipper Chip.

1995: Netscape goes public; its crypto-enabled browser establishes need for secure e-commerce.

1999: Fed surrender: Al Gore signs off on regulations, finally allowing the export of strong crypto.

Source: Excerpted from Steven Levy, "Crypto," *Newsweek,* January 15, 2001, 48–49.

Public-key infrastructure (PKI) creates the ability to authenticate users, maintain privacy, ensure data integrity, and process transactions without the risk of repudiation. It satisfies four e-security needs.

1. **Authentication.** Identifies or verifies that the senders of messages are, in fact, who they claim to be. For example, Jane, an e-customer, wants to be sure that she is dealing with a legitimate vendor. Likewise, the vendor wants to make sure that Jane is really Jane. (An imposter who sends a false message is **spoofing.**) For example, a hacker can concoct a fake Web site and, through a security hole in the genuine Web site, allow his Web site IP address to substitute for that of the real one. Then innocent traffic going to the legitimate Web site is funneled to the fake site. When orders or queries arrive, the hacker can make all kinds of alterations — direct the traffic to a third Web site, change the nature of the orders, and so on.

> **spoofing:** the act of sending a message while pretending to be the authorized user.

2. **Integrity.** Verifies that neither the purchase amount nor the goods bought are changed or lost during transmission. Integrity also means the message has not reached the recipient twice. In the case of Jane, she and the vendor want to

ensure that attackers cannot change the price, purchase amount, or quantity. A nonelectronic mechanism example of integrity is indelible ink or a hologram on a credit card.

3. **Nonrepudiation.** Prevents sender and vendor in a transaction or communication activity from later falsely denying that the transaction occurred. **Nonrepudiation** is like sending a certified letter with a return receipt via the U.S. postal system. Like a receipt accompanying the registered letter, because a digital signature accompanies the transfer of data, the originator cannot deny having sent the message. In our example, the vendor wants to make sure that Jane cannot deny having placed the order. A nonelectronic mechanism of nonrepudiation is knowledge of mother's maiden name or a photo ID card.

nonrepudiation: procedure that prevents sender and vendor from credibly denying that they sent or received a specific message, file, or transmission.

4. **Privacy.** Shields communications from unauthorized viewing or access. Jane might not want her spouse or any other person to know what she is transacting, nor does the vendor want to reveal the special deal he has made for that particular customer. Privacy protection implies confidentiality and anonymity. *Confidentiality,* or message content security, means that during the transmission from sender to receiver, no third party can access the contents of the message or identify the sender and receiver. *Anonymity* means outsiders cannot trace, link or observe the contents of the message. An anonymous record is one that cannot be associated with a particular individual, either from the data itself or by combining the record with other records.

THE BASIC ALGORITHM SYSTEM

Cryptographic techniques are a means of securely transferring data over Internet applications. It is the science of applying complex mathematics to increase the security of electronic transactions. The techniques provide assurance that the data will be viewed only by the intended parties. Basic encryption relies on two components: an algorithm and a key. Encrypting information is simple: A computer program is used that has an encryption algorithm. The algorithm converts data, documents, credit card numbers, and other information into an encoded message using a key.

For encryption to work, both sender and receiver have to know the rules used to transform the original message or transaction into its coded form. A set of rules for encoding and decoding messages is called a **cipher** (or cypher). The encoded message is called a **ciphertext.** A message can be **decrypted** only if the decryption key matches the encryption key. For most algorithms, the keys are the same.

cipher: a set of rules for encoding and decoding messages.

ciphertext: an encoded message; the result of transforming a plaintext via encryption.

decrypt: transform a ciphertext into plaintext.

How many possible keys can each algorithm support? This depends on the number of bits in the key. For example, a 6-bit key allows for only 64 possible numeric combinations (2^6), each called a key. The greater the number of possible keys, the more complex the key becomes and the more difficult it is to crack an encrypted message. A hacker using the brute-force method would potentially have to try every combination before finding the right key. The key could also be guessed correctly on the first try.

The standard 56-bit DES encryption code can be cracked on a high-speed computer in a few hours. Even Certicom Corporation's encryption code, which took the power of 10,000 computers running continuously for 549 days to protect digital data, was cracked by Notre Dame researcher Chris Monico in 2000. With a 100-bit (2^{100}) key, it could take a computer, guessing at 1 million keys every second, years to discover the right key. The security of an encryption algorithm, therefore, is related to the length of the key. Knowing the key length gives you an idea of how much time it will take to break the code.

Late in 2002, a quantum encryption prototype was developed by two Northwestern University professors to encode entire high-speed data streams moving at 250 Mbits/ second. Professors Prem Kumar and Horace Yuen use quantum codes to encrypt the signal sent down the Internet's optical fiber backbone.

CLASSES OF ALGORITHMS

secret-key (symmetric) encryption: encryption system in which sender and receiver possess the same key; the key used to encrypt a message also can be used to decrypt it.

There are two classes of key-based algorithms: **secret key or symmetric,** and public key or asymmetric. In secret-key, or symmetric encryption, sender and recipient possess the same *single* key. Both parties can encrypt and decrypt messages with the same key. (See Figure 14.1.) This can pose two problems: One, the key must be delivered securely to the two parties involved. Hand delivery or generating a complex network-based scheme makes key distribution an awkard process. The second problem is that if a business has 10 business vendors, it needs 10 different single keys unique to each vendor. Key distribution for multiple keys can be a hassle.

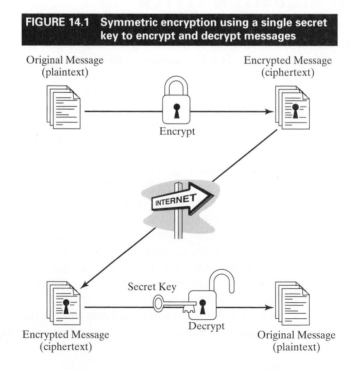

FIGURE 14.1   Symmetric encryption using a single secret key to encrypt and decrypt messages

Original Message (plaintext)

Encrypted Message (ciphertext)

Encrypt

INTERNET

Encrypted Message (ciphertext)

Secret Key

Decrypt

Original Message (plaintext)

However, symmetric encryption satisfies the requirement of message content security, because the content cannot be read without the shared secret key. The process of providing a secure mechanism for creating and passing on the secret key is called *key management*. This topic will be covered later in the chapter.

stream cipher: a symmetric algorithm that encrypts a single bit of plaintext at a time.

Symmetric algorithms can be divided into stream ciphers and block ciphers. **Stream ciphers** encrypt a single bit of plaintext at a time, whereas **block ciphers** encrypt a number of bits (normally 64) as a single unit.

block cipher: a symmetric algorithm thatencrypts a number of bits as a single unit.

Public-key, or asymmetric, encryption involves two related keys called a *key-pair* or *dual key*: one public key that anyone can know and one private key that only the owner knows. One half of the pair (public key) can encrypt information that only the other half (private key or secret key) can decrypt (see Figure 14.2). The private key is assigned to one designated owner, but the public key can be announced to the world. It can be published in a newspaper, on a server, on a Web site, or via a service provider so that anyone can encrypt with it.

public-key (asymmetric) encryption: encoding/ decoding using two mathematically related keys or key-pairs: one public key and one private key.

The key-pairs can be used in two different ways.

1. **To provide message confidentiality.** The sender uses the recipient's public key to encrypt a message to remain confidential until decoded by the recipient with the private key. Suppose Jay wants to send a confidential message to Ellen. He would first acquire Ellen's public key. Then he would use that key to encrypt the message and send it to her. If a third party intercepts the message and tries to decode

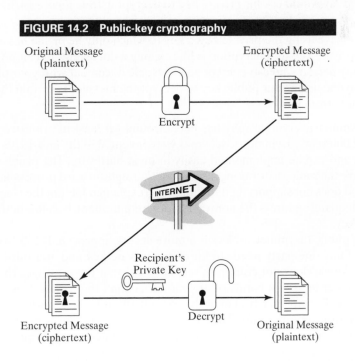

FIGURE 14.2   Public-key cryptography

Original Message (plaintext)

Encrypted Message (ciphertext)

Encrypt

INTERNET

Recipient's Private Key

Encrypted Message (ciphertext)

Decrypt

Original Message (plaintext)

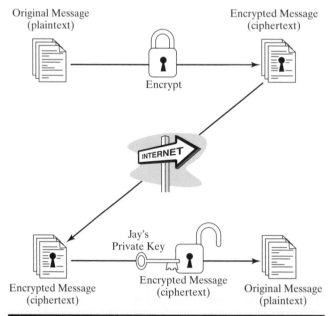

Original Message
(plaintext)

Encrypt

Encrypted Message
(ciphertext)

INTERNET

Encrypted Message
(ciphertext)

Jay's
Private Key

Encrypted Message
(ciphertext)

Original Message
(plaintext)

FIGURE 14.3 Message confidentiality using a key-pair

it using Ellen's public key, it won't work. Because only Ellen has the private key, only she can decrypt it. Were Ellen to send a reply, she would use Jay's public key, and Jay would use his private key to decrypt it. (See Figure 14.3.)

2. **To prove the authenticity of the message originator.** The sender encrypts a message using the private key, a key to which only he or she has access. Using a private key for encryption is like signing a document. Because you are the only person who can encrypt an electronic document with your private key, anyone using your public key to decrypt the message is certain that the message came from you.

Symmetric cryptography has been around (at least in primitive forms) for more than 2,000 years; asymmetric schemes were invented in the mid-1970s. Asymmetric key is fast and can be implemented easily in most hardware. The problems are that both keys are the same, distributing keys is not a straightforward process, and the symmetric method does not support digital signatures (explained later in the chapter). It also does not adequately address the nonrepudiation requirement, because both parties have the same key.

A public (asymmetric) key is a more secure approach. It has two distinct advantages: Only one party needs to know the private key and, if a third party knows the public key, it does not compromise the security of the message. The decryption key need never be in the hands of anyone other than the owner. It is easy to distribute the keys. The approach also addresses all the integrity, authentication, and non-repudiation requirements. The main disadvantage is that it takes time to compute. Currently, a 1,024-bit asymmetric key length is necessary to provide security. This

TABLE 14.1 Estimated time and cost of breaking different key lengths				
	Key Length (Bits)			
Estimated Cost to Break Key	*40*	*64*	*80*	*128*
$100,000	2 sec	1 year	70,000 years	10^{19} years
$1 million	0.2 sec	37 days	7,000 years	10^{18} years
$100 million	2 millisec	9 hours	70 years	10^{16} years
$1 billion	0.2 millisec	1 hour	7 years	10^{15} years

Source: Bruce Schneier, *Applied Cryptography* (2nd ed.), New York: John Wiley & Sons, 1997, 153.

requires a lot of processing power, resulting in delays when large volumes of messages are sent.

The choice of an encryption method depends on the sensitivity of the data to be protected and the duration of the protection. Typically, the encryption method and key length chosen should take longer to break than the time the data stay sensitive. Table 14.1 summarizes sample key lengths and the time it takes to break a key, using a brute-force attack.

COMMON CRYPTOSYSTEMS

Symmetric algorithms use the same key for encryption and decryption. The key is not to be leaked to outsiders and should be changed often to ensure security. This means that a longer key means higher security. Symmetric algorithms are generally faster than asymmetric ones and use shorter keys. In the following section, we summarize the key public- and secret-key algorithms. No better or more powerful ones have been introduced to date.

RSA ALGORITHM.   **RSA** is the most commonly used public-key algorithm, although it is vulnerable to attack. Named after its inventors, Ron **R**ivest, Adi **S**hamir, and Len **A**dleman of the Massachusetts Institute of Technology (MIT), RSA was first published in 1978. It is used for encryption as well as for electronic signatures. RSA lets you choose the size of your public key. The 512-bit keys are considered insecure or weak. The 768-bit keys are secure from everything but the National Security Administration (NSA). The 1,024-bit keys are secure from virtually anything. The U.S. patent on this algorithm expired in the year 2000. RSA is embedded in major products such as Windows, Netscape Navigator, Intuit's Quicken, and Lotus Notes.

RSA: the most commonly used public-key algorithm.

How strong is RSA? Its strength depends on the time and the cost of the equipment performing the decryption. To illustrate, an international team of scientists was asked to break a 129-digit RSA block cipher in 1994. The total processing power used was comparable to the processing power of a single Pentium 100-MHz computer running nonstop for 46 years. With improvements in computing power and cost, RSA's vulnerability has increased. It is estimated that an attacker with $20,000 to spend will be able to break a 425-bit block cipher.

DATA ENCRYPTION STANDARDS (DES).

Data Encryption Standards (DES): a popular secret-key encryption system; the first to be widely adopted commercially.

Data Encryption Standards (DES) was developed by IBM in 1974 in response to a public solicitation from the U.S. Department of Commerce. It was adopted as a U.S. federal standard in 1977 and as a financial industry standard in 1981.

DES is the first symmetric system to be widely adopted commercially. Any change to a message encrypted with DES turns the message into a mess of unintelligible characters. As a block cipher with 64-bit size, DES uses a 56-bit key to encrypt a 64-bit plaintext block into a 64-bit ciphertext. A 56-bit key might seem easy to crack, but it is strong enough to give most random hackers a run for their money.

DES messages can be decrypted by a huge computer mainframe or by thousands of small ones working together. DES is known to be a good block cipher design because no practical attack more efficient than exhaustive key search is known to threaten the integrity of the algorithm. In an exhaustive key search, the attacker systematically attempts to decrypt a ciphertext block against all possible key values until it runs into the value that will decrypt the message. To do this type of search requires powerful computing resources.

3DES.

triple DES (3DES): a stronger version of DES that uses three 56-bit keys to encrypt each block of plaintext.

A stronger version of DES, called **Triple DES (3DES),** uses three 56-bit keys to encrypt each block. The first key encrypts the data block, the second key decrypts the data block, and the third key encrypts the same data block again. The 3DES version requires a 168-bit key that makes the process quite secure and much safer than plain DES. It can secure the most valuable data, even that of large corporations.

RC4.

RC4: variable-length cipher widely used on the Internet as a bulk encryption cipher in SSL protocol.

RC4 was designed by Ron Rivest RSA Data Security Inc. This variable-length cipher is widely used on the Internet as the bulk encryption cipher in the Secure Sockets Layer (SSL) protocol, with key lengths ranging from 40 to 128 bits. RC4 has a reputation of being fast, although its security is unknown. The U.S. government routinely approves RC4 with 40-bit keys for export, but keys this small can be broken easily by criminals, amateurs, and governments. (SSL is explained later in the chapter.)

INTERNATIONAL DATA ENCRYPTION ALGORITHM (IDEA).

IDEA: a strong encryption algorithm using a 128-bit key to encrypt 64-bit blocks; resistant to brute-force attack.

International Data Encryption Algorithm (IDEA) was created in Switzerland in 1991. It offers strong encryption using a 128-bit key to encrypt 64-bit blocks, which makes it resistant to brute-force attacks. This system is widely used as the bulk encryption cipher in older versions of Pretty Good Privacy (PGP) systems, covered later in the chapter.

ISSUES IN PUBLIC-KEY CRYPTOGRAPHY

The choice of who generates key-pairs is an issue that has plagued the security industry. The choices are the key owner, a service organization of the owner's choice, or a government agency. In the case of the owner, the private key never travels outside the owner's computer, and the owner must have the technical competence to perform the necessary mathematical functions. In the case of a service organization, the private key resides with the service organization and must travel to the owner. The owner has to trust the organization not to keep a copy.

In the case of a government agency generating key-pairs, the private key has to travel, trust must exist, and the location of all private keys is known to the state agency. If individual organizations lose their private keys, they will be unable to encrypt messages with the private keys or read messages sent to them encrypted with their own public keys.

Any system, especially a system that involves customers' private information, the merchant's vital customer profile, and the financial transactions that are crucial for successful e-commerce, must be secure, well documented, and scalable any time an upgrade is required. In theory, any cryptographic method with a key can be broken by trying various possible keys in sequence. If brute force is the only alternative, the likelihood of cracking the system depends on the length of the key. For example, a 32-bit key can be broken on any home computer. In contrast, a system with a 56-bit key (such as DES) takes special hardware to crack. Although expensive to acquire, such hardware is within the reach of major corporations and most governments. Keys with 128 bits are presently impossible to crack by brute force.

MAJOR ATTACKS ON CRYPTOSYSTEMS

cryptoanalysis: the science of deciphering encrypted messages without knowing the right key.

Cryptoanalysis is the science of deciphering encrypted messages without knowing the right key. Here are some common cryptoan-alytic attacks.

1. **Chosen-plaintext attack.** The attacker uses an unknown key to encrypt any text or document. The challenge is to find the key that is known only to the attacker. An e-payment system should be designed so that an attacker could never succeed in encrypting chosen plaintext.

2. **Known-plaintext attack.** In this technique, the attacker knows the plaintext for part(s) of the ciphertext. He or she uses this information to decrypt the rest of the ciphertext.

3. **Ciphertext-only attack.** In this approach, the attacker has no idea what the message contains and works primarily from ciphertext, making guesses about the plaintext. Some ciphertext data might contain a common word as a starter. Certain documents begin in a predictable way that often gives away the contents.

4. **Third-party attack.** In this technique, an adversary breaks into the communication line between two parties (e.g., buyer and vendor). He or she uses a separate key with each party. Each party uses a different key that is easily known to the adversary. The adversary, in turn, decrypts the transmitted documents with the right key and encrypts it with the other key before it is sent to the recipient. Neither party has any idea that their communication system has been intercepted.

For more on cryptosystem attacks, see www.ssh.fi/tech/crypto/intro.html.

AUTHENTICATION AND TRUST

DIGITAL SIGNATURES

One way to implement public-key authentication on a per-message basis is to send a **digital signature** with each message. As shown in Figure 14.4, when you sign a letter, you authenticate it by adding your signature at the end of the message.

digital signature: a special signature for signing electronic correspondence, produced by encrypting the message digest with the sender's private key.

A digital signature is added at the end of each message you send. The U.S Postal Service now issues digital signatures on smart cards through post offices nationwide, using "in-person proofing" as part of the process. A digital signature, first proposed in 1976 by Whitfield Diffie of Stanford University, transforms the message that is signed so that anyone who reads it can be sure of the real sender. It is a block of data or a sample of the message content (called a **message digest**) that represents a private key.

message digest: a block of data or a sample of the message content that represents a private key.

Encrypting a message digest with a private key creates a digital signature. A public key can be used to verify that the signature was, in fact, generated using the corresponding private key. If John encrypts a message to Hillary with his own private key, Hillary decrypts the message with John's public key and knows that John generated the message.

authentication: verifying that a message or document, in fact, comes from the claimed sender.

A digital signature's main function is to verify that a message or a document, in fact, comes from the claimed sender. This is called **authentication.** It can be used also to time-stamp documents when a trusted party *signs* the document and its time stamp with his or her secret key. This process attests that the document was present at the stated time.

hash function: formula that converts a message of a given length into a string of digits called a message digest.

When making a digital signature, cryptographic hash functions are generally used to construct the message digest. A **hash function** is a formula that converts a message of a given length into a string of digits (128 or more), called a *message digest.* Once the message digest is encrypted with the sender's private key, it becomes a digital signature. (See Box 14.3.)

Suppose Jay (sender) generates a message digest for his message to Ellen, encrypts it with his private key, and sends that digital signature along with the plaintext message. Ellen uses Jay's public key to decrypt the digital signature and receives a copy of the

---

FIGURE 14.4 The digital signature process

1. Sender generates a message.
2. Sender creates a "digest" of the message.
3. Sender encrypts message digest with his/her private key for authentication. This is the *digital signature.*
4. Sender attaches the digital signature to the end of the message.
5. Sender encrypts both message and signature with the recipient's public key.
6. Recipient decrypts entire message with his/her private key.
7. Recipient verifies digest for accuracy.

BOX 14.3

Hashing

Hashing is producing hash values for accessing data or for security. A hash value (or simply hash) is a number generated from a string of text. The hash is substantially smaller than the text itself, and is generated by a formula in such a way that it is extremely unlikely that some other text will produce the same hash value.

Hashes play a role in security systems where they're used to ensure that transmitted messages have not been tampered with. The sender generates a hash of the message, encrypts it, and sends it with the message itself. The recipient then decrypts both the message and the hash, produces another hash from the received message, and compares the two hashes. If they're the same, there is a very high probability that the message was transmitted intact.

Hashing is also a common method of accessing data records. Consider, for example, a list of names:

- John Smith
- Sarah Jones
- Roger Adams

To create an index, called a *hash table*, for these records, you would apply a formula to each name to produce a unique numeric value. So you might get something like:

- 1345873 John Smith
- 3097905 Sarah Jones
- 4060964 Roger Adams

Then to search for the record containing *Sarah Jones*, you just need to reapply the formula, which directly yields the index key to the record. This is much more efficient than searching through all the records till the matching record is found.

Source: Excerpted from www.webopedia.com/ TERM/h/hashing.html.

---

message that Jay encoded. Because Jay's public key decrypted his digital signature, she is certain that the message was Jay's. This authenticates the sender as genuine. Ellen then uses the same hash function (known to her and to Jay in advance) to *encode* her own message digest of Jay's plaintext message. If the encoded message digest turns out the same as the one Jay sent, the digital signature is considered authentic and the message has not been tampered with. (See Figure 14.5.)

DIGITAL CERTIFICATES

In many ways, digital certificates are the heart of secure online transactions. In shopping on the Internet, buyers need evidence that they can trust the vendor. Some infrastructures use digital signatures, and others use digital certificates to establish a merchant's identity. A digital certificate is an electronic "credit card" that establishes one's credentials when doing business on the Web.

A digital certificate is a software program that can be installed in a browser. Once there, your digital certificate identifies you to Web sites equipped to check it automatically. Such a tool has distinctive benefits. It eliminates multiple passwords and enhances security, because your certificate cannot be guessed, forgotten, forged, or intercepted. It also lets you send and receive secure e-mail using almost any e-mail program, including Netscape Messenger. (See home.netscape.com/security/ basics/getperscert.html.)

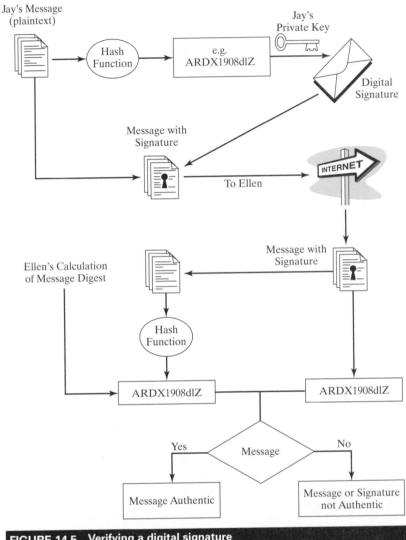

FIGURE 14.5 Verifying a digital signature

digital certificate: an electronic document issued by a certificate authority to establish a merchant's identity.

certificate authority (CA): a trusted entity that issues and revokes public-key certificates and manages key-pairs.

Digital signatures and digital certificates are related. As noted previously, a *digital signature* is a special signature for signing electronic correspondence, produced by encrypting the message digest with the buyer's private key. A **digital certificate** is an electronic document issued by a **certificate authority (CA)** to establish a merchant's identity by verifying its name and public key. It is more like the electronic version of a driver's license. (See Box 14.4)

Once you generate a public key and a private key, it is your job to keep the private key secure and distribute your public key to those with whom you intend to correspond. Because sending

---

BOX 14.4

The Keys to Safe Shopping

Digital certificates provide an easy and convenient way to ensure that the participants in an electronic commerce transaction can trust each other. This trust is established through a common third party such as Visa. For example, Visa will provide digital certificates to the card-issuing financial institution, and the institution will then provide a digital certificate to the cardholder. A similar process takes place for the merchant.

At the time of the transaction, each party's SET-compliant software validates both merchant and cardholder before any information is exchanged. The validation takes place by checking the digital certificates, which were both issued by an authorized trusted third party.

The basis for digital certificates is secret codes. . . . The procedure is simple. A message can be converted into code using a "key," which is a means of translating the message's characters into other characters that make no sense to the uninvited interceptor. . . . A simple example of a key might be replacing each letter with the next letter in the alphabet. Thus, Visa would become WJTB. To decipher the message, or "decrypt" it, the recipient simply needs to know the secret key.

Source: Excerpted from Visa, "The Keys to Safe Shopping," www.visa.com/nt/ecomm/set/ setsafe.html.

---

the key to each correspondent (say, by e-mail) is time consuming, a more efficient and trusted way is to use a certificate authority such as Verisign, Cybertrust, or the U.S. Postal Service to manage the availability and use of your public key. It also provides information about certificates that were lost or stolen or, in the case of employees issued certificates to conduct business for an employer, certificates that once belonged to employees no longer with the firm.

A digital certificate includes the holder's name, name of the certificate authority, the public key for cryptographic use, the duration of the certificate (usually six months to one year), the class of the certificate, and the certificate's ID number. (See Figure 14.6.)

The certificate can be issued (for a fee) in one of four classes. The fee for obtaining a digital certificate increases with higher classes.

1. Class 1 certificates are the quickest and simplest to issue because they contain minimum checks on the user's background. Only the name of the user, the address, and the e-mail address are checked. Think of it as a library card.

2. Class 2 certificates check for information like real name, Social Security number, and date of birth. They require proof of physical address, locale, and e-mail, as well. This is more like a credit card, because the company giving

User's basic ID information (name, address, SSN, etc.)

Digital signature and ID information of issuing authority

User's public key

Dates of validity and expiration of the digital ID

Class of certification (class 1–4)

Certificate number of digital ID

FIGURE 14.6   Contents of a digital certificate

out the certificate will consult with a credit database for verification with a third party.

3. Class 3 certificates are the strongest type in terms of specifics. They are like a driver's license: To get them, you need to prove exactly who you are and that you are responsible. Organizations whose specialty is the security business foresee class 3 certificates being used for things like loans acquired online and other sensitive transactions.

4. Class 4 certificates are the most thorough. In addition to class 3 requirements, the certificate authority checks on things like the user's position at work.

Electronic IDs with digital certificates may soon pack enough security to power the next generation of IDs for e-commerce. These credentials are beginning to appear in Web browsers and PKI software for data-sensitive sectors such as banking and government. Windows 2000, for example, comes with a digital certificate and PKI embedded in the operating system. This feature allows the Windows 2000 server to be a certificate authority, registering users and issuing and revoking certificates. In fact, digital certificates are getting smart: They can now be moved to smart cards instead of being stored on hard disks.

MANAGING CRYPTOGRAPHIC KEYS

Management of cryptographic keys is crucial to ensuring security in e-commerce transaction processing. **Key management** involves making keys known to the systems that

key management: making keys known to the systems that need them and making sure keys are protected against disclosure or substitution.

need them and making sure that the keys are protected at all times against disclosure and substitution. In other words, the strength inherent in a cryptographic system lies in the fact that nobody knows the value of the key, nor the complexity of its algorithm. How keys are managed depends on whether the keys are symmetric cryptosystems or public-key cryptosystems.

KEY LIFE CYCLE

Like passwords, all keys have limited lifetimes. The life of a key is limited for two reasons: The more keys are used, the greater the opportunity is for attackers to gather ciphertext on which they can work. Because most keys can be compromised over time, limiting the lifetime of a key means limiting the damage that can occur.

From generation to termination, a key life cycle includes the following phases: key generation and registration, key distribution, key backup/recovery/escrow, and key revocation and destruction.

KEY GENERATION AND REGISTRATION. This phase involves choosing a random number source for key-pairs and key length that cannot be guessed by an attacker using an exhaustive approach. The registration part involves linking the generated key with its special-purpose use. For example, if the key is used to authenticate a digital signature, then such a link becomes the basis for registering it with a certificate authority.

KEY DISTRIBUTION.   This phase operates through a key distribution center in situations when two or more persons located some distance apart must exchange keys. For example, when system X needs to establish a key with system Y, system X requests the key from the key distribution center. The center generates the key and returns it to system X in two forms: the first under a master key shared between system X and the center, and the second under the master key shared between system Y and the center. System X retains the first form for its own use and passes the second form to system Y for Y's use.

KEY BACKUP AND RECOVERY.   A critical aspect of key management is the ability to recover a key after failure. If an encrypted message, for example, is stored on disk and a key is needed to decrypt it, the loss of the key could mean the loss of the message. A copy of a secret or private key should be recoverable in the event the original is accidentally lost, or an employee assigned a special key suddenly leaves the firm, or the key is destroyed. Someone must hold copies of sensitive keys and be available to release them when needed. If the key(s) is held in trust by a third party, the location where keys reside is referred to as **key escrow.**

key escrow: location where keys held in trust by a third party reside.

notary service: company that provides encryption-oriented services including key escrow, key recovery, time stamping, trusted intermediary, and archiving.

Trusted Information Systems (TIS, www.tis.com) has a key escrow system that takes businesses' keys and stores them in escrow. This way, law enforcement agencies can access keys with a search warrant. The company (also called a **notary service**) provides a kind of insurance: If you lose the key to an encrypted file, you can get it back. Or, if an employee does not remember the key, it can be recovered through the escrow agency.

KEY REVOCATION AND DESTRUCTION.   Sometimes the key must be revoked. Maybe one information system must be replaced with another, or a change occurs in the security classification of a key, or suspicion arises that a key has been compromised. In all of these cases, the best policy is to terminate and replace the key. In key destruction, all traces of a key are wiped clean. A revocation list is maintained by the certification authority, which includes the date and the reason(s) for the revocation.

A PKI must provide a way for a certificate to be revoked. Once revoked, the certificate must be added to a revocation list available to all users. A specific mechanism also must be provided to verify that revocation list and refuse to use a revoked certificate at any time.

In general, it is important to ensure proper and effective protection of a key throughout its lifetime. The focus is on integrity of the security and encryption process. All keys, except public keys in public-key cryptosystems, also should be protected to ensure the privacy and confidentiality of the e-commerce traffic.

THIRD-PARTY SERVICES

Throughout the chapter, we have mentioned a "third party." This is a certificate authority that verifies certificates intended for use by other distinct legal entities. Third-party services include two main parts: certificate authority and directory services. A certificate authority (CA) is a trusted independent legal entity. It issues and revokes public-key certificates and manages key-pairs. The actual verification of the person or entity tagged to that key is done at the time of application. This means that the CA has a formal arrangement with a financial institution (e.g., a credit card company), which provides it with information to ensure an individual's claimed identity. In essence, CAs guarantee that the two parties exchanging information are in fact who they claim to be.

A CA also provides policies, practices, and procedures for certifying keys. A **certificate policy** is a set of rules that identifies how, when, and for what reasons certificates are used within the assigned organization.

certificate policy: a set of rules that identifies how, when, and for what reasons certificates are used within the assigned organization.

CAs also offer different classes of certificates, depending on the type of initial identification provided by the person. The certificate revocation list, along with the valid certificates issued, are posted in the **directory service**—a repository that distributes certificates as requested by message originators.

directory service: a repository that distributes certificates as requested by message originators.

INTERNET SECURITY PROTOCOLS AND STANDARDS

As stressed throughout the chapter, a successful e-commerce environment is built on trust in the integrity of the communication network that links a buyer and a merchant. Many types of threats can compromise the security of the business process. With the open exchange of information on the Internet, more security measures are needed to minimize vulnerability. Among these measures are security for Web applications (SSL and S-HTTP), security for e-commerce transactions (SET), and security for e-mail (PGP, S/MIME).

SSL: WEB APPLICATIONS

Transaction security has become a challenge. Most browsers and computers already can exchange *secure* transactions across the Internet, making it difficult for unauthorized people to intercept data such as credit card numbers. Even if a transmission is intercepted, the encrypted message cannot be read. The two key protocols for secure World Wide Web transactions are **Secure Socket Layers (SSLs)** and Secure Hypertext Transfer Protocol (S-HTTP).

Secure Socket Layer (SSL): a key protocol for secure Web transactions; secures data packets at the network layer.

Originally developed by Netscape, SSL is the most widely used standard for encrypting data on the Internet. It is used by all of Netscape's browser products, as well as Microsoft's Internet Explorer 3.0 or higher. In addition, it is built into products such as Apache and Internet Information Server. Technically, SSL protocol operates on its own layer, between the application layer and the transport layer (see Chapter 3 for details), meaning it is compatible with hypertext transfer protocol (HTTP). (See developer.netscape.com/ docs/ manuals/security/sslin.)

One requirement for proper use of SSL is that the merchant's Web server and the customer's Web browser must use the same security system. Because SSLs are used by all URLs that begin with *http*, no problem should arise with interfacing online. SSL is included free with Netscape 2.0 or higher, Internet Explorer 3.0 or higher, and America Online 3.0 or higher.

SSL provides three basic services: server authentication, client authentication, and an encrypted SSL connection. SSL server authentication uses public-key cryptography to validate the server's digital certificate and public key on the client's machine. (See "How SSL Works," at developer.netscape.com/tech/security/ssl/howitworks.html.)

Client authentication is performed in the same way on the server machine. During the authentication process, SSL allows client and server machines to jointly select an encryption algorithm to be used for the secure connection. The key to this algorithm is transmitted using public-key cryptography, after which client and server may communicate using the secret key. Although this technology has not yet matured, Netscape is turning it over to the Internet Engineering Task Force (IETF) to make it a standard for other applications. The IETF is responsible for coordinating Internet design, Internet standards, and short-term engineering issues. The committee already has renamed the technology Transport Layer Security protocol (TLS) and plans to standardize and improve the protocol. All Netscape browsers support the 128-bit encryption for the domestic version, as well as the 40-bit encryption for the international/export version. Currently, Netscape does not support SSL for Java browser applets. Microsoft's version 3 (and above) browsers also use this technology.

S-HTTP: WEB APPLICATIONS

Hypertext transfer protocol (HTTP) is a "request-response" type language spoken between a Web browser (client software) and a Web server (server software) somewhere on the Internet to allow communication with each other and to exchange files. The function of **Secure HTTP (S-HTTP)** is to secure Web transactions and nothing else. It secures transaction confidentiality and authenticity/integrity, and it ensures nonrepudiation of origin. In many ways, this protocol is more robust than SSL, although it is less widely used due to Netscape's market penetration. You can use S-HTTP with SSL for increased protection. After an encrypted S-HTTP transaction arrives, it can be decrypted on another computer, separated from your Web server by a firewall.

Secure HTTP (S-HTTP): a protocol that secures Web transactions and nothing else.

The power of S-HTTP lies in its compatibility with HTTP and its ability to integrate with HTTP applications. It provides application-level security and is mainly used for intranet communications (Rodriguez 1996, p. 41). S-HTTP allows a client machine and a server machine to communicate securely using HTTP, to provide immediate transmission of secure data over the Internet. (See ftp.ietf.org/rfc/rfc2660.txt.) The protocol supports only symmetric key cryptography and, therefore, does not require digital certificates or public keys. In addition, because it operates on the application layer, S-HTTP provides user authentication and is capable of securing parts of a document.

The newest security standard in e-commerce is the **Secure Electronic Transaction (SET)** specification developed by Visa, MasterCard, and Europay. SET is used for handling funds transfers from credit card issuers to a merchant's bank account. It is an accepted and well-known payment model, signature based, and exploits existing banking infrastructure. SET's goal is to provide confidentiality, authentication, and integrity of payment card transmissions. To do this, it uses a variety of encryption techniques, digital signatures, and certificates.

Secure Electronic Transaction (SET): a protocol used for handling funds transfers from credit card issuers to a merchant's bank account.

From its beginning in 1970, Visa has worked with the banking industry to make the Visa card the safest way to purchase goods and services anywhere in the world. In the 1970s, Visa introduced the magnetic stripe for quick authorization. In the 1980s, it established an International Standard Organization (ISO) message format to provide an efficient way to process purchases and payments. On February 1, 1996, Visa and MasterCard, with participation from companies like Microsoft, IBM, Netscape, RSA, and VeriSign, established a single technical standard for safeguarding payment card purchases made over open networks, including the Internet, covering 13 million Visa-acceptance merchants in the physical world.

Called SET specification, this standard uses digital certificates to authenticate all parties involved in the purchase process. SET requires consumers to register their accounts once with the card-issuing bank so it can provide the appropriate digital certificate.

Two things are needed for customers to use SET.

1. A digital certificate customers can request from their issuing bank by filling out a form on the bank's Web site.

2. A **digital wallet** (also called an encrypted envelope) to seal personal information such as bank account number, credit card numbers and expiration dates, shipping and handling details, billing addresses, and the digital ID. The wallet is a free plug-in that can be downloaded from the Web or that is included in today's Netscape Navigator or Internet Explorer. The customer invokes the plug-in when making a purchase. This eliminates having to retype credit card information in future transactions. Because card numbers and addresses are stored in the wallet, consumers can select payment methods and shipping addresses to consummate the purchase with a single click.

digital wallet: online shopping device that seals personal information in a free plug-in that can be invoked when making a purchase.

Let us assume that you have decided to make a purchase and your software has passed the round of certificate exchanges. From the certificate exchange, you have the e-merchant's public key, the payment processor's key, and a unique transaction identifier issued by the merchant. How does SET deliver your purchase securely?

The first step is to create the necessary order information and payment instructions; each includes the e-merchant's assigned transaction identifier. Next, you execute a one-way hashing function to make digests of the two items (order information [OI] and payment instructions [PI]). Once done, you generate a "dual signature," which allows the merchant and payment processor to verify independently that your order information and payment instructions are related together. SET's dual signature is the link of order information and payment instructions message digests encrypted with your private key. When finished, you have a message containing the following.

1. OI, including the merchant's transaction identifier
2. A digest of the order information
3. PI, including merchant's transaction identifier, encrypted with a random symmetric key
4. A digest of the payment instructions

5. A dual-signature digest (OI digest + PI digest) encrypted with your private key

6. Your account number plus the random symmetric key encrypted with the payment processor's public key

On paper, SET has gone a long way toward making payment card purchases more secure than they've ever been.

Pretty Good Privacy (PGP): protocol that encrypts the data with a one-time algorithm and then encrypts the key to the algorithm using public-key cryptography.

Three main protocols govern secure communication through e-mail: Pretty Good Privacy (PGP), Secure Multipurpose Internet Mail Extensions (S/MIME), and Message Security Protocol (MSP). **Pretty Good Privacy (PGP)** is a file-based product developed by software engineer Phil Zimmerman in 1991. Zimmerman used it to encrypt his own messages and those of his friends (pgpi.org/doc/overview).

What made him well known is that he released the tool kit on the Internet (web.mit.edu/network/pgp.html; accessed June 2003), allowing anyone to create private keys and encrypt their own messages. When PGP first came out, it was wrapped in a web of controversy because it used 128-bit encryption and was available on the Internet, actions of which the U.S. government did not approve. In 1996, after the government decided against prosecuting him, Zimmerman founded PGP, Inc. in San Mateo, California, to commercialize the technology. A year later, the company was sold to Network Associates.

PGP competes head-to-head with protocols like S/MIME, but it is used mostly for personal e-mail security. PGP supports public-key and symmetric-key encryption, as well as digital signatures. It operates by encrypting the data with a one-time algorithm and then encrypting the key to the algorithm using public-key cryptography. PGP also supports other standards, such as SSL and Lightweight Directory Access Protocol (LDAP). LDAP is a standard for accessing specific information, including stored public-key certificates.

S/MIME (Multipurpose Internet Mail Extension): powerful protocol that provides security for different data types and attachments to e-mails.

S/MIME (Multipurpose Internet Mail Extensions) was developed by RSA in 1996 as a security enhancement to the old MIME standard for Internet e-mail. It is built on public-key cryptography standards. S/MIME is considered powerful because it provides security for different data types and for e-mail attachments. It has two key attributes: a digital signature and a digital envelope. The signature is created by using a hashing algorithm that constructs a message digest.

The message digest is then encrypted using public key cryptography. The signature ensures that nothing is done to the message during transmission. The digital wallet then ensures that the message remains private. It uses an algorithm such as DES, 3DES, or RC4 to encrypt the message. The key is then encrypted using public key cryptography. In addition to these two functions, S/MIME also performs authentication.

Message Security Protocol (MSP): protocol that secures e-mail attachments across multiple platforms.

Message Security Protocol (MSP) is a protocol used mainly by the U.S. government and government agencies to provide security for e-mail. Its function is securing e-mail attachments across multiple platforms. It operates at the application level of the Internet and does not involve the intermediate message transfer system. An MSP message includes the original message content and specific security parameters required by the recipients to decrypt or validate the message when received.

OTHER ENCRYPTION ISSUES

GOVERNMENT REGULATION

Several U.S. government organizations are authorized to control encryption enforcement. The best known is the National Security Agency (NSA), which has the power to monitor, intercept, and retain any information that might be damaging to national security. The agency also conducts research in cryptography, both in designing algorithms to protect U.S. communications and in cryptoanalytic techniques for listening in on non-U.S. communications. It is known to be the largest employer of mathematicians in the United States and the largest buyer of computer hardware and software.

The National Computer Security Center (NCSC), a branch of the NSA, is responsible for listing government-trusted computer programs. The center evaluates products and recommends standards. Its *Orange Book* presents criteria for evaluating trusted computer systems. The center also publishes a number of other books on the subject, commonly called the "Rainbow Books."

A third government agency, the National Institute of Standards and Technology (NIST), is a division of the Department of Commerce that promotes standards among different commercial systems. The agency develops and issues standards, including those for cryptographic functions and export rules.

U.S. Export Rules lists cryptography in the same category as munitions and treats the technology just like a missile or a tank. The Office of Defense Trade Controls (DTC), which is authorized by the International Traffic in Arms Regulations (ITAR) office from the State Department, receives recommendations from the NSA on the level of encryption that can be exported.

Although the encryption field is saturated with robust solutions designed by the brightest minds, advances are being held back by national interests and governmental control, as well as the available computing power.

With increased security risks facing today's businesses, security specialists are in high demand. Many IT consultants have barely a business card to attest to their specialty; good security specialists require attributes beyond mere certifications. You need to look at their experience (good and bad), the technology they worked with, and the problems they solved. In other words, candidates must be balanced with real-world experience.

Anyone in the security business for the long haul is expected to constantly read up on new viruses, evaluate new products, and attend conferences and training. A combination of real-world skills, state-of-the-art training, and vendor-based certifications like Cisco certification are a true measure of a security candidate's ability and potential.

Most successful security gurus start as IT professionals, with knowledge about how networking is designed and managed, how to authenticate to the network, how to monitor e-mail and other traffic, what tools to use to fight viruses and other threats to a company's capital assets, and how to drive routers and firewalls for maximum security and protection. A security guru is now expected to be well versed in the algorithm related to protocol analyzers and wireless network discovery tools, and perform forensic investigations on networks—a tall order.

The problem with all these qualifications is getting someone with this much experience to be willing to work for small or midsize companies. Most of them carry a six-digit salary, which is out of line with the affordability of smaller firms. The alternative has been for smaller businesses to send a talented IT-oriented person for training with known vendors in the hope of addressing the security challenges in the firm.

IMPLICATIONS FOR E-COMMERCE

Developing high-powered and reliable encryption methods is a top priority for many organizations. It also raises serious issues for society. Imagine airlines keeping specific data on passenger flights that could be dangerous in the wrong hands. Think of the danger that could arise if the U.S. president's travel itinerary landed in an unsecured computerized document. Hospitals collect and protect sensitive patient information, and patients trust their doctors to keep the records confidential. Imagine the damage if a patient's employer or a health insurance provider accesses a patient's files and finds confidential data that could be used for blackmail or for intimidation.

Most encryption systems have prevention as the sole means of defense against theft, cheating, or abuse, but sooner or later every system will be attacked successfully. A good system must protect against every possible attack.

With these vulnerabilities and the increasing volume of online traffic, intranets and encryption have become necessary, even when financial transactions are not involved. In terms of online business security, any credit card traffic must be tamperproof. Internet and e-mail messages should be secure, as well. Otherwise businesses can be sued for negligence or violation of the trust inherent in a customer-merchant relationship.

Merchants face a number of choices when considering encryption methods. Messages or transactions must be encrypted to a level at which the cost for a criminal to break into the system would be greater than the benefits the criminal would receive by obtaining the information in that system. A multinational banking institution must have unbreakable encryption because criminals will go to great lengths to obtain that information.

Of major concern is the cost associated with different encryption methods: The more powerful the method is, the higher the cost is. More powerful methods also generally consume more power. It is important for merchants to take into consideration the size of their business, the sensitivity of the information transacted, the power of their technical infrastructure, and the amount of money they are willing to spend when choosing an encryption method.

Government regulations present considerable problems for businesses, as well. Until September 1998, the government did not allow most effective types of encryption to be exported. In late 1999, it relaxed the regulation and began allowing 56-bit encryption methods to be used overseas. This was an important victory for businesses. In the past, international companies had to struggle to secure their transactions. Internal versions of software packages had weaker encryption due to U.S. regulations. Companies had to bundle different types of encryption to achieve the requisite level of security.

THE FUTURE

The current public-key model of encryption fits well with the open nature of the Internet, where the growth of applications using technology such as SSL and SET is greatest. Many recent and current cryptographic innovations relate to strengthening public-key cryptography or breaking its security. Among the key developments for the future are elliptic-curve cryptography and quantum computing.

The future of PKI will hinge on a variety of factors. The technology continues to be criticized for its lack of interoperability. PKI products from different suppliers have yet to be made compatible with one another, because PKI does not employ a universal standard. In addition, the cost and complexity of PKI systems, whether or not you are outsourcing services to firms like VeriSign, remains extremely high. This explains in part why worldwide adoption of PKI technology has been slow.

ELLIPTIC-CURVE CRYPTOGRAPHY. This cryptographic technique is an alternative to using large prime numbers to generate keys. Elliptic curves are simple functions that can be thought of as gently curving lines (not ellipses) on a simple graph. The goal is to use elliptic curves to define special mathematical operations (e.g., addition or multiplication) that can be used to generate public keys. Proponents of this method argue that it can provide smaller keys in less time while providing an equivalent level of security. As shown in Figure 14.7, elliptic curves are functions that can be drawn as looping lines in the (x,y) plane. Interesting things happen when one studies the points where the curve exactly crosses integer (x,y) coordinates.

The mathematics of elliptic-curve cryptography are too advanced to include in this section. In order to derive the private key from the public key, the mathematics behind the elliptic curve used must be understood. Described as "elliptic-curve group discrete log technique," the mathematics behind cracking elliptic-curve encryption have not been the focus of much research and have seen little improvement in the last 20 years. This is in stark contrast to the continuous efforts to break the popular RSA scheme. However, supporters acknowledge that as elliptic-curve cryptography increases in popularity, new techniques also might be found to compromise its current advantages.

qubit: a unit of quantum information that can store many levels of information and whose information is destroyed automatically once it is viewed.

Quantum information theory is a completely new area of scientific research born in the 1990s. Essentially, it is the application of quantum physics to information theory and, ultimately, to cryptography. Benjamin Schumacher coined the term *qubit*, a unit of quantum information. The most important property of **qubits** is that they can store many levels of information. They also possess

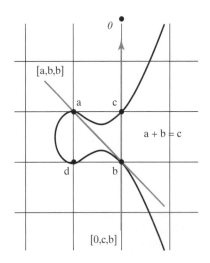

FIGURE 14.7 Quantum computing

another unique property: Looking at a qubit automatically destroys its information; therefore, quantum information cannot be copied.

Suppose a man left his bag somewhere in a given building—let's call it Monroe Hall. Suppose computers could somehow electronically search each room for the bag. An ordinary computer would search from room to room, stopping only when it found the bag. Quantum computing has a much more efficient search method. It has the ability to divide the task up such that all rooms are searched *simultaneously*, so it finds the bag almost instantly.

Peter Shor, of then-AT&T Bell Labs, found that quantum computing could be used to perform certain mathematical operations at an astonishingly faster rate than ordinary computers. Applying his findings to public-key encryption, he determined that a quantum computer could easily crack popular public-key encryption methods such as RSA. Yet at the same time, quantum cryptography solves its own problem by taking advantage of the property whereby looking at quantum information destroys it. Eavesdroppers can crack public-key encryption only if they can see what the public key is. If a quantum-encoded public key falls prey to an eavesdropper, the break can be detected, because the public key would be damaged and the quantum-encoded public key would simply be retransmitted until it went through unscathed.

At present, quantum computing is still very much a theoretical entity. A working model of the system has been developed by MagiQ Technologies. The system allows a code's keys to be transmitted as a stream of photons over fiber-optic cable. Because of the laws of quantum physics, the act of observing the transmission will alter the photons, rendering the information they contain useless to any eavesdroppers. At present, the method will work only over dedicated cables, in which photon transmission can be controlled. To see more about this technology, go to www.vnunet.com.

Summary

1. Encryption addresses message transmission security requirements. An algorithm converts the data into an encoded message using a key to decode or decipher the message.
2. In addition to ensuring privacy, encryption satisfies other e-security requirements: authentication, integrity, and nonrepudiation.
3. There are two classes of key-based algorithms: secret key and public key. For public-key algorithms, RSA is the most commonly used, although vulnerable to chosen-plaintext attacks. As a secret-key system, DES and RC4 are the most popular. DES is the first symmetric cryptosystem to be widely adopted commercially. A stronger version of DES is 3DES—based on using DES three times.

RC4 has key lengths ranging from 40 bits to 128 bits. IDEA offers strong encryption, using a 128-bit key to encrypt 64-bit blocks, which makes it resistant to brute-force attacks.
4. Cryptoanalysis is the science of deciphering encrypted messages without knowing the right key. Cryptoanalytic attacks include chosen-plaintext attack, known-plaintext attack, ciphertext-only attack, and third-party attack.
5. One way to implement public-key authentication on a per-message basis is to send a digital signature with each message. A digital signature's main function is to verify that a message or a document in fact comes from the claimed sender. This is called authentication.

6. A digital certificate is an electronic document issued by a certificate authority (CA) to establish a merchant's identity by verifying its name and public key. The CA manages the availability and use of a public key and provides information about lost or stolen certificates. The certificate can be issued in one of four classes.

7. With the Internet dependent on open standards and open exchange of information, various security measures have been installed to minimize vulnerability to the exchange. They include SSL and SHTTP, SET, and S/MIME. The overall goal is to secure Web transactions for confidentiality, authenticity, integrity, and nonrepudiability of origin.

Key Terms

- **authentication** (p. 460)
- **block cipher** (p. 455)
- **certificate authority (CA)** (p. 462)
- **certificate policy** (p. 466)
- **cipher** (p. 453)
- **ciphertext** (p. 453)
- **cryptoanalysis** (p. 459)
- **Data Encryption Standards (DES)** (p. 458)
- **decrypt** (p. 453)
- **digital certificate** (p. 462)
- **digital signature** (p. 460)
- **digital wallet** (p. 468)
- **directory service** (p. 466)
- **encrypt (encipher)** (p. 449)
- **encryption** (p. 449)

- **hash function** (p. 460)
- **International Data Encryption Algorithm (IDEA)** (p. 458)
- **key** (p. 450)
- **key escrow** (p. 465)
- **key management** (p. 464)
- **message digest** (p. 460)
- **Message Security Protocol (MSP)** (p. 469)
- **nonrepudiation** (p. 453)
- **notary service** (p. 465)
- **plaintext (cleartext)** (p. 450)
- **Pretty Good Privacy (PGP)** (p. 469)
- **public key (asymmetric encryption)** (p. 455)

- **qubit** (p. 472)
- **RC4** (p. 458)
- **RSA** (p. 457)
- **secret key (symmetric encryption)** (p. 454)
- **Secure Electronic Transaction (SET)** (p. 467)
- **Secure HTTP (S-HTTP)** (p. 467)
- **Secure Socket Layer (SSL)** (p. 466)
- **S/MIME (Multipurpose Internet Mail Extension)** (p. 469)
- **spoofing** (p. 452)
- **stream cipher** (p. 455)
- **Triple DES (3DES)** (p. 458)

Test Your Understanding

1. According to the text, encryption is intended to satisfy a number of e-security requirements. List and briefly explain each requirement.
2. Distinguish between:
   a. Authentication and nonrepudiation
   b. Integrity and privacy
   c. Nonrepudiation and integrity
   d. Cipher and ciphertext
   e. Stream cipher and block cipher
3. Explain the basic concept of how information is encrypted.
4. What is so unique about a secret key? A public key? Is one key more secure than the other? Be specific.
5. Briefly elaborate on the key features of the following cryptosystems:
   a. RSA algorithm
   b. DES and 3DES
   c. IDEA

6. What is a digital signature? How does it work? How does it differ from a digital certificate? Be specific.
7. Briefly review some of the cryptoanalytic attacks that an e-merchant can expect in day-to-day e-traffic.
8. In what way(s) does a certificate authority perform a vital role in cryptography?
9. What is so important about key backup, recovery, and escrow?
10. List and briefly describe three major third-party services.
11. Elaborate on the main services of SSL.
12. In e-mail technology, three main protocols are employed to govern secure communication through e-mail. Briefly explain each protocol.

Discussion Questions

1. In your own words, what implications does encryption have for managing e-commerce traffic?
2. Do you think electronic messaging has seriously affected the integrity of messages? Review material on the Internet and bring information to class on this issue.
3. Which do you think is better legal evidence—an electronic legal document with a digital signature or a handwritten signature? In other words, knowing the legality of a digital signature, which one would be considered more valid in a court of law? Why?
4. Under what conditions or for what reason(s) would a company opt to manage its own keys and certificates in-house rather than using a public certificate authority?
5. Because the purpose of certification authorities is to authenticate the identities of individuals and organizations, who vouches for the certificate authorities? Look on the Internet under "certificate authority," "encryption regulations," and so on and see what is available on this subject.

Web Exercises

1. Use your Web browser to research the contents of a digital certificate. Find out what is new about this area that has not been covered in the text. Write a two-page report on the subject.
2. Use your Web browser to access information about the hash algorithm—its function, how it works, and how it differs from private-key or public-key encryption. Report your findings in class.
3. A simple cipher replaces B with A, C with B, D with C, and so on until Z is replaced with Y. With this in mind, decrypt the following statement: BMM NFO BSF DSFBUFE FRVBM.
4. Visit www.amazon.com, www.fedex.com, and www.ibm.com. Investigate the following:

    a. Type of server (e.g., HTTPS) each Web site uses
    b. SSL cipher type
    c. Validity period
    d. Certification authority's name

CHAPTER 15

GETTING THE MONEY

Learning Objectives

The focus of this chapter is on several learning objectives:

- ▇ Real-world and electronic cash and their unique features and uses
- ▇ The key requirements for Internet-based payments
- ▇ The many ways people pay to purchase goods and services on the Internet
- ▇ Business-to-business methods of payment
- ▇ Paying for goods and services via the mobile phone
- ▇ Issues and implications behind electronic money transactions and payments

IN A NUTSHELL

The final step before shipment is making payment—*getting the money*. The business might be a small shop selling candy or a multibillion-dollar corporation selling computers, homes, or automobiles. The business could have a simple Web page advertising products using an in-house database, or a business-to-consumer environment supported by databases linked to vendors and suppliers around the world, around the clock. Regardless of the setup, for e-commerce to happen the consumer must have a way to hit the *buy* button and make a payment.

In the real world, we have three ways to pay for goods: cash, check, or credit card. Cards can be smart cards, debit cards, automated teller machine (ATM) cards, and any kind of credit card. They all serve a special purpose: allow consumers to pay without cash. They are online electronic payment media.

Any e-commerce environment with a payment system needs a complex design. A payment system means ensuring payment security, transaction privacy, system integrity, customer authentication, and the purchaser's promise to pay. These systems were covered in Chapters 13 and 14. In this chapter, we discuss payment options using real-world systems and see how they can be emulated in an online electronic payment system. Finally, we look at micro transactions and how payments are carried out.

REAL-WORLD CASH

For centuries, we have known money as a *medium of exchange* to simplify transactions, a *standard of value* to make it easier to decide on the worth of goods, and a *store of value* to facilitate the concept of saving. In e-commerce, electronic money must fulfill the first function. Payment online (using credit cards and the like) is not very different from cash transactions made in the real world, except for speed of transfer, ease of handling, and the safety of not having to carry cash.

Outside the Internet, cash continues to be the most widely used form of payment. It offers several features:

1. Convenience: Easy to use, easy to carry, and easy to handle in small quantities.
2. Wide acceptance: The U.S. dollar is the most widely accepted paper currency in the world because of its stability and durability.
3. Anonymity: No identification is needed to pay in cash.
4. No cost of use: For customers who use cash, there are no hidden costs, overhead, or processing fees. For the merchant, it means transporting cash to the bank for safekeeping on a daily basis.
5. No audit trail: Lack of traceability means you can do what you want with your cash. In countries where trust in the currency, the banking system, or the government is in question, cash is used to buy all kinds of products, including homes, automobiles, and other big-ticket items. Trust is the basis of electronic payment systems.

Despite these features, the credit system is more attractive for conducting business in the real world. Cash is easy to lose; difficult to trace; cumbersome to carry; and time consuming to count, organize, and manage.

ELECTRONIC MONEY (E-MONEY)

e-money: an electronic medium for making payments.

identified e-money (digital cash): notational money system that generates an audit trail and can be traced.

anonymous e-money: notational money system that cannot be traced.

E-money is an electronic medium for making payments and is the trend today. It includes credit cards, smart cards, debit cards, electronic funds transfer, and Automated Clearinghouse (ACH) systems. (These systems are discussed later in the chapter.) It is a notational money system that may be online or off-line, identified or anonymous. **Identified e-money** (also called **digital cash**) contains information that makes it possible to identify the person who withdrew the money from the bank. The process generates an audit trail. **Anonymous e-money** works like paper money and leaves no trail. With the online option, each transaction is verified and approved by the issuing institution (such as a bank) before payment is made. Off-line e-money requires no validation.

There are four types of e-money.

1. Identified and online (+I+L)—unique to credit card and debit card transactions. The buyer is clearly identified and the card is validated against the issuing bank's computer before payment is made. Making a deposit at the teller window is another example of a transaction that is identified and online. The teller asks for a picture ID to identify the customer and uses the workstation to credit (or debit) the account online.

2. Identified and off-line (+I−L)—purchasing by check, traveler's check, or postal service money order. The merchant asks for ID to make sure the identity of the purchaser is known, but no verification is made against the account. If the check bounces, the merchant has to call the purchaser, backtrack through the issuing bank, and chase the purchaser for payment—a messy procedure.

3. Anonymous and online (−I+L)—cash payments where the identity of the purchaser is anonymous and a purchase is made on the spot for cash. The same applies to automated teller machine (ATM) transactions such as withdrawals from savings, checking, or special accounts. In the case of deposits, however, the transaction is off-line. The account records the amount of the deposit, but the bank does not make the money available until the deposited check clears.

4. Anonymous and off-line (−I−L)—electronic cash, which includes transactions such as making deposits in one's account via ATM and using a credit card with a merchant who does not have an online connection to the Visa/MasterCard network.

ANALYZING CASH, CHECKS, AND CREDIT CARDS

ACID test: set of properties of a money transfer that include atomicity, consistency, isolation, and durability.

Regardless of the form of money, two distinct sets of properties should be considered in a money transfer: the **ACID test** (atomicity, consistency, isolation, durability) and the **ICES test** (interoperability, conservation, economy, **scalability**).

THE ACID TEST.

ICES test: set of properties of a money transfer that include interoperability, conservation, economy, and scalability.

1. Atomicity: A transaction must occur completely or not at all. When you transfer $100 from savings to checking, the full amount must be debited from the savings account and credited to the checking account before the transfer is considered successful.

scalability: ability of a system to handle multiple users at the same time.

2. Consistency: All parties involved in the transaction must agree to the exchange. In a customer-retailer relationship involving a purchase, the customer must agree to purchase the goods for a specific price, and the merchant must agree to sell it at that price; otherwise, there is no basis for exchange.

3. Isolation: Each transaction must be independent of any other transaction and be treated as a stand-alone episode.

4. Durability: It must always be possible to recover the last consistent state or reverse the facts of the exchange. This means reversing charges in the event that customers change their mind.

THE ICES TEST.   The ICES test addresses four important properties of money transfer.

1. Interoperability: Ability to move back and forth between different systems.
2. Conservation: How well money holds its value over time (temporal consistency) and how easy money is to store and access (temporal durability).
3. Economy: Processing a transaction should be inexpensive and affordable. This property has a direct relationship to the size of the transaction. A $10,000 purchase costing only $0.90 to process is economical. If the charge is the same for a $5 item, it would be considered expensive. In banking, wiring money from one bank to another usually generates a fee (say, $25), regardless of the amount of money transferred.
4. Scalability: This test refers to the ability of the system to handle multiple users at the same time.

Cash has all the ICES properties except conservation; checks and credit cards as electronic methods of payment do not. A check transaction is not isolated, because anyone can write a check and proceed to withdraw the money from the bank well before the check is cleared; the check writer also can put a stop on the check. Checks are money-transfer atomic, although there is usually a one- to three-day delay in clearing the check for final payment.

In the case of cash, the ACID properties are fulfilled. The problem with cash is transportability and storage of large amounts. Credit cards may appear atomic to the seller, but they are not. The seller is guaranteed payment, but the credit card issuer may lose out if the card is stolen or used fraudulently. Also, the question of storing and retrieving value is not applicable in a credit-based system.

Cash is the most anonymous form of payment. Anyone can walk up, purchase an item, and pay in cash without having to show identification. Checks and credit card transactions are less anonymous than cash, although some forms of digital transactions can hide the identity of the buyer from the seller and vice versa.

REQUIREMENTS FOR INTERNET-BASED PAYMENTS

Electronic payments are financial transactions made without the use of paper documents such as cash or checks. Having your paycheck deposited directly to your checking or savings account, having your telephone bill paid electronically, and having transactions handled via point-of-sale or debit card are all electronic payments.

electronic payment: financial transaction made without the use of paper documents.

INTERNET-BASED PAYMENT SYSTEMS MODELS

Four main models illustrate Internet-based payment systems: electronic currency, credit cards, debit cards, and smart cards. **Electronic currency** is the network equivalent of cash. For example, electronic funds transfer (EFT) moves cash from one account, such as the employer's payroll account, to another account, such as the employee's checking account, regardless of bank type or

electronic currency: the Internet equivalent of cash.

debit card: a payment card that transfers funds directly from the consumer's bank account to the merchant's.

location. Credit and **debit cards** are the electronic equivalent of checks: They require the user to have an account on a server or at an issuing bank equipped with the proper Internet network. Smart cards are cards equipped with a memory chip.

In addition to the ACID and ICES tests, other properties are important to an electronic payment system.

1. Acceptability: For electronic payment to work, the system must be widely accepted by, and acceptable to, merchants. Merchants must have the technical ability and the processes to expedite a sale without delay.

2. Ease of integration: The Web site interface must be effective and well integrated into the total network environment. It also should be independent of any other payment instrument.

3. Customer base: Enough users and enough traffic must be present to justify investing in the electronic payment mechanism.

4. Ease of use and ease of access: Users don't like to wait. Using a payment system should be as easy as pressing a button on the screen.

ELECTRONIC TRANSACTION SYSTEMS

An electronic transaction system makes it possible to process transactions over the Internet, whether the customer uses Visa, MasterCard, Discover, American Express, or any other form of card. As mentioned in Chapter 9, the elements required to do business on the Internet are a storefront, a shopping cart, a merchant account, and an electronic transaction processing system to pay the merchant against the customer's credit or debit card. Several systems can do this job. The following examples illustrate how the bulk of Internet payment systems work.

CYBERCASH. Bill Melton and Dan Lynch founded CyberCash, Inc. (www. cybercash.com.) in 1994; it is now part of VeriSign. The company offers a range of e-commerce solutions, from credit card–based payment systems to secure micropayment systems. One unique service is a gateway that ties Internet merchants to an existing electronic payment system. Another is the CyberCoin mechanism designed to support online micropayments (less than $1). The main CyberCash transaction system centers on secure credit card payments.

CyberCash servers act as a gateway between the merchant on the Internet and the bank's secure financial networks. Using dedicated secure lines, a typical sale transaction via the merchant's Web site involves several steps.

1. Customer places an order on merchant's Web site, then enters the payment and shipping information to initiate purchase process.

2. Consumer verifies the information and clicks the appropriate button to submit the packet of information back to the merchant.

3. Merchant ships the order (packet of information) and forwards payment information, which has been digitally signed and encrypted, to the CyberCash server.

4. CyberCash server receives the packet, moves the transaction behind its firewall and off the Internet, unwraps the packets within a hardware-based crypto box

(the same technology banks use to handle PINs as they are shipped from an ATM network), reformats the transaction, and forwards it to the merchant's bank over secure, dedicated lines.

5. Merchant's bank forwards authorization request to issuing bank via the card association that settles credit card transactions (or directly to Visa, American Express, Discover, and so on) for approval. The decision is sent back to the CyberCash server.

6. CyberCash transmits approval or denial code back to merchant, who presents it to consumer. Merchant proceeds with the fulfillment phase (shipping the order).

Typically, a transaction goes through the payment processing cycle in less than 15 seconds. Because CyberCash uses an e-wallet, no one except the customer and the banks ever sees the customer's credit card number. An e-wallet is an electronic payment system that operates like a carrier of e-cash and information in the same way a real-world wallet does. CyberCash merely acts as an intermediary. Because the merchant is charged on a per transaction basis, the system is not economical for small payments. (See Figure 15.1.)

NETBILL.   This product is a secure and economical payment method for purchasing digital goods and services via the Internet. The Netbill server maintains accounts for consumers and merchants, which allows customers to pay merchants for goods to be delivered. The goods are delivered in encrypted form to the consumer's machine. The Money Tool (consumer software) verifies receipt, and the goods are displayed automatically for the consumer. The Netbill protocols enable

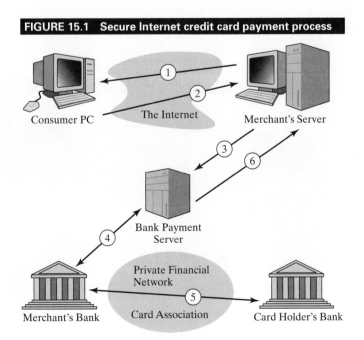

FIGURE 15.1   Secure Internet credit card payment process

Consumer PC   The Internet   Merchant's Server

Bank Payment Server

Private Financial Network

Merchant's Bank   Card Association   Card Holder's Bank

communication among the Money Tool, the merchant server, and the NetBill server. The goal is to ensure that all transactions are completed successfully.

The general configuration of NetBill operations is shown in Figure 15.2. The eight major steps are as follows.

1. A consumer requests a price quote by clicking on the URL in his or her browser.

2. The merchant responds with a price quote.

3. The consumer accepts (or declines) the price via a Money Tool pop-up window.

4. The merchant delivers the goods in encrypted form.

5. The Money Tool acknowledges receipt of the goods.

6. The merchant contacts NetBill's transaction server to record the transaction and transfer funds.

7. The NetBill transaction server confirms that funds have been transferred and stores the decryption key.

8. The merchant sends the decryption key to the Money Tool, which displays the goods in the consumer's browser.

The accounts on the NetBill server are linked to a financial institution—a bank. Consumers can replenish funds in their NetBill account using a credit card or bank account. Likewise, a merchant can transfer funds from its NetBill account to its bank account with each sale. When consumers create a NetBill account, they receive a unique user ID and generate a public key-pair associated with that ID. The key-pair is used for signatures and **authentication** within the NetBill system. As explained in Chapter 14, these electronic signatures prove that the person who ordered the merchandise is, in fact, the person authorized to do so. (See Figure 15.2.)

authentication: making sure that a cardholder is, in fact, the person authorized to use the card.

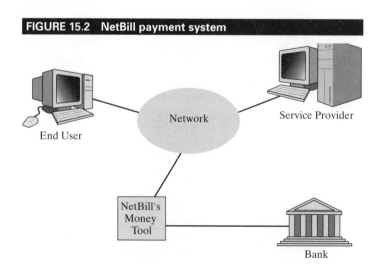

FIGURE 15.2   NetBill payment system

End User

Network

Service Provider

NetBill's Money Tool

Bank

SECURE ELECTRONIC TRANSACTIONS (SET). The **Secure Electronic Transactions (SET)** protocol is a proven standard for handling transactions on the Internet. The system is administered jointly by Visa and MasterCard to ensure reliable, secure transaction processing in the electronic payment medium. It covers every aspect of online commerce from initial registration of a cardholder with an online agency through the actual details of payment.

Secure Electronic Transactions (SET): protocol for handling transactions on the Internet administered jointly by Visa and MasterCard.

Among the services are cardholder and merchant registration, purchase request, payment authorization, payment capture, purchase notification, authorization reversal, and credit reversal. It authenticates the identification of the parties involved in the transaction by using a combination of cryptography systems, along with a *trust hierarchy* of digital certificates. SET was developed with four important goals in mind.

1. Confidentiality of payment as it is processed electronically.

2. Integrity of transmitted data. This means data will not be corrupted during transmission or processing.

3. Authentication that a cardholder is, in fact, the person authorized to use the card. It also verifies that the merchant handling a sale can accept an authorized card via the acquiring bank.

4. Interoperability across network providers. This implies a more encompassing or comprehensive way of making electronic payments over the Internet 24 hours a day, seven days a week, without delay.

The protocol defined by SET is thorough and complex. For example, each purchase request transaction requires exchanging four messages between customer and merchant. Figure 15.3 shows the classic SET transaction.

HOW WOULD YOU LIKE TO PAY?

TYPES OF ELECTRONIC PAYMENT MEDIA

Dozens of electronic payment media are already in use. Electronic payment media can be grouped into three types, depending on the information being transferred online.

1. Trusted third-party type: This type maintains all sensitive information. Banks maintain bank accounts and credit card numbers for customers, who may be buyers and sellers. No real financial transaction is done online and the information need not be encrypted because financial transactions are updated completely off-line.

2. Notational fund transfer-related type: This is the Visa/MasterCard SET-based transaction. The customer submits a credit card to a merchant for payment. The merchant transmits the credit card number via a phone line to the issuing bank for confirmation. The issuing bank, in turn, adjusts the customer's and the merchant's accounts accordingly. Because it is all done online, the information

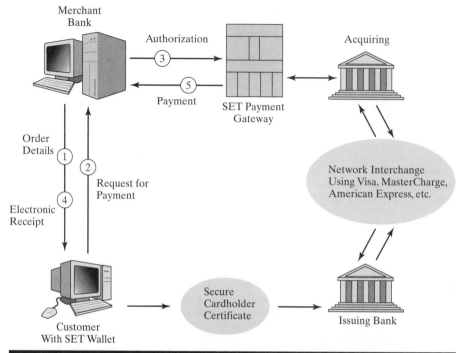

FIGURE 15.3 Classical flow of a SET transaction

transmitted is encrypted for security. Unfortunately, a hacker can still tap an account by intercepting a message or credit card number and run up charges before any electronic system detects it.

Despite these issues, this medium has been the core of online payment systems for years and now is being extended to the Internet. More sophisticated protocols are being tested to ensure transaction integrity.

3. Digital cash or electronic money: This type allows the transfer of money itself, which carries value. In this case, serial numbers representing actual money are encrypted all the way to their destination and can then be converted into real money such as U.S. dollars.

It took years for people to accept paper money; it will take time before people will accept a digital economy as a replacement for a paper-based economy. In the long run, digital money is necessary if we are to operate effectively in the digital marketplace. Digital money is effective in the sense that it is adaptable and can be manipulated to act like electronic checks or anonymous cash, depending on the situation and regardless of location or distance.

CREDIT CARDS

To sell things on the Web, a merchant must accept credit cards. A huge processing industry exists to handle the multibillion-dollar traffic that credit cards generate each year. Companies like Bank of America, First Data Corporation, and National Data

---
BOX 15.1

Credit/Debit Card Use Gaining Among Teens

A recent poll of teenagers who participate in the Junior Achievement program found that more than 11 percent are carrying credit cards, and some of them are as young as 13 or 14 years old. In addition, three out of 10 teenagers have checking accounts, and many are likely linked to automated teller machines with debit cards.

While 82 percent of the teen credit card users said they paid their bills in full every month, 18 percent said they carried balances over—a practice that has gotten a lot of their parents in trouble. The act of giving kids a credit card or a debit card isn't going to give them good money management habits. There has to be teaching and practicing.

Myron Pristino, First Heritage's business development officer, said teenagers who handle their accounts responsibly "get a start at building a level of confidence with their parents." They'll need that, he pointed out, when they're seeking parental help for an auto loan or college financing.

Source: Excerpted from Eileen Alt Powell, "More Teens Carrying Credit, Debit Cards." *Yahoo!*, April 13, 2005, Business—AP Consumer Columns.

Corporation handle the technology-based infrastructure for hundreds of banks, their merchants, and credit card holders 24 hours a day. Stores around the country swipe credit cards, enter codes, issue receipts, and move merchandise quickly and efficiently with no actual cash changing hands. See Box 15.1.

To accept a credit card payment on the Internet, you must first open a merchant account with your bank. You can work with your bank or search Yahoo! for credit card merchant services. A merchant account allows sellers to accept and process credit card transactions. In these transactions, the card number and transaction details are processed with no identification of the buyer, as there is when the customer signs a payment slip in person.

Charges the merchant pays for online transactions are equivalent to the charges for phoning in the transaction. The average charge for a transaction making its way through a terminal is anywhere from 2 cents to 5 cents, depending on the volume of business the merchant generates per time period. Fees include a few hundred dollars for setup plus 2 to 4 percent of each credit card transaction processed. Some banks may also charge statement fees and a monthly minimum charge of $20 to $50.

To accept credit card payments over the Internet, the Web merchant needs some form of secure and encrypted line, usually employing the Secure Sockets Layer (SSL)—a standard on Netscape and Microsoft browsers. All the merchant's server needs is an encryption key.

To complete the cycle, the merchant needs a shopping cart program that allows users to collect their purchases. The shopping cart interfaces with a payment-processing system such as CyberCash, calculates the costs and taxes, and delivers a complete bill for customer approval. To improve fraud detection, CyberCash offers its online merchant customers a real-time fraud-detection service to show when a customer is trying to make fraudulent online purchases using credit cards.

Because credit cards are so widely used, you might get the false impression that the billing process is straightforward. In reality, credit cards are just the most convenient way to get online payments. Credit cards work around the globe, regardless of the location or country of the issuing bank. They also handle multiple currencies and clear transactions through a series of clearinghouses or consortiums.

Credit card processing is not, however, simple.

1. Most card issuers charge interest from the day a charge is posted to the account if payment is not made in full monthly. Some charge interest from the date of purchase, several days before they have even paid the store on your behalf.

2. For the merchant, credit card transactions result in immediate credit to the merchant's bank account. They have the same effect as cash.

3. By law, the cardholder's risk of losing a credit card amounts to $50. A cardholder is expected to notify the issuing bank immediately upon discovering the loss of the card.

4. A cardholder can dispute charges or purchases to the card issuer. In this case, the merchant's acquiring bank can reverse payments or adjust payments as the situation warrants.

Despite their widespread use in e-commerce, credit cards leave a complete audit trail and continue to be an incredibly insecure form of payment. No signature gets verified, and no face-to-face clues are available to interpret. A merchant can't tell whether the card is in the hands of the actual cardholder, a 10-year-old child, one's spouse, or a thief. Getting a merchant account is not a straightforward procedure either. If your online storefront is your first business venture on the Web, banks invariably examine your company's financial records and the history of the business. They try to assess how serious your commitment is to the Web store, how long you plan to stay with it should it not do well at the outset, and so on.

If a merchant can't get a merchant account, credit cards can be accepted in other ways. The most common way is to find a company that will subcontract the payment collection process as a third party. In terms of the mechanics of processing credit card purchases, Figure 15.3 illustrates the five-step process as it relates to purchases over the Internet.

CREDIT CARD LAUNDERING

As a merchant, would you extend an unsecured line of credit to another merchant who could not get credit from a financial institution on its own? If you agree to deposit another seller's credit card sales into your merchant account, you're taking more than a financial risk. Although you'll be charging a fee, this type of credit card *laundering* is a violation of your merchant agreement with the bank or credit card company. It seems like a simple procedure for earning extra cash, but it can turn into a nightmare. The guaranteed easy income often turns into losses beyond all commissions. Merchants that are turned down for credit often have a bad credit history or bad management.

Many disreputable telemarketers use credit card–processing merchants to bill consumers for their sales. Once they have received payment from the processing merchants, they close their operations or move to new and undisclosed locations without ever sending any merchandise to the customer. When consumers find out, they contact their credit card company and dispute the charges. In these cases, everyone loses. The customer loses time chasing the false charges, the credit card company might have to write off the amount to bad debt, and the telemarketer has blood on its hands.

DEBIT CARDS

Payments can be made on a Web site in two ways: debit cards and credit cards. Most ATM cards are debit cards with a Visa or MasterCard logo. They look exactly like credit cards, except they directly tap your checking account every time you make a purchase or a withdrawal. They are easier, more convenient, less burdensome, and offer greater access to your money than do checks, ATMs, or credit cards. They are descendants of the ATM cards that became popular in the early 1980s.

Debit cards are different, however, because transactions are processed through the issuing bank's credit card network. Debit cards can be used with or without a personal identification number (PIN) almost everywhere—retail stores, gasoline stations, restaurants, and pay phones. When used without a PIN (called an *off-line* transaction), the procedure is simple. The merchant's terminal reads the card and identifies it as a debit card that creates a debit against the cardholder's bank account. Because the transaction is off-line, instead of debiting the account immediately, there is a two- to three-day wait before final processing.

When a debit card is used for off-line transactions, as in the case of retail purchases, a thief can drain an account simply by getting hold of a receipt. The thief does not need the card; the card number is sufficient to commit the fraud. Unlike credit cards, for which a cardholder's liability for a stolen card under the law is $50, the liability for debit card fraud is higher. It is $50 if one notifies the bank within two days of learning of the fraud, and $500 or more after two days, up to the entire amount stolen under certain circumstances.

Worse, regardless of the liability, the thief has the victim's money and the victim might have to fight to get it back from the bank. In the case of credit card fraud, the victim simply talks with the bank about getting disputed charges taken off the bill.

When a debit card is used with a PIN, as in using an ATM machine, it is called an *online* transaction. The cardholder simply inserts the card in the machine, enters the PIN number, and proceeds as when using an ATM card.

Today's banks are pushing hard to replace the ATM card with a debit card without asking customers if they want one. The reasons are obvious. More merchants have credit card readers than PIN-based readers. Banks also make more money through off-line debit cards in percentage fees or discounts from the merchant. Banks and merchants make more money and have lower risks than when a consumer writes a check because there are no check-clearing costs, there is less float time, and no checks bounce.

All debit card purchases are reflected in the monthly hard copy statement the bank mails each customer for reconciliation.

According to the National Consumers' League, here is what consumers need to know about debit cards.

1. Using a debit card frees you from having to carry cash or a checkbook. You don't have to carry traveler's checks, show identification, or give out personal information at the time of the transaction.

2. Debit cards are more readily accepted by merchants than are checks, especially in countries where check cashing and check processing are not widely used.

3. It is generally easier to get a debit card than a credit card. You can get a debit card the moment you have a checking or a savings account.

4. Returned debit card purchases are treated just like returns for items purchased by cash or check.

5. The debit card is a quick *pay now* process. No grace period is given as for credit card payments.

6. A major problem at this time is that using a debit card may mean less protection for items that are never delivered, for defective items, or for items that were misrepresented. With credit card purchases, you can contest the charge and put a hold on payment within 60 days.

7. Cardholders might overspend their limit before anyone finds out. Retailers do not have verification machines to see a bank account balance before the sale. During busy times, most retailers process small sales on faith.

SMART CARDS

Imagine discarding your wallet full of plastic—credit cards, debit cards, frequent-flyer cards, gas company cards, and a special card to get into your company building—in favor of one smart card that can do all these functions in a swipe. A **smart card,** first produced in 1977 by Motorola, is a thin, credit card–sized piece of plastic that contains a half-inch-square area that serves as the card's input/output system.

smart card: a card with a built-in chip capable of storing information in its memory.

This is its interface with the outside world, and it handles a variety of applications. A smart card contains a programmable chip, a combination of RAM and ROM storage, and an operating system of sorts, all embedded in the plastic. It encrypts digital cash on a chip and can be refilled by connecting to a bank. A smart card carries more information than can be accommodated on a card with a magnetic stripe. The chip's ability to store information in its memory makes the card *smart*. It can make a decision, because it has relatively powerful processing capabilities. A brief summary of smart card evolution is shown in Table 15.1.

Among its many uses and applications are the following.

1. Provides users with the ability to make a purchase. It contains stored value the cardholder can spend at retailers.

2. Holds cash, ID information, and a key to a house or an office.

3. Provides three categories of applications. The first is information to authenticate an individual's claim of personal identification using either token-based (e.g., a passport, driver's license, credit card) or knowledge-based (e.g., PIN numbers or passwords) authentication approaches. The second category is authorization for things like drug prescription fulfillment and voting purposes. The third category is transaction processing. The smart card could be loaded with cash value in ATM machines and used as a credit card. A more recent development in smart card design is capturing fingerprints for improved authentication.

TABLE 15.1   A summary of smart card evolution

Date	Technology	Architecture	Application Memory	Program Memory
Late 1970s	Memory	State machine*	100 bit	Serial number
1980s	Memory	State machine	Up to 1 KB	Serial number
Early 1990s	Microprocessor and secure microprocessor	8-bit	1 KB–16 KB	8 KB–32 KB
Late 1990s	Microprocessor with cryptographic coprocessor	16-bit	256 bytes–64 KB	8 KB–136 KB
Today	Microprocessor with cryptographic coprocessor	32-bit (RISC)	80 KB–512 KB	240 KB–512 KB

Year**	Event
1968	2 Germans invented smart card
1970	Arimura invents in Japan
1974	Roland Moreno invents in France
1976	Bull (France) first licenses smart card
1980	1st trials in 3 French cities
1982	1st U.S. trials in N. Dakota & N.J.
1996	1st university campus deployment

*A state machine is a device that performs a single function.

**Shelter and Procaccino, 2002, 84.

Source: Nancy Gohring, "Get Smart," *Interactive Week,* January 14, 2001, 45.

integrity: ensuring that transmitted data will not be corrupted during transmission or processing.

confidentiality: privacy of message transmission or reception.

4. Provides encryption and decryption of messages to ensure security, **integrity,** and **confidentiality.** Though not inherently anonymous, smart cards can be designed to share no transaction information.

5. Acts as a carrier of value in a system, similar to what is called an *electronic purse.* For example, Visa Cash allows a customer to use a smart card for small purchases by storing specific cash value that can be replenished once the amount is used up. The standard technology is to allow transfer from a smart card to an authorized merchant.

Known smart card applications include the following.

1. Government: Smart cards are gaining importance with government agencies around the world. They often are used to control areas of access for government employees. (See Box 15.2.) Postal workers in France carry smart cards to gain access to apartment buildings. The cards are programmed daily with the postal workers' predefined schedules. This card allows access only at

---

BOX 15.2

Smart Cards in Defense

The Defense Department's Common Access Card (CAC) program, through which smart cards will be issued to more than 4 million military personnel, civilian DOD employees, and contractors, is the largest smart card project currently under way.

Deployed in March 2004, the 32KB chip-based cards that incorporate Java technology will serve as military ID cards and provide access to physical facilities and government networks,. Apart from the standard credential information, each ID card has up to 7KB of space reserved for use by military services as needed, for functions such as tracking troop deployment readiness or paying for food at the commissary.

The card infrastructure is based on technology from Axalto and Oberthur Card Systems, and has been a crucial enabler of the Pentagon's e-business initiatives, including the use of digital signatures for electronic documents. So far, about 3.5 million cards have been deployed at a rate of more than 10,000 cards a day from 900 centers worldwide.

The DOD effort has been a big catalyst for the smart card industry. There has been a significant increase in the shipment of smart cards to corporate and government programs in the last three years. The most visible has been the DOD effort. We expect to see similar initiatives in the future from other agencies, including the Department of Homeland Security and the Transportation Security Agency, which is expected to roll out 10 million cards.

Source: Excerpted from Jaikumar Vijayan, "Defense Leads the Way." *Computerworld*, February 9, 2004, 31.

---

certain times, facilitating easy access to appropriate individuals and discouraging intruders.

2. Identification: The identification market benefits greatly from the security associated with smart cards. Examples are driver's licenses, immigration cards, and college campus IDs. Florida State University uses a smart card for its official student identification card. It is a multi-application card and offers a variety of conveniences and services to university students. Students use this card to gain access to certain facilities and events. If a student wishes to activate these features, the card can serve as a debit card on and off campus, a prepaid vending card, and a long-distance calling card.

3. Health care: Countries with national health care systems, such as Germany and France, have employed smart cards to reduce service costs associated with the health care industry. Germany and France have issued national smart cards for the purpose of collecting payments. In France, the smart card focuses on an insurance payment system, including features such as electronic signature abilities and built-in encryption. These smart cards assure confidentiality, security, authentication, and integrity and are being piloted in four major French cities.

4. Loyalty: The retail industry widely uses applications of the smart card; more specifically, to identify and reward customers. The Boots Advantage Card in Britain is one such example of a loyalty card retailers use to capture customer information and better cater promotions processes to them. Currently, more than

5 million Boots Advantage Cards have been issued in Britain. Each British pound a customer spends in the Boots convenience store is worth four points on the Advantage Card. Each point amounts to 1 penny available to spend in any Boots store. Most often, the stores offer extra points with the purchase of certain products, which allows customers to collect points even faster.

5. Telecommunications: Smart cards are widely used in the telecommunications industry. The Global Standard for Mobile Communicators (GSM) has been adopted in Hong Kong, Singapore, Australia, New Zealand, India, South Africa, and the Persian Gulf states. A smart card called a Subscriber Information Module contains the information necessary to access the network. This card can be inserted into any GSM phone, and the user is billed automatically. The user's location is detected, and any incoming phone calls are directed to that phone.

6. Transportation: Contactless smart card technology is quickly gaining acceptance in the transportation industry throughout the world. Hong Kong uses a single smart card, the Octopus Card, in most of its public transportation systems. Octopus equipment has been installed in all buses in the city. Passengers also are able to travel franchised trams, coaches, and railways in Hong Kong using the Octopus Card.

7. Financial: Financial institutions were one of the first to adopt smart cards for various applications. There are several common uses of smart cards within the industry, including electronic purses, credit and debit cards, and payment associations. Electronic purses attempt to eliminate the costs associated with small change at the point of sale. The electronic cents purse is a smart card that stores a maximum value of 99 cents. When a customer presents this card at the point of sale, the transaction is rounded up or down to the nearest whole number and the card is either credited or debited to account for the difference.

As can be seen, smart cards benefit consumers in several ways, depending on the application. In general, smart card–based applications benefit consumers where their life and business habits intersect with payment-processing technologies. This includes managing expenditures more effectively, reducing paperwork, and being able to access multiple services and the Internet. A multiple application card can support services like health care, travel, and financial data access. Some smart cards also link directly to the Internet.

HOW SMART CARDS WORK.   Operationally, smart cards require a special reader to connect the card with a computer system programmed for this purpose. Smart cards have special contacts that match those in the reader when the card is inserted into the slot for processing. The newest smart cards are "contactless." Infrared communication technology allows the reader to exchange data. In a retail store, the reader normally is attached to a cash register. In buildings, authorized users scan the smart card across a reader attached to the door and programmed to a computer-based recognition system. With remote contactless cards, the card can be read from a distance. This is how tollbooth electronic payment readers work.

How secure and confidential are smart cards? Smart cards offer more security and confidentiality than any other financial or transaction storage card on the market. They are a safe place to store sensitive information (keys, passwords) or personal information.

Smart cards have their share of problems. First, they are vulnerable to hardware hacking, which means data stored in the card can be altered or corrupted. Left undetected for long, these alterations could bankrupt the card backer. According to one report, smart cards are broken routinely, in spite of their reputation as the most secure processor available.

HOW DOES A SMART CARD RELATE TO THE INTERNET?   A smart card can be used in Internet applications in several ways. First, it can help an Internet client support an established protocol such as SSL or SET. For example, the smart card can authenticate access to encrypted transactions or files stored on a personal computer. It also can be used for cryptographic functions such as digital signatures and storing the key(s) and certificate(s) for the specified protocol. Key storage is an important function that can be relegated to a smart card. Also, secret keys in the chip let the card authenticate its communication with any device sharing the same keys. In the absence of ready availability of card readers, smart cards in Internet systems are confined to special-purpose processes such as "electronic cash" for low-value payments, telebanking, and authentication of a transaction.

THE FUTURE OF SMART CARDS.   The future of smart cards is promising. Smart cards are expected to be used in 95 percent of the digital wireless phone services offered worldwide. Asia, Latin America, and North America are countries where smart cards have the greatest potential in the next five years. The main uses to date are for pay telephones, wireless telephony, Internet access, banking, and pay TV.

With the proliferation of smart cards and other payment media in e-commerce, one big headache a customer will encounter is keeping track of passwords for different cards.

A single card could replace all these passwords and be activated simply by pressing your thumb on the card. This is called **biometrics** (see Chapter 13), or the use of a body part such as the thumb to authenticate identity. The card would carry a digital fingerprint. Many ATM machines already scan the customer's retina for a few seconds in lieu of the traditional password.

biometrics: the use of a body part such as the thumb to authenticate identity.

The problem with the retinal scan is the storing of a customer's physical characteristics in a database, which brings up the privacy issue. With the fingerprint, the characteristic is known only to the customer and is activated only when the owner presses it into action. This eases the privacy concern and eventually could be cheaper, especially when the retailer no longer needs elaborate equipment to match the thumbprint.

The next wave in smart cards is their use in place of keys as a way of opening doors. The card is already programmed to allow mail deliverers into a building at certain times of the day or during certain periods of the year. In the lab, scientists are trying to put a screen resembling a tiny computer on a smart card. Scientists are even trying to make it possible for this wallet-sized computer to process voice commands.

In terms of obstacles, smart card use in the United States faces resistance because of the privacy issue. Aside from housing all applications on a single card, smart card infrastructure also must achieve interoperability. Even then, with massive personal information on one card, concerns have surfaced about businesses gaining access to such information for marketing purposes. In situations where organizations use smart cards to give employees access control, the smart card keeps a log of where the employee is at all times. This is an obvious invasion of privacy for many Americans.

Another obstacle is culture. Because Americans do not feel deprived by not having to use smart cards, no incentive exists to use them. In the U.S. culture, greater emphasis is placed on privacy than by individuals in other parts of the world. The bottom line is that consumers are reluctant to purchase smart cards until enough privacy and security features are embedded in the infrastructure to address this concern.

DigiCash, E-Cash, and the E-Wallet

Credit cards leave a complete audit trail, which makes them more open to pervasive eavesdropping than the mail or the telephone network. Credit cards also have other drawbacks. They are not well suited for impulse buying, because an element of deliberation goes with using them. In addition, they are not that convenient for making small purchases.

Some tech designers see a solution in digital cash. Unlike credit card transactions, digital cash leaves no audit trail. It offers a true digital economy—one in which anyone can pay $5 or $5,000 directly as if it were a real cash payment in person.

One such digital cash system is CyberCoin. To use CyberCoin, you first open an account at a bank that handles e-cash (Mark Twain Bank in St. Louis, Missouri, was the first U.S. e-cash bank). Next, you make a withdrawal in the form of e-cash coins stored in a digital wallet or an e-wallet on your PC's hard disk. You can spend the e-cash at the business of any merchant that also has an e-cash account at a bank.

E-cash was an electronic currency service till 2002, when it was acquired by InfoSpace Technologies. This service requires a client-server interaction, whereby the customer buys electronic cash with a secure credit card transaction. The customer does not have to possess an open account with e-cash. Although this service requires an intermediary, it is the safest in terms of fraud protection.

From a regulatory point of view, digital cash is not any different from any other kind of electronic financial payment medium. Just as the IRS often suspects independent contractors' reporting because of the possibility of tax fraud, the Treasury Department is likely to resist minters of digital cash because of the confusion that resulted in early America when each bank printed its own notes.

viral product: a product offered as a giveaway or a special promotion to encourage receivers to pass on the word to others, creating the potential for exponential growth in the product sale (sale spreading like a virus); a communications product.

One new development in early 2000 was combining e-mail and the credit card network to send real cash. A new online payment system called PayPal.com allows registered users to send a payment to anybody with an e-mail address just by writing a dollar amount into an online form. When the e-mail is sent, the payment is charged to the sender's credit card or bank account. Registration takes less than five minutes. If the person on the other end is not registered, that person simply fills out a form attached to the e-payment to "tag" the money, which is already available in a PayPal.com account in the receiver's name. This is called a **viral product.** See Box 15.3.

e-wallet: an electronic payment system that operates like a carrier of e-cash and information in the same way a real-world wallet functions.

THE E-WALLET.   The **e-wallet** is another payment scheme that operates like a *carrier* of e-cash and other information in the same way a wallet carries real cash and various IDs. The aim is to give shoppers a single, simple, and secure way of carrying currency electronically. Trust is the basis of the e-wallet as a form of electronic payment. The procedure for using an e-wallet is easy.

BOX 15.3

PayPal Pushes On

Cybersource and PayPal are teaming up to push PayPal's service. The idea is that retailers would let people use a payment system in addition to credit cards for online buying. PayPal is the leading service for consumers to make payments online without using a credit card. It is owned by eBay. PayPal ended the third quarter with 35 million accounts worldwide, up from just under 20 million a year ago. Cybersource helps retailers manage several different payment services, including credit cards and electronic payments.

PayPal's growth among users made it a natural addition to the list of payment services processed by Cybersource. Cybersource plans to bundle PayPal with other payment methods, such as credit cards and electronic debit services. The partners are also hoping retailers will heed the fact that many consumers are wary of using credit cards online because they fear personal information being stolen.

When making a purchase, PayPal makes users submit a personal identification number and the balance of their PayPal account. PayPal works by providing consumers with a variety of payment methods. A user can pay with a credit card without having to type in the account numbers during the transaction. Consumers can also set up the PayPal service to draw funds directly from their bank account.

PayPal charges business sellers 2.9 percent of each transaction. But firms such as Home Depot, which process thousands of transactions daily, likely get better rates from credit card companies. The question is whether there's enough value and whether PayPal is going to be cheaper.

Source: Excerpted from Pete Barlas, "PayPal Pushes for Business Use." *Yahoo! News*, October 27, 2003, Business.

---

1. Decide on an online site where you would like to shop.

2. Download a wallet from the merchant's Web site where you intend to shop. The special form requires the buyer to fill in some personal information.

3. Fill in the personal information such as your credit card number, name, address, and phone number, and where merchandise should be shipped.

4. When you're ready to buy, click on the wallet button and the buying process is fully executed. Billing information is filled out automatically. Another option is to drag information out of the wallet and drop it into the online form.

Suppose a discount stockbroker offers electronic trading for customers with a cash or margin account. To trade (buy/sell) electronically on the Web for the first time, you are asked to fill out a short form on the screen with your name, account number, address, phone number, and so on, and enter a preassigned password. Once the system accepts the form, it asks if you want to replace the assigned password with one of your own. This completes setting up your electronic trading profile. Your cash or margin account is the e-wallet. It carries cash value. Every trade you make will affect the wallet as a credit or as a debit; it either takes e-cash out of your e-wallet or puts e-cash into it.

Some wallets sit on your PC's hard disk for privacy; others sit on the computer of a host if you want to reach your wallet from several different locations. The big online shopping sites like Amazon.com (amazon.com) have their own internal wallets.

FIGURE 15.4 The most popular wallets	
Wallet Vendor	Service Details
America Online	Works within America Online shopping only
Brodia.com	Direct-marketing tool: travels with a consumer across sites
CyberCash	Marketed to the CyberCash merchant customer base as an added service
eWallet	Client-based desktop application: shopping bots
Galtor.com	Direct-marketing tool, dubbed an "online companion" for storing passwords and credit cards
IBM	Part of the IBM Payment Suite of products for corporate customer
Trintech	Single card resides on the desktop or a toolbar; multiple-card service can reside on a server or desktop
Yahoo!	Works within Yahoo! shopping only

You can buy and pay with a single click. Other Web sites store your name, address, and credit card number so you don't have to enter them again. Banks like MBNA, NextCard, and First USA already are offering their customers digital wallets. Microsoft offers Microsoft Passport, and IBM has its Consumer Wallet.

A popular site-based wallet is Amazon.com's 1-Click system, which builds on an established relationship of trust with the customer. The problem with e-wallets today is that they are tied to specific retailers. Can you imagine having an e-wallet for each retailer you deal with? Eventually, a way will be devised to have one wallet communicate across retailers. The most popular wallets available to date are shown in Figure 15.4.

A recent joint protocol called Electronic Common Modeling Language (ECML), announced in 1998, was designed to make it easier to build multisite electronic wallets. ECML-compiled e-wallets, backed by American Express, IBM, Microsoft, Sun Microsystems, Visa, SETCo, and MasterCard, are designed to fill out forms. They read a list of field names and fill them with information provided previously by the consumer. There is a question of how quickly they will be adopted because security mechanisms have been left out of the specifications. A physical wallet is on your person. You trust yourself, and experience tells you that you can protect it. For e-wallets to be trusted, e-wallet companies need to work jointly with banks to promote trust and establish reliable protection.

electronic funds transfer (EFT): a computer-based system that facilitates the transfer of money or the processing of financial transactions between two financial institutions.

Automated Clearinghouse (ACH): where bank transactions involving more than one institution are routed to debit and credit the correct accounts.

ELECTRONIC FUNDS TRANSFER AND AUTOMATED CLEARINGHOUSE

Electronic funds transfer (EFT) is a computer-based system that facilitates the transfer of money or processing financial transactions between two financial institutions the same day or overnight. Interbank transfer is one of the earliest forms of electronic payment systems on private networks.

The **Automated Clearinghouse (ACH)** routes bank transactions among financial institutions so that accounts held by respective financial institutions can be debited and credited. Suppose your present checking account shows a balance of $100 in Bank A. You walk up to the teller one morning to deposit a payroll check for $280 written on your employer's Bank B in your checking account. The teller deposits the "not on us" check in your checking account and gives you a receipt showing a total balance of $380, but the amount available is still $100. The teller places a "hold" on the payroll check because it has to clear ACH before the money becomes available for your use. Here is the generic processing cycle for clearing the check.

- Your bank (A) sends the payroll check to ACH for processing. The check sorter/reader scans the check and, based on the bank code, determines that it is drawn on an account at Bank B.
- ACH queries Bank B's network to determine whether it will honor the payroll check in the amount of $280.
- Bank B's computer system, which is linked to ACH, examines the check and the checking account against which it is drawn. If approved, the amount of $280 is credited to Bank A.
- Bank A routes the money to your checking account. (See Figure 15.5.)

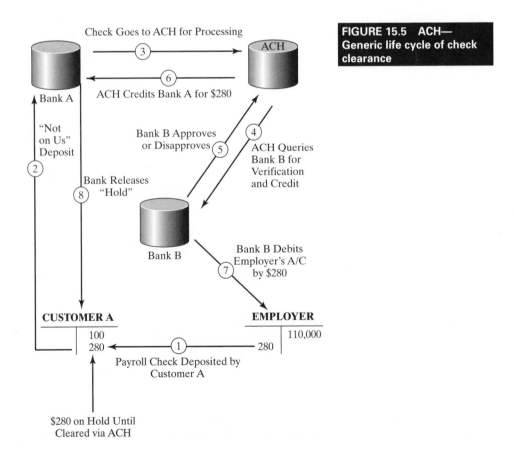

FIGURE 15.5 ACH— Generic life cycle of check clearance

B2B AND E-PAYMENT

One area drawing attention is the dawn of business-to-business e-payment systems that can save processing costs and improve the overall efficiency of financial transactions between businesses. This area is part of electronic invoice presentment and payment (EIPP) systems. The goal of such systems is to automate everything from how the seller presents the invoice to how the other business pays the invoice. The most significant advantage comes from savings in staff, postage, and handling. Some sources estimate as much as 85 percent of the benefits result from manual handling of invoices and settling billing disputes and the resulting writing of refund checks.

Connecticut-based Gartner Inc. estimated up to 15 percent of the invoices mailed by large businesses resulted in a dispute that cost between \$20 and \$40 per invoice to settle. With EIPP, customers can scan bill details on their screen, submit disputes, and can opt to make partial payments online.

Every time the subject of e-payment comes up, concern over fraudulent orders is bound to come up. Before expecting e-payment online (in fact, any payment) to be finalized, online merchants should heed several warning signs regarding online orders:

- Expensive items. Be careful with big orders, especially for high-priced brand-name items.

- Ordering multiple items to be shipped to more than one verifiable address.

- Different addresses, where one address is given for shipping the products and another address for sending the bill. Very likely the latter address is questionable.

- Providing e-mail addresses that are difficult to trace. Free e-mail services are usually the ones that are hard to trace.

- Overseas addresses. Romania, Belarus, Pakistan, Egypt, Nigeria, Indonesia, Malaysia, and other countries have been known to have a high incident of fraud, unverifiable addresses, or names that simply do not exist.

- Instructing the e-merchant to have an expensive order left at the door or in front of a given store.

In summary, the most obvious savings of EIPP are more efficient invoicing, quicker receipt of payments, easier processing of receipts, and reduced customer service that once handled such things as invoices and complaints. It will be interesting to see how well the technology establishes roots in ongoing businesses in the next two to five years.

M-COMMERCE AND M-PAYMENT

The ability to secure payments over wireless devices like mobile phones and personal digital assistants is the major focus of m-commerce and e-commerce today. The success of m-commerce depends on its payment infrastructure, delivering confidential data safely and reliably. With the growing mobility of consumers worldwide, the infrastructure also must be capable of handling payments between authorized parties anywhere and at any time in a consistent and interoperable manner.

Taking the lead in this endeavor is MasterCard International, working with financial institutions and technology organizations to build standards for mobile transactions. Through the Global Mobile Commerce Interoperability Group (see www.gmcig.org), the goal is to establish secure payment standards for the evolving m-commerce market.

Security and convenience are two important motivations for using mobile devices for transactions. Electronic means of authorizations are based on account-holder authentication by the payment system, but it can fail in a number of ways. Existing systems do not always distinguish among fraud by the user. Damages resulting from fraud are resolved through legal and administrative means rather than through technical means. Credit card purchases and electronic generated money transfers must be cancelled, because the bank cannot prove that the rightful card holder was in fact the one who made the purchases.

On the convenience side, cell phones can be used when paying for goods and services, whether on foot, in the car, aboard planes or trains. The user can view balances and logs of transactions. It is also easy for a single cell phone to support several applications like investment, retail payments, micropayments, and banking in general.

Figure 15.6 is a graphic representation of the transactions architecture via the mobile phone. The key players are the user, the mobile device, and a mobile transaction provider—a bank, a cellular operator, or both. Each transaction goes through three independent processes:

• Identification of the user via passwords, biometrics, etc.

• Authentication of the transaction via encryption mechanisms like digital signatures

• Secure performance of the total transaction process via secure payment protocols like Secure Electronic Transactions (SET)

FIGURE 15.6   Mobile-specific transaction architecture

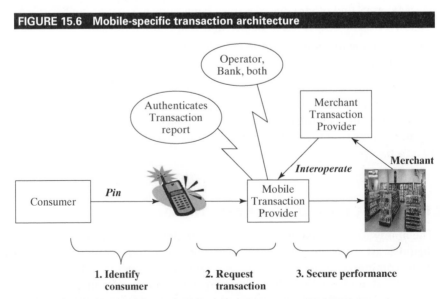

Source: Adapted from Amir Herzberg, "Payments and Banking with Mobile Personal Devices." *Communications of the ACM,* May 2003, 54.

GENERAL GUIDE TO E-PAYMENT

With all the options, procedures, and technical support available, there are general rules and tips to consider before paying for goods or services on the Internet.

- **Use a secure Web browser.** In today's security-threatened Internet, a browser must have the most up-to-date encryption capabilities. When submitting payment information, make sure the "lock" icon is visible on the browser's status bar.

- **Read the Web site's privacy policy carefully.** Specifically, find out how the site will use or share any personal information you provide.

- **Figure out the merchant's refund and return policies in advance of the final purchase.** These are tough areas to figure out should you decide to return merchandise for refund.

- **Investigate the trustworthiness of the merchant before you initiate a purchase.** You should know by now that not every Web merchant is reliable or long-lasting.

- **Keep a record of all online transactions and check e-mail and other contacts regularly.** After the purchase is finalized, most merchants will e-mail you a confirmation with specific information that acts like a receipt.

- **Review your credit card statements line by line to ensure authenticity.** Be sure to notify the proper issuing bank of any unauthorized purchases or irregularities in your account.

In addition to the FTC, there are several other agencies that can help with fraud and dishonest transactions. They include financial institutions, local consumer protection agencies, and law enforcement agencies like your state's attorney general's office. An important telephone number to remember is 1–877-FTC-HELP (382–4357).

ISSUES AND IMPLICATIONS

With the Internet's increasing traffic and congestion resulting from growing e-commerce, there are issues regarding electronic payment methods and methodologies of which you should be aware. The issues can be grouped as follows.

1. Consumer needs: What features will make electronic payment cheaper and more secure for the consumer and the merchant?

2. Corporate processes: How will today's increasing e-commerce business affect the way tomorrow's corporation operates in the marketplace? Will small- and medium-size businesses be harmed or helped by the electronic payment system?

3. Corporate strategy: Will the electronic payment system end up in the hands of fewer financial institutions, or will it generate a number of smaller banks that cater specifically to clearing and processing digital business transactions?

4. Regulation of competition: How does the government ensure fair play among companies doing business on the Internet? What standardization can be

expected? How can we be sure that financial service providers will behave in the public's best interests? How will the government levy taxes on electronic funds flowing over open networks like the Internet, especially with the increasing sophistication of encryption?

5. Economics and social processes: Will the government pull out of the cash-making business? If so, what are the consequences for business and society? If taxing goods and services over the Internet ends up being a big job to control, will the government find new ways to tax the working public?

In principle, the present technology seems to do the job of securing electronic payment over the Internet. Micropayments (say, less than $1) and high-value payments have different security and cost requirements. Based on all indicators, smart card readers will become widely available to expedite payments of small amounts. Ultimately, smart cards and e-wallets will provide better security, allowing the customer to use unfamiliar workstations without endangering the security of the transaction.

A FINAL WORD

The payment systems that will be used in the digital world for e-commerce are virtually the same types of payment systems used in the paper world. They are cash (for small and anonymous payments), checks, credit cards, and systems involving vouchers and coupons. It is the same business model, has the same look and feel, is at least as cost-effective, and is at least as secure as that used in the paper world. The implementation is simply different.

In terms of integrity for the customer, the merchant, and the payment system, nothing happens without authorization. Nobody gives up money without an explicit agreement, stating all necessary payment details. Nothing happens without generating convincing pieces of evidence. That is, if person A receives money, A can prove this fact. If A has not given any money, no one can prove the contrary. Rules and technical procedures for handling disputes are part of the payment system.

In terms of privacy, outsiders must not know payment details (customer, merchant, account numbers, amounts, date and time, payment information, and so on). In the same manner, payment anonymity should be preserved. Customers should be anonymous, and the merchant should not be able to link any two payments by the same customer. Also, the payment system should not trace payments back to the customer.

Finally, the future of privacy, money, banking, and finance is cryptography. But because encryption can make communications immune from legal interception, it threatens a key law enforcement tool. Electronic payment messages between banks are now mostly encrypted to safeguard against unauthorized interception. Of course, the more security is embedded in a transaction, the longer it will take to reach its destination. This is counter to the key feature of electronic payments, which is speed and efficiency of exchange. But that is the way it is going in today's e-payment industry.

Summary

1. Cash offers unique features of convenience, wide acceptance, anonymity, no cost of use, and no audit trail, but e-money is becoming more attractive for making payments and conducting business in the real world. On the negative side, cash is easy to lose; difficult to trace; cumbersome to carry; and time consuming to count, organize, and manage.

2. There are four types of e-money: (1) identified and online—credit and debit card transactions; (2) identified and off-line—purchasing by check, traveler's checks, or postal money order; (3) anonymous and online—cash payments; and (4) anonymous and off-line—electronic cash such as making deposits in one's account via ATM.

3. Regardless of the type or form of money, there are two distinct sets of properties to consider in money transfer: the ACID test (atomicity, consistency, isolation, durability) and the ICES test (interoperability, conservation, economy, scalability).

4. Electronic currency, credit cards, debit cards, and smart cards are the four main models for Internet-based payment systems. In addition to the ACID and ICES properties, several nontechnical properties are relevant to an electronic payment system: acceptability, ease of integration, customer base, and ease of use and access.

5. Payment systems via the Internet include CyberCash and First Virtual. Secure Electronic Transactions (SET) is a standard for handling transactions on the Internet and was developed with four important goals: confidentiality of payment, integrity of the transmitted data, authentication of the person using the card, and interoperability across network providers.

6. Electronic payment media can be grouped into three types, depending on the type of information being transferred online: (1) trusted third party (e.g., banks) that maintains all sensitive information; (2) notational fund transfer-related type, such as Visa/MasterCard's SET-based transaction, where customers submit their credit card to a merchant for payment; and (3) digital cash or electronic money—this allows the transfer of money itself, which carries value.

7. Debit cards and credit cards are the two ways to make payments on a Web site. Debit cards directly transfer funds from the consumer's bank account to the merchant's. Credit cards leave a complete audit trail, are not well suited for impulse buying, and are not convenient for making small purchases.

8. A smart card is a card with a built-in chip capable of storing information in its memory. It contains stored value that the cardholder can spend at retailers and provides identification of the cardholder. It also provides data portability and helps businesses expand their products and services.

9. One alternative method of payment is digital cash. It leaves no audit trail and offers true digital economy. From a regulatory view, digital cash in transit is not any different from any other kind of electronic financial payment media. The e-wallet gives the shopper a single, simple, and secure way of carrying currency electronically.

10. EFT is a computer-based system that facilitates the electronic transfer of money or the processing of financial transactions between financial institutions. ACH is an automated clearinghouse where bank transactions are routed to debit and credit the correct

accounts held by the correct financial institution.

11. Cryptography is the future of privacy and represents the future of money, banking, and finance. Money is digital information. The way to hide digital information is through cryptography.

Key Terms

- **ACID test** (p. 478)
- **anonymous e-money** (p. 477)
- **authentication** (p. 482)
- **Automated Clearinghouse (ACH)** (p. 495)
- **biometrics** (p. 492)
- **confidentiality** (p. 489)
- **debit card** (p. 480)
- **electronic currency** (p. 479)
- **electronic funds transfer (EFT)** (p. 495)
- **electronic payment** (p. 479)
- **e-money** (p. 477)
- **e-wallet** (p. 493)
- **ICES test** (p. 478)
- **identified e-money (digital cash)** (p. 477)
- **integrity** (p. 489)
- **scalability** (p. 478)
- **Secure Electronic Transactions (SET)** (p. 483)
- **smart card** (p. 488)
- **viral product** (p. 493)

Test Your Understanding

1. List and briefly explain the unique features of cash.
2. Explain the key characteristics of e-money.
3. Distinguish between:
   a. Atomicity and isolation
   b. Scalability and interoperability
   c. Consistency and durability
   d. Authentication and interoperability
4. If you were to point out two problems with cash, what would they be? Be specific.
5. What are the requirements for Internet-based payments? Explain each briefly.
6. What is the main difference between credit cards and debit cards? Why is one type of card favored over the other?
7. What is credit card laundering? How do you think it can be prevented?
8. Explain the unique features and uses of smart cards.
9. What is unique about the e-wallet? How does it differ from real money? How does it work?

Discussion Questions

1. Why would anyone with a credit card want to use an electronic cash system on the Web?
2. What are some of the security requirements for safe electronic payment systems? Do you think the systems are safe enough?
3. Why do you think traditional payment systems are inadequate for e-commerce?
4. Of the electronic payment systems covered in the chapter, which ones do you think would be appropriate for business-to-business transactions? Justify your answer.

Web Exercises

1. Look up the homepages of Amazon.com and Dell.com. Identify each e-merchant's payment methods and the kinds of security measures incorporated in each site.

2. Review the homepages of Bank of America (www.bankamerica.com), Wells Fargo Bank (www.wellsfargo.com), and Wachovia Bank (www.wachovia.com). Evaluate and compare the payment systems on each site.

3. John wants to pay his mom, Jean, who lives in another city, by e-cash. How can he do this?

4. You have been asked to give a 15-minute presentation on the structure of electronic payment systems and the procedure for implementing them in small retailing stores. Prepare an outline of what you plan to cover. What highlights would you focus on?

5. Look up the Web site of CyberCash (www.cybercash.com) and write a report about the company: its electronic payment system, basic infrastructure, prices, and so on.

CHAPTER

GOING ONLINE

Learning Objectives

The focus of this chapter is on several learning objectives:

■ How to build a business on the Internet—from beginning to end

■ What it takes to plan effectively

■ The hardware, software, security, and setup considerations in e-commerce infrastructure

■ The critical elements in the design of an e-business

■ How to market e-presence

■ How to manage customer feedback

IN A NUTSHELL

Launching a business on the Internet requires careful planning, understanding the target customer base, and choosing the right products and services. Planning means resolving IT infrastructure issues and linking to the Internet service provider before going online. The site should make e-marketing a breeze. It should capture customers' attention and retain them long enough to result in a sale. The ultimate goal is to build repeat customers.

Product delivery is critical. The process should include a tracking system to let the shopper know when and who received the product. A follow-up e-mail to confirm the sale is a tactful way to thank the customer and confirm the commitment.

Customer service contributes a great deal to creating customer loyalty. The shopping experience should be risk free for the merchant and the customer. That means implementing powerful security measures for the Web site and the servers to protect them and the transactions from hackers.

Electronic business is no longer an alternative; it is becoming an imperative. Individuals and businesses by the thousands are building Web presence, from personal Web pages to storefronts. New Web participants range from established companies like

General Motors to individuals starting online mail-order businesses from scratch, and they all hope to make money. It is almost impossible to count the kinds and types of businesses now on the Internet. Whether your business is an auction, selling baseball caps or groceries, or trading stocks, there is a procedure to follow before you attempt to go online.

Planning your new site, marketing the business, providing good services, and maintaining security take on new meaning when applied to e-commerce. We will focus on these issues in the chapter.

THE LIFE CYCLE APPROACH

Here and throughout the book, we have followed a life cycle approach. (See Figure 16.1.) Each phase has been explored in detail in separate chapters.

1. The business planning and strategizing phase: having a vision, preparing a business plan, defining the target market, and setting immediate and long-range goals.

2. The Web infrastructure, security, and setup phase: deciding on how to go online.

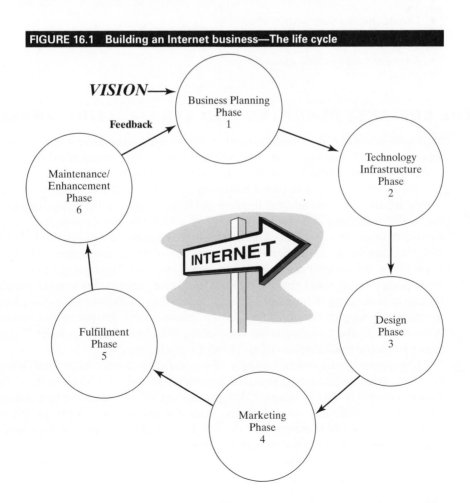

FIGURE 16.1   Building an Internet business—The life cycle

VISION→

Business Planning Phase 1

Feedback

Technology Infrastructure Phase 2

Maintenance/ Enhancement Phase 6

INTERNET

Design Phase 3

Fulfillment Phase 5

Marketing Phase 4

3. The design phase: building the site and placing it on the Internet.

4. The marketing phase: advertising the site, setting up feedback mechanisms, and providing customer service.

5. The fulfillment phase: selling and shipping the product.

6. The maintenance and enhancement phase: retaining and growing the business.

The sheer number of things to think about when going online is daunting, but the number one issue is planning and thinking in advance about the process before committing resources to the launch.

Here are some specific goals that make or break an e-commerce venture.

- Create and maintain a competitive edge.
- Reduce operational costs.
- Improve employee communication and satisfaction.
- Find new markets for products or services.
- Improve relationships with partners who provide the goods (e-business).
- Create distinct distribution channels.
- Ensure customer satisfaction (customer relations management).
- Improve supply-chain management.

THE BUSINESS PLANNING AND STRATEGIZING PHASE

New companies that do business on the Internet must plan, have a vision, and obtain financial support. Small merchants can sell online for an investment of as little as $500 per year, but to be successful, they need to do careful planning beforehand. (See Box 16.1).

Planning means evaluating a company's position and its competition, setting a course for the years ahead, and figuring out how to achieve the goals. This process is especially important in e-commerce. Having a Web site does not make a brick-and-mortar business an e-business. Unlike traditional operations where the business controls the channels, in e-commerce, customers control the channels, demand innovations in products, and expect personalized one-on-one service. Any strategic plans are likely to be good for only short periods of time. Traditional approaches to strategic planning that include devising the mission statement, deciding on objectives, and implementing a strategy to achieve the objectives are too cumbersome: By the time a business has gotten through these phases, some competitor will have "stolen its lunch." Table 16.1 summarizes the traditional and the e-way of strategizing.

Companies going online struggle with several basic problems: First, what is the best way to launch the business on the Internet? Second, how much of the company's business should be on the Internet? Simply loading a Web site on the Net and getting a surge of visitors to buy your products does not just happen: Strategic planning is needed. This kind of planning includes top management support and a *champion* at that level who is going to sponsor and support the push into the Internet. As National Semiconductor's Jim Gibson said, "There has to be an executive sponsor from the top that has the e-business religion."

BOX 16.1

Launching an E-Commerce Site, Cheap

When Leslie Gordon started looking for a way to sell products from the Hudson Valley online, she didn't have a lot of money, time, or computer expertise. What she had were high expectations for an e-commerce site that would be classy, powerful, and adaptable. "Most important to us was finding a low-cost [solution] without sacrificing quality, sophistication, or flexibility," says Gordon, 31.

Gordon found her low-cost e-commerce Web site solution at Homestead.com, which charges her $150 a month to host Madeinthehudsonvalley.com. She used the Web design tool supplied by Homestead to create the site herself, and also takes advantage of the marketing services the host provides.

Start-ups in search of a low-cost solution for an e-commerce Web site don't have as many options as they did three years ago, says Kneko Burney, director of business infrastructure and services at In-Stat MDR, a research firm. But that's not necessarily bad. Those providers that are left, Burney says, tend to be larger and stronger companies that have well-defined offerings and will probably be around for the long haul.

Besides saving the $10,000 she estimates it would have cost to have a programmer custom-build her site, Gordon is also happy with the results. "Their functionality mirrored the functionality of, say, an Amazon.com in its look and feel," she says. Selling online is still an excellent idea for many small businesses, and inexpensive options for setting up your own online store are plentiful and effective. To help you decide, we checked out five popular low-cost e-commerce Web site solutions.

Source: Excerpted from Mark Henricks, "How Low?" *Entrepreneur's Be Your Own Boss Magazine,* June 2003, 17.

TABLE 16.1   Traditional business versus e-business

Factor	Traditional Business	E-Business
Barriers to entry	Location requirements (i.e., build where the raw materials and market are)	Time and space limits; limited financial capital; unique products, special skills
Basis of competition	Improved products; bigger products	Smarter products; innovations in products and services, like a loran on a boat
Basis of control	Manufacturer	Customer
Organization	Hierarchical departments	Specialized teams connected to the Web
Marketing/sales	Mass advertising	Mass personalization
Pricing	Based on cost of raw materials	Transaction costs on a sliding scale; for example, a stock trade can cost $35 through a retail stockbroker, $23 through a discount broker, and $6 through the Internet

Another problem a first-time entrant faces is the *when* factor. When should the business go on the Web? Many people might encourage waiting, but if Henry Ford had waited to manufacture cars until air bags had been developed, he would not have been known as "the father of the automobile." One of the key points in launching your business on the Internet is competitive advantage—the jump you will have on the competition. Careful planning, knowing what is involved up front, ensuring management support, and proper funding should lower risks of entry.

What we have emphasized so far is the ultimate goal of your e-commerce setup: to connect users with content. It is so important to review the information requirements of your Web site's users and to inventory content assets that you wish to serve: text, applications, databases, and so on. Without a clear picture of the type of model that will drive the project, problems will arise. It is risky to plunge ahead before strategizing in the following areas.

- Vision: What is your business trying to achieve? How will the goals be met? How will the Web site help fulfill these goals? How will you measure success?

- Resources: How much can your business afford to build the right Web site? Are people available within the company who can turn the vision into reality?

- Culture: Is your business politically amenable to coordinating efforts to support this new approach to selling? Who will ultimately control the Web site's content and user feedback?

Some of the questions we ask new clients are:

- What is the key product or service at stake?

- What is the main goal of going online? To gain new customers? Help existing customers? Promote an existing brick-and-mortar business? See Box 16.2.

BOX 16.2

Role of Planning

... Our client that I have worked with is an online bridal registry. The company is called 1000Mabrouk.com and it is an online/off-line business, dealing with a network of the most prestigious shops in Lebanon and offering services for couples who are about to get married. By registering on the Web site, these couples can select their "wish list" from the items proposed by the various ... shops. Guests who are invited to these couples' weddings can buy them any gift from their wish list or any other gift from the Web site or simply by contributing a certain amount of money, a "Gift Certificate."

During the analysis of this project, I found out that the [number] of ... couples, guests, and orders will [be] relatively large ... and thus will require an SQL database linked to this e-commerce site.

Creating a flow diagram up front can save a lot of time and money later on when the development has already progressed. The flow diagram usually begins with the homepage and includes all of the various pieces that will eventually be on the site.

Source: Shireen Halawani, "Going Online," a partial quote from a practical Web site project, Spring 2004, 3.

With these areas in mind, it is important to consider the role of leadership and how leaders with a vision can turn the possible into the practical. Outstanding organizations have visionaries with the ability to recognize and shepherd great ideas through the organizational maze.

THE PLANNING PROCESS: STRATEGY

THE PLAN.   The most critical part of going online is the plan—the blueprint. For people to invest in your business, they need to believe in your business model and your management team before they focus on your concept or product. The business model should show a realistic and sizable revenue stream, a sustainable proprietary advantage, a well-conceived growth strategy, and a reliable financial backbone to support growth and profitability.

What goes into a blueprint? Here are some practical ideas:

- What is the online business about? What does it do? Where is it heading?
- How does the business work? Where does it plan to derive its revenues?
- How does the company compare to the competition?
- What market is the company intending to enter?
- How much money is involved in executing the master plan?

As you can see, an online plan is a tool with communication, management, and planning in mind. It is also your firm's resume. As a communication tool, it is supposed to attract investment capital, secure loans, convince workers to join, and attract strategic business partners. It is also a prerequisite for attracting business in general. As a management tool, the plan helps you track, monitor, and evaluate your progress. The plan is a living document that will have built-in flexibility for future modifications to reflect change, progress, and potential. As a planning tool, the plan guides you through various phases of the business. It should help identify roadblocks and obstacles so that you can avoid them and establish alternatives.

THE PROCESS.   An e-commerce Internet business provides a unique opportunity for an organization to do business from anywhere, anytime. Companies can expand their customer base, generate growth, and improve profitability. Because of its potential, establishing an e-commerce business may be among the most important business moves a company can make. This is all the more reason why the first step should be strategic planning.

You want to be an online retailer. How do you proceed? The first step is deciding what is to be done within a given time horizon. You also need to think about what you want to sell, the target audience, what visitors will do once they access your Web site, and so forth. Certain products or services that don't stand a chance in the so-called brick-and-mortar world may be tailor-made for the Web—for example, rare and old books. You have to choose products and services that will meet the needs of a new breed of Web-based consumer and a sales medium that offers unique opportunities. In a way, the planning step is all about the products or services you sell and how you address the needs of that product or service's consumer.

Here are strategic planning questions the online merchant should consider.

1. **How familiar are you with the Internet?** The added uncertainty and the undisciplined nature of the Web make a new venture a challenge. The key to reducing risk is to focus on what you know and the type of customers to visit your site. The Internet has generated a new breed of savvy consumers. More and more online visitors conduct extensive research on a product before buying it. You should have as much knowledge about the competition as visitors do. Losing customers to the competition means they click away.

2. **Who will buy the product?** Knowing your market is critical. A new online retailer must know the segment of the Web market the product will attract and how well the product will meet the specific needs of the customer. Once the market is identified, then your focus is servicing it 24 hours a day.

3. **Are you planning to be a short-term presence or a long-term presence?** Are you approaching the Internet for a quick killing or for sustained growth? A commodity item like T-shirts or socks is a good bet on the Web because customers buy these everyday products without trying them on. Information-intensive products (stocks, securities transactions, travel services) are also good bets for long-term selling. Short-term items such as baseball caps could be a lasting business, but you should have enough staying power to weather seasonal changes.

4. **Who are your competitors?** It is rare that a product is left alone without competition creeping up on it. Take the example of selling books on the Internet. The books might be old and rare, and the Web might be the ideal vehicle, but it is likely that Amazon.com or Barnesandnoble.com will find a way to meet the challenge and divert your Web traffic.

5. **How good will your products look?** In today's multimedia world, looks are important. Because customers cannot feel or touch the product, the way it is displayed on the monitor is crucial. If you sell clothing, for example, you might use real-life models when photographing clothing, then edit out the face and body parts of the model to make the product look more realistic.

6. **How will you present your product offers?** This question deals with the range of products that you plan to offer, the pricing, substitution if an item is not in stock, and building customer orders. Do you customize a product around customers' requirements? Can you handle incoming e-mail with the expertise your customers expect? Remember to abide by the Truth in Advertising requirements that essentially require you not to be misleading in your ads.

7. **How will you manage and process transactions?** Are all items taxable? Should taxes and shipping be added automatically to the total cost for a customer to accept the order? In what states is tax applicable to sales? What types of payment (credit card, digital cash) will you accept?

8. **How will the product be shipped?** The product has been paid for and now it is ready to be shipped to the customer. How will the product be packed and delivered? Selling birds, for example, might be a great idea until you begin to figure out how to ship them around the country. Size, weight, durability of the product, speed of delivery, and cost are all factors to think about in the planning phase.

Remember that the Federal Trade Commission passed a rule in 1975 requiring you to ship merchandise within 30 days of receipt of payment.

9. **How will you handle unexpected change?** Unexpected online change is a way of life. The technology, the users, the competition, and shopping trends are constantly on the move. Entering a Web business thinking it has a one-time development cost is a mistake. You need to plan for maintenance, upgrade, and performance of the site around the clock. Funds should be available to implement those changes when the time comes.

10. **How will you handle CRM?** Web site owners should plan on fine-tuning the communication channel between the Web site and the user for feedback and follow-up. CRM is becoming extremely critical for ensuring a repeat customer base. It is also important to consider how to make use of what customers do and learn from their surfing pattern.

capacity planning: determining in advance the capacity of the bandwidth (pipeline) that will accommodate the traffic to and from the Web site.

Capacity planning is related to strategizing about feedback. Imagine that you're already on the Internet and everything looks, feels, and works fine. Your customers are delighted, and the business begins to snowball. Suddenly, your site begins to slow down. Response time is now 20 seconds instead of 1 to 2 seconds. The site is functional but no longer works in the real world.

America Online (AOL) found this out the hard way. After offering unlimited monthly access to its online service, system overload led to millions of unhappy customers. It was only after round-the-clock work to upgrade that AOL began to regain normal service. It issued refunds in the millions to restore its integrity with its customer base.

This and other examples highlight the importance of planning for scalability. It is difficult to patch in solutions later. The objective at this phase is to ensure that your customers do not go somewhere else. After meeting demands for round-the-clock availability, your business must make certain that traffic flow continues uninterrupted through a reliable network. If a network cannot scale quickly to meet sudden surges in traffic, consumers simply won't wait. For mission-critical e-commerce applications, any breakdown or slowdown is unacceptable.

GOING GLOBAL

Strategic planning means considering the politics of going global. Pursuing a global strategy means more for information technology than setting up foreign branches or hiring foreign information technology specialists in their foreign domain. It is essential to research the customs, delivery costs, and employment laws in those countries.

A lot of questions and queries into the ramifications of going global come up and must be addressed before going any further. In the end, Web content must be customized to avoid conflict with customs and perceptions of each host country. Even Web marketing has to be tailored to local holidays and events.

Adopting a global strategy means setting up foreign distribution with IT talent abroad. The first thing to do for international presence is to research the customs, delivery costs, and employment laws in those nations, or global expansion could spell global disaster.

An important item to keep in mind is adopting an international role in new ways. How will the content of your Web page be interpreted in each country? Will shipping costs drain your profit margin? Will you be able to place your own work procedures without running afoul of laws of the host country?

It is important to think like a local. International marketing can do a great job if your Web content is not misinterpreted. Think of the Web page ad that showed a hiker next to a car in Mexico, where hikers are viewed as poor people who cannot afford cars. Cultural sensitivity should be weighed carefully in deciding on a marketing strategy.

Related to the global issues, there are supply-chain factors to consider. You should decide early whether e-commerce IT infrastructure can handle your international traffic. You also need to know the real cost of shipping of goods worldwide ordered via the Web. It is often the case that local delivery expense makes online product purchase prohibitive. This raises the question whether the e-commerce would be profitable in certain countries.

DECIDING ON TYPE OF WEB SITE

An important step in the planning phase is to decide on the type of e-commerce model that fits the products or services you will sell on the Internet. One way to classify e-commerce business models is by community, content, and commerce. Message boards and chat rooms are examples of community-type sites. Information content sites provide a wide variety of data such as stock quotes. Commerce sites involve consumers or organizations paying to purchase physical goods, information, or services advertised online. All organizations with the Internet address *company.com* are commerce-type sites.

Table 16.2 lists sample sites by type of product (commerce or content) and by type of market (business-to-consumer, business-to-business, or consumer-to-consumer). In business-to-consumer commerce, the Web site is the interface between the merchant with goods and services to sell and the consumer who orders them via the Web site. In business-to-business commerce, one company orders supplies or products from another company in order to make a product that is then sold to the consumer. Consumer-to-consumer e-commerce is a market like an auction, where one consumer contacts another to transact business.

Any way you look at it, to ensure that your site benefits your business and its customers, you need to clearly define your site goals from the beginning. Focus on a primary function and develop your site around delivering that to your customers. Clearly defined goals always help keep your priorities in perspective as you manage the building of your online presence. Some of the main goals for Web sites are:

- Marketing: If your main business is delivering an off-line service, you probably should have an online brochure describing the service.
- Online sales and service: If your main business is selling physical goods, then focus on creating an online store that gives customers a sense of place and makes purchasing simple and convenient.
- Information delivery: If your main business is publishing and disseminating information, then the site should provide some form of online publication. You should specify how to charge a fee for content, through subscription or a per-use basis.

TABLE 16.2	Types of e-commerce strategies		
E-Commerce Site	**Type of Market**	**Information Type of Product**	**Content**
Amazon.com	Business-to-consumer	**Physical goods:** books, music, home goods	Articles, chat, customer feedback
Barnesandnoble.com	Business-to-consumer	**Physical goods:** books, music, magazines	Articles, chat
Cisco.com	Business-to-business	**Physical goods:** net-working products, Web-based services	Company-related
Dell.com	Business-to-consumer Business-to-business	**Physical goods:** hardware, software, applications	Chat, company related
eBay.com	Consumer-to-consumer Business-to-consumer	**Services:** Advertisements, online auctions	
TDWaterhouse.com	Business-to-consumer Business-to-business	**Services:** Discount broker, financial	Stock quotes, investment information, services

- Customer support: You should provide tips and tricks for using your product and a page for frequently asked questions (FAQs) that makes it easy for customers to access the information they need. These functions can easily be automated.

Once you have a clear idea of the goals of the online business—who your customer is, what product you're going to promote, and the nature of the competition—you need to organize the Web site and decide whether you want to develop it in stages or all at once. You also need to decide whether you will develop the site yourself (using in-house staff) or outsource the project.

Another aspect of planning is to make a detailed list of requirements against which you compare the solutions. One approach is the *summit* approach: Set up a committee that holds strategic meetings to generate the master plan. A sample Web site development plan created using Web Strategy Pro was published by Palo Alto Software. See www.paloalto.com

HARDWARE, SOFTWARE, SECURITY, AND SETUP PHASE

You cannot use the information highway without the proper tools. In this phase of building an Internet presence, decisions are made regarding the hardware needed to cruise the Web, the software that will be used, and the security required to ensure reliable exchanges between customers and your business. The first set of questions deals with what hardware to buy. How fast should it be? What about quality, reliability, and durability? What type of modem do you need? What brand should you buy? Do you buy through magazines or from stores? Do you buy from big companies or small ones?

HARDWARE

Computer hardware is constantly getting faster, smarter, smaller, and cheaper. There are certain components to consider for the Internet. First, you need a computer with a lot of memory, a powerful central processing unit (CPU), and a fast link to the Internet. No matter what platform your computer runs on, you will be able to find a browser for it. Web browsers make it possible to connect with Web servers anywhere on the Internet. Browsers cache (store) images and, therefore, need a lot of disk space. As the browser accesses a page, it stores the images in a temporary directory (**cache memory**) on the visitor's hard disk. When a request is made to access or retrieve the image, the browser takes it from cache memory instead of requesting it from the network again. The browser clears its cache memory when you exit or after a preset time period. To allow for adequate caching, there should be at least 60 megabytes of hard drive storage space. The larger the disk space is, the quicker the access is to stored data.

cache memory: a highspeed memory dedicated to storing Web pages.

Processor speed is measured in megahertz (MHz). On today's Internet, it is risky to work with processing speeds of less than 100 MHz. Images gobble up a lot of storage and take longer to download than text. A lot of random access memory (RAM) also is needed for the Web browser program. Again, because most PCs use Windows, the larger the RAM storage, the quicker the processing. A minimum of 64 megabytes of RAM is required for navigation.

Other hardware includes a monitor, a mouse, and a modem. In choosing a monitor, color is a basic requirement. You should take care to ensure crisp, clean color and clarity of displayed information. For PCs, the monitor should be super VGA to make best use of extensive combination of colors.

A **mouse** allows you to navigate through a Web site with ease. You almost never need to use the keyboard. The **modem** is the *translator*. Modems come in varying speeds: The faster the modem is, the more bandwidth (speed) it will provide.

mouse: a point-and-click device that allows you to navigate a Web site or screen with ease.

modem: device that converts an outgoing message into bits for transmission and converts incoming bits into a human-readable message.

SOFTWARE

To be competitive online, you must identify the software that will help you manage your products, promotions, customers, and orders. Programs are available to handle tax calculations (Taxware), shipping, and payment processing (Cybercash or OpenMarket). Do you want to pick a design and insert your products, or do you want to customize the way your storefront will look and feel? Do you want a template so you can just fill in the blanks, or do you want to go with programs like Microsoft's Site Server Enterprise or IBM's Net.Commerce?

Surfing the Internet requires basic software.

- File transfer protocol (FTP)—transfer files to and from remote computers.
- Telnet—allows you to log onto a remote computer to access remote accounts.

- Archie—a program that finds files on the Net according to a search word you supply.
- NetNews—a newsreader that allows you to leaf through thousands of special-interest newsgroups on the Internet.
- E-mail—receives and sends electronic mail to anyone, anywhere, and anytime.
- Serial Line Interface Protocol (SLIP)—a program that connects with your modem to access the Internet.
- A browser—allows you to surf the Internet.

FINDING AN INTERNET SERVICE PROVIDER

Finding an ISP can be difficult, depending on where the business is located, the nature and volume of the business on the Web site, and so on. ISPs do not advertise aggressively: You must look for them, evaluate their services, decide on the fees, and agree on the final linkup. InterNIC is an Internet organization that maintains a list of ISPs around the nation. Other systems are available, such as that maintained by AOL, although they provide somewhat limited access.

SECURITY

security: protection of data, software, or hardware against accidental or intentional damage from a defined threat.

shopping cart: a utility that keeps track of items selected for purchase and automates the purchasing process.

If we were to compress the construction phase of going online to its essence, four essentials would result: security, shopping carts, payment, and marketing. **Security** is the critical backdrop that must be in place for every step to work. From strategic planning to fulfillment, from the moment the merchant begins to envision the Web site until it begins to handle transactions, the Web site must be absolutely secure. A **shopping cart** takes the products off the virtual shelves and puts them into a virtual waiting area. An electronic form of payment (primarily credit cards) must be used in order to sell on the Web.

When it comes to security, Web site planners look at three overlapping types of risk: document security, privacy, and system security. *Document security* entails the integrity of the Web site and its information. There must be security features in Web design that ensure that no one can corrupt the integrity of the site itself, let alone the information in its content or its layout. *Customer privacy* has to do with embedding devices in the visitor's hard disk to track site usage. The visitor should be aware of such marketing tactics and should be able to choose whether the merchant is allowed to secure such a link. *System security* deals with the way the network, the Web server, and the e-commerce infrastructure prevent unauthorized access and tampering with e-commerce traffic. System security was covered in detail in Chapter 13. Encryption was covered in Chapter 14.

Promoting security in an online business means adhering to a few simple rules.

- Control access to the Web server.
- Update server software and encode security measures to ensure server–Web site integrity.

firewall: a network node consisting of hardware and software to protect or filter certain information entering the company's databases or to keep select information from leaving the company.

Webmaster: a specialist in designing, maintaining, and managing Web sites.

- Use **firewalls** to protect the merchant's internal network.
- Monitor the traffic and detect irregularities in time to minimize damage.
- Assign Web security to a qualified **Webmaster.**
- Ensure a hot standby for every piece of hardware and software. Every router, program, Web application, and firewall must have a ready backup at all times. If a site is not available to end users at all times, companies may lose business and even their reputation.

EXPERTISE

Knowing what to do to ensure network performance is far more important than knowing how to do it. To ensure technical expertise, the trend is for more and more businesses to outsource network solutions rather than having to tackle its complexity on their own. In this sense, outsourcing is cost-efficient, because it helps the e-business concentrate on what it is best known for.

To ensure reliability and integrity, dedicated staff must have practical expertise. To resolve issues on-site, e-commerce requires security expertise, a network and telecommunications specialist, and competence in server software and architecture. When choosing a provider for e-commerce network traffic, a business must consider expertise as the top priority. A well-designed network infrastructure breaks down quickly without the staff required to maintain and upgrade it at all times.

THE DESIGN PHASE

In this phase, the focus is on designing a Web site to represent your products or services in the best way. The site also promotes your company to customers who normally would not visit your store. As a Web store manager, you should consider how much technology you need, to whom your site will be geared, and who will create the site. Once it is up and running, you will need a Webmaster to keep the site up to date and a network administrator to keep the hardware and software running.

To become familiar with Web site design, you have access to resources on the Internet, in magazines, and via consultants who help in the planning. Most of these sources are updated on a regular basis. Some search services also have topics of interest. Planning content and navigation system should consider:

- Limiting vertical scrolling to one and one-half pages
- Providing links (anchors) when using long text-intensive pages to subsections within the page, and at the end of each subsection providing a link to the top of the page
- Creating useful organizational structures to help users locate information
- Using structured navigational aids that reveal the organization and make it easy to access both the homepage and other main areas within the site

THE WEB STOREFRONT

storefront: a technology infrastructure that includes the Web site, the supportive hardware, the server, and security and payment systems that work together to provide the business-to-consumer interface.

search engine: Web software that locates Web pages based on matching keywords.

banner: a graphic display on a Web page for advertising or promoting a Web store or service.

The intention of a Web **storefront** is to make sales. The Web site should load quickly and be simple to navigate. It should provide lots of information about your business. It should include your physical address, phone, and fax numbers, and be registered with VeriSign's Secure Site program or InterNIC—both nonprofit privacy organizations. In addition to registering the site with numerous **search engines** (Yahoo!, Google, and so on), you can generate traffic by the way you announce your new online store in magazines, books that list Web sites, online newsgroups, or newsletters. **Banner** exchange services are also a low-cost way to generate site traffic and make your site look professional. A storefront should have four attributes.

1. Customers should be able to find the product quickly. There is an eight-second guideline: Customers who can't find what they're looking for during that time will click out of the site and go to alternative sites.

2. The site should have mechanisms to process the order and send it to the fulfillment center for quick and secure packing and shipping.

3. The site should have mechanisms to generate a summary of the order and produce a printable receipt.

4. The site should have mechanisms to send a confirming e-mail to customers.

Behind every Web site is a cluster of programs stored on the server to present your application to site visitors, and the hardware that will host your server and application. Included in the program cluster are the following.

- Database server: Provides secure access to shared data for client applications.

- Store administrator: Decides on items such as how the store is opened and closed, manages product information and site appearance, configures shipping options, adds and edits product information, makes pricing changes, and creates product promotions.

- Catalog builder: Presents the product information the customer must see. This feature should allow customers to search for products.

- Shopping cart: Similar to a physical shopping cart, this allows customers to gather items they are buying and hold them until the actual purchase function is executed. Customers can add or remove items at will as they browse through a product catalog or database.

- Order-processing system: Handles the purchase order. This includes totaling the order, calculating state and other taxes, shipping costs, and shipping information. It also determines the method of payment (credit card, digital cash) and generates detailed sales and customer reports.

For a small to medium-size business launching its storefront on the Internet for the first time, the easiest option is a prepackaged e-commerce system such as Microsoft Commerce. Larger businesses such as the nationwide mail-order store Crutchfield

Corporation (www. crutchfield.com) or Dell (www.dell.com) design their own storefronts from scratch. The main advantage of doing your own design is full control over the site.

DOING IT YOURSELF OR OUTSOURCING

One of the issues raised at the planning stage is whether the IT department of the business should design the Web site or whether it should it be assigned to an outside Web designer. The advantage of doing the work in-house is control over the entire project. Company staff assigned to the project will be familiar with what it takes to represent the company's image and product. The flip side of the coin is that effective Web design requires experience and expertise that often is not available in-house.

Giving the Web design to an outside consultant has definite advantages. The consultant can help you determine the audience, shop for the right Internet service provider, set up the Web site, design and post the Web pages, advertise the pages, and provide a variety of solutions dealing with logistics and traffic congestion, as well as Web performance monitoring.

Whether you design in-house or outsource the project has much to do with how long it takes your in-house people to do the work well, and how quickly the job can be done. If the Web project is going to be handled piecemeal and you have a ready audience, you need to think of the opportunity cost of customers going elsewhere to buy competitive products while your site is under construction. Professional firms are available to evaluate your site and help you make the necessary changes to improve overall performance. (See Box 16.3.)

BOX 16.3

Web Site Testing, Delivery, Tracking

Webking is an automated Web testing product that automates the most critical Web verification practices: static analysis, functional/regression testing, and load testing. The product improves the functionality, security, performance, reliability, accessibility, and presentation of a Web application. To verify functionality, Webking allows users to record critical user click paths by following them in a browser, then it automatically configures and executes functional/regression tests that verify paths and page contents while ignoring insignificant differences.

To verify how the application handles realistic traffic levels, patterns, and combinations, Webking provides intelligent virtual users and sophisticated ready-to-run load test scenarios. Users can easily customize these initial tests to the different paths, tools, traffic combinations, load distributions, and so on. To verify that the application's front end is constructed properly, Webking's static analysis identifies client-side code that does not comply with development rules known to prevent functionality, security, presentation, and portability problems, pages that do not comply with project/organizational branding, content, and design rules, pages that do not comply with Section 508 accessibility rules, and pages with broken links and spelling errors. For security verification, Webking's security module statically analyzes code to enforce the organization's security policy from the client side, then performs penetration testing to confirm that the policy has been implemented correctly and operates properly on the server side.

Source: Excerpted from www.parasoft.com/webking.

If you want a site to attract users and crush the competition; if you want a slick, bells-and-whistles site, there is a price to pay. The cost of the design is only the beginning. Depending on the approach a business takes, you need to consider setup costs, establishing a merchant bank account to which purchases are credited, credit card verification services and software, monthly site hosting fees, fees for a site designer, and support personnel.

WHAT SERVICES WILL YOU OFFER?

The basic infrastructure of a Web site consists of pages with text, graphics, audio, and links to other pages. The entry point is called the **homepage.** It is the first thing users see, and it creates a first and lasting impression about the content of the Web site. It determines whether the visitor will browse through the succeeding pages or simply leave and go to the competition. Homepages should be simple, use the right colors, and have well-organized **buttons** and minimum text.

homepage: the opening screen of the site.

button: a link with a label that, when you click on it, will take you to the intended destination site.

The next level in a Web site is the ability to input data into the system—for example, filling out a form, sending an e-mail message to the company regarding a product, or sending comments about the product or the site. For this to be possible, you must have a server that is capable of receiving the content and processing it. Other considerations for this aspect of Web site design include the following.

- User control and freedom: Users should be able to undo and redo paths they have taken by mistake and get back on track within your site. All pages should allow customers to navigate within the site from any page to any other page.

- Consistency and standards: Users should not have to wonder whether different words or actions mean different things on different Web pages.

- Recognition rather than recall: Objects and options should be visible, requiring no memorization or explanation.

- Efficient design: Dialogs should not have information that is either unrelated to the segment or rarely needed.

- Recovery from error: Error messages should be displayed in plain language, indicate the source of the problem, and describe ways to correct it.

- Help desk: The Web site should have a feature where the user can go for help on activities related to the product, service, how to order, and so on.

The outcome of the design phase is a balance between designers' innovations and users' expectations. (Web design was covered in Chapter 8.)

Once a decision is made on what to include in the Web site and how to format it, the next step is where to store the pages. If you are a small business and you have limited networking technology, you will have the Internet service provider load the Web site on its server, as well as update the site and manage the traffic the site generates. The main drawback of this approach is limited control over sensitive data. Because the ISP has many other businesses to manage, there is a chance that your business data may be vulnerable; on the other hand, if you set up your Web site on your own in-house server, you need to consider the cost of maintaining, monitoring, and updating the site.

THE MARKETING PHASE

The generic term **e-marketing** is used to describe all marketing channels facilitated by the Web; it is growing at an amazing rate. Selling products and services on the Web differs substantially from in-store sales, because a customer may view your offering for only a few seconds. The importance of physical location is significantly diminished. However, one should be alert to cultural differences when selling items in different countries and on restrictions other countries place on certain items.

e-marketing: all electronic-based activities that facilitate production of goods and services to satisfy customer demand.

For example, General Motors' Nova did not do well in Latin America, because *no va* in Spanish means "it will not go." Pepsi's advertisement in China fizzled, because in China the interpretation was "it brings back your ancestors from their grave." Baby jars sold by an American company in Africa featured a picture of a cute baby. The product did not do well, because food products in Africa always carried a picture of their containers.

Despite the differences between brick-and-mortar and e-commerce storefronts, many of the factors important for in-store sales remain important to a Web start-up. Accurate information, a good reputation and appearance, stability of service, good advertising, and knowledge of your customers contribute to online success. The essence of the marketing phase is providing good service, having enticing advertising, knowing the customer, selling the products or services, and following up after the sale. Inventory issues and stock control are also relevant items in this phase. (See Figure 16.2.)

FIGURE 16.2 The marketing phase

Providing Good Site Service

Maintaining accurate information is a major step in marketing. Too many businesses put up a Web site without fully understanding the amount of maintenance required to keep information current. Outdated information can cause a potential customer to lose interest and trust in the site and the product. Customers often expect particularly good service, with perhaps a demonstration of how something works or how it will look in different situations, because in many cases they are buying items online that they cannot touch or physically see. The service and products provided must be consistent and competitive in price. Failing to meet consumer expectations is the beginning of marketing failure.

Advertising

One important aspect of placing a new Web company in the marketplace is the ad campaign. The Web site should be a mirror image of the real business. Among the techniques for promoting the Web business are the following.

- Announcing the Web site through Internet search engines like Yahoo! and Netscape
- Issuing a press release
- Obtaining links from other Web sites
- Purchasing ad banners from other Web sites
- Announcing the new site in newsgroups
- Advertising via e-mail

Internet search engines provide the easiest access to your site when a customer has had no contact with your company before. By registering with the engines and by keeping your site at the top of their search lists, you dramatically increase your chances of receiving customer *hits*. Because the size of the Web makes random encounters somewhat unlikely, search engines provide the connection between your business and customers seeking your product or service.

Advertising through press releases, e-mail, and newsgroups also can be productive. Getting the company name and Web address out can be invaluable. New technology in direct marketing via e-mail is gaining momentum with products such as Broadc@st, an e-mail marketing tool. Broadc@st and similar products use customer information in your database, either purchased or gathered, to send consumers personalized adver-

spamming: sending unwanted advertising to users.

tisements via e-mail. Although techniques such as this can be productive, marketers should be wary of **spamming,** which can alienate potential customers and also create legal problems.

In addition to these media, you can use television, radio, and print ads. The channel your company chooses should fit your business needs and reach your target audience without exceeding the budget.

Know Your Customer

Part of the marketing function involves understanding the customer base. This tenet of good marketing does not change, even when your business moves into the electronic landscape. The goal is to zero in on target customers who fit your demographic criteria. Familiarity with who is buying the product or service and viewing the site allows the company to determine how to change the business to better meet customer needs. Information about who makes up your customer base can be obtained in various ways, including demographics, counters, e-mail and forms, or the use of **cookies.**

cookie: bits of information stored on users' hard disks that identify the users the next time they access the Web site that triggered the cookie.

When a person visits your site, a database can automatically put a small text file, called a *cookie*, onto the visitor's hard disk, allowing the company to gain information about the customer's visits to the site. You could then store purchase information or purchase demographic profiles of regions, thereby refining your knowledge of your customers. Cookies and other tracking devices are explained in detail in Chapter 10.

The first step in gauging your customer base is finding out how many hits your site gets in a given day, week, or month. This can be achieved through devices called hit counters, which are usually provided by the Internet service provider. Many companies conduct more specific consumer research by placing surveys on their sites, either through forms attached to a database or simple information e-mailed from the site to a company employee responsible for sorting the data. These surveys can be accompanied by incentives, so customers are more likely to fill them out.

No matter how a business gets to know the customer, profiling customers and tracking their data is an essential tool in online marketing. It is a prerequisite for deciding what products to offer and the inventory to keep, for managing the sale regardless of the traffic, and for updating the Web site.

MAKING THE SALE

To keep buyers on track toward making a purchase, the Web site must provide an easy-to-use purchasing function. This means installing a shopping cart and setting up automatic tax and shipping calculation software. Merchants also might want to make special discounts and product bundles available to Web buyers, and allow buyers to decide on shipping and payment methods. In addition, although privacy is important before the sale, encryption technologies become critical when making the sale.

Simplified ordering is closely related to making the sale. The ideal ordering process gets customers to the merchandise and their purchases into a shopping cart as fast as possible. Recalling customers' past orders and their recipients adds value because it helps buyers avoid reentering information and tracking down addresses for family and friends. For example, Amazon.com and Virtual Vineyards remind visitors what products they have ordered previously. Although this tracking system is not easy to implement, the benefits are immeasurable. Customers feel valued and return in the future. The marketing function is covered more completely in Chapter 11.

Securely storing the user's address and credit card data speeds the purchasing process. Depending on the depth of the product selection, pop-up menus can be used to aid in product selection. The L.L. Bean Web site speeds the process of browsing for its customers by using drop-down menus to offer instant access to literally hundreds of product names on a single page. Many sites, on the other hand, simply run long text listings or ask customers to click through multiple levels to see the complete product line.

STOCK CONTROL.   Stock control is also important in making the sale, and is especially critical in complicated orders such as the custom-built computers sold online by Dell. Even if the status of the stock is updated regularly, customers might not be able to find the items they want. In order for the merchant to offer alternatives, the Web server needs to know how these products are related. For example, if the merchant runs out of pretzels, the shopper might be willing to accept potato chips instead. Unfortunately, this type of feature is not built into most database structures. A well-designed e-commerce structure should let the company add such attributes to each product.

Once a customer places an item in a shopping cart, a simple stock check is not enough. Some customers might put something in the shopping cart one day and come back later to order it. What should a company do if the product goes out of stock in the meantime? A good strategy is to use a cookie or a user name and password to track when customers place items in the cart. If the customer is away from the site for more than a few hours, the company can check to make sure the selection is still available when the customer returns.

COLLECTING THE CASH.   E-commerce sites should accept as many credit cards as possible. Many sites require a fax order, a call to an 800 number, or some other off-line process to complete the sale. These methods are undoubtedly easier to implement, but they do not meet customer expectations of shopping on the Web. Some business could be lost if the consumer breaks the Web connection to write down the order and then picks up the phone to buy the product. As discussed in Chapter 15, MasterCard and Visa are the two cards shoppers use most, but smart sites will offer as many options as possible, including American Express, Discover, and digital cash.

Before jumping in and accepting credit cards, the online merchant needs an acquiring bank to handle the credit card processing. A regular commercial bank often can do this, although the merchant needs an intermediary company like CyberCash to do the verification of the card and authentication of the transaction, resulting in proper credit to the merchant's account at a designated bank. Storing credit card data helps make purchasing easier for the e-commerce site and for the consumer. To do this, the business needs a well-thought-out plan and a secure communication line using software such as Secure Electronic Transactions (SET). (These security measures are explained in detail in Chapter 14.)

DELIVERING THE GOODS AND FOLLOWING UP

After a buyer has made selections and paid for them, the merchant must deliver the goods promptly. Speed of delivery is critical. If the products are soft goods downloaded via the Internet, like music or a software package, buyers expect immediate delivery. If the products are hard goods (clothing, books), buyers expect shipment at least as fast as if they had ordered by phone. This means tight synchronization between the merchant's stockroom and the supplier. The electronic relationship between a merchant and a supplier falls under business-to-business (B2B). In either case, for any request by the customer regarding the status of the order, the merchant's Web site should recognize the customer and provide a quick report.

In this marketing step, the focus is on following up with the customer to ensure satisfaction with the product and the order process. As in traditional marketing, word of mouth can make a big difference. Over time, merchants can build ongoing personal relationships with their Web customers.

In the final analysis, the goal of the marketing function is to give site visitors a quality experience. Technical support can make or break the business-to-consumer interface for any business. As you analyze the electronic marketplace, you need to consider several marketing essentials for any online business.

- Have a niche-market focus—narrow your target customer.
- Know your visitors—ask them what they are looking for.
- Integrate the online sales with other sales channels.
- Provide a fast, easy payment process that puts convenience and spontaneity back into the process. A trusted payment environment guarantees security and privacy.

THE FULFILLMENT PHASE

All e-companies must face one simple truth—you can't send a package over the Internet. Solving shipping (fulfillment) problems can make the difference between e-business success and failure. Online shoppers expect quick, timely delivery. **Fulfillment** is what happens after a sale is made. Typically, it includes the following.

fulfillment: honoring a commitment to deliver goods or services after payment has been assured.

- Packing up the merchandise
- Shipping the merchandise
- Answering questions about the order
- Sending out the bill or verifying e-payment
- Following up to see if the customer is satisfied

Most e-business merchants are putting extraordinary pressure on their vendors and shippers to deliver merchandise just in time. Customers also want to be able to initiate, track, and acknowledge their orders online. More and more of today's fulfillment effort is part of an integrated chain—customers, warehouses, suppliers, drivers, rail partners—that makes it possible to have online shipping information within seconds.

The critical aspect of the fulfillment phase is having real people in real warehouses to get products into customers' hands. Good computers help, because coordinating an electronic business can be more complicated than operating a brick-and-mortar shop. E-merchants have a lot at stake. The competition is getting stronger as more businesses rush to get online, and every botched order creates a dissatisfied customer with a big mouth. For example, Toys R Us's known failure to deliver items ordered for Christmas 1999 wreaked havoc with the company's online retail effort. It turned out to be a costly mistake.

From the customer's viewpoint, order fulfillment is the most important business activity of all. Concerns about delivery delays have some of the biggest e-players beefing up their fulfillment systems. For example, in 1999, Amazon.com Inc. spent $300 million to build 3 million square feet of warehouse space. Shipper.com is building fulfillment centers to warehouse goods for e-tailers in nine metropolitan areas.

Customers also should be offered as many options as possible, and the options should be explained in detail, including the cost of each option and how long each will take.

The tax angle is also part of the fulfillment phase. Special software should keep track of the tax rules and exceptions, and know how much to charge. For example, New Jersey levies no sales tax on clothing, but California does. California levies no tax on food, but Virginia does. State tax, city tax, and county tax also must be considered. A service that automates tax calculations, like Taxware or CyberSource, is necessary. Another part of the fulfillment phase includes integrating fulfillment with inventory. Several issues must be addressed in this category.

- Product availability: Are the products for sale only items in your immediate inventory?
- Matching the products for sale to the products in the inventory: Is there a compatible linking of back-end inventory systems with the Web site?
- Out-of-stock notice: When should customers be notified that the items they selected are out of stock, not available for immediate delivery, or can be back-ordered?
- Back orders: When should the customer be notified of a back order?
- Processing orders: How often should orders be sent to order entry?
- Controls: Should the customer be notified of a back order when inventory count is at a minimum or when stock in the warehouse is gone?

THE MAINTENANCE AND ENHANCEMENT PHASE

maintenance: keeping a system or a business on course based on the initial design or plan.

enhancement: implementing upgrades or changes that are designed to improve the system's productivity.

Maintenance means keeping a system or a business on course, based on the initial design or plan. **Enhancement** means implementing upgrades or changes that are designed to improve the system's productivity. The focus in this phase is on managing the e-business. When customer messages pile up unanswered, something is wrong. The source of the pileup could be a poor Web site, a congested communication line, or an understaffed e-merchant.

Regardless of the reasons or circumstances, the goal of maintenance is to ensure the usability of the Web site. The goal of enhancement is to upgrade the Web site and the business-to-consumer connection to meet the latest standards and customer expectations. The bottom line is customer attraction and retention.

It is a known fact that when people are in a room for any length of time, they tend to go toward the light. People are biologically phototropic, so they tend to place themselves where the light is. Also, if they are in a room for any length of time, they tend to sit down and make themselves comfortable. You expect the same thing to happen when customers hit your site. If it is usable, they begin to scroll, surf, and search for things to buy. The feedback the merchant gets through the Web site should be the input for maintenance and enhancement of the merchant-customer interface.

Implied in the terms *maintenance* and *enhancement* is management of the Web site. Part of the management process is establishing online customer support that can help keep Internet customers loyal. It also can make them less likely to pick up the phone. Many companies use their customer service efforts as a selling point on the Internet. Customer queries by e-mail should be answered in hours rather than days, depending on the business and the time-sensitive nature of the product. Companies like Amazon.com have a set quota in terms of the number of e-mail queries customer service representatives must answer.

MANAGING CUSTOMER FEEDBACK

Here are some important tips on managing customer feedback.

- Set up a list of frequently asked questions (FAQs) and post it in a prominent location on the homepage.
- Make sure the information can be accessed easily and quickly.
- Make sure any page downloads within eight seconds and test it on slow, older computers to be sure the site loads quickly on all makes and models.
- Avoid unnecessarily large images or bandwidth-hogging elements.
- Answer e-mail. Be careful about inappropriate content: Any e-mail is a binding, legal document.

MANAGING CUSTOMER SERVICE

In terms of customer service, here are several items to consider:

- Updating orders: How will the fulfillment center let the system know that an order has been shipped?
- Order status: Will customers be able to look up the shipping status of their orders online? Do you want to send customers notification upon acceptance of their orders?
- Technical support: Will there be online support for the products you sell?
- Localization: Do you plan to support multiple languages and/or multiple currencies on your Web site?
- Handling customer expectations: What do you want to tell customers about fulfillment? Will you provide same-day delivery? Two-day? Will you charge a premium for such services? How much?

ROLE OF THE WEBMASTER

Finally, we need to consider the role of the Webmaster. The Webmaster's practical role is to create, implement, and manage the Web site. He or she acts also as visionary, business strategist, and manager of the merchant's expectations. One of the Webmaster's key roles is helping company executives understand what is possible and what works, and what can and cannot be done in e-commerce as it relates to the company's products and services.

A Webmaster often has to guide the company in setting realistic goals for the Web endeavor. This can be crucial in sizing up resource needs, budgeting, knowing what actual costs and opportunity costs are acceptable, and what return the company can expect on those costs. Managing expectations begins with setting general goals and deciding where and how a Web site can achieve a number of specific goals — informing, promoting, selling directly, distributing certain product information, and distributing products. Managing also involves prioritizing goals and ensuring their achievement in time to be of use to the organization. Managing expectations is not easy. The site's goals must support company goals that were set before the e-business was even considered.

Summary

1. Launching a business on the Internet involves a life cycle that includes the business planning and strategizing phase; the hardware, software, security, and setup phase; the design phase; the marketing phase; the fulfillment phase; and the maintenance and enhancement phase.

2. Strategizing means evaluating a company's position and the competition, setting a course for the years ahead, and figuring out how to get it done.

3. Specific goals need to be considered when planning an e-business: creating and maintaining a competitive edge, reducing operational costs, improving employee communication and satisfaction, finding new markets for products or services, improving relationships with partners who provide the goods, creating distinct distribution channels, ensuring customer satisfaction, and improving supply-chain management.

4. The hardware, software, security, and setup phase focuses on the hardware to buy; whether to buy through magazines or from stores; and what software to buy. Among the software needed are FTP, Telnet, Archie, NetNews, e-mail, SLIP, and a Web browser, plus the security programs.

5. The four essentials of launching a business on the Internet are security, shopping carts, payment, and marketing.

6. Behind every Web site are programs stored on the Web server to present your application to site visitors and the hardware that will host your server and application. These programs include the database server, the store administrator, the catalog builder, the shopping cart, and the order-processing system.

7. In Web design, the focus is on user control and freedom, consistency and standards, recognition rather than recall, aesthetic design, recovery from error, and a help desk to handle customer queries and complaints.

8. The marketing phase includes advertising, knowing the customer, making the sale, getting the goods, and follow-up procedures after the sale. The critical aspect is knowing the customers and finding ways to keep them at the site long enough to make a sale. The ideal is to cultivate recurring customers rather than one-time customers.

9. The fulfillment phase typically includes packing up the merchandise, shipping the goods, answering questions about the order, and sending out the bill or a copy of the bill. There is also a follow-up to see if the customer is satisfied. From the customer's view, this phase is the most important business activity.

10. The maintenance and enhancement phase addresses the need to keep the Web storefront up to date and to make any changes that will enhance the use and effectiveness of the Web site. Managing the business-to-consumer environment is essential and can be a full-time commitment.

Key Terms

- **banner** (p. 517)
- **button** (p. 519)
- **cache memory** (p. 514)
- **capacity planning** (p. 511)
- **cookie** (p. 522)
- **e-marketing** (p. 520)
- **enhancement** (p. 525)

- **firewall** (p. 516)
- **fulfillment** (p. 524)
- **homepage** (p. 519)
- **maintenance** (p. 525)
- **modem** (p. 514)
- **mouse** (p. 514)
- **search engine** (p. 517)

- **security** (p. 515)
- **shopping cart** (p. 515)
- **spamming** (p. 521)
- **storefront** (p. 517)
- **Webmaster** (p. 516)

Test Your Understanding

1. Is there a difference between vision and mission? Elaborate. How do they relate to starting an online business? Be specific.
2. Identify the key steps of the Internet business life cycle. What step is the most critical? Why?
3. When you hear someone talking about strategic planning, what is the person focusing on? In terms of e-commerce, what questions does an online merchant consider when strategizing? Explain.
4. The chapter brings up specific goals that a merchant should consider when planning an e-business. Elaborate on the key goals.
5. Elaborate on the distinctive types of hardware and software necessary to launch a business on the Internet.
6. Distinguish between:

   a. A browser and a Web server
   b. A mouse and a modem
   c. Telnet and file transfer protocol (FTP)
   d. Marketing phase and fulfillment phase

7. In what way(s) is security critical in e-commerce? Explain.
8. Discuss the basic rules when promoting security in online business.
9. If you were to design a Web storefront, what factors, constraints, or parameters would you consider? Explain.
10. How would one decide whether to design the Web site in-house or outsource it to an outside agency?
11. If you were assigned the job of locating a Web site developer, what factors would you consider to locate the right one? Explain.
12. Elaborate on the key considerations in Web site design.
13. What is involved in collecting payment for the products that customers order through a merchant's Web site? Be specific.
14. Explain the key steps of the fulfillment phase. How important is this phase? Why?
15. Distinguish between maintenance and enhancement. Which one assures compliance with the original plan?

Discussion Questions

1. If you were asked to give a five-minute talk to a gathering of local small business merchants about launching a business on the Internet, what would you say?
2. Take a close look at the marketing phase with a business the size of your community bank in mind. Assume that the bank wants to establish a presence on the Internet. How would you proceed in planning the marketing phase?
3. Advertising presence is part of the marketing function for a first-time merchant on the Internet. How would one advertise such a presence? Write a one-minute scenario advertising the bank's presence. See Discussion Question 2.
4. If you were searching for an ISP, what type of service would you expect it to provide? If you're unsure, go to a search engine and enter the subject "Internet service provider." Write a two-page report on your findings.
5. What benefits might a business measure in an electronic commerce business plan?
6. Why do you think some firms plunge into e-commerce without assessing their return on investment? Discuss.

Web Exercises

1. Aunt Sarah's Glendora Candy is a family-owned candy-manufacturing plant in western Pennsylvania. Although candy making is fully automated, the company employs 96 people and 21 salespeople on a full-time basis. The company makes more than 60 brands of chocolate, chocolate cakes, candy bars, and specialized chocolate-based products for Halloween, Christmas, and other occasions. Since it was founded in 1945, the company has sold its products directly to retailers and filled phone orders from customers as far west as Colorado and all the way to the Eastern seaboard.

    You are the consultant for Aunt Sarah. The CEO has been seeing screaming headlines in business journals that just cannot be ignored—"E-Commerce Will Jump to $32 Billion by 2007" and "U.S. Online Business Trade Will Soar to $1.9 Trillion by 2008." The competition is catching up with Aunt Sarah. Smaller candy makers are slowly entering e-business. The chairman of the board tells you they want to open Aunt Sarah's cyberdoors in two months. That should be plenty of time, he insists. After all, his daughter (a college freshman) built her own online store in three days using Microsoft Front Page as a Web design tool. She was selling baseball caps to make enough money to pay her tuition.

    What will you say? How will you start? What procedure will you follow? Map out a plan of attack and explain to the chairman of the board the long road ahead "from vision to implementation." Think of planning. Remember the life cycle of launching this business on the Internet.

2. The First National Bank of Elwood City is a small, regional, family-owned bank founded in 1947 with assets of about $46 million; 43 full-time employees; 9,000 checking accounts; 6,400 savings accounts; and a full-service operation including commercial and personal loans, trusts, safe deposit boxes, bookkeeping, and mortgage loans. In the early 1990s, the city grew larger, attracting larger banks to handle the growth in the community. With the surge of banking traffic on the Internet, almost every large bank has an interactive Web site. Two of the online banks even issue

loans, with the customer simply filling out a form on the screen and clicking on the "submit" button. The information goes directly to the bank's database for processing. The resulting loan amount is either mailed to customers the next day in the form of a check or electronically transmitted to a destination of the customer's choice.

The bank president calls you and asks for a meeting to assess the bank's readiness to be on the Internet. After a brief session with senior management, you discover the following: (a) very few of the bank's employees are computer literate; (b) the bank has a small local area network in the loan department only; 42 stand-alone PCs are used primarily for Word and Excel; and (c) there is no e-mail system.

a. What general plan can you introduce that shows how to put the bank on the Internet?
b. If you were to give senior management a 30-minute presentation on what must be done to be on the Internet, what would you cover?
c. Present a brief summary of the building life cycle, and explain where and in what way management should be involved in seeing the Web site through to fulfillment.

REFERENCES

CHAPTER 1

Athitakis, M. "How to Make Money on the Net: The Second Internet Book Is Quietly Taking Shape," *Business,* May 2003, 83–90.

Dandapani, Krishnan. "Success and Failure in Web-Based Financial Services." *Communications of the ACM,* May 2004, 31–36.

Drickhamer, D. "EDI Is Dead! Long Live EDI!" *Industry Week,* April 2003, 31–35.

Johnson, C. "U.S. E-Commerce: The Year in Review." Cambridge, MA: *Forrester Research,* 2003.

Kristof, Nicholas D. "Blogs Are Strangling Chinese Communism." *Herald International Tribune,* July 25, 2005, 8.

LaMonica, Martin. "Academia Gets Creative with Web Services." http://news.com.com/2100-7345-5096702.html.

Mackey, C. "The Evolution of E-Business." *Darwin,* May 1, 2003. www.darwinmag.com/read/050103/ebiz.html.

Murphy, C. "Five Internet Myths: An Interview with Jeff Bezos." *Information Week,* June 11, 2003. www.informationweek.com/story/showArticle.jhtml?articleID=10300770.

Porter, Michael. *Competitive Advantage.* New York: Free Press, 1985.

Rush, L. "U.S. E-Commerce to See Significant Growth by 2008." *CyberAtlas,* August 7. http://cyberatlas.internet.com/markets/retailing/article/0,1323,6061_22 46041,00.html.

Spangler, Todd. "Internet Telephony: A Sound Move?" *eWeek,* July 12, 2004, 43.

Sturdevant, Cameron. "How to Make the Move to JP Telephony." *eWeek,* July 12, 2004, 44ff.

Werthner, Hannes, and Francesco Ricci. "E-Commerce and Tourism." *Communications of the ACM,* December 2004, 101–103.

CHAPTER 2

Anthes, Gary H. "Search for Tomorrow." *Computerworld,* April 5, 2004, 26.

Associated Press. "Yahoo! Touts Search Engine as the Biggest on the Web." *Daily Progress,* August 9, 2005, A7.

Blake, Brian F., and Kimberly Neuendorf. "Cross-National Differences in Website Appeal: A Framework for Assessment." www.ascusc.org/icmc/vol9/issue4/blakeneuendorf.html. July 2004.

Bolton, Ruth N. "Marketing Challenges of E-Services." *Communications of the ACM.* June, 2003, 43–44.

Coyle, Frank. "Web Services, Simply Put." *Computerworld,* May 19, 2003, 38–39.

Dunn, Bob. "A Manager's Guide to Web Services." *eAI Journal,* January 2003, 15–17.

Ferris, Christopher, and Joel Farrel. "What Are Web Services?" *Communications of the ACM,* June, 2003, 31.

Green, Heather. "The Web Collaboration." *BusinessWeek,* November 24, 2003, 82ff.

Hall, Mark. "Overcoming Web Services Insecurities." *Computerworld,* December 22, 2003, 23.

Hoffman, Douglas K. "Marketing + MIS = E-Service." *Communications of the ACM,* June 2003, 53–55.

Kannan, P. K., and Roland T Rust. "E-Service: A New Paradigm for Business in the Electronic Environment." *Communications of the ACM,* June 2003, 37ff.

Kreger, Heather. "Fulfilling the Web Services Promise." *Communications of the ACM,* June 2003, 29–30.

Kuchinskas, Susan. "Trust Issues Loom over E-Commerce." www.abiz.com.au/Trust_Issues_Loom_Over_E-Commerce.htm.

Mullaney, Timothy J. "At Last, the Web Hits 100 MPH." *BusinessWeek,* June 23, 2003, 80–81.

Singh, R., A. Salom, and L. Iyer. "Agents in E-Supply Chains." *Communications of the ACM,* June 25, 2005, 190–115.

Song, Hongjun. "E-Services at FedEx." *Communications of the ACM,* June 2003, 45–46.

Stafford, Thomas E. "E-Services." *Communications of the ACM*, June 2003, 27–28.

Thillairajah, Velan, and Senthil Ramia. "Hailing a Web Service." *Business Integration Journal*, July 2003, 44–46.

Violino, Bob. "Waves of Change." *Computerworld*, May 19, 2003, 33.

Walker, Leslie. "Searching and Shopping." *Washington Post*, September 25, 2003, E1.

Watson, Sharon. "End of Job Loyalty?" *Computerworld*, May 15, 2000, 52–53.

Wingfield, Nick. "Internet Companies See Value in Misaddressed Web Traffic." *Wall Street Journal*, September 5, 2003, B1ff.

Wolf, Christopher. "Internet Infrastructure Issues: Regulation and Un-Regulation of the 'Pipes' That Provide the Internet." http://library.1p.findlaw.com/articles/file/00086/002196/title/Subject/topic.

CHAPTER 3

Berinato, Scott. "The ABCs of Security." *CIO Magazine*, February 20, 2002, 16ff.

Braden, Bob. "Architectural Principles of the Internet." *IPAM Tutorial*, March 2002.

Brewin, B. "Michigan City Turns on Citywide Wi-Fi." *Computerworld*, July 30, 2004, www.computerworld.com/mobiletopics/mobile/wifi/story/0,10801,94928,00.html.

Dornan, A. "Unwiring the Last Mile." *Network Magazine*, January 2003, 34–37.

Duffy, J. "RBOCs and Cable Wage Turf War." *Network World*, August 18, 2003, 11–14.

Fitchard, K. "Covad's Quiet Authority." *Telephony*, June 7, 2004, 34–39.

Floyd, S. "Congestion Control Principles." Network Working Group, University of Tennessee, February 2002.

Gurtov, A., and R. Ludwig. "Lifetime Packet Discard for Efficient Real-Time Transport over Cellular Links." *ACM Mobile Computing and Communications Review*, October 2003, 37–45.

Gurtov, A., and J. Korhonen. "Effect of Vertical Handovers on Performance of TCP-Friendly Rate Control." *ACM Mobile Computing and Communications Review*, October 2004, 19–31.

Hadzic, I., and J. M. Smith. "Balancing Performance and Flexibility with Hardware Support for Network Architecture." *ACM Transactions on Systems* 21(4), November 2003, 375–411.

Huston, G. "Commentary on Inter-Domain Routing on the Internet." *Internet Architectural Board*, 2000, www.potaroo.net/papers/ietf/draft-iab-bgparch-02.html.

Kaven, O. "Wired Ethernet and 802.11g Outpace the Rest." *PC Magazine*, April 6, 2004, 104.

Lais, Sami. "MPEG Standards." *Computerworld*, October 7, 2002, 36.

Lowry, G. T. "Satellite's Hot Pursuit of Cable." *Business Week*, May 24, 2004, 46.

Marsan, C. "It's a New Domain-Name Game." *Network World*, March 1, 2004, 1, 14.

Moore, K. "On the Use of HTTP As a Substrate." Network Working Group, University of Tennessee, February 2002.

Panko, Raymond R. *Business Data Communications and Networking*, 6th edition. Upper Saddle River, NJ: Prentice Hall, 2006.

Richtel, M. "Where Entrepreneurs Go and the Internet is Free." *New York Times*, June 7, 2004, www.nytimes.com/2004/06/07/technology/07wifi.html.

Vogelstein, F. "The Cisco Kid Rides Again." *Fortune*, July 26, 2004, 132–137.

Witte, G. "Bringing Broadband over the Mountain: Roadstar Puts Wireless Technology to the Test." *Washington Post*, September 15, 2003, E1.

Zhang, M. and R. Wolff. "Crossing the Digital Divide: Cost-Effective Broadband Wireless Access for Rural and Remote Areas." *IEEE Communications Magazine*, February 2004, 99–105.

CHAPTER 4

Cho, David. "Politicians Deal with Newcomer, the Blog." *Washington Post*, June 5, 2005, B1ff.

Definitions of *Spyware* on the Web. www.google.com/search?hl=en&lr=&oi=defmore&q=define:Spyware.

Editorial. "Intelligence Czar Has Tough Task." http://news.enquirer.com/apps/pbcs.dll/article?AID=/20050218/EDIT01/502180348.

Kay, Russell. "Fighting Spam." *Computerworld*, May 12, 2003, 33.

Maney, Kevin. "Once Blogs 'Change Everything,' Fascination with Them Will Chill." *USA Today*, May 25, 2005, 3B.

Mangalindan, Mylene. "Web Vigilantes Give Spammers a Big Dose of Their Medicine." *Wall Street Journal,* May 19, 2003, A13.

Murphy, Brian. "Iran Wraps Up Western-Style Presidential Race." *Indianapolis Star,* June 17, 2005, A7.

Saint-Cyr, Yosie. "Employees Disciplined for Inappropriate Use of the Internet and Email." www.hrmguide.net/canada/law/inappropriate-use.htm.

Shadid, Anthony. "Syria's Voices of Change." *Washington Post,* June 25, 2005, A1.

CHAPTER 5

Angwin, Julia. "Speed Kills." *Wall Street Journal,* May 19, 2003, R10.

Better Business Bureau. "Choosing the Right Internet Service Provider." www.bbb.org/alerts/article.asp?ID=180.

Cohen, Laura. "How to Connect to the Internet." http://Library.Albany.edu/internet/connect.html.

Definitions of *ASP* on the Web. www.google.com/search?h1=en&1r=oi=defmore&q=define:asp.

IBM. "Building Your ISP/ASP Infrastructure." www-1.ibm.com/servers/eserver/pseries/hardware/tour/briefs/asp_isp.html.

McGatney, Dawn, and Dog Wolf. "How an ISP Really Works." http://dogwolf.seagull.net/ispwork2 .html.

NetZero. ISP Comparison. http://my.netzero.net/s/signup?r=isp-fmf&refed=GOOAW0403NXP_isp.

Panko, Raymond R. *Business Data Networks and Telecommunications,* 5th edition. Upper Saddle River, NJ: Prentice Hall, 2005.

Patterson, Zachary. "Serve-Level Agreements." *Computerworld,* January 22, 2001, 53.

Rosoff, Matt. "Rate Your ISP." http://home.cnet .com/category/0-3765-7-285302.html1–2.

The List: The Definitive Internet Services Buyer's Guide. http://thelist.iworld.com.

Walsh, Kenneth R. "Analyzing the Application ASP Concept: Technologies, Economies, and Strategies." *Communications of the ACM,* August 2003, 103–107.

Welden, Amelie. "Broadening Horizons: Broadband Developments on the WWW and Interactive Advertising." www.ciadvertising .org/studies/student/00_summer/welden/paper/overall.htm.

Wilson, Ralph. "How to Choose a Web Hosting Service (ISP) for Your Business Web Pages." www.wilsonweb.com/articles/webhost.htm.

ZDNet Australia. "Small Businesses Still Confused Over ISP Offerings: ACA." www.zdnet. com.au/news/business/0,39023166,39161676,00.htm.

CHAPTER 6

Berghel, Hal, and Jacob Uecker. "Wireless Infidelity II: Airjacking." *Communications of the ACM,* December 2004, 15–20.

Bethoney, Herb. "Bluetooth's Buzz Seemingly Fizzled." www.zdnet.com/eweek/stories/general/0,11011.2649006,00.html.

Brain, Marshall, and Jeff Tyson. "How Cell Phones Work—From Cell to Cell." www. howst uffworks.com/cell-phone2.htm.

Brewin, Bob. "Wireless LANs Find Their Voice." *Computerworld,* May 17, 2004.

Brewin, Bob. "Wireless Nets Go Regional." *Computerworld,* March 3, 2003, 26.

——. "WorldCom Wins $20M Bid to Build Baghdad Cell Network." *Computerworld,* May 26, 2003.

Brooks, Jason. "Bluetooth Update Shows Maturity." *eWeek,* July 12, 2004, 60.

Cambridge Consultants, Ltd. "Bluetooth Products." www.cambridge-consultants. com/html.

Cauley, Leslie. "AT&T Rolls Out Super-Speedy Internet Service." *USA Today,* July 21, 2004, 5B.

Courson, Paul. "Crackdown Targets Work-at-Home Scams." www.cnn.com. February 22, 2005.

Culler, David E., and Wei Hong. "Wireless Sensor Networks." *Communications of the ACM,* June 2004, 28–40.

Dunn, Danielle, and Lee Pender. "Glossary." www.cio.com/research/communications/edit/glossary.htm

Enbysk, Monte. "7 Tips for Going Wireless." www .bcentral.com/articles/enbysk/127.asp.

Farley, Tom. "Cellular Telephone Basics." *TelecomWriting.com,* www.privateline.com/cellbasics/cellbasics.html.

Freudenrich, Craig. "How Personal Digital Assistants (PDAs) Work." www.howstuffworks .com/pda.htm.

Green, Heather. "Winging Info Wireless." *Business Week*, February 18, 2002, EB9.

Hamblin, Matt. "Taking the Leap." *Computerworld ROI,* www.computerworld. com/roi/.

Henderson, Peter. "Super-Fast Wireless Heads to Homes." www.msnbc.com/news/877268.asp, February 25, 2003.

Jarvenpaa, Sirkka L., Karl R. Lang, Yoko Takeda, and V. K. Tuunainen. "Mobile Commerce at Crossroad." *Communications of the ACM,* December 2003, 41–44.

Johnston, Britton. "Government and Mobile Applications." www.wwpi.com/sg/articles/Aug Sep03_3.asp.

Kessler, Michelle. "Wi-Fi Could Let Iraq Skip Steps to Leap into Broadband." *USA Today,* April 17, 2003, 1B.

——. "Wireless Web Changes the Way We Use the Internet." *USA Today,* February 19, 2004, 6Aff.

Mathews, Guy. "Insecurity in a Wireless World." www.vnunet.com/Analysis/1119074.

Mallat, Nina, Matti Rossi, and Virpi K. Tuunainen. "Mobile Banking Services." *Communications of the ACM,* May 2004, 42–46.

Nicopolitidis, Petros, and Georgios Papadimitriou. "The Economics of Wireless Networks." *Communications of the ACM,* April 2004, 83–86.

Perrig, Adrian, John Stankovic, and David Wagner. "Security in Wireless Sensor Networks." *Communications of the ACM,* June 2004, 53–57.

Proxim White Paper. "802.11a: A Very High-Speed, Highly Scalable Wireless LAN Standard." www.proxim.com/learn/library/whitepapers/pdf/80211a.pdf.

Rao, Bharat, and Louis Minkakis. "Evolution of Mobile Location-Based Services." *Communications of the ACM,* December 2003, 61–65.

Robb, Drew. "Managing over the Airwaves." *Computerworld,* October 20, 2003, 36ff.

Rosencrance, Linda. "E-Commerce on the Fly." *Computerworld,* May 26, 2003, 34.

Rubin, Aviel D. "Wireless Networking Security." *Communications of the ACM,* May 2003, 29–39.

San Filippo, Michael. "Marconi: Grandfather of Wireless." *History of Italians,* http://italian.about.com/library/weekly/aa111099a.htm.

Schmidt, Terry, and Anthony Townsend. "Why Wi-Fi Wants to Be Free." *Communications of the ACM,* May 2004, 47–52.

Siau, Keng, and Ziking Shen. "Building Customer Trust in Mobile Commerce." *Communications of the ACM,* April 2003, 91–94.

Solheim, Shelley, and Carmen Nobel. "Connecting Nets?" *eWeek,* August 30, 2004, 29.

Songini, Marc L. "Army Uses Mobile Technology, Satellite Link to Track Supplies." *Computerworld,* March 31, 2003, 6.

Sun, Jun. "Information Requirement Elicitation in Mobile Commerce." *Communications of the ACM,* December 2003, 45–47.

Tarasewich, Peter. "Designing Mobile Commerce Applications." *Communications of the ACM,* December 2003, 57–60.

3COM White Paper. "What Is Wireless Networking and Why Consider It?" www.3com.com/corpinfo/en_US/technology/tech_paper.jsp?DOC_ID=5377.

Tuesday, Vince. "New Job Brings Back Old Problems." *Computerworld,* October 13, 2003, 36.

——. "Wireless Hackers Leave No Tracks." *Computerworld,* June 7, 2004, 42.

Urbaczewski, Andrew, Joseph S. Valacich, and Leonard M. Jessup. "Mobile Commerce: Opportunities and Challenges." *Communications of the ACM,* December 2003, 31–40.

Venkatesh, Viswanath, V. Ramesh, and Anne P. Masswey. "Understanding Usability in Mobile Commerce." *Communications of the ACM,* December 2003, 53.

Washington Post. "Wi-Fi Vulnerable to Hackers." *The Daily Progress,* August 1, 2003, B3.

Wexler, Joanie. "Wi-Fi Plays Defense." *Computerworld,* August 23, 2004, 23–24.

Wingfield, Nick. "Wi-Fi Anytime, Anywhere." *Wall Street Journal,* March 31, 2003, R6.

www.beststuff.com/articles/737.

www.corp.cellmania.com/newsroom/whitepapers/whitepapers_local.html, 1.

www.howstuffworks.com/cell-phone2.htm.

www.palowireless.com/bluetooth/products.asp.

www.zdnet.com/filters/printerfriendly/0,6061, 2704389-2,00.html.

Yan, Xu. "Mobile Data Communications in China." *Communications of the ACM,* December 2003, 81–85.

Yuan, Li. "Dancing to Japan's Mobile Tune." *Asian Wall Street Journal,* September 19, 2005, A9.

CHAPTER 7

Canter, Sheryl. "No-Cost Ad Blocking." www.pcmag.com/article2/0.1759.1674956.00.asp.

——. "Managing Web Traffic Spikes." www.savetz.com/articles/newarch spikes.php.

——. "IPN Survey: Web Site Design Criteria." www.tbchad.com/ipngweb.html.

Chau, P., M. Cole, A. Massey, M. Montoya-Weiss, and R. O'Keefe. "Cultural Differences in the Online Behavior of Consumers." *Communications of the ACM,* October 2002, 138–143.

Daisay, Karine. "What Makes a Web Site Popular?" *Communications of the ACM.* February 2004, 51–55.

Lightner, Nancy J. "Evaluating E-Commerce Functionality with a Focus on Customer Service." *Communications of the ACM,* October 2004, 88–92.

Loiacono, Eleanor. "Cyberaccess: Web Accessibility and Corporate America." *Communications of the ACM,* December 2004, 83–87.

Olsen, Stefanie. "Internet Explorer to Stomp Pop-Ups." http://news.com.com/2100-1032_3-5105139.html?tag=nefd_top.

Pratt, Mary K. "Who Owns the Web?" *Computerworld,* August 30, 2004, 31–32.

Rothman, Johanna. "Hiring Nerds." *Computerworld,* November 8, 2004, 58.

Sanford, Susan. "The Art of E-Biz Web-Site Design." *InformationWeek,* February 14, 2000, 42–44ff.

CHAPTER 8

Arditi, Aries. "Effective Color Contrast." www.llighthouse.org/color_contrast.htm.

Awad, Elias M. "How Effective Is Your Bank's Web Presence?" Unpublished manuscript, 2005.

Bailor, Coreen. "Checking in with E-Commerce." *Customer Relationship Management,* July 2005, 57.

Bruene, Jim. "Website Usability: Homepage." www.onlinebankingreport.com.

Clarke, Arthur. "The Anatomy of a Web Site." http://riccistreet.net/gizmos/toolkit/webmaking/websiteanatomy.htm.

Festa, Paul. "Report Slams Web Personalization." http://news.com.com/2100-1038-5090716.html?tag=cd_top.

Gilhooly, Kym. "Getting Personal." *Computerworld,* August 16, 2004, 23–24.

He, Kang. "How to Receive Web Awards." www.pageresource.com/zine/award1.htm.

Holzschlag, Molley E. "Color My World." www.webtechniques.com/archives/2000/09/desi/.

——. "Satisfying Customers with Color, Shape, and Type." www.newarchitectmag.com/archives/1999/11/desi/.

Johnson, David. "Psychology of Color." www.infoplease.com/spot/colors1.html.

Kravatz, Harris. "Designing Web Personalization Features." Boca Raton, FL: HK Interface Design.

Kyrnin, Jennifer. "Color Symbolism." http://webdesign.about.com/od/color/a/aa072604.htm.

Lais, Sami. "How to Stop Web Shopper Flight." *Computerworld,* June 17, 2002, 44–45.

Lightner, Nancy J. "Evaluating E-Commerce Functionality with a Focus on Customer Service." *Communications of the ACM,* October 2004, 88–92.

Marcus, Aaron. "Cultural Dimensions and Global Web User-Interface Design: What? So What? Now What?" www.tri.sbc.com/hfweb/marcus/hfweb00_marcus.html.

Martin, Mike. "The Seven Habits of Highly Effective Web Sites." www.ecommercetimes.com/perl/printer/19270.

Mordkovich, Boris. "Build Your Site in 9 Steps." www.pageresource.com/zine/des01.htm.

Morris, Charlie. "Amateur Web Sites—The Top Ten Signs." www.webdevelopersjournal.com/columns/abc_mistakes.html.

Morris, Charlie. "How to Build Lame Web Sites." www.webdevelopersjournal.com/columns/perpend1.html.

Muler, Thomas. "Shades of Meaning." *Wall Street Journal,* April 15, 2002, R4.

Newman, Chuck. "Considering the Color-Blind." http://webtechniques.com/archives/2000/08/newman/.

Ouellette, Tim. "Web Personalization." *Computerworld,* December 20, 1999, 1–4.

Pamatat, Scott. "Your Choice of Web Site Color." www.pageresource.com/zine/webcolors.htm.

Pollock, John. "A Quick Loading Site." www.pageresource.com/zine/quick.htm.

Ricci, Christian. "Personalization Is Not Technology: Using Web Personalization to Promote Your Business Goal." www.boxesandarrows.com/archives/personalization_is_not_technology.html.

Rutledge, Patrice-Anne. "Let's Get Personal: Enhancing the Customer Experience with Web Personalization." www.patricerutledge.com/Art_pers.htm.

Schmitt, Christopher. "Color Your Web." http://old.alistapart.com/stories/color.

Schroeder, D. "The Key to Effective Design." www.pageresource.com/zine/keydes.htm.

Seffah, Ahmed, and Eduard Metzker. "The Obstacles and Myths of Usability and Software Engineering." *Communications of the ACM*, December 2004, 71–75.

Singh, Vaishall. "Color Design for the Web." www.coolhomepages.com/cda/color.

Spool, Jared. "Web Site Usability: The Big Picture." June 2003, www.webreview.com/wr/pub/web98east/23/spoolx.html.

Wilson, Diane. "Color Vision, Color Deficiency." www.firelily.com/opinions/color.html.

CHAPTER 9

Bruxvoort, Tim. "Viral Marketing Methods and Applications." www.businessandlaw.com/articles/node/35.

Data Media Group. "Modern e-Commerce: Future Trends." www.dtmedia.lv/raksti/EN/BIT/200005/00052207.stm.

Dodge, Bernie. "Specialized Search Engines and Directories." http://edweb.sdsu.edu/webquest/searching/specialized.html.

Gates, Patrick. "T-commerce Expected to Go Far Beyond the 'Existing Shopping Networks.'" *USA Today*, May 25, 2005, 5Aff.

Grant, Lorrie. "T-commerce Poised to Offer New Alternative to Mall." *USA Today*, May 25, 2005, 1Bff.

Hill, Jeromy. "Creating Banner Ads for Wireless Sites." http://gethelp.devx.com/techtips/wireless_pro/10min/10min0900.asp.

Hobson, Katherine. "Ads That Just Don't Click-No, Literally." www.usnews.com/usnews/nvcu/tech/articles/010312/ads.htm.

Kaplan, Fred. "The End of History: How E-Mail Is Wrecking Our National Archive." http://slate.msn.com/id/2083920.

Komperda, Jack. "Buying Time Online." *U.S. News & World Report*, October 6, 2003, 42.

Mangalindan, Mylene. "Web Ads on the Rebound." *Wall Street Journal*, August 25, 2003, B1ff.

Mark, Roy. "FTC to Host SPAM Forum." www. internetnews.com.

McGovern, Gerry. "Website Content Management Consulting." www.gerryntcgovern.com/content-management-consulting.htm.

Jupiter Media Corporation. "Banner Ad Placement Story." www.webreference.com/dev/banners/research.html.

Morrissey, Brian. "Pop-Ups Work." http://itmanagement.earthweb.com/ecom/print.php/2213861.

Otten, Luo. "Price Is Not Everything." *News.com*, December 13, 2004.

Sipior, Janice C., Burke T. Ward, and Gregory Bonner. "Should Spam Be on the Menu?" *Communications of the ACM*, June 2004, 59–63.

Sliwa, Carol. "Electronic Retailers Hurt by Spam Flood." *Computerworld*, August 18, 2003, 10.

Spencer, Jane. "I Ordered That? Web Retailers Make It Easier to Return Goods." *Wall Street Journal*, September 4, 2003, D1ff.

Spinosa, Charles. "Viral Marketing: Strategies for Viral Marketing." www.vision.com/thinking/white_papers/cs0403.html.

Sturdevant, Cameron. "Fighting Spam on Different Fronts." *E-Week*, November 29, 2004, 45–46.

Sundsted, Todd. "Agents on the Move." www.javaworld.com/javaworld/jw-07-1998/jw-07-howto.html.

Tejada, Carlos. "The Best Way to Start a Blog." *Wall Street Journal*, September 15, 2003, R10.

White, Colin J. "Leveraging the Power of the Web Using E-Intelligence." *Database Associates*, 1–15.

Wingfield, Nick, and Brian Steinberg. "Ads Aim to Sell That Tune." *Wall Street Journal*, November 10, 2003, B1ff.

CHAPTER 10

Collins, Heidi. "Enterprise Knowledge Portals." www.amanet.org/books/catalog/0814407080.htm.

Enterprise Knowledge Portal, www.askmecorp.com.

"Enterprise Knowledge Portals to Become the Shared Desktop of the Future." www.itweb.co.za/office/bmi/9903300919.htm.

Firestone, Joe. "Portal Progress and Knowledge Management: Hummingbird Enterprise." *KMWorld*, May 2003, 20–21.

Harney, John. "Delivering on the Promise of Enterprise Portals—Part 1." *KMWorld*, February 2005, 10–11.

Hoffman, Douglas. "Marketing + MIS = E-Service." *Communications of the ACM*, June 2003, 53–55.

Jansen, Christoph M. "Knowledge Portals: Using the Internet to Enable Business Transformation." www.isoc.org/inet2000/cdproceedings/7d/7d_2.htm.

Mack, R., Y. Ravin, and R. J. Byrd. "Knowledge Portals and the Emerging Digital Knowledge Workflow." www.research.ibm.com/journal/si/404/mack.html.

LaMonica, Martin. "Academia Gets Creative with Web Services." http://news.com.com/2102-7345 3-5096702.html?tag=st_utll print.

McDonough, Brian. "The State of Enterprise Portal Initiatives: Portal Adoption Trends 2003." www.portalsmag.com/articles/default.asp?ArticleID=4861.

Monte, Catherine. "To Portal or Not to Portal—That Is the Question." www.llrx.com/features/portals.htm.

Motsenigos, Alex, and Brian McDonough. "Globalizing and Localizing Your Portal Site." *KMWorld*, May 2003, 16–17.

Novell Consulting. "Transforming Service Delivery through Next-Generation Portals." www.novell.com.

O'Toole, Annrai. "A Tectonic Shift for Integration?" *Business Integration Journal*, July 2003, 17–20.

Pickering, Chris. "Portals: An E-Business Success Story." *Software Magazine*, October 2002, 22–27.

"Portals: An Overview." www.1.ibm.com/services/kcm/cm_portal.html.

"Portals, Knowledge," and "Content Management." www.1.ibm.com/services/kcm/know_mngt_com.html.

Walsh, Norman. "What Is XML?" www.xml.com/pub/a/98/10/guide0.html?page=2.

———. "Validity." ww.xml.com/pub/a/98/10/guide0.html?page=4.

———. "What Do XML Documents Look Like?" www.xml.com/pub/a/98/10/guide0.html?page=3.

Wastervelt, Robert. "Web Services Skills a Must for 2005." http://searchwebservices.techtarget.com/originalContent/0.289142.sid_26 gci1036730.00.html.

Williams, Joseph. "The Web Services Debate." *Communications of the ACM*, June 2003, 59–63.

Youman, Mark, and Matthew Thompson. "Next Generation Portals: Catalyst for Government Transformation." *AMS*, white paper.

Zimmerman, Kim A. "Portals Help Insurers and Their Customers." *KM World*, September 2002, 23.

CHAPTER 11

Fairchild, Alea M., and Ryan R. Peterson. "Business-to-Business Value Drivers and eBusiness Infrastructures in Financial Services: Collaborative Commerce Across Global Markets and Networks." *Proceedings of the 36th Hawaii Interntional Conference on System Sciences (HICSS '03)*, May 2003, 1–5.

Ferguson, Renee Boucher. "Teaming Up on PLM." *eWeek*, November 29, 2004, 36.

———. "B2B: Supply Chain Management: Build or Buy?" *eWeek* July 12, 2004, 29.

Fisher, Michael, Thomas Kunstner, and Klaus Mattern. "Ten Success Factors in e-Business." *Insights*, Vol. 7(1), 1–6.

Groves, Varun, and James Teng. "E-Commerce and the Information Market." *Communications of the ACM*, April 2001, 81.

Paul, Lauren G. "SCM: A Matter of Trust." www.managingautomation.com/maonline/magazine/read.ispx?id=925.

Sarma, Brig. "Trust Factors in SCM." *Supply Chain Management Forum*, June 29, 2004.

Schragenheim, Eli. "Measures and Trust in SCM." www.elyakim@netvision.net.il.

Swindle, Orson. "Antitrust in the Emerging B2B Marketplace." www.fic.gov/speeches/swindle/princetonclub2k.htm.

Taylor, David A. "Supply Chain." *Computerworld*, November 10, 2003, 44–45.

Yuva, J. "Knowledge Management: The Supply Chain Nerve Center." *Knowledge Management*, July 2002, 34–43.

CHAPTER 12

ACM Council. "ACM Code of Ethics and Professional Conduct." www.acm.org/constitution/code.html.

ACM Council. "Trust, Safety, and Privacy." http://pages.ebay.com/community/aboutebay/overview/trust.html.

———. "Computer Crime and Intellectual Property Section" (CCIPS). www.usdoj.gov/criminal/cybercrime/Patriot.redline.htm.

Carlson, Caron. "No Spying, Please." www.eweek.com , August 23, 2004, 31.

Cha, Ariana Eunjung. "After Death, a Struggle for Their Digital Memories." *Washington Post*, February 3, 2005, Alff.

Darlington, Roger. "Internet Ethics: Oxymoron or Orthodoxy?" www.rogerdarlington.co.uk/Internetethics.html.

Floridi, Luciano. "Information Ethics: On the Philosophical Foundation of Computer Ethics." www.wolfson.ox.ac.uk/~floridi/ie.htm.

———. "Hi Ethics." www.hiethics.com/Principles/index.asp.

Harris, Frances J. "Zippy Scenario for Teaching Internet Ethics." www.uni.uluc.edu/library/computerlit/scenarios.html.

Johnson, Maryfran. "Ethics and Influence." *Computerworld*, October 20, 2003, 24.

Kay, Russell. "Digital Rights Management." *Computerworld*, June 23, 2003, 33.

Mariano, Gwendylon. "Hollings Pulls Together Net Privacy Bill." http://news.com.com/2100-1023-886679.html.

McCullagh, Declan. "Are Taxes on the Way for Net Access?" *MSNBC*, November 3, 2003.

Newman, Matthew. "So Many Countries, So Many Laws." *Wall Street Journal*, April 28, 2003, R8.

Panko, Raymond R., and Hazel G. Beh. "Monitoring for Pornography and Sexual Harrassment." *Communications of the ACM*, January 2002, 84–87.

Regan, Keith, "Taxation and the Future of Online Commerce." *E-Business*, September 28, 2003, www.ecommercetimes.com/perlstory/31668.html.

Spencer, Jane. "Shirk Ethic: How to Fake a Hard Day at the Office." *Wall Street Journal*, May 15, 2003, D1ff.

Sullivan, Andy. "New Spam Law Has Little Initial Impact—Net Providers," http://story.news.yahoo.com/news?tmpl=story&cid=581&ncid=581&e=9&u=/nm/20040107/tc.

Swartz, Jon. "More Firms Keep an Eye on Outgoing E-Mail." *USA Today*, July 14, 2004, B1.

Tedeschi, Bob. "The Battle over Online Sales Tax Turns Acrimonious." *New York Times*, February 17, 2003, 17E.

Thibodeau, Patrick. "Trade Secret Theft." *Computerworld*, November 15, 2004, 44.

Times Report, "An Army of One and His 50 Fiancees." www.msnbc.com/news/925113.asp?vts=061120031145&ep1=1.

Ulfelder, Steve. "CPOs: Hot or Not?" *Computerworld*, March 15, 2004, 40.

Volokh, Eugene. "Does Pfc. Jessica Lynch Own the Movie Rights to Her Life?" http://slate.msn.com/id/2081488 April 14, 2003, 1–4.

Wiener, Leonard. "No Longer a Tax-Free Zone." *U.S. News & World Report*, November 3, 2003, 40.

Yahoo! Auction Help, "What Am I Not Allowed to Sell?" http://help.yahoo.com/help/auct/asell/asell-21.html.

CHAPTER 13

Acohido, Byron, and Jon Swartz. "MyDoom. M Virus Slams Search Sites." *USA Today*, July 27, 2004, 1B.

Associated Press. "Biometrics Security Improved." *The Daily Progress*, August 28, 2005, B1.

Associated Press. "Government Targets Spyware in Crackdown." *The Daily Progress*, October 6, 2005, B3.

Awad, Elias M. "Money Laundering—The Basics." Unpublished manuscript, April 2005.

Baker, Stephen. "How Spammers Are Fighting Back." *BusinessWeek*, December 15, 2003, 82.

Biba, Erin. "Biometric Passports Set to Take Flight." *PCWorld*, March 21, 2004, 57.

Brewin, Bob. "Security Threats Raise Concerns about Bluetooth." *Computerworld*, May 10, 2004, 43ff.

Brooks, Jason. "In Operating Systems We Trust." *eWeek*, September 6, 2004, 43–45ff.

Cha, Ariana. "Fixes Only Temporary for Infected Internet." *Washington Post*, June 26, 2005, A1ff.

Coffee, Peter. "Security Is Shaping IT Pros' Roles." *eWeek*, June 14, 2004, 47–48.

Enbysk, Monte. "Should You Monitor Your Employees' Web Use?" www.bcentral.com/articles/enbysk/156.asp.

Foix, Roger. "Secure E-Mail Stops at Corporate Borders." *Computerworld*, September 6, 2004, 32.

Fisher, Dennis. "Changing the Face of Passwords." *eWeek*, September 20, 2004, 1ff.

———. "Pair Mulls OS Security." *eWeek*, July 12, 2004, 32.

———. "Phishing Gets Savvier." *eWeek*, May 3, 2004, 14.

———. "Tales of Cyber Crime." *eWeek*, May 24, 2004, 1ff.

Glanz, William. "Internet Scams Getting Banking Users Rise in June." *Washington Times*, August 2, 2004, A9ff.

Hall, Mark. "Winning Ways to Stop Spam." *Computerworld*, March 1, 2004, 21ff.

Hamblen, Matt. "Outsourcing IT Security Functions Can Succeed . . ." *Computerworld*, January 19, 2004, 38–39.

Hodges, Arthur. "Intelligence and Terrorism Information." www.intelligence.org.il/eng/sib/8_internet.htm.

Hulmes, George V. "Hack in Progress." *Information Week*, September 8, 2003, 33–35ff.

Ives, Blake, Kenneth R. Walsh, and Helmut Schneider. "The Domino Effect of Password Reuse." *Communications of the ACM*, April 2004, 75–78.

Johnson, Maryfran. "Spyware Wake-Up Call." *Computerworld*, May 3, 2004, 20.

Krebs, Brian. "Hackers to Face Tougher Sentences." www.washingtonpost.com/wp-dvn/articles/A35261-2003Oct2.html.

Krim, Jonathan. "Senate Votes 97–0 to Restrict E-Mail Ads." *Washington Post*, October 23, 2003, A01.

Lamb, Gregory M. "ID Stolen? Call a Privacy Gumshoe." *CS Monitor*, March 9, 2005, 16.

Levy, Steven, and Brad Stone. "Grand Theft Identity." *Newsweek*, July 4, 2005, 38ff.

Lundquist, Eric. "Insecure on Insecurity." *eWeek*, July 12, 2004, 28.

MacMillan, Robert. "Phear of Pharming." *Washington Post*, March 14, 2005, B1ff.

McGuire, Russ. "How Microsoft Fuels Internet Terrorism." www.worldnetdaily.com/news/article.asp?ARTICLE_ID=34231.

Mitchell, Robert L. "Spyware Sneaks into the Office." *Computerworld*, May 3, 2004, 23–24.

Monash, Curt A. "Invest in an Antispam System Now." *Computerworld*, April 26, 2004, 29.

———. "The Real Risks." *Computerworld*, July 19, 2004, 26.

Murali, D. "Don't Let Security Slip Through Your Fingers." *Business Line*, July 12, 2004, 17–18.

Newman, Aaron C. "6 Security Secrets Attackers Don't Want You to Know." *DB2 Magazine*, Quarter 2, 2004, 32–37.

Di Pietro, Robert, and Luigi V. Mancini. "Security and Privacy Issues." *Communications of the ACM*, September 2003, 75–79.

Popp, Robert, Thomas Armour, Ted Senator, and Kristen Numryeh. "Countering Terrorism through Information Technology." *Communications of the ACM*, March 2004, 36–40.

Richmond, Riva. "How to Find Your Weak Spots." *Wall Street Journal*, September 29, 2003, R3.

Rohde, Laura. "Shopkeepers Get High-Tech Help." www.pcworld.com/news/article/0.aid.114610.00.asp.

Rothke, Ben. "E-Voting: It's Security, Stupid," *eWeek*, August 23, 2004.

Smith, Edward. "The Changing Face of Information Security." *Computerworld*, August 23, 2004, 33.

Solomon, Alan, and Robert M. Slade. "Virus History." www.cknow.com/vtutor/vthistory.htm.

Sturdevant, Cameron. "Keeping Up with CAN-SPAM Act." *eWeek*, February 2, 2004, 43–47.

Swartz, Jon. "Spam Can Hurt in More Ways Than One." *USA Today*, Section B1.

———. "Survey: ID Theft Takes Time to Wipe Clean." *USA Today*, July 29, 2005, 1B.

Thompson, Roger. "We Must Beat Spyware." *eWeek*, August 9, 2004, 37.

Thurman, Mathias. "Company Secrets Hit the Exits." *Computerworld*, August 30, 2004, 27.

———. "IP Telephony Changes Security Equation." *Computerworld*, September 27, 2004, 36.

Tuesday, Vince. "This Is Your Attacker Calling." *Computerworld*, March 8, 2004, 36.

Ubois, Jeff, and Mitch Betts. "Dural Curses." *Computerworld*, February 2, 2004, 29.

Verton, Dan. "Organized Crime Invades Cyberspace." *Computerworld*, August 30, 2004, 20ff.

Weitzner, Daniel J. "The Need to Know What We're Missing." *Computerworld*, September 27, 2004, 38.

Whitman, Michael E. "Enemy at the Gate: Threats to Information Security." *Communications of the ACM*, August 2003, 91–95.

CHAPTER 14

Abelson, H., R. Anderson, S. Bellovin, J. Benaloh, M. Blaze, W. Diffle, J. Gilmore, P. Neumann, R. Rivest, J. Schiller, and B. Schneier. "The Risks of Key Recovery, Key Escrow, and Trusted Third-Party Encryption." www.cdt.org/crypto/risks98/.

Aumont, Marcel. "Public Key." *CGI Group, Inc*, 2002, 1–14.

Banisar, David. "U.S. State Department Reports Worldwide Privacy Abuses." *Privacy International*, www.privacy.org/pi/reports/1995_hranalysis.html.

Blaze, Matt. "Crypto.com." www.crypto.com.

Center for Democracy. "Cryptography." www.cdt.org/crypto.

Connolly, P.J. "Policing User Identities." *Infoworld*, August 13, 2001, 43.

"Getting Your Own Digital Certificate." http://webopedia.internet.com/TERM/d/digital_certificate.html.

Johnson, Colin R. "Quantum Encryption Secures High-Speed Data Stream." *Etimes*, November 7, 2002, 1.

Johnston, Margret, "U.S. Postal Service Taps Digital Authentication." *Infoworld*, March 9, 2001, www.infoworld.com/articles/hn/xml/01/03/07/010307hnusps.html.

Levy, Steven. "Did Encryption Empower These Terrorists?" *Newsweek*, November 11, 2002, 1–5.

Litterio, Francis. "The Mathematical Guts of RSA Encryption." http://world.std.com/~fran1crypto/rsa-guts.html.

Petreley, Nicholas. "Secrecy Is an Illusion." *Computerworld*, March 25, 2002, 43ff.

Reinhold, Arnold G. "Diceware for Passphrase Generation and Other Cryptographic Applications." July 28, 1995, http://world.std.com/~reinhold/diceware.txt.

Rivest, Ronald L. "Chaffing and Winnowing: Confidentiality Without Encryption." *MIT Lab for Computer Science*, March 18, 1998.

Rivest, Ronald L. "Cryptography and Security." http://theory.lcs.mit.edu/~rivest/crypto-security.html.

Rodriquez, Karen. "SHTTP, SSL Big Hits in Web Ware." *Communications Week*, January 29, 1996, 41.

Scheier, Robert L. "Sorry, Only Authentic Users Need Apply." *Computerworld*, January 8, 2001, 62.

SSH Communications Security. "Cryptography De-Mystified." www.ssh.fi/tech/crypto/intro.htm.

Thurman, Mathias. "Authentication Rollout Turns into Control Issue." *Computerworld*, March 4, 2002, 50.

———. "Stalking Elusive Access Points." *Computerworld*, November 11, 2002, 40.

Verton, Dan. "Feds Plan Biometrics for Border Control." *Computerworld*, May 26, 2003, 12.

Visa International Service Association. "For Businesses." www.international.visa.com/fb/main.jsp.

"What Is Hashing?" A Word Definition from the Webopedia Computer Dictionary. http://webopedia.com/TERM/h/. hashing.html.

Ylonen, Tatu. "Introduction to Cryptography." SSH Communications Security. http://home-netscape.com/security/basics/ getperscert.html.

CHAPTER 15

Barlas, Pete. "PayPal Pushes for Business Use." *Yahoo! News*, October 27, 2003.

Federal Trade Commission. "A Consumer's Guide to E-Payments." www.ftc.gov/bcp/conline/pubs/online/payments.htm.

Goodwin, Bill. "Biometric ID Cards Do Little to Cut Fraud." ComputerWeekly.com, July 13, 2004.

Grabbe, Orlin. "The End of Ordinary Money, Part I." www.aoi.net/kzilliste/money1.htm.

Herzberg, Amir. "Payments and Banking with Mobile Personal Devices." *Communications of the ACM*, May 2003, 53–58.

Powell, Eileen Alt. "More Teens Carrying Credit, Debit Cards." *Yahoo!*, April 13, 2005, Business—AP Consumer Columns.

Scheier, Robert L. "The Price of E-Payment." *Computerworld*, May 26, 2003.

Shelfer, Katherine M., and J. Drew Procaccine. "Smart Card Evolution." *Communications of the ACM*, July 2002, 83–88.

Vijayan, Jaikumar. "Low Draw for Smart Cards." *Computerworld*, February 9, 2004, 30–31.

INDEX

■ 550 Index

THE LEARNING CENTRE
HAMMERSMITH AND WEST
LONDON COLLEGE
GLIDDON ROAD
LONDON W14 9BL